The Status of Tibet

About the Book and Author

For centuries, Tibet, located at the strategic heart of Asia, has been coveted by the continent's great empires, including those of the Mongols, the Russians, the Manchus, the British, and the Chinese. This study reviews the history of the Tibetan state from the nation's unification in the seventh century to its present disputed incorporation into the People's Republic of China. A definitive record of the legal status of Tibet, the book provides a much-needed basis for understanding the unresolved Sino-Tibetan conflict and its importance in the broader issues of Asian politics. In particular, it addresses questions of statehood, the effects of interstate relations on independence, acquisition of territory, and self-determination. This overview is especially timely in light of the present negotiations between representatives of the PRC and the Dalai Lama's Tibetan government-in-exile.

Michael C. van Walt van Praag practices international law in Washington, D.C., and London. He has taught international law and Tibetan studies at the Monterey Institute of International Studies and is a former director of the Tibetan Affairs Coordination Office in the Netherlands.

The Status of Tibet

History, Rights, and Prospects in International Law

Michael C. van Walt van Praag,
with a Foreword by Franz Michael
and an Introduction by Rikhi Jaipal

Westview Press / Boulder, Colorado

Copyright © 1987 by Michael C. van Walt van Praag

Published in 1987 in the United States of America by Westview Press, Inc.; Frederick A. Praeger, Publisher; 5500 Central Avenue, Boulder, Colorado 80301

Library of Congress Cataloging-in-Publication Data
Van Walt van Praag, Michael C.
  The status of Tibet.
  Bibliography: p.
  Includes index.
  1. Tibet (China)—International status. 2. Tibet
(China)—Foreign relations—China. 3. China—Foreign
relations—Tibet (China). 4. Tibet (China)—Politics
and government—1951–   . I. Title.
JX4084.T45V36 1987   341.2'9'09515   86-11197
ISBN 0-8133-0394-X

Composition for this book was created by conversion of the author's computer tapes or word-processor disks.

Printed and bound in the United States of America

⊗ The paper used in this publication meets the requirements of the American National Standard
    for Permanence of Paper for Printed Library Materials Z39.48-1984.

6   5   4   3   2   1

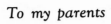

To my parents

Contents

Maps

Foreword

In this book, Michael C. van Walt van Praag deals with an issue treated less than adequately in the pertinent literature of Tibet: the legal status of Tibet, past and present. For Peking, Tibet is simply a part of China, called officially "Tibet, Region of China"—a relationship that supposedly existed throughout history. Tibetans maintain that Tibet was always wholly independent and separate from China. It is time to set the record straight and provide the well-documented, carefully reasoned, objective account of the legal past and present that this study represents.

In its early history, from the seventh to the ninth centuries, Tibet was ruled with a strong hand by King Songtsen Gampo and his successors, who unified the country and expanded their control over a large part of Central Asia, including Chinese territory. In this period, Tibetan kings were certainly equal in their power to any ruler in Asia. Years later, when their military supremacy was lost, Tibetan rulers developed varying and at times close relationships with the rulers of neighboring states. At issue, in particular, is the relationship between the Tibetan rulers and the emperors of China.

A singular relationship developed between a Tibetan incarnation—first of the Sakya sect of Tibetan Buddhism in the thirteenth century and later the Dalai Lamas of the Gelug sect—and the Mongol Khans and emperors of the Yuan Dynasty, and the Chinese and Manchu emperors of the Ming and Ch'ing Dynasties, respectively. This relationship, under which the Khans and emperors provided protection and support for the religious and political authority of the Dalai Lama—who ruled Tibet from the seventeenth century— in exchange for assumed religious blessing and succor, was not one of dependence any more than was at its time the relationship between the popes and the emperors of the medieval Holy Roman Empire in Europe.

To describe the European situation, historians devised the "two sword" theory. In the Tibetan case the Chö-yön (priest-patron) concept was applied to the relationship between the Dalai Lamas and the secular emperors. However, both concepts are difficult to define in modern terms of sovereign State authority and, as with the "two sword" system in Europe, the substance of the Chö-yön relationship shifted as power relations changed.

The Manchu emperors' power in Tibet reached its height when a Ch'ing army defended Tibet against a Nepalese invasion in the so-called Gorkha war in 1788–1792. In this volume, Michael C. van Walt van Praag recounts the role of the Manchu representatives, the two Ambans who with Manchu

xiii

garrisons were stationed in Tibet from the eighteenth century on. Some scholars have interpreted this situation as a Manchu "protectorate" or Manchu "suzerainty" over Tibet, concepts that have remained vague and that, as van Walt van Praag points out, cannot be translated in terms of modern state relations. In fact, no treaty between the Ch'ing emperor and the Tibetan ruler indicated any legal change in their relationship. As it happened, the magnified Manchu influence of the last two centuries had eroded by the end of the nineteenth century, and it ended altogether with the Chinese revolution of 1911, after which the Manchus were driven out of Tibet.

The ensuing Tibetan struggle to assert independence in modern terms, the international strategems and machinations and their legal expression in the treaties of the time, and, finally, the 1949 communist invasion and its consequences make up the major part of van Walt van Praag's study, which concludes with a discussion of the Tibetan claim to self-determination and alternative solutions.

A historical account makes evident the fact that the communist Chinese claim that Tibet was an integral part of China throughout history is largely based on a misinterpretation of the premodern relationship between a religio-political powerholder and a secular powerholder. The Chinese historical interpretation goes beyond that, however, for it also misconstrues the ideological foundation of the Chinese Empire by ignoring the fundamental difference between it and a modern nation State. The Chinese Empire was conceptually a world State; indeed, it covered "all under Heaven" under the sway of the "Middle Kingdom," in which the emperor, as the holder of the "Mandate of Heaven" for mankind, assumed his placement above all other worldly kings and rulers or even emperors who might, voluntarily, wish to "participate in Our beneficence," as emperor Ch'ien Lung wrote to the British King George III. It would be anachronistic, to say the least, to translate whatever connections existed in the past, outside of China proper, between the emperor and other heads of polities in terms of modern national bonds. The Chinese reinterpretation of medieval imperial relations in terms of a modern nation State in order to advance the claim that the Tibetan people—who were never a part of the Chinese people—were in the past and are today a "minority" within the Chinese "nation," is part of an attempt to justify what is, in effect, a new form of Chinese imperialism.

The communist leaders in China have also attempted to justify the invasion of Tibet in terms of the need to "liberate" the Tibetan people from what is described in propaganda terms as "medieval feudalism" and "slavery." Thus, an entire body of propagandistic literature has been dedicated to the effort to paint the darkest picture of Tibet's pre-occupation past. Van Walt van Praag does not address this issue, as it is not immediately relevant to the question of Tibet's legal status. It should, nevertheless, be pointed out that traditional Tibet was not "feudal" in the sense that this term is used by political and historical analysts. Tibet was ruled by an incarnation, the Dalai Lama, and by a predominantly clerical bureaucracy largely made up of monks from common, often peasant, backgrounds. This system provided great social mobility. Aristocracy, insofar as it survived from an earlier time, was a service aristocracy that provided one son per family for the small number of appointed government positions left for lay officials. A large number of commoners, almost a third, were traders or private entrepreneurs in the towns—a middle class, as it were. In the rural areas the land was divided into state, monastic, and aristocratic estates, but the farmers and herders were not serfs in a feudal system. Those obligated to work estate land or herds made up slightly over half of the rural population, owned their own inheritable land or animals, were well off, and constituted the "upper" group from which local headmen and leaders were taken. The large number of laborers were free to sell their labor and to move onto their own private enterprises in town or, as many did, into rural communities.

Whatever the traditional system's merits or defects, it is significant to note that Tibet had experienced neither famines nor "peasant rebellions" prior to the Chinese take-over in 1950 and it had no police and no army of any significance (the military forces that did exist were used exclusively for defense against outside attack). By contrast, since its occupation by China and the imposition of "socialist reforms," Tibet has experienced both famines and numerous popular rebellions and the army's presence is all pervasive. Moreover, the modernization of the traditional Tibetan system, which was started inside Tibet by the Tibetans themselves but was curbed and then replaced by Chinese socialist reforms there, has since been highly successful in exile where it has been implemented by the Tibetan refugee community under the Dalai Lama in the Indian diaspora.

Since 1950, the Chinese have attempted to destroy the national culture of Tibet in the name of progress toward socialist utopianism. As a result, over a million Tibetans out of a total of 6 million have lost their lives, and of the more than 6,000 original temples and monasteries fewer than two dozen have escaped destruction. Sadly, this has been largely ignored in international discussions. All the more important then, that van Walt van Praag's detailed scholarly study provides the definitive legal record upon which to base Tibet's future self-determination.

Franz Michael

Preface

International law is a body of principles, customs, and rules that are recognized as effectively binding obligations by sovereign States and international persons in their mutual relations. Although no one disputes the fact that States frequently violate international law in the same way that individuals violate national laws, the respect that international law commands, together with its observance and invocation by most States most of the time, justifies a positive, optimistic, and constructive view of the role of law in international relations. It is the belief in justice and truth, and in the law embodying those principles, that has contributed to humankind's advancement in the past; so also can today's efforts in furtherance of that law contribute to a more peaceful, equitable, and dignified human existence in the future.

On a pragmatic level, international law is an instrument for the resolution of conflicts, primarily among States. The conflict that impels the writing of the present volume is one that affects the lives of millions of people, the destiny of nations, and even the stability of a continent: It is the Sino-Tibetan dispute over the status, rights, and prospects of the world's highest plateau, Tibet, and its inhabitants, the Tibetans.

Tibet, though known mostly for its unique culture and rich philosophical tradition and often portrayed as a land of mystery and magic, has been and still is regarded as an area of great strategic importance by the major powers in Asia. The plateau's geographic location, in the heart of Asia and between the continent's three giants—China, the Soviet Union (formerly the Russian Empire), and the Indian subcontinent—has frequently caused Tibet to be the object of international political rivalry.

This study is concerned neither with strategic considerations nor with questions of a purely political or ideological nature. Neither is it the intention of the author to deal with the socioeconomic arguments advanced by both sides in the conflict to support or condemn a Chinese presence in Tibet. What the present volume does attempt is a comprehensive analysis of the legal questions that have been raised by the Tibetan-Chinese conflict.

When Chinese armies first marched into Tibet in 1949, soon after the communist victory in China, the government of the new People's Republic of China claimed the right to incorporate the plateau on the grounds that Tibet was and had been for centuries an integral part of China. The Tibetan government, in Lhasa, repudiated the Chinese allegation and accused China of aggression and violation of Tibet's territorial integrity and independence.

These diametrically opposed stands have not been modified in the last decades; on the contrary, at least until recently, they have posed unsurmountable obstacles to any hope of resolving the conflict, which has caused massive outbreaks of violence in Tibet and the flight to India of the Dalai Lama, Tibet's head of State, and his government.

Today, some improvement is taking place. As a dialogue has been established between the Tibetan government-in-exile and the leadership in Beijing, the prospects for some kind of reconciliation in the future are not quite so remote. What remains unresolved, however, is the principal issue of contention—the question of Tibet's past and present legal status.

As noted earlier, both the Chinese and the Tibetans use historical arguments to support their respective claims to sovereignty over Tibet. The People's Republic of China makes no claim to sovereign rights over Tibet as a result of its military subjugation and occupation of Tibet since 1950. Thus, China does not allege that it acquired legal title to Tibet by means of conquest, annexation or prescription in this period. Instead, China bases its claim solely on the theory that Tibet was an integral part of China for centuries. The Tibetan claim to independence is similarly based on its historical status prior to 1950. That being the case, it should be sufficient to limit the discussion of the contending claims regarding the status of Tibet to the period prior to 1950. However, some political and legal analysts have suggested that China's military intervention in Tibet in 1950, followed by close to 35 years of Chinese domination, may have resulted in a transfer of sovereignty over Tibet to China regardless of Tibet's historical status. This author, therefore, examines the historical evolution of Tibet since the seventh century, when Tibet's status and its relations with other States, including China, were clear and unambiguous, as well as the developments in Tibet since 1950.

The student of Tibet's past legal status inevitably confronts the problem of finding legal categories and terms appropriate to describe and define the position of this Central Asian country in relation to its neighbors. The existing system of international law, with its concepts and definitions, owes its genesis and growth in large part to the interaction among European States during the past four centuries. Only in the present century has international law been significantly influenced and modified by non-Western members of the family of nations.

In the past, other systems of law governed inter-State relations in various regions of the world. Relations among the States of the Indian subcontinent, for example, were regulated to a large extent by ancient codes such as the Smiritis, the code of Manyu, and the Dharmasastra. Similarly, from the standpoint of the rulers of the Chinese Empire, all international relations were based on ancient philosophic perceptions of the world, generally attributed to Confucius, according to which the Emperor—the center and apex of the world order—possessed a mandate from Heaven to rule all peoples, Chinese and "barbarians" alike.

In order to determine Tibet's historical status, we must understand the peculiar position of that Central Asian country at any given time in terms of both the actual political developments inside Tibet and in its relations with other States and peoples. Such an understanding can be reached if we take into account the perceptions of the contemporary rulers and historians of Tibet and of other States with whom it maintained relations. In addition, our perspective must be rendered in terms applicable to a no longer Eurocentric international law.

The source materials available to today's scholar of Tibet's historical position are fairly extensive. The early history of Tibet has been researched and documented by numerous eminent Tibetologists, Sinologists, and historians, with the help of official records and chronicles found in Tibet, China, and other parts of Asia (in particular Central Asia), which date at least as far back as the seventh century, the point of departure for the present study. Excellent sources of information regarding the more recent history include the collections of documents—comprising public and secret diplomatic correspondence and other communications, memoranda, and reports—contained in the India Office and Foreign Office archives in London and the National Archives in New Delhi. In addition to British documents, these archives contain Tibetan, Manchu, Chinese, and Nepalese documents, among others. Information can also be obtained from the documents that Tibetan officials managed to take with them on their flight from Tibet, as well as from published and unpublished Chinese sources that the author has been able to consult only through the kind assistance of translators. In addition, eyewitness accounts and press reports are useful sources. Foremost among the sources used in the present study are the treaties and other agreements concerning Tibet and/or concluded by Tibet or by other States, many of which are reproduced in the appendixes. Classified documents to which the author has had access are generally not cited.

Whatever the limitations to which the researchers of this subject, and this author in particular, may have been subject, the aggregate of evidence presented in the present volume is, I believe, sufficiently compelling to support the conclusions arrived at in Chapter 8, regarding the legal status of Tibet prior to the Chinese actions initiated in 1949, and in Chapter 10, regarding the present status of Tibet.

A detailed examination of alternatives for future Tibetan-Chinese relations is not within the scope of this study (although it should form the subject of a separate one). Nevertheless, the last chapter touches on certain suggestions and prospects for a resolution of the conflict, thus completing the present investigation of the principal legal issues of the Sino-Tibetan conflict.

Tibetan names and terms are rendered phonetically in the text, and their correct orthographic transcription (based on the Wylie system) are included in the index. Chinese names and terms are rendered in the pinyin system. Where sources are cited, the romanization used in those sources is left unchanged.

Michael C. van Walt van Praag

Acknowledgments

So numerous are the people who, in varying ways, contributed time and effort to this book that I am unable to name and thank them all individually. My gratitude goes out to all of them.

I will, however, specify the Threshold Foundation (London), the Menil Fund (Houston, Texas), the Stichting Dr. Hendrik Muller's Vaderlandsch Fonds (The Hague), and the Tibet Fund (New York), without whose generous funding the research could never have been done. I also thank the Library of Tibetan Works and Archives; Thribuvan University; the Institute for Sino-Soviet Studies at George Washington University; the Research Institute for Inner Asian Studies and the Department of Uralic and Altaic Studies of Indiana University; Stanford Law School; the Department of Oriental Languages and Boalt Hall at the University of California, Berkeley; the Monterey Institute of International Studies; and Wilmer, Cutler & Pickering for their provision of the extensive facilities and support indispensable to the research, writing, and completion of my manuscript. I am particularly indebted to Gyatsho Tshering, Dr. Gaston J. Sigur, Professors Thubten J. Norbu, Stephen A. Halkovic, and Paul A. Draghi, and the late Dean Joseph Leininger.

Many friends have given invaluable help in the various stages of preparation of the manuscript. I am particularly grateful to Cat Hennings, Vajra Kilgour, Paul Turco, Kimberly Greco, and my wife, Lynn, for their help in editing, proofing, citation-checking and typing; Professor L. J. Bouchez, Professor David L. Snellgrove, Lobsang Lhalungpa, Dr. Elliot Sperling, Professor Franz Michael, and Dr. Jan Anderson for their comments on the manuscript, which were much appreciated; Dr. T. R. Onta, Dr. Niranjan Bhattarai, Ambassador H. Leopold, Kalon Tenzin Geyche Tethong, Kalon Tashi Wangdi, Ngari Rimpoche, Samdung Rimpoche, Tempa Tsering, Rinchen Dharlo, and Kesang Tseten for their kind assistance in my research efforts; Tsepon W. D. Shakabpa and Lobsang Lhalungpa for sharing their documents and their vast historical knowledge with me; Tsering Youdon, Douglas Ngo, Guy M. Newland, Miriam Lutz, and many others for translating documents and other materials and for their help in connection with the romanization of Chinese and Tibetan words; and John F. Avedon, Tenzin Namgyal Tethong, Professor and Mrs. M. L. Sondhi, Tsering Wangyal, and Professor John Barton for their encouragement and knowledgeable advice.

Finally, I am indebted to Lynn, my parents, and His Holiness the Dalai Lama for their unwavering support and inspiration.

Michael C. van Walt van Praag

Introduction

Many people only know of Tibet as the land of mystery and magic perched on the roof of the world, once known as the forbidden land. Many have no doubt seen on their television sets the familiar figure of Tibet's self-exiled leader, the Dalai Lama, who also represents the unique religion and philosophy of Tibetan Buddhism. But what is generally not known, even to policymakers of many countries, is the legal status of Tibet and the curious historical relationship between the Dalai Lama and the Mongol and Manchu emperors.

This book by Michael C. van Walt van Praag is a seriously researched and objective study of important developments in Tibet's history and especially of its legal status in relation to China. It is a fascinating account based on a wealth of evidence and documentation from the seventh century onward. The author's conclusions are well reasoned, based on adequate evidence, and invariably carry conviction.

According to his analysis, throughout its history Tibet possessed the essential attributes of statehood, never ceased to be a separate entity, was never an integral part of any other State, and though subjected to invasions by outsiders, always maintained its independence.

With the advent of Buddhism in Tibet, the source of sovereignty came to be vested in the person and position of the Dalai Lama, and that inevitably imparted to governmental authority a nonviolent character. For protection against external invaders, however, it became expedient for Tibet to have friendly relations with a State that understood the compulsions of its religion and would willingly respond to its requests for assistance. Thus developed the Chö-yön relationship between the Dalai Lama and the Mongol emperors and later the Manchu emperors.

This was a sui generis relationship without precedent or parallel, and its scope and relevance has to be appreciated in its own historical context. Any attempt to relate it to other similar arrangements will not make for its better understanding. By and large it served Tibet in times of peril, and it began to decline gradually as Tibet, under pressure of circumstances, acquired its own small defense force and also developed relations with other foreign countries. It finally ceased when the Manchu emperor was overthrown in 1911.

For the Chinese to interpret Tibet's special relationship with the Manchu emperors as conferring on China sovereignty over Tibet is to distort history in order to further nationalist and communist expansionary purposes. In

1950 China invaded and occupied Tibet in the name of "liberating" its people, and incorporated the country by force, claiming it to be part of Chinese territory.

Tibet appealed to the United Nations for help; the failure of the UN to take any action was deplorable. The UN was then engaged in Korea against Chinese forces and was evidently reluctant to start another front in Tibet. However, there was no reason why the UN should not at least have condemned China's aggression against Tibet. With the benefit of hindsight those countries that were unwilling in 1950 to press for UN action may now wonder at the wisdom of their policies. Especially India, which had been misled by the Chinese Note of 16 November 1950 saying that a peaceful resolution of the Tibetan question was still possible, would have done well to press for UN action.

Van Walt van Praag concludes his study of facts and law with irrefutable logic: "China's presence in Tibet constitutes a continued serious violation of international law." His book is an important contribution toward an understanding of the international status of Tibet, which (as Mr. Aiken, the representative of Ireland, pointed out at the UN) was for "two thousand years free and fully in control of its own affairs and a thousand times more free than many members of the UN."

Rikhi Jaipal
Former Indian Ambassador
to the United Nations

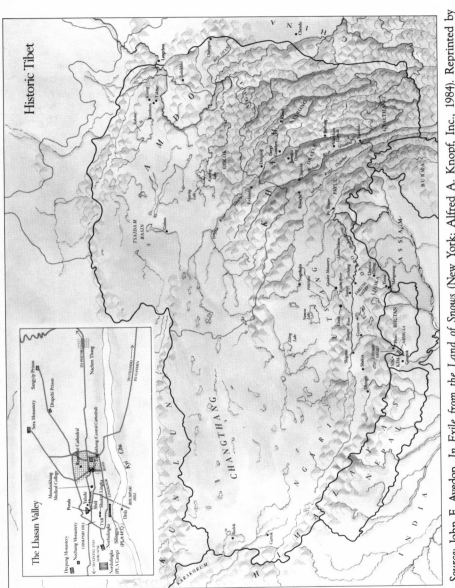

Historic Tibet

The Lhasan Valley

Source: John F. Avedon, In Exile from the Land of Snows (New York: Alfred A. Knopf, Inc., 1984). Reprinted by permission.

1

The Early
Political History

The Tibet-China Treaty of A.D. 821
and the Imperial Age

The treaty, sworn to by "the Ministers of Great Tibet" and "the Ministers of Great China" in the name of their sovereigns, the Tibetan *Tsanpo* (Emperor),[1] Tritsug Detsen Ralpachen and the Tang Emperor Mu Zong in A.D. 821,[2] was not the first treaty concluded between Tibet and China. Tibet had already concluded at least seven bilateral treaties with China,[3] as well as with other powers such as Siam and the Caliphate.[4] The 821 agreement was a peace treaty meant to end almost two centuries of fighting. It is most significant because it reveals, in clear and unambiguous language, the nature of Sino-Tibetan relations at the time.

The text of the Tibet-China Treaty was recorded in Tibetan and Chinese on three pillars in the Tibetan capital, Lhasa; in the Chinese capital, Chang'an; and at the border in Gugu Meru. The Lhasa pillar still stands in front of the Jo-khang cathedral, and the text carved on it is, for the most part, legible:

> The great king of Tibet, the Divine Manifestation, the bTsan-po and the great king of China, the Chinese ruler Hwang Te, Nephew and Uncle,[5] having consulted about the alliance of their dominions have made a great treaty and ratified the agreement. . . .
> Both Tibet and China shall keep the country and frontiers of which they now are in possession. The whole region to the east of that being the country of Great China and the whole region to the west being assuredly the country of Great Tibet, from either side of that frontier there shall be no warfare, no hostile invasions, and no seizure of territory. . . .
> Now that the dominions are allied and a great treaty of peace has been made in this way, since it is necessary also to continue the communication of pleasant messages between Nephew and Uncle, envoys setting out from either side shall follow the old established route. . . .
> According to the close and friendly relationship between Nephew and Uncle the customary courtesy and respect shall be practiced. Between the two countries, no smoke or dust shall appear. Not even a word of sudden

1

alarm or of enmity shall be spoken and from those who guard the frontier upwards, all shall live at ease without suspicion or fear, their land being their land and their bed their bed. . . . And in order that this agreement establishing a great era when Tibetans shall be happy in Tibet and Chinese shall be happy in China shall never be changed, the Three Jewels, the body of Saints, the sun and the moon, planets and stars have been invoked as witnesses.[6]

On the east face of the pillar, an edict of the Tsanpo Tritsug Detsen[7] describes the growth of the Tibetan Empire from its birth in the seventh century A.D. In this edict, in Tibetan histories (particularly those in the annals and chronicles found in Dunhuang), and in the Tang Dynastic histories (the *Jiu Tang Shu* and the *Xin Tang Shu*), Tibet between the seventh and the mid-ninth century is portrayed not only as a strong, independent, and expansionist power but also as a serious rival to China in Central Asia.[8] As the *Jiu Tang Shu*, for example, reveals in Chapter 196B: "The Tibetans founded their kingdom on our western borders a great number of years ago; like silkworms, they gnawed away at their barbarian neighbors in order to expand their own territory. In Gao Zong's time, their territory comprised 10,000 li and they were competing with us for supremacy; in more recent times, no one has proved more powerful than they."[9]

Tsanpo Songtsen Gampo (ca. 620–649) unified the nomadic tribes that populated the Tibetan plateau in the early seventh century. He is thus considered to be the father of the nation.[10] Tibet's era of politico-military greatness and territorial expansion began under his rule and lasted nearly three centuries. Songtsen Gampo also had a lasting influence on the subsequent evolution of Tibet: Under him the Tibetan script was created, a code of law was promulgated, and histories were written.

Songtsen Gampo conquered or subdued most of the peoples and States on Tibet's borders and entered into matrimonial alliances with neighboring rulers.[11] Two of the most significant weddings were those involving the Nepalese Princess Bhrikuti in 637 and the Chinese Imperial Princess Wen Cheng in 641, both reluctantly given in marriage in the face of threats from the Tsanpo.[12] These weddings had a lasting impact on Tibet's cultural and religious development, for it was these princesses who first introduced Buddhism to Tibet.[13]

Aside from Songtsen Gampo, the Emperors Trisong Detsen (755–797) and Tritsug Detsen Ralpachen (817–836) are remembered as great and powerful rulers. Under the former, the Tibetan Empire reached its apogee. Its influence extended across the Pamirs up to the empires of the Arabs and Turks in the west and over Turkestan in the north as well as Nepal in the south. In the east, Tibetan armies overran Gansu and large parts of Sichuan,[14] exacted a yearly tribute from the Chinese, and even took their capital, Chang'an, in 763.[15] A treaty was concluded in 783 which laid down the frontier between China and Tibet and incorporated practically all of the Tibetan conquests. These borders had not changed much when the new peace treaty was concluded in 821.[16]

3

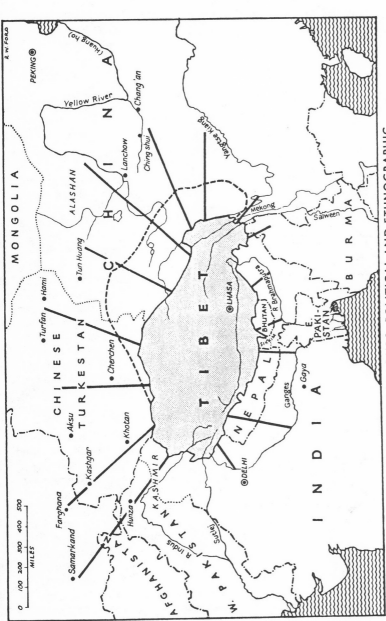

TIBET AND ITS NEIGHBOURS: POLITICAL AND ETHNOGRAPHIC

Shaded area: **Political Tibet**
Broken line: **Limits of Ethnographic Tibet**
Radiating lines: **Extent of Tibetan influence in 6th to 10th centuries**

Source: Hugh M. Richardson, *Tibet and Its History*, 2nd ed. (Boston: Shambhala Publications, 1962). Reprinted by permission.

The Imperial Age of Tibet, which lasted two centuries, ended soon after the assassination of Tsanpo Ralpachen in 836. It witnessed both the creation of a unified Tibetan State, which engaged in active relations with neighboring States, and the dawn of a unique Tibetan and predominantly Buddhist civilization.

Tibet and the Mongols: The Rise of Religious Power

Tsanpo Langdarma (836–842) met with the same fate as that of his predecessor. He was assassinated in 842, after a short reign that is remembered primarily for his ruthless persecution of Buddhism. A schism in the royal lineage followed his death, and the Nyatri Dynasty of Tibet terminated with him. The Empire collapsed and fragmented into a number of principalities constantly warring against or allying with one another.[17]

In the subsequent "Age of Disintegration," as it is sometimes referred to, the emphasis of Tibet's foreign relations shifted from China to India and Nepal, whence came fresh and strong impulses to stimulate the spiritual and cultural life of the country. A Buddhist revival, known to Tibetans as "the second (or later) spreading of the Law," gained momentum with the arrival in Tibet of accomplished Indian masters such as Atisha.

Great monasteries were built, especially for two new schools of Tibetan Buddhism, the Sakyapa and the Kagyupa. A new monastic aristocracy emerged to challenge the economic, social, and political monopoly of the feudal nobility.[18] This movement was more than a spiritual and intellectual renaissance: It reshaped Tibet's social, economic, and political infrastructure and even transformed the very character of the nation. The Tibetans' interest "turned away from political and military exploits and produced that strong feeling for religious and spiritual life which henceforth totally permeated the life of the people."[19]

In the south and the west, the Tibetans retreated or were forced back from their imperial borders to the confines of the Tibetan plateau, bounded by the Karakoram, the Kuen Lun, and the Himalayan ranges, never again to expand beyond those limits. Their fighting spirit and aggressiveness had been neutralized; indeed, as F. W. Thomas has remarked, "probably no religion is more potent than Buddhism in damping the fighting spirit."[20]

The Tang Dynasty of China survived the Nyatri Dynasty by a generation. By the time it fell in 907, China had recovered most of its territory from the Tibetans.[21] The fall of the Tang precipitated the Empire's disintegration, and control was lost over the western provinces of China bordering Tibet. A "no man's land" was created between China and Tibet, and governed by local chieftains.[22] Consequently, dealings between the two peoples, throughout the periods known in China as those of the Five Dynasties (907–960) and the Song Dynasty (960–1276), were limited to courtesies and skirmishes among the border tribes. Practically no exchanges took place between the Tibetan and Chinese governments.[23] The situation remained so until contacts were reestablished through the conquest of both countries by a third Central Asian power, the Mongols.

Chingis (1167–1227), having been elected Khan of all the Mongols in 1206, initiated a series of conquests "which eventually led to the creation of the greatest empire the world has ever known."[24] He subjugated the Tangut Empire (Chinese: Xixia; Tibetan: Mi-nyag) in 1207 and Korea in 1218, and then advanced against the Junchen (or Nuzhen) State of Jin, which had controlled North China since 1126. The latter State was conquered by his successor, Ogodei Khagan (1229–1241), in 1234. A year later Ogodei Khagan launched offensives to the west, toward Europe, and to the east into Song China, which was finally conquered by the Mongols in 1279.[25]

This expansion, in particular the conquest of Tangut, Tibet's northern neighbor, caused concern among the Tibetans, who thought it best to open friendly contacts with the Mongols. Although Tibetan chronicles record the submission to Chingis Khan of some Tibetan leaders as early as 1207, this traditional account of the establishment of Mongol supremacy is now disputed.[26] It has nevertheless been established that Prince Goden, Chingis Khan's grandson and the ruler of Kokonor, dispatched an expedition to Tibet in 1240 and summoned one of Tibet's leading religious hierarchs, Sakya Pandita (1182–1251), to his court. The Tibetan Lama of the powerful Sakya School of Tibetan Buddhism heeded the summons and, once arrived at Prince Goden's Court, introduced the Mongols to Buddhism and the Tibetan culture.[27]

In return for Sakya Pandita's loyalty, Prince Goden invested him with temporal authority over all of Tibet, which, at the time, was still predominantly disunited.[28] Although this investiture had little real impact, as neither Prince Goden nor Sakya Pandita could claim authority over all Mongols or all Tibetans respectively, it was significant in that it established a sui generis relationship known in Tibetan as the Chö-yön (spelt mChod-Yon), or "Priest-Patron," relationship. This relationship formed the basis for the future unique relation not only between the Yuan Emperors and the Tibetan Sakya Lamas but also, in more recent history, between the Manchu Emperors and the Dalai Lamas. The Fifth Dalai Lama in his chronicle later described this investiture as follows:

> This Tibet, country of snows, and the great Tibet, all of it,* by the order of 'Jam-dbyams Gong-ma-se chen-gan, the great King invested from heaven, was offered to the glorious Sa-skya-pa, and they [the Mongol Emperors and the hierarchs of the Sakya school] like the sun and the moon in the sky, jointly, were known the former as patrons and the latter as chaplains.[29]

More will be said about the Chö-yön relation in the following chapter. It suffices at present to draw attention to the personal nature of the relationship, underlined here by the fact that neither the Prince nor the

---

*Here Bod is considered distinct from Bod-chen—that is, Central Tibet from Greater Tibet.

Lama represented the supreme power of his country. In the later, more politically oriented Chö-yön relationships, the Patron typically was expected to provide military power to protect the Lama and his Teachings (or his Church) and, at times, even his temporal prerogatives, in return for the Lama's devotion to the religious needs of his Patron.[30]

In reality, only Kubilai Khagan (1259–1294) had been able to establish a real degree of authority over Tibet by the mid-thirteenth century, through Sakya Pandita's successor and nephew, Pagpa (1235–1280).[31] The Khagan became so devoted to his religious master that he bestowed upon him the title of State Preceptor (or "National Master"), and then Imperial Preceptor (Tibetan: Tishri, Chinese: Dishi), a title borne also by Pagpa's successors. Thus, Buddhism became the State religion in the whole eastern part of the Mongol Empire, and the Tibetan Sakya Lama became its highest spiritual authority.[32] In return for the title bestowed upon him, the Lama provided the legitimation required by the "barbarian" Mongol conquerors in order to rule over China and their world Empire, thereby creating a unique interdependent relationship between the Mongol Emperors and the Tibetans.[33] Tishri Pagpa developed a theory of dual temporal and religious responsibility by which the Emperor was the supreme temporal sovereign, ruling for the benefit of all sentient beings, whereas the Tibetan Lama was the supreme spiritual ruler and sovereign in all religious matters. Each was dependent on the other in the Empire's dual order.[34] By this theory, the Mongol emperors were to be regarded as the legitimate successors of the line of Buddhist Universal Emperors, not of a Chinese dynasty. Thus Chingis Khan and Kubilai Khagan were ranked among the Chakravartirajas of India, the holy Tibetan kings, and the mythical Mahasamadhi. This, and the sacralization conferred upon the Imperial family by the Tibetan Lamas, provided the Mongol rulers with a sacral kingship that served to legitimize their dominion not only over Mongolia, Tibet, and China, but over the entire world.[35]

In addition to his spiritual role, the Tishri had been granted by the Emperor, as Sakya Pandita had been earlier, temporal rule over all of Tibet (comprising the three regions (chol-kha) of U and Tsang (or U-Tsang), Kham, and Amdo. He ruled Tibet through an office for Buddhist and Tibetan affairs (the Ministry for the Spread of Government, Xuan Zheng Yuan) and a Ponchen (Great Minister) entrusted with the administration of civil and military affairs.[36]

Throughout its domination by the Mongols, Tibet remained a unique part of the Empire and was never fully integrated into it. Thus, for example, licensed border markets continued to exist for trade between China and Tibet, as they existed nowhere in Yuan China.[37] Tibet regained its actual independence from the Mongols by 1350, under the lay myriarch Changchub Gyaltsen (1350–1364), who effectively established himself as ruler of a newly unified and centralized Tibet,[38] thus leaving only a nominal bond between him and the person of the Mongol Emperor.

Kubilai's victory over Song China in 1279 had marked the end of independent China. For eighty-nine years, China was a part of the Eastern

Mongol Empire, which comprised at one time or another the whole of Mongolia, Tibet, China, parts of Korea, and Siberia (from the Amur estuary to the Irtych), and portions of Annam and Upper Burma. The Chinese overthrew the alien Yuan Dynasty and regained their independence in 1368.[39]

Tibet had come under Kubilai Khagan's domination before his conquest of China; it had also regained its actual independence before China did. The Mongol subjugations of Tibet and China were therefore unrelated. The Mongol-Tibetan relationship was, moreover, an expression of a racial, cultural, and, above all, religious affinity between the two peoples—an affinity that neither shared with the Chinese. That bond remained even after the fall of the Yuan Dynasty and has been a determining factor in Central Asian politics ever since.

From Secular Nationalism
Toward Theocratic Rule: The Dalai Lamas

In freeing Tibet from Mongol domination, Changchub Gyaltsen also terminated the Sakya hegemony by starting a hereditary, predominantly secular rule, inspired by a desire to restore to Tibet the glories of its Imperial Age. He replaced the system of administration introduced by the Mongols with a new and distinctly Tibetan one, enacted a code of law by which justice would be administered in Tibet well into the twentieth century, and promoted the revival of national culture and traditions. His was, in G. Tucci's words, "a national claim and a statement of independence."[40]

The Chinese, who under the leadership of Zhu Yuanzhang overthrew and expelled the Mongols from their country a couple of decades later, also initiated a nationalistic renaissance of sorts. Confucian tradition once again predominated at the Imperial Court, and with the exception of a few emperors, the Ming did not display the preference for Buddhism that characterized the Yuan Court.[41]

Once established in China, the Ming did not take over the Mongol Empire in its entirety and showed little interest in Tibet.[42] The first Emperor, Tai Zu (formerly Zhu Yuanzhang), initially did attempt to revive some of the connections that had existed between the Yuan Court and local Tibetan ecclesiastic and lay rulers. The Ming Shi has recorded the following:

In the beginning of the Hung Wu [1368] T'ai tsu, fearing the disturbances [caused by] Tibet in the T'ang's times [might be repeated], decided to put these matters in order. Conforming to their customs, he made use of the monks and their disciples to educate them and then guide them towards good. He also sent envoys with the order that they should submit. Moreover he arranged that Hsu Yunte, Yuan Wai-lang of the provincial government of Shen-si, should go into that country, and he ordered that those who were invested with old offices conferred upon them by the Yuan, should come to court and be [again] confirmed in their posts.[43]

In reality, nothing came of this attempt by the Chinese to revert to the rights and privileges of their former Mongol conquerors, and Ming Emperors were content to maintain friendly relations and exchange diplomatic missions with Tibetan rulers. True to Confucian interpretation of relations with foreigners, Sino-Tibetan contacts were nevertheless rendered later in terms of tributary relations by Chinese court historians. Thus, the numerous economically motivated Tibetan missions to the Ming Court are referred to as "tributary missions" in the *Ming Shih*.[44] In fact, most missions were prompted by China's continuous, at times urgent, need for horses. As Chinese armies were still fighting the Mongols in the north, the Mongol horse markets were closed to them; as a result, it was the Tibetans who supplied them with horses.[45]

While they maintained friendly relations with the Ming, the Tibetans, in particular religious leaders, continued to have ties with the Mongolian ruling families who often patronized them. Tibet had extensive diplomatic and trade relations with the Kingdoms of Nepal and Kashmir and was at times engaged in armed confrontation with them.[46] Thus, Tibet carried on active religious, diplomatic, and trade relations with all its neighbors.

In Central Asia, it is difficult, if not impossible, to draw the line between religion and politics. In Tibet, the influence of Buddhism and its institutions was pervasive and blurred all distinction between the two. The founding by the religious reformer Tsonkapa (1357-1419) of a new Tibetan Buddhist school, the Gelugpa, was a religious reformation[47] and not a political movement. Nevertheless, the Gelugpa quickly became a strong political force that challenged and ultimately replaced the most powerful school of the time, the Kagyupa.

In the space of a few years, the "yellow church," as the Gelugpa came to be called, extended all over the central Tibetan district of U, where Tibet's largest and most powerful monasteries, Ganden, Drepung, and Sera, were founded.

When Tsonkapa's principal disciple, Gedun Trupa (1391-1474), died, he was believed to have reincarnated in a newborn child, Gedun Gyatso (1475-1542). Gedun Trupa and Gedun Gyatso were posthumously considered to be the First and Second Dalai Lamas respectively, and the forerunners of Tibet's supreme spiritual and temporal rulers.[48]

The discovery of Gedun Trupa's rebirth and of all his subsequent rebirths as Dalai Lama was based on the belief that human beings who have attained a very high degree of enlightenment can reincarnate voluntarily and out of compassion, in order to help all living beings on their path to final liberation. The Dalai Lama was furthermore recognized to be the embodiment of Chenrezig (the Bodhisattva or emanation of compassion), and the protector of Tibet.

The Dalai Lama's next incarnation, Sonam Gyatso (1534-1588), traveled to the Mongol Court of Altan Khan (1543-1583) and set in motion the conversion of the Mongols.[49] It was Altan Khan who, translating the incarnate Lama's name "Gyatso" (meaning "ocean" in Tibetan) into the

Mongolian language, called him "Dalai" (or *Tale*) for the first time. As the Dalai Lama became his spiritual teacher, the *Chö-yön* relationship was once again established between a Tibetan Lama and a Mongol ruler.[50] To this day, Mongolians are among the most devout followers of the Gelugpa and the Dalai Lama.

Recognizing the growing influence of Tsonkapa, the Chinese Emperor Yongle invited him to his court. Tsonkapa declined, but at the Emperor's insistence he sent one of his students and accepted an offer of patronage.[51] Tibetan chroniclers recorded the Chinese Emperor's embassies sent to honor the Dalai Lama, and Chinese historians acknowledged in the *Ming Shi* the Lama's authority over the "foreigners of the western countries."[52] It was with the Mongols, however, that the Gelugpas chose to associate themselves closely.

Once again, Mongol-Tibetan ties assumed political significance. The bond between the two peoples was sealed firmly when the Fourth Dalai Lama, Yonten Gyatso (1589–1617), was discovered to have been reborn in Altan Khan's own family, as his great-grandson.[53] The Mongols then helped the Fifth Dalai Lama to attain supreme religious and political power in Tibet and thereby changed the course of Central Asian history.

2

Government by Dalai Lama: Mongol, Manchu, and Gorkha Intervention

A study of the seventeenth and eighteenth centuries is crucial to an understanding of later relations between the Tibetans and the Chinese, for it is primarily on the evolution of Tibetan-Manchu relations of this period that the People's Republic of China bases its claims to Tibet.

The period is marked, on the one hand, by the emergence of the strong unifying force of the Dalai Lama in Tibet and, on the other, by the establishment of a degree of Manchu authority there. The dominant theme of the time, however, was the conflict between the Manchu Empire and Mongol tribes striving to recreate an empire of their own.

The Dalai Lama's Supremacy

Although the successive Dalai Lamas had acquired an important religious authority in Tibet and among the Mongols by the end of the sixteenth century, it was not until the rise to power of the fifth incarnation, Ngawang Lobsang Gyatso (1617–1682), that the Dalai Lama came to wield uncontested supreme spiritual and temporal power in Tibet.[1]

The Great Fifth, as he is usually remembered, called upon his Qoshot Mongol Patron, Gushri Khan, to intervene on his behalf in the religious and regional power struggle in which Tibet was immersed.[2] Fulfilling the Patron's duty, Gushri Khan advanced into Tibet and, after protracted fighting, defeated the rival Tsang armies and presented the whole of Tibet to the Dalai Lama in 1642.[3] The Chö-yön relationship could once again be applied to the temporal governance of Tibet.

The Great Fifth ruled both as the sole sovereign of a unified and independent State of Tibet and as the spiritual head of the dominant State religion, until his retirement in 1679.[4] In order not to have to concern himself directly with the administration of the country, the Dalai Lama created the office of Regent, or Desi (sDe-srid or sDe-pa), to administer in his name. As the Qoshot Khan continued to perform the function of protecting the Dalai Lama, he retained control over the armed forces and was granted, by the Dalai Lama, the title of Chökyi Gyalpo (King-according-to-the-Faith).[5] His inferiority in status vis-à-vis the Dalai Lama, however, was never questioned. In fact, the Dalai Lama's position was unparalleled by any ruler before him since the great tsanpos of the Imperial Age. His prestige and power was recognized far beyond Tibet's borders—by the Manchu Emperor, the Mongolian Khans and Princes, and the rulers of Ladakh, Nepal, India, Bhutan, and Sikkim.[6]

When China's Ming Dynasty was overthrown in 1644, that country was once again invaded and conquered, this time by the Manchus from the North, who established the Qing Dynasty (1644–1912).[7]

Much confusion has resulted from the careless and, at times, intentional practice of calling the Qing Empire Chinese, when, as Owen Lattimore rightly points out, "what existed in fact was a Manchu Empire, of which China formed only one part."[8] The distinction was certainly made at the time: The Emperors either appointed Manchus to all commanding military and bureaucratic positions or set them alongside Chinese officials, and intermarriage between the two peoples was prohibited. These Manchu rulers were as foreign in China as the Mongols of the earlier Yuan Dynasty had been, and they were regarded and resented by the Chinese as alien conquerors. The anti-Manchu feeling in China, always latent, intensified near the end of the nineteenth century and ultimately found expression in the 1911 Revolution, when the Chinese overthrew the Qing to set up their own native regime.[9]

The first official contact with the Tibetans was initiated in 1693 by the Manchu Emperor Tai Zong, who invited the Dalai Lama to Mukden, his capital.[10] The Dalai Lama, unable to accept the invitation personally, sent envoys to the Manchu Court and accepted Tai Zong's offer to patronize him and his church. The Emperor received the Dalai Lama's delegation with exceptionally high honors and loaded it with gifts, in a display of respect.[11]

In 1644, Tai Zong's successor, Shunzhi (1644–1661), became ruler of the empire, which now included China.[12] He also invited the Dalai Lama to his court, which had been moved to Beijing. This time the Tibetan ruler did accept the invitation,[13] and, as a result of the visit that took place in 1653, a close relationship developed between the two sovereigns.

The reception accorded to the Dalai Lama by the Emperor and the meetings of the two men have been recorded in Tibetan as well as Chinese sources.[14] Tibetan sources tend to emphasize the religious significance, whereas Chinese documents are primarily concerned with the protocol of the meetings. The protocol observed on the occasion of these meetings is significant given the importance accorded it by the Imperial Court. It is therefore indicative of the state of Manchu-Tibetan relations at the time that, in an uncommon gesture, the Emperor traveled outside Beijing to receive the Dalai Lama; that he descended from his throne and walked 20 yards to greet his guest at their first meeting; and that both sovereigns seated themselves at the same time and drank tea together.[15]

W.W. Rockhill, an American scholar and diplomat in China, has concluded that

> [The Dalai Lama] had been treated with all the ceremony which could have been accorded to any independent sovereign, and nothing can be found in Chinese works to indicate that he was looked upon in any other light; at this period of China's relations with Tibet, the temporal power of the Lama backed by the arms of Gushri Khan and the devotion of all Mongolia, was not a thing for the Emperor of China to question.[16]

Indeed, it is evident from these accounts that the Fifth Dalai Lama and the Shunzhi Emperor respected each other as sovereigns over their own territories and subjects.[17]

As a mark of mutual respect, the Manchu Emperor and the Dalai Lama bestowed upon each other unprecedented high titles, which reaffirmed the *Chö-yön* relationship established a decade earlier.[18] As the *Chö-yön* remained the basis for Tibetan-Manchu relations throughout the Qing Dynasty, its nature should be clarified. A *Chö-yön* relationship first came into being between the Sakya Lamas and the Mongol Khans—later Yuan Emperors— in the thirteenth and fourteenth centuries. The Ming Emperors chose to patronize the Karmapa Lamas, whereas Altan Khan and the Manchu Emperors patronized the Dalai Lamas of the Gelugpa.[19]

Two principal constitutive elements make up the *Chö-yön*: The first is evident from the term itself: *Chö-yön (mChod-yon)* is a contraction of (a) *Chö-ne (mChod-gnas)*, meaning "the object worthy of religious offering"— that is, a deity, *Lha*, a Bodhisattva, an Arhat, and so on, or a Buddhist saint or sage, *Jetsun (rJe-btsum)*; and (b) *Yön-daq (Yon-bDaq)*, meaning "the dispenser of offerings to a religious person or object"—that is, a lay person manifesting his piety by making religious offerings to the object of his worship.

Thus, the first element is that of the Lama as *Chö-ne*, the object of worship and offerings, and the respective Khans and Emperors as *Yön-daq*, the Patron, the worshipper, and the giver-of-alms.

The second element is that of protection: The Patron in the *Chö-yön* relation is bound to protect his Priest and Spiritual Teacher from the "enemies of the Faith" or those of his Teaching. The Lama, in turn, sees to the spiritual well-being of the Patron and his subjects, and he prays and conducts religious services for their benefit. That such protection did not imply the superiority of the Protector over the protected (as characterized in European medieval relationships) is obvious from the fact that the protected was, above all, the object of worship. It is also evidenced by the fact that the protected was "entitled, as of right, to call on the assistance, including the military services, of his Protector; and that the Protector was obliged, as of duty, to provide these services."[20]

From this brief survey it is plain that the religious *Chö-yön* relationship cannot be categorized or defined adequately in current international legal terms and must be regarded as a *sui generis* relationship. At the same time, recognition of the Chö-yön relationship as a religious one does not justify overlooking its political implications: Just as Gushri Khan's "protection" had helped the Dalai Lama to secure the position of uncontested sovereign of Tibet, Manchu Patrons later also intervened in the name of the Chö-yön relationship to safeguard political interests.

The Manchu Emperor Tai Zong and all his successors were recognized by the Dalai Lamas as the incarnation of the Bodhisattva Manjushri, one of the most important Bodhisattvas in Buddhism (he is the embodiment of the intellect of the Buddha, just as Chenrezig [Avalokiteshvara] embodies his compassion). Although this recognition did not affect the Priest-Patron relation, the respect shown for the Manchu Emperors by the deeply religious Tibetans in the two-and-one-half centuries that followed must largely be attributed to it.[21]

From Chinese records it is clear that beyond the religious significance of the meeting between the Dalai Lama and the Shunzhi Emperor, the meeting was especially important in view of the Emperor's concern for the Mongol menace on the Empire's northern and western borders. The grand reception accorded to the Dalai Lama was therefore as much a reflection of his unsurpassed authority over the Mongols as a token of respect for the Tibetan sovereign and spiritual master.[22]

The fear of the Mongolians was a determining factor in Manchu foreign policy throughout the seventeenth and the greater part of the eighteenth centuries. The effort to contain the expanding Empire of the Dzungar Mongols (or Kalmucks), in particular, underscored the importance to the Manchus of maintaining close relations with the Dalai Lama. This policy proved beneficial, for the Dalai Lama used his authority on a number of occasions to quell or prevent the outbreak of conflicts among the Mongols and between them and the Manchus. For a period of time, the Qing Emperor and the Dalai Lama pursued a joint policy for preserving the peace among the Mongols and containing Dzungar expansion. The Dalai Lama, however, turned down the Emperor's request for military support against the anti-Manchu rebels in Yunnan, thereby showing that their policies did not necessarily coincide on other fronts.[23]

During the last years of his life, the Dalai Lama left the administration of the country to his able and trusted Depa, Sangye Gyatso (1679–1703), and retired in meditation. The Great Fifth had successfully rebuilt a strong and united Tibet. His personal and religious power and influence stretched far beyond the confines of his country, and Tibet gained a commanding, if not controlling, influence over Central Asian affairs.

By concealing the Dalai Lama's death from the Manchus and Mongols for some fifteen years, Sangye Gyatso was able to pursue the active foreign policy of his late sovereign using the latter's ongoing prestige.[24] To the north, he maintained a degree of authority over the Mongols. To the west, he waged war with Ladakh in 1681. In 1684 he concluded the peace treaty of Tingmosgang,[25] which permanently fixed the borders and regulated trade between Tibet and Ladakh. To the south, a series of conflicts broke out with Bhutan that were fought with varying degrees of success. Sangye Gyatso maintained diplomatic relations with other neighboring countries as well and received embassies in Lhasa from rulers in Sikkim, India, and Nepal.[26]

Manchu Intervention in Tibet

A new phase in Tibetan-Manchu relations set in when, in 1720, Manchu armies entered Lhasa. The Imperial troops came both as liberators to expel the Dzungar Mongols, who had invaded and occupied Tibet three years earlier, and as protectors of the Seventh Dalai Lama, whom they escorted to Lhasa. But along with the armies, Imperial officials arrived in the capital to reorganize the administration of Tibet and to establish some form of Imperial supervision in order to curb Dzungar activity.

Tibet had been in political turmoil since the turn of the century. To the Manchus, Depa Sangye Gyatso's apparent ties with the Dzungar leaders, Galdan and Tsewang Rabten, were too close for comfort.[27] Thus, when the Qoshot Mongol Lhazang Khan (1703–1717), who had become the Chögyal of Tibet, successfully carried out a coup d'état against the Depa, the Emperor was pleased.[28] Not only was the Depa executed, but the young Sixth Dalai Lama, Tsangyang Gyatso (1683–1706), was exiled by the Khan with help from his Manchu allies, and was possibly even executed by them.[29]

Lhazang Khan proceeded to declare his own protege, Ngawang Yeshe Gyatso, to be the true Dalai Lama, arguing that the Sixth Dalai Lama's alleged misconduct proved that he no longer embodied the true spirit of the Dalai Lama.[30] The Manchu Emperor Kangxi favored this new regime, which was friendly to his interests, and sent an experienced administrator to help the Khan strengthen his position in Tibet.[31]

Both Lhazang Khan and Kangxi had committed a serious error, one proven disastrous each time it has been repeated: They attacked the Dalai Lama himself and in doing so incurred the condemnation of the whole Tibetan people. Few issues can arouse such unity and solidarity among Tibetans as an assault on the Dalai Lama. Disregarding the Khan's declaration and also the Emperor's edict ordering obeisance to the new puppet Dalai Lama, the Tibetans soon found a child whom they considered to be the true reincarnation of the deceased Sixth Dalai Lama. The Emperor quickly saw to it that the child, born in Litang near the Chinese border, was taken to Kumbum in Amdo, where he could be interned under Imperial sur-veillance.[32]

The Dzungars, taking advantage of the Tibetans' growing hatred for Lhazang Khan, particularly among the powerful clergy, set out to break the influence the Manchus had gained in Tibet through the Khan and to take power. Their invasion of Lhasa in 1717 was made particularly easy by the clergy's cooperation, which the Dzungars had secured by announcing that they would bring the true Seventh Dalai Lama with them from Kumbum. Once it became clear that the Dzungars were in no position to fulfill that promise, the clergy withdrew its support. Moreover, the invading armies proceeded to commit some of the worst plundering and destruction Lhasa had ever known.[33] By 1720, Tibetan troops under the leadership of Polhanas had regained control over most of the country. When the Manchu armies— whose help Polhanas had requested—arrived in Tibet, they came in time only to help consolidate the position the Tibetan leader had already secured. At the same time, the anticipation of their intervention probably had a decisive impact on Polhanas's success.[34]

The Imperial Armies brought with them the Seventh Dalai Lama, Kelsang Gyatso (1708-1757), whom the Emperor now saw fit to use as a pawn in his strategy. After keeping him interned in Kumbum for over ten years and recognizing Lhazang Khan's usurper, the Emperor now recognized Kelsang Gyatso to be the true Dalai Lama. He thus counterbalanced his earlier malfeasance and won the overwhelming support of the Tibetans and Mongolians for fulfilling his duty as Patron and Protector in reuniting the Dalai Lama with his people and restoring to him his rightful position in Tibet.[35]

The first Manchu intervention was not so much a conquest of Tibet as a response to the Tibetan need for help in overthrowing the Dzungar occupation. In effect, the Emperor at this stage was doing no more than fulfilling the obligation that arose out of the *Chö-yön* relationship.[36]

The purpose of the Manchu intervention in helping Polhanas was to oust the Dzungars from Tibet and to eliminate all remnants of their rule. To that end, the commanding officers of the Imperial troops installed a provisional administration in Lhasa with the Tibetans and the Mongols.[37] This joint administration held office until the spring of 1721, when it was replaced by a regular government formed under the active guidance of the Manchu officers.

The new government was led by a Council of Ministers, or Kalons, which operated under the supervision of an Imperial representative, who himself had no administrative powers.[38] Furthermore, a small garrison under the representative's command was stationed at Lhasa, and other such garrisons remained in the east and northwest of the country.[39] The Dalai Lama, obviously too young to exercise power, was—at least initially—left with little more than a ceremonial role, notwithstanding the Emperor's recognition of his temporal sovereignty. He nonetheless commanded the unquestioned highest respect of the Imperial representatives and the numerous envoys sent to honor him by the Nepalese, Bhutanese, Sikkimese, and, of course, the Mongolian rulers.[40]

The Tibetan-Manchu Relationship Takes Shape

Following the death of the Kangxi Emperor, his successor, Yong Zheng (1723-1735), withdrew virtually all remaining Imperial troops from Tibet, as part of a general policy of retrenchment. At the same time, he replaced his military representative with a civilian adviser. These changes marked an end to the first short period of direct and close Manchu involvement in the Tibetan administration.[41]

This is not to say that the Emperor no longer played a role. In some instances, particularly where the defense of Tibet against possible Dzungar threats was concerned, he even issued direct orders to Tibetan ministers.[42] In addition, following a rebellion of some Kokonor Mongol chiefs, the Emperor established control over the Kokonor region in the northeastern province of Amdo, which he renamed Qinghai.[43]

The relative stability in Tibet did not last long. Political rivalry led to a short civil war (1727-1728), from which Polhanas emerged victorious.[44] The Emperor's role during the war was both dubious and limited. To both parties in the conflict, who appealed to him for aid (by now the Tibetan custom of asking foreign rulers for assistance in their internal power struggles seems to have been well established), he gave the impression that he supported them and would send help. As a result, continuation of the conflict was encouraged and mediated settlement was discouraged. When the Emperor did finally send troops, they typically arrived in Lhasa only in time to congratulate Polhanas on his victory and to severely punish the leaders of the vanquished party.[45]

Yong Zheng issued an edict supporting Polhanas and approving the government he had formed. The Emperor, fearing the possible disturbing influence of the Dalai Lama—and especially that of his father, who had sided with the vanquished faction—succeeded in having both exiled from Lhasa to Kham in east Tibet. In 1728, two Manchu representatives were once again left behind in Lhasa with a military escort. These were the first Imperial Residents in Tibet, commonly called by their Manchu title of "Amban."[46] The function of the Ambans was to report to their Emperor on events in Tibet and to supervise its defense, but not to participate in the government of Tibet.[47]

As if to complete a now almost familiar cycle, this veritable Manchu supremacy was reduced to a matter of form by 1735. Once Polhanas had succeeded in inspiring sufficient confidence at the Imperial Court, the Amban's escort was reduced to only five hundred men and the Dalai Lama was allowed to return to Lhasa two years later in 1735. As the Dalai Lama was to refrain from all political activity, his return did not alter Polhanas' full power.[48]

Luciano Petech characterizes the power distribution in Tibet at this time as follows: "The power of P'o-lha-nas was absolute, the authority of the Dalai Lama was in abeyance, the supervision by the Chinese [Manchus] nominal only. Truly P'o-lha-nas was a king, the first Tibetan king after the tragic end of the last gTsan ruler in 1642."[49] Manchu and Chinese sources as well as European missionary accounts supported this conclusion. A document in the *Gao Zong Shilu*, for example, states that "the Dalai Lama presides over Buddhism in the western countries, while P'o-lha-nas governs the Tibetan people."[50]

The situation changed once again, dramatically, following Polhanas's death in 1747. His son and successor, Gyume Namgyal (1747-1750), imprudently attempted to throw off even this token Manchu authority, and presumably hoped for Dzungar support.[51] The Manchus were understandably alarmed, and the Ambans assassinated the Tibetan ruler. The disorder that followed, which led to the lynching of the Ambans, was quickly put to an end by the Dalai Lama's personal intervention. He took over the reins of government as the country's only undisputed leader, abolished the secular government, and drew all power to himself.[52]

The Emperor had no choice but to recognize the supreme position the Dalai Lama had recovered—a position similar to that assumed by the Great Fifth a century earlier. Upon the arrival of the new Ambans, Tibet's administration was once again reorganized along the lines suggested by the Dalai Lama. The Council of Ministers, the Kashag, was reinstated to carry out the administration of the government, and the Seventh Dalai Lama was again referred to as "Lord of Tibet." As in the time of the Fifth Dalai Lama, the Ministers were made to obey him as his subordinates. An Imperial edict confirming these governmental changes and describing the extensive powers of the Dalai Lama amounted to a recognition by the Manchu Court of the Dalai Lama's newly recovered temporal sovereignty.[53]

The Ambans' powers also increased. Aside from commanding the garrison and directing the postal services, these Manchu officials were now made advisers to the Kashag. Although they did not interfere directly in the administration of government, their new role gave the Ambans broad supervisory authority and served as a certain reminder of the Patron's "protection" and perhaps supremacy.[54]

A characteristic of the foreign relations of Tibet throughout this period was its missionary aspect. Tibetan colonization and missionary activities in Bhutan, Sikkim, Nepal, and Ladakh were carried out by all of the major schools of Tibetan Buddhism.[55] On numerous occasions Tibetan armies intervened in Bhutan.[56] Relations with Tibet's other neighbors were generally good, and the rulers of Sikkim, Nepal, India, and Ladakh continued to send embassies to Lhasa to pay their respects to the Dalai Lamas and their Regents (*Gyaltsab*).[57] It is significant that in all these foreign relations, the Manchu Emperor and his Ambans had no part whatsoever, for the Manchus concerned themselves only with Tibetan-Mongol relations.

For nearly 150 years following the death of the Seventh Dalai Lama in 1757, until the assumption of full temporal power by the Thirteenth incarnation in 1895, Tibet was ruled almost uninterruptedly by successive Regents because of the Dalai Lamas' premature deaths. The fate of these successive Dalai Lamas was probably not entirely accidental, for the Regents and Ambans might well have had a hand in these deaths. On at least one occasion, a Regent was found to have been involved.[58]

The interest of the Manchus in Tibet dwindled as a result of the final defeat and submission of the Dzungars in 1757. The last threat of the rise of a Mongol Empire on the Central Asian steppes was finally eliminated, and consequently little further attention was paid to Tibetan affairs. Furthermore, since the Patron was no longer called upon to protect his Priest, his role and influence diminished and was hardly felt in Tibet until the outbreak of war with Nepal, which precipitated yet another Imperial intervention forty years later.[59]

Conditions in Tibet and the state of Manchu-Tibetan relations in this period can best be understood through the reports of two British officers sent to Tibet as envoys of the Governor General of Bengal, Warren Hastings (1772-1785). The first of these envoys, George Bogle, spent six months at the court of the Panchen Lama, Palden Yeshe, in 1774.[60]

The Panchen Lama or Tashi Lama, as he is also called, a Gelugpa Lama, is generally regarded as the most important clerical authority in Tibet after the Dalai Lama. He is the abbot of the Tashi Lhunpo monastery near the major southern city of Shigatse, and at one time autonomously governed the immediate region around this city.[61]

At the time of Bogle's visit, Tibet was ruled by the Regent, Demo Tulku (1757-1777). However, since the Seventh Dalai Lama's death, the Third Panchen Lama was considered by the people to be the foremost leader in both spiritual and worldly affairs. His influence and power proceeded chiefly from the veneration he inspired by his remarkable character and exceptional abilities. The Qianlong Emperor (1736-1796), who was a religious man, also held the Panchen Lama in the highest esteem and consulted him frequently.[62]

Bogle reported that although the Manchu Emperor's temporal supremacy was reluctantly acknowledged by many Tibetans, the internal administration of Tibet was entirely in the hands of the Tibetans themselves and a Manchu presence was felt only in Lhasa, where the Ambans were stationed with an escort of approximately 1,000 men. The Panchen Lama himself admitted to Bogle that his country was subject to the Manchu Emperor. At the same time, he declined to concede that Tibet was completely dependent on the Qing Court and labored all his life to enhance the temporal authority of the Dalai Lama and his government and to restrict Manchu interference in the affairs of Tibet. During a visit to Beijing in 1780, the Lama in fact secured the Emperor's promise to further reduce the Manchu presence in Lhasa and fully restore sovereignty to the Dalai Lama. Nevertheless, when the Panchen Lama died a few months later, this promise was conveniently disregarded.[63]

Captain Samuel Turner was the second British envoy to the Panchen Lama's Court, in 1783. His observations were very similar to those of his predecessor. He believed that the Tibetans were intimidated by the influence of the Qing Court but asserted that they did not "bend under the immediate authority of that Court" and that "they were adverse to own any immediate dependence upon the Chinese."[64]

What emerges from the accounts of both envoys and from their correspondence with the Panchen Lama and the Regent is the existence of an apparently ill-defined relationship between the Manchu Court and the government in Lhasa. On the one hand, the Qing Emperor exercised a vague supremacy, which the Tibetan authorities acknowledged. In addition, some Ambans derived considerable influence in Lhasa from the Emperor's prestige. On the other hand, the Tibetans certainly did not consider themselves truly dependent on the emperor, nor did they submit directly to his authority. They jealously guarded against any interference in Tibet by the governance of the Ambans who, Bogle confirmed, "seldom interfere[d] in the management of the country."[65]

The Tibetan attitude was ambiguous, however, for the authorities in Lhasa were frequently prepared to invoke the guise of Manchu overlordship and the Amban's authority in their dealings with foreigners (especially the British and Nepalese) when it seemed advantageous for them to do so.[66] By this opportunistic attitude, which prevailed for over a century, Tibetans not only contributed to the subsequent confusion and misrepresentation of Tibet's status vis-à-vis the Qing Empire but, in effect, also attributed a role to the Emperor in their foreign relations even before the latter claimed it in 1793, following the Tibet-Nepal war.

The Gorkha Invasion
and the Last Manchu Intervention

The long-standing relations between Tibet and the Kingdoms of Nepal, particularly of Kathmandu, intensified in the early seventeenth century. This development was the result not only of increased trade but, more especially, of an arrangement whereby the Malla Newari rulers of Kathmandu minted coins for use as Tibetan currency.[67] Bilateral relations were formalized in a treaty concluded by representatives of the Dalai Lama and of Pratap Malla (1624–1674) of Kathmandu around 1645.[68] The significant clauses of the treaty secured for the Kathmandu Court the right to post a representative (*naya*) in Lhasa; it also permitted merchants to establish trading houses there and confirmed the right of Kathmandu to mint coins for Tibet. The treaty further guaranteed that all trade with India would be channeled through Kathmandu rather than other routes through Sikkim, Bhutan, or Towang.[69]

The ruler of the Nepalese kingdom of Gorkha, Prithvinarayan Shah (1743–1775), conquered Kathmandu and most of the other kingdoms constituting modern-day Nepal; by 1769 he had unified most of the country. Gorkha's expansionistic program, which aimed at total control of the Central Himalayas, brought that aggressive State in conflict with all of its neighboring countries, including Tibet.[70]

A serious problem arose out of disagreement over the value of coins which the Mallas had debased. It was fueled by the annoyance of both Prithvinarayan Shah and his successor Pratap Singh Shah (1775–1777) over the establishment of direct trade relations between Bengal and Tibet. Finally, Tibet's support for Sikkim in its war with Gorkha in 1775 brought Gorkha in direct conflict with Tibet.[71] When an attempt to patch up differences by concluding another treaty failed, the Gorkha armies invaded Tibet in 1788.[72] Fighting was severe, even after their occupation of Kuti, Kyrong, Jhunga, and Rongsar, but the invaders kept the upper hand. In an effort to ward off any Manchu intervention, the Tibetans negotiated a treaty with Nepal in 1789, the terms of which were humiliating. As Tibet did not abide by its provisions, hostilities were renewed late in 1791: The Gorkhas plundered the city of Shigatse and the Panchen Lama's monastery, Tashi Lhunpo.[73]

After much procrastination, the Qianlong Emperor sent a large army under Manchu General Fu Kangan to help Tibet drive the Nepalese back. Although he officially invoked his role as Protector or Patron, the Emperor admitted that the campaign was being undertaken in the interest of his own Dynasty's security, in order to maintain the Dalai Lama's status among the Mongols.[74]

The joint Tibetan-Manchu-Chinese army pushed the Gorkhas back to within a few miles of Kathmandu by the summer of 1792. A peace treaty between Nepal and Tibet, mediated by General Fu Kangan, was concluded that same year. It included the following terms:

1. Nepal and Tibet pledged to maintain fraternal relations and to refrain from engaging in hostilities, and agreed that future disputes would be submitted to the Amban in Lhasa for arbitration. In addition, the boundary between Nepal and Tibet would be demarcated by Imperial officials.

2. Nepal agreed to send a quinquennial mission to Beijing with gifts for the Emperor. The Imperial government agreed to bear the costs of this mission, to facilitate its travel, and to send gifts to the rulers of Nepal in return. (Nepalese documents refer to *sauqauli*, or "gifts," whereas Chinese sources refer to "tribute" where the Nepalese gifts are concerned.) Significantly, the "gifts" sent by the Emperor in return were more valuable.

3. The Emperor pledged to come to Nepal's assistance in the event of an attack by a foreign power. Nepal agreed to return the articles seized from Tashi Lhunpo monastery and to never again raise claims based upon either the 1789 Treaty or the coinage question.[75]

The 1792 Treaty represented the Manchus as the overlords, arbiters, and protectors of both Nepal and Tibet, a vision certainly held by the Qing Court at the height of the Manchus' imperial power. The Nepalese historian, Prem Uprety, rightly concludes that no one emerged victorious from this war.[76] The Tibetans suffered the greater defeat, however, for their dependence on the Manchus increased as a direct consequence of the war. For the Manchus, the cost of the expedition had been financially, politically, and militarily prohibitive. It was the fourth time in seventy-five years that the Qing Emperor had been called on to intervene in Tibet, and he was determined that this would be the last. He thus imposed important reforms on the administration of Tibet in order to bring the country's government, particularly the conduct of its foreign relations, under his direct supervision.[77]

Among the most significant reforms was the authority given to the Ambans to take part, albeit in a limited way, in the administration of Tibet.

Tibetan officials were to submit all matters of importance to the Ambans, whose position was further enhanced by the requirement that the Dalai Lama and the Panchen Lama communicate with the Emperor indirectly through the Ambans. The latter were also required to control Tibet's foreign relations, trade, and defense. The new policy was to be implemented with the help of Imperial officials to be posted in Shigatse, Tingri, and Phari in the south, and in Chamdo and Draya in the east of Tibet.[78]

Another significant reform concerned the method of choosing the great incarnate lamas—namely, the leaders of the ecclesiastical hierarchy in Tibet and Mongolia, including the Dalai and Panchen Lamas. That selection had always been the responsibility of the high lamas and the government of Tibet, and it was carried out in accordance with prescribed religious regulations. The Imperial Edict invoked the Emperor's obligation "as Protector of the Yellow Church" (i.e., the Gelugpa) to protect that church from alleged corruption and nepotism, and prescribed the drawing of lots from a golden urn as the new selection procedure.[79] The reform did not give the Emperor any influence in the selection of incarnate lamas; on the face of it, nevertheless, the implications of such intervention in an important traditional religious process were potentially serious.[80]

In taking control of Tibet's foreign relations, the Manchus effectively imposed on Tibet a "forbidden land" policy, which closed the borders to most foreigners, especially the British and the Russians. The Tibetan authorities were led to believe by their Manchu Protector that Tibet and its religion would surely be endangered if foreigners were allowed to enter the country.[81] The Ambans had earlier shown concern over contacts that the Tibetans maintained with the British, but they were unsuccessful in putting a stop to them. Now, Tibetans were gradually being led to become xenophobes—a development that effectively closed the borders to almost all Westerners for a century. Ultimately, this reform was the only one actually fully carried out.[82]

On paper, the Imperial reforms represented an imporant loss of autonomy for the Tibetan government and the imposition of an unprecedented degree of control by any foreign power in Tibet. In reality, as two factors rendered these reforms with the exception of the "closed land" policy virtually ineffective, there was little increase in actual Imperial authority in 1793 and, in fact, even a decrease thereof soon after.[83] One factor concerned simply the difficulty with which Imperial orders were executed in distant Tibet— orders that were wholly dependent on the individual Amban's effectiveness. Following a few initial years of enthusiasm, the role of these often corrupt representatives dwindled fast and was eventually reduced to little more than a formality during the government of the Regent Tsemöling (1819–1844), a nearly absolute ruler. But the main reason for the ineffectiveness of the reforms was the drastic dynastic decline that set in shortly after this last successful foreign military campaign of the Qing Dynasty. After the death of the great Qianlong Emperor, "China entered upon one of the most ruinous centuries of her whole history."[84]

In Tibet, the decline of Imperial influence was steady and irreversible. After the initial zeal by Amban He Lin to make his presence felt, Manchu authority increasingly took on the character of a purely nominal supremacy. Thus, on the first occasion Tibetans had for selecting a new Dalai Lama, only twelve years after the Imperial reform was decreed, they did so in the traditional manner and disregarded the procedure prescribed by the Emperor.[85]

By the mid-nineteenth century, Manchu influence had ebbed to so low a point that the Tibetans could have expelled the Amban and other Manchus from Tibet had they agreed to do so. This did not happen until much later, however, because there were always powerful factions of the Tibetan nobility and religious hierarchy who chose to use the remaining link with the Imperial Court to their advantage. Moreover, though reluctant to recognize any Manchu authority in Tibet, government officials continued to invoke such authority in foreign dealings, especially with the British, when they considered that feigning inability to take responsibility might be to their immediate advantage.[86] Abbé Huc, a French missionary who traveled in Tibet and lived in Lhasa at the time, confirms this assessment of Manchu authority in Tibet. He concluded, for example, that the Amban, whom he regarded as a mere ambassador, no longer held any real authority. He further observed that the Tibetan Ministers, the Kalons, would not tolerate any interference in Tibetan affairs by the Manchus.

That having been said, we must recognize that the person of the Emperor was always held in high esteem by the Tibetans, particularly because they considered him to be a reincarnation of the Bodhisattva Manjushri. Thus his decision, and to some extent those of his representative, the Amban, must still have carried some weight in Lhasa. Abbé Huc made an interesting observation about the Amban's "permanent embassy" whose real purpose, he noted, was solely "to flatter the religious beliefs of the Mongols and to rally the people behind the reigning dynasty by leading them to believe that the Beijing government was a devout believer in the deity of the Bouddha-La [i.e. the Dalai Lama]."[87]

The Manchu's Abandonment of Their Protective Role and Nepal's Challenge to It

The total abandonment of the Qing Emperor's role as Protector of the Dalai Lama, his Teaching (or church), and his country—and therefore of the very essence of the relationship that had existed between the Manchu Court and Tibet—was indisputable by the middle of the nineteenth century. The Emperor, preoccupied with encroachments of the Western imperialist powers in China—leading to the devastating Anglo-Chinese war of 1840— and with the internal threats to his Empire "tottering under a corrupt regime," was unable to send assistance to Tibet when it was again attacked.

In 1842, Raja Gulab Singh of Jammu, after conquering Ladakh, sent his Dogra troops under General Zorawar Singh across the borders into Western

Tibet. They were eventually driven back by the Tibetans with no foreign assistance whatsoever,[88] and a peace treaty was concluded in the form of two documents exchanged by the Dogra and Tibetan Plenipotentiaries on September 17 and 20, respectively.[89] Ten years later, a new treaty was signed between Tibet and Kashmir, reaffirming the boundaries between Tibet and Ladakh and regulating mutual trade.[90]

When the Gorkhas of Nepal once again invaded Tibet in 1854, the Emperor made no move to come to the assistance of Tibet. Tibet-Nepal relations normalized after the 1792 war, but they were strained on occasion. Both countries, on such occasions, had used the "good offices" of a neutral party, the Amban, to mediate—not arbitrate—when disputes arose.[91] Tibet's apparent weakness and the Qing Empire's own struggle for survival prompted Jung Bahadur Rana, the powerful Prime Minister of Nepal, to go to war with Tibet over some of the same claims that had led to the previous war (in particular, Nepal's claims to the border districts of Kuti and Kyrong). Domestic reasons also led Nepal's rulers to launch a foreign campaign, but most important was Jung Bahadur Rana's ambition to replace the special position the Manchus enjoyed in Tibet by some form of Nepalese supremacy. Thus, the Nepalese suggested that once the tottering Manchu government was toppled, Nepal would help the Tibetans to expel the remaining Manchus and Chinese from Tibet.[92]

The war that broke out was fought exclusively by Nepalese and Tibetan troops, as no foreign assistance was available to either side. The British refused to help Nepal despite the latter's request for same,[93] and Manchu assistance to Tibet was never even contemplated. The war claimed an exceedingly high toll and ended in a military stalemate. Politically, however, the Nepalese emerged on top, and Jung Bahadur Rana secured numerous privileges for Nepal, including at least the nominal role of protector of Tibet.[94]

Nepal's stand regarding the future status of Tibet at the start of the negotiations was clear: It wanted total independence of Tibet from the Qing Empire, the payment of tribute to Nepal, and the acceptance of Nepal's protection. This position and Tibet's acceptance of it was reflected in a treaty signed by the two countries' plenipotentiaries in Kathmandu on March 24, 1856.[95]

At the insistence of the Amban, who was anxious to preserve for his Emperor some semblance of authority over Tibet—at least in the form of a face-saving declaration of respect—one of the treaty's clauses was modified, though not substantively.[96] Moreover, a preamble was added in which the parties to the treaty (Tibet and Nepal, or Gorkha) declared that "they have agreed to regard the Chinese Emperor as heretofore with respect."[97] The second clause of the treaty, which had simply held a promise by Nepal to help Tibet in the event of foreign attack, was now modified to read: "Gorkha and Tibet have been regarding the Great Emperor with respect. Tibet being the country of monasteries, hermits, and celibates, devoted to religion, the Gorkha Government have agreed henceforth to afford help and protection to it as far as they can if any foreign country attacks it."[98] This clause, it was felt, could be interpreted to each party's advantage; and the Manchus, who had pressed for the modification, probably saw in it not only a face-saver but also an exemption from Nepal's obligation to help Tibet, should the "foreign power" be either China or the Quing Empire.[99] The treaty also contained important stipulations whereby the Tibetan government agreed (1) to pay an annual sum of Rs. 10,000 to the Nepalese government; (2) not to levy customs duties on commodities imported by Nepalese subjects; (3) to permit the Nepalese government to raise the status of their *Vakil* (Ambassador) at Lhasa from a Newar to a Bahadar;[100] (4) to permit the Nepalese to establish shops in Lhasa for trading; and (5) to allow Nepal to exercise jurisdiction over its own subjects in Tibet. Nepal agreed to withdraw its troops from occupied territories, and the last clause provided for mutual extradition of criminals.

By the terms of the Tibet-Nepal Treaty, Nepal exacted a form of tribute from Tibet and assumed protection over it, thus replacing the Manchus to some extent. At the same time, the declaration of respect for the Emperor contained in the Preamble created the acceptable, and typically oriental, recognition of an almost mystical regard for the person of the Emperor— a respect that transcended, although it did not interfere with, the Tibet-Nepal relationship.

In practice, the extent of Nepal's new protective role was wholly insignificant. Only once in the decades that followed was its implementation ever suggested. In 1862, the Tibetan government applied to the Nepalese government for military assistance to crush a rebellion in Eastern Tibet. Although eager to comply by supplying troops, the Nepalese were ultimately asked only to lend a number of mountain guns.[101] By contrast, the economic and jurisdictional privileges secured by Nepal were implemented and led to an increased tension between the two countries that, in the latter part of the century, even brought them to the brink of war. The crises were nevertheless resolved peacefully. At times, the Amban was also asked to help resolve disputes by playing a mediating role.[102]

In practice, Tibet and Nepal functioned as independent States, maintaining direct diplomatic relations with each other on an equal, though not reciprocal, basis. It is noteworthy that when Kalon Shatra came to power and established a new government in Tibet in 1862, it was to the Nepalese Court that he turned for official recognition, and not to Beijing.[103] It was then that Tibet had the most intensive dealings with Nepal. Relations with the Manchus were reduced to ceremonial gestures. The Emperor, for example, sent presents and unsolicited titles when new Tibetan officials were appointed and a plaque when new monasteries or temples were built, as evidence of his patronage. The only remaining evidence of Manchu influence was the presence in Lhasa of the Amban along with his small escort of some 100 men, most of whom were born in Tibet of mixed parentage and had no real military duties to perform.[104] The Nepalese historian Uprety concludes that the "sweeping erosion" of this influence "had turned [the Emperor's] traditional suzerainty over Tibet into a constitutional myth."[105]

Indeed, the Manchu intervention in Tibetan affairs, which had started in 1720, came to a virtual end. Since the passing away of the Great Fifth Dalai Lama, the Tibetans had experienced Mongolian, Manchu, Gorkha, and even Dogra interventions in their country, in addition to frequent internal dissension. How these interventions affected the international status of Tibet will be discussed in a later chapter. We should note here, however, that all of these interventions were essentially short-lived, although the Manchus maintained a formal Chö-yön link with Tibet for over two centuries. Equally important, whatever supremacy the Manchus exercised over Tibet, they did so in a manner quite different and separate from that by which they ruled China. Accordingly, the statutes of the Imperial office in charge of Tibetan affairs, the Li Fan Yuan, reveal both that the Manchus certainly never combined the administration of China with that of their other dominions, and that "the Manchus by and large imposed special imperialistic organs of control upon the indigenous Tibetan bureaucracy leaving it largely intact and free in internal matters."[106]

By the time the Thirteenth Dalai Lama took over the reins of government in 1895, no Asian State could escape the attention of the Great Powers of Europe competing for influence and power. With the erosion of Manchu influence in Tibet, the interest of other empires increased, for a power vacuum could not exist in the very heart of Asia.

3

Tibet in the "Great Game"

In the late nineteenth and early twentieth century, Tibet became the unwilling object of contention among the three great empires of Asia: the Russian, British, and Manchu Empires. Their relations with Tibet were conditioned primarily by their ambitions and fears. Thus, Tibet was treated in much the same way as smaller countries are today by the demands of "superpower" rivalry.

Tibetan Isolationism: The Forbidden Land

Before the frontiers of Tibet were closed in 1793, the British Colonial Government of Bengal had established some contact with Tibetan authorities. The Panchen Lama, Palden Yeshe, initiated these contacts in 1774, when he wrote to the Governor of Bengal, Warren Hastings (1772–1785), urging him to cease hostilities against Bhutan. Hastings grasped at the opportunity offered, and, after withdrawing his troops from Bhutan, he sent a diplomatic good-will mission to the Lama in that year, and again in 1782.[1]

The British believed that trade with Tibet could be very beneficial to the East India Company. Existing trade, though limited, was profitable and provided a balance of payment in highly valued gold and silver, in the Company's favor. In addition, they hoped that contacts with the Panchen Lama might lead eventually to some access to the Qing Court in Beijing, with whom the British had no means of communicating directly.[2]

Although the missions of Bogle and Turner were well received by the Panchen Lama and his Regent (the Lama had died in 1780), nothing was secured beyond promises by the Panchen Lama and his court that they would encourage trade.[3] After Warren Hastings' departure from India in 1785, little was done to continue this active policy. It was under very changed circumstances that official interest in Tibet was revived almost a century later.

India's interest in developing trade with Tibet still persisted in the second half of the nineteenth century, but since the British victory in China in 1842, the Government of India had maintained direct contact with the Qing Court, where it had a diplomatic agent.[4]

Although the "forbidden land" policy was initiated and encouraged in Tibet by the Manchus, it presently became an essential element of Tibet's own foreign and defense policies.[5] The British were regarded with particular suspicion, after rumors of British help to the Gorkhas in the 1792 war spread in Tibet.[6] The treaties the British concluded with Nepal in 1792 and 1816 did little to dissipate this suspicion. In 1854 the British not only refused to assist Tibet against the Gorkha invaders from Nepal but, in fact, supplied the latter with arms and allowed them to pass through Indian territory to reach Tibet.[7]

The British had bound all the Himalayan States, most of which had close religious, commercial, and political ties with Lhasa, to the expanding British Empire by means of a series of wars, annexations, and agreements, and the Tibetans feared an imminent advance into Tibet.[8] The treaties of 1817 and 1861, whereby the British established their protectorate over Sikkim, provided them with direct access to the Tibetan border, on the shortest route to Lhasa; similar treaties with Gulab Singh of Lahore in 1846 and with Bhutan in 1865, as well as the earlier annexation of Assam in 1826, strengthened the British position south and west of Tibet.[9]

Lacking any access to the authorities in Tibet, and under the mistaken assumption that the Manchu government exercised effective authority in Tibet, the British government attempted half-heartedly to secure concessions from Beijing to open up Tibet to British trade.[10] From the Manchus' perspective, any European involvement in Tibet, so close to their borders, created the prospect of yet another base from which the British, Russians, or French might approach their disintegrating empire. They were therefore not eager to help the British gain rights or concessions in Tibet. Nevertheless, given the weak position in which the Qing Court found itself after the disastrous Opium war and the subsequent pressure caused by Western imperialist encroachment in China, concessions were made.

In 1876, the governments of Great Britain and the Qing Empire concluded the treaty known as the Chefoo Convention, to which was added a special article, wholly unrelated to the subject of the treaty. This article granted the British the right to send a mission of exploration to Tibet, for which they would be issued the necessary passports.[11] The inclusion of this article in the treaty was but the forerunner of a series of treaties concerning Tibet concluded between these two governments. It demonstrated, first, that neither the British government nor the Qing Court considered Tibet to form part of the Qing Empire itself, for, by the Treaty of Tien-tsin (Tianjin) of 1858, British subjects were already authorized to travel throughout the Emperor's dominions under passports issued by their consuls and counter-signed by the local authorities.[12] In fact, neither that treaty nor any of the other treaties concluded with the Imperial government in Beijing was ever considered applicable in Tibet.[13] Second, this treaty clause implied British recognition of an undefined authority of the Imperial government over Tibet. This recognition went so far as to include the right of the Emperor to make treaties on behalf of Tibet with regard to that country's foreign affairs. On the other hand, it clearly did not include the applicability to Tibet of treaties concluded for the empire as a whole.

No attempt was made to implement the special article in the Chefoo Convention until 1885, when a British expedition to Tibet was first seriously contemplated. The Tibetan government was alarmed by the treaty clause and determined to resist attempts at the implementation of its provisions. The Tsongdu (National Assembly), in emergency session, reiterated that the Manchu Emperor and his government had no authority to give anyone permission to pass through Tibet. After further deliberations in the Kashag and the Tsongdu, directives were sent to all border posts notifying officials that Tibet could not recognize passports issued in China for travel through Tibet. When a mission to Lhasa, under the leadership of Colman Macaulay, finally did get under way in 1885, the Tibetans reacted determinedly by sending a detachment of soldiers to block its passage into Tibet.[14]

The Manchus dreaded the prospect of open Tibetan opposition to a mission traveling on passports issued by their Imperial government, because it would expose the Emperor's total lack of authority over the Tibetan government. Moreover, an armed clash would undoubtedly be won by the British, who would bring Tibet under their influence.[15] The Qing government therefore offered the British an immediate settlement over Burma in exchange for the permanent abandonment of the Macaulay mission. The British agreed in return for assurances of "full facilities for trade between India and Tibet."[16] In July 1886, the "Convention Relating to Burmah and Tibet" was signed, which in fact obligated the Manchus only to "adopt measures to exhort and encourage the people [of Tibet] with a view to the promotion and development of trade. Should it be practicable, the Chinese Government shall then proceed carefully to consider trade regulations; but if insuperable obstacles should be found to exist, the British Government will not press the matter unduly."[17] The importance of this article lies in the fact that, unlike the clause of the Chefoo Convention, it was an affirmation of the principle that negotiations about Tibet were to be carried out through the Imperial government—which, indeed, they were. Within the next few years the British and Manchu Plenipotentiaries were at the negotiating table once again, this time to define the status and boundaries of Sikkim.[18]

Following the abandonment of the Macaulay mission, the Tibetans still refused to withdraw the troops they had stationed in Lingtu (which the British claimed was inside Sikkim territory) to stop the mission. They flatly rejected the Amban's insistence that the town be evacuated, but the British finally pushed them out in 1888. Once again, it was the prospect of further British confrontations with the Tibetans, coupled with an obvious loss of prestige, that frightened the Manchus into negotiating.[19]

In March of 1890, the "Convention Relating to Sikkim and Tibet" was signed in Calcutta by the Viceroy, Lord Lansdowne, and the Amban, Sheng Tai, with no Tibetan participating.[20] The treaty recognized the British protectorate over Sikkim as well as Great Britian's "direct and exclusive control over the internal administration and foreign relations of that State."[21]

It further provided for the delimitation of the boundary between Sikkim and Tibet. The treaty was followed some three years later by the conclusion of the "Regulations Regarding Trade, Communication, and Pasturage to be Appended to the Sikkim-Tibet Treaty."[22] These regulations secured for the British the right to trade with Tibet at a trade mart that was to be established in the Southern Tibetan town of Dromo (or Yatung), 13 miles north of Sikkim, and to station their officers there.[23]

As might have been expected, the Tibetan government repudiated both parts of the treaty and expressly rejected the authority of the Imperial government to make treaties on Tibet's behalf.[24] The Tibetans succeeded in making the treaty unenforceable: A wall was built north of Dromo to make it impossible to use that town effectively as a trade mart; pillars erected by the British on the Sikkim-Tibet frontier were destroyed; and a Tibetan military post was set up at Giagong, south of the border agreed upon in the treaty.[25] The British complained bitterly about the Tibetans' systematic obstructions. A period of frustration followed, for the British recognized Manchu authority over a people whom the Manchus themselves now confessed they had no power to control, and they were bound to deal only with an impotent government in Beijing.[26]

The crux of the matter was that Manchu authority in Tibet was purely nominal during the second half of the nineteenth century. Thus, the British Political officer J.C. White concluded while in Tibet, after discussions with Tibetan and Manchu officials in 1894, that the Manchus had no authority whatever there: "Though rulers in name, [they] have no power and can enforce no order." He further wrote that their officials "hated the Tibetans, and do not scruple openly to say so. This, I take it, is caused by the knowledge of their impotence, knowing full well that they have no real power, though to all outward appearance they receive a great deal of respect."[27] It was not until the Manchu and Chinese defeat at the hands of Japan in 1895, however, that the British in India and at home fully realized the weakness of the Qing Dynasty's power, particularly in Tibet. The war also showed the Tibetans, especially the Thirteenth Dalai Lama, who took control of the Government of Tibet in 1894, that the Patron's power could no longer be relied on for protection against an invader.[28] These realizations brought Tibet out of isolation.

Diplomatic Relations with Russia and Treaty Relations with Great Britain

What had started as a half-hearted attempt to open up Tibet for trade with British India, turned into a major international issue by the turn of the century. Tibet by then had become the object of expansionism and of a mutual fear for such expansionism, among the Russian, British, and Manchu Empires.[29] Edmund Candler's observation that, "jealousy and suspicion make nations willfully blind"[30] is poignantly applicable in this connection.

Anglo-Russion Rivalry over Tibet

The Russian Empire had expanded well into Asia, especially Central Asia, in the same way as the British Empire had expanded into South Asia, by safeguarding its frontiers in that continent and striving to prevent situations from arising that would endanger its position in the newly acquired territory.[31] The Russian government realized—as the Manchus had for centuries—that in Tibet lay the key to influence over most peoples of Central Asia. Russian friendship and perhaps influence over the Dalai Lama could mean a certain degree of influence and even control over the Mongols, Kalmucks, Buriats, and other Buddhist peoples now within the Russian Empire's borders or sphere of interest.[32]

The Manchus, though apparently still capable of crushing a major rebellion in Gansu and northwest China as late as 1895, were fast losing their hold on the Empire and their influence over its dependencies. The Taiping rebellion, followed by the encroachments of the Western imperialist powers, had drastically weakened the Qing Dynasty, and the Sino-Japanese war (1895) dealt a fatal blow to its prestige at home and abroad. The Manchus thus saw any involvement of European powers in Tibet as a possible threat to the Empire's western borders, and the Emperor was anxious to prevent any situation from arising that would demonstrate his lack of authority in Tibet and create a "power vacuum" for the Russians, the British, or even the French to fill.[33]

British advances in the Himalayan States traditionally in Tibet's sphere of influence, as well as their overtures toward the Tibetans themselves, caused anxiety in Russia and China. British authorities in India and at home had finally come to the realization that, as the Foreign Secretary the Marquess of Salisbury put it, "if the Chinese [i.e., Manchus] ever had any authority in Tibet, they certainly have none now."[34] This realization prompted the not unfounded fear that the Russians would attempt to fill the "power vacuum" left in Tibet. Such an extension of Russian influence to Tibet would be felt on the very borders of India, and would threaten the British Empire as well. Lord George N. Curzon, Viceroy of India (1899–1905), felt that the Empire could not permit "the creation of a rival or hostile influence in such a position so close to the India border and so pregnant with possibilities of mischief."[35] Trade considerations were now only of secondary importance in the face of this new threat, which became the principal determinant of Britain's Tibet policy.[36]

The British authorities, having realized the extent of Manchu impotence with respect to the Tibetans, were determined to establish direct contacts with the Dalai Lama and his government. At the same time, the Home Government in London favored the continued recognition of some degree of Manchu responsibility for Tibet, in the interest of preserving friendly relations with Beijing.[37]

The Thirteenth Dalai Lama, Thubten Gyatso (1876–1934), assumed full spiritual and temporal power over Tibet in 1894. This was an event of immense political importance, for—as Sir Charles Bell pointed out and as

Manchu officials reluctantly admitted—"a Dalai Lama's position among the Tibetans is such that no Chinese [i.e., Manchu] authority in Tibet, however eminent, can oppose him on equal terms."[38] Indeed, the young dynamic ruler steered Tibet on an independent course, refusing to recognize any Manchu authority in or over Tibet. He regarded his relationship with the Qing Emperor, as had the Fifth Dalai Lama, as nothing more than a personal one between the Dalai Lama, the Priest, and the Emperor, his Patron. He consequently would not tolerate any intervention in Tibetan affairs by the Ambans or other Imperial officials.[39] As Lord Curzon remarked in 1903: "For the first time for nearly a century [Tibet] is under the rule of a Dalai Lama, who is neither an infant nor a puppet, but a young man some 28 years of age, who is believed to exercise a greater personal authority than any of his predecessors, and to be *de facto* as well as *de jure* sovereign of the country."[40]

The Manchu Emperor had demonstrated his inability to protect Tibet in the Dogra and Nepal wars, and his weakness was equally apparent from the outcome of his wars with the British and the Japanese: The Tibetans felt he could no longer be relied on to fulfill the Patron's fundamental duty to protect the Dalai Lama, his Faith, and his people. The Dalai Lama himself took measures to improve the country's defenses. He also kept the borders of his country tightly closed, especially to the British, whose intentions were feared more than those of the relatively distant Russians (a fact the British found hard to understand).[41] It was with the Russians that the Dalai Lama first established contacts.

Mongols, Kalmucks, and Buriat Buddhists from Russian Central Asia had long been coming to Lhasa on pilgrimages, to study in Tibet's renowned monastic universities, or to carry out trade, just as all Central Asian peoples had done. Little is known of the purpose of the first mission headed by a certain Baranoff that visited Lhasa in 1898. Through the services of Ngawang Lobsang Dorjieff, a highly learned Buriat Mongol monk who had studied at Drepung monastery in Lhasa and had had the singular privilege of tutoring the young Dalai Lama,[42] diplomatic relations took on a significant character.

In October 1900, the *Journal de Saint-Petersbourg* reported that in the Imperial palace the Czar had received from the Dalai Lama a mission led by Dorjieff.[43] Less than a year later, a second Tibetan mission, also headed by Dorjieff, was once again received by the Czar. The British government was particularly alarmed by the official character attributed by Russia to this latter mission. According to the Russian *Messager Officiel* of 25 June/ 8 July 1901: "On Saturday, 23 June, at the Grand Palace of Peterhof, His Majesty the Emperor received the Envoys Extraordinary from the Dalai Lama of Tibet: Hambo Akhuan Dorgeviev and Loubsan Kaintchok Hambo Donir. . . . On the same day, the Tibetan mission was received by Her Majesty the Empress Maria Feodorovna."[44] The envoys were also reported to have visited the Foreign Minister.[45]

Despite assurances by the Russian Foreign Minister, Count Lamsdorff, that his government's contacts with the Tibetans were of a religious nature and "could not be regarded as having any political or diplomatic character"[46] (a distinction difficult, if not impossible, to make in Central Asian relations, especially given the Dalai Lama's immense influence), the British authorities, especially those in India, were not reassured.[47] At the same time, Lord Curzon, who was appointed Viceroy of India in 1899, became increasingly frustrated, both by the continuing obstructiveness of the Tibetans over the execution of the 1890–1893 Sikkim-Tibet Treaty and Trade Regulations and by his own failure to establish any kind of direct communication with the Tibetan authorities.[48]

Ever since his arrival in India, Curzon had tried to initiate some contact with Lhasa, for he had decided that dealing with Tibet through the Manchu authorities was "most ignominious" and "an admitted farce."[49] He sent a number of letters to the Dalai Lama through different channels, expressing his government's desire to establish friendly and good-neighborly relations with Tibet, and assuring the Dalai Lama that "the British Government [has] no desire to interfere in any way in the internal administration of Tibet. That is a matter that concerns the people and the ruler of Tibet."[50] The letters were returned unanswered and the Dalai Lama and his government remained resolved not to enter into a dialogue with the British.[51]

The excuse often given by Tibetan officials that they did not wish to displease the Amban or the Emperor, who had forbidden all contact with foreign governments, was now recognized for what it was—namely, an instance of the Tibetan diplomatic method of using one power as a shield against another. When it served their purpose, Tibetans were quick to use Manchu overlordship as such a shield, not realizing that this attitude would harm them in the future.[52] Describing this "solemn farce" in a report to London, in 1903, Lord Curzon stated that the Government of India now regarded

> the so-called suzerainty of China over Tibet as a constitutional fiction—a political affectation which has only been maintained because of its convenience to both parties. China is always ready to break down the barriers of ignorance and obstruction and to open up Tibet to the civilizing influence of trade; but her pious wishes are defeated by the short-sighted stupidity of the Lamas. In the same way Tibet is only too anxious to meet our advances, but she is prevented from doing so by the despotic veto of the suzerain. This solemn farce has been re-enacted with a frequency that seems never to deprive it of its attractions or its power to impose. As a matter of fact, the two Chinese [i.e. Manchu] Ambans at Lhasa are there not as Viceroys, but as Ambassadors; and the entire Chinese soldiery by whom the figment of Chinese suzerainty is sustained in Tibet consists of less than 500 ill-armed men.[53]

In that same detailed report, the Viceroy advocated a more forceful policy toward Tibet. He suggested sending a mission to Lhasa, using force if necessary, to compel the Tibetans to deal directly with his government and to conclude a treaty covering all aspects of Anglo-Tibetan relations and providing for the appointment of a permanent British representative in Lhasa. This the Government of India considered to be the only remedy for breaking "the wall of Tibetan impassivity."[54] The predictable reply of His Majesty's Government was that, aside from the Indo-Tibetan frontier problems, "the wider point of view of the relations of Great Britain to other Powers, both European and Asiatic, had to be considered."[55] China was considered, much as it is today, an important trade partner and the main bulwark against Russian expansion in Asia. A forward policy in Tibet might provoke undesired action by the Manchus or Nepalese to safeguard their interests and might drive the Dalai Lama further toward Russia.[56] Furthermore, the British government was already tied down by a so-called "self-denying ordinance" with respect to Tibet. In statements of February and April 1903, Britain and Russia had exchanged denials of any intention to alter the status quo in Tibet and specifically disclaimed any intention of establishing representatives in Lhasa. Russia recognized only Britain's special interest and "local predominance" in Tibet, for geographical reasons[57]— hence the British government's reluctance to sanction a mission to Lhasa and its preference for the continuation of diplomatic efforts with both St. Petersburg and Beijing.[58] Ultimately, Great Britain pursued a double policy: It continued negotiations with the Manchus, but also sanctioned a mission to Tibet.[59]

The British Mission to Lhasa

The declared purpose of the British "commercial mission" was to discuss the enforcement of the 1890–1893 treaty and trade regulations on Tibetan soil.[60] In reality, it was Lord Curzon's hope, shared by the leader of the mission appointed by him, Colonel Francis Younghusband, that the mission would be able to establish a channel for continuing direct communication with Lhasa, secure trade marts with British officers in or close to Lhasa, and reach agreement for the appointment of a British agent in Lhasa or at least in the major southern city of Gyantse. In short, the Government of India expected to achieve the "formal recognition of exclusive political influence" of the British in Tibet to thwart Russian intentions.[61]

In July 1903 the Younghusband mission arrived in Khamba Dzong, a few miles across the Tibetan border, with two hundred soldiers. It was presently evident that no fruitful negotiations would take place there: Despite a Manchu desire that negotiations be conducted in Khamba Dzong, the Tibetan government insisted that the mission leave Tibetan territory before any discussions could take place.[62] The Dalai Lama ignored the Amban's high-handed instructions "to select a barbarian official of fairly high standing" to go to Khamba Dzong to negotiate, and prevented the Amban himself from leaving Lhasa. Younghusband used this obstruction and other pretexts to advance further into Tibet, with the approval of the Government of India and the reluctant acquiescence of the Home Government.[63]

Thus it was that the mission, reinforced with some 3000 soldiers and twice that number of men to support them, occupied the Chumbi Valley and marched on to Gyantse and ultimately to Lhasa, where it arrived on

3 August 1904. Along the way, the British encountered ineffective but determined opposition from the Tibetan army and had to fight a number of battles.

The Tibetans were badly shaken by their defeat and heavy losses, as well as by the lack of aid from the Manchus, the Russians, and the Nepalese.[64] The Dalai Lama and the Tibetan National Assembly had appealed to the Qing Emperor for assistance on the basis of both the long-standing *Chö-yön* relationship and an alleged agreement made around 1840, whereby any Manchu troops in Tibet would be made available to the Tibetan government in case of need. Wishing to avoid another confrontation with the British, the Manchus refused to consider the request and demanded instead that the Tibetans negotiate a settlement.[65] The Amban wrote condescendingly to the Dalai Lama: "If you do not know how to do this, I will show you."[66] There is also evidence to show that the Manchus hoped to use the situation to establish their own authority in Tibet: The Amban requested the Nepalese to send troops to assist him to establish Imperial authority in Tibet and to strip the obstructive Dalai Lama of his temporal powers.[67] The Nepalese, who were bound to help Tibet by the Treaty of 1856, prized their relationship with the British greatly and hence offered only to mediate in the dispute.[68] To the very last, the Tibetans hoped to stop Younghusband from entering Lhasa, and to this end the Dalai Lama sent delegates to negotiate with him in July 1904.[69] The advance on Lhasa was nevertheless undertaken.

The Anglo-Tibetan Treaty

As British troops entered Lhasa, the Dalai Lama fled his capital, leaving his seal with Ganden Tri Rimpoche, whom he appointed Regent during his absence. The Amban, with British encouragement, took this opportunity to try to assert Imperial authority in Tibet and to remove the independent-minded Dalai Lama. He secured from his government an Imperial Decree denouncing and deposing the Dalai Lama. This action elicited angry reactions from the people of Lhasa and was considered *ultra vires* by the Tibetan authorities, who continued to refer to the Dalai Lama for all decisions.[70]

London resolved to authorize Younghusband to conclude a bilateral treaty directly with the Tibetan government. The Imperial government in Beijing would be asked to recognize this treaty in a separate adhesion agreement rather than being regarded as a party to the treaty itself. Negotiations were thus opened with the Regent and other Tibetan officials in Lhasa and on 7 September 1904 the "Lhasa Convention" was signed and sealed by Younghusband on behalf of the British government and by the Regent, the Kashag, the Tsongdu, and the Big Three monasteries (Ganden, Sera, Drepung) for Tibet. It was ratified on 11 November of the same year. Following the conclusion of the treaty, the British troops withdrew.[71]

The most important articles of the Lhasa Convention provided for direct relations between the two contracting parties and required Tibet to secure the consent of the British government for most agreements it might wish to enter into with other States.[72] Thus Article 9 of the treaty states:

The Government of Tibet engages that, without the previous consent of the British Government—

(a) no portion of Tibetan territory shall be ceded, sold, leased, mortgaged or otherwise given for occupation, to any Foreign Power;

(b) no such Power shall be permitted to intervene in Tibetan affairs;

(c) no Representatives or Agents of any Foreign Power shall be admitted to Tibet;

(d) no concessions for railways, roads, telegraphs, mining or other rights, shall be granted to any Foreign Power, or to the subject of any Power. In the event of consent to such concessions being granted, similar or equivalent concessions shall be granted to the British Government;

(e) no Tibetan revenues, whether in kind or in cash, shall be pledged or assigned to any Foreign Power, or to the subject of any Foreign Power.

Nowhere in that or any other article of the treaty is there any reference— explicit or implicit—of the right of the Qing Emperor or his government to interfere in any way in the affairs of Tibet. In fact, the agreement does not even acknowledge the existence of any privileged position or special relationship between the Manchu Emperor and Tibet.

Younghusband's own reports suggest that he clarified that he did not consider that Article 9 implied a restriction of the Imperial government's special privileges over Tibet and declared Britain's continuing recognition of its "suzerainty" over Tibet—a term never before officially used to describe that relationship. This *eclaircissement*, however, was not included in the treaty itself, nor was it laid down in notes or other written communications between the treaty parties; indeed, it was never accepted by the Tibetans.[73] The most that can be said is that the signatories presumably were aware, in a general way, that the British government recognized an undefined privileged position to the Manchus in Tibet. It was in fact precisely because the treaty itself did not recognize any form of Manchu supremacy over Tibet that the Amban was instructed by his government not to conclude any agreement recognizing it: "On no account are you to sign it, as it robs China of her suzerainty over Tibet."[74] The Manchus actually saw the treaty as a "conversion of Tibet into a vassal state of Great Britain."[75] It is undeniable that the Lhasa Convention placed Great Britain closer than the Qing government to the position of "suzerain" of Tibet for, as the British Minister in Beijing pointed out: "It is evident that the freedom of action previously enjoyed by the Suzerain with regard to the Vassal is limited in our favour by the requirement of the previous consent of the British Government to steps enumerated in Art. 9."[76]

The great importance of the Lhasa Convention lies in the recognition, which the British government expressed therein, of the Tibetan government's full capacity to enter into treaty relations independent of the Qing Emperor. Conversely, that treaty denied the prerogative of the Imperial government to treat on behalf of Tibet. Indeed, the Government of India held that the privileged and predominant position of the Manchus in Tibet "which it may be held to amount to an undefined suzerainty, cannot be regarded as comprising the power of preventing or regulating the separate relations of Tibet, commercial and political, with limitrophe States."[77] In this statement, the Government of India made the further point that, in fact, only the treaties concluded by Tibet itself—such as those with Kashmir, Ladakh, Nepal, Bhutan, and now Britain—were valid. By the very terms of the Lhasa Convention, the only restriction to the Tibetan government's otherwise exclusive right to handle its foreign relations now resulted from privileges granted to the British government.

Tibet: The Subject of Great Power Treaties

Following Younghusband's withdrawal from Lhasa, the Anglo-Tibetan treaty provisions were put into effect. In accordance with Article 3, the Chumbi Valley was occupied and put under British administration until the three trade marts at Dromo, Gyantse, and Gartok had been effectively opened for three years and payment of the indemnity provided for in Article 6 was completed.[78]

The international reaction to the mission to Lhasa and the Lhasa Convention was not favorable. Germany complained that Article 9 contravened the Most Favored Nation status of Western powers in the Qing Empire.[79] Russia regarded the treaty, and especially the occupation of the Chumbi Valley that followed it, as constituting interference in Tibetan affairs in violation of British assurances to the Russian government. The Manchus officially refused to accept a treaty that did not explicitly recognize their overlordship over Tibet. They had badly lost face and were determined to reverse the gains secured by the British.[80]

The Adhesion Agreement

In the face of criticism, Britain regarded Manchu adhesion to the Anglo-Tibetan treaty with renewed importance, nonetheless maintaining that the Lhasa Convention was fully valid regardless of such adhesion. In the long and difficult negotiations that preceded the signing of the "Adhesion Agreement," the central issue and chief obstacle proved, not unpredictably, to be the status of Tibet vis-à-vis the Qing Empire. Initially, the Waiwu Bu (Foreign Ministry in Beijing) insisted that the Empire's suzerainty be expressly recognized in the agreement. The British government was inclined to do so but pointed out that by asking for the Imperial government's adhesion to the treaty they were already implicitly recognizing their suzerainty.[81]

The Manchu point of view was best represented in the telegrams sent by the Waiwu Bu to the Amban in September 1904:

> Tibet is a Chinese dependency. The negotiations of 1890 and 1893 were
> carried on by officers appointed by Great Britain and China, and the treaties

concluded in those years were treaties between Great Britain and China. The present Treaty [i.e., the Lhasa Convention] also should be one between Great Britain and China, while the Tibetan Government should be instructed to agree to it and sign it. The British should not make a treaty with Tibet direct, as such an arrangement robs China of her suzerainty; and Chinese admonitions to the Tibetans will be unavailing, once her suzerainty is lost.[82]

Thus, the Emperor claimed responsibility for Tibet's external affairs, including the making and execution of treaties. In November, this stand was modified and the Waiwu Bu insisted on the recognition of its government's sovereignty instead of suzerainty over Tibet.[83] This unprecedented claim must have been prompted by the realization that the British did not define suzerainty in such a way as to leave the Manchus much authority in Tibet.

To claims of sovereignty, the British government would under no circumstances give way.[84] The Government of India emphasized that, whereas Tibet was not one of the eighteen provinces of the Chinese Empire, and was not even "under the direct administration of the Imperial government," treaties concluded by the latter were invalid and unenforceable in Tibet. The Tibetans, the Viceroy pointed out, "consistently refused to recognize the Chinese [Manchu] right to make such treaties on their behalf," and British experience proved that Beijing was "unable to enforce [a] treaty made with [them] as to Thibet, and it is now admitted by the Chinese Government, as well as by the Amban, that for a Convention to be valid in Thibet it requires to be signed by Thibetan authorities." As to the Most Favored Nation treatment, the Viceroy added, "[the] question cannot arise, since treaties made with China alone are not valid in Thibet. . . . Treaties with the limitrophe States (Kashmir, Nepal and, it is believed, Bhutan also) are the only valid treaties which have, up to the present, been made with Thibet; to none of these was China a signatory, and they were concluded without Chinese intervention." In further support of his government's view of Tibet's virtual independence, the Viceroy cited the fact that the Imperial government received no regular revenue from, and levied no taxes in, Tibet; that, as was admitted by the Amban, China did not enjoy full freedom of trade in Tibet and even had to pay a tax on Chinese goods entering the country; and that the Amban did not even have the power to leave the capital against the wishes of the Tibetans.[85] London, while concurring with this view, felt that arguments based on it should be used with caution— particularly the argument concerning Tibet's right to maintain diplomatic relations and conclude treaties independent of its suzerain: "Though no doubt it is historically true that this [right] has been exercised by Tibet, [it] is hardly one which it would be expedient for His Majesty's Government to urge in view of the position which they claim in regard to the foreign relations of Afghanistan."[86]

On 27 April 1906, the Adhesion Agreement was finally signed in Beijing. It represented a compromise whereby Britain not only lost much of what Younghusband had secured but Tibet was also disadvantaged.[87] The terms "suzerainty" and "sovereignty" were not used in the treaty in accordance with the Waiwu Bu's request—despite British concern that their omission would lead to repeated claims to sovereignty in the future.[88] The Emperor's special position in Tibet was nevertheless recognized: Article 1, for example, obliged both High Contracting Parties "to take such steps as might be necessary to secure the due fulfillment of the terms of the Lhasa Convention," thus shifting that responsibility from the Tibetan government to the Imperial government; Article 3 specifically excluded China from the term "Foreign Power" where it appeared in Article 9 of the Lhasa Convention, whereas Article 2 stated: "The Government of Great Britain engages not to annex Tibetan territory or to interfere in the administration of Tibet. The Government of China also undertakes not to permit any other foreign state to interfere with the territory or internal administration of Tibet."

The effect of the agreement between its signatories was to modify the Lhasa Convention (recogized as valid in Article 1 of the Adhesion Agreement) to the extent that it was now the Qing Emperor rather than the British government who was made responsible for preserving Tibet's integrity.[89] In fact, the Manchus and Chinese later looked upon the Adhesion Agreement as a rectification or revision of the Lhasa Convention and interpreted it so as to theoretically eliminate the autonomous rights of Tibet that it recognized.[90]

The Tibetan government, far from being requested to assent to the modifications implied by the Adhesion Agreement, was never formally informed of the agreement's conclusion. The government in Lhasa protested and, quite legitimately, declared that it did not consider Tibet bound by the Anglo-Chinese agreement. In a communication to the British, the Tibetan government first reminded the latter that "the Treaty enacted in 1904 . . . was contracted between the British and the Tibetans as the contracting parties" and then accused the Imperial government in Beijing of having engaged in "premeditated intrigues" to enact "a new treaty regarding Tibet, in which neither His Holiness the Dalai Lama nor the Tibetan people have been consulted." Instead of performing their role as lay Patron of the Dalai Lama, which bound the Imperial government "to respect and preserve the integrity and independence of Tibet, and to treat them as a separate but friendly nation, the Manchus presumptuously posed as being fully authorized to treat with other powers in Tibetan matters." The Tibetan government therefore concluded: "This Treaty cannot be regarded as binding by anyone."[91]

The Anglo-Russian Treaty

In the Russian government's view, Britain's involvement in Tibet, especially the conclusion of the Lhasa Convention, amounted to the establishment by Britian of a virtual protectorate. The Russians asserted that as this involvement was a departure from British assurances made in 1903 and 1904, it created an obstruction to a possible rapprochement between themselves and the British.[92] To allay Russian displeasure, but, more important, to forestall possible retaliatory expansionistic moves, the British negotiated a treaty with Russia concerning Persia, Afghanistan, and Tibet in which they defined the limits of each other's sphere of influence.[93]

This treaty, signed at St. Petersburg on 31 August 1907, insofar as it concerned Tibet, provided generally for the preservation of the status quo and included a mutual pledge "to respect the territorial integrity of Thibet and to abstain from all interference in [its] internal administration." The contracting parties recognized the suzerainty of China over Tibet and engaged "not to enter into negotiations with Thibet except through the intermediary of the Chinese government." They also agreed not to send representatives to Lhasa. In short, the treaty was designed to exclude all but limited Manchu and British influences in Tibet.

The Anglo-Russian treaty admittedly could not affect the status of Manchu-Tibetan relations, for as Russian Foreign Minister Alexander Isvolsky pointed out, there could be no question of the two contracting parties concluding a convention relative to the sovereign rights of Persia or Tibet given that "the two contracting parties have no sovereign rights to use at their will over these regions." Hence the parties could do no more than agree to "a declaration, arrangement, or agreement, stating purely and simply the line of conduct which the two states mutually pledge to observe henceforth concerning the Persian and Tibetan issues."[94]

With the conclusion of the treaties in Beijing and St. Petersburg, Britain and Russia in effect recognized that the Manchu Empire's sphere of influence included Tibet, largely to the exclusion of other powers, except the British Empire. The immediate result of their conclusion was to encourage the Manchus and Chinese to fill the power vacuum the British had created by first defeating the Tibetans and then by withdrawing their influence and protection from them. The British official Charles Bell remarked: "By going in and then coming out again, we knocked the Tibetans down and left them there for the first-comer to kick."[95] The Manchus lost no time in filling the vacuum, made the more pronounced by the Dalai Lama's continued absence,[96] and they pursued an aggressive policy toward Tibet on all fronts.

Manchu Forward Policy

Even before the Adhesion Agreement was concluded, the Waiwu Bu announced that the Emperor himself would settle the indemnity Tibet had agreed to pay the British under Article 6 of the Lhasa Convention. The object was to emphasize and provide evidence of his responsibility for Tibet's foreign relations, to limit occasions for direct Anglo-Tibetan intercourse, and to secure the early retirement of British forces from Chumbi.[97] The Foreign Office in London was reluctant to accept this payment on behalf of Tibet, thereby admitting Beijing's intervention in this matter, particularly given the complete inability shown by that government in the past "to exercise effectual control over the Tibetan authorities." It consequently seemed to the Foreign Secretary "that it would be highly inadvisable to agree to any settlement which might be regarded as an admission that responsibility for the future rests upon the Chinese Government."[98] Shortly before the first installment was due, Sir Ernest Satow, the British Minister in Beijing, informed Prince Qing that unless the agreement of adhesion to the Lhasa Convention was concluded, "the arrangement proposed of payment on behalf of Tibet cannot be entertained."[99] Ultimately, the British did not hold firmly even to that condition, insisting only on the formality that the money, regardless of where it came from, be handed over to them by a Tibetan government official. After the signing of the Adhesion Agreement, that formality was also dropped for the second and third installments, which were paid directly from Beijing.[100]

The Tibetans, who increasingly succumbed to pressure exerted on them by a newly appointed Amban, unwisely accepted the Emperor's offer of payment and displayed little awareness of the implications of such acceptance. By January 1908, the Manchus had paid all three installments, and in the next month the Chumbi Valley was evacuated. The Manchus thus gained some ground in their strategy for the subjection of Tibet.[101]

Another element of Manchu forward policy was the dispatch to Tibet of a powerful "Special Commissioner," Zhang Yintang, "to investigate and conduct affairs" there, in the autumn of 1906.[102] Commissioner Zhang's work was facilitated by the weakness of the Tibetan administration during the Dalai Lama's absence and by the inactivity of the British. As soon as he arrived, he set about the task of destroying the position the latter had secured in Tibet and put the Tibetans under pressure to desist from all communications with them. He launched anti-British propaganda, harassed British officials in Tibet, and succeeded in having most of the Tibetan officials who had negotiated the Lhasa Convention, as well as Amban You Tai, who was in Lhasa when the treaty was concluded, dismissed, degraded, or arrested.[103] The British government delivered repeated, but mild, protests in Beijing against these and other activities, which they claimed constituted violations of the Adhesion Agreement.[104] The Tibetans, though highly resentful of the special commissioner's high-handedness, were intimidated by him and dared do little in the absence of the Dalai Lama, whose return they anxiously awaited.[105]

Meanwhile, Imperial armies advanced deep into the eastern Tibetan province of Kham, bringing parts of it under the provincial administration of Sichuan. Attempts to impose Manchu control over parts of Kham bordering China, including Dartsedo (Chinese: Dajianlu or Kangding), had led to serious resistance in early 1905.[106] In view of the seriousness of the situation, the Manchu General Zhao Erfeng was appointed Imperial Commissioner in Charge of the Frontier Districts in April of that year and was sent into Tibet. He advanced westward with a sizable army, annexed Batang in 1906, and Derge, Draya, and even the capital of Kham (i.e., Chamdo) within the next three years. The campaigns of General Zhao were dreadful, and his administration was oppressive. His troops destroyed or desecrated religious monuments, temples, and monasteries, and killed and abused the local population. It is no wonder that, when Zhao's Imperial appointment to Lhasa as Amban was announced in April 1908, the Tsongdu was determined to prevent his coming and immediately sent orders to the troops in the east to oppose his advance resolutely.[107]

An additional component of the Manchu strategy for gaining control over Tibet concerned the Dalai Lama, who had remained in exile in Urga (Mongolia) and Kumbum (Amdo) since his departure from Lhasa in 1904. The Tibetan officials and people alike were anxiously awaiting his return to Lhasa and sent delegations to him to secure his early return.[108] The Dalai Lama's future was not wholly in his own hands, however, for it was being discussed in St. Petersburg, Beijing, and London. While all three Imperial governments were professing that they would oppose his return to Lhasa on the grounds that it might destabilize the situation, the Manchus and the Russians were secretly urging the Dalai Lama to go back.[109]

The Manchu Court had come to the conclusion that in order to exert effective control over Tibet and to subdue the rebellious population of Kham, the Dalai Lama's cooperation was indispensable. The Empress Dowager and the Emperor therefore sent him several pressing invitations to come to Beijing before returning to Lhasa. The Dalai Lama, whose relations with the Manchus and Chinese were far from cordial, reluctantly accepted the invitation in late 1908, in the hope that he could persuade the Manchu Court to put an end to its aggressive policy in Tibet, particularly in Kham.[110]

In Beijing, the Dalai Lama secured from the Empress Dowager only the promise that the court would not interfere with his power and position as Dalai Lama and that no harm would be done to the Tibetan people. The Tibetan leader's attempt to enlist the support of Western governments to combat the forward policy of the Manchus in Tibet was no more successful.[111]

The Dalai Lama was much offended by the inferior treatment to which he was subjected by the court. The tone of his visit was set when the Dalai Lama was informed that he would be required to perform the *ketou* (or *"kowtow,"* the three kneelings and nine prostrations) before the Emperor, in disregard of precedent for such meetings. The Dalai Lama refused to see the Emperor and Empress Dowager under such a condition, so the requirement had to be countermanded. Despite the compromise that was arrived at regarding the protocol of the meetings and the many honors shown to the Dalai Lama, he was treated by the Qing Court as a subordinate.[112] As if to leave no doubt in this respect the Empress Dowager issued an edict announcing the bestowal on the Dalai Lama of a new honorific title, to replace the one withdrawn from him at the time of his "deposition":

> The Dalai Lama already, by the Imperial commands of former times, bears the title of Hsi-T'ien-Ta-Shan-Tzu-Tsai-Fo [pinyin: *Xitian Da Shan Zizai Fo*], the Great, Good Self-existent Buddha of Heaven. We now expressly conferred upon him the addition to his title of Ch'eng-Shun-Tsan-Hua-Hsi-T'ien-Ta-Shan-Tzu-Tsai-Fo, [*Chengxuo Zanhua Xitian Da Shan Zizai Fo*], the Loyally Submissive Vice-Regent, the Great, Good, Self-existent Buddha of Heaven.[113]

The Empress Dowager's Edict, issued on her birthday, specified that "when he [the Dalai Lama] has arrived in Tibet, he must carefully obey the laws

and ordinances of the Sovereign State, and make known to all the good-
will of the Chinese Court."[114] The Dalai Lama was further denied the right
to memorialize the throne directly, being instructed to communicate via the
Amban in Lhasa instead. This last measure particularly displeased the Dalai
Lama, who reminded the court that he had been the ruler of Tibet before
the Manchu Dynasty ever came to power in China.[115]

The Dalai Lama was far from having been influenced in favor of closer
ties with the Manchu Court. As W. Rockhill reported to President Theodore
Roosevelt at the time, "[the Dalai Lama] leaves Peking with his dislike for
the Chinese intensified. I fear that he will not cooperate with the Chinese
in the difficult work they now propose to undertake of governing Tibet
like a Chinese province, and that serious trouble may yet be in store for
my friend the Dalai Lama, if not for China."[116] Bad news greeted the Dalai
Lama when he returned to Tibet at the end of 1909. Zhao Erfeng had
advanced far into Kham and even proposed to the Emperor the creation
of a new Chinese province, Xikang, that would incorporate parts of Sichuan
and the area of Kham under his occupation.[117] Furthermore, Zhang Yintang
and the Amban in Lhasa had succeeded in gaining much power during his
absence, and the former had even negotiated trade regulations for Tibet
with the British in the previous year, without active participation of the
Tibetan government.

The Tibet Trade Regulations

The Lhasa Convention stipulated in Article 3 that "the question of the
amendment of the regulations of 1893 is reserved for seperate consideration,
and the Tibetan Government undertakes to appoint fully authorized delegates
to negotiate with representatives of the British Government as to the details
of the amendments required."[118] The intention was clearly to negotiate and
conclude the Trade Regulations exclusively with the Tibetan government.[119]
However, once the Adhesion Agreement had been signed and it became
apparent that Zhang Yintang was doing his best to frustrate the execution
of the Lhasa Convention in Tibet, the British government, anxious for an
early settlement, did not insist on Anglo-Tibetan negotiations. Instead, it
agreed to Manchu participation on the condition that the Tibetan government
appoint its own delegate with full powers. In principle, the Waiwu Bu
agreed to the presence of a Tibetan representative if he were associated
with Special Commissioner Zhang, but throughout the negotiations for the
Regulations, the Manchus took pains to make his participation—and even
the formality of it—meaningless in order to emphasize, in Zhang's words,
that the negotiations were being conducted between his government and
the British: "Tibet having no voice in [the] matter except through China."[120]

Thus, for example, the Manchus maintained that the Tibetan delegate
Kalon Tsarong was appointed by their Emperor and not by the Tibetan
government; that no Tibetan translation of the draft of the Trade Regulations
under discussion nor of their final version was necessary or desirable; that
the Tibetan delegate should not sign the Trade Regulations, as it would

impair the Emperor's "sovereign rights"; and that the texts of the Regulations and the instruments of ratification should leave out any mention of the Tibetan government.[121] This attitude was unacceptable to the British, who, remembering the uselessness of earlier treaties concluded with the Manchus concerning Tibet, insisted on formal Tibetan participation in the conclusion of the treaty. As it turned out, however, the British gave in to most of the Manchu demands. The role of the Tibetans in the conclusion of the Trade Regulations is amply evident from the Preamble to that agreement.[122] Whereas the British and Manchu representatives are referred to as Plenipotentiaries named by their respective sovereigns, the Tibetan delegate is regarded only as a "fully authorized representative to act under the directions" of Zhang Yintang and to take part in the negotiations, named by "the High Authorities of Tibet."[123]

Substantively, the provisions of the agreement arrived at reflected the acceptance of a large measure of Manchu responsibility for Tibet's relations with the British, including the fulfillment of the Lhasa Convention and the Trade Regulations appended thereto; they subjected Tibet to a degree of Manchu authority unacceptable to the Tibetans. This was particularly true of the provisions that gave Imperial officials supervisory authority over the trade marts and responsibility for policing the marts and trade routes; it was also true of Article 3, which stipulated, in part, that "questions which cannot be decided by agreement between the Government of India and the Tibetan High Authorities at Lhasa shall, in accordance with the terms of Article 1 of the Peking Convention of 1906, be referred for settlement to the Governments of Great Britain and China." The Trade Regulations were signed by the two Imperial Plenipotentiaries on 20 April 1908 and ratified by their respective governments in October.[124] The Tibetan Delegate, Kalon Tsarong, merely signed the regulations.

It is questionable whether Kalon Tsarong should be regarded as having been fully authorized to represent Tibet and sign the Trade Regulations, for he had not been appointed by the Dalai Lama.[125] His credentials, issued by the Regent and presented to the British Plenipotentiary, Sir Louis Dane, were, formally speaking, regarded as sufficient authorization.[126] The Tibetan government, however, had been reluctant to give the Kalon full powers; therefore, the Regent had reserved the right to make the final decisions. It was only under pressure from the British that the reservation was withdrawn.[127] Kalon Tsarong was nevertheless tried and executed by his government for having signed the agreement against the interests of Tibet and, more specifically, for having done so without authorization.[128]

Although the Kalon's credentials may have been formally acceptable to the other delegates to the negotiations, it is clear from all accounts that he lacked proper authorization from the Dalai Lama and his government; that the delegate was only Commissioner Zhang's subordinate and puppet; and that he took no part whatsoever in the negotiations.[129] As indicated earlier, the Manchus actually insisted that Kalon Tsarong was appointed by them and not by the Tibetans, and the Tibetans claim he was coerced into accompanying Zhang.[130] Both these claims are likely to be true. At any rate, it is evident that the Tibet Trade Regulations were in fact negotiated by delegates from London and Beijing, the Tibetans "having no voice in the matter." Furthermore, ratifications were exchanged only between the British and the Manchus, as the latter objected even at the mention of Tibet in those instruments.[131]

The Dalai Lama, who was in Beijing when the Trade Regulations were signed, was not officially advised of the terms of the agreement for some time. To foreign diplomats he spoke favorably of measures to promote international trade, but he expressed his disapproval of any encroachments on Tibetan autonomy that the new agreement might entail.[132]

When the Dalai Lama returned to Lhasa, the situation in Tibet had become so critical that his primary task became to stop the imminent invasion by Imperial armies from Sichuan.

Manchu Invasion and Flight of the Dalai Lama

The dangerous situation in East Tibet turned critical shortly after the Dalai Lama's return to Lhasa in December 1909. General Zhao Erfeng's troops were advancing toward Lhasa, leaving behind them a trail of destruction.[133] The official explanation from Beijing was that troops were being sent to Tibet to police the trade marts and routes, in accordance with the Tibet Trade Regulations. The Manchus even asked the British to allow the passage of their troops through India for this purpose, but permission was refused.[134]

In Lhasa, tension mounted as the government mobilized troops and distributed arms and ammunition. The Dalai Lama sent urgent pleas for help to Great Britain, Russia, France, and Japan, but the only result was a weak and ineffective British protest in Beijing. Meanwhile, the Kashag turned to Nepal, which was bound to assist Tibet by the 1856 Treaty, and requested the Prime Minister's intervention in Beijing; it also demanded guns.[135] None of these pleas were effective, however.

The Tibetan government broke off all relations with the Amban in Lhasa, stating that relations with him "as guardian and ward" had become impossible. His refusal to call for a halt to the military advance could hardly be called consistent with his duty "to watch and promote the welfare of this Country, [the reason for which] His Majesty the Emperor of China has kept the Ambans here."[136]

Believing that the Emperor was not truly being informed of the situation, the Dalai Lama sent a messenger to India to telegraph directly to the Emperor and request his intervention.[137] In order to avert unnecessary bloodshed, knowing full well that armed opposition to the superior Imperial troops would be fruitless, the Dalai Lama made a last attempt to come to some agreement with Lian Amban. An agreement was indeed arrived at and confirmed in writing: The Amban promised that no more than 1,000 troops would enter Lhasa; that they would presently be distributed to the marts and the borders; and that no Tibetans would be harmed. The Dalai Lama, in turn, agreed not to oppose the Imperial troops and to demobilize.[138]

Two days later, a vanguard of some 2,000 soldiers charged through Lhasa, shooting at unarmed crowds even though, in accordance with the Dalai Lama's word, they encountered no opposition. Once again, the Dalai Lama was constrained to flee, this time to India.[139] In the Chumbi Valley he handed the British trade agent a letter in which he stated,

> The Chinese have been greatly oppressing the Tibetan people at Lhasa. Mounted infantry arrived there. They fired at the inhabitants, killing and wounding them. I was obliged, together with my six ministers, to make good my escape. My intention now is to go to India for the purpose of consulting the British Government. . . . I have left the Regent and Acting Ministers at Lhasa, but I and the Ministers who accompany me have brought our seals with us. . . . I now look to you for protection, and trust that the relations between the British Government and Tibet will be that of a father to his children. Wishing to be guided by you, I hope to give full information on my arrival in India.[140]

Once again, the Qing Emperor issued an edict "deposing" the Dalai Lama on 25 February 1910 and announcing the search for a successor. Once again, this Manchu interference angered the Tibetans, and the latter ignored the deposition, which they considered to be *ultra vires*.[141] Commissioner Zhang and the commander of the invading forces, General Zhong Yin, took over the reins of government, leaving no power to the Tibetans. Zhao Erfeng even suggested that Tibet be converted into a province of China.[142]

This was the first Manchu invasion of Tibet. The Manchu interventions in the eighteenth century (1720, 1728, 1750, and 1792) had all been measures taken at the request or with the support of the Tibetans to restore order or to protect Tibet from foreign aggressors. The 1910 invasion marked a turning point in Manchu-Tibetan relations. The Patron/Protector was now invading the country of his Priest, destroying the religion of the Protected, and deposing the Lama, who was the object of his worship and protection! Thus, the *Chö-yön* relationship that had existed with the Qing Emperors came to an end.

The Dalai Lama declared as much in Darjeeling, where he was in exile. He and his ministers formally renounced the Manchu/Chinese claims to any form of overlordship over Tibet, including suzerainty, and once again repudiated the treaties that Tibet had not been a party to. The only relationship the Dalai Lama did recognize was the *Chö-yön*, which, he declared, had now come to an end, so that all ties with the Manchus were broken.[143]

In Lhasa, despite the presence of some 3,000 troops, General Zhong Yin and the Amban were not able to achieve their political aims, for they were facing resistance and obstinate noncooperation from all quarters of the population—including the Panchen Lama, who refused to head a temporary government. Once the Manchus had reached the inevitable conclusion that Tibet could be ruled only with the cooperation of the Dalai Lama, they urged him to return and accept a spiritual role. The Dalai Lama declined.[144] The violent upset of the status quo in Tibet created concern in India. Yet the British attitude was surprisingly passive and somewhat ambiguous. On the surface, they were neutral, claiming to recognize only the *de facto* authority in Tibet.[145] On the other hand, the developments in Tibet endangered the safety of India's northern borders. According to a Foreign Office communication, the Government of India "attached particular importance to the maintenance of an effective Tibetan Government, since they considered that the disappearance of such a government, and the substitution for it of a strong Chinese administration would be likely to complicate relations between China and British India, and between China and Nepal, Bhutan and Sikkim [where they had a special interest]."[146] Moreover, the British considered the interference of the Manchus in Tibet's internal affairs to be a breach of the 1904, 1906, and 1908 treaties that they had concluded with both powers.[147] Thus, the British Minister in Beijing was ordered, on several occasions, to deliver strong protests at the Imperial Court. The replies always contained denials of any intention to alter the status quo, to interfere in Tibet's internal affairs, or to convert Tibet into a province of China.[148] Nepal, Bhutan, and Sikkim also lodged protests with the Manchu government, but to no avail.[149]

With the fall of the Manchu Empire and the establishment of the Chinese Republic, the situation changed. Imperial troops stationed in Tibet mutinied, were attacked by Tibetans, and surrendered.[150] The Dalai Lama returned and issued a declaration of independence. Tibet entered a new phase in its modern history and, against great odds, asserted its independence in the world of the twentieth century.

4

Tibet Asserts Its
Independence

Expulsion of the Manchus
and Reassertion of Independence

The British Consular officer in Sichuan, Eric Teichman, remarked that during the Thirteenth Dalai Lama's two-year exile in India (1910–1912), "the rule of the Chinese military officials in Tibet succeeded in uniting all the Tibetan factions in common detestation of everything Chinese."[1] Both Amban Lian Yu and his assistant Wen Zongyao shared this opinion.[2] Thus, when the Imperial garrisons in Lhasa, Dromo, and Gyantse mutinied on hearing the news of the October revolution in China, the Tibetans rose up in arms against them.[3]

In China, the Chinese revolted against their alien Manchu rulers and inaugurated their own native provisional government in October 1911. By February of the next year, the Qing Dynasty had fallen, and China became a Chinese republic.[4] Manchu officials were replaced by Chinese and were made scapegoats for the former Empire's troubles. Thus, within a few months Amban Lian Yu was recalled from Lhasa and blamed for the disasters that had befallen the Manchus and Chinese in Tibet. The Chinese General Zhong Yin, who had entered Lhasa at the head of the invading armies in 1910, was appointed Xizang Banshi Zhanguan (Senior Officer on Duty in Tibet) by the President. This appointment was strongly resented by the Tibetans, who refused to recognize it and ordered both the General and ex-Amban Lian out of the country.[5]

The Tibetans soon gained the upper hand against the disorganized Imperial troops. After a series of successful military engagements they insisted that all Imperial troops surrender their arms and ammunition and return to China via India without delay. One of the first official acts of the Dalai Lama after he crossed into Tibet in June 1912 was to demand of Zhong and Lian "that all Chinese soldiers should return to China and that arms should be taken charge of by representatives of myself and of themselves."[6]

The British government was asked to help secure the departure of the occupation troops, but it declined any involvement for fear either of incurring new responsibilities or of displeasing the Russians.[7] On the other hand, the Nepalese government, whose "earnest desire" it was "to see Tibet restored to its proper status of practical independence," was willing to aid Tibet and restore peace.[8]

In the summer of 1912 the Chinese and Tibetans accepted Nepalese mediation to reach agreement on terms for the surrender of the Manchu and Chinese troops and their expulsion from Tibet. Through the good offices of the Nepal Vakil, Lieutenant Lal Bahadur, an agreement was signed and sealed by the representatives of the Dalai Lama and of General Zhong Yin and former Amban Lian Yu, on 12 August 1912.[9] This "Three Point Agreement" provided for the surrender and total withdrawal of all Manchu and Chinese soldiers and officials from Tibet within fifteen days; for the protection of the departing soldiers and officials on their journey to India, whence they would be repatriated to China; and for the surrender to the Tibetan government of all their arms and ammunition.

On secret instructions from Beijing, General Zhong delayed his departure from Lhasa, in violation of the Three Point Agreement. The Tibetan government threatened to use force to expel him and Lian, and fighting once again broke out. A new truce and agreement for the surrender of all remaining soldiers was signed on 14 December, and the last contingent of troops under General Zhong left Lhasa on 6 January 1913.[10]

With all foreign troops out of Central Tibet and Tibetan forces regaining control over most of Eastern Tibet, the Dalai Lama returned to Lhasa to a grand reception.[11] On 13 February 1913, the Dalai Lama issued a proclamation from the Potala Palace reaffirming Tibet's independence, which he ordered "to be posted and proclaimed in every district of Tibet, and a copy kept in the records of the offices in every district."[12]

In this proclamation the Dalai Lama reaffirmed his position as supreme spiritual and temporal ruler of Tibet:

> I, the Dalai Lama, most ominiscient possessor of the Buddhist faith, whose title was conferred by the Lord Buddha's command from the glorious land of India, speaks to you as follows: I am speaking to all classes of Tibetan people. Lord Buddha from the glorious country of India, prophesied that the reincarnations of Avalokitesvara, through successive rulers from the early religious Kings to the present day, would look after the welfare of Tibet.

Regarding Tibet's relations with the Mongols, the Chinese, and the Manchus, the declaration clarified as follows:

> During the time of Genghis Khan and Althan Khan of the Mongols, the Ming dynasty of the Chinese, and the Ch'ing dynasty of the Manchus, Tibet and China co-operated on the basis of the benefactor and priest [Chö-yön] relationship. A few years ago, the Chinese authorities in Szechuan [Sichuan] and Yunnan endeavored to colonize our territory. They brought a large number of troops into Central Tibet on the pretext of policing the trade marts. I, therefore, left Lhasa with my ministers for the Indo-Tibetan border, hoping to clarify to the Manchu Emperor by wire that the existing relationship

between Tibet and China had been that of patron and priest and had not been based on the subordination of one to the other. There was no other choice for me but to cross the border, because Chinese troops were following with the intention of taking me alive or dead.

Meanwhile, the Manchu Empire collapsed. The Tibetans were encouraged to expel the Chinese from central Tibet. I, too, returned safely to my rightful and sacred country, and am now in the course of driving out the remnants of Chinese troops from Dokham [Amdo and Kham provinces] in Eastern Tibet. Now, the Chinese intention of colonizing Tibet under the patron-priest relationship has faded like a rainbow in the sky. Having once again achieved for ourselves a period of happiness and peace, I have now allotted to all of you the following duties. . . .

The Dalai Lama then exhorted his people to diligently practice and preserve Buddhism; he called on his officials to deal justly and fairly with the people; he encouraged measures for productive cultivation of land and fair taxation policies; and he announced a land reform whereby the land would belong to the cultivator.

With regard to the maintenance of Tibetan independence, the Dalai Lama proclaimed: "We are a small, religious, and independent nation. To keep up with the rest of the world we must defend our country. In view of past invasions by foreigners, our people may have to face certain difficulties, which they must disregard. To safeguard and maintain the independence of our country, one and all should voluntarily work hard." To Tibet's neighbors the Dalai Lama and his government had already reaffirmed the country's independence.

As early as September 1910, the Dalai Lama, while in exile in India, denounced the Manchu invasion of Tibet and declared all of his country's ties with the former Patron to be broken. He informed a Manchu envoy sent to negotiate his return to Tibet that, owing to the Manchu authorities' disregard for "the independence of Tibet and the religious relationship between the two countries," he had lost confidence in them and was constrained to discontinue the past relationship.[13]

In October 1912, the Viceroy of India received a letter from the Chief Ministers of Tibet, sealed by the National Assembly and the Monasteries of Ganden, Sera, and Drepung, declaring the Tibetan government's resolve to separate entirely from China. The Dalai Lama himself wrote to the British government asking for a British representative to be sent to Lhasa and for help in securing the withdrawal of all Chinese officials and troops— "there being no hope of continuance of [the] relationship formerly existing between Tibet and China."[14]

To the Czar of Russia the Dalai Lama wrote similar letters, requesting his support, "so that all the Chinese officials and soldiers may be withdrawn from Tibet and that the Kingdom of Tibet may be restored to us."[15]

The Dalai Lama made his stand unmistakably clear to the President of the new Chinese Republic when the latter sent communications to the Dalai Lama at the end of 1912 "to announce and explain the Republic and ask for its acceptance by Tibet."[16] The Tibetan ruler sent the Chinese

President a telegram, which, the British Minister remarked, "though courteously worded, is recognized as distinctly hostile to the Republic."[17] The Dalai Lama telegraphed as follows:

> The Republic has only just been proclaimed and the national foundations are far from strong. It behooves the President to exert his energies towards the maintenance of order. As for Thibet, the Thibetans are quite capable of preserving their existence intact and there is no occasion for the President to worry himself at this distance or to be discomposed. The reason why the Thibetans do not approve of the Central Government is entirely due to the excessive ill-treatment inflicted upon them by the Chinese troops in Thibet. Their indignation has been roused. How many, to take an instance, of the temples and shrines have been set on fire or demolished by the Chinese troops, while the officers in command have been quite powerless! How could the Thibetans fail to oppose China?[18]

When the President, expressing regret for the excesses of the Manchu regime, announced the "restoration" of the rank and titles taken from the Dalai Lama by the Manchu Emperor in 1910, the Dalai Lama and his Cabinet replied that he did not desire any rank or titles from the Chinese government, that he had resumed both temporal and spiritual rule of his country, and that "although Tibet and China were previously on terms of mutual friendship, on account of the relationship of the Priest and the Lay [Patron], lately they have not been on good terms. The Tibetans have now regained their power."[19]

With the northern neighbor, Mongolia, which formally declared its independence on 28 December 1911, Tibet concluded a "Treaty of Friendship and Alliance" on 11 January 1913, in Urga.[20] In the Preamble, Mongolia and Tibet declared to have freed themselves from Manchu dominion, to have become independent States, and to have allied themselves in view of the community of religion. In Articles 1 and 2 each State recognized the other's independence. The other articles of the treaty contained pledges to work together for the advancement of Buddhism as well as an engagement to assist each other against external and internal dangers.

In order to further underscore Tibet's independence, the Dalai Lama introduced new paper currency, gold and silver coins, and postage stamps, all of which were used in Tibet until 1959. Those Tibetans who had openly collaborated with the Manchus and the Chinese during the Dalai Lama's exile were punished, and the Dalai Lama conferred titles on patriotic Tibetans. The British official and friend of the Dalai Lama, Sir Charles Bell, wrote that at this time the Tibetan leader's absolute power brought order throughout Tibet, which he unified as none other had done in the country's recent history.[21]

The Tibetan resolve to break off all ties with China and to reaffirm its independence was, in fact, a logical consequence of both the Manchu invasion of Tibet in 1910 and the fall of the Qing Dynasty. As the relationship that existed between the Qing Empire and Tibet was based on the personal

Chö-yön bond between the Dalai Lama as the Priest and Teacher, and the Emperor as the Patron and Protector, the Emperor's invasion of Tibet in 1910 and denunciation of the Dalai Lama ended that relationship. Moreover, when the Qing Empire was overthrown and replaced by a Chinese Republic, no basis was left for a relationship between the two States.[22]

Emergence of New Chinese and British Policies

It was humiliating for the Chinese to look on powerlessly as Manchu and Chinese troops were being defeated by the Tibetans and forcibly expelled from Tibet. The new Republican government were understandably alarmed at the turn of events in Tibet and Mongolia. But China's President, Yuan Shikai, issued an order, presumably for domestic consumption, that totally ignored the unpleasant reality of the situation:

> Now that the Five Races [the Chinese, Manchus, Mongolians, Tibetans, and Turkiks (or Moslems)] are joined in democratic union, the lands comprised within the confines of Mongolia, Tibet and Turkestan all become a part of the territory of the Republic of China, and the races inhabiting these lands are all equally citizens of the Republic of China. The term "Dependencies," as used under the Monarchy, must therefore cease to be used, and henceforth, as regards Mongolia, Tibet, and Turkestan, a complete scheme must be devised to arrive at a unified system of administration and so promote the unity in general among all races of the Republic. The reason why the Republican Government did not create a special Ministry to deal with dependencies was Mongolia, Tibet and Turkestan are regarded as on an equal footing with the provinces of China proper. For the future all administrative matters in connection with these territories will come within the sphere of internal administration.[23]

Presidential orders carried "little weight even in the neighborhood of Peking," as the British Minister in that city remarked, and were even less likely to penetrate Tibet or Mongolia.[24] Yet this new grand design for the unification of the "Five Races," symbolized in the new national flag and laid down in the provisional constitution, represented a major departure from previous Imperial policy: For the first time in history, it was proposed that Tibet and Mongolia were to become parts of the territory of China, and their populations, its citizens.[25]

The Government of China acknowledged the Dalai Lama's Declaration of Independence and his expressed "disapproval" of the Republic, but they would not abandon efforts to induce him to form a union.[26] The Central Government policy was reinforced, perhaps even surpassed, by that of the zealous military governors of Sichuan, who saw Tibet as "a buttress on [China's] national frontiers—the hand, as it were, which protects the face"— and who feared the "foreign peril" from British India.[27]

The British government also feared a "foreign peril," but in the form of a strong Chinese presence on their Imperial borders. Sir John Jordan was instructed to lodge a formal protest with the Chinese government over the presidential order declaring Tibet to be a part of China, and accused them of having "arrogated to [China] a position in Tibet which conflicted with the international obligations it had inherited from the Manchus and with the autonomy which the country had always enjoyed."[28] Jordan told the Chinese President that the British government wanted to see "an autonomous Tibet lying between the territories of Great Britain and China," for they had always held that Tibet was not a part of China, a view supported by the fact that the Chinese treaties with foreign powers were not valid in Tibet.[29] The British government was eager that Tibet should remain "really independent and free from extraneous influence." As the government noted, "The present position is that, by the unaided efforts of the Tibetans, the Chinese have been ejected," but the Chinese were claiming sovereignty while failing "to make good their claim at arms." With the recent experiences of a Chinese and Manchu occupation still vivid, an official British report concluded "it is unnecessary to argue that we cannot, in our interests, allow the attempt to be repeated."[30]

In early September a Chinese mission arrived in Darjeeling hoping to proceed to Tibet to meet with the Dalai Lama "to announce and explain the Republic and ask for its acceptance by Tibet."[31] As the Tibetans insisted on keeping their borders closed to the Chinese, a measure the British were willing to help enforce, the mission was refused permission to proceed to the Tibetan border.[32] The Chinese nevertheless persisted in their attempts to establish direct negotiations with Tibetans and to gain a foothold there: A new mission was sent to invest the Dalai Lama with his newly "restored" title; then, a commissioner was appointed to "conduct investigations in Tibet in a conciliatory spirit";[33] Lu Xingji, a Chinese already in India, was deputed by the President to negotiate peace and restore Chinese influence in Tibet; and, meanwhile, Yang Fen, leader of the first abortive mission, continued his efforts to enter Tibet from Darjeeling. None of the missions succeeded in entering Tibet, however. As the patience of the Chinese was running low, attempts to enter the country were soon accompanied by threats of invasion.[34]

Already by October 1912, Chinese forces had advanced at least as far west as Litang and were consolidating positions in the Zayul district of Tibet. The Tibetans were meeting the threat by speeding up military recruitment and sending reinforcements to the eastern front; a new Governor was appointed in Kham province, with overall civil and military authority; and in Lhasa, a Japanese military expert was employed to train a section of the Tibetan army, and apparently Buriat and Mongolian instructors trained others.[35] In addition, the Tibetan government repeatedly appealed to the British to exert pressure on the authorities in Beijing to cease hostilities in East Tibet.[36]

The fears and ambitions of the British and Chinese clashed over Tibet. British protests over China's declared policies and military operations continued, as did China's formal denials that it had any intention of interfering in Tibet's internal affairs or using force against that country.[37] The apparent contradictions between these reassuring statements and the actions of the Chinese prompted the British both to define their position on Tibet more clearly and to demand written assurances in the form of a bilateral agreement from China. On 17 August 1912, the British Minister handed the Waijiao Bu (Foreign Ministry, formerly Waiwu Bu) a carefully worded memorandum, which was to become the basis for discussion.[38]

The first clause stipulated that "His Majesty's Government, while they have formally recognized the 'suzerain rights' of China in Thibet, have never recognized, and are not prepared to recognize, the right of China to intervene actively in the internal administration of Tibet." The second clause rejected the presidential decree of 21 April, whereby Tibet was declared to be on an equal footing with China's provinces; and the third recognized China's right to station a representative, with escort, in Lhasa. The conclusion of a written agreement on these lines was then declared by the British to be a precondition to their recognition of the Chinese Republic. When the Chinese failed to reply, Sir Edward Grey instructed his Minister, Sir John Jordan, to issue the following stern warning: "His Majesty's Government will regard the Anglo-Chinese Convention of 1906 as no longer holding good, and will hold themselves free to enter into direct negotiations with Tibet. Moreover, should the Chinese troops enter Tibet, they would be prepared to give active assistance to the Tibetans in resisting their advance and in establishing and maintaining Tibetan independence."[39] Precisely at the time Sir John received his instructions, the Waijiao Bu handed him a written reply: The 1906 Anglo-Chinese Convention, they claimed, recognized China's exclusive right to intervene in the internal affairs of Tibet, and there was thus no need for a new agreement.[40] Rejecting this argument, Jordan again warned China that its "policy of aggression, which impaired the integrity of a country which had independent treaty relations with Great Britain, could no longer be tolerated."[41] Later, he stressed "the extremely advantageous nature" of the terms being offered: His government, he pointed out, was "contemplating the reestablishment of China's former position in Tibet at a moment when both position and authority had been completely effaced."[42]

While Anglo-Chinese discussions were taking place, the Chinese government increased its pressure on the Dalai Lama to enter into direct negotiations. The Dalai Lama in turn demanded that the President order a complete halt to the military aggression in East Tibet. After that, he suggested, a meeting might be organized in India, on neutral ground.[43] When the Dalai Lama also asked the British to participate in bringing about a solution along these lines, the seed for a tripartite conference was planted.[44]

The British, realizing that the Tibetans would resent the conclusion, without previous reference to them, of an agreement between Britain and China "as curtailing the independence which they have already gained by their own efforts," and concerned that they might be excluded from a Tibetan-Chinese settlement, favored (as did the Tibetans) tripartite negotiations.[45] The Chinese, however, opposed the idea. Their strategy was to settle the issue of Tibet separately with Tibet and then with Britain, and they opposed the notion that the parties to the negotiations would have equal status.[46] At the same time, they feared separate Anglo-Tibetan negotiations; thus, the Chinese government ultimately agreed to take part and accepted the equal status of all plenipotentiaries.[47] Virtually until the last minute, however, they were secretly doing their utmost to induce Tibet to conclude a separate agreement with them. To this end, they adopted an openly conciliatory attitude toward Tibet while engaging in subversive activities and attempting military advances in eastern Tibet.[48]

President Yuan Shikai, nevertheless, finally sent Zhen Yifan to join the British and Tibetan Plenipotentiaries in Simla. In October 1913, the Simla Conference was finally able to commence.[49]

The Three Power Conference and the Anglo-Tibetan Agreement of 1914

The Plenipotentiaries of Great Britain, Tibet, and China assembled in Simla on 13 October 1913, in the hope of ending the state of war that existed between Tibet and China and of defining the relations between the three powers.

On that day the British delegate and Secretary of State of the Government of India, Sir Henry McMahon; the Tibetan delegate, Lochen Paljor Dorje Shatra (who was also Prime Minister); and the Chinese delegate, Zhen Yifan (commonly called Ivan Chen) examined each others' credentials and, finding them in order, formally recognized one another as Plenipotentiaries of their respective governments.[50] Sir Henry McMahon was elected President of the Conference—a logical step, as Tibet and China were at war and the British were intended to mediate.

The actual business of the Three-Power Conference started with the presentation by Lochen Shatra of the proposal of his government.[51] The Tibetan statement clarified as *Chö-yön* the historical relationship between the Dalai Lamas and the Manchu Emperors and stated:

> Tibet and China have never been under each other and will never associate with each other in the future. It is decided that Tibet is an independent State and that the Precious Protector, the Dalai Lama, is the Ruler of Tibet, in all Temporal as well as spiritual affairs. Tibet repudiates the Anglo-Chinese Convention concluded at Peking on the 27th April 1906 . . . as she did not send a representative for this Convention nor did she affix her seal on it. It is therefore decided that this is not binding on the three governments.

The statement indicated further that the Tibet Trade Regulations of 1893 and 1908 were to be revised by Great Britain and Tibet, as "China . . . no longer [had] any concern with the afore'said Trade Regulations," and that the claimed territory stretched eastward as far as Dartsedo. It added that "In order therefore to ensure peace beween the two countries in future no Chinese soldiers or colonists will be permitted to enter or reside in Tibet. Chinese traders shall be admitted to Tibet when so authorized by permits issued by or under the authority of the Tibetan Government."

Ivan Chen presented the counterproposals of his government on 30 October.[52] The Chinese government claimed to have established sovereignty over Tibet in 1793, after the Imperial armies had protected Tibet from foreign invaders.

It is evident, the statement continued, "that the claims presented in the Tibetan statement are inadmissible." In answer to them, the Chinese made the following demands "as the only basis for the negotiation of the Tibetan question":

1. Tibet was to form "an integral part of the territory of the Republic of China," and China's rights in this regard would be recognized and respected by all parties; China would engage not to convert Tibet into a province, whereas Great Britain would agree not to annex any portion of Tibet.
2. The Chinese would have the right to appoint a Resident in Lhasa with an escort of 2,600 Chinese soldiers.
3. Tibet would be guided by China in foreign affairs and defense matters and enter into negotiations with other powers only through the intermediary of China.

In addition, the Chinese claimed territory stretching as far west as Giamda, close to Lhasa, and included all of Amdo and much of Kham.[53]

While a British compromise proposal was being prepared, the Tibetan and Chinese delegates presented documentary evidence for their respective territorial claims. The weight of documentary evidence produced on the Tibetan side was overwhelming, and it was evident from the outset that the Tibetans were in a more favorable position in that respect.[54] Having made an exhaustive study of the well-authenticated records presented for his arbitration by both sides, McMahon, the British Plenipotentiary, "saw no alternative but to recognize the traditional and historical Tibetan frontier, which coincided generally with the claim put forward by Lochen Shatra." At the same time, McMahon recognized that the Chinese had "succeeded to some extent in consolidating their position over a considerable tract" of country in Eastern Tibet, between Batang and Dartsedo.[55]

In order to meet both claims, McMahon proposed the division of Tibet into two zones: an Outer one and an Inner one taking Mongolia as a precedent. "Outer Tibet" would correspond roughly to Central and Western Tibet, whereas "Inner Tibet," bordering on China, would incorporate Amdo and part of Kham—that is, the East and Northeastern parts of the country. The full autonomy of Outer Tibet would be recognized, but so would "the right of the Chinese to reestablish such a measure of control in Inner Tibet as will restore and safeguard their historic position there, without in any way infringing the integrity of Tibet as a geographical and political entity."[56] The problem, as Hugh Richardson has explained it, "was to ensure the reality of Tibetan autonomy but still to leave the Chinese with a position of sufficient dignity."[57]

Both the Tibetans and the Chinese objected to the British proposal. The Tibetans refused to accept any form of Chinese overlordship, inasmuch as they had only recently regained their full independence. The Chinese objected to a proposal that recognized only their nominal suzerainty and not their sovereignty over Tibet and that failed to restore to them any effective control.[58]

The British put pressure on both parties to accept a convention along the lines of their proposal and urged them to make concessions. The tripartite convention finally placed on the conference table for initialing by the three Plenipotentiaries on 27 April 1914 can be summarized as follows.[59]

Tibet was to be divided into two zones, Inner and Outer Tibet. Within the former zone, which could be considered as a buffer region for China, the Chinese were accorded the right to establish a measure of control— but without in any way infringing the integrity of Tibet as a geographical and political entity. China's suzerainty over Tibet would be recognized by the convention, in exchange for the similar recognition of the autonomy of Outer Tibet. China would agree to abstain from interfering in the administration of Outer Tibet and would be precluded from sending troops or officials and from establishing colonies there. It would be permitted only to send one high official with a personal escort, not to exceed 300 men, to reside at Lhasa.[60] China was not to convert the country into a province, whereas Great Britain pledged not to annex any portions of Tibet. The convention explicitly provided for direct Anglo-Tibetan relations on matters affecting the two countries, including the settlement of mutual boundaries and the regulation of trade and commerce. Moreover, provision was made for the British Trade Agent at Gyantse to travel to Lhasa from time to time.[61] China's insistence upon the recognition that Tibet formed a part of its territory was resolutely opposed by the Tibetans. In an effort to persuade China to accept the convention, however, the three parties agreed to add a note to follow the convention by which Tibet was understood to form a part of Chinese territory[62]—a notion curiously inconsistent with the recognition of Tibetan autonomy and Chinese suzerainty. Other notes were similarly to be appended to the convention. They included the understanding that the selection and appointment of all officers in Outer Tibet would rest solely with the Tibetan government, and that Outer Tibet should not be represented in the Chinese Parliament or any similar body.

The Tibetans succumbed to British pressure after securing concessions on the Sino-Tibetan border issue and securing the total exclusion of Chinese interference in Tibetan affairs in the area to be designated as Outer Tibet. The price Tibet would have to pay was the recognition of nominal Chinese suzerainty over Outer Tibet, and a large measure of Chinese interference in Inner Tibet.[63] That the Tibetans would have agreed to these terms can be explained mainly by their anxiety over Chinese military advances in

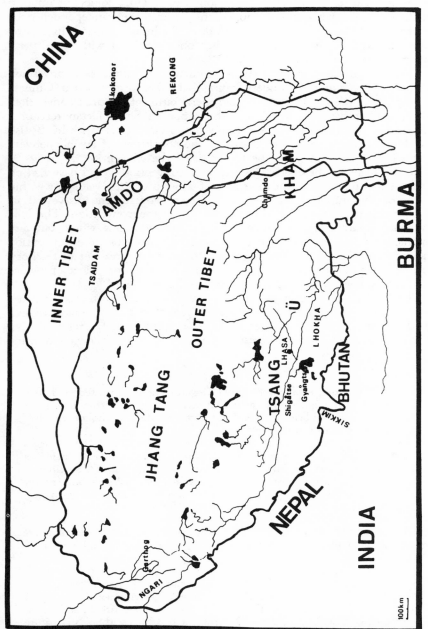

Boundaries proposed at the Simla Convention, 1914. Map drawn by the author.

Kham and the fear of an all-out invasion, which Tibet could not hope to resist. The Tibetans primarily hoped to preserve their independence by securing their Eastern borders and excluding all Chinese influence in Central Tibet. In addition, they were counting on closer ties with the British government to help them maintain it.[64]

The Chinese, after securing the attachment to the proposed convention of the note containing the understanding that Tibet formed part of Chinese territory, were prepared to accept the general terms of the draft convention. On the other hand, they rejected the proposed Sino-Tibetan territorial boundaries.[65] At the last moment, Ivan Chen decided to act with his British and Tibetan colleagues rather than risk the conclusion of an independent Anglo-Tibetan agreement, so he too initialed the convention.[66]

To speculate on the effects this tripartite convention would have had on Sino-Tibetan relations or on the status of Tibet is of little value, for within a day of the initialing thereof, the Chinese government disavowed its Plenipotentiary's action and declined to accept the convention. The government repeated its acceptance of the convention as a whole but also reiterated its inability to make the boundary concessions the convention entailed.[67] As Richardson has suggested "the formal surrender of territory, however acquired, and the prohibition against making Inner Tibet a province may have seemed too great an affront to Chinese pride."[68]

The Tibetan and British governments were not prepared to make further concessions to the Chinese, and warned them that if they refused to sign the convention, Britain and Tibet would do so independently after modifying its terms to protect their interests.[69] On 25 June, the following warning was sent:

> As it is, the patience of His Majesty's Government is exhausted, and they have no alternative but to inform the Chinese Government that, unless the Convention is signed before the end of the month, they will hold themselves free to sign separately with Tibet.
>
> In that case the Chinese Government will of course lose all the privileges and advantages which the tripartite convention secures to them, including recognition of Chinese suzerainty over Tibet; while the return of the Chinese Resident at Lhasa will be postponed indefinitely, and His Majesty's Government will render the Tibetans all possible assistance in resisting Chinese aggression.[70]

After a further warning, Great Britain and Tibet concluded a bilateral agreement on 3 July, consisting of a formal declaration as follows:

> We, the Plenipotentiaries of Great Britain and Tibet, hereby record the following Declaration to the effect that we acknowledge the annexed Convention as initialled to be binding on the Governments of Great Britain and Tibet, and we agree that so long as the Government of China withholds signature of the afore'said convention, she will be debarred from the enjoyment of all privileges accruing therefrom.[71]

To this document, duly signed and sealed by the two Plenipotentiaries, were attached copies of the convention, duly initialed and sealed by the same, and the accompanying map of Tibet similarly initialed and sealed.[72] This procedure, of initialing the treaty and signing the declaration, was explained by McMahon as having been done in order to "avoid a dual signature of the document drawn up on a tripartite basis, whilst at the same time the covering Declaration would assure to Great Britain and Tibet, and would preclude from China so long as she refused to sign, the privileges contemplated by the Convention."[73]

In addition, the two Plenipotentiaries signed and sealed new Tibetan Trade Regulations to supersede those of 1893 and 1908, for which provision had been made under Article 7(b) of the new convention, and which had already been initialed on 27 April. In these regulations there was no mention of China.[74] The British and Tibetan delegates also concluded an agreement defining their long common boundary, in the form of a map showing the Indo-Tibetan boundary, signed and sealed by both Plenipotentiaries. The Chinese were not invited to take part in these boundary negotiations, and their acceptance was never sought.[75]

Chen told his colleagues on 3 July that he was instructed to declare before the conference that his government would not recognize any treaty or similar document that might be signed between Great Britain and Tibet.[76] Moreover, in a written note of 6 July, the Chinese government, reiterating this position, stated: "The Government of China have no right whatever to alienate any portion of her territory and this accounts for their inability to sign the proposed Tripartite Convention and to recognize any convention or other similar documents that have been signed between Great Britain and Tibet."[77]

Meanwhile, McMahon conveyed to the Tibetan delegate on behalf of the British government a formal assurance that the government of Tibet "might depend upon the diplomatic support of His Majesty's Government, and on reasonable assistance in the way of munitions of war, in the event of a continuation of aggression on the part of the Chinese."[78]

On balance, by not signing the convention, the Chinese gained nothing but the retention of a relatively small territory between the Salween and Mekong formerly administered by the Tibetan government but occupied by Zhao Erfeng in 1908–1909. The state of war between Tibet and China was continued. But, as Richardson has noted, "China reserved, in its own opinion, the right to settle with Tibet in its own time."[79]

The British government secured the existence of a friendly northern neighbor, the delimitation of the Indo-Tibetan boundary, favorable regulations for Indo-Tibetan trade, and the right of the British Trade Agent at Gyantse to proceed to Lhasa and negotiate directly with the Tibetan government there.[80]

Tibet emerged from the conference only slightly more secure than it had entered. Its position vis-à-vis China had not improved, and the state of war still existed. On the other hand, Tibet's international personality, recognized at the start of the conference, remained intact and buttressed by British assurances—for what they were worth. In addition, the distinction between Inner and Outer Tibet having been virtually invalidated by China's refusal to adhere left a geographical and political delineation of Tibet, including both zones, recognized by Great Britain.

The major task that lay ahead, as the Tibetans saw it, was the preservation and protection of their independence and the conclusion of, at least, a regional peace on their eastern border with China.

5

Policies of
National Survival

Had the tripartite Simla Agreement been signed by all three governments, it might have provided Tibet with an acceptable degree of security. The Chinese refusal to sign left Tibet and China in a state of intermittent and undeclared war. This was a dangerous situation for Tibet. The Chinese forces were superior to the Tibetan army, and the disunity that had weakened China could not be counted on to last.[1] Thus, for the next decade, Tibet's principal foreign policy objective was the avoidance of a major military confrontation.

At the close of the Simla Conference, the British delegate gave his Tibetan counterpart formal assurances that Tibet might depend on his government for diplomatic support and for assistance in obtaining munitions of war to resist Chinese aggression.[2] It was not unusual for Tibet to look to an outside power for protection. Now, it looked to the British Empire for help.[3]

Tibetan Reliance on the British

No sooner had the negotiators left Simla in the summer of 1914 then the Chinese resumed their efforts to arrive at a separate settlement with the Tibetan government.[4] When China's overtures were met with Tibet's obstinate refusal to negotiate without British participation and with the insistence that the former sign the Simla Convention, the Chinese threatened to invade.[5]

During the Simla Conference, the Tibetan government purchased small quantities of arms and ammunition from India with the tacit approval of the British government.[6] In addition, the British presented the Dalai Lama with 5,000 obsolete rifles and 500,000 rounds of ammunition and promised the loan of four Indian army instructors.[7] The arms received by the Tibetan government, however, were not adequate. Tibet was left to fend for itself, for Britain's attention was now focused on the world war that had broken out in Europe.[8] The Dalai Lama offered 1,000 of his best troops to support the British in the war,[9] but British military supplies for Tibet were not forthcoming.

Britain's reluctance to provide Tibet with military assistance did not indicate total disinterest. On numerous occasions, the British lodged protests with the Chinese government against the latter's hostile policy toward Tibet and warned that they would "afford all possible assistance to Tibet in resisting Chinese aggression."[10] The British also agreed to exert pressure on the Chinese to effect their adhesion to the Simla Convention, and when the Chinese proposed a separate agreement with Britain, the Foreign Secretary, Sir Edward Grey, replied:

> The agreement recently reached between the British and Tibetan delegates at Simla represents the settled views of His Majesty's Government on the question, as stated by the British plenipotentiary at the final meeting of the conference. His Majesty's Government accordingly see no object in reopening the discussion of questions which have already been exhaustively dealt with and as to which they have come to a final decision. They must consequently decline to reopen negotiations either at Peking or in London, except for the purpose of recording the signature of the Chinese Government to the convention in its present form.[11]

By the end of 1917, it had become clear that the Chinese would never willingly accept the Simla Convention. That year, tension on the Sino-Tibetan border was high, and the Chinese made plans for an invasion. But, these had to be temporarily abandoned when serious rebellions broke out in China.[12] With order restored, attention was focused again on Tibet. The newly appointed military commander on the western border, General Peng Risheng, decided to advance to Lhasa in January 1918. He used a minor border incident to break the fragile truce and rejected Tibetan attempts at conciliation.[13]

Tibetan troops were now much better armed and trained than those Zhao Erfeng had faced in 1910, and thus they were a good match for Peng.[14] To his surprise and humiliation, the Tibetans crossed the Mekong River and drove the invading columns back. After months of fighting, General Peng surrendered. Three thousand prisoners were sent to Lhasa to be repatriated to China by way of India. Tibetan troops took Draya, Markam, Gonjo, and Derge and advanced so far that, as Eric Teichman, the British Consular Officer in Dartsedo (Dajianlu), reported, "[a]nother month or two would possibly have seen several thousand more Chinese prisoners in Tibetan hands, and the Lhasa forces in possession of all the country up to Ta Chien-lu."[15] At this juncture, the Chinese called on the British to mediate.[16] Eric Teichman was deputed to the border for that purpose, and, once again, tripartite negotiations were opened.

On August 19, a peace treaty was signed by the Tibetan and Chinese delegates.[17] It provided for a truce of one year and the acceptance of a provisional boundary, roughly along the course of the upper Yangtze, except that Derge and Beyul, east of the river, remained under Tibetan control.

A supplementary agreement was signed at Rongbatsa to arrange for the withdrawal of troops in that area.[18] Despite Teichman's stern warning at the opening of the negotiations that "if any agreement which we might come to were not immediately ratified by the Chinese Government, the Tibetans would have no option but to resume hostilities and advance on Batang,"[19] the treaty was never ratified by Beijing. Nevertheless, both parties respected its provisions for the next twelve years, and Tibet remained in full control of most of the newly occupied territories until 1949.

In Beijing, meanwhile, the British Minister, Sir John Jordan, again explored avenues for a comprehensive tripartite settlement. He complained that the attitude of the foreign ministry official he met with was "typical of that of all Chinese officials who approach this question. . . . He knew little about Tibet, except that it had once belonged to China, and foresaw that public opinion would not tolerate any cession of Chinese territory."[20] The talks were soon broken off, and the Chinese Premier suggested that the issue be decided by an international tribunal. Jordan, however, was persistent in his attempt to negotiate, and to this the Chinese eventually agreed.[21]

On 30 May 1919, the Waijiao Bu (Chinese Foreign Ministry) presented Jordan with a set of proposals. Though based on the Simla Convention, they suggested a Sino-Tibetan boundary more favorable to China and demanded the inclusion in the text of any agreement of two—apparently contradictory—statements: that Tibet formed a part of Chinese territory and that Tibet recognized China's suzerainty.[22] The talks were not pursued, however, for the Chinese broke them off in a matter of months. Once they had crossed into Mongolia and taken control there in November, they were in no mood for compromise.[23]

The Tibetan government's frustration with Britain's failure to deliver the promised military supplies and the resulting loss of faith in Britain as a protecting power raised the possibility that Tibet might look elsewhere for help.[24] The feeling of uneasiness that this prospect caused in London was aggravated by the Tibetan government's reception of a Chinese mission in Lhasa for the first time since 1911. This mission consisted of lamas and provincial officials from Gansu sent by the Governor of that province, ostensibly to present religious offerings to the Dalai Lama but in actuality to urge him to negotiate an agreement with China.[25] The Dalai Lama rejected the overture and, instead, called for tripartite negotiations in Lhasa.[26] The British government presently authorized Charles Bell, the Political Officer in Sikkim, who had long argued for a policy of active support to Tibet, to lead an official mission to Lhasa, the first since the military invasion of Tibet in 1903.[27] At the same time, London proposed to notify the Chinese government that, unless negotiations were resumed, Tibet would be given "material support against external aggression."[28]

The British mission was warmly received in Lhasa—an outcome that reflected both the Tibetan government's desire to improve relations with the British and the special friendship and trust the Thirteenth Dalai Lama felt for Charles Bell. Meanwhile, on 26 August 1921, the British handed the Chinese government an ultimatum.[29] The communication, presented simultaneously in London and Beijing, invited the Chinese to resume negotiations without delay and warned:

> In view of the commitments of His Majesty's Government to the Tibetan Government arising out of the tripartite negotiations of 1914 and in view of the fact that the Chinese Government accepted, with the exception of the boundary clause, the draft convention of 1914, providing for Tibetan autonomy under Chinese suzerainty, and formally reaffirmed their attitude in this respect in their offer of 1919, His Majesty's Government do not feel justified, failing a resumption of the negotiations in the immediate future, in withholding any longer their recognition of the status of Tibet as an autonomous State under the suzerainty of China, and intend dealing on this basis with Tibet in the future.

Hence the Marquess Curzon of Kendleston, as the British Foreign Minister, was compelled to inform the Chinese government:

> We [shall] regard ourselves as at liberty to deal with Tibet, if necessary, without again referring to China; to enter into closer relations with the Tibetans; to send an officer to Lhasa from time to time to consult the Tibetan Government; to open up increased trading intercourse between India and Tibet; and to give the Tibetans any reasonable assistance they might require in the development and protection of their country.[30]

As Hugh Richardson has noted, the communication clearly showed a new determination by the British government to recognize and treat Tibet as a fully autonomous State and to deal with it without further reference to China. He also rightly pointed out that it failed to give an accurate interpretation of British commitments to the Tibetan government;[31] in fact, any recognition of Chinese suzerainty was a direct contravention of the Anglo-Tibetan Declaration of 1914 and a violation of that agreement.

The language of the British ultimatum was not communicated to the Tibetans, however, and when no positive response from China was forthcoming, the British government authorized Charles Bell to enter into a bilateral agreement with Tibet that would provide for closer relations with that country.[32] By the terms of this new agreement, concluded in October of 1921, Britain undertook to "grant to the Tibetan Government reasonable assistance in the protection and development of Tibet . . . [and] therefore permit the Tibetan Government to import on payment munitions in installments at adequate intervals, provided that the Tibetan's Government gives an assurance in writing that such munitions will be used solely for self-defense and for internal police work."[33] In addition, the British were to provide assistance in the training of the Tibetan forces and in the development of Tibet. It was also agreed that the British would periodically dispatch an officer to Lhasa.

The new Anglo-Tibetan agreement had the effect of reviving mutual friendship and trust, without causing a reversion to undue Tibetan reliance on the British. But with the retirement of Charles Bell from government service at the end of 1921, and with the passing away of his friend the Tibetan Minister Shatra a year later, the personal quality that had characterized Anglo-Tibetan relations was replaced by a more formal relationship.

By the time the next British mission arrived in Lhasa in 1924, Major F. M. Bailey, its leader, found the country in an independent mood:

> It would not, I think, be correct to say that the attitude of the Tibetan Government is in any way less friendly to the Government of India than previously, but I think the attitude has somewhat changed. I think that it would be nearer the mark to say that, having been relieved of the threat of Chinese invasion owing to the disturbed state of that country, the Tibetan Government are able to moderate the attitude of dependence on the Government of India, which they have adopted since the Dalai Lama's flight in 1910. In fact the attitude now adopted would appear to be the more normal one for Tibet which was temporarily altered by our action in 1904, and by the subsequent action of the Chinese.[34]

Tibet had embarked on a policy of independent and equal diplomatic relations with its two giant neighbors—a policy of balance of power by which the Dalai Lama wished to demonstrate his independence as well as that of his country.

Striking a Balance with China

The Tibetan government was cautious in resuming contact with China, for there remained major obstacles to improved relations. The first was China's declared intent to subjugate Tibet; the second, the unresolved boundary dispute; and the third, a rift between the Dalai Lama and the Panchen Lama.

In 1922, the Dalai Lama had appointed Konchok Jungne to be abbot of the Yungong Monastery in Beijing, but formal contacts with the Chinese government only occurred seven years later, when Konchok Jungne returned to bring a letter from President Chiang Kai-shek. The Chinese President called for better relations between the two countries, suggested that the Dalai Lama might consider sending representatives to China, and offered Tibet assistance. In the same letter, however, he also urged Tibet to join the Republic as one of its "five races."[35]

The Dalai Lama welcomed this first communication from Chiang Kai-shek. He expressed a desire to improve bilateral relations but indicated that the main obstacle was the fundamental question of Tibet's status. Although a move might therefore be made toward close diplomatic ties between the two countries, the Dalai Lama left no doubt that he expected Tibet to be treated as an independent State. To the President's offer of assistance he responded only by suggesting that "for the purpose of protecting itself against aggression," Tibet might be supplied with arms.[36] The Dalai Lama did, however, send Konchok Jungne with a small staff to represent him in Nanjing, the seat of China's Nationalist government.[37]

Chiang Kai-shek did not propose to send a representative to Lhasa. But in November 1929, the official *Tibet-Mongolia Weekly News* announced that "the Chinese government, for the benefit of Tibet and Mongolia, will depute special officials to conduct state affairs."[38] The following year the Waijiao Bu warned that "inasmuch as both Mongolia and Tibet are integral parts of the Chinese Republic, the local authorities there should take care to avoid establishing direct diplomatic relations with any foreign government."[39]

These pronouncements could be no more than mere reflections of the wishes of the Chinese government, as the latter possessed neither the authority nor the means to implement such policies. Beyond that, the statements appear to have contributed to a systematic effort to misrepresent facts, with two ostensible objectives in mind: First, it was important that the Chinese government save face and appear more powerful than it was. The reality of China's powerlessness in and over Tibet, and the humiliation of military defeat at the hands of the Tibetan army and of Tibet's blunt refusal to join the Republic, could not be admitted openly to the Chinese public. As the Chinese Foreign Minister, T.V. Song, later explained: "[A]ll Chinese who have had any schooling have learned in their study of geography that Tibet is a part of China; that it has never occurred to them that there is any question about this as a matter of simple fact; and that these are, politically speaking, the Chinese people."[40] Second, as some observers have maintained, the misrepresentation of facts was part of a strategy to accumulate documents, first-hand reports, and correspondence that could serve as contemporary evidence to substantiate a future Chinese claim.[41]

In its dealings with the British government, as well, the Chinese kept up the fiction of authority over Tibet. After 1919, however, they no longer sought an agreement with the British to further their ambitions in Tibet. The British Ministers in Beijing—J. Jordan and his successor, B. Alston— concluded that China had "decided to wait until [the] Tibetans grow weary of the situation and of [Britain's] failure to obtain a settlement then to endeavour to win them back to Chinese allegiance by assurances of autonomy and favourable treatment."[42]

On the Sino-Tibetan border, reports and rumors of impending Chinese offensives and charges and countercharges of border violations characterized the situation after the 1918 truce. In 1931, open fighting again broke out and resulted in further Tibetan territorial gains. A truce was concluded, and both sides once again agreed to respect existing borders.[43] Although it did not provide a permanent solution to the boundary dispute, the truce agreement proved effective in preventing further major clashes until the communist advance of 1949.

The third cause of Sino-Tibetan friction, the dispute between the Panchen Lama of Tashi Lhunpo and the Tibetan government, arose in 1922 out of the Panchen Lama's refusal to contribute toward Tibet's costly defenses.[44]

The Panchen Lama, it will be recalled, was given his position by his pupil, the Fifth Dalai Lama; moreover, the relationship between the successive incarnations of the Dalai Lamas and Panchen Lamas was an interchangeable one between teacher and pupil, depending on their relative ages.[45] On both the religious and the personal levels, there was no animosity between the two foremost spiritual leaders; and in the worldly sphere, the Panchen Lama possessed no authority beyond his monastery and extensive estates.[46] Friction nevertheless arose at times between the courts of the two lamas, which outsiders—the Manchus, the Chinese, and the British—tried to use to their advantage.[47]

The present dispute was exploited by the Chinese in order to gain a foothold in Tibet. It had taken on such serious proportions that the Panchen Lama felt constrained to flee to Mongolia and then to China, where he remained almost until his death in 1937. The Chinese government pressed for his return to Tibet, suggesting that he should be escorted by Chinese troops. Though never objecting to the Lama's return, the Tibetan government stubbornly resisted Chinese attempts to send in troops to accompany him.[48] The Dalai Lama also rejected British offers of mediation, reminding the British of their undertaking not to interfere in the internal affairs of Tibet.[49]

The Absence of the Dalai Lama:
A Test of Strength

In December 1933, the Thirteenth Dalai Lama died at the age of 58. He had led Tibet through some of the most turbulent periods of its history: Twice he was forced to flee before invaders; at home, he fought corruption and enforced justice; and, most significant, he reasserted the independence of Tibet and steered his country toward self-reliance. Shortly before his death, the Dalai Lama wrote a testament in which he laid down the duties and responsibilities of his subjects and the policy they should follow during his temporary absence.[50] In particular, he warned against the threat of communism and instructed that "you must develop a good diplomatic relationship with our two powerful neighbors: India and China. Efficient and well-equipped troops must be stationed even on the minor frontiers bordering hostile forces. Such an army must be well trained in warfare as a sure deterrent against any adversaries."

The Dalai Lama's death left Tibet in a state of political insecurity. A young and inexperienced lama, Rating Rimpoche, was selected to be Regent of Tibet until the reincarnation of the "Precious Sovereign" of Tibet could be found and had come of age. Tibet felt vulnerable, and the ruling officials resolved not to deviate from the late Dalai Lama's policies of independence and self-reliance. This they conveyed in no uncertain terms to the President and Government of China:

Although experiencing the greatest bereavement owing to the temporary passing away of His Holiness the Dalai Lama, the Selon (head of the Government) [i.e., Prime Minister], the Kashag, and the State Council are conducting all affairs as before. As the representatives Khimpo Kunchok Jungney [Kongchok Jungne], Ngagwang Dakpa, Ngawang Gyaltsen, and Thobten Chuphel are in China, please refer to them all matters, so as to bring about the most amicable relations. On the other hand, should any steps be taken as a result of the influence of persons who want to create trouble between the two countries, such action will never be tolerated [by Tibet] even if reduced to the last man in this country. Please give this matter your most careful consideration, and send us a reply.[51]

The Chinese government expressed grief at the loss of the Dalai Lama and conferred a posthumous title on him: "Great Priest, Protector of the State, Propagator of Culture, Spacious in Benevolence, Perfect in Immaculate Intelligence."[52] A special mission of condolence, headed by General Huang Musong, a member of the National Military Council and the head of the Mongolian and Tibetan Affairs Commission, was promptly dispatched to Lhasa.[53]

General Huang had a political mission to accomplish. He handed to the Kashag China's terms for a settlement with Tibet—namely, that the Tibetan government must declare that Tibet is a part of the Republic of China, obey the instructions of the Chinese government, and set up a republic. In return, Tibet would be protected from aggression. The Kashag and the Tsongdu immediately rejected these terms, replying that Tibet had been ruled by thirteen successive Dalai Lamas and would never declare a republic or become a part of the Chinese Republic; and that Tibet would defend its independence to the last man against any invader. General Huang's suggestion that China might use force prompted the Tsongdu to pass a solemn resolution, sealed by all its members, reaffirming the position that under no circumstances would Tibet join the Chinese Republic.[54]

Having failed in his mission, General Huang was recalled to Nanjing. Before leaving, however, he tried to gain at least some concessions. First, he watered down his demands, insisting only that the Tibetans should admit that they are one of the five races of the Republic. The important thing, he explained, was that the Tibetans must recognize their subordinate position and rely solely on China. The Tibetan government reiterated its stand and pointed out that the only country Tibet had to fear was China.[55]

Next, General Huang's deputy handed the Kashag a fourteen-point proposal for an agreement, to which both the Kashag and the Tsongdu replied point by point:[56] To the suggestion that the Chinese and Tibetan governments should help each other on the basis of a Chö-yön relationship and that Tibet should always be respected as a holy and religious country, the Tibetans had no objection. They also readily agreed to the propositions that "China should consider Tibet to be independent and should not interfere in the internal administration of Tibet," and that "no Chinese troops should be kept on any of the frontiers of Tibet."

On the other hand, the Kashag and the Tsongdu entirely rejected the proposals, that they should "consult the Chinese Government before corresponding with other nations about external affairs"; that they should consult with the Chinese before appointing government officials to the highest ranks; and that China should have any responsibility to protect Tibet from invasion, arguing that Tibet was an independent State and capable of dealing with such matters itself. On the question of posting a Chinese representative in Lhasa, the Tibetans replied that the possibility could be entertained only if such an officer would strictly observe the independence of Tibet and refrain from all interference. The Chinese also asked to be informed of the discovery of new incarnations of the Dalai Lama, which the Tibetans agreed to do only after the installation had taken place, to ensure that the Chinese would be in no position to interfere in the matter. As to the suggestion that the Tibetan representative in China be paid by the Chinese government, the Tibetans were indifferent. And although they raised no objection to the return of the Panchen Lama, they did insist that he should not be accompanied by Chinese troops. Finally, they rejected the Chinese government's demand for extraterritorial jurisdiction over persons of mixed Chinese and Tibetan parentage.

At General Huang's further insistence, the Tibetans indicated only that, should an agreement be reached on all major matters, they might be prepared to consider accepting a degree of Chinese suzerainty along the lines contemplated in the Simla Convention. In order that the dialogue should not be totally broken off, a Chinese officer was allowed to remain in Lhasa with a wireless transmitter.

Summing up the outcome of Huang Musong's mission, Basil Gould, the British Political Officer, concluded that "Tibet conceded nothing. All that the Tibetan Government did was to indicate what were the points which they would be willing to concede in return for a satisfactory settlement."[57] Britain reacted to Huang Musong's visit by sending its Political Officer to Lhasa, where a mission, headed by Hugh Richardson and equipped with a wireless transmitter, was established.[58]

Following the death of the exiled Panchen Lama in 1937, the tension between China and Tibet, which had been aggravated by Chinese threats of invasion in 1935 and 1936, eased somewhat. The Lama's body was brought back to Tashi Lhunpo with a minimum of complications, and the dispute that had affected Sino-Tibetan relations for over a decade dissolved in the new excitement over the discovery of the reincarnation of the Dalai Lama.

In 1937, the fourteenth incarnation of the Dalai Lama, Tenzin Gyatso, was discovered in the village of Taktser, in Amdo province, by an official search party from Lhasa. Much of Amdo was at that time controlled by a practically independent Chinese Muslim Governor, General Ma Bufang, who demanded a ransom of 400,000 Chinese dollars from the Tibetan government before allowing the young incarnate lama to travel to Lhasa.[59] The Fourteenth Dalai Lama was officially recognized by the Tibetan government in July 1939, and a proclamation to that effect was issued by the authority of the Regent, the Kashag, and the Tsongdu. On 22 February 1940, the new Dalai Lama ascended the *Sengtri*, the Lion Throne.[60]

Official announcements of the Dalai Lama's recognition and invitations to the enthronement ceremony were sent to the King of Nepal, the Maharajas of Bhutan and Sikkim, and the governments of India and China. In response, representatives from all of these countries were deputed to attend the installation and to pay respects to the young ruler and protector of Tibet. "The keynote of the ceremonies," as Basil Gould described them, "was the public celebration of the return of the Dalai Lama to a throne which was already his own."[61]

The reports of the installation proceedings, and even of the discovery of the Dalai Lama, written by the Chinese representative, Wu Zhongxin, were misleading in their effort to present events in such a way as to substantiate the Chinese claim to supremacy over Tibet. Consequently, official Chinese accounts based on Wu's reports contain misrepresentations of the events and especially of Wu's own participation in the ceremonies. Indeed, substantiated records show that the Chinese representative was treated no differently than the representatives of the other foreign governments.[62]

As had likewise been the case during Huang's visit, Wu also broached the subject of Sino-Tibetan relations with the Kashag, and tried in vain to persuade its members to accept the appointment to Lhasa of a High Commissioner for China. Wu later complained that he had offered the Tibetans various forms of aid on behalf of the Chinese government but that they had refused it.[63]

During the absence of the Dalai Lama, the Tibetan government successfully withstood Chinese pressures. With the establishment of Chinese and British missions in Lhasa, in addition to the Nepalese legation and Bhutanese representation already there, Tibet was moving toward a fuller participation in the family of nations. The Dalai Lama's return strengthened the resolve to pursue this policy of self-reliance. As Basil Gould reported to his Viceroy: "The Thirteenth Dalai Lama was the outstanding influence in making the Tibet of today. Now that his throne is occupied by a child one sees more clearly than before that the existence of the Dalai Lama and the national existence of Tibet come very near to being one and the same thing."[64]

Neutrality in War

World War II broke out in 1939. Unlike any war in history, it left hardly a country untouched or unaffected. Tibet was no exception, although it remained neutral throughout the war and was therefore never directly involved. Nonetheless, the external circumstances of the war, at a time when a shift in attitude toward international relations was taking place inside Tibet, had an important impact on the international position of that country.

When Japan entered the war, Great Britain, China, and later the United States became close allies in the Asian war theater. By 1940, the Chinese had experienced serious setbacks against the Japanese and suffered greatly from the closing of coastal ports and the Indochina supply route. In that year, the Burma Road, the only other major supply route to China, was also closed, and the Allies were compelled to find alternative routes.[65]

The British and Chinese believed that supplies could best be transported from India to China by road through Tibet, a route far removed from likely Japanese attack. The Chinese government handed the British Ambassador a proposal for the construction of the "Xikang-India Highway," which would join Sichuan with India through Tibet. They were eager to begin construction at once. The British, though sharing the Chinese government's sense of urgency and aware of the importance of the project, foresaw both physical and political obstacles.[66] The following reply was accordingly delivered to the Chinese government:

> His Majesty's Government and the Government of India welcome in principle the Chinese proposal for a through road linking China with India, but in view of their traditional friendly relations with Tibet, they could not be parties to any scheme for the construction of a road that would pass through territory under the jurisdiction of the Tibetan Government without the full and willing assent of the Tibetan authorities. As a first step therefore the Government of India are obtaining the Tibetan Government's views. Owing however to the immense difficulties of the terrain it is obvious that the project can only be at the survey stage for the present. The Government of India suggest that air survey would be the most practical method of rapid progress and would be glad to cooperate with the Chinese Government in conducting an air survey from Assam if the Tibetan Government agree.[67]

The Tibetan government had no objection to the aerial survey the British requested, in view of the very friendly relations between the two countries, but it could not permit the construction of a road through Tibetan territory. When the Chinese simply announced to the Tibetan government that "it has been decided between the British and Chinese Governments to construct a motor road for the benefit of Tibetans" and asked permission to construct it through Tibetan territory, the Kashag replied: "The British and Chinese Governments may have decided to construct the road for their own convenience, but it is of no concern to the Tibetan Government, [which] cannot allow the Chinese to construct a road in Tibetan territory."[68]

The British, embarrassed by the tactlessness of the Chinese approach and angered by reports of the uninvited arrival on the Sino-Tibetan border of Chinese surveying parties, delivered a strong protest in Chongqing. Meanwhile, the Tibetan National Assembly also resolved not to allow the road construction under any circumstance and informed the Chinese government accordingly.[69]

In February 1942, Chiang Kai-shek visited India and, among other things, pressed for the opening of new supply routes. In view of the obstacles involved, the British and Chinese leaders agreed to abandon the China-India highway project for the time being. Instead, the two governments now proposed to approach the Tibetan government about allowing passage of essential supplies through existing trade routes, to be carried by pack animals. The Tibetan government refused to consider the new plan because it wished to preserve its neutrality and feared that the war would extend to Tibet if it acquiesced to the Anglo-Chinese request.[70]

The Tibetan refusal was not taken well by the Allies. The British Ambassador and the General Officer Commanding in China urged their government "that action should now be taken with the Tibetan government to induce them to agree to immediate exploration and development of all possible routes by land and air across Tibet and that the Chinese Government should be openly associated with us in these representations."[71] The War Cabinet in London agreed, but it also cautioned that the Tibetan position was motivated out of the Tibetans' fear not only that the supply route would violate their neutrality but also that it would facilitate Chinese encroachment on their independence: According to the British Foreign Office, "The Tibetans have every moral right to their independence for which they have fought successfully in the past and we are committed to support them in maintaining it."[72] The British government therefore considered exerting pressure on Lhasa, possibly by threatening economic sanctions, in order to change the Tibetan attitude, but only on the condition that the Chinese government would give a definite and public undertaking of its intention to respect Tibetan autonomy and to refrain from interfering in Tibet's internal affairs.[73] The Chinese declined to do so, but strong pressure was nonetheless brought to bear on the Tibetan government. In its response of July 1942, the Tibetan Foreign Office informed the British that, since the passage of war materials through Tibet would violate Tibet's neutrality, the government had decided to allow the transport of nonmilitary supplies only, in the interest of preserving the good relations that existed between the two governments. The concession was minimal, but both Britain and China accepted the Tibetan terms.[74]

This was not the end of the matter, however, for the Chinese then decided to station their own technicians along the supply route to supervise the transportation. Despite assurances to the Tibetan government that such personnel would refrain from all political activity, the Chinese technicians were refused entry. As the Tibetan Foreign Office asserted, "The Tibetan Government cannot agree to the Chinese Ministry of Communications establishing stations in any part of Tibet, or their representatives travelling all over the country."[75]

For the same reason, subsequent Chinese proposals to set up a joint Chinese-Tibetan-Indian commercial company to handle the transport were doomed from the start. The Tibetans felt, as did the British, that the Chinese were more interested in using a supply route to extend their influence in Eastern Tibet than they were in getting supplies over it. The issue came to a head when the Kashag, determined to thwart any such attempt, ordered all goods destined for the Chinese government to be held up; as a result, Chiang Kai-shek ordered Chinese troops to the Tibetan borders. The British, fearing that the Chinese might attempt to use the recalcitrant Tibetan attitude as an excuse for aggression, persuaded the Kashag to rescind the order. In April, the latter issued new directives, once again permitting the entry of Chinese goods, but on the condition that they "not be military stores and that no person of foreign nationality endeavours to obtain admission into Tibetan territory with the goods."[76] A serious crisis was thus averted, but the dispute was left unresolved.

Since the collapse of Burma in early 1942, the United States, as well, had taken an active interest in the question of supply routes to China, in particular the trans-Tibet route.[77]

The government in Washington decided to send an official United States mission to discuss the question of supply routes with the Tibetans in Lhasa. The United States government obtained permission for the visit from the Tibetan government through the good offices of the Government of India. The leaders of the mission, Captain Ilia Tolstoy and Lieutenant Brooke Dolan, both officers of the Office of Strategic Services, were designated official envoys of President Franklin D. Roosevelt to the Tibetan government. Accordingly, they bore a letter and official presents from the President to the Dalai Lama and were received in Tibet with due ceremony as official presidential emissaries.[78]

President Roosevelt's letter was carefully worded, so as to avoid giving any possible offense to the Chinese allies. The President expressed his great interest in Tibet and explained how the United States and its allies were fighting a war "which has been thrust upon the world by nations bent on conquest who are intent upon destroying freedom of thought, of religion, and of action everywhere. The United Nations are fighting today in defense of and for the preservation of freedom."[79] This reference to freedom and, of course, to religion was much appreciated in Tibet. Thus, the Dalai Lama emphasized in his reply to the President that "Tibet also values her freedom and independence enjoyed from time immemorial," and the Regent noted that "Tibet, which has been free and independent from her earliest history, devotes her entire resources in the cause of religion and being the great seat of Buddhism, we are striving to maintain and strengthen our national and religious status."[80]

The head of the Tibetan Foreign Office, Surkang Shape, took pains to explain to the United States envoys that Tibet was fully independent and had never recognized Chinese suzerainty. Tolstoy and Dolan were highly impressed by the Tibetan officials they met and by the Tibetan case for independence. They suggested that Tibet should be represented at the coming peace conference, a proposal that the Tibetan Government immediately approved. Generally, the latter were well pleased with the visit and with the strong support the Americans had expressed for the maintenance of Tibetan freedom.[81] As a result, the Kashag granted the envoys special permission to travel through Eastern Tibet to China, explaining: "This is the first time that friendly relations were established between Tibet and the United States of America and Mr. Franklin D. Roosevelt also sent a letter and presents to the Dalai Lama. For [the] above reasons the Tibetan Government allows you to go through [but] will not set a precedent which other foreigners can claim."[82]

As for the military supply route, none was ever opened. For a time, nonmilitary needs were partly met by air-lifting supplies from India to China; then, once a new Burma road was opened in 1944, the pressure on Tibet was eased.[83]

Expanding International Relations

In 1942, the Tibetan government created a Foreign Office to deal with all matters pertaining to Tibet's foreign affairs. The importance given to the conduct of international relations was reflected in the ministerial rank of the Office's directors, who were made directly responsible to the Kashag and had immediate access, unlike the Kashag, to the National Assembly. Henceforth, the Foreign Office became the only proper channel for communication between the representatives of foreign governments and the Tibetan government. The Chinese, reluctant to admit their position as a foreign power, instructed their representative in Lhasa, Gong Qingzong, not to deal through the Foreign Office. As the Kashag did not permit another channel for communication, however, Gong was put in a position of practical isolation and ineffectiveness. In fact, he was able to communicate with the government only through the intermediary of a low-ranking Tibetan interpreter attached to his mission.[84]

Relations with Mongolia and the Soviet Union

Mongol-Tibetan relations were close throughout history. Their religious and cultural bonds were especially strong, because it was the Tibetan lamas who had converted the Mongols to Tibetan Buddhism; in turn, the Mongols became the Dalai Lama's most devout followers.

The bond was also a politico-religious one. The Tibetan and Mongolian people alike acknowledged the spiritual supremacy of the Dalai Lama. The Bogdo Khan (i.e., the Holy Prince, or Grand Lama, of Urga and thus the immediate head of the Mongolian Church) was traditionally appointed by the Dalai Lama and was invariably a Tibetan. The Mongol Khans, on their part, had patronized the Dalai Lamas for centuries and had also occupied positions of influence in Tibet.[85] The Tibet-Mongolia Treaty of 1913 was but a reflection and formalization of existing ties. The treaty was of little consequence, inasmuch as the Tibetans and Mongolians were bound, with or without it, by much stronger historic bonds and mutual pledges than such a treaty could ever create. Thus, when the British marched on Lhasa in 1903, it was in Mongolia that the Dalai Lama naturally sought a home in exile.[86]

The connection between the two countries was traditionally maintained by trade, pilgrimages, the residence of some 800 Mongolian monks and scholars in monastic universities around Lhasa, and the appointment of Tibetan lamas to monasteries in Mongolia. When the Dalai Lama left Urga in 1908, he retained an agent there to look after his interests, including a bank that he had opened. The Tibetan government was in constant touch with this agent, who in turn maintained contact with the Mongolian government. It was this agent who, together with Dorjieff, negotiated and signed the 1913 Treaty, and it was through him that arms and ammunition were purchased in Mongolia by the Tibetan government.[87]

Mongolian autonomy, secured as the result of a declaration of independence and a series of treaty arrangements made with Russia and China in 1912, 1913, and 1915, was formally canceled by the Chinese in 1919. Taking advantage of the Bolshevik scare, General Xu Shucheng moved troops into Mongolia and took power by a coup d'état. A forged document was prepared, purporting to be a petition from the Mongolian leaders for the abrogation of their country's autonomy, and all Mongolians in positions of authority were replaced by Chinese.[88]

Two years later, the Mongolians took advantage of the weakness caused by the civil war in China to oust the Chinese from Mongolia and to recover their autonomy with the assistance of Russian reactionary forces.[89] At the end of the year, Soviet Russian troops intervened in Mongolia and set up a communist government with whom they concluded a treaty. Mongolia once again became independent and was recognized as such by the Soviet Union in 1924, although it remained under Soviet influence. The Soviet intervention was dramatic for the lamas and monks, who were now persecuted in the communist drive to eradicate religion and the class system.[90]

In May 1927, a Mongolian delegation arrived in Lhasa to discuss relations between the two countries. The envoys proposed the exchange of diplomatic representatives between Lhasa and Urga, establishment of telegraph communications between the two capitals, and an increase in trade.[91] The Tibetan government, much alarmed by the socialist revolution and religious persecution that had occurred in Mongolia, felt unable to entertain any of the Mongolians' proposals, which if fulfilled, they feared might lead to Bolshevik infiltration. Moreover, the fact that the Bogdo Khan was under house arrest in Urga, that some of Tibet's assets in Mongolia had been nationalized, and that travel restrictions were being imposed on Tibetan traders traveling in and out of that country did not encourage the Tibetans to seek closer ties with the Mongolian government. Despite these misgivings, the Mongolian delegation was generally well received and was granted an audience with the Dalai Lama.[92]

The delegation also requested on behalf of the Soviet government the establishment of a diplomatic agent for the USSR in Lhasa. In support of this request, the Dalai Lama was shown a document he had signed in Mongolia in 1904 with Russian officials, by which he had agreed to the establishment of such an agent in Lhasa. The Dalai Lama rejected the Russian request, pointing out that the agreement had been made with the Czarist government and not with that of the Bolsheviks.[93]

A year later, a joint Soviet-Mongolian delegation, led by a Soviet Buriat military officer, arrived in Lhasa. Despite British pressure on the Tibetans to expel the delegation, they were once again courteously received and granted an audience with the Dalai Lama. The envoys suggested that relations be improved between Tibet and both Mongolia and the Soviet Union, but the Tibetans still felt compelled to decline the overtures.[94] The talks with the Mongolian missions nevertheless had some effect, for in October 1930 the Dalai Lama deputed a high-ranking official to replace his agent in Urga.[95]

Relations with Nepal

In 1911, when the Tibetans fought the Manchu troops in Tibet, it was Nepalese mediation that eventually led to the Sino-Tibetan agreements of August and December 1912. At no time while the Nepalese mediated, nor in the settlements that resulted, was there any suggestion that Nepal acknowledged the existence of any form of suzerainty either between China and Tibet or between China and Nepal.[96] The governments of Nepal and Tibet actually felt much the same way about their ties with China. Both States had declared their "respect" for the Manchu Emperor in the 1856 Treaty and had sent tributary missions to him since 1792. But the Chinese revolution against the Manchus in 1911 changed all that. Tibet declared its independence, and Nepal also conveyed to China expressions of total independence. The Chinese General Zhong Yin had sent the Nepalese ruler a communication very similar to the one sent to the Dalai Lama:

Inasmuch as the relations between Nepal and China have always been most intimate and cordial . . . it is desirable that at least the same relationship should exist as heretofore, and, if a union of Nepal with the five affiliated races of China could be effected, China may be regarded as Nepalese China; the needs of one part will be felt and responded to by the rest of the nation, and the powers of China, thus united, may be so multiplied that it will be difficult to draw a parallel. . . . It is expected that it may please Your Highness to dispatch a special delegation with congratulations to Peking for orders and advice.[97]

A union with "the last of our subject states,"[98] General Zhong argued, was of great importance, as "the relations between China and Nepal during the past several hundred years have been unceasingly more intimate than between China and Tibet."[99]

The Nepalese Prime Minister rejected the Chinese attempt to claim and establish authority over Nepal:

Nepal has no other wish but to ever remain in peace and amity with her friends and neighbours so long as her independence is respected, and, as her friendly relations with China are of such a long date, it is only natural that she should be glad at the continuance of the same. . . . As Nepal is an ancient Hindu Kingdom, desirous of preserving her independence and her separate existence, she cannot entertain the idea of a union with the five affiliated races said to constitute the Republic of China.[100]

Since 1911, Nepal had stopped sending missions to Beijing, and relations with China were limited to the reception of Chinese missions to Kathmandu (in 1930, 1932, 1934, and 1946) sent to confer titles and to present ceremonial robes to the Kings and Prime Ministers of Nepal.[101]

In contrast with former times, when the Manchu Amban in Lhasa helped to mediate disputes, no outside power was involved in Tibet-Nepal relations after 1911. Those relations officially remained based on the 1856 Treaty.

Thus, the Nepalese Government had a permanent legation at Lhasa, headed by an ambassador (the Vakil). As the Tibetan government had no legation in Kathmandu, all relations between the two countries were conducted through the Vakil, or, in exceptional circumstances, directly beween the Dalai Lama or Kashag and the Nepalese King or his Prime Minister. The generally friendly relations between the two countries, demonstrated by Nepal's role in resolving the Sino-Tibetan conflict in 1912, were briefly disrupted by a diplomatic incident in 1929.

For some time prior to the incident there existed among the Tibetans a good deal of resentment about the privileged position Nepal had acquired in Tibet through the 1856 Treaty: It had a trading colony with its own officers in Lhasa and elsewhere; its subjects were exempt from trade duties; and its own magistrates adjudicated quarrels among Nepalese subjects. Furthermore, Tibet still paid a yearly sum of Rs. 10,000 to Nepal, whereas Nepal had failed to come to the assistance of Tibet against the British in 1904 and the Manchus in 1910, although it had been bound to do so by treaty. The Nepalese, for their part, resented the unfriendly and at times unfair way in which many of them were treated in Tibet.[102] There were some seven hundred Nepalese traders and over a thousand persons of mixed Nepalese and Tibetan parentage (referred to as *Kachcharas*) in Lhasa alone. Large numbers of Nepalese and Kachchara traders also lived in Shigatse and other southern Tibetan cities and villages. They generally dressed, lived, and worshipped as the Tibetans did, but there was no close feeling of brotherliness such as that between the Mongolians and the Tibetans; hence, friction between the two peoples was not infrequent.[103]

The diplomatic confrontation itself occurred in August 1929, when an alleged criminal, whose nationality the Tibetan and Nepalese authorities disputed, was forcibly arrested by the Tibetan police at the Nepalese legation where he had received asylum. The question at issue, as the Nepalese and British governments had complained to the Dalai Lama, was the "violation of [the Nepalese] legation, an act opposed to all international law and custom."[104] The Prime Minister of Nepal demanded both a public apology and the punishment of the officials responsible for violating the legation's diplomatic immunity. The British advised the Tibetans, in view of the seriousness of their violation of international law, to acquiesce to the Nepalese demand. The Dalai Lama did so, and the crisis was resolved.[105]

Two other problems preoccupied the Tibetan and Nepalese governments. One concerned jurisdiction over the Kachcharas, the other, minor perennial boundary disputes. The Kashag sent the Commander-in-Chief Tsarong Shape to Kathmandu in early 1925 to discuss these problems and the improvement of bilateral relations. By 1931, both issues had been amicably resolved without the interference of third parties, and good relations were reestablished.[106]

The Chinese President deputed an envoy to Kathmandu in 1930 with a letter to the Nepalese King, in which he announced: "To the end that peace and security may be maintained, the National Government [of China] will assume the responsibility to settle the boundary dispute between Nepal and Tibet."[107] The Nepalese ruler's reply, in which he "repudiated in *toto* any claim of the Chinese Government to interfere in any question of this nature,"[108] served to emphasize yet again that China had no role whatsoever to play in Tibet-Nepal relations after 1911.

Relations with the United States

Until World War II, the United States government had had little occasion to maintain official contacts with Lhasa. It had little interest in a country in which there were no United States residents, or even travelers, and in which no United States property existed.[109] Consequently, the United States government had not found it necessary to formulate a stand on the question of Tibet's status.

An early reference to Tibet can be found in a State Department memorandum of June 1942 entitled, "China's War Potential," in which Tibet was included in a description of the "total area of Chinese territory."[110] The British Foreign Office reacted to this memorandum with surprise, and protested that "in point of fact the Tibetans not only claim to be but actually are an independent people, and they have in recent years fought successfully to maintain their freedom against Chinese attempts at domination."[111]

This response prompted the first statement of United States policy regarding the question of Tibet's status. The United States government did not believe that "a useful purpose would be served" by opening a detailed discussion of this issue at the time, but they did point out that "suzerainty over Tibet has long been claimed by the Chinese Government, . . . Tibet is listed in the Chinese Constitution among areas constituting the territory of the Republic of China, and . . . this Government has at no time raised question concerning either of these claims."[112] In an internal communication, the Assistant Secretary of State explained to the Director of the Office of Strategic Services that

> the susceptibilities of the Chinese Government are of importance to this country and to the United Nations [i.e., the Allies] in connection with the war effort as a whole. It therefore is desirable, in any relations which we may have with the Tibetan authorities or in any action which we may take vis-à-vis them, to avoid gratuitously or inadvertently giving offense to the Chinese Government.[113]

Despite these considerations, the United States did deal with Tibet directly and without reference to China;[114] indeed, it even contemplated sending a representative from the embassy in Delhi to Lhasa from time to time, to maintain the direct relations with Tibet that had been established by Ilia Tolstoy and Brooke Dolan.[115]

Relations with Great Britain

During World War II, Britain reverted to the position regarding Chinese claims over Tibet that it had held at the Simla Conference and maintained that position at least until 1951. In an official communication to the U.S. government, the British government formulated its stand as follows:

> The Government of India have always held that Tibet is a separate country in full enjoyment of local autonomy, entitled to exchange diplomatic representatives with other powers. The relationship between China and Tibet is not a matter which can be unilaterally decided by China, but one on which Tibet is entitled to negotiate, and on which she can, if necessary, count on the diplomatic support of the British Government along the lines shown above.[116]

The British government decided that whereas Tibet had been independent in practice since 1911, any recognition of Chinese suzerainty over Tibet should be rejected "unless and until Tibet recognizes it herself as part of a general and peaceful settlement of her relations with China."[117] Britain's policy was conveyed officially to the governments of Canada, Australia, New Zealand, and South Africa in June 1943 as follows:

> Tibetans are a different race from Chinese and have a different religion, language, and culture. They have never been absorbed culturally by the Chinese; on the contrary, Chinese in Tibet have often become more Tibetan than Chinese. For over thirty years they have enjoyed *de facto* independence and do not wish to be resubjugated. Their memories of Chinese rule are those of disorder and incompetence, whereas the Dalai Lama's administration has great moral authority. Chinese nationalists claim all territories formerly incorporated in the Manchu dynastic empire, but as the new China is based on a purely Chinese nationalism there appear to be few grounds on which China can justifiably assert unqualified control over a nation isolated by geography, already self-governing and determined to retain the same independence which China advocates for other countries of the Far East such as Burma and the Malay States.[118]

The British Ambassador in Chongqing was instructed to make it clear in his discussions with the Chinese government that "His Majesty's Government do not feel themselves committed to regard China as the suzerain unless she in turn agrees to Tibetan autonomy."[119] A memorandum to that effect was handed to the Chinese Foreign Minister by his British counterpart, Anthony Eden;[120] and to the Tibetan government, Political Officer Basil Gould reiterated Britain's preparedness to do all it could to help Tibet maintain its autonomy.[121]

Relations with Other States

With Bhutan and Sikkim, Tibet continued its traditionally friendly relations. These were based not only on the religious and cultural bond between the countries in question, but also on the numerous family ties between the Tibetan nobility and the Bhutanese and Sikkimese ruling families. The King of Bhutan, or Maharaja, kept a representative in Lhasa, known as the Druk Lochawa or "Interpreter of Bhutan."[122]

A number of Japanese travelers had reached Lhasa in the first decades of the century, and some lived there for prolonged periods of time. When the Dalai Lama visited China in 1908, the Japanese Colonial Minister, Sonyo Otani, went to see him. As a result of their meeting, the two countries concluded an agreement of mutual cooperation, referred to as the "Buddhist Alliance."[123] Following the return of the Dalai Lama to Tibet in 1912, his Government employed a retired Japanese army officer to train one of the Tibetan regiments. Some years later, the Commander in Chief of Tibet's army visited Japan, and in 1921 the Japanese agreed to supply Tibet with arms, which it did for a number of years.[124] In 1942, a Tibetan government delegate was received in Japan by senior government officials who hoped to win the Tibetans over to the Japanese war cause.[125] Tibet, however, maintained its neutrality toward the Japanese just as it did toward the Americans, the Chinese, and the British.[126]

World War II proved to be a test of the Tibetan government's ability not only to maintain the country's independence but also to follow a foreign policy wholly distinct from that of its two giant neighbors. It was now some thirty-three years since Tibet had regained its independence, and in that time, the country had successfully opposed Chinese attempts to assert control. Although the Chinese government had not given up, it was compelled to admit failure and to conduct its relations with Tibet as other foreign governments did. Tibet maintained direct relations with numerous States. Its relations with Great Britain were once again stabilized when the latter reverted to the position that it was bound to maintain by the Anglo-Tibetan agreement of 1914—that is, to refuse any recognition of Chinese suzerainty over Tibet unless and until the Tibetans themselves agreed to do so.

Tibet did not take part in the Peace Conference after World War II, as the Allies believed that its presence as a nonbelligerent party would be inappropriate.[127] Immediately following the war, however, the Tibetan government dispatched high-level delegations to India and China, as well as to the United Kingdom and the United States: Hence, Tibet had embarked on a policy of unprecedented diplomatic activity.

6

From Independence to Invasion

On 12 August 1945, Japan surrendered, and the World War ended in an Allied victory. For Tibet, this was a mixed blessing. It was clearly in Tibet's interests that Great Britain and its allies should have emerged victorious. But an ascendant China could mean a renewed threat to Tibetan security. Tibet nevertheless emerged more self-confident from the World War period for having succeeded in maintaining its independent policy of neutrality. The Tibetan government was now ready to embark upon an active foreign policy.

Active Diplomacy

In late 1945, Regent Takdra Rimpoche decided to send a Good Will Mission to India and China.[1] Its official purpose was to convey the Tibetan government's congratulations to the allies for their victory over Germany and Japan. Its primary objective, however, was to emphasize Tibetan independence. Thus, the Government of India reported:

> The Tibetan Government informed us at the end of October last year that with the avowed intention of asserting the independence of Tibet (which is recognized by [the British Government] but not by China) they proposed to send to New Delhi and Chungking a Mission of high officials—though not of Cabinet rank—to offer congratulations to the Viceroy on the achievement of victory, and to present gifts from the Dalai Lama and the Regent to H.M. The King and to His Excellency. The Mission would also bring greetings to the President of the U.S.A. with a ceremonial scarf, and would then proceed to Chungking on a complimentary visit to Generalissimo Chiang Kai-shek.[2]

The Mission, led by Dzasak Thubten Samphel and Dzasak Khemey Sonam Wangdu, both of ministerial rank, was extremely well received by the British in India, who "welcome[d] this evidence of Tibet's desire to assert her independence" and took the opportunity to publicize in the world press the facts concerning Tibet's international status.[3] The Mission was invited to attend the Victory Week Celebrations in New Delhi and its members were received officially by the Viceroy, through whom a message was conveyed to the King. They also called on the U.S. Commissioner, G. Merrell, as planned, to deliver letters from the Dalai Lama, the Regent, and the Kashag to President Harry S. Truman, expressing the hope that the good relations that had been established between the two States and their governments would be strengthened.

On 5 April, the Tibetan Mission arrived in Nanjing. The Chinese press reported that the Tibetan officials had come to attend the National Assembly and also "to represent Tibetans in paying respects to President Chiang Kai-shek for his leadership in the war of resistance against Japanese aggression."[4] The Chinese authorities went to great lengths to represent the Tibetan Mission as a delegation to the Chinese National Assembly.[5] This should have come as no surprise, for ever since the formation of the Republic, the Chinese had tried to secure some form of Tibetan representation in their Parliament, as such representation might imply acceptance by Tibet that it formed a part of the Republic. When these efforts failed, the Chinese authorities appointed ethnic Tibetans living in China, especially in the border areas of Sichuan, Yunnan, and Gansu, to act as representatives of Tibet.[6]

The British warned the Tibetan government of the danger that, once in Nanjing, their Mission would be pressured to attend the National Assembly. The Tibetan government was grateful for the British expressions of concern but gave formal assurances that the Mission had been instructed not to take part in the Assembly, that it was purely complimentary, and that it would not embark on political discussions with the Chinese.[7] The truth was slightly different. The Tibetan Mission was indeed given instructions not to participate in the Assembly, but aside from delivering a congratulatory message to Chiang Kai-shek, the Mission was also instructed to present demands for the return to Tibet of territories still occupied by the Chinese.[8]

In Nanjing, the Mission delivered a letter from the Tibetan government and National Assembly to Chiang Kai-shek and his government. It contained a "nine-point" proposal for the improvement of relations between the two countries, in keeping with the Tibetan government's response to Huang Musong's proposals made in 1934.[9] The first point made was that the Tibetans would "continue to maintain the independence of Tibet as a nation ruled by the successive Dalai Lamas through an authentic religious-political rule." The second was the desire to establish "an unstrained relationship" between the two countries on the basis of the Priest-Patron (Chö-yön) relationship. Third, the Tibetans demanded the return of territories in Kham and Amdo under Chinese control.

On the question of Tibetan independence, the proposal emphatically stated in numerous places that "Tibet has been an independent state, managing its own domestic and foreign, civil and military affairs" and that this should remain the case in the future. Consequently, the Tibetans demanded that the Chinese respect the boundaries and laws of Tibet and that they recognize Tibetan passports. The letter, however, was somewhat ambiguous with respect to the Chö-yön relationship. In keeping with its earlier position, the Tibetan government expressed a willingness to establish friendly relations with the Chinese government, "which has its precedent" in the Chö-yön relationship. At times, the phrasing of the letter suggests that the Chö-yön relationship still existed between Tibet and China and had been interrupted ("deteriorated to the point of hostility") only after 1908. From the context of the message, however, it is clear that the Tibetan government was proposing a normalization of relations between the two countries for which the Chö-yön relationship, which had existed between the Dalai Lama and the Manchu Emperor, could serve as a basis. It is also clear that those relations were conditioned upon agreement on other essential issues, such as the boundary question and the respect for Tibetan independence. The only concession the Tibetans were prepared to make, in keeping with the references to the Chö-yön, was to ask for China's "support" should Tibet be invaded by foreign forces.

On the boundary question, the Tibetans claimed that the three provinces of U-Tsang, Kham, and Amdo had been "a territory unmistakably under the control and protection of the Dalai Lama" and demanded the return of the Tibetan areas forcibly taken by the Chinese. "[T]he annexation by force of small nations and territories by big ones," the letter complained, "is against well-known international rules."

As the British had feared, the Tibetans, once in Nanjing, were no longer free agents but were virtually kept hostage. When the National Assembly meeting was postponed for a number of months owing to domestic troubles and it became clear in Lhasa that the Chinese authorities had no intention of letting the Tibetan officials leave before then, the Kashag sent their mission instructions to return to Tibet at once and to plead ill health if necessary. But this was to no avail, for the Chinese refused to make the necessary travel arrangements[10] and kept the Tibetans waiting to receive a reply to their letter from the President and to take official leave from him. They were then informed that the issues raised in their letter could be dealt with only by the National Assembly. The Tibetans were thus persuaded to attend the Assembly, which opened in November 1946.[11] The Tibetans took the position, however, that they had no authority to discuss matters concerning China or its draft constituion, which was the main item on the Assembly's agenda.[12]

The agenda circulated at the Assembly's opening indicated that the participants would be called on to declare that "all the people of the countries whose delegates are present in this assembly are subjects of the Chinese Kuomintang government."[13] The Mission reported this matter to Lhasa, whereupon the alarmed Kashag wired back immediately, ordering its officials to state that they could never accept such a resolution; that they had only been sent on a congratulatory mission to Nanjing; that, in order to remove misunderstandings, they had also been deputed to hand a letter to Chiang Kai-shek stating the Tibetan stand on a number of outstanding issues of Sino-Tibetan relations; that, as they had received no response to this communication, they had attended the National Assembly with a view to securing from that body a reply to the points raised in the letter; and that, if the Assembly chose to pass the resolution in accordance with the agenda instead of giving the Tibetan officials an opportunity to say what they had come to say, the latter would have no alternative but to leave the meeting. The Kashag further instructed the Mission to make it plain that no one but the members of the Mission were authorized to represent the Tibetan government.[14] The resolution was apparently not passed. The Tibetans still made a public demonstration of their refusal to vote on or sign any resolutions, including the newly drafted constitution, maintaining as before that they were not authorized to do more than simply attend the meeting.[15] This behavior clearly displeased the Chinese hosts, who, following the Tibetans' return to Lhasa, once again urged the Tibetan government to send another delegation to Nanjing to attend the Chinese Constituent Assembly. The Tibetans, all the wiser from past experience, declined the invitation.

The Tibetan Mission accomplished little by airing the government's views and grievances to the National Assembly and to the President of China. At best, the Tibetans reaffirmed the resolve to continue to run their affairs without Chinese interference. As to the possible adverse affects of the Tibetan presence at the Assembly and of the misleading Chinese publicity in this regard, there was apparently no need for undue concern, as L. H. Lamb, of the British Embassy in Nanjing, advised his government:

> I rather wonder if we are not taking the matter too seriously. The Chinese love of self-deception is well known (and their own public can have few illusions as to the fiction of their boasted suzerainty over Tibet), while the rest of the world can scarcely be taken in by such pretensions, whether aired in the press or more solemnly in the National Assembly. And the effect or significance of the presence of Tibetan representatives in the Assembly must be appreciably discounted by the fact that delegates also came from the United Kingdom and other parts of the world which no one is likely to credit as being part of China.[16]

Indian Independence

On the eve of India's independence, Pandit Jawaharlal Nehru and the Congress Party of India organized the Asian Relations Conference in March 1947. The Tibetan government accepted an invitation to send a delegation to New Delhi, as did the governments of other Asian States. The national flag of Tibet was flown alongside those of the other participating countries, including China, and in every respect Tibet was treated in the same way as the other independent Asian States. In fact China's delegates lodged a protest against this official recognition of the Tibetan delegation and even demanded the removal of a map of Asia displayed in the conference building that showed Tibet as a country politically separate from China.[17] But the spirit of the conference was expressed in Nehru's opening speech: "In this Conference . . . there are no leaders and no followers. All countries of Asia have to meet together on an equal basis in a common task and endeavor."[18] While in India, the Tibetan delegates met with Mahatma Gandhi and Pandit Nehru, thereby establishing the first formal contacts with the leaders of independent India. India became fully independent on 15 August 1947, and the Tibetan government telegraphed its good wishes on the occasion. On that day also, the British Mission at Lhasa formally became the Indian Mission, and the flag of India thenceforth flew over its compound. Until a suitable replacement could be found, the Head of the Mission, Hugh Richardson, who joined the Indian government service, retained his post.

Shortly before the transfer of power, the British government and the Government of India communicated formal statements to Lhasa concerning the future of Anglo-Tibetan and Indo-Tibetan relations. The Tibetan government was informed that "after August 15th the close and cordial relations which have existed for so many years with themselves and the Government of India will continue with the successor Indian Governments upon whom alone rights and obligations arising from existing Treaty provisions will thereafter be devolved."[19]

The British further assured the Tibetans that the United Kingdom would continue to take a friendly interest in the future prosperity of the Tibetan people and the maintenance of the autonomy of their country and suggested that contact might be maintained by periodic visits to Tibet from the British High Commissioner in New Delhi. The Tibetan government responded by welcoming the continued British interest in the maintenance of Tibetan independence. To the Indian government the Kashag sent a message asking for the return of territories that had been incorporated into India by the British, possibly to test India's stand on the matter or, once again, to show all concerned that Tibet followed an independent policy.[20]

In response to the Tibetan note, the Government of India sent the following communication to the Tibetan Foreign Office:

> The Government of India would be glad to have an assurance that it is the intention of the Tibetan Government to continue relations on the existing basis until new agreements are reached on matters that either party may wish to take up. This is the procedure adopted by all other countries with which India has inherited treaty relations from His Majesty's Government.[21]

There can be no question, therefore, that the Indian government recognized the treaty relations that existed between the Tibetans and the British and accepted these as binding on India.[22]

Hugh Richardson assessed the consequences of the transfer of power in India on that country's relations with Tibet thus:

> The effect of the devolution of British obligations and rights upon the new Government of India was that the Indian Government, besides inheriting the British frontier with Tibet, became bound by the Simla Convention of 1914 as between India and Tibet, subject to the modifications introduced by the joint British and Tibetan declarations of the same year. The relationship thus

accepted had been most recently defined in the memorandum of 1943, referred
to earlier, which had made it clear that there was no unconditional British
recognition of Chinese suzerainty over Tibet. The Indian Government also
acquired the extraterritorial privileges enjoyed under agreements with Tibet—
the right to maintain Trade Agents at Gyantse, Yatung, and Gartok (the last
was never a permanent post) with small military escorts; to try cases occurring
in the Trade Marts between British subjects; and to hold joint inquiries with
the Tibetan authorities into disputes between British subjects and Tibetan or
other nationals. A further inheritance was the post and telegraph service and
the staging bungalows between the Indian border and Gyantse which had for
some time been paid for out of Indian revenues.[23]

The Tibetan Trade Mission

In keeping with Tibet's opening up to the world, the government at
Lhasa decided to send an official Trade Mission to India, China, the United
States, and the United Kingdom. The purpose of this Mission, led by the
Secretary of Finance, Tsepon Shakabpa, was to promote the expansion of
direct trade, to improve relations with other countries and to demonstrate
Tibet's independence.[24]

The Mission arrived in India in December of 1947. The delegates' principal
task was to negotiate the relaxation of controls on Tibetan exports passing
through India. Discussions centered on their request for access to the
foreign exchange received for Tibetan exports to third countries that had
been held by the Indian government. The Mission also took up the matter
of customs duties collected by the Indians on imports into Tibet passing
through India. While in India, the delegates were received officially by Lord
Mountbatten, Prime Minister Nehru, and Mahatma Gandhi.

Early the following year, the Trade Mission traveled to Nanjing, where
they once again tried to secure from the Chinese government an allocation
of foreign exchange for the Tibetan exports shipped through China to the
United States and other countries. The delegates met with little success,
despite high-level discussion with Chiang Kai-shek, members of the Executive
Yuan, and other officials.[25]

At the time of the Tibetans' visit, the Chinese National Assembly once
again met to elect the President and Vice-President. Contrary to some
Chinese reports, the Mission did not attend this Assembly. The only
Tibetans present at this meeting were the Tibetan envoy in Nanjing, who
attended solely as an observer, and a number of ethnic Tibetans selected
by the Chinese from among those long resident in China.[26]

In the United States, the Mission's reception was friendly but reserved.
The United States government's handling of the visit was marked by a
desire "to avoid offending the Chinese government by taking any action
which the latter might choose to interpret as a reflection on its claim to
sovereignty over Tibet"; but its objective, at the same time, was to extend
a friendly welcome to the Tibetans without offending their sensibilities.[27]
In answer to protests from the Chinese government over the reception
accorded the Mission and over the proposed meeting of the Tibetans with

President Truman, the State Department reassured the Chinese that the United States government had no intention of calling into question China's *de jure* sovereignty over Tibet but also pointed out that the Chinese government exerted no *de facto* authority over that country:[28]

> The Department does not desire to offend the sensibilities of either China or Tibet, but is of the opinion that Tibetans could rightly be affronted if they were not received by the President. They come bearing a photograph from the Dalai Lama and letters from the Lama and Regent.
>
> The Press is showing considerable interest in the Tibetans' visit, and if it should become known that their intended call on the President was frustrated by the Chinese Government, [the Department] believes that the press would make most of the situation to China's disadvantage. Such a story might also be raised in light of self-determination, which is a popular concept among the American people.
>
> The President has expressed personal interest in greeting the Tibetans.[29]

China's displeasure, nevertheless, compelled the formulation of a face-saving compromise allowing the Chinese Ambassador to accompany the Mission on its meeting with the President. The Tibetans informed the State Department, however, that they preferred to cancel the meeting with the President rather than agree to Chinese interference in the matter.[30] Although the State Department claimed that it did not feel bound to have the Chinese government's concurrence, the matter was dropped; the Tibetan delegation was received instead by the Secretary of State, who forwarded the letters and presents to the President.[31]

In Washington and New York, Tsepon Shakabpa raised the question of purchase of gold by the Tibetan government from the United States. The matter was not a simple one, for the Gold Reserve Act of 1934 prohibited the purchase of gold except on foreign government accounts, thus raising the question of the independent status of Tibet. Although the U.S. government did consent to the sale of gold, it nonetheless held that this transaction should not affect their recognition of China's *de jure* position.[32]

The Tibetan Trade Mission crossed the Atlantic on the *Queen Elizabeth*, arriving in London at the end of November 1948. The British government received the Tibetans warmly and treated them in every respect as they would any official trade mission of an independent country they recognized and had friendly relations with. In anticipation of Chinese protests, Sir Paul Patrick, head of the Commonwealth Relations Office, explained Britain's policy:

> Both we and the Government of India have, for over 30 years, insisted on maintaining direct diplomatic relations with the Tibetan Government, and so far as we can recall, have on no occasion admitted the frequently expressed claim of the Chinese Government that they are responsible for the conduct of Tibet's external relations. The 1914 Convention, which governs the relations between India, ourselves, and probably Pakistan, on the one hand, and Tibet on the other was negotiated in the name of the King, on behalf of the United

Kingdom as well as India. As we regard Tibet as capable of entering into Treaties, it is difficult to see why we should at the present juncture be chary of receiving a Tibetan Trade Mission in this country or of recognizing Tibetan passports. Nor would we be in favour of admitting the claim of the Chinese Embassy that our official contacts with the Mission should be through them. It is hardly the moment for the Chinese to press their claims when the present instability of the Nanking Government so belies them.[33]

As the Mission was to be officially received by the King, the Prime Minister, the Foreign Secretary, and other high officials, interference by the Chinese Embassy in these matters was not tolerated.[34] The Tibetans were very pleased at the reception accorded them and for the help they were provided in matters of trade.

The Trade Mission's year-long travels were probably as successful as could have been expected from a first delegation of this kind. Shakabpa had been authorized by his government not to conclude important trade agreements but only to explore the opportunities for expanded trade. This he and his colleagues had done. Moreover, the foreign exchange problem was eventually resolved with India, as was the question of the payment of duty on goods in transit through that country. An important result of the Mission's work was the suggestion to Tibet to establish permanent trade representations in the United Kingdom, the United States, and India.[35] Also significant was the fact that the members of the Mission traveled on official Tibetan government passports, to which gratis official or diplomatic visas were affixed by all countries, including India, the United Kingdom, the United States, Switzerland, Iraq, Italy, France, and Saudi Arabia, but not China.[36]

The Communist Chinese Threat:
Imminent Invasion

Communist Chinese armies entered Beijing on 3 February, 1949, following a series of victories against the Nationalist Kuomintang, or KMT (pinyin: Guomindang) forces in a civil war that had lasted almost two decades. As attempts at reaching a negotiated peace failed, Mao Zedong and Zhu De, the Commander-in-Chief of the communist forces, issued orders to the People's Liberation Army (PLA) "to wipe out" all KMT resistance, "liberate the entire people, and defend the sovereignty and territorial integrity of the country." Thus, by the end of the year, "all territories on the mainland except Tibet were liberated."[37]

The communists' intention to "liberate" Tibet, as they had China, was already apparent in the earliest declarations of policy of the Chinese Communist Party (CCP). The Manifesto of the party's second National Congress, held in 1922, listed among the communists' principal aims (aside from the unification of China) the "achievement of a genuine republic by the liberation of Mongolia, Tibet, and Sinkiang."[38] The intention to liberate those areas bordering on China remained an important component of Mao's declared policy for the next thirty years. This policy was undoubtedly governed primarily by strategic and security considerations. Thus, Mao declared: "The point of departure for the [Chinese] Soviet national policy is the capture of all the oppressed minorities around the Soviets [of China] as a means to increase the strength of the revolution against imperialism and KMT."[39]

The Tibetan people, their government, and their religious leaders were fervently opposed to communism, fearing more than anything else the religious prosecution it inevitably brought with it. Events in Mongolia served as a warning to Tibet, and the late Dalai Lama, in his testament, had made no secret of the fate Tibet would suffer under communism.

In a decisive move in the early summer of 1949, the Tibetan government asked the Chinese officer in Lhasa to leave the country within two weeks, with his staff and some Chinese suspected of communist sympathies. The Kashag sent telegrams to Chiang Kai-shek and President Li Zongren explaining that the measure was taken for fear that communist elements might attach themselves to the Chinese Mission, and the evacuees were given an official and friendly send-off by the Tibetan government.[40] The Chinese Mission in Lhasa, established for the purpose of settling pending disputes, had always been considered a temporary one by the Tibetans. In 1946, Chiang Kai-shek had already been asked by the Good Will Mission to close it down.

The immediacy of the new Chinese threat was brought home in the latter part of 1949, when communist armies marched into Amdo, which was traditionally considered to be Tibetan and was the home of the Dalai Lama. Beijing Radio broadcasts in September and October announced that, whereas the People's Liberation Army had liberated the Chinese and Inner Mongolian peoples and was in the process of liberating the Moslem peoples of Xinjiang, they would presently liberate the Tibetans, to enable them to throw off the yoke of foreign imperialism. The Chinese warned:

> The PLA must liberate all Chinese territory including Tibet, Sinkiang Hainan and Taiwan. Tibet is Chinese territory and no foreign aggression is allowed; the Tibetan people are an indivisible part of the Chinese people. Any aggressor who fails to recognize this point will "crack his skull against the mailed fist of the PLA."[41]

The Tibetan government reacted decisively to the Chinese allegations and announcements. The Foreign Office at Lhasa wrote to Mao Zedong, as follows:

> Tibet is a peculiar country where the Buddist religion is widely flourishing and which is predestined to be ruled by the Living Buddha of Mercy, Chenresig. [i.e., the Dalai Lama]. As such, Tibet has from the earliest times up to now, been an independent Country whose political administration had never been taken over by any Foreign Country; and Tibet also defended her own territories from Foreign invasions and always remained a religious nation.

In view of the fact that Chinghai and Sinkiang etc. are situated on the borders of Tibet, we would like to have an assurance that no Chinese troops would cross the Tibetan frontier from the Sino-Tibetan border, or any such Military action. Therefore please issue strict orders to those Civil and Military Officers stationed on the Sino-Tibetan border in accordance with the above request, and kindly have an early reply so that we can be assured.

As regards those Tibetan territories annexed as part of Chinese territories some years back, the Government of Tibet would desire to open negotiations after the settlement of the Chinese Civil War.[42]

The Tibetan government sent a copy of the letter to the British, United States, and Indian governments and expressed the hope that Mao would react favorably, but it also warned that if "the Chinese Communist leader ignores our letter, and takes an aggressive attitude and sends his troops toward Tibet, then the Government of Tibet will be obliged to defend her own country by all possible means. Therefore the Government of Tibet would earnestly desire to request every possible help from your Government."[43]

All three governments reacted in a somewhat similar fashion to the Tibetan appeal. They were anxious not to see the establishment of Chinese influence in Tibet, much less communist Chinese influence, as this would present a serious threat to South Asia, especially Nepal, India, and Pakistan.[44] Nevertheless, they did not wish to embark on a new military adventure and were extremely concerned not to provoke the Chinese to invade Tibet. The only course of action open to them, these governments felt, was to maintain at a high level the morale of the Tibetans to resist communist infiltration, but without creating the impression that they would be prepared to provide significant military aid.[45]

The basis of Indian policy, as Foreign Minister K. Menon explained, would remain unchanged: India was still prepared to recognize Chinese suzerainty provided that China recognized the autonomy of Tibet (presumably as defined in the Simla Convention); India would give diplomatic support to Tibet to enable it to maintain its present position; and it would continue to supply small quantities of arms. But India would raise the question of Tibet's political status only if compelled to do so by Chinese actions. An overriding concern, however, was the Indian government's desire to avoid provoking such actions in any way.[46] The Indian government was apparently much influenced by its Ambassador in China, Sardar Panikkar, who did not wish the Tibetan question to harm the possibility of cordial Sino-Indian relations. He did not regard the threat to India as seriously as did some of his colleagues and encouraged the feeling in India that nothing could be done to deter China from enforcing its claims over Tibet.[47]

The British were annoyed at India's attitude but did no more themselves than urge New Delhi to take a more active stand.[48] Their policy was explained in a directive to all of their diplomatic representatives abroad:[49] It declared Britain's continued interest in Tibet as communicated to the Kashag in 1947 and reiterated its willingness to recognize Chinese suzerainty only if and when China recognized Tibet's full autonomy. No military action was envisaged, for the government took the view that "Tibet's best hope appears to lie in the probability that more urgent problems will cause the Chinese Communists to postpone their attack on Tibet." British diplomats were cautioned not to give this policy unnecessary publicity, so as to avoid provoking China, but they were instructed that, in dealing with inquiries, "chief emphasis should be given to the fact that the Tibetans have successfully maintained their virtual independence for over thirty-five years and to their opposition to the imperialistic claims of the Chinese."

The United States government, though decidedly opposed to the spread of communism in that part of the world, tended to follow the British and Indian lead with regard to Tibet. They wished to encourage Tibetan resistance to communist advance but were anxious to avoid provoking China. Thus, the State Department canceled a visit to Lhasa by an official U.S. Mission and decided against the extension of formal recognition of Tibet's independence.[50]

The Kashag appealed to the British, United States, and Indian governments to support the country's application for membership of the United Nations. The Kashag also announced that it was sending a special mission in this connection. The two Western powers and India advised Tibet of the impracticability of the proposal, as the Soviet Union and the Republic of China, both permanent members of the Security Council, would be certain to veto the application. They also asked that the proposed mission be suspended, as all overt action by or on behalf of Tibet might well precipitate a Chinese reaction.[51]

Discouraged by the lack of effective diplomatic and military support, the Tibetans decided to send a mission to Moscow, Hong Kong, or Singapore, to negotiate with the communists there.[52] The credentials issued to the leaders of the mission, Tsepon Shakabpa and Tsechag Gyalpo, were summarized by the former as follows:

Tibet, the Abode of Snow, ruled by the successive reincarnations of Chenresi (Avalokitesvara) is an independent and peace loving country dedicated to religion. The country's peace is being disturbed and endangered by possible infiltration of defeated Chinese soldiers during the civil war in China, and though the Foreign Bureau of the government of Tibet has addressed a letter dated the twelfth day of the ninth month of the Earth-Ox year [1950] to Mao Tse-tung, Chairman of Communist China, to use his authority in checking Chinese troops from crossing into Tibetan territory, the Chinese have kept the request unanswered. Instead, radio announcements from Sining and Peking claimed Tibet as part of China and instigated the people to the liberation of Tibet. The Delegation, with full authority to deal with matters concerning Tibet, is to proceed for negotiations on the following subjects: (1) concerning the unanswered letter to Chairman Mao Tse-tung from the Foreign Bureau of the Government of Tibet; (2) concerning the atrocious radio announcements from Sining and Peking; (3) to secure an assurance that the territorial integrity of Tibet will not be violated; and (4) to inform the government of China that the people and Government of Tibet will not tolerate any interference in the successive rule of the Dalai Lama, and they will maintain their independence. The Delegation is instructed to negotiate on the above subjects with a Chinese representative at a place close to China.[53]

While the delegates sought the necessary visas to proceed on their mission from India, the Chinese informed them that their ambassador was due to arrive in New Delhi shortly, and that talks should be opened with him. In the meantime, Shakabpa, who was worried that the Indian government might come to an understanding with China regarding Tibet, urged Pandit Nehru to take a firm stand in favor of Tibet, not only because India was obliged to do so by the 1914 agreement but also because the recognition and maintenance of Tibet as a buffer State between the two great powers of Asia was essential to India's security.[54]

Around this time, India, Britain, and the United States began to show a more active interest in helping Tibet. The Indian government increased the supply of arms and ammunition to Tibet somewhat, while Britian and the United States considered collaborating in this effort.[55] When reports of the Tibetan intention to depute representatives for talks in Moscow or Hong Kong reached the State Department, the United States Ambassador in New Delhi was instructed to make it clear to the Tibetans that the inability of the United States to help more actively should not be misinterpreted as disinterest or lack of sympathy for their predicament.[56] It wasn't until after the outbreak of fighting in Korea, on 23 June, 1950, that the United States government decided actively to counter Chinese communist expansion. For the first time, President Truman sanctioned United States military involvement to protect Taiwan from communist attack. A month later, in response to renewed Tibetan appeals, an Embassy official in New Delhi informed Shakabpa that the United States was not prepared to assist Tibet in procuring war materials and in financing such acquisition.[57]

The Government of India instructed Ambassador K.M. Panikkar to urge the Chinese to avoid the use of force, and decided to take up the matter in the Security Council in the event of an armed attack. The Foreign Ministry in Beijing replied, on 25 August, that although China must maintain its sovereignty over Tibet, it did not wish to have an armed conflict and had thus instructed Ambassador Yuan Zhongxian to enter into tentative conversations with the Tibetan representative in New Delhi.[58] Meetings were indeed held in the Indian capital soon after the Chinese Ambassador's arrival there. He demanded from Shakabpa as a preliminary to further negotiations that Tibet be recognized as part of China and that China should handle all matters concerning Tibetan national defense.[59]

Before Shakabpa could convey his government's unfavorable response to these demands, the People's Liberation Army unexpectedly attacked Eastern Tibet:[60] The full-scale invasion of Tibet had begun.

7

The Legal Status
of Political Entities

In preceding chapters much has been said about the Tibetan government's perception of the status of Tibet at various times in the country's history, as well as about the perceptions of the Mongol, Manchu, and Chinese governments. The views of the present Dalai Lama (now in exile) and his government, and of the Chinese communists since their assumption of power, are diametrically opposed. The former hold that Tibet has always been a fully independent State. The communist Chinese authorities claim that Tibet has been an integral part of China for centuries.

In order to assess the status of Tibet on the eve of the Chinese military intervention in 1949–1950, we must review the law on the status of political entities—that is, we must analyze what factors determine that status.

Statehood

The notion of statehood is central to the determination of the status of political entities. In international law, statehood denotes international personality and the State is considered not merely an organized community but one possessing certain attributes that are deemed essential to the maintenance of international relations. The determination of a political entity's statehood or lack of statehood is thus central to the determination of that entity's legal status, which may vary from complete independence to total absence of international personality.[1]

For a State to exist according to international law, it must have a defined territory and population, a government possessing authority over the territory and population independent of other international persons, and the capacity to enter into relations with other subjects of international law.[2] Although these criteria are clearly interrelated, we shall examine them individually at first.

The State's territory is the framework within which the State exercises its competence. According to the Permanent Court of Arbitration, "One of the essential elements of [State] sovereignty is that it is to be exercised within territorial limits, and that, failing proof to the contrary, the territory is coterminous with the sovereignty. . . ."[3] As the size of the territory is irrelevant to the existence of the State, no precise delimitations of its borders, which can undergo considerable changes, is necessary.[4] In some cases a State may continue to exist even despite claims to all of its territory.[5]

That the territory of a State must be inhabited by a population (defined as an aggregate of individuals living together in a community) is evident.[6]

The requirement that the political entity have an effective government may be regarded as central to its claim for statehood. By government (or legal order) is meant the exercise of authority with respect to the population and the defined territory.[7] The scope of government typically includes the exercise of jurisdiction over the population and territory of the State, the collection of taxes, promulgation of laws, maintenance of order, dispensation of justice, and conduct of social affairs.[8]

Government is the prerequisite for the other central requirement of statehood: independence. In fact, the requirements of government and independence, or the exercise of power and the absence of superior control, are only different aspects of the same central constitutive element of statehood, also described as the requirement of effective and separate control.[9]

The existence of a government exercising effective authority over the territory of a putative State is in general a precondition for statehood. But as will be shown below, the degree of effectiveness required is minimal where the possession of an undisputed title to the exercise of governmental authority exists. Even so, the continued absence of an effective government will tend toward the dissolution of the State.[10]

Government is also a precondition for the conduct of international relations, inasmuch as, in normal circumstances, only the government can represent and bind the State in its external relations. It is the possession and enjoyment of the capacity to enter into distinctive relations with members of the international community that characterizes the State as an international person. In principle, States determine their relations with other States independently—that is, free from interference of or subordination to other States.[11] A "State proper," to use L. Oppenheim's definition, is therefore one that, while fulfilling the requirements regarding to territory, population, government, and the capacity to conduct international relations, is also separate and independent of external control.[12] Some publicists, including Oppenheim, use the term "sovereignty" to denote this central element of statehood.

For a State to be sovereign in international law, it is sufficient to establish that the sovereign power is possessed in the State and not outside of it:[13]

Sovereignty in the relations between States signifies independence. Independence in regard to a portion of the globe is the right to exercise therein, to the exclusion of any other State, the functions of a State. The development of national organization of States during the last few centuries, and, as a corollary, the development of international law, have established this principle of the exclusive competence of the State in regard to its own territory in such a way as to make it the point of departure in settling most questions that concern international relations.[14]

Lest this statement be interpreted as a requirement of absolute independence for statehood, it must be pointed out that no State is independent in an absolute sense: General international law and conventional law impose restrictions on a State's ability to act independently of other States. For example, States restrict their independence by joining international organizations, alliances, or economic communities; by accepting the jurisdiction of international tribunals; and by concluding bilateral and multilateral agreements.[15]

The degree of independence possessed by States may vary considerably. The absence of independence can be so complete that the entity concerned cannot properly be regarded as a State. On the other hand, a State can be regarded as independent even when it is subjected to a considerable degree of control by another State.[16] To quote Judge D. Anzilotti: "The restrictions upon a State's liberty, whether arising out of ordinary international law or contractual engagements, do not as such in the least affect its independence. As long as these restrictions do not place the State under the legal authority of another state, the former remains an independent State however extensive and burdensome those obligations may be."[17]

The distinction Judge Anzilotti has made is that between formal and actual independence. Formal independence exists where the source of a State's governmental authority is vested within the State. It does not exist where a political entity derives its governmental authority from the government of another State as a matter of international law. Such governmental authority is legally merely an extension of the dominant State's government. When a State delegates functions of government to another State, however significant these may be, its formal independence is not affected. A State may, for instance, agree to have its foreign relations or defense conducted by another State on its behalf without thereby losing its formal independence. The same is true of a State's consent to the existence of foreign military bases on its territory. On the other hand, when the dominant State has discretionary authority, as a matter of right, to intervene in the internal affairs of a political entity, the latter cannot properly be considered an independent State.[18]

Treaty obligations do not derogate from formal independence. Thus, in the *Wimbledon Case*, the International Court "decline[d] to see in the conclusion of any treaty by which a State undertakes to perform or refrain from performing a particular act an abandonment of its sovereignty." The court further held that "no doubt any convention creating an obligation of this kind places a restriction upon the exercise of the sovereign rights of the State, in the sense that it requires them to be exercised in a certain way. But the right to enter into international agreements is an attribute of State sovereignty."[19] A good example is provided by the extensive territorial privileges granted by Imperial and Republican China to colonial powers in the "capitulation treaties," despite which China maintained its "territorial integrity and political independence."[20] Even the possession of joint organs to carry out certain governmental functions is not inconsistent with formal independence.[21]

The point is that in these situations the source of governmental authority, regardless of who exercises that authority, lies within the State and that restrictions to its exercise are presumed to be based on consent. In contrast, where the exercise of governmental authority is derived as a matter of law from a foreign State and is thus merely a delegation of that State's authority, there is no formal independence. Nevertheless, in extreme cases even consensual limitations on the exercise of sovereignty can become so extensive that, to use Judge Manley O. Hudson's characterization in the *Lighthouses in Crete and Samos* case, "a ghost of a hollow sovereignty cannot be permitted to obscure the realities of [the] situation."[22]

By actual independence is meant the exercise of effective governmental authority independent of an outside power. Actual independence is, in principle, a matter of political fact. A presumption follows from the mere exercise of actual independence: As G. Schwartzenberger has noted, "Unless another State can produce a better title, the actual display of territorial sovereignty is evidence of the right of sovereignty over the territory in question"—that is, formal independence.[23] What the exercise of actual independence entails was indicated by the British courts in the *Charkieh* case, in *Mighell v. Sultan of Johore*, and by Judge Stelio Seferiades in a dissenting opinion in the *Lighthouses in Crete and Samos* case.[24] Among the factors taken into consideration by these authorities, aside from the independent exercise of normal governmental functions, prominence was given to the maintenance of separate armed forces, the independent right of making peace, war, and treaties, and the possession of a separate flag and *jus legationis*.

The extent of actual independence required in order to retain statehood is minimal where the formal existence of the State is legally undisputed. On the other hand, when a political entity comes into existence by revolutionary means or in violation of certain basic rules of international law, such that its title to statehood is at issue, a considerable amount of actual independence is a necessary precondition to the acquisition of statehood.[25] Thus, when a new State acquires independence through devolution, as was the case with India in 1947, there is no need to question its legal independence. This was plainly demonstrated by the United Nations' intervention in 1960 on behalf of the newly independent Republic of Congo. The self-dismemberment of that Republic, with a bankrupt and divided government hardly able to control even the capital, was avoided only by international intervention on its behalf. Despite this state of affairs, the Congo remained a State and was widely recognized as such.[26]

The legal independence of a State remains intact also when it is occupied by foreign forces. Pending a final settlement of the conflict in question, belligerent occupation does not affect the continuity of the State, even when the latter's government has become totally ineffective in the whole of its territory and has been driven into exile or silenced.[27]

By contrast, when a State is formed by a war of secession or as a result of the abandonment of control by the prior sovereign and the seizure of power by the inhabitants, effective exercise of government authority is central to the acquisition of statehood.[28] A good example is provided by the position of Finland in 1917–1918. Following World War I, Finland declared its independence.[29] The Commission of Jurists investigating Finland's position for the League of Nations concluded that it was difficult to say

> at what exact date the Finnish Republic, in the legal sense of the term, actually became a definitely constituted sovereign State. This certainly did not take place until a stable political organization had been created, and until the public authorities had become strong enough to assert themselves throughout the territories or the State without the assistance of foreign [i.e., German and Russian] troops.[30]

The much stricter application of the effectiveness test to the Finnish government's exercise of authority than was required in the Congolese situation is explained by the fact that the Republic of Congo possessed the uncontested title to exercise governmental authority, whereas Finland did not.

In the case of a State possessing formal independence, actual independence is presumed: To establish lack of actual independence one must show "foreign control overbearing the decision-making of the entity concerned on a wide range of matters of high policy and doing so systematically and on a permanent basis."[31] In determining whether control is "substantial," the extent to which important decisions with respect to the State are made outside it and whether its government is staffed, especially in more important positions, by nationals of a dominant State are crucial considerations. Also critical is the question of whether separate State organs continue to exist or whether they have disappeared or are effectively submerged in those of another State.[32]

External control may be exercised on the basis of an agreement among States, in which case it is not inconsistent with independence. Such control may also result from political or economic domination, such as that between the Soviet Union and a number of Eastern European "satellite" States. Although such domination may be extensive in practice, it does not affect the legal independence of those countries.[33] Iran's occupation by the Allies from 1941 to 1946 is certainly an outstanding illustration of the extent to which statehood may coexist with very little exercise of independent governmental authority.[34]

A given State may have a very brief existence, but this fact cannot divest it of its statehood for as long as it exists. On the other hand, the continuance of an independently functioning entity over a period of time can be an important piece of evidence in support of statehood and in practice has led to effective recognition of independence.[35] Similarly, the conduct of other States, though not a determining factor in ascertaining the status of an entity, can provide evidence of that status. The extension of recognition by other States is an important example of such conduct.[36]

Such recognition, though of considerable political importance, has only evidentiary value with regard to an entity's international legal status. Recognition is "the act by which another state acknowledges that the political entity recognized possesses the attributes of statehood."[37] If a political community actually possesses those attributes, recognition is not essential to the acquisition or maintenance of independence.[38] To concede to recognition more than an evidential role, as supporters of the constitutive theory of recognition have done, transfers "the vital problem of the legal existence of States" from the realm of objective law to the province of politically motivated third States.[39] Moreover, as many writers have pointed out, the use of recognition as a constitutive element of statehood has no practical value, as it provides no help where third States do not adopt a uniform attitude toward a putative State. This situation inevitably leads to the absurd contention that a State does and does not exist at the same time.[40]

As the Montevideo Convention[41] states in Article 3: "The political existence of the state is independent of recognition by other states. Even before recognition the state has the right to defend its integrity and independence, to provide for its conservation and prosperity, and consequently to organize itself as it sees fit, to legislate upon its interests, [to] administer its services, and to define the jurisdiction and competence of its courts." And in Article 6: "The recognition of a State merely signifies that the State which recognizes it accepts the personality of the other with all the rights and duties determined by international law. Recognition is unconditional and irrevocable."

The act of recognition of a State may be express or tacit. Express recognition consists of a formal act such as a unilateral declaration or other formal notification clearly announcing the intention of recognition. Tacit or implied recognition results from any act that implies the intention of recognizing a State. The presumption, in that case, is against recognition by inference.[42] Certain unequivocal acts do, however, imply recognition. Among the most important of these is the conclusion of a bilateral treaty, for the treaty-making power of States is "the highest manifestation of external sovereignty."[43] Hans Kelsen has emphatically made the point that "a treaty entered into with a State which, legally, does not yet exist is a completely inconceivable thing. . . . In order to conclude treaties, a State must already possess international legal personality. In other words, it must exist within the sphere of international law."[44] Other acts that imply recognition are the formal initiation of diplomatic relations, the formal opening of treaty negotiations and the issue of consular exequatur. In addition, it would seem that the establishment of a trade mission and particularly of a consular service with extensive powers could be interpreted as a first step toward recognition.[45]

Recognition is opposable to the recognizing State only, and its legal effect is to create estoppel. By granting recognition, States debar themselves from challenging in the future what they previously acknowledged. As the World Court stressed in the *Eastern Greenland* case, "Norway reaffirmed that she recognized the whole of Greenland as Danish, and thereby she has debarred herself from contesting Danish sovereignty over the whole of Greenland."[46]

The distinction between *de facto* and *dejure* recognition of States has occasionally been made. From the foregoing discussion of statehood it is evident that a State cannot exist in fact (i.e., possess all the attributes of statehood) without existing in a juridical sense. Consequently, the distinction between *de facto* and *de jure* statehood or independence is inadmissible in international law. The terms *de facto* and *de jure* serve in the process of recognition only when conflicting claims to sovereignty over territory remain unresolved and the recognizing State is anxious not to commit itself in favor of either claimant.[47]

Apart from recognition, there are other forms of conduct of States that can have evidential value. The conduct of direct and separate relations with the government of a putative State, particularly if such intercourse covers a wide range of affairs, tends to support that entity's claim to statehood, for such conduct constitutes at least an acknowledgment of the State's existence.[48] The same is true of the conduct of official bilateral relations, especially the sending and receiving of official government envoys, the negotiation and conclusion of agreements, mediation, the insistence upon the international responsibility of the entity in question, and the extension of military aid and other governmental assistance, or the conduct of trade. Consideration should also be given to the population's own will and conviction. The evidential value of an entity's own perception of its status, especially when such perception is held consistently over a period of time and its conduct is in accordance with this perception, should not be discounted.[49] The issue of self-determination will be touched on below. Suffice to say here that, whereas the creation of a State in accordance with the principle of self-determination lends support to a claim to independent statehood, the creation of such an entity in violation of that principle may constitute an obstacle thereto.[50]

Once the existence of a State is established, there is a strong presumption in favor of its continuation. To establish loss of independence is, consequently, "to overcome a formidable burden of proof."[51] This presumption follows from the central position of independence and sovereignty in the system of international law, created and maintained by sovereign States for their protection. Any restrictions on a State's independence can be accepted only with strong and unequivocal evidence and must be interpreted restrictively. In the absence of such evidence, full independence must be presumed; hence the burden of proof is on the party claiming the existence of restrictions.[52]

A State claiming to have established sovereign rights over another State must show convincing proof of the transfer of sovereignty by a consensual transaction or the undisputed and effective exercise of authority for a prolonged period of time. The test of effectiveness should be applied at least as strictly as it is when a putative State claims independence on the basis of secession or other revolutionary changes.[53] Furthermore, the presumption in favor of continued statehood prevails over the principle of effectiveness in the case of belligerent occupation. In addition, statehood is not lost when a State has established control over another in contravention of general principles of international law. Thus, acts of illegal intervention, including military aggression and occupation, cannot in themselves cause the extinction of a State.[54]

According to traditional legal doctrine, in force at least until the early part of this century, the temporary physical suppression of a State under belligerent occupation and illegal intervention could reach a final resolution either by the liberation of the held territory or by its annexation. Annexation, in turn, could have a legal effect only if it was undertaken after hostilities ended and "the defeat of the occupied state [was] so decisive and the enemy's victory so final, that the possibility of his expulsion [could] reasonably be excluded."[55] Premature annexations were consequently invalid. The State was safeguarded not by an act of will of the occupying power but by a clear, objective rule of international law.[56] The modern law on conquest and annexation will be discussed in a later chapter.

Conclusion

The general principles developed in the preceding paragraphs may be summarized as follows, subject to the exceptions and specifications discussed above:

A political entity that fulfills the criteria with respect to territory, population, and government is considered to be an independent State in international law, when it possesses formal independence (i.e., when the source or validity of its government is situated within that State) and, generally, a minimal measure of actual independence. Where deficiency exists in the formal independence of an entity claiming statehood, it may nonetheless be regarded as a State if it possesses a considerable measure of actual independence. This does not hold true, however, when another State possesses a better title to sovereignty over this entity and also exercises a measure of actual control over it.

Once established, a State is presumed to be independent and to remain so, despite extensive loss of actual governmental authority, as sometimes occurs. This presumption in favor of continued independent statehood is so strong that it may prevail over the principle of effectiveness, especially in the face of belligerent occupation, revolution, illegal actions of other States, and analogous situations. Nevertheless, a final resolution of such situations in favor of the dominant State either by way of a legal settlement or forcible total subjugation can still lead, at least according to the traditional view, to the extinction of the State as an international person.

Restrictions on State Sovereignty

The term "dependence" is generally used to describe relationships that restrict an entity's exercise of sovereignty. The choice of that term is unfortunate, however, insofar as it suggests incompatibility with independence,[57] whereas considerable subjection to and control by an outside power is compatible with legal independence. The delegation of governmental functions to another State does not imply a loss of independence, although such delegation may result in a degree of external restraint and deprivation of freedom. On the other hand, a State would not retain its legal independence when, as a result of its dependence, "it ceased itself to exercise within its own territory the *summa potestas* or sovereignty, i.e., if it lost the right to exercise its own judgment in coming to decisions which the government of its territory entails."[58]

Characteristic of relationships of dependence or reliance of one State upon another is the inequality of the entities involved. The classical conception of international relations that prevailed in Europe until the nineteenth century, expounded by Grotius and others, was based on the notion that States, though sovereign, need not be equal in all respects and that relations among them could be established on the basis of inequality.[59] "Unequal alliances," which established relationships of reliance of a weaker State on a stronger one, did not necessarily infringe on the sovereignty of either State. The classical writers held that even important limitations upon the exercise of political power were consistent with the enjoyment of international personality and sovereignty.[60] Inter-State relations in Asia, at least until the mid-nineteenth century, were also typically conceived in terms of superiority and inferiority of States: Equality was rare unless States were too distant to be in contact.[61] The principle of equality of States in international law started to gain acceptance in Europe only in the second half of the eighteenth century[62] and did not make an impact in Asia until more than a century later.

A recurrent problem in the law of territorial status has been the categorization of the various types of dependent or restrained entities, only one of which is the protectorate, another the tributary State, yet another the vassal. It is very difficult to give precise juristic significance to these terms, particularly because they have been used to describe a broad scale of permutations of rights and powers, ranging from virtual independence to practical incorporation in another State. The resulting confusion in the use of terms such as "protectorate," "suzerainty," or "tributary" is further aggravated by the changes in the relationships they attempt to describe after their inception, which may render once appropriate terms quite inadequate. To make matters worse, these terms have regularly been used inaccurately to describe inter-State relationships, at times for political reasons. An example is provided by Britain's use of the term "suzerainty" to describe its position vis-à-vis Transvaal in the Treaty of Pretoria, in 1881, when that treaty in fact established a protectorate over the African State.[63] The resulting confusion is evident in Lord Derby's statement in the British House of Lords (on the occasion of the modification of the treaty in 1884):

> The word Suzerainty was a very vague word, and I do not think it capable of any precise legal definition. Whatever we may understand by it, it is not very easy to define. But I apprehend, whether you call it a Protectorate, or a Suzerainty, or the recognition of England as a paramount Power, the fact is that a certain controlling power is retained. . . .[64]

Another example is provided by Article 1 of the treaty between France and Cayor (Senegal) of 16 January 1883, stipulating that "the inhabitants of Cayor place themselves under the protectorate of France and accept her suzerainty."[65] What France established by that agreement was in fact neither a protectorate nor suzerainty, but a form of colonial administration.

Not suprisingly, international law publicists stress, as James Crawford has done, that "it is therefore a cardinal principle that the legal incidents of a given relation are to be determined not by an inference from the label attached to it ('protectorate,' 'suzerain,' 'vassal,' etc.), but from an examination of the constituent documents and the circumstances of the case."[66] Indeed, none of these relationships, whether they be termed protectorate, suzerainty, or otherwise, can be described by reference to a single, general rule, inasmuch as the mutual relationships of the States in question vary according to the particular agreements arrived at, and consequently must be considered on their own merits.[67] Nonetheless, a number of basic elements can be identified as constituting either the protectorate, the suzerainty, or the tributary arrangement.

In order to assess the effects of various forms of subordination and reliance on the international status of political entities, we must distinguish between the formal and actual aspects of independence or governmental authority: First, the source of the restraint on the exercise of State sovereignty must be identified—particularly with respect to whether it is situated within the State or outside of it. Second, the actual nature and extent of external control and intervention by the stronger State in relation to the exercise of governmental authority by the weaker State must be examined. The first question pertains to the title or formal source of the relationship in question, whereas the second is essentially a question of political fact.[68]

Protectorate

The International Court, in the *Nationality Decrees in Tunisia and Morocco* case, held that "in spite of common features possessed by Protectorates under international law, they have individual legal characteristics resulting from the special conditions under which they were created, and the stage of their development."[69] In fact, there are as many differences among protectorate relationships as there are instruments establishing them.[70] The common elements of the protectorate relationships that the International

Court refers to can essentially be reduced to the following distinctive features: A protectorate is a consensual relationship between two subjects of international law, whereby one (or more) State is legally bound to protect another State from external threat and whereby that same State is made responsible for the external relations of the protected State.[71]

Protectorates are established by a consensual transaction, which is generally accomplished in the form of a treaty. There are no formal requirements in this regard, however. An agreement could therefore be arrived at verbally and perhaps even inferred from a factual situation. Because the conclusion of the protectorate agreement is itself an act of sovereignty, most publicists emphasize the sovereign status of the parties entering the agreement.[72]

The protectorate relationship consists of two substantive elements: The first is the legal obligation of the stronger State to protect the weaker one against foreign aggression and intervention.[73] A mere right to come to the protection of a State without the legal obligation to do so is insufficient to satisfy the requirements of the protectorate relationship.[74] A pledge to extend the protection against internal threats to the established regime, though frequently included in protectorate agreements, is not a necessary feature of it.[75]

The second element is the transference of the management of the protected State's foreign relations to the protector State[76]—a logical corollary to the obligation to protect.[77] A relationship between two States in which one State provides protection for the other, and in which the protector State does not take control of the more important facets of the protected State's foreign relations, does not qualify as a protectorate. Such a relationship is instead generally known as "simple protection."[78]

The extensiveness of the powers exercised by the protector vary considerably. In some cases, they entail no more than a right of approval or veto of the international acts of the protected State.[79] In most cases, the protector is granted the exclusive authority to represent the protected State in international affairs.[80] But in other cases, protectorate agreements go even further—that is, in granting the protector an active role, as well, in the supervision or management of the protected State's internal affairs, typically with regard to the enactment of administrative, judicial, or military reforms.[81] Such agreements also often grant the protector extensive military facilities[82] and provide for the appointment by that State of a high-ranking resident officer to act as intermediary between the government of the protected State and that of the protector, and to represent the former in dealings with third States.[83] This intervention does not, however, result in the merging of the two States' governmental organs, which remain separate and distinct.[84]

Despite sometimes far-reaching concessions of governing powers to the protecting State in relation to the protected State, a distinctive feature of the protectorate is that the latter retains its statehood and international personality.[85] This feature follows logically from the nature of the protectorate. In the first place, the conclusion of the agreement establishing the protectorate is an act of State sovereignty and is consequently governed solely by international law. The agreement is an international instrument that is internationally binding. Furthermore, as restrictions or obligations relative to the exercise of sovereignty arising out of ordinary international law and contractual relations do not derogate from independence, relations between the protected and the protector continue to be governed by international and not municipal law.[86] The transfer of the management of specific governmental functions to the protector State is properly a delegation and not a cession by the protected State of governmental authority. Delegation of governmental authority does not entail its loss but, rather, only authorizes another State to exercise certain functions on behalf of, and in the name of, the delegating State.[87]

As the source of governmental authority or legal order remains within the protected State, the latter retains its formal independence.[88] Thus, the International Court held in the *Rights of Nationals of the United States of America in Morocco* case,

> it is not disputed by the French Government that Morocco, even under the Protectorate, has retained its personality as a State in international law. . . . Under [the] Treaty [of Fez of 1912], Morocco remained a sovereign State but it made an arrangement of a contractual character whereby France undertook to exercise certain sovereign powers in the name and on behalf of Morocco. . . .[89]

The extinction of the protectorate relationship is also governed by the rules pertaining to conventional relationships. Two situations have generally led to the extinction of protectorates: The first is the incorporation of the protected into the protecting State—for example, by progressively converting the administration of the protected State into a colonial one. Once the source of governmental authority is transferred to a State outside the protected State, its independence is lost.[90]

The other situation leading to the extinction of protectorates—namely, the progressive removal of the restrictions upon the protected State's exercise of sovereignty in its relations with third States, the erosion of the protector's effective power, or the loss of its ability or commitment to protect (a condition *sine qua non* of the protectorate relationship)—invariably results in the restoration of the protected State's full exercise of sovereignty.[91] In addition, the outbreak of war between the protector and the protected State, irrespective of its outcome, ends the protectorate relationship: Not only does the *raison d'être* of the relationship disappear, but the state of war also implies a denunciation of the agreement on which it is based.[92]

Suzerainty

Suzerainty was originally an institution of feudal law that defined the relationship between the lord and his vassal or liege man.[93] The use of the concepts of suzerainty and vassalage to describe inter-State relations has been the source of much confusion. At first, these concepts were used to refer to the application of the feudal relationship to States. Suzerainty in Europe had much in common with the protectorate relationship, from which it was at times hard to distinguish. But in the nineteenth century they came to be used to describe the condition of States breaking away from disintegrating empires, such as the Ottoman Empire.[94] There are even fewer common characteristics of suzerainty than of protectorate relationships.

According to J.H.W. Verzijl, "[the] feudal system was characterized by a number of traditional elements such as: a solemn investiture of the liege man by the liege lord, a pledge of fealty on the side of the vassal, a promise of protection by the suzerain, an annual tribute due to him, possible forfeiture of the feif on the ground of felony, etc."[95]

The concept of suzerainty was first applied to inter-State relations in the period of inter-dynastic relationships, when rulers, and not their people, were endowed with legal as well as political sovereignty and were capable of receiving and giving allegiance to one another. Examples of its application to relations among separate States is furnished by the Holy Roman Empire and the treaties among European States in the fourteenth and fifteenth centuries.[96] The Peace of Westphalia (1648) formally accorded to the princes and potentates of the Empire a qualified international status. The religious settlement stipulated an exact and reciprocal equality among them in ecclesiastical affairs, thus ensuring their independence from imperial control in this respect. The political settlement divided international capacity between the Empire as a whole and its component States, which "were internationally accepted as sovereign States, and were so called, while they recognized the empire as their suzerain power."[97] The Pope also established relationships between himself as liege lord and the rulers of various secular kingdoms inside and outside Italy—including the Emperor—as liege men. Bonds of suzerainty were complex relationships in which rulers might be both suzerain and vassal at the same time.[98]

At the inter-State level, the basic features of the feudal relationship were preserved: The ruler of the vassal State was invested with autonomous powers by a solemn act of investiture by the suzerain ruler, to whom he was bound by an oath of allegiance; the suzerain was obliged to protect his vassal; and the latter was bound to give military assistance to his suzerain in case of war. In addition, the vassal paid an annual tribute and had to pay personal homage in order to receive his investiture.[99]

F. Despagnet has distinguished two modes of establishing suzerainty among States. Suzerainty may be established by a victorious State over a defeated State when it allows the latter to retain its independent existence in exchange for the recognition that it does so only by virtue of the good will or generosity of the former. It may also be established when a State concedes the exercise of sovereign rights as a fief to its feudatory, reserving the right to be regarded as the author of this concession and to be treated as the suzerain by the latter.[100] Thus, a distinctive element of the feudal suzerainty relationship is that the suzerain holds the source of the governmental authority of the vassal State whose ruler he grants the right to exercise the authority autonomously.[101] The regular payment of homage and tribute and the solemn investiture serves as a periodic reaffirmation of this characteristic of suzerainty. This symbolic reaffirmation may be replaced by the continuous exercise of sufficient effective authority by the suzerain to leave no doubt as to the relationship's continuation. Conversely, suzerain rights cannot be claimed where the suzerain-vassal relationship has not been maintained formally or in fact.[102] Where there is suzerainty, it would appear from the analysis of statehood that the vassal could not be properly termed independent. It should be pointed out, however, that this conclusion was not necessarily drawn by the classical doctrine, which recognized the inequality of States. Furthermore, a distinction must be made between purely symbolic relationships, on the one hand, and those entailing substantive elements, on the other. Nominal suzerainty entails nothing more than the expression of respect for the suzerain, and possibly an acknowledgment of his higher status.[103]

Nominal suzerainty did not involve exercise by the suzerain of the vassal's governmental functions. It also did not entail the granting of any rights by the suzerain to the vassal with respect to the exercise of authority. Rather, the source of governmental authority was actually situated within the nominal vassal State (sometimes referred to as "autonomous" vassal). Although it might originally have been vested in the suzerain and transferred in the modes described by Despagnet, the exercise of authority no longer remained an extension of the suzerain's power. An example of such a symbolic relationship in the feudal period was that between the Holy See and the Kingdom of Naples until 1818.[104] More recent examples are the relationship of the Barbary States to the Porte, and the Crimean Tartars to the Sultan in Constantinople.[105]

When the suzerain, while conceding the autonomous exercise of most governmental functions to the vassal, reserves for himself the right to exercise important ones such as the conduct of foreign affairs, the relationship entails actual submission such that the vassal might be regarded as being only "semi-sovereign."[106] Although this relationship has much in common with the protectorate, suzerainty is not necessarily based on an international agreement, and the authority exercised by the suzerain cannot properly be regarded as a delegation of governmental authority by the vassal. Whereas the autonomous vassal in a nominal suzerainty relationship should therefore be regarded as a State with international personality, the vassal in a relationship entailing formal as well as effective suzerainty does not possess full independence.

In the late nineteenth century, the term "suzerainty" was revived to describe the residue of authority of the Sultan of the Ottoman Empire over the autonomous components of his disintegrating empire and similar situations. The suzerainty relationship was by then typically a stage in the progressive devolution of an empire's component entities toward full participation in the family of nations.[107] Oppenheim described "modern suzerainty" in the following terms:

Suzerainty is by no means sovereignty. It is a kind of international guardianship, since the vassal State is either absolutely or mainly represented internationally by the suzerain State. . . . The fact that the relation between the suzerain and the vassal always depends upon the special case, excludes the possibility of laying down a general rule as to the international position of vassal States.[108]

In principle, the "modern" suzerain was entirely responsible for the international relations and acts of the vassal.[109] The suzerain acted for the vassal in the conclusion of treaties, especially when these treaties had a bearing on the vassal's political relations with third States. Furthermore, "all international treaties concluded by the suzerain State [were] *ipso facto* concluded for the vassal."[110] The sending and receiving of diplomatic and consular officers was in general denied to a vassal,[111] as was the right to declare war;[112] but the outbreak of war between the suzerain and a third power was "*ipso facto* war of the vassal," such that the latter could not remain neutral.[113]

The international personality of the vassal in a true "modern suzerainty" relationship was thus clearly limited. As J.B. Moore cautions, however, "the extent of the authority or subordination comprehended by [the term suzerainty] is not determined by general rules, but by the facts of the particular case."[114] Thus, the term was used to denote purely symbolic or nominal relationships, but also to describe relationships that, in reality, were protectorates or colonial in nature.[115]

It would appear that a relationship entered into by means of a consensual transaction at the initiative of a weaker State (the vassal-to-be), primarily in order to safeguard its independence from external threats, should not be categorized as one of suzerainty when it displays elements more characteristic of a protectorate relationship.[116] In such cases, Despagnet has concluded, the relationship is in reality one of protection, "which does not necessarily involve the relegation of the protected State to semi-sovereign status."[117]

A further cautionary remark is necessary with regard to the characterization by the Western colonial governments of relations among African or Asian States, especially when concepts such as suzerainty—which developed in relation to political circumstances particular to the European continent— were used. (The most prominent system of Asian relationships—the one utilized by the Emperors of China—will be discussed in a separate section because of its particular relevance to this study.)

We must conclude, then, that the use of the term "suzerainty" to describe an inter-State relationship does not by itself imply the existence or lack of international personality. Whereas true suzerainty—in a formal as well as an actual sense—does imply the absence of such personality, nominal suzerainty need not affect the vassal's international status. Therefore, rather than basing an evaluation of an entity's international status on the terminology used, we must carefully consider that entity's formal and actual relationship with its suzerain and with other States.[118]

Sphere of Influence

As was true of the restrictions on State sovereignty examined above, the concept of "sphere of influence" is not easily definable. This concept was used in the past specifically to characterize the control by imperialist powers of portions of Asia and Africa, certain islands in the Caribbean, and regions in Central America. In these areas, the imperialist powers exerted political influence that varied greatly in degree and intensity over existing states— an influence that had been established by treaties, unilateral declarations, or simply effective penetration. By such arrangements the influencing States and their citizens enjoyed advantages and privileges in the influenced regions without exercising sovereign control.[119]

James Crawford defines "sphere of influence" rather narrowly—that is, as an agreement between States delimiting the areas of territory within which each party would be permitted by the other party to operate. He emphasizes that the force of this agreement was strictly contractual between those parties and, furthermore, that the agreement did not give legal rights to those parties over the territory in question.[120] G. Rutherford, in his study of spheres of influence, uses the concept more broadly to include agreements between the "influencing" and the "influenced" States. He also distinguishes negative and positive characteristics and privileges constituting this concept.[121]

The influencing power's aim to prevent any other powers from exerting influence over a country or region can be considered the "principal negative" characteristic. This aim is described by Rutherford as "the exclusion of the activities of other Powers, the consequent reservation by the privileged State of certain privileges and, in some cases, obligations, and a determination, on the Power exercising the influence, to enforce if need be these stipulations by military measures."[122] Typical of the provisions of instruments establishing the sphere of influence were those barring the influenced State from alienating any part of its territory to other Powers, and those reserving for the dominating State a supervisory role in the conduct of the former's foreign relations. Often the aim of these negative stipulations was to secure the existence of a buffer State on the periphery of an empire in order to check the ambitions of other major powers in the region, without incurring the direct responsibilities that would normally follow from the establishment of a protectorate and that might occur in the case of suzerainty.[123]

In the positive sense, on the other hand, the influencing power typically claimed a special interest, and consequently a privileged position, in regions of strategic importance to its empire, especially in those areas coterminous with its dominions.[124] In practice, the influencing power's privileges led to the exercise of varying degrees of interference in the affairs of the influenced State, ranging from occasionally acting in a supervisory role as an intermediary in the latter's foreign relations to interference even in the conduct of its internal affairs. A stipulation often found in sphere-of-influence relationships included the obligation by the influenced State not to enter into treaty relations impairing its own sovereignty and the obligation to consult with the influencing power in matters of foreign relations. In some cases, the influencing power was even made responsible for the enforcement of treaties concluded by the influenced State and for the conduct of some of its foreign relations.[125]

It is important, however, to emphasize the distinction between political influence, which is characteristic of the sphere of influence relationship, and the direct exercise of authority found in the relationships discussed earlier.[126] The legal consequences for the influenced State of being drawn into another State's sphere of influence was limited to those arising out of the agreement establishing the sphere of influence.[127] Even when the relationship was recognized by third States, it did not, however, entail the formal loss of independence or sovereignty of the influenced State.[128]

Other Relationships Entailing Reliance or Restraint

The status of dominions in the British Commonwealth was touched upon in a previous chapter. Whereas most dominions were originally administered as part of colonial empires, they became progressively more self-governing in the latter part of the nineteenth century and the early twentieth century, such that by 1918 most enjoyed independence from their "parent" State.[129] Thus, the dominion members of the British Commonwealth were described in the Balfour Report of the Inter-Imperial Relations Committee of the Imperial Conference of 1926 as "autonomous Communities within the British Empire, equal in Status, in no way subordinate one to another in any aspect of their domestic or external affairs, though united by a common allegiance to the Crown, and freely associated as members of the British Commonwealth of Nations."[130] This description contains the essence of the dominion relationship. Even the allegiance to the Crown mentioned therein is little more than a symbolic one, in no way impairing the dominion government's exercise of the State's independence in internal as well as external affairs.[131] This is not to say, however, that the dominions were not subjected to any influence from the United Kingdom. The degree of influence a particular dominion was subjected to varied depending on its specific relations with the British government and the substantive issues involved.[132]

The independent members of the Commonwealth may be regarded as united by what is termed a personal union.[133] But there are more examples of such unions "where States which are wholly separate and distinct, have the same ruling prince."[134] Although the relations between the States thus united may vary considerably, those States remain separate international entities.[135] On the other hand, a real union exists where two States, each retaining its international personality, share joint institutions—as, for example, for the purposes of foreign affairs, defense, and/or finance.[136] The union of Austria and Hungary from 1867 to 1918 was just such a real union. With respect to that union, however, the International Court held that "although Austria and Hungary had common institutions based on analogous laws passed by their legislatures, they were none the less distinct international units."[137]

Some forms of reliance by one State on another entailing restrictions of the former's exercise of sovereignty are difficult to classify or categorize. The United Netherlands Provinces' voluntary subordination to Queen Elizabeth I of England in 1585 in order to secure her "protection" in their struggle for definite independence from Spain cannot, for example, properly be called vassalage, nor did the Netherlands become a protectorate of the British Crown.[138] This situation could more accurately be classified as one of "simple protection," a concept used to describe the relations of Monaco to France and San Marino to Italy. In the simple protection relationship, a State promises to protect another State without taking over the control of the foreign relations of the protected State. By such an agreement, the protected State does not lose it statehood.[139] Yet another variation on the theme of protection is the relationship entailing the protector's right to intervene in order to protect another State, but not the obligation to do so. This quasi-protectorate relationship also does not involve the transfer or delegation of governmental functions to the protector. G. Venturini cites the relationship established between the United States and Cuba in 1903, giving the former the right to intervene for the preservation of Cuban independence, as an example of a quasi-protectorate.[140]

There are other relationships of reliance in international law, but not all are relevant to this study. Thus, for example, the territories mandated by the League of Nations and the United Nations trusteeship arrangements need not be discussed here.

The survey of relationships among States and similar entities presented in this study is intended to provide guidelines in determining the international status of political entities bound in varying degrees by relationships with other States. Such a survey cannot go much beyond this, however, for, as has already been stressed, the legal status of a political entity can be determined only on the basis of an analysis of the particular circumstances of each case.

Before turning to the status of Tibet, we shall briefly review the system governing the international relations of Imperial China as well as the attitudes of Republican China and the People's Republic of China.

China and International Law

International Relations of Imperial China

The international relations of the Ming and Qing Empires must be understood in the context of the Chinese tributary system, which the Manchus inherited together with almost the entire administrative system, from the Ming Dynasty. The tributary system of the Confucian world order formally continued in existence until the very end of the nineteenth century. In practice, it was only gradually replaced by treaties with the British and other Western powers following the Anglo-Chinese war of 1842.[141]

The most authoritative work on this tributary system, written by John Fairbank and Ssu-yu Teng, is chiefly based on the various editions of the *Huidian* [Collected Statutes], the foremost official source for the system.[142] Much of the analysis that follows is therefore based on this work.

The Chinese tributary system developed from the age-old tradition of Chinese cultural superiority over all "barbarians," a term that was synonymous for non-Chinese.[143] Fairbank and Teng, among others, point to the following basic assumptions underlying the system:

> First, that Chinese superiority over the barbarians had a cultural rather than a mere political basis; it rested less upon force than upon the Chinese way of life embodied in such things as the Confucian code of conduct and the use of the Chinese written language; the sign of the barbarian was not race or origin so much as non-adherence to this way of life. From this it followed, secondly, that those barbarians who wished to "come to be transformed" (lai-hua), and so participate in the benefits of (Chinese) civilization, must recognize the supreme position of the Emperor; for the Son of Heaven represented all mankind, both Chinese and barbarian, in his ritual sacrifices before the forces of nature. Adherence to the Chinese way of life automatically entailed the recognition of the Emperor's mandate to rule all men. This supremacy of the Emperor as mediator between Heaven and Earth was most obviously acknowledged in the performance of the Kowtow, the three kneelings and nine prostrations to which European envoys later objected. It was also acknowledged by the bringing of a tribute of local produce, by the formal bestowal of a seal, comparable to the investiture of a vassal in medieval Europe, and in other ways. Thus the tributary system, as the sum total of these formalities, was the mechanism by which barbarous non-Chinese regions were given their place in the all-embracing Chinese political, and therefore ethical scheme of things.[144]

The Manchus, once they initiated the Qing Dynasty, adopted the Chinese way of life. The Manchu Emperor himself, in fact, became the son of Heaven, the apex of the pyramid of the Confucian world order.

As noted earlier, "barbarian" States entered into nominal tributary relations with the Ming Empire chiefly in order to trade with China. Although this was true in the early part of the Qing Empire, it may have become less so when other forms of economic intercourse became possible. From the viewpoint of the Imperial Court, the major reason for adherence to the tributary system was national security, as ideally, whoever wished to enter into relations with China was compelled to do so as the Emperor's tributary, thus ruling out all possibility of international intercourse on terms of equality.[145] Furthermore, as Jung points out:

> To a universal ruler, the ideological necessity of external peace was closely related to internal order: if barbarians were not submissive abroad, this would give the lie to the Emperor's universal rule, and might encourage rebels to rise up within the Empire. Every Emperor was therefore under compulsion to keep peace with foreign courts, but on a proper tributary basis.[146]

Aside from commercial and security considerations, an important aspect of the tributary system was its function as a diplomatic medium. As Fairbank and Teng have noted, "since all foreign relations in the Chinese view were *ipso facto* tributary relations, if they occurred at all in the experience of China, [they] had to be fitted into the tributary system."[147]

The absurdity to which this dogma eventually led can been seen from the list of vassals who allegedly paid tribute regularly to the Emperor, as recorded in the Qing edition of the Collected Statutes and the *Da Qing Lichao Shilu* [The Veritable Records of the Great Qing Dynasty]. Aside from China's neighbors—for example, Tibet, Turfan, Korea, Annam, Siam, Burma, and the Mongol States—these "tributaries" included such diverse countries as Laos, Portugal, the Papacy (the Pope was actually reported to have presented tribute in 1725), Russia, Nepal, Java, England, and Holland.[148] The last-named country is particularly conspicuous in the Kangxi edition of the Statutes, which notes with satisfaction that the country of Holland asked the privilege of sending tribute to the Emperor in 1653. Holland's allegiance was gratefully acknowledged, moreover, after the country reportedly assisted the Imperial troops in defeating rebels and pirates off the coast of Taiwan. In actual fact, however, the Dutch were defending their trading outpost from pirates, who had captured a Dutch trading outpost. Similar misrepresentations of history may be found especially in regard to Portugal and England (the latter of which is elsewhere described as a dependency of Holland).[149]

As also noted earlier, the relationship established under the tributary system required the ritual performance of the presentation of tribute by the so-called tributary. In return, the Emperor generally contributed to the travel expenses and provided hospitality to the members of the tributary mission while they were present in his capital; he also proffered gifts, usually of a value higher than those given to him as a tribute.[150] In principle, the tributary relationship implied neither the Emperor's protection of the tributary State nor any interference in the latter's internal affairs. In actuality, however, the implication held true in some cases, as revealed in the Manchu Emperor's Statement concerning Korea in the Declaration of War against Japan of 1894:

> Korea has been our tributary for the past two hundred odd years. She has given us tribute all this time, which is a matter known to the world. For the past dozen years or so, Korea has been troubled by repeated insurrections and we, in sympathy with our small tributary, have repeatedly sent succor to her aid, eventually placing a Resident in her capital to protect Korea's interest. . . . [We] sent troops to Korea to put down a rebellion. . . . Although we have been in the habit of assisting our tributaries, we have never interfered with their internal government.[151]

It is also interesting to note that tributary relationships in Asia were by no means exclusive. Thus, some of the Qing Emperor's tributaries established similar relations with other rulers, either as "suzerains" or "vassals."

China was first exposed to Western international law during the early years of the Qing Dynasty (1644–1911).[152] Despite the isolated application of international law in two treaties with Russia in 1689 and 1727, however, it wasn't until after the Opium war (1839–1842) that the Manchus reluctantly began to take an interest in and apply it, albeit in a limited way. By the end of the century the Qing Court was not only systematically using international law to check the expansionism of Western Powers in China, but it was also applying it in its relations to some Asian States. Finally, when China participated in the Hague Peace Conferences in 1899 and 1907, adhered to a number of multilateral conventions, and joined international organizations at the beginning of this century, it was in fact also playing a role in the growth of international law.[153]

The Republic of China and International Law

Upon the inauguration of the Republic of China on 1 January 1912, the country's founder, Sun Yat-sen, declared that the goal of the Republic was "to obtain [for China] the rights of a civilized State" and "to place China in a respectable place in international society."[154] A principal instrument in achieving this goal was recognized to be international law. The frequent references to international law in the Republic's statutes as well as in the opinions of the country's courts, judicial organs, and publicists leave little doubt as to the Republic of China's adherence to and application of customary as well as conventional international law.[155]

In 1945, China became one of the founding members of the United Nations and contributed to the formulation of international law as it was codified in the Charter of that organization. Furthermore, the Republic of China's undivided adhesion to and promotion of international law was clearly demonstrated when it proposed that all States should be required to accept the International Court of Justice's compulsory jurisdiction.[156] The Republic of China itself did accept the court's compulsory jurisdiction vis-à-vis those States making a reciprocal acceptance.[157] To quote Jerome Cohen and Hungdah Chiu, the Republic of China can indeed be said to have "contributed to the evolutionary process by which international law is being transformed from an exclusively Western product to one that more truly reflects the composition of the world."[158]

Regarding the specific question of the existence of States, the accepted view, as formulated by Huang Zhenming, is that this is a factual question that is not dependent upon recognition. Huang adds that "a State, in executing its policy, must choose a way favorable to itself. The maintenance of its right to self-preservation is a basic right to the State and also a prerequisite for the existence of the community of nations."[159] It should also be noted that the Republic has consistently supported the right of colonized States to independence.[160]

The People's Republic and International Law

In 1971, the People's Republic of China (PRC) formally adhered to the Charter of the United Nations when its government replaced that of the

Republic of China at the United Nations. Furthermore, in 1984, Ni Zhengyu, a prominent international jurist from the PRC, was elected to the International Court of Justice. Even before the PRC thus formally demonstrated its adhesion to existing international law, it had shown its recognition thereof, particularly in the conduct of its foreign relations.[161]

Until recently, there was much criticism of specific legal theories and norms by Chinese communist politicians and jurists, who classified them as "bourgeois." But never did they reject existing international law as a whole.[162] In fact, the Communist party and government of the PRC have consistently expressed strong support for the principles laid down in the Charter of the United Nations, to which the former were signatories in San Francisco and to which the latter formally referred in a number of international treaties.[163] At the same time, communist Chinese jurists have always accepted the validity of generally recognized international law as a means of regulating relations between States, even where differences did exist in their respective social systems.[164]

In recent years, the study of international law has been encouraged in the PRC, and major books on the subject have appeared.[165] For the purposes of this study, a review of communist China's stand regarding the principles and doctrines of international law already discussed in this chapter will be helpful.

The PRC regards sovereignty, self-determination, true equality, and peaceful co-existence as among the foremost principles of contemporary international law.[166] Even the central concept of statehood is determined with the help of these principles. Chinese communist legal doctrine holds that,

> according to the principles of sovereignty and national self-determination, the emergence of a State and its becoming a subject of international law should be decided by the will of the people in that State, that is to say, in accordance with the fact of their establishment as a State. It should not be decided by the will of other States, nor should the new State's qualifications as a subject of international law be conferred upon it by other States. As soon as a new State comes into existence, it is a subject of international law, and it enjoys rights and undertakes duties in international society, regardless of whether or not it is recognized by another State and regardless of how many States recognize it. Recognition in international law merely confirms the fact of the existence of a new State by the existing States . . . it cannot create a subject of international law.[167]

The actual or *de facto* existence of a State, based on the will of the people constituting it, is therefore determinative of the legal existence of a State as a subject of international law.[168] In keeping with this view, recognition can have no more than evidential value. The principle of effectiveness underlying this doctrine also determines the independence of governments: According to Kong Meng, "From the viewpoint of international law, the government which in fact independently exercises power within a country is the representative of that country in international relations."[169] Quoting Soviet as well as Western sources, Shao Jinfu elaborates on this view, which regards actual independence or effective governmental control to be the decisive element:

> According to international law, "In such single States there is one central political authority as government, which represents the State, within its borders as well as without, in its international intercourse with other International Persons." "It [international law] recognizes the government which actually and independently exercises power on the territory of the State as representative of that State in international relations." To quote the Italian jurist Anzilotti, "He who actually holds the power of command has the quality of organ of international personality in international relations; he who in fact loses this power ceases to represent the State internationally." Whether the government of a State is legal or not, only the people of that State can decide.[170]

The traditional Soviet view that State sovereignty is "the keystone of international law" and is illimitable, which the Soviet Union has now abandoned, is still the point of departure for communist Chinese legal thinking.[171] Thus, publicists and politicians in the PRC always stress legal instruments or parts thereof that safeguard the sovereignty of States, such as Article 2, paragraph 4 of the UN Charter, which provides that States shall "refrain in their international relations from the threat or use of force against the territorial integrity or political independence of any State."[172] State sovereignty is defined by Jin Fu as

> the inherent right of a State, which manifests itself internally as supreme authority, namely the exclusive jurisdiction of a State over its territory and all the persons and material on the territory and, externally, as the right of independence, namely, the complete independent exercise of right by a State in international relations from any outside interference. . . . The power of a State to rule in its territory [administrative power]. . . . is a concrete expression of sovereignty.[173]

According to a Soviet textbook on international law, the illimitability of sovereignity also means that

> the forcible restriction of the sovereignty of States which are members of the international community is impermissible, except following aggression [by those States]. The subjection of small States to the will of large States, or the subordination of the former by the latter, is also impermissible. This is often cloaked by hypocritical reference to the weak States' "voluntary restriction of sovereignty."[174]

This definition, in turn, leads to the principle of true equality of States as subjects of international law and its corollary, the rejection of "unequal treaties."

The communist Chinese notion of equality of States goes beyond the generally accepted concept of equality before the law. According to jurists in the PRC, inter-State relations must be conducted on the basis not only of legal equality but also of "true equality," so that the sovereign rights of weaker States are safeguarded against attempts by the stronger ones to dictate the terms of such relations.[175] A textbook on international trade treaties used by the Beijing Foreign Trade Institute thus states:

> The classical writers of Marxism-Leninism confirmed an important principle concerning international treaties, namely, the genuine sovereign equality between all parties concerned should become the foundation of international treaties. Lenin said: "Negotiations can only be conducted between equals and, therefore, genuine equality between both sides is an essential condition for reaching a genuine agreement."

The same text then goes on to make the following distinction:

> [I]n accordance with Marxism-Leninism, there are equal treaties and unequal treaties, and, therefore, progressive mankind takes a fundamentally different attitude towards different kinds of treaties. Equal treaties should be strictly observed. Unequal treaties are in violation of international law and without legal validity.[176]

A spokesman of the Information Department of the Chinese Foreign Ministry's recent statement with regard to the status of Hong Kong is consistent with this distinction:

> The treaties concerning the Xianggang [Hong Kong] area signed by the British Government and the government of the Qing Dynasty of China are unequal treaties which have never been accepted by the Chinese people. The consistent position of the Government of the People's Republic of China has been that China is not bound by these unequal treaties.[177]

China's emphasis on this point must certainly be attributed, in part, to its own "unequal" status from the 1840s to the 1940s, during which time Western powers "enjoyed extraterritorial and other privileges in China guaranteed by treaties signed under unequal circumstances."[178]

In fact, China's effort to erase its "unequal" status started well before the 1949 revolution. The Nationalist government called for the abolition of unequal treaties as early as 1913.[179] But that government and its jurists did not argue that unequal treaties were invalid in international law. Instead, they held that such agreements should be revised or abrogated in accordance with the principle of *rebus sic stantibus*.[180] Communist China's opposition to unequal treaties is not limited to its own experience; for the principle of true equality is often given prominence in that country's treaties and other instruments, particularly in its relations with African and Asian States.[181]

The impermissibility of subjecting small or weak States to the will of large ones or subordinating the former to the latter is a logical corollary to the principal concept of State sovereignty, as well as that of true equality, in the Chinese legal doctrine. Chinese jurists thus criticize the "bourgeois doctrine" whereby sovereignty over territory can be transferred through cession on the grounds that

> countries which ceded their territories were all under compulsion and that they were either weak, small, or defeated countries. Countries which acquired ceded territories were all imperialistic countries engaging in territorial expansion. Bourgeois international law writings have never been able to cite a single case in which an imperialist power ceded its territory to a weak or small country.
>
> Therefore, it can be said that cession of territory is a method of plundering the territories of weak and small or defeated countries used by imperialist countries through the use of war and threat of force. The special characteristic of cession is that the "transfer" of territorial sovereignty is fixed through the use of the formality of the unequal treaty.[182]

Such exploitation of the weakness of States by imperialist or other strong States is not limited to cession of territory, however. Any surrender of sovereignty to a stronger State necessarily results from the use of pressure, force, or other forms of coercion. Thus, according to this viewpoint, annexation of territory following conquest or by prescription (i.e., through prolonged occupation) clearly cannot give the annexing State a legal title to the territory.[183] But, by the same reasoning, this doctrine also considers the delegation of sovereignty by one State to another to be inadmissible, even when this action is taken for a definite period of time and is limited to specific governmental functions.[184] This doctrine leaves no room for those relationships analyzed earlier in this chapter, such as the protectorate or sphere-of-influence relationships, as they necessarily involve what would be considered an illegal infringement of the weaker State's sovereignty by expansionistic powers.[185]

As for the suzerainty relationship, it is regarded by Chinese jurists as

> a special form of rule used by a big State to control a small State during the feudalistic period. . . . Under this relationship the external affairs of the vassal State were generally administered by the suzerain State. Internally, the vassal State enjoyed a certain degree of self-governing authority or self-government, but it had to fulfill a definite obligation to the suzerain State, particularly the obligation to pay tribute. The unequal relationship between the suzerain State and the vassal State fully expressed the characteristic of international relations in the feudal period, and thus suzerainty can also be called feudal ruling authority.[186]

The Chinese scholar Yu Fan agrees with the view that the use of the suzerainty institution by colonial powers in more recent history, as in the case of the British in India, was only a tool for the expansion of imperial or colonial administration, which cannot properly be termed suzerainty.[187]

That writer similarly considers those so-called suzerainty relationships in which the suzerain's sovereignty over the vassal is denied in fact—such that the former maintains only "the empty title of suzerain State"—a fictitious title, then, devoid of legal significance. He uses Turkey's nominal suzerainty over Egypt until 1914 as an example of such a hollow suzerainty. In fact, the recognition of this kind of suzerainty by imperialists, Yu Fan claims, is only a device used by them to safeguard or to further their own interests with regard to the so-called vassal State.[188]

In addition, under no circumstances can an agreement between two or more States by which they recognize the suzerainty of a third State over another one, or any other such relationship with regard to the status of entities, create such a relationship or in any way legally affect the latter States' relations. This follows, writes Yu Fan, from the principle of *pacta tertiis nec nocent nec prosunt* of the law of treaties, whereby conventions cannot bind third parties.[189]

The principles discussed thus far do not imply that the present situation regarding territorial status is "absolutely stabilized." According to the practice of modern international law, Chinese scholars maintain, the following changes may occur:

> (1) According to the international law principle of national self-determination, colonial people have the right of political self-determination, including the right to determine the destiny of the territory they inhabit. . . . (2) In order to rectify the unjust situation created by history, a State must recover sovereignty over its own territory. . . . (3) It is also possible that neighboring States may exchange a part of their frontier area in accordance with generally accepted principles of international law.[190]

Later chapters will also touch on the views held in the PRC regarding specific legal questions; hence, for the moment, the above survey should suffice.

8

The Historical Status
of Tibet: Conclusions

From a Secular Empire
to a Religious State

During its imperial era, Tibet was undoubtedly one of the mightiest powers in Asia. Even the Chinese court historians, writing their dynastic histories to the glorification of the Tang Emperors, were compelled to admit that Tibet, China's foremost rival at the time, had become the most powerful State in Asia by the eighth century.[1] Tibet's independence and, indeed, preeminence in this period of its history is not seriously disputed.

In some recent political writings, Songtsen Gampo's wedding to the Tang Princess Wen Cheng and his receptiveness to Chinese cultural influences are cited as evidence of Tibet's alleged political unification with, or subordination to, China.[2] In light of the circumstances surrounding the wedding and the Tibetan Emperor's five other recorded marriages, this suggestion is absurd. If anything, Songtsen Gampo's securement of the Chinese ruler's reluctant consent to give a princess in marriage demonstrated Tibet's preponderance in Asia at the time. The status of Sino-Tibetan relations during this Imperial era is well documented and is reflected in the Tibetan-Chinese treaties of 783 and 821 A.D.[3] Even Li Tieh-Tseng (pinyin: Li Diezeng), in his serious treatise in defense of China's historical claims over Tibet, dismisses the suggestion that Tibet was subordinate to China at the time. He quotes an interesting passage from the *Tang Shu*, referring to the Tang Emperor's embassy to the Tibetan Emperor in 781, as evidence of the actual relations between the two empires:

> When Ch'ang lu, with the envoy [of Tang Emperor T'e Tsung] Ts'ui Han-heng, first arrived at their hotel (781), the [Tibetan Emperor, Tsanpo Trisong Detsen] ordered them to stop, and made them first produce the official despatch [from their Emperor]. That having been done, [the Tsanpo] sent this message to Han-heng: "The imperial despatch you bring says, 'The things offered as tribute have all been accepted and now we bestow upon our son-in-law a few presents for him to take when they arrive.' Our great Fan [Tibetan] and Tang nations are allied by marriages, and how is it that we are treated with

the rites due to a subject? . . . Let, then, Han-heng send a messenger to report to the Emperor that he may act."

Lu was sent back and the imperial despatch was accordingly altered, the words "offered as tribute" changed to "presented," "bestowed" to "given" and "for him to take" to "for his acceptance." The following words were added, "The former minister, Yang Yen, departed from the old practice and is responsible for these errors."[4]

Almost three hundred years after the birth of the unified State, the Tibetan Empire disintegrated. Although the principalities that remained were united by a common history and by racial, linguistic, and, to some extent, religious bonds, the Tibetan historian W.D. Shakabpa concedes that "nothing approaching central authority" remained.[5] The Tibetans were left to deal with their internal problems without foreign interference, and their external relations were sporadic and of little significance.

To speak in terms of statehood in describing what was in fact a collection of principalities and hegemonies of varying sizes and power, only partly united by shifting sets of alliances, would be inconsistent with the analysis of statehood presented earlier in this book. At the same time, when Tibet was reunited by clerical rulers under the shadow of Mongol supremacy, in the mid-thirteenth century, a sense of identification and continuity with the Tibetan State of the Imperial age clearly existed.

The agreement reached between the Mongol Prince Goden and Sakya Pandita in 1240 might be regarded as the original foundation of the Mongol-Tibetan relationship that developed in the following century.[6] Goden invested Sakya Pandita with temporal authority over Tibet and pledged his protection in return for the latter's loyalty to him. This personal relationship, however, did not extend beyond the relatively small areas controlled by either hierach, and it is to the subsequent relationship between Kubilai Khagan, ruler of the eastern half of the Mongol Empire, and Pagpa, who came to exercise supreme authority over Tibet, that one must turn to determine the nature of Mongol-Tibetan relations during the Yuan dynastic rule.

The investiture of Pagpa with supreme temporal authority over Tibet by the Khagan and the personal nature of the relationship between the two are elements common to feudal suzerainty. The Mongol-Tibetan bond was markedly different from the feudal counterparts, however, in that it lacked the element of superiority and subservience characteristic of suzerain-vassal relations. Indeed, an essential element of the Chö-yön (Priest-Patron) relationship established between the Lama and the Khagan was the Patron's devotion to and even worship of his spiritual Teacher. Furthermore, the protection that the Patron provided his Lama was given in return not for the latter's allegiance but for his religious teachings and prayers. The Mongol-Tibetan relationship is best defined by the doctrine of dual responsibility, which formed the theoretical foundation for it. This doctrine provided for dual political and religious paramountcy of the Emperor and the Tishri (Imperial preceptor) on the basis of equality, interdependence, and mutual respect and reverence.

Thus, from a formal point of view, the source of the Lama's temporal authority over Tibet was vested outside Tibet, with the Mongol Khagan. The Khagan, in turn, derived the legitimacy of his Imperial rule from the religious position or mandate recognized by the Tibetan Lama.

In practice, the Tishri and his subjects owed a degree of temporal allegiance to the Mongol Emperor, and the Mongolian presence was at times felt in Tibet. At the same time, the Mongol, Tibetan, Chinese, and other Buddhist peoples of the Empire acknowledged the religious leadership of the Tishri.

Beyond these formal and practical elements, the close racial and cultural affinity between the Mongol and Tibetan peoples was unique. Thus, although Tibet was never fully integrated into the Mongol Empire—in contrast with most territories, including China, which were directly ruled by the Mongols— the bond between the Mongols and the Tibetans was much closer than that between the former and the Chinese or other peoples populating the Empire. This bond, which exists to this day, was symbolized by the dual temporal and religious leadership of the Yuan Empire by the Mongol Khagan and the Tibetan Tishri.

No standard legal categorization can describe the unique position of the Tibetans in relation to the Mongols and the Yuan Empire. Although Tibet was bound to the Mongol Empire, it was so bound not by simple subjection to Mongol rule but by a combination of religious, cultural, racial, and political relationships unique to that Empire.

It may seem superfluous, given the historical evolution and distinctiveness of the Mongol-Tibetan relationship, to point out that this relationship was legally unrelated to the Mongol rule over China and other parts of the Empire. The Mongol-Tibetan and Mongol-Chinese relationships were sep- arate matters. Nevertheless, because it has been suggested that the Emperor's supremacy over Tibet and his conquest of China effectively turned Tibet into a part, or at least into a vassal, of the Chinese State, the point should once again be emphasized: The Mongol-Tibetan relationship and the system put in place for the administration of Tibet was established before Kubilai's conquest of China, and for the duration of the Mongolian Empire the administration of the two countries was always kept separate. Tibet was administered by Tibetans under the supervision of the Mongol Court, and separate organs were created under the direction of the Tishri for this purpose. At no time was Tibet administered as part of China or vice versa, and no Chinese were involved in the administration of Tibet. Beyond that, as the affinity that existed and was felt between the Mongols and Tibetans did not exist between either of these peoples and the Chinese, the very nature of the Mongol-Chinese relationship, established by conquest, was totally different and separate. Tibet also effectively broke away from the Empire before China regained its independence from its Mongol rulers.

Changchub Gyaltsen's rise to power and replacement of the Sakya hegemony in 1349 was coupled with a nationalistic move away from Mongol domination. The new Tibetan ruler effectively broke away from the declining

Yuan Empire and established control over Tibet without outside help and without the need for outside approval. When the Yuan Dynasty was ousted by the Chinese and fell, no bonds of political significance remained between the Tibetan ruling dynasty of the Pamogrupa and any outside ruler.

In contrast with the governmental authority exercised by the Sakya rulers of Tibet, who derived their authority from the Mongolian Emperors, Changchub Gyaltsen seized power and he and his successors maintained control over the State in their own right: The source of their governing authority lay within the State, and its exercise was not dependent on an outside power. Under the new regime, the administrative, military, and other governmental organs introduced or reformed under the influence of the Mongols were replaced by distinctly Tibetan ones; a new code of laws was enacted by which justice was administered throughout the country; and until civil war broke out, in the seventeenth century, the public authorities asserted themselves without the assistance of foreign troops. Tibet conducted diplomatic and treaty relations with its neighbors, including the Nepalese Kingdoms, China and Kashmir, without foreign interference.

The Ming Dynasty, which ruled over the Chinese Empire for the next two and three-quarter centuries, was Chinese. The Tibetans had no ethnic or close cultural affinity with China's rulers or their subjects; and as the Chinese were generally not Buddhist, no special bond existed. Autonomous relationships between individual Tibetan priests and noblemen or traders on the one hand, and wealthy patrons, including Mongolian or Chinese princes and chieftains and even Ming Emperors, on the other, did exist during this period. These relationships did not, however, affect the independent government of Tibet: They were maintained for personal, generally economic, gain and did not involve any measure of effective subjection to foreign rulers.[7]

For some three hundred years after the fall of the joint Mongol-Sakya rule, Tibet was left to reassert itself as an independent State. It was not until the early seventeenth century, however, that Tibet had a significant political role to play in Asia.

The Fifth Dalai Lama's rise to power and his enthronement as the supreme ruler of Tibet in 1642 marked the beginning of an era in which the religious influence of the Gelugpa, and especially of the Dalai Lama, was so immense in Central Asia that Tibet once again rose to become, in a sense, a great power. This period also marked the end of an essentially religious war that had raged since 1603 between the Gelugpa and the rulers of Tsang province, who supported the rival Karmapa.[8] Tibet reemerged from that war in 1642 a more united and powerful State, with the Dalai Lama as sovereign.

Gushri Khan's role in the civil war and the Dalai Lama's assumption of supreme authority must be seen in the light of the *Chö-yön* relationship that existed between them: The Qoshot Chieftain's response to the Dalai Lama's request for intervention was a fulfillment of his obligation as the Lama's protector and an act of devotion as his worshipper; his delivery of all the vanquished territory to the Dalai Lama was an offering to his Priest.

The Fifth Dalai Lama's sovereign authority over Tibet, inherited by his successive incarnations, was described by Ippolito Desideri, a Jesuit scholar who resided in Tibet until 1721, as follows:

> The hierarchy existing in Thibet is not secular but superior to all temporal and regular government. Head of all is the Grand Lama of Thibet. . . . [He] is recognized and venerated not only by all Thibetans. . . . but by Nepalese, Tartars and Chinese, and is regarded as their Chief, Master, Protector, and Pontiff. . . . He rules not only over religious, but over temporal matters, as he is really the absolute master of all Thibet.[9]

During the Fifth Dalai Lama's reign and, upon his death, under the government of his Regent, Sangye Gyatso, the Tibetan government conducted its international relations actively and independently with neighboring rulers, including the Mongol Khans and Manchu Emperors. Tibet concluded treaties with the Kings of Nepal and fought a war and signed a peace treaty with Ladakh.[10]

The Dalai Lama's relations with the Manchu Emperors of the Qing Dynasty preceded his rise to political power. Emperor Tai Zong sent envoys to invite the Dalai Lama to Mukden as early as 1639, "in order to propagate the growth of the Buddhist Faith and to benefit all living beings."[11] Although the Dalai Lama did not go to Mukden himself, he accepted the Emperor's wish to patronize his church; from the reply he sent, it is clear that he regarded the relationship he had opened with the Qing Emperor as "in no way different from his relationship with any other Worshipper-Patron-and-Protector."[12] The Dalai Lama regarded the Emperor as, "simply, one of the many rulers of Tibet, Mongolia and (now) Manchuria, who were his Worshippers, Patrons and Protectors. A very well-known relationship between Dalai Lama and the secular rulers was now being extended to Manchuria."[13]

The Chö-yön relationship thus became the formal basis for Tibet's relations with the Manchus, who came to rule over China in 1644.[14] The Chö-yön is a uniquely Buddhist and Central Asian religio-political institution, which cannot be categorized or defined adequately in current international legal terms and must therefore be regarded as a *sui generis* relationship. As earlier noted, it is a personal bond consisting of the elements of protection by the Patron of his Priest and of his devotion to him, and the Priest's commitment to fulfill the Patron's spiritual needs. No subservience is implied in the relationship.

When, some ten years later, the Dalai Lama traveled to the Qing Court in response to a renewed invitation, he did so essentially to reaffirm this religious relationship with Emperor Tai Zong's successor, Shunzhi. The religious nature of the relationship is evident from the complimentary titles the two sovereigns exchanged.[15] Nothing in this relationship suggests, as some recent Chinese authors would have it,[16] that the Dalai Lama accepted or recognized a position of vassalage with respect to the Manchu Emperor at the time, or that the latter asserted a form of suzerainty over his Spiritual Teacher.[17]

<h2 style="text-align:center">Tibetan-Manchu Relations
in the Eighteenth Century</h2>

When Imperial Manchu troops came to the assistance of the Tibetans against the Dzungar invaders in 1720, a new dimension was added to Manchu-Tibetan relations. For the first time, the Qing Emperor intervened openly in Tibetan affairs[18] and, for roughly a century afterward, continued to do so at various times—that is, in defending Tibet from foreign invaders or internal disorders and in exerting varying degrees of influence over its government. The question is to what extent this intervention affected the status of Tibet.

In 1720, when the Imperial armies first entered Tibet, that country's independence was not in question.[19] Tibet's only ties with the Manchu Emperor were those arising out of the *Chö-yön* relationship between the Dalai Lama and the Emperor. This relationship was never as close as it had been between the Sakya Lamas and the Mongol Emperors. It did not involve, as it had done at the time of the Yuan Dynasty, the dual temporal-religious leadership of the Empires and there was no formal role for a Tibetan Lama at the Manchu Court. Only a personal religious bond existed between the Dalai Lama and the Manchu Emperor, similar to that between the Lama and various Mongolian and Tibetan Patrons. Although the Manchus had more affinity with the Tibetans than with the Chinese, the two peoples were never as close as the Tibetans and Mongols had been. Furthermore, the Qing Emperors and their court adopted Chinese ways once they had conquered China, and the Emperors conducted their relations with other States and peoples according to the Confucian system, which they inherited from the Ming.

When the Manchu Emperor intervened in 1720, he officially invoked the *Chö-yön* by way of justification.[20] The fact that his action was undertaken in response to requests from the Tibetans for help in expelling the invaders, and that Imperial troops escorted the Dalai Lama to his rightful place in Lhasa, served to emphasize the Emperor's role as the Patron and Protector fulfilling his obligations arising out of the *Chö-yön* relationship. The temporary appointment of an Imperial representative to "supervise" the restoration of effective administration in Tibet was in keeping with the protective role, for that official's primary task was to protect the Dalai Lama and to advise on measures taken to ensure peace and stability in Tibet.[21] Following this first intervention, Tibet continued to conduct most of its affairs, including foreign relations, as it had done previously—that is, without Manchu interference; and even in matters of defense Manchu "supervision" was minimal.

Hence, the first Imperial intervention brought about no fundamental changes, either formal or actual, in Manchu-Tibetan relations.[22] We must question, however, whether this assertion applies to the development of those relations in the decades that followed. For with each new Manchu intervention, in 1728, 1750, and, finally, 1793, Imperial influence in Lhasa increased.

The principal features of the Manchu-Tibetan relationship, as it evolved from 1720 to the early nineteenth century, can be described in formal as well as actual terms.

The formal basis for the Emperor's interventions in Tibet was the Chö-yön relationship. Each time he intervened, he did so at the request or with the consent of the Tibetan authorities, and the justification for these actions was always the protection of Tibet from external or internal threats. This justification was just as obvious in 1792, when Imperial troops were sent to help the Tibetans drive back the Gorkha invaders, as it had been in 1720.[23] But even in 1728, when the Dalai Lama was exiled to Kham, the Emperor officially justified his action in terms of protection from the renewed danger of Dzungar attack. Only in 1750 was the situation different, in that the threat was an internal one. On that occasion, the Emperor's intervention was in effect limited to supporting the Dalai Lama in his efforts to consolidate the government's power and to restore its stability. Even the 1793 reforms proclaimed by the Emperor, concerning the formalities for recognizing High Lamas in Tibet, were prescribed officially by "the Protector of the Yellow Church [i.e., The Gelugpa]" to protect the latter from harmful abuse.[24]

In practice, Manchu involvement in Tibetan affairs in the eighteenth century was effective only during its peaks, which immediately followed each military intervention. In between those times, the Tibetans were left to conduct their own affairs virtually without interference, except after 1793, when the Ambans played a role in Tibet's foreign relations.

An important feature of the Manchu-Tibetan relationship was the appointment by the Emperor of representatives to Lhasa. In 1728, two "Residents" were appointed in Lhasa (generally referred to by their title, that of Amban). Their duties before 1751 were limited to commanding the small Imperial garrison, ensuring communications with their court, and reporting to the Emperor on developments in Tibet. As a rule, there was no interference in the Tibetan government.[25] After 1751, their role increased, for they were authorized to give advice to the Kashag on important matters. The most far-reaching changes took place in 1793, following the Manchu and Tibetan victory over Gorkha. The reforms enacted at that time empowered the Ambans to exercise control over the external affairs of Tibet, to consult with the Dalai Lama and his Ministers on these and other important matters on a footing of equality, and to act as intermediary between the Tibetan sovereign and the Emperor.[26]

The Emperor's 1793 edict, insofar as it represented the involvement of the Emperor in things religious, was less significant than it appeared. The official justification for the directive, as an action of the "Protector of the Yellow Church," indicated that it did not necessarily represent an unwarranted intrusion in Tibetan religious affairs, and the prescription of the use of lots for choosing High Lamas among candidates already selected by traditional Tibetan procedures was not new to the Tibetans, nor did it give the Emperor any influence over either the selection of candidates or the final choice from among those candidates. Furthermore, as the Tibetans totally ignored the Emperor's wishes the very next time a Dalai Lama was selected, the edict had virtually no effect.

The following conclusions may be drawn concerning the status of Tibet in the eighteenth century. Throughout the period under examination, Tibet possessed the essential attributes of statehood and never ceased being considered a separate entity. Before 1793, it conducted its international relations independently; but even after that time, when those relations were controlled or supervised by an Amban, they were conducted either by Tibet or on its behalf. This development became clearer in the nineteenth century, but it was plain already from the terms of the Tibet-Nepal Treaty of 1792, which, although it respectfully mentioned the Emperor, referred to both Tibet and Nepal as separate entities.[27]

The source of governmental authority remained in Tibet or, more precisely, in the person and office of the Dalai Lama, and not outside the State. The Dalai Lama's sovereignty was formally uncontested, even when it was not exercised by the Dalai Lama himself. His sovereignty was not derived from an outside power but inherited, as it were, from the previous incarnation and, originally, from the Fifth Dalai Lama. Consecutive Dalai Lamas were born with sovereign authority because they were believed to be the same spiritual entity as the Great Fifth. Thus, when the Seventh Dalai Lama actually exercised sovereign control again in 1751, he was merely restoring the situation that had existed at the time of the Great Fifth, not creating a new one. As L. Petech has noted, this sovereign right was "considered [by the Chinese] as having been always exercised, even if through deputies."[28]

Relations between Tibet and the Manchu Emperor were formally based on the Chö-yön relationship throughout this period. As the Kangxi Emperor himself professed: "There has always existed a relationship of religious patronage between the Manchu Emperor and the Dalai Lama."[29] That relationship did not imply the political subordination of one party to the other. Little significance can be attributed to the reference in Qing documents or histories to the vassal status of either country or even to the tributary missions sent by them, given that all of the Empire's relations were of necessity conducted in terms of tributary relationships.[30] In fact, the only conclusion that can be drawn from such references is that relations between the Qing Empire and Tibet or Nepal were at least of a semi-international nature. For if those two countries were regarded as forming integral parts of the Qing Empire (as, for example, were China and Manchuria), they could not at the same time maintain "tributary relations" with that Empire (as, for example, Annam or Korea had done).

The principal features of the Tibetan-Manchu relationship, as it developed and reached its culmination in 1793, bore a striking similarity to those of the protectorate, which was examined earlier—hence Petech's consistent references to the Qing "Protectorate" in his, the foremost, scholarly study of this period.[31] First, the formal basis for the relationship, the *Chö-yön*, was established by means of a consensual transaction, creating an obligation for the Patron to protect his Priest, church, and country. This obligation was also the basic element of the protectorate arrangement. The other necessary ingredient in that arrangement was the protector's involvement in and responsibility for the conduct of the protected State's foreign relations. The 1793 reforms specifically provided for this aspect of the Manchu-Tibetan relationship. Moreover, the nature and extent of Manchu intervention, including the appointment of an Amban (i.e., a "Resident") to act as intermediary between the Tibetan sovereign and the Emperor and to take charge of the former's international relations was also typical of protectorate arrangements.

Beyond the similarity between the Manchu-Tibetan relationship in the eighteenth century and the protectorate, categorization becomes difficult. Both the personal nature of the *Chö-yön* relationship and the payment of tribute by the Tibetans suggest a similarity with feudal suzerainty as well. This can be no more than a similarity, however, primarily because the *Chö-yön* relationship was established outside the traditional tributary framework; in other words, it was a typically Buddhist institution that could not be placed within the Confucian Order. Furthermore, as the essential elements of the suzerainty relationship—the investiture of governing authority by the suzerain and the inferiority and submission of the vassal to the suzerain—were absent from the Manchu-Tibetan relationship, it is hardly appropriate to regard the Manchu Emperor as the suzerain of the Dalai Lama.

The conclusion that must be reached, therefore, is that Manchu-Tibetan relations in the eighteenth century, while formally and solely based on the *Chö-yön* relationship, included features primarily characteristic of protectorate arrangements—though they were often conceived in terms of tributary relations by the Qing Court.[32] As the formal source of government remained in Tibet; as Tibet was not conquered or annexed by the Emperor but, rather, was taken under his protection; and as the nature of Manchu interference in Tibetan affairs, specifically its foreign affairs, did not differ from that characteristic of protectorate relationships and the extent of actual interference was limited and by no means continuous, the State of Tibet never ceased to exist. The exercise of sovereignty by the Tibetans was restricted by the Manchu involvement in the affairs of Tibet, but that did not result in the extinction of the independent State, which continued to possess the essential attributes of statehood. This conclusion is supported by the strong presumption in favor of the continued existence of States in international law. Hence the analyst is compelled to interpret restrictively the instruments and other evidence indicating the establishment of outside control over Tibet, for the evidence to support the contention that Tibet, as a State, ceased to exist in the eighteenth century is, indeed, insufficient.

The Nineteenth and Early Twentieth Centuries

Manchu authority in and over Tibet reached its apogee in 1793 and the years immediately following. By the beginning of the nineteenth century that authority had waned considerably, and by the middle of that century hardly any Manchu influence remained. Abbé Huc's remark that the Amban's position in Lhasa was essentially reduced to that of a foreign ambassador is illustrative of Manchu-Tibetan relations at the time.[33] Indeed, Li Tieh-tseng, citing the Imperial Qing records (*Xuan Zong Shilu*), has also commented on this sharp decline in Manchu influence.[34] Even where Tibet's foreign affairs were concerned, the Imperial role was reduced to a merely nominal one, as is clearly evidenced by the following set of circumstances.

Tibet waged war with the Dogras and the Gorkhas and concluded peace treaties with them in 1842 and 1856, respectively, without Imperial assistance or intervention.[35] First, Tibet could not have waged these wars on its own had it been bound to the Qing Emperor as his vassal or protectorate, for the right to do so was reserved for the suzerain or protector. Second, the Emperor defaulted, on both occasions, in his obligation to protect Tibet from foreign invaders. As such protection is an essential element of the protectorate, suzerainty, and the Chö-yön relationship, such Imperial inactivity signified an abandonment by the Emperor of his protector's role, at least in practice. This abandonment was not just temporary either, for never again did the Imperial armies come to the assistance of Tibet. Third, the conclusion by the Tibetan government of treaties with the Dogras and the Gorkhas, as well as with Kashmir, was inconsistent with the Manchu protectorate or suzerainty over Tibet. This was especially true given that those treaties were comprehensive and dealt with Tibet's territorial, commercial, and diplomatic as well as political international relations.[36] Moreover, by concluding these treaties with Tibet, its neighbors recognized Tibet's statehood and international personality. The commercial, diplomatic, and even extraterritorial and judicial privileges conceded to Nepal in the 1856 treaty, for example, presupposed the full exercise of sovereignty by the Government of Tibet.[37] In addition, inasmuch as a distinctive element of the protectorate and suzerainty relationships was the conception that an attack on the protected State was considered to be an attack on the protecting State, the Amban's request that Nepal affirm that it had attacked only Tibet and not the Empire was inconsistent with the existence of either relationship.

On the other hand, Tibet did recognize the continuance of the Qing Emperor's nominal role—a recognition consistent with the Chö-yön relationship. This is evident from references to the Emperor in the Nepal-Tibet Treaty, whom both parties agreed to regard "as heretofore with respect."[38] The nature and extent of Imperial influence in Tibet is poignantly attested by the following characterization of the position of the Amban in Lhasa, given at the time by the Abbot of Tashi Lhunpo Monastery: "Where Chinese policy was in accordance with their own views, the Tibetans were ready enough to accept the Amban's advice; but . . . if this advice ran counter in any respect to their national prejudices, the Chinese Emperor himself would be powerless to influence them."[39]

The Manchu "protectorate" over Tibet, if the term can be used loosely here to describe the relationship established in the mid-eighteenth century, thus appeared to have virtually ceased to exist by the mid-nineteenth century. What remained was a nominal relationship but without the effective protection it would otherwise have entailed; that is, it was still formally based on the Chö-yön relationship and was at times viewed by the Manchus in terms of tributary (i.e., at least semi-international) relations.

Whereas the role of the Manchus was thus reduced to a nominal one, through the 1856 Treaty Nepal secured rights and privileges in Tibet for itself, in addition to a nominal role there. The relationship created between the two countries by that treaty cannot be regarded as a protectorate, however, for the agreement provided only for Nepal's assistance in the event of a foreign invasion of Tibet and not, as is the case in protectorate arrangements, for the former's involvement in Tibet's foreign relations or defense. The relationship should be regarded, instead, as a simple protection arrangement. At the same time, Nepal was given a special position in Tibet involving commercial and jurisdictional privileges similar to those granted by some Asian and African States to Western imperialist powers. These privileges, though forming an intrusion in the Tibetan government's exercise of territorial or personal jurisdiction, did not, however, affect Tibet's statehood, just as the so-called capitulation treaties concluded by Western powers with China and other Asian or African States did not affect theirs. Nepal's protective role, it must be added, was never an effective one, for that country never came to the assistance of Tibet: not when the British invaded in 1903, nor when the Manchus did so in 1910 and the Chinese in 1950.

Great Britain's interest in Tibet brought renewed strain in Manchu-Tibetan relations. The early British contacts with Tibet were not of an official intergovernmental nature, for the Panchen Lama did not represent the government at Lhasa. Their significance is thus limited to the fact that they took place at a time when the British had not yet established any relations with the Qing Emperor. Once these relations had been established, the British attempted to use the dominant position they had secured for themselves in China by means of the 1842 "unequal treaties" in order to gain access to Tibet with the help of the Qing Emperor.

The significance of the series of agreements concluded by those two powers in the late nineteenth century, beginning with the special clause appended to the Chefoo Convention and ending with the Trade Regulations of 1893,[40] can be summarized in the following terms: First, Tibet was regarded by both parties as a political entity distinct from the Qing Empire. In all of the agreements reference is made to Tibet in this sense. Thus, for example, the 1886 Convention is entitled "Convention Relating to Burmah and Thibet" and that of 1890, "Convention Between Great Britain and China Relating to Sikkim and Tibet." Thus, neither Burma, Sikkim, nor Tibet was considered to be an integral part of either the Qing or the British Empire. Second, these agreements constituted recognition by Britain of the Manchu Emperor's right to enter into international agreements on behalf of Tibet. That this right was not considered by Britain to belong to the Emperor exclusively was demonstrated by the conclusion, in 1904, of a bilateral Anglo-Tibetan Treaty without the intermediary of the Manchu Emperor.[41] Third, these agreements also confirmed that treaties with foreign powers concluded by the Qing Emperor or his government were not valid in Tibet unless they were entered into specifically for Tibet.[42] The special agreement granting the British permission to send an exploratory expedition to Tibet (added to the Chefoo Convention) amply illustrates this point, for it would have been wholly unnecessary had previous agreements granting them such rights in the Qing Empire been applicable to Tibet also.

These factors point to recognition by the British government of the Qing Emperor's protectorate, but not suzerainty, over Tibet. Although in either situation the Emperor would have had the authority to enter into agreements on Tibet's behalf, had he been the suzerain all treaties concluded by him would automatically have been valid in Tibet.[43] This recognition, it should be emphasized, was opposable only to Britain, in its dealings with Beijing and Lhasa, and could not create mutual rights or obligations for the Manchus or Tibetans.[44]

The Tibetans, for their part, never recognized the Emperor's authority to conclude treaties on their behalf and, until the Chefoo Convention was drawn up, had been party to all treaties concerning them. Consequently, the Tibetan authorities rejected the agreements reached by the Manchus and the British without their participation, and made their implementation impossible by actively opposing all attempts to enforce the treaty provisions.

Given the Emperor's claim to authority with regard to Tibet's foreign relations, based on the 1793 reforms, and the British recognition thereof on the one hand, and the abandonment of the Emperor's protective role and the repudiation of his claim by the Tibetans on the other, the question concerning the actual exercise of the contested authority must be asked.

The evidence presented in Chapter 3 leads to the following conclusions: The Tibetan government exercised effective control in Tibet, free from Manchu interference, throughout this period; it conducted Tibet's relations with neighboring States, waged wars and concluded treaties on its own; it opened relations with the Russian government without Beijing's participation or approval; and it effectively obstructed the implementation of the agreements concluded by the Imperial government on its behalf. Nothing demonstrated the total ineffectiveness of Imperial authority over Tibet more clearly than the Manchus' utter inability to enforce those treaty provisions. It was indeed the absence of actual control over Tibet by the Manchus and the futility of treating with the government in Beijing with regard to Tibet that prompted the British mission to Lhasa and the opening of direct relations with the Tibetan government there on a basis similar to that of Nepal's direct relations with Tibet.

The 1904 Anglo-Tibetan Treaty and the military invasion that preceded it were significant, particularly for the following two reasons: The Emperor did not come to the assistance of Tibet when it was invaded, and he refused responsibility for the actions of the Tibetans, thus confirming the previous abandonment of his protecting role; and the conclusion of a bilateral treaty between the British and Tibetan governments constituted implicit recognition by Britain of Tibet as a State and a subject of international law, and of the Dalai Lama's government as the legitimate government of Tibet, competent to represent that country internationally as well as conclude treaties. The provisions of the Lhasa Convention, especially Article 9, necessarily presupposed the unrestricted sovereignty of Tibet in internal and external matters, as otherwise the Government of Tibet could not legitimately have transferred to Great Britain the extensive powers specified therein.

In signing the Lhasa Convention, which made no mention of the Manchu Emperor or his government, the British did not necessarily reject the existence of some kind of relationship between the Emperor and Lhasa. On the contrary, verbal statements made by Colonel Younghusband in 1904, and the conclusion two years later of the Beijing Adhesion Agreement, indicated Britain's continued acknowledgment thereof.[45] But the relationship the British government thus recognized was a purely nominal one, for it impaired neither their own direct relations with Tibet nor the execution of the Lhasa Convention, the validity of which was confirmed by both parties to the Adhesion Agreement. In other words, the relationship did not restrict Tibet's international personality, nor did it hinder the inclusion of Tibet in the British Empire's sphere of influence.

The terms of the Anglo-Tibetan Treaty of 1904 are characteristic of instruments establishing a power's sphere of influence. The principal purpose of this treaty was to effectuate the exclusion of other powers from Tibet, particularly Russia, and, in a positive sense, to secure for the British a privileged position in what was hoped could remain a buffer State between the three Empires of Asia. The stipulations restricting the Tibetan government's right to alienate Tibetan territory or requiring consultation with the British for other specific international acts were typical for the sphere-of-influence arrangement. The British had therefore established a relationship with Tibet that was inconsistent with their recognition of anything more than a purely nominal Manchu overlordship in relation to that country.[46] At that same time, that relationship was not at all inconsistent with Tibet's continued sovereignty, for not only did the conclusion of the Anglo-Tibetan Treaty itself signify Britain's recognition of Tibet's international personality, but the transfer or delegation of certain specified attributes of sovereignty to the British by that agreement could not affect the continued statehood of Tibet.

The 1906 and 1907 treaties concluded by the British with the governments in Beijing and St. Petersburg, respectively, modified the situation insofar as Great Britain denied itself some of the privileges it had secured from the Tibetans.[47] These treaties could not alter the status either of Tibet or of its relations with the Qing Emperor as Yu Fan emphasizes, for, to quote the International Court, "a treaty only creates law as between the States which are parties to it; in case of doubt, no rights can be deduced from it in favour of third States."[48]

Regarding Tibet, the 1906 and 1907 treaties were *res inter alios acta*. The Government of Great Britain had recognized the capacity of Tibet to conclude treaties wholly independent of the Manchu authorities. This recognition was made unmistakably clear to the Waiwu Bu throughout the Adhesion Agreement negotiations.[49] Great Britain could not consider the Lhasa Convention "fully valid and complete" in itself[50] and, at the same time, conclude a treaty with another State (despite its recognition of that State's nominal suzerainty) creating rights for the State in and over Tibet without the latter's consent.[51]

The following conclusions may be drawn with respect to the status of Tibet from the early nineteenth century until 1907. Throughout this period, Tibet possessed actual independence and maintained its statehood. The Dalai Lama and his government did recognize the continuing existence of the *Chö-yön* relationship with the Manchu Emperor, but they refused to accept the latter's interference in Tibetan affairs, including external relations. The Manchu Emperor claimed the authority to treat on behalf of Tibet but was unable to exercise any actual control over that country to enforce treaties. The neighboring States that concluded treaties with Tibet, including Nepal and the British Empire, thereby recognized Tibet's capacity to conclude treaties and, hence, its international personality or statehood and they treated the Lhasa government as the legitimate government of Tibet. At the same time, the Nepalese, the British, and the Russians also recognized the nominal overlordship of the Qing Emperor over Tibet to the extent consistent with its independence.

By conceding extensive privileges to both Nepal and Great Britain, Tibet restricted the government's exercise of sovereignty, but not sufficiently to affect thereby the continuity of the State. The granting of privileges could, by the "unequal treaties" doctrine adhered to by the People's Republic of China, be considered invalid, but only if Tibet had repudiated the 1856 and 1904 treaties itself. This Tibet did not do, preferring instead to press for the revision of certain clauses only.

Tibet during this period was therefore no longer bound to the Qing Emperor, as it had been in the latter part of the eighteenth century, by a relationship resembling that of the protectorate arrangement. Instead, as Tibet had regained its actual independence, it was linked with the Emperor only by a nominal *Chö-yön* relationship, which the latter at times perceived in terms of the traditional tributary system. The use of the term "suzerainty" by the British and the Russians to describe this link is justified only where that term is understood to mean "nominal suzerainty" or, as Yu Fan describes it, the "empty title" of suzerainty, neither of which involves the impairment of the formal or actual independence of a State.[52]

The short period from 1908 to 1911 represented an eclipse in the trend of Tibetan history. The preceding century saw the progressive detachment of Tibet from the overlordship of the Manchus established in the mid-eighteenth century, leading to the complete breaking off of ties with Beijing following the revolution of 1911. For those last three years, however, Tibet was brought under the effective domination of the Empire and, part of the time, was under military occupation. The Manchus' attempt to establish effective authority in Tibet started in 1906, during the absence from Lhasa of the Dalai Lama. By the end of 1908 their influence was unmistakable, and once again, the Emperor's role in Tibet's foreign relations was, for a brief time, reestablished.

The following are the main developments relevant to the status of Tibet. On the one hand, there was the Manchu forward policy, the terms of which pertained to military invasion, political pressure, and unilateral assumption of responsibility for Tibet's foreign relations. The latter was demonstrated particularly by Beijing's conduct of the 1908 Trade Regulations negotiations and the payment by the Emperor of the Tibetan indemnity to the British. On the other hand, there was the Tibetan government's inability to oppose this policy effectively, as illustrated by the role played by the Tibetan delegate during the Calcutta negotiations of 1908. Then, in 1910, there was the denunciation of the Dalai Lama by the Emperor, the total repudiation of the Manchu actions by the Dalai Lama and his government, and their flight into exile following the invasion and occupation of Lhasa in the same year. Tibet remained under military occupation for over a year, but the Manchus were unable either to secure the cooperation of the Tibetan officials left in Lhasa or to effectively suppress Tibetan resistance.

The Manchus' actions were violations of the Emperor's obligations under the Chö-yön relationship, already much watered down by his failure to protect Tibet against invasion, for the Emperor had attacked and denounced the very object of his protection and worship. The "deposition" of the Dalai Lama was considered by the Tibetans to be *ultra vires*, for neither the Amban nor the Emperor himself ever possessed any authority to depose a Dalai Lama. The Dalai Lama's position and title were not granted to him by the Manchu Emperor, as is sometimes claimed by Chinese authors, but, rather, were secured by the Fifth Dalai Lama himself with the aid of the Mongol Gushri Khan, at a time when Tibet was fully independent of the Qing Emperor. The Shunzhi Emperor did no more than exchange honorific titles with the Great Fifth as a sign of mutual respect and recognition. Hence the Tibetan government declared:

> The Emperor of China never conquered Tibet or gave it to the Dalai Lama. Titles given by the Emperor to the Dalai Lama are complimentary; the Dalai Lama's power and position does not depend on them. . . . The deposing of the Dalai Lama is as if the Dalai Lama would try to depose the Emperor by withholding the usual title of "Celestial Emperor Manjushri Incarnate of China."[53]

The military invasion of Tibet, the destruction of temples, and the pursuit of the fleeing Dalai Lama were flagrant violations of the Emperor's duty imposed by the *Chö-yön* relationship, to protect the Priest, his religion, and his people. The Dalai Lama's revocation of the *Chö-yön* relationship was therefore a legitimate reaction. The Dalai Lama emphasized that in doing so he was severing all remaining ties between Tibet and the Qing Court.

Belligerent occupation, it was established earlier, does not affect the continuity of the occupied State, even when the government of that State exercises no effective control over its territory or is driven into exile. Hence the occupation of Tibet in 1910 and the flight into exile of the Dalai Lama and his government did not affect the continuity of the Tibetan State. Resistance to Manchu occupation continued throughout its duration, and the Tibetan War Department, set up by the exiled government, coordinated the military campaigns that contributed to the final defeat of the Imperial forces and their expulsion.

The outcome of this three-year crisis, the expulsion of all Imperial troops and officials from Tibet, was the termination of all ties with the Manchus. Thus, aside from the fact that the temporary occupation did not affect the continuity of the Tibetan State, it marked the severance of the country's remaining nominal relationship with the Qing Court.

The Status of Tibet
on the Eve of the Invasion

The second decade of the twentieth century marked a new phase in the political history of Tibet, for the Tibetans largely shed the vestiges of the anachronistic Central Asian conception of interstate relations in order to take their place among modern States. The events that occurred from 1911 to 1913 set the direction of Tibet's development for the next forty years. Three other important occurrences helped determine the international status of Tibet: The Simla Conference and the Anglo-Tibetan agreements of 1914 were the first of these, and the position taken by Tibet during the Second World War and the active diplomacy that its government pursued following the war constitute the other two. The legal interpretation of these and other factors presented below compels us to draw the conclusion that Tibet had fully recovered its independence by 1913 and was, throughout the four decades that followed, a State in international law in the fullest sense of that term.

The period from 1911 to 1913 saw the expulsion of Imperial troops and officials from Tibet and the severance of ties with the Manchus; the return of the Dalai Lama to Lhasa and the reestablishment of effective control by his government; and the relinquishment of Tibet's extreme isolationist policies in favor of close relations with Great Britain.

The legal significance of the first of these occurrences, the formal and actual severance of ties with the Manchus, needs some explanation. First, the very existence of the relationship between the Manchu Emperors and the Dalai Lamas depended on the continued commitment of both parties to the Chö-yön relationship. Thus, Shen Zonglian, the Chinese government representative in Lhasa from 1944 to 1949 and the adviser of Chiang Kai-shek, wrote: "The patron-chaplain partnership lasted only as long as the patron was capable of being a patron and the chaplain was willing to remain a chaplain."[54] The Manchu invasion of Tibet and the Emperor's denunciation of the Dalai Lama in 1910 were, as noted earlier, obvious violations of the Patron's obligation to protect the Priest, the very *raison d'être* of their relationship. When the Dalai Lama, in reaction to these events, denounced the Emperor and explicitly revoked all remaining ties with him, the Chö-yön relationship ceased to exist. To paraphrase Shen, the Patron was no longer capable (or willing) to be the Patron, and the Chaplain was no longer willing to be the Chaplain.

If the consensual Manchu-Tibetan relationship were considered in light of the accepted general rules of international law governing conventional relations, the same conclusion would be reached. A fundamental rule of the law governing such relations is the *exceptio non ad impleti contractus*, which is formulated in Article 60 of the Vienna Convention on the Law of Treaties as follows: "A material breach of bilateral treaty by one of the parties entitles the other to invoke the breach as a ground for terminating the treaty," where a material breach is defined as "the violation of a provision essential to the accomplishment of the object or purpose of the treaty."[55] Needless to say, the Emperor's actions consisted of such a violation.

Second, it should once again be stressed that the Tibetan-Manchu relationship was a personal and religious one, established between the Fifth Dalai Lama and his successive reincarnations on the one hand, and the Manchu Emperor Tai Zong and his heirs on the other. The Manchu Emperors were considered by the Tibetans to be both the Emperors of China and the Patrons of the Dalai Lama; that is, they were not the Patrons of the Dalai Lamas because of their position as Emperors of China. The fact that the Priest-Patron relationship was established before the Qing Emperors became Emperors of China amply demonstrates this point, as does the fact that, up until the last days of the Qing Dynasty, the Emperor was represented at Lhasa by a Manchu and not by a Chinese. In other words, as Eric Teichman and most other scholars have pointed out, it was the Manchu Emperors, the incarnations of Manjushri, and not the Chinese government, who were recognized in some sense as overlords. In addition, as J. Escarra has noted, this relationship was an expression of the closer affinity between the Tibetans and the Manchus than between either of these peoples and the Chinese.[56] The logical consequence of the nature of the Chö-yön relationship was its automatic extinction along with the passing away of the last Qing Emperor.

Once again, viewed from the perspective of the law governing conventional relationships, the fall of the Manchu Qing Dynasty inevitably resulted in the extinction of the Manchu-Tibetan relationship; for when one of the parties to a bilateral agreement or relationship ceases to exist the relationship itself also ceases to exist. In addition, because the outbreak of war between the protector and protected States in a protectorate arrangement extinguishes the relationship, as it would other similar conventional arrangements,[57] it stands to reason that the same was true of the Manchu-Tibetan relationship in 1910, when the Manchus sent troops to invade Tibet. And by 1913, with the expulsion of the last Imperial troops and officials from Tibet, the formal severance of ties also became effective, so that no connections remained between Lhasa and Beijing.

Even if one were to accept the notion that the Tibetan-Manchu relationship either implied a form of vassalage of the Dalai Lama with respect to the Qing Emperor or resulted in a degree of political dependence, it is clear that neither survived the 1911 revolution in China. Such relationships never resulted in Tibet's incorporation into the Qing Empire, much less into China. Hence, no ties existed between China and Tibet, or between the new Chinese President and the Dalai Lama, in 1911.

As no legal or political Sino-Tibetan ties existed when the Manchu Empire collapsed, and as none were inherited by the Chinese from the Manchus after the 1911 revolution, if a relationship did exist between the Tibetan government and the Republican Chinese government between 1911 and 1951, it must have been established after 1911. There is ample documentation of Chinese attempts to establish some form of authority over Tibet by negotiation or by the use of force, and there is at least as much evidence of the rejection by the Tibetans of all Chinese overtures and of their determined and successful resistance to Chinese incursions on Tibetan territory; however, there is no evidence whatsoever of the establishment between the two States of any relationship at all after 1911. This point is well demonstrated by the repeated Chinese demands in numerous official communications to the Tibetan government throughout that period that Tibet "approve," "accept," or "join" the Republic.

Regarding the return of the Dalai Lama to Lhasa and the re-establishment of effective control by his government; the Dalai Lama's Proclamation of January 1913 and other declarations of independence inaugurated a long period of stable and effective government free from unwanted foreign interference. For almost four decades, Tibet was governed exclusively by the Dalai Lama and his Regents, with the help of the Kashag and the Tsongdu. Franz Michael recently completed a study of the unique Tibetan system of government and administration that leaves no doubt as to the effectiveness of this government throughout Tibet,[58]—a conclusion supported by all of the important studies of the period as well as by first-hand accounts by Tibetan, Chinese, British, and other officials.[59] Tibet had a distinct form of government, Ganden Phodrang, based on the unification of the religious and temporal governances of the country. It also maintained an extensive civil service; an army of 10,000–15,000 men, who were mainly deployed on the eastern borders with China; a judicial system based on that introduced by Changchub Gyaltsen in the fourteenth century; a system of taxation; a telegraph and postal service; and a currency of its own. Eric Teichman reported in 1922, after living in the Tibetan-Chinese border areas for many years, that Tibet enjoyed internal peace and prosperity under the Lhasa government.[60] He added: "It seems indeed paradoxical that the Chinese, who have so signally failed to maintain law and order in their own country, should put forward any claim to have a hand in the administration of peaceful and orderly Tibet."[61]

Finally, we turn to the issue of the changing attitude of the Tibetans toward international relations, which resulted from the close friendship that the Dalai Lama had developed with the British during his exile.

With its neighbors to the immediate south, Nepal, Bhutan, and Sikkim, Tibet maintained relations on the same basis as before, with one exception: With the fall of the Qing Dynasty, neither Nepal nor Tibet acknowledged even a nominal role for an outside ruler. With Mongolia, Tibet initiated formal relations on a more modern basis with the conclusion of the Treaty of Urga.[62] With the British, Tibet developed the closest relations, formally still based on the Lhasa Convention of 1904. And with China, no official relations were opened for a number of years, whereas war was being waged on the Sino-Tibetan border. The war lasted until 1918, when the Rongbatsa peace agreement was signed.

The Simla Conference was the first serious attempt at resolving Sino-Tibetan differences. The proceedings of that conference and the conclusion of the Anglo-Tibetan agreements at Simla had an important impact on the position of Tibet at the time.

The formal recognition of the Tibetan delegate to the conference as a Plenipotentiary of his government to participate in the negotiations and conclude a treaty on an equal footing with Great Britain and China was the first, albeit implicit, recognition by the governments of those countries since 1911 of Tibet's independent treaty-making powers and unimpaired international personality. The meaning of this recognition could not have been more clearly formulated than by the British negotiator, who told his Chinese counterpart that "until the seal of the Tibetan Plenipotentiary had actually been affixed to an agreement such as was now under consideration, the status of Tibet was that of an independent nation recognizing no allegiance to China."[63]

Indeed, one of the arguments advanced by the Arbitral Tribunal in the *Deutsche Continental Gas Gesellschaft v. Poland* case in support of Germany's implied recognition of Poland, namely, that when Poland was admitted to the Peace Conference on 15 January 1919, "the full powers of [Poland's] delegation were, without reservation, recognized, admitted and accepted as being in order and valid by the delegation which negotiated in the name of Germany and represented that State,"[64] could equally well be quoted with respect to Great Britain and China's recognition of Tibet.[65]

The status of Tibet would have changed had the draft Simla Convention been signed by all three governments. China's suzerainty over Tibet would then have been recognized, as would have been the full autonomy of so-called Outer Tibet. But the convention, as it stood when the delegates initialed it, was an ambiguous instrument, to say the least. On the one hand, Outer and Inner Tibet were recognized to be geographically and politically one State. Yet China was only a nominal suzerain in Outer Tibet whereas it was granted extensive privileges in Inner Tibet—a fact hardly consistent with suzerainty. An even more peculiar ambiguity would have resulted from the proposed exchange of notes whereby Tibet would have been understood to form "a part of Chinese territory," for suzerainty is not exercised over one's own territory. The note, had it been exchanged, could have been accepted only in the context of the convention as a reservation on the part of China. But even that would seem to be inconsistent with the reason given by the Chinese government for its refusal to sign the convention—namely, its inability "to alienate any portion of [Chinese] territory" on the Sino-Tibetan border in favor of Tibet.[66] As it happened, the notes proposed during the negotiations were never exchanged between the three governments; neither was the convention itself ever signed on a tripartite basis: As the initialing act of the Chinese plenipotentiary was immediately and formally repudiated by his government, China never became a signatory.

The outcome of the Simla Conference was significant in that the three agreements concluded between Great Britain and Tibet comprehensively regulated their mutual relations.[67] By these agreements the previous treaties concluded between Britain and the Qing Empire were superseded, and henceforth Anglo-Tibetan relations were regulated solely by the 1904 Lhasa Convention and the 1914 agreements, which modified it in some respects. Furthermore, the Anglo-Tibetan Declaration, by which the Simla Convention became binding upon the two governments, denied China all the privileges it would have accrued by the terms of the convention, specifically the recognition of nominal suzerainty over Tibet, unless and until it affixed its signature to the convention, which China never did.[68]

The legal effect of Great Britain's recognition of Tibet's full independence (and of its refusal to recognize Chinese suzerainty) was to preclude itself from challenging that independence in the future; in other words, it created an estoppel.[69] This is an important point, in view of the ambiguous and contradictory statements made by Great Britain and, later, by India with respect to Chinese suzerainty.[70] Following the Simla Conference, no significant changes took place in the status of Tibet and its relations with China sufficient to warrant a modification of the British recognition of Tibetan independence.

The conclusions reached in the preceding paragraphs are confirmed by an official communication of the Indian government, sent to the government of the People's Republic of China many years later in 1960, in which the Chinese government's questioning of the validity of the 1914 agreements between the British (and, therefore, Indian) and Tibetan governments were protested:

This was not the first time that Tibet conducted negotiations and concluded treaties, in her own right, with foreign states. On several occasions before 1914 Tibet had conducted negotiations and concluded treaties with other states. For example, Tibet concluded a Treaty with Nepal in 1856 and another with Great Britain in 1904. These treaties were never objected to by China and were fully operative. At the Simla Conference, the Tibetan and Chinese plenipotentiaries met on an equal footing. This position was explicitly and unequivocally accepted by the Chinese Government. The three Plenipotentiaries exchanged copies of their credentials at the first session of the Conference on October 13, 1913. The credentials of the Tibetan representative issued by the Dalai Lama made it clear that Tibet was an equal party at the Conference with the right "to decide all matters that may be beneficial to Tibet," and the Chinese representative accepted the credentials of the Tibetan representative as being in order. The credentials of the British Indian representative, which were also accepted by the Chinese representative, confirmed that all the three representatives were of equal status, and that the Conference was meeting "to regulate the relations between the several Governments."[71]

Tibet successfully maintained its independence following the Simla Conference. Although it initially relied substantially on the British for diplomatic and military assistance, Tibet gained increasing self-reliance in the 1930s. This development was demonstrated by Lhasa's handling of Tibet's relations with the British and the Chinese and, unquestionably, by the position Tibet took during the Second World War: By effectively maintaining its neutrality throughout the war, despite strong pressure from the Allied Powers, Tibet demonstrated its ability to pursue a nonaligned and independent foreign policy.

After the war, events moved quickly. Tibet's foreign policy became more active and the British attitude less ambiguous. Although the British had at no time questioned Tibet's actual independence, the government in London had on various occasions made statements acknowledging China's suzerainty over Tibet, in violation of the Simla agreements. In 1943, Britain reverted to its original, and only legally permissible, position—namely, that it would be prepared to recognize China's suzerainty only subject to China's acceptance of the conditions laid down in the Simla Convention. This was also the position taken by India when, upon its independence, it succeeded Great Britain as a party to the Simla agreements. The United States, which had never before committed itself to an official view on the status of Tibet, took a cautious political attitude. Washington supported Tibet and treated it as an independent State, even recognizing its *de facto* independence, but, in an effort to avoid offending China, chose to recognize as well the latter's *de jure* sovereignty (or suzerainty) over Tibet until 1949.

Nepal's recognition of Tibetan independence was confirmed by the Nepalese government in 1949, in documents presented to the United Nations in support of that government's application for membership. Prominent among the arguments advanced by Nepal to prove the kingdom's sovereignty were the references to Nepal's power to make war and peace with Tibet, and to its power to conclude treaties, specifically the 1856 treaty with Tibet.

Nepal listed Tibet among the six countries with which it had "established diplomatic relations" and in which it maintained legations; the other countries named were the United Kingdom, France, the United States, India, and Burma. It should also be noted that, whereas Nepal maintained full diplomatic relations with Tibet throughout this period, it never established diplomatic relations with the Republic of China.[72]

The fact that foreign governments conducted their relations with Tibet through the Tibetan Foreign Office in Lhasa, the extensive recognition accorded by numerous governments to the official Tibetan travel documents issued to the Trade Mission to Europe and the United States, and the reception accorded to that and earlier delegations abroad (the 1946–1947 Complimentary Mission and the 1947 delegation to the Asian Conference) serve as supporting evidence of the recognition of Tibet's independent status.

An examination of the events between 1911 and 1950 thus leads to the inevitable conclusion that, throughout this period, Tibet was a fully independent State possessing all the attributes of statehood. Few scholars seriously challenge the notion that Tibet possessed actual independence *at least* between 1911 and 1950. Thus, for example, the International Commission of Jurists, the legal scholar C.H. Alexandrowicz, and even the last official Chinese Representative in Tibet, Shen Zonglian, who conceded that "since 1911 Lhasa [i.e., Tibet] has to all practical purposes enjoyed full independence," support this conclusion.[73]

What the present study shows is that Tibet possessed both actual and formal independence throughout this period and, indeed, was indisputably a separate State throughout its history, despite the sometimes considerable foreign interference in its affairs.[74] Since the reunification of Tibet under the Sakya hierarchs backed by the Mongolian Emperors in the mid-thirteenth century and its reemergence as a fully independent State under the rule of Changchub Gyaltsen less than a century later, the State of Tibet never ceased to exist. Neither the protection exercised by the Manchu Emperors, nor their intervention in Tibetan affairs, nor even their temporary occupation of Lhasa immediately prior to the 1911 revolution can constitute proof of the extinction of the Tibetan State. The same must be said of the Nepalese and British invasions and the subsequent ties those States established with Tibet. This conclusion follows logically in international law from the presumption of continued statehood. Any other conclusion would necessarily lead to the legally incorrect and politically unacceptable notion that a State such as Bhutan, which is formally bound to India by a protectorate arrangement, has lost its independence, or that, for example, Czechoslovakia and East Germany cannot be considered independent States because the Soviet Union exerts considerable actual influence over their affairs and maintains troops on their soil. Above all, whatever influence the Manchus ever did exert in and over Tibet had totally eroded by the beginning of the twentieth century. Thus, in 1950, Tibet was no more bound to China than The Netherlands is to Spain or France, whose rulers asserted their authority over The Netherlands in past centuries. Indeed, whatever the role of the Manchu Emperors at the peak of their authority in the eighteenth century, the largely uninterrupted separate existence of the Tibetan State throughout history and the Tibetans' full reassertion of independence since 1911 (following the brief military occupation) amply justify the conclusion that on the eve of the Chinese Communist invasion, officially launched in October 1950, Tibet was a State independent both in fact and in law.

9

The "Peaceful Liberation," or Invasion, of Tibet

On 7 October 1950, troops of the People's Liberation Army crossed into Tibet. Two and a half weeks later, the Chinese government announced publicly that "People's army units have been ordered to advance into Tibet to free three million Tibetans from imperialist oppression and to consolidate national defenses on the western borders of China."[1] The total defeat of the Tibetan army was soon followed by the signing in Beijing of a peace treaty, the terms of which called for the Tibetan government to "actively assist the PLA to enter Tibet and consolidate the National defences" and provided for the incorporation of Tibet into the PRC.

The immediate effect of the military invasion and the signing of the treaty on the legal status of Tibet form the subject of the present chapter.

Military Invasion

Early in October, about 40,000 troops under command of General Zhang Guohua crossed into Tibet at eight points on the border and attacked the provincial capital of Chamdo. Tibetan troops numbering only 8,000 and much inferior in training to the Chinese were defeated. The communist forces took Chamdo on 19 October, and captured the Governor of Kham, Kalon Ngapo Ngawang Jigme. In the first two weeks of fighting, a total of 4,000 Tibetan Army officers and men were killed and the remainder of the Tibetan army was forced to surrender.[2] In the face of such a defeat, Lhasa ordered the Tibetan delegation in India, which had held preliminary talks with the Chinese Ambassador in New Delhi, to make arrangements to proceed immediately to Beijing.[3]

The Indians were not only shocked at China's unprovoked military action; they were also much offended in view of the explicit assurances the Chinese government had given them.[4] The feeling in New Delhi was best expressed by India's Deputy Prime Minister, Vallabhai Patel, in a note to Nehru:

The Chinese government have tried to delude us by professions of peaceful intentions. My own feeling is that at a crucial period they managed to instil in our Ambassador [Panikkar] a false sense of confidence in their so-called desire to settle the Tibetan problem by peaceful means. There can be no doubt that during the period covered by this correspondence the Chinese must have been concentrating for an onslaught on Tibet. The final action of the Chinese, in my judgement, is little short of perfidy.[5]

In a sharp note to the Chinese government, the Indian Foreign Ministry expressed deep regret and suprise at the decision to send troops into Tibet just after the Tibetans had initiated negotiations with China's Ambassador in New Delhi and were preparing to proceed to Beijing.[6] The note went on to complain:

Now that the invasion of Tibet has been ordered by the Chinese government, peaceful negotiations can hardly be synchronised with it and there naturally will be fear on the part of Tibetans that negotiations will be under duress. In the present context of world events, invasion by Chinese troops of Tibet cannot but be regarded as deplorable and in the considered judgement of the Government of India, not in the interest of China or Peace.

The United States and British governments expressed their support for the Indian position, and the former informed New Delhi of its desire to help Tibet by whatever means possible. The Americans recognized that, in view of geographic and historic factors, the main burden of the problem rested on India and that its cooperation was needed in any attempt to help Tibet effectively. The Indian Foreign Ministry, however, dissuaded the United States government from supplying militiary aid to Tibet. Prime Minister Nehru even requested that Washington refrain from publicly condemning China for its actions in Tibet for fear that such condemnation might give credence to China's claims that Western powers had an interest in Tibet and that they exerted influence over Indian policy.[7] He explained his policy thus:

We cannot save Tibet, as we should have liked to do, and our very attempts to save it might bring greater trouble to it. It would be unfair to Tibet for us to bring this trouble upon her without having the capacity to help her effectively. It may be possible, however, that we might be able to help Tibet to retain a large measure of her automony. That would be good for Tibet and good for India. As far as I can see, this can only be done on the diplomatic level and by avoidance of making the present tension between India and China worse.[8]

The main consideration, however, was Nehru's belief that friendly relations between the two biggest Asian countries, each of which had "expansive tendencies," was essential to their welfare and to the security of Asia as a whole.[9] Whatever the consideration, India's attitude of "washing its hands of Tibet," as the Nepalese Ambassador in New Delhi described it, deeply

144   The "Peaceful Liberation"

discouraged the Tibetans and contributed to the ease with which China
was able to force its will upon them.[10]

In marked contrast to India's cautious attitude, the Chinese government
made little effort to appear conciliatory. In its reply to the Indian protest
notes, it accused India and other powers of harboring expansionistic designs
on Tibet and of interfering in China's domestic affairs. The Chinese argued
that they were only excercising their sovereign rights in Tibet by performing
the "sacred duty" to "liberate the Tibetan people and drive out foreign
forces and influences to ensure that the Tibetan people will be free from
aggression and will realise regional autonomy and religious freedom."[11] The
Chinese further stated in their note that they had not abandoned the desire
of settling the problem of Tibet peacefully, but that Tibetan troops, who
were resisting the advance of the PLA, and foreign influences, including
those from India, were obstructing China's efforts. The note warned: "But
regardless of whether the local authorities of Tibet wish to proceed with
peace negotiations, and regardless of whatever results may be achieved by
negotations, no foreign intervention will be permitted. The entry into Tibet
of the Chinese People's Liberation Army and the liberation of the Tibetan
people are decided."

They were indeed so decided: Chinese armies were consolidating their
position in Eastern Tibet and the military high command issued directives
for the completion of the "glorious task" of liberating Tibet.[12] One such
proclamation is worth quoting at some length, for it represented China's
terms for the incorporation of Tibet:

> Now that the People's Liberation Army has entered Tibet, they will protect
> the lives and property of all the religious bodies and people, protect the
> freedom of religious belief for all the people of Tibet, protect the lamaseries
> and temples, and help the Tibetan people to develop their education, agriculture,
> animal husbandry, industry and commerce, so as to improve the livelihood
> of the people. The existing political system and military system in Tibet will
> not be changed. The existing armed forces of Tibet will become part of the
> national defense forces of the People's Repulic of China. All members of the
> religious bodies of all classes, government officials, and headmen will perform
> their duties as usual. All matters concerning reform of any kind in Tibet
> will be settled completely in accordance with the wishes of the Tibetan people
> and through consultation between the Tibetan people and the leader personnel
> in Tibet. Government officials who were formerly pro-imperialism and pro-
> Kuomintang will remain at their posts and no action will be taken concerning
> their past actions, provided that subsequent facts prove that they have severed
> relations with imperialism and the Kuomintang, and that they do not carry
> out acts of sabotage and resistance.[13]

The members of the Tibetan National Assembly, far from being reassured
by the proclamations, resolved to take the exceptional measure: They
requested the Dalai Lama, still a minor at the age of fifteen, to accept full
ruling powers over Tibet.[14] Only the Divine Emanation of Chenrezig, the
Precious Protector of Tibet, could be trusted to lead his people in the face

of such adversity. The Dalai Lama reluctantly accepted this heavy burden and became the supreme ruler of Tibet on 17 November. His Foreign Secretary issued the following public statement:

> Tibet is united as one man behind the Dalai Lama who has taken over full powers and there is no possibility of a fifth column operating in Tibet proper; we have appealed to the world for peaceful intervention in [the face of this] clear case of unprovoked aggression but should no help be forth-coming we are determined to fight for our independence; if necessary we are even prepared to remove the government and the Dalai Lama to other parts [in order] to continue the fight. Tibet is a large and difficult country regarding the terrain, and as we have men and ammunition we can continue the warfare indefinitely.[15]

A few weeks later, the Tsongdu advised the Dalai Lama to leave Lhasa and set up temporary headquarters in Dromo, near the Indian border.[16]

In the meantime, the Tibetan government sent the first of two appeals to the United Nations. In a letter to the Secretary General it explained:

> Tibet recognizes that it is in no position to resist the Chinese advance. It is thus that it agreed to negotiate on friendly terms with the Chinese Government.
> We can assure you, Mr. Secretary General, that Tibet will not go down without a fight. Though there is little hope that a nation dedicated to peace will be able to resist the brutal effort of men trained to war, we understand that the United Nations has decided to stop aggression wherever it takes place.[17]

The letter also appealed to the United Nations to intervene and entrusted the problem of Tibet to the U.N.'s ultimate decision.

El Salvador asked the General Assembly to consider the appeal, and the United States and India decided to lend their support to the Salvadoran initiative.[18] The Salvadoran delegate, Hector David Castro, stated that unprovoked aggression had been committed against Tibet, a country that, although at one time a protectorate of China, had enjoyed complete independence at least since 1912. He considered that the Assembly would be neglecting its responsibilities if it failed to condemn this international act of aggression, and called for the adoption of a resolution to that effect.[19]

The General Assembly was much preoccupied with the Korean question. Two days before the Tibetan appeal, it was confirmed that communist Chinese forces had intervened in Korea; then, on the day that the El Salvador resolution was considered by the General Committee, General Douglas MacArthur launched a massive offensive in Korea. By that time the Indian representative to the U.N., Sir Benegal N. Rau, persuaded his government not to support a discussion of Tibet in the General Assembly, as Indian criticism of communist China would adversely affect India's mediation efforts in the Korean conflict and also might jeopardize what little hope remained that the Sino-Tibetan problems could be resolved by negotiation.[20] The Indian representative consequently advised the General Committee that, in view of the fact that the latest Chinese note received by his government hinted that a peaceful resolution of the Tibetan question was still possible, India believed that the best chance of achieving this objective was by refraining, for the time being, from including this item in the agenda of the General Assembly.[21] The British representative expressed much the same opinion, and his United States counterpart joined the other members of the General Committee in supporting the Indian and British suggestion to adjourn the discussion. The United States representative pointed out, however, that he did so only because his government had recognized India's primary interest in the question: "In accordance with its traditional policy the United States would in any other circumstances have voted for the inclusion of the item in the General Assembly agenda."[22]

Upon hearing the disappointing news, the Tibetan delegation to the United Nations, which was preparing to leave India for Lake Success, sent a fresh appeal to the Secretary General. The Tibetans expressed surprise and dismay at the General Committee's decision and invited the United Nations to send a fact-finding commission to Tibet to carry out an investigation of the contending claims on the spot.[23] But no action was taken in the United Nations.

Despite this setback, the United States government was still anxious to support Tibetan resistance to communist domination but found it increasingly difficult to secure any degree of cooperation from Nehru's government. The United States was now "faced with [the] choice [of] supporting some power other than India taking iniative or of continuing [to] postpone hearing Tibetan pleas until autonomous Tibet ceases [to] exist." "Is it logical," U.S. Ambassador Lloyd W. Henderson asked, "for [the] U.N. which gave Indonesia, which was under Dutch sovereignty, [a] hearing to ignore Tibet?"[24] The State Department renewed efforts to provide Tibet with help[25] and, for the first time, officially declared its position on the status of Tibet in December of 1950:

> The United States, which was one of the early supporters of the principle of self-determination of peoples, believes that the Tibetan people has the same inherent right as any other to have the determining voice in its political destiny. It is believed further that, should developments warrant, consideration could be given to recognition of Tibet as an independent State. The Department of State would not at this time desire to formulate a definitive legal positon to be taken by the United States Government relative to Tibet. It would appear adequate for present purposes to state that the United States Government recognizes the de facto autonomy that Tibet has exercised since the fall of the Manchu Dynasty, and particularly since the Simla Conference. It is believed that, should the Tibetan case be introduced into the United Nations, there would be an ample basis for international concern regarding Chinese Communist intentions toward Tibet, to justify under the United Nations Charter a hearing of Tibet's case in either the U.N. Security Council or the U.N. General Assembly.[26]

While the United States was searching for an effective, though limited, course of action, events in Tibet and China had already reached the critical stage.

Sino-Tibetan Agreement:
Incorporation on China's Terms

In February 1951, the Tibetan government sent a fifteen-man delegation to Beijing, via Chamdo, led by Kalon Ngapo Ngawang Jigme, who had been released and appointed Vice-Chairman of the so-called Chamdo Liberation Committee by the Chinese, after a short period of imprisonment and indoctrination. Upon its arrival in the Chinese capital, the delegation was joined by the first mission, led by Dzasa Khemey Sonam Wangdi and Khenchung Thupten Tendar. The mission had traveled via India and Hong Kong. On 29 April, negotiations started with the Chinese Plenipotentiaries, Li Weihan, Zhang Jingwu, Zhang Guohua, and Sun Zhiyuan.[27]

It was with great reluctance that the Dalai Lama had sent negotiators to Beijing. The Indian government, though initially in favor of the negotiations, had warned that with the military conquest of Tibet under way the negotiators would be under considerable duress. On the other hand, there was little else Tibet could do. It had suffered a decisive military defeat in Kham and a diplomatic setback at the United Nations, and there was little prospect of obtaining effective outside aid at this stage. To pursue negotiations as best it could seemed to be the only viable course of action.[28] The Dalai Lama did not, however, give the delegates plenipotentiary powers, for he feared that they might yield to Chinese pressures in Beijing. Instead, the delegates were instructed to refer all important matters to Lhasa and the temporary government headquarters in Dromo for decision.[29]

Negotiations were opened with the presentation of a draft agreement by the chief Chinese negotiator. It was totally rejected by the Tibetans. During several days of heated debates, both sides held firmly to their positions, and negotiations were deadlocked. The Chinese then put on the table a modified draft that was no more acceptable to the Tibetans than the first one had been, because it failed to acknowledge the independence of Tibet and conceded control over Tibet's defense and foreign affairs to China. The Chinese negotiators, Li Weihan and Zhang Jingwu, made it plain that the terms as they now stood were final and in effect represented an ultimatum. The Tibetans were addressed in harsh and insulting terms, threatened with personal violence, and virtually kept prisoners. No further discussion was permitted, and the Tibetans were not allowed to contact their government for instructions. They were simply given the choice of signing or accepting responsibility for the immediate and unconditional military advance on Lhasa.[30]

As the Dalai Lama had feared, the delegates succumbed to Chinese pressure and signed what came to be known as the "Seventeen-Point Agreement." Before doing so they warned the Chinese that they were signing only on behalf of the delegation and had no authority to bind either the Dalai Lama or the Tibetan government and people. In addition, the Tibetan negotiators did not have with them the official government seal required for the conclusion of a treaty by Tibet. The seals that were affixed to the document were therefore copies of Tibetan government seals allegedly forged in Beijing by the Chinese authorities.[31]

The full text of the "Agreement of the Central People's Government and the Local Government of Tibet on Measures for the Peaceful Liberation of Tibet" was broadcast by Radio Peking on 27 May and was the first the Tibetan government had heard of it.[32] The Preamble to the agreement opened with the following crucial statement: "The Tibetan nationality is one of the nationalities with a long history within the boundaries of China, and like many other nationalities, it has done its glorious duty in the course of the creation and development of the great Motherland." The Preamble then declared:

In order that the influences of agressive imperialist forces in Tibet might be successfully eliminated, the unification of the territory and sovereignty of the CPR [Chinese People's Republic] accomplished, and national defense safeguarded; in order that the Tibetan nationality and people might be freed and return to the big family of the CPR to enjoy the same rights of national equality as all other nationalities in the country and develop their political, economic, cultural and educational work, the CPG [Chinese People's Government], when it ordered the People's Liberation Army (PLA) to march into Tibet, notified the local government of Tibet to send delegates to the central authorities to conduct talks for the conclusion of an agreement on measures for the peaceful liberation of Tibet. In the latter part of April 1951 the delegates with full powers of the local government of Tibet arrived in Peking. The CPG appointed representatives with full powers to conduct talks on a friendly basis with the delegates with full powers of the local government of Tibet. As a result of the talks both parties agreed to establish this agreement and ensure that it be carried into effect.

The seventeen clauses that followed authorized the entry into Tibet of Chinese forces and empowered the Beijing government to handle the external affairs and defense of Tibet. China agreed not to alter the existing political system in Tibet and not to interfere with the established status, functions, and powers of the Dalai Lama or the Panchen Lama.[33] The Tibetan people were to have regional autonomy, and their religious beliefs and customs were to be respected. Internal reforms in Tibet would be effected after consultation with leading Tibetans, without compulsion. A committee that would include "patriotic Tibetans" would be set up to ensure the implementation of the agreement.

The reaction in Dromo and Lhasa was one of shock and disbelief. Instructions were immediately sent to the delegation in Beijing to inform the Chinese government that the agreement was unacceptable. The Dalai Lama telegraphed his representative in India, Tsepon Shakabpa, that he and his government did not recognize the agreement, which the Tibetan negotiators had had no authority to sign. The Dalai Lama decided to postpone a public repudiation of the agreement until he had obtained a full report from his delegates and until he had had an opportunity to meet with General Zhang Jingwu, who apparently was accompanying them to Dromo.[34]

The United States government urged the Dalai Lama in secret communications to repudiate the agreement publicly, leave Tibet, and lead the Tibetan resistance from exile with United States assistance.[35] India took a fatalistic attitude toward the events in Tibet and was prepared to accept the new situation created by the Seventeen-Point Agreement as a *fait accompli*.[36] The British, though convinced that India's bowing to communist "blackmail" could only lead to further blackmail by China in Burma, Bhutan, Nepal, Sikkim, Kashmir, and Assam, merely adhered to their policy of following India's lead in the matter.[37]

Thus, despite United States sympathy for Tibet, there was little the Dalai Lama or his government could realistically count on in the way of effective outside assistance to stop the Chinese conquest. The Dalai Lama was seriously considering fleeing to India, but finally decided to follow the advice of his ministers and religious guides to await the arrival of General Zhang and to discuss matters with him and other officials before making a final decision. After a brief meeting with General Zhang in Dromo, the Dalai Lama returned to Lhasa on 17 August in the hope of renegotiating a treaty with the Chinese himself.[38]

On 9 September, 3,000 Chinese troops marched into Lhasa, and, soon afterward, some 20,000 more arrived under the command of Generals Zhang Guohua and Dan Guansan. Chinese troops, which had also entered Tibet from Xinjiang to the northwest, took the principal cities of Rudok and Gartok, and then Gyantse and Shigatse near Lhasa. With the occupation of all the major cities of Tibet, including Lhasa, and large concentrations of troops throughout eastern and western Tibet, the military control of Tibet was virtually complete.[39]

Under the circumstances, the Chinese were not willing to renegotiate the terms of an agreement with Tibet: The Dalai Lama and his government had effectively lost their freedom to accept or reject the Sino-Tibetan agreement and felt compelled to acquiesce in it. Their "acceptance" was communicated to Chairman Mao Zedong on the Dalai Lama's behalf.[40] On the first occasion the Dalai Lama had to express himself freely again, which came only after his flight from Tibet in 1959, he made the following declaration in an official statement: "While I and my government did not voluntarily accept the Agreement, we were obliged to aquiesce in it and decided to abide by the terms and conditions in order to save my people and country from the danger of total destruction."[41]

The Validity of Tibet's Incorporation

Two factors are crucial to an understanding of the effect that the invasion of Tibet and the signing of the Seventeen-Point Agreement had on the legal status of Tibet: first, the extent—if any—to which China was violating international law when the People's Liberation Army marched into Tibet and occupied Tibetan territory; and, second, the effect of the signing of the Seventeen-Point Agreement in Beijing, following the Chinese military advance.

The Use of Force

Wars of aggrandizement and self-interest, "even if promoted under the guise of a defensive war," were outlawed in the General Treaty for the Renunciation of War (otherwise known as the Kellogg-Briand Pact or the Pact of Paris), signed in 1928.[42] Almost all States in the world, including China, became parties to this treaty, which provided as follows:

> Article 1. The High Contracting Parties solemnly declare . . . that they condemn recourse to war for the solution of international controversies, and renounce it as an instrument of national policy in their relations with one another.

> Article 2. The High Contracting Parties agree that the settlement or solution of all disputes or conflicts of whatever nature or of whatever origin they may be which may arise among them, shall never be sought except by pacific means.

The pact thus prohibited war both as a means of settling international controversies and as an instrument of national policy.[43]

As a result of the disastrous experiences of World War II, the waging of agressive war was condemned by the principal Allied Powers as a "war crime" and "a crime against the peace" in the Charter attached to the London Agreement of 8 August 1945.[44] Article 6, paragraph (a) of the Charter provided the following definition of crimes against peace: "planning, preparation, initiation or waging of a war of agression, or a war in violation of international treaties, agreements or assurances, or participation in a common plan or conspiracy for the accomplishment of any of the foregoing."[45] Not just States but individuals as well were held responsible under international law and were tried for war crimes by the International Military Tribunals at Nuremberg and Tokyo.[46]

China was among the eleven Allied Powers that set up the Military Tribunal for the Far East in Tokyo. The People's Republic of China has supported its establishment, and Chinese political and legal authorities have consistently condemned wars of agression as unjust and unlawful and as international crimes.[47] This stand was expressed authoritatively in 1951 by Shen Chun-ju, the President of the Supreme People's Court, as follows:

> After World War II the concept of "war crime" witnessed a noteworthy development by the adding of crimes against peace. In other words, aggressive war is recognized as a crime in international law. According to Article 6 of the Nuremberg Tribunal regulations, crimes against peace include the "planning, preparing, initiating, or carrying out of aggressive war or a kind of war

violating international treaties, agreements, or assurances, or taking part in the planning of the above forms of war." The regulations of the Tokyo Tribunal are in the main similar (see Article 6, Section 1, item 2). These crimes against peace are the most serious of war crimes. As is stated in the Nuremberg Tribunal verdict, aggressive war is the greatest crime because it includes and produces many other crimes; it is the embodiment of all kinds of crime. The Tokyo Tribunal was in complete agreement with this decision. This decision has already become an influential principle of international law.

Therefore, I hold that the decision to define "agressive war as an international crime" is the greatest contribution made by the two great international tribunals after World War II and represents a great development in the concept of war criminals in international law. . . .

"Aggression," as we have repeatedly pointed out above, is now in international law one of the most serious crimes committed by war criminals. Agression is the "biggest crime." All those who take part in this crime should be indicted and punished as "Class A war criminals."[48]

The adherence of nineteen States and the subsequent affirmation by the United Nations General Assembly of the principles of the charters and judgments of the International Military Tribunals underscored the essential illegality of the use of force as an instrument of national policy.[49] In addition, the United Nations Charter has added new dimensions to the prohibitions against the use of force by totally outlawing not only recourse to war but *all* threat or use of force. Article 2, Paragraph 4, provides that "All members shall refrain in their international relations from the threat or use of force against the territorial integrity or political independence of any state, or in any other manner inconsistent with the purposes of the United Nations."[50] Moreover, justifications of the use of force must be regarded as exceptional and should therefore be restrictively interpreted: Coercive measures are legally permissible only in cases of collective self-defense, individual self-defense when the Security Council has failed to take the necessary steps to maintain international peace and security, or upon the Council's recommendation to apply coersion against an aggressor.[51]

In 1970 the principle laid down in the United Nations Charter was reiterated in the "Declaration on Principles of International Law Concerning Friendly Relations and Co-operation Among States," which also reaffirmed that "[a] war of aggression constitutes a crime against the peace, for which there is responsibility under international law."[52]

In the period since 1954, a considerable number of States have concluded agreements embodying or otherwise approving principles that subsequently became known as the *Panch Shila*, or Five Principles of Peaceful Coexistence. These principles, initiated by India, the PRC, and Burma in 1954, are as follows:

1. Mutual respect for each other's territorial integrity and sovereignty,
2. Non-aggression,

3. Non-interference in each other's internal affairs for any reason of an economic, political or ideological character,
4. Equality and mutual benefit, and
5. Peaceful co-existence.[53]

In bilateral or multilateral agreements, these principles are often linked with an undertaking by signatories to observe the principles of the United Nations Charter. In relation to existing obligations under international law, including the charter, they are declaratory. As numerous States, both members and nonmembers of the United Nations, have subscribed to the Five Principles, "they now rank with and supplement the United Nations Charter and the Kellogg-Briand Pact."[54]

The prohibition of the threat or use of force in the Charter of the United Nations, reiterated and strengthened in other multilateral and bilateral instruments, is of universal validity and should be broadly interpreted.[55] Its validity was confirmed by the International Court of Justice in the *Corfu Channel* case (1949):

> The court can only regard the alleged right of intervention as the manifestation of a policy of force, such as has, in the past, given rise to most serious abuses and such as cannot, whatever be the present defects in international organization, find a place in international law. . . .
>   Between independent states, respect for territorial sovereignty is an essential foundation of international relations.[56]

Even when States act in self-defense, the burden of proving the legality of the resort to force rests on the State asserting the necessity of self-defense.[57]

In his authoritative volume, *International Law and the Use of Force by States*, Ian Brownlie reached the conclusion that, at least since 1945, "the fundamental proposition of law is the illegality, and in some cases criminality of the use of force by states";[58] he then added:

> The general acceptance, by membership or otherwise, of the obligations of the Charter of the United Nations has rendered a treatment of the Charter as "particular international law" unrealistic and has reinforced the pre-existing law. In particular the acceptance by the majority of states of the criminal character of illegal resort to force, or at least the major forms of resort to force, has considerable significance in supporting, and raising to a higher power, the norm of illegality. It is suggested that this basic norm is so powerful and so widely expressed in the relevant instruments that any justifications for resort to force by individual states, acting without the authority of the appropriate organ, or organs, of the United Nations must be regarded as exceptional.[59]

This conclusion has been supported by Chinese jurists, one of whom has been known to declare "An encroachment on the territorial integrity of a state is an infringement of its sovereignty and is an aggressive act in violation of international law."[60]

The Imposition of Treaties

The law governing international agreements is based, as is contract law, on the universally recognized principle that the foundation of conventional obligations is the free and mutual consent of contracting parties and, conversely, that freedom of consent is essential to the validity of agreements. An "agreement" imposed on a weaker party by coercion would therefore lack validity.[61]

Traditional law, in force until the early part of this century, regarded as invalid only the expression of consent procured by the coercion of the party's representative,[62] but it did not generally consider agreements to be void where force was used or threatened against the State itself.[63] Of course, the traditional doctrine was established at a time when the use of force as an instrument of national policy was not outlawed. With the prohibition of the illegal resort to force early in the century, now embodied in Article 2 (4) of the United Nations Charter, the foundations of that doctrine were shaken.[64] The U.N. International Law Commission, in its commentary to what is now Article 52 of the Vienna Convention on the Law of Treaties, stated:

> With the Covenant [of the League of Nations] and the Pact of Paris there began to develop a strong body of opinion which held that treaties [brought about by the threat or use of force] should no longer be recognized as legally valid. The endorsement of the criminality of aggressive war in the Charters of the Allied Military Tribunals for the trial of the Axis War criminals, the clear-cut prohibition of the threat or use of force in Article 2(4) of the Charter of the United Nations, together with the practice of the United Nations itself, have reinforced and consolidated this development in the law. The Commission considers that these developments justify the conclusion that the invalidity of a treaty procured by the illegal threat or use of force is a principle which is *lex lata* in the international law of today.[65]

The same Article 52 contains an accurate statement of the modern law governing international agreements,[66] for it provides that "a treaty is void if its conclusion has been procured by the threat or use of force in violation of the principles of international law embodied in the Charter of the United Nations."[67]

Although it is difficult to ascertain the precise point in time at which the rule prohibiting the illegal resort to force and the procurement of consent by coercion is considered as having entered into force, there can be no question as to its universal validity since the adoption of the United Nations Charter.[68] The Chinese communists, though not signatories to the Vienna Convention, have consistently held that all treaties imposed by the threat or use of force are invalid, even those concluded in the previous century.[69]

If a treaty has been procured by force, the "victim State" is never estopped from alleging its invalidity. A State may invoke two types of invalidity: relative and absolute. Relative nullity may be invoked if the State has been the victim of error, fraud, or corruption or if its representative acted *ultra vires*; and express agreement or subsequent acquiescence cures relative nullity. In contrast, absolute nullity voids an agreement entirely in cases where a State's representative was coerced into signing the agreement or where the State itself was coerced by the threat or use of force into concluding it.[70] Finally, an agreement imposed on a State by another State whose superior armed forces have or are in the process of occupying, invading, or threatening the territory of the other in violation of international law is *ipso facto* procured by the illegal threat or use of force and, consequently, is without any legal effect.[71]

The Legal Effect of Tibet's Incorporation

The invasion of Tibet by the armies of the People's Republic of China was an illegal act under both customary and conventional international law. The Chinese action constituted a violation of all the basic principles of customary international law, such as the principles of State sovereignty, independence, and territorial integrity; the prohibition of intervention; and the prohibition of the threat or use of force. The invasion also ran directly counter to the letter and spirit of the Covenant of the League of Nations, the Kellogg-Briand Pact, and the Charter of the United Nations as well as to other agreements to which the PRC is a party and to assurances given by the PRC.

In addition, the invasion of Tibet constituted an act of aggression within the meaning of Article 2 (2) of the Conventions for the Definition of Agression of 1933[72] and a crime against the peace within the meaning of Article 6 (a) and 5 of the Charters of the International Military Tribunals at Nuremberg and Tokyo, respectively.

The conditions under which the Tibetans were made to sign the "Agreement on Measures for the Peaceful Liberation of Tibet" unquestionably amounted to coercion. The very terms of the treaty, whereby the Tibetan government was to "actively assist" the Chinese army to enter and occupy Tibet, leave little doubt in this regard.[73] Preceding the opening of the negotiations on 29 April 1951, some 40,000 Chinese troops had entered Tibet, defeated the small Tibetan army, killing over half its officers and troops, and captured the provincial capital of Chamdo. By the time the Tibetan and Chinese delegates had met in Beijing, the greater parts of Amdo and Kham were under effective Chinese occupation. At the same time, proclamations had been and were still being issued by the Chinese authorities declaring their intention to take control of all of Tibet, by force if necessary.

The terms for a settlement presented to the Tibetan negotiators were more in the nature of an ultimatum than a basis for a negotiated agreement. This is evident both from the accounts of the negotiations and from the fact that the principal terms had already been unilaterally proclaimed by the Chinese five months before the start of the talks. Members of the Tibetan delegation have claimed that their Chinese counterparts threatened to make an immediate advance on Lhasa if the terms proposed by them were not agreed to. There is little reason to disbelieve these allegations, given the uncompromising stand taken by the Chinese authorities on the question of the "reunification" of Tibet with China throughout that period.[74] At any rate, the position the Tibetans found themselves in was clearly one in which consent cannot be presumed to have been freely given. The Dalai Lama formulated the choice facing the Tibetans as being essentially that between "peaceful liberation," meaning the more or less orderly occupation of the country and the maintenance of some form of autonomy provided for by the Seventeen-Point Agreement, and the immediate and forceful advance of the Chinese army to Lhasa with the unilateral imposition of even harsher terms by the occupiers:[75] "The consent of the [Tibetan] Government was secured under duress and at the point of the bayonet. My representatives were compelled to sign the agreement under threat of further military operations against Tibet by the invading armies of China leading to utter ravage and ruin of the country."[76]

Hence, whether or not one accepts a broad or more limited interpretation of the prohibition of the use of force, the facts of the present case necessarily lead to the conclusion that Tibet was coerced into concluding the Seventeen-Point Agreement in 1951. That agreement was consequently devoid *ab initio* of any legal effect.[77] This conclusion is only reinforced by the fact that the Tibetan delegates to the negotiations were not authorized by their government to sign the agreement, let alone affix any official seals to it, as well as by the fact that they declared that they were unable to bind their Head of State or government.

10

Tibet and the People's Republic: Decades of Turmoil

Since 1950, Tibet has undergone major changes, both socialeconomic and political. The position of the country within the People's Republic of China has also undergone various transformations between the time of the conclusion of the Seventeen-Point Agreement and the recent twentieth anniversary of the establishment of the "Tibet Autonomous Region of China."

The government of the PRC claims that the present status of Tibet is that of an autonomous region of China. As "the People's Republic of China is a unitary multinational state built up jointly by the people of all its nationalities,"[1] it follows that Tibet—that is, the Tibet Autonomous Region and the Tibetan autonomous prefectures and counties incorporated in the provinces of Yunnan, Sichuan, Gansu, and Qinghai[2]—forms an integral part of the People's Republic. This conclusion is confirmed by Article 4 of the Constitution of the PRC, which states that "all the national autonomous areas are inalienable parts of the People's Republic of China." The same article provides for the establishment of organs of self-government "for the exercise of the right of autonomy" in "areas where people of minority nationalities live in compact communities." A little more light is shed on the meaning of that provision in Section 6 of the Constitution and in the Law on Regional Autonomy for Minority Nationalities, adopted on May 31, 1984,[3] the essence of which is explained by Ngapo Ngawang Jigme, currently Vice-Chairman of the National People's Congress (NPC) Standing Committee and Chairman of the NPC Nationalities Committee, as follows: "The unified leadership of the Central People's Government must be guaranteed and its general principles, policies and plans must be implemented. On the other hand, the full power of autonomy of the organizations of self-government of national autonomous areas must be guaranteed and consideration must be given to their special characteristics and needs."[4] According to Ngapo, the autonomous organizations of government are, in fact, "both ordinary local state organizations and organizations of self-government."[5] Basically, both the Constitution and the Autonomy Law grant local organs of government a little more flexibility in implementing Central Government policies than is possessed by similar provincial authorities.

If Chinese claims to Tibet are found to be valid, Tibet today would be considered an integral part of the PRC, and the "autonomy" of the region would represent no more than a limited delegation of governmental authority from the Central Government, in Beijing, to the local authorities.[6] It is precisely the legality of China's claims that forms the subject of the present investigation.

The Chinese presence in Tibet has not gone unchallenged. Mounting popular resistance to the Chinese presence culminated in the eruption of open rebellion in Lhasa, the Tibetan capital, in 1959. The revolt was put down swiftly in the city, but not before the Dalai Lama and most of his ministers had succeeded in escaping toward India, where he and over 80,000 refugees have since been granted asylum. The guerrilla warfare, which had started in Eastern and Northeastern Tibet as early as 1954, continued at least until 1974, when it was replaced by a state of armed hostility—a struggle of attrition marked by cycles of harassment and repression. Over fifty major revolts have occurred in different parts of Tibet in the last twenty-five years, and, by some estimates, over 1 million Tibetans have lost their lives to this day, as a result of the Chinese occupation of Tibet.

In order to determine the present legal status of Tibet and the rights of the Tibetan people, we must examine the significance of the events that took place in the decade following the signing of the Seventeen-Point Agreement, those leading up to the 1959 revolt, and those following it. The intention here is not to delineate the sequence of events in Tibet since 1950; that has been done admirably by other authors. Nevertheless, we shall briefly review the developments of relevance to the present inquiry.

Cooperation, Resistance, and Rebellion

The Dalai Lama and his government never formally ratified or sealed the Seventeen-Point Agreement. Expressions of approval were conveyed to the Chinese authorities,[7] but the Dalai Lama and other Tibetan officials have since declared that these were not free expressions of the Tibetan government's consent. All official speeches and communications were prepared by the Chinese officials, and the Tibetan officials had no alternative but to deliver them as instructed.[8] On the other hand, the Tibetans made no secret of their opposition to the agreement. Thus, the two Tibetan Prime Ministers, who jointly headed the Cabinet, unambiguously conveyed their rejection to the Chinese Generals upon their arrival in Lhasa.[9]

The question still arises as to whether the conduct of the Dalai Lama, as Head of State, or that of his government in the years that followed the conclusion of the Seventeen-Point Agreement can be interpreted as conduct manifesting an intention to accept the agreement as valid and binding on Tibet—and, if so, whether this interpretation could give the agreement legal effect despite its original nullity.

At the time of the Dalai Lama's return to Lhasa, in August of 1951, the Chinese army was moving to occupy all strategic points in the country. On 9 September 3,000 troops of the 18th Route Army marched into Lhasa, and within three months the occupation force in the capital alone numbered some 20,000 troops.[10]

The main thrust of the Chinese policy in the first years of occupation was the so-called united front work: a policy aimed at consolidating the Communist Party's influence by giving special attention to the "prominent members" of the non-Chinese nationalities, so as to use the influence and prestige they commanded among their own people "to facilitate the successful performance of the mass work."[11]

The principal target for the united front work in Tibet was "the Dalai group," the Tibetan government. Paradoxically, it was also this group that was viewed as the main obstacle to the policy's success.[12]

On the surface, the Chinese authorities initially honored their pledge to leave unchanged the status, functions, and powers of the Dalai Lama and his government. Almost immediately following the entrance of the Chinese troops in Lhasa, however, a concerted effort was launched to undermine their actual authority. This was done in three ways: First, the existing political and regional divisions among the Tibetans were exploited and even institutionalized in order to diminish, where possible, the authority of the Tibetan government as well as that of the Dalai Lama himself. Second, various organs of the Central Government and new bodies under their authority were set up alongside the existing Tibetan institutions and were vested by Beijing with real power, thus hollowing out the actual authority of the Tibetan government. And, third, certain social and economic reforms, calculated to change the fabric of Tibetan society, were instituted so as to reduce once again the traditional authority of Tibet's political and religious institutions.[13]

The Beijing government set out to redefine the authority of what was now called the "Local Government of Tibet" by carving up the country's territory along regional lines. Although there is no historical basis for its partition, Tibet was now presented as an area composed of three separate and, for all intents and purposes, equal autonomous territorial parts: the Chamdo area (comprising most of Kham province—that is, those regions not already incorporated into the Chinese provinces of Sichuan and Yunnan), the Panchen Lama's district of Shigatse, and Central Tibet. The Chamdo Area People's Liberation Committee was set up by the Chinese to govern the first area; a pro-Chinese Council of Kenpo (*mKhan-po*) of the Panchen Lama was to govern the second; and the Local Government of Tibet was recognized as having administrative authority over Central Tibet only.[14] The Chinese then claimed that the terms of the Seventeen-Point Agreement applied to Central Tibet only and moved to consolidate political control and to institute socialist reform in the other two areas.[15]

One of the first demands made of the Lhasa government was to dissolve the Tibetan Foreign Office. All foreign relations were henceforth conducted

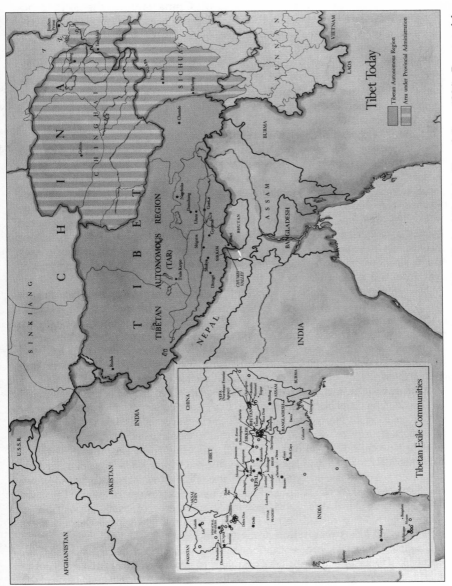

Source: John F. Avedon, *In Exile from the Land of Snows* (New York: Alfred A. Knopf, Inc., 1984). Reprinted by permission.

by the Chinese government. Furthermore, with the establishment in Lhasa and other cities of the People's Bank of China and of the joint Sino-Tibetan syndicate under its authority, all trade was monopolized and the Chinese gained a controlling influence over Tibet's economy, which was made dependent upon that of China.[16] Another major step in the integration of Tibet in the People's Republic was the establishment, in February 1952, of the "Military District of Tibet," thereby bringing the country's defense directly under the central authority in Beijing.[17]

The Seventeen-Point Agreement called for social and economic reforms in accordance with local conditions and the wishes of the Tibetan government. Consistent with Beijing's contention that its terms applied only to Central Tibet, socialist reforms were initiated at once in Eastern Tibet, without any consultation with the government in Lhasa. Thousands of Chinese settlers arrived in the Chamdo area to work the land along socialist lines.[18] Land reform was also thrust on the local Tibetan people, who showed obvious reluctance to exchange their ways for imposed alien ones. The mounting impatience and belligerence of the Chinese administrators, directed at the fiercely independent Khamba population, provoked violent reactions and rapidly degenerated into armed conflict in a widening spiral of attack and military repression that engulfed the entire province and then spilled over into the adjacent areas of the plateau.[19]

The country's unification with China was accelerated by the opening of the Xikang-Tibet and Qinghai-Tibet highways to Lhasa in 1954.[20] Organizations such as the Cultural Society of Patriotic Youth and the Lhasa Association of Patriotic Women were instituted with the help of the PLA;[21] a number of primary schools and hospitals were opened, starting in 1952; and indoctrination, especially of the young, was systematically undertaken, with thousands of children taken to China for education.[22]

Within nine months of the Chinese occupation, the first crisis occurred in Lhasa. The appropriation by the PLA of thousands of tons of barley and other foodstuffs pushed the region to the verge of famine and prompted protest meetings in Lhasa. The first major popular resistance group, the Mimang Tsongdu (or Mimang Tsoba), meaning the "People's Assembly," spontaneously formed and handed the Chinese Military Command a petition demanding both the withdrawal of the PLA and an end to Chinese interference in Tibetan affairs. The Chinese reaction was swift: The two Tibetan Prime Ministers, who had made no secret of their opposition to Chinese rule, were forced to resign and five Mimang Tsongdu leaders were jailed, driving the organization underground.[23]

The extension of Chinese influence into the social, cultural, and religious aspects of Tibetan life did not take on major proportions until the government of the country had been radically reformed, thus bringing it under the more direct control of the Central Government in 1955. The "special" autonomous position of Tibet recognized in the Seventeen-Point Agreement was formally abolished when the People's Congress, China's legislative body, adopted a Constitution in 1954. Tibetan delegations, headed by the Dalai

Lama, the Panchen Lama, and Ngapo Ngawang Jigme, representing Central Tibet, the Shigatse, and the Chamdo areas, respectively, attended the Congress.[24] By the terms of the Constitution, China was to be a multinational, unitary State, and "autonomous" regions were considered integral parts of the Chinese People's Republic.[25]

Although the new Constitution did not purport to supersede the 1951 agreement, its immediate result was the adoption by the Chinese State Council of the "Resolution on the Establishment of the Preparatory Committee for the Autonomous Region of Tibet" in order to further integrate the administration of Tibet with that of the PRC.[26]

With the Dalai Lama as Chairman, the Panchen Lama and Zhang Guohua as Vice-Chairmen, and Ngapo Ngawang Jigme as Secretary General, the Preparatory Committee (PCART) was to function as the central administration of Tibet and to direct the work of the so-called Local Government of Tibet, the Shigatse Council of Kenpos, and the Chamdo People's Liberation Committee. The PCART derived its authority directly from the State Council of the PRC and was wholly dependent on it. Most of its members were Tibetan. The majority, however, especially the delegates from Chamdo and Shigatse, owed their position solely to the Chinese authorities' support, and all appointments were subject to the approval of the Chinese government.[27] In fact, rather than serving as a vehicle for compromise, as the Dalai Lama had hoped it might, the Preparatory Committee directly subverted Tibet's government. The committee's several subordinate administrative agencies dealt with civil administration, economy and finance, health, culture and education, the judiciary, agriculture, industry and commerce, communications and construction, and even religious affairs—in short, all functions of government. All of these agencies were dominated by Chinese personnel; the committee itself was headed by General Zhang Guohua.[28] Although decisions were taken formally by the PCART under the Dalai Lama's chairmanship, neither he nor the other Tibetan officials felt they had any measure of real authority or influence over the decisionmaking process. Thus, as the Dalai Lama stated: "The Committee was powerless—a mere facade of Tibetan representation behind which all the effective power was exercised by the Chinese. In fact, all basic policy was decided by another body called the Committee of the Chinese Communist Party in Tibet, which had no Tibetan members."[29] This form of distribution of actual power is fairly typical of all levels of government throughout the People's Republic and, indeed, in most communist States.[30]

While these changes were taking place at the governmental level, social, political, and agrarian reforms imposed by the Chinese in Amdo and Kham and, to a much lesser degree, in the rest of the country, coupled with frequent attacks on religious personages and monasteries, led to increasingly violent reactions.[31] Whereas in Lhasa the widespread popular resentment was voiced through the underground organization Mimang Tsongdu,[32] in Kham and Amdo full-scale guerrilla warfare broke out in the summer of 1956.[33] Refugees from Eastern and Northeastern Tibet began to arrive in Lhasa that summer, adding to the tension in the capital.[34]

During the Dalai Lama's absence from Tibet in the winter of 1956–1957, when he was visiting India to take part in the Buddha Jayanti celebrations at the invitation of Prime Minister Jawaharlal Nehru, the situation rapidly deteriorated.[35] The Chinese authorities were no longer able to conceal the rebellions that had been breaking out in various parts of Eastern and Northeastern Tibet (especially in the Tibetan areas of Qinghai, Gansu, and Sichuan), and over 150,000 troops were dispatched to crush them. During meetings with Nehru and Zhou Enlai in Delhi, the Dalai Lama expressed his deep concern at the explosive situation in his homeland and even contemplated seeking political asylum.[36] The Chinese government promptly announced that reform would be postponed in Tibet for the time being because "facts have proved that only a few of the upper-strata personages support [the reforms] while the majority still harbour varying degrees of doubt and are actually against it; and that although a small portion of the masses enthusiastically demand reform, the large portion of the masses still lack much enthusiasm."[37]

The withdrawal of most of the Chinese civilian personnel from Tibet was announced, and a "Retrenchment Committee" was installed to implement the new policy.[38] While the Chinese Communist party was issuing its "Programme for Propaganda on the Non-Institution of Democratic Reforms in the Tibet Region,"[39] Tibetans were being warned that "if any imperialist element or any separatist takes advantage of the reduction of our establishment, or under any pretext in the future, to try to conduct sabotaging activities and manufacture revolts," the Liberation Army would deal "firm and telling blows to the rebellious elements."[40]

China's new policy came too late. Within a year the revolt had spread to central Tibet with the founding of Tensung Dhanglang Magar, the National Volunteer Defense Army (NVDA), a union of the Mimang Tsongdu and Gushri Gangdruk. By the autumn of 1958, this popular army, estimated at 80,000 men, was in control of most districts of Southern Tibet and parts of Eastern Tibet.[41]

A "Manifesto by Tibetan Leaders" was forwarded to Prime Minister Nehru by members of the Mimang Tsongdu in exile in India, in an attempt to obtain some help from the outside world.[42] The Chinese intensified campaigns and purges against "local nationalists" engaged in activities for "independence"[43] and sent considerable army reinforcements to Tibet, thus more than offsetting the earlier modest reduction of Chinese cadres. The Chinese, it seemed, were preparing for a major emergency.[44]

The inevitable showdown occurred in March 1959. It was the culmination of years of resistance and repression, and it erupted into an open and all-out revolt in the Tibetan capital. Starting on March 10, daily mass meetings held in Lhasa called on the Chinese to quit Tibet and to restore its full independence. While Tibetan guerrilla troops consolidated their positions in Southern and Eastern Tibet and the Lhasans, their ranks swelled by Khamba refugees and soldiers, staged mass demonstrations, government officials held meetings and issued proclamations, including one in the name of the Cabinet that repudiated the Seventeen-Point Agreement and pro-claimed Tibet's full independence.[45] Open fighting broke out in Lhasa soon afterward.[46] Tens of thousands of Tibetans were imprisoned and, according to Chinese sources, 87,000 were killed.[47] The Dalai Lama and most of his ministers managed to escape in the night of March 17; two weeks later they arrived in India, where they were followed by tens of thousands of refugees. Several months passed before the PLA recovered control over the southern and southeastern parts of the country, in particular the Lokha area, and one and a half decades before the organized guerrilla warfare was reduced to insignificant proportions.

On 28 March 1959, while Chinese forces were regaining control over Lhasa, Premier Zhou Enlai issued an Order of State Council dissolving the Government of Tibet.[48]

The Dalai Lama and his ministers, en route to the Indian border, reacted promptly by formally inaugurating a provisional government in Lhuntse Dzong, to be the sole legitimate government of independent Tibet.[49] As for the new administration installed in Lhasa, the Dalai Lama claimed that it was totally controlled by the Chinese and that the people of Tibet would never recognize it. Upon his arrival in India, the Dalai Lama publicly denounced the Seventeen-Point Agreement and declared: "Wherever I am, accompanied by my government, the Tibetan people recognize us as the Government of Tibet."[50] With that, he and his government-in-exile set up their headquarters in the foothills of the Himalayas, in Northeast India.

From the factual evidence two principal elements emerge. The first is the apparent, albeit reluctant, acquiescence of the Dalai Lama and his officials to the new state of affairs and their participation in some of the new organs of government established by the Chinese. The second is the widespread opposition to the Chinese presence in Tibet and to the terms of the Seventeen-Point Agreement, as well as the expression of this opposition. These two elements did not represent opposing views among the Tibetans; on the contrary, they represented different and complementary reactions to the continued coercion to which the Tibetans were subjected.

The Dalai Lama's general attitude, as expressed, for example, in his public speeches between 1951 and 1959, was conciliatory. Indeed, he has since described his policy, aimed at avoiding unnecessary violence and preserving for Tibet at least some autonomy, as one of cooperation with the Chinese wherever possible and passive resistance wherever it was not. That very attitude, however, was dictated by the coercive nature of the Sino-Tibetan relationship: The number of Chinese troops in the country was close to 150,000; opposition to the Chinese policies had been met with violent repression in Eastern Tibet; the expression of hostility toward the Chinese occupation by the Dalai Lama's highest officials, his Prime Ministers, led to their dismissal and exile; and even before the Chinese entered Lhasa, the Dalai Lama himself had been warned of their intention to assassinate him if he resisted them.[51]

In short, Tibet was under military occupation, and the position secured by the Chinese through armed invasion was being maintained by the continued use and threat of force. The Dalai Lama was able to express his opinion openly only when he reached India; where he unequivocally rejected the Sino-Tibetan agreement and all Chinese claims over Tibet. The degree of duress he had felt until then was underscored by his desire to seek political asylum in India during his visit there three years earlier. He told Nehru at that time that he felt unable to do anything for his people by staying in Lhasa, where his role in the PCART was no more than "a facade of Tibetan representation."[52]

Under these conditions, the Dalai Lama's conduct and that of his officials between 1951 and 1959 certainly cannot be regarded as constituting free expressions of agreement or consent. Throughout this period Tibet was under military occupation and no Tibetan was in a position to express any opposition to the Chinese without incurring the risk of serious repercussions.

Furthermore, the Dalai Lama and his government's opposition to the Chinese invasion, to the terms of the imposed agreement, and to the subsequent interference in Tibetan affairs was very apparent throughout. The Tibetan Prime Ministers' open opposition to the Chinese has been but one of the more obvious manifestations. The Dalai Lama himself had returned to Lhasa after the Seventeen-Point Agreement had been announced in the hope of renegotiating an agreement with Chinese officials there, but he was unable to do so as the PLA was only a few days' march from the capital.[53] Mao himself conceded that "apparently not only the two Prime Ministers but also the Dalai Lama and most of his clique were reluctant to accept the agreement."[54]

Furthermore, that the Chinese were fully aware of the continued opposition to their presence and to the Seventeen-Point Agreement is evident from the following official Chinese statement made in 1959: "Since the Chinese People's Liberation Army entered Tibet and the Central People's Government and Tibetan Local Government concluded the 17-Article Agreement on measures for the peaceful liberation of Tibet in 1951, they have been plotting to tear up this agreement and preparing armed rebellion."[55] General Zhang Guohua also admitted that from the outset "some reactionary elements of the upper strata groups of Tibet [i.e., the ruling class] cried 'we do not recognize the agreement signed in Beijing'" and that the PLA had to take immediate measures "against the attempt to scrap the agreement" when they entered Lhasa.[56] Zhang Guohua then concluded that "it is clear that the traitorous clique in Tibet do not have the slightest intention to bring about the realization of a democratic, national regional autonomy with the participation of the people; all they want is the so-called 'independence of Tibet.'"[57]

In 1958, many government employees joined the ranks of the guerrilla Volunteer Army, and twenty senior officials became involved in the Mimang Tsongdu organization. Shortly thereafter, eighteen members of the PCART joined the rebels and the major monasteries, and the Tibetan army, only partly integrated into the PLA, openly sided with them.[58]

The Effect on the Seventeen-Point Agreement

It was established in the previous chapter that the 1951 Seventeen-Point Agreement was null and void *ab initio*, leaving the legal independence of Tibet intact at the time of its conclusion.

To the extent that the agreement was void because the Tibetan delegates had no authority to sign on behalf of their government or because the seal affixed to the document was, allegedly, a forgery, this relative nullity of the agreement could subsequently have been undone and the agreement validated "by means of a specific confirmation or by conduct manifesting an unmistakable intention" to adopt the agents' unauthorized acts as the government's own.[59] Insofar as the treaty was imposed upon the Tibetan State by coercion, however, the situation is different because of the absolute nullity of agreements imposed by the illegal threat or use of force. The President of the International Court of Justice, Eduardo Jimenez de Arechaga, distinguished the two as follows:

> If the treaty is tainted with relative nullity by reason of a defect of capacity, error, fraud or corruption, the injured party is free to invoke or not to invoke the invalidity of its consent, and it could agree to confirm the act—expressly or impliedly. On the other hand, if a treaty has been procured by force or is in breach of a rule of *jus cogens* there is no question of waiver or of estoppel resulting from the conduct of the state victim. This state or any other state may at any time allege the invalidity of a treaty obtained through duress or in violation of *jus cogens*.[60]

It might still be argued that a treaty imposed by coercion could nevertheless acquire validity if the legitimate government of the coerced State subsequently expressly accepted the treaty and this acceptance was unquestionably a free expression of consent. Under no circumstances, however, can the mere fact that a State enforces the terms of an illegal and void agreement by means of force or the threat of force validate the treaty. As Fairborz Nozari has noted, "the *de facto* enforcement of such a treaty does not change its *de jure* invalidity. As soon as the means of force disappear, the situation must be brought back to the state which existed before the treaty was put into operation."[61]

Accordingly, the Seventeen-Point Agreement, which had no legal validity when it was signed in 1951, also did not acquire legal validity thereafter. Between the time of its conclusion and the public denunciation thereof in 1959, nothing occurred to give it validity. In the first place, as the state of coercion by which the treaty was imposed continued throughout that period, the Dalai Lama and his government were at no time in a position to freely express their acceptance or rejection of the terms of the Seventeen-Point Agreement. Second, Chinese enforcement of those terms by the continued threat and use of force could not have legitimized what was originally an illegal act and a void treaty. Third, the Dalai Lama's conduct in seeking a compromise and avoiding confrontation could not be interpreted as acquiescence or estoppel by conduct, because he and his government, to paraphrase Judge Jimenez de Arechaga, could at any time have alleged the invalidity of the treaty imposed on them by force. This they did, of course, at the first opportunity they had of publicly repudiating it.

Hence the Seventeen-Point Agreement was at no time valid under international law; therefore, it could not affect *per se* the independent legal status of Tibet. As Nozari, in his comprehensive study of such treaties, has concluded:

> The conditions of time and place cannot change the illegal nature of such treaties; no matter in which place they have been concluded and put into operation, and no matter how long [a] time by reason of force they have been in operation. As soon as the means of force establishing the treaty relations disappear, the situation must be brought back to the state which existed before the conclusion of such treaties.[62]

The question of whether other factors did affect the status of Tibet remains to be answered in the following two sections, the first of which presents a review of some relevant developments since 1959.

The Lhasa-Beijing-Dharmsala Triangle

Following the abortive 1959 uprising, the struggle for the restoration of Tibet's independence took on a new character as did the Chinese efforts to gain total control over the country. The Chinese policy was aimed primarily at erasing the distinctive Tibetan national identity and fully incorporating and integrating the plateau with China. The Tibetans' efforts were aimed at preserving their identity, to which end an effective exile community had to be set up and the resistance to the Chinese sustained.

Tibet in Exile

The most immediate concern of the Tibetan authorities in exile and of their host governments was the relief and rehabilitation of some 80,000 refugees who had arrived in and were still fleeing to India, Nepal, Bhutan, and Sikkim. This monumental task claimed all of the exiles' energy and resources in the first decade. By 1970, 38 settlements harbored almost 60,000 refugees, and a decade later 45 settlements, mostly agricultural, were flourishing throughout the subcontinent. The majority of some 100,000 refugees live in these settlements; the remaining few are concentrated in towns and villages in the Himalayan foothills or have emigrated to countries around the world.[63] The exiled Tibetans are linked by strong commercial, political, and religious ties. They look to the Dalai Lama and his administration as their government and to Dharmsala, a hill station in Northwest India that serves as the seat of the exile government, as their capital.[64]

Upon his arrival in India, the Dalai Lama lost no time in establishing an effective government-in-exile. At first, this consisted of his Cabinet, the Kashag, with six portfolios: Home Affairs, Foreign Affairs, Religion and Culture, Education, Finance, and Security. A bureau was opened in New

Delhi to serve as a link with the Indian government, foreign diplomatic missions, and the various international relief agencies. Offices were subsequently opened in New York, Geneva, Kathmandu, Gangtok, and later in Tokyo and London, to act as unofficial embassies for the government-in-exile.[65]

In 1960, the Dalai Lama called the first democratic elections for a newly created representative body, the Commission of People's Deputies.[66] A year later he announced the outline for a new democratic constitution, and on 10 March 1963, the Dalai Lama promulgated the "Constitution of Tibet," an instrument combining the principles of Buddhism with those of popular democracy. The Constitution is called a "draft" pending the return to Tibet, at which time it is to be given final shape in accordance with the wishes of the Tibetans there. The drafting of a democratic Constitution, the Dalai Lama felt, was important in order to give to the Tibetan people both a new hope and "a new conception of how Tibet should be governed when she regained her freedom and independence."[67] For, the Tibetan leader explains, "just to criticize China was not sufficient. We had to have a definite alternative of our own."[68] And that alternative was to serve as the basis for the present government-in-exile.

The Constitution, in its Preliminary Articles, specifically recognizes the supremacy of international law, the United Nations Charter, and the Universal Declaration of Human Rights; it also renounces the use of force as an instrument of national policy. The main body of the document provides for a system of government not unlike a constitutional monarchy, with the executive power vested in the Head of State, the Dalai Lama, and the Kashag; the legislative authority vested in the elected National Assembly; and the judicial authority vested in an independent Supreme Court. In exile, there is no separate Tibetan judicial system, and a smaller elected body, the Commission of People's Deputies, essentially fulfills the function of a parliament-in-exile.[69] Below the Kashag, the governmental functions are now organized under the following departments: the Councils for Home Affairs, for Religious and Cultural Affairs, and for Education; the Finance Office, the Security Office, and the Information Office; and the Departments of Health, of Service Management, and of Audit. One of the Kashag Ministers, assisted by a small staff, is responsible for International Affairs and Security. In that capacity, he supervises the activities of the government's representatives abroad. The government is financed primarily by means of a voluntary tax from the Tibetan refugees around the world and from Tibetan business organizations, as well as through small enterprises run by the Finance Office.[70]

The government has established or encouraged the establishment of a number of institutions to preserve and promote the Tibetan heritage and to enhance the exile community's cultural life. Among the most important are the National Library of Tibetan Works and Archives, the Tibetan Medical Center and Hospital, Tibet House in New Delhi, and the Tibetan Institute of Performing Arts. Religious institutions, including all the major monasteries of Tibet, have also been reestablished in India and Nepal. But perhaps the most significant factor of all in the reconstruction of the community in exile, (as well as that, eventually, of Tibet as a whole) is the modern Tibetan educational system. This system comprises over fifty residential and day schools, numerous vocational training centers, and a graduate academic institution, the Central Insitute for Higher Tibetan Studies.[71] Already, the education of the young generation of exiled Tibetans has contributed greatly to the success of the experiment in democracy.

In 1970, the Tibetan Youth Congress was founded to enlist the active participation of younger Tibetans in issues of national interest and to further the cause of Tibetan independence. With well over 10,000 members, the Congress is both the largest and the most democratic Tibetan political party. Significantly, it counts among its members 75 percent of all Tibetan government officials.[72]

On the international plane, the Dalai Lama's efforts have not yet been wholly successful. International reaction to the events of 1959, it is true, was extremely sympathetic to the Tibetans, but no government went so far as to formally recognize the Tibetan government-in-exile.[73] Shortly after the Dalai Lama's arrival in India, for instance, Prime Minister Nehru informed him of the Indian government's inability to extend such recognition. Although Nehru sympathized with the Tibetans and considered the subjection of Tibet to China to be "an unhealthy relationship" that had brought about much suffering, he also felt that in welcoming the Dalai Lama and the refugees to settle in India and allowing the establishment, at least *de facto*, of a government-in-exile, India was doing as much as possible without risking open conflict with an already irritable China.[74] Many criticized Nehru's stand as one of appeasement to China, and the government faced stiff opposition in Parliament and the press.[75] But, by 1954, India had already concluded with China the "Agreement on Trade and Intercourse Between the Tibet Region of China and India," whereby India had at least implicitly recognized the status quo in Tibet.[76] Under these circumstances, New Delhi felt that recognition of the exile government would seriously endanger Sino-Indian relations. Nepal was in much the same position in that it had established diplomatic relations with the PRC in 1955 and a year later had also concluded a "trade and intercourse" agreement whereby all previous Sino-Nepalese and Tibeto-Nepalese treaties were abrogated.[77] But in Nepal, as in India, the Congress deplored the events in Tibet and called for the restoration of Tibet's full autonomy and self-determination.[78]

In London, the Foreign Office reiterated that the United Kingdom recognized China's suzerainty over Tibet only on the understanding that the latter was autonomous. It now felt compelled to reconsider such recognition in light of the statements made by the Dalai Lama, whom they still regarded as the head of the Tibetan government.[79] The United States strongly condemned China's intervention, its ruthless repression in Tibet, and the dissolution of "the legitimate Tibetan government" in place of which it had established "direct military rule."[80] They had never "recognize[d] nor condone[d] the so-called 'agreement' of May 1951 under which the Chinese Communists deprived the Tibetan people of the *de facto* political autonomy which they had long enjoyed." And again, as a State Department spokesman stated at a press conference on 11 September 1959: "The United States has never recognized the pretensions to sovereignty over Tibet put foreward by the Chinese Communist regime."[81] Most other non-communist governments and political parties condemned the Chinese action also,[82] and support for Tibet was further voiced at the Afro-Asian Convention on Tibet and Against Colonialism in Asia and Africa, convened in Delhi by the Afro-Asian Council in April of 1960.[83]

In the summer of 1959, the International Commission of Jurists, a nongovernmental organization associated with the United Nations, found *prima facie* evidence of genocide in Tibet. The Commission instructed its Legal Inquiry Committee to fully investigate the evidence and recommended that the matter be taken up by the United Nations.[84] Bolstered by the findings of these distinguished jurists, the Dalai Lama appealed directly to the Secretary General, Dag Hammarskjold, for the immediate intervention of the United Nations to stop the crimes against humanity being perpetrated against his people.[85]

The Federation of Malaya and the Republic of Ireland cosponsored Tibet's case at the fourteenth session of the General Assembly. A year later, Malaya and Thailand again brought the question to the attention of the Assembly; at the sixteenth session El Salvador and Ireland joined them in proposing the adoption of a resolution; and the question was once again discussed in 1965, when Nicaragua and the Philippines joined the list of sponsors. The resulting resolutions adopted by the General Assembly in 1959, 1961, and 1965 called for an end to the violation of fundamental human rights of the Tibetan people, the suppression of their distinctive identity, and the deprivation of their right to self-determination.[86]

In the late 1960s the Dalai Lama himself traveled to Thailand and Japan, and in 1973 he visited eleven European countries. These visits were followed by many more to Europe and Asia, and in 1979, by his first visits to the United States, the Soviet Union, and Mongolia. During these visits, the Dalai Lama was often received by government officials (sometimes heads of states) and municipal authorities, as well as by religious leaders. Most governments, however, especially those having good relations with the PRC, were careful not to treat the Dalai Lama in such a way as to imply recognition of his political status.[87] Despite this caution, the Chinese government has always protested with the governments of the States he was visiting. Thus, for example, the New China News Agency reacted to the first such visit abroad, to Japan, as follows: "The reactionary State Government's action to drag the Dalai Lama, the anti-China tool of the Indian reactionaries to Japan for criminal manoeuvers is another serious provocation."[88] Fifteen years later, the Chinese were still sending protest notes and releasing statements when the Dalai Lama was, once again, being received officially by the Mayors of Rome and Paris, complaining that "the Dalai Lama is not only a religious personality, but an exile engaged in political activities abroad."[89] The Dalai Lama's travels abroad have always officially been undertaken for cultural and religious purposes, but as Beijing is plainly aware, they cannot fail to have political impact.

Despite the fact that the Tibetan government-in-exile remains politically unrecognized except by its own people, it effectively administers all affairs pertaining to refugees in India and, to a lesser extent, elsewhere. Furthermore, the Dalai Lama's government enjoys a special status in India. New Delhi, for example, refers all matters relating to Tibetan refugees to Dharmsala, or at least handles them in consultation with the exile government. International governmental or nongovernmental agencies also work with the Dharmsala administration.[90] In addition, the Government of India and other governments have encouraged, supported, and even organized Tibetan armed forces in exile, a subject dealt with elsewhere in this study.

The Dalai Lama's objective, to reconstruct a viable and even successful community in exile, has succeeded remarkably well. Indeed, the Tibetans have been called "the world's most well settled refugees."[91] Moreover, as Franz Michael concludes: "In India, the Tibetan polity, its settlements, its enterprises, and its religio-political structure have not only flourished but have transformed and developed from the prototype in Tibet into an active part of the modern world."[92]

"Tibet Region of China"

In Tibet, the PLA's suppression of the 1959 revolt was violent and brutal and had serious repercussions for the decades that followed—decades characterized by China's continuing struggle for undisputed mastery of Tibet.

Much of the inhuman treatment the Tibetans were subjected to during the years following the rebellion has been documented by the International Commission of Jurists, whose Legal Inquiry Committee found China guilty of genocide "in [its] attempt to destroy the Tibetans as a religious group."[93] This is not the place to discuss the human rights violations documented in that and other reports, except to point out that they were both a result and a manifestation of the broader Chinese policy for Tibet: Tibet was to come under the undisputed and effective control of the Central Government in Beijing and was to be fully integrated with China. The elimination of the distinct Tibetan national identity, a principal obstacle to "unity with the Motherland," was essential for the achievement of these objectives.[94] As that identity was so closely and indistinguishably tied to the culture and religious beliefs of the people, those manifestations became the primary targets for eradication.[95] Although, the immediate purpose of China's policy was to ensure its absolute control, Beijing also pursued the further objective of refashioning Tibet socially and economically into an integrated and indistinguishable component of the socialized Chinese State.[96]

Immediately following the army's restoration of authority over Lhasa and the imposition of martial law, the local government of Tibet was dissolved and Military Control Committees were established. The PCART was expanded with the addition of a Public Security department and entrusted with the exercise of all governmental functions, under the leadership and control of the CCP Working Committee and the Tibet Area Military Command.[97] Zhou Enlai declared at the Second National People's Congress, in April, that the action of the Tibetan rebels "in destroying themselves" had created "extremely favorable conditions for the democratization of Tibet."[98] In accordance with the directives from Beijing, the Panchen Lama, who was now named Acting Chairman of the PCART to replace the "abducted" Dalai Lama, and Zhang Guohua, the Vice-Chairman, announced the implementation of "democratic reforms" on 28 June. The first stage, General Zhang declared, "would consist of thoroughly suppressing the rebellion and campaigns to oppose rebellion, unpaid forced labor and slavery, and reduce rent and interest," and "the second stage would be the redistribution of land."[99]

In order to implement the "Three Cleanliness Campaign," as the first stage was called, "offices to suppress the uprising" were set up. All persons suspected of having taken part in or sympathized with the rebellion and all those who were connected with the now dissolved government were classified as "reactionaries" and "enemies of the people" and arrested, imprisoned, executed, or "re-educated" in forced-labor camps. The population was further divided into "big serf-owners," their agents, and the middle and the poor classes; the first two categories, together with most members of the clergy, suffered the same fate as the "reactionaries." In Lhasa, for example, this meant the disappearance of practically all adult males.[100] For the next twenty-five years, campaign after campaign was launched by the Chinese authorities to "weed out" Tibetan nationalists and to strengthen Chinese control on the plateau.[101] The second phase of "democratic reforms," the social and economic revolution, started with the redistribution of the land of "class enemies" and "reactionaries" and the organization of Mutual Aid Teams, the first step toward collectivization of agriculture and animal husbandry.[102]

Despite initial increases in agricultural production, opposition to the Chinese reforms was widespread, for Tibetans saw none of the benefits of the increases, which were used to relieve disastrous food shortages in China. Conditions in Tibet itself deteriorated so rapidly that by 1961, the country suffered an unprecedented famine that lasted for three years then and, again, from 1968 to 1973.[103]

Although it was Beijing's policy that was being implemented in Tibet, the Chinese were careful to preserve some appearance of Tibetan autonomy. Thus, G. Ginsburgs and M. Mathos have characterized the new political order established in Tibet following the revolt as "one in which the outward trappings of regional autonomy were to some extent maintained, but merely served to camouflage the reality of Peking's final authority, as supreme here as elsewhere throughout the country."[104] With the Dalai Lama in exile, the Panchen Lama's role as a symbol not only of Tibetan autonomy but even of the legitimacy of China's rule over Tibet became exceedingly important.

The Chinese now demanded of the Panchen Lama that he denounce the Dalai Lama and take over his position of religious and political leadership, a situation reminiscent of that of 1904 and 1910. As was the case in both of those years, the Panchen Lama, though he may have been sympathetic to China in earlier years, could not bring himself, as a Tibetan and a Buddhist, to usurp or challenge the authority of the Dalai Lama. In 1962 and 1963, he declined to assume the latter's place in the PCART and, in 1964, he used a mass public meeting to defy the Chinese and openly declare his loyalty to the Dalai Lama and his support for the cause of Tibetan independence. He was immediately arrested, tried, and charged as an antirevolutionary and traitor. The Panchen Lama spent the next fifteen years in prisons, labor or re-education camps, and under house arrest. Meanwhile, the Dalai and Panchen Lamas were both officially dismissed from their posts in the PCART, leaving Ngapo Ngawang Jigme as the only prominent Tibetan in a position of leadership.[105]

At lower levels of the administration, the Chinese did employ Tibetan cadres. Following the abortive uprising, over 3,000 Tibetan youths who had been taken to China for training were hastily sent back to Tibet to become cadres, in an effort to reduce the popular hostility toward the Chinese administration. As it turned out, it was these Chinese-educated and politically conscious Tibetans who shortly afterward led Tibet's burgeoning underground resistance and undermined the Chinese administration and policy at every level. Thus, by 1962, almost all of them had been dismissed from their posts as unreliable.[106] This is not to say that there were no Tibetan collaborators. In 1965, between thirty and forty thousand mostly uneducated Tibetans were reportedly employed by the Chinese in administration, and half of these were considered to be collaborators. Nevertheless, few seemed to have inspired much confidence, for each of them had to report directly to a Chinese Party member and none had any say in government.[107]

With the removal of the "big rock on the road to socialism," as Zhang Jinwu called the Panchen Lama,[108] and the Dalai Lama and his government out of the country, the Central Government felt sufficiently confident to launch the Tibet Autonomous Region (TAR) and impose upon Tibet a political structure that conformed to the rest of the People's Republic. Thus, on 9 September 1965, the TAR was officially inaugurated, with Ngapo Ngawang Jigme as its chairman. At the same time, the CCP Tibet Work Committee was reorganized as the Chinese Communist Party Tibet Autonomous Regional Committee. General Zhang Guohua was appointed First Secretary of this all-Chinese body, thus maintaining the position of actual leadership in Tibet.[109]

The inauguration of the Tibet Autonomous Region was considered to be a significant step forward in terms of Tibet's integration with the People's Republic of China.[110] In Zhang Guohua's words, expressed during the course of the inauguration:

> This represents another great victory of the Party's policy of national regional autonomy. The national regional autonomy is part of the people's democratic

dictatorship. As far as Tibet is concerned, this means the working class, the peasantry and herdsmen, other working people, patriotic elements, and all those in support of socialism, all rallied under the leadership of the Party, establish a people's democratic national regional autonomy. It imposes dicta-torship on the self-owner class, reactionary serf-owners and their agents, counter-revolutionaries who resist the socialist revolution and sabotage the socialist construction, elements who took part in the rebellion and other bad elements. The formal establishment of the Tibet Autonomous Region signifies the further consolidation of the people's power.[111]

It also signified that after six years of "democratic reform," Tibet was now ready for "socialist Revolution and Construction."[112] Whatever the new phase of reform was to entail for Tibet, however, it was disrupted violently, as in all of China, by the outbreak of the so-called Great Proletarian Cultural Revolution.

The Cultural Revolution was, in essence, Mao's attempt to wipe out, once and for all, the conservative and moderate elements within the CCP and the government: It was to be the violent "cleaning" of China's "rotten core." Red Guards were urged to seize power on behalf of Mao, to purge the "capitalist roaders" and "rightists," and to thoroughly destroy the "Four Olds" (old ideology, old culture, old custom, and old habits). Minority areas were particularly vulnerable to the new directives, especially the "Destroy the Four Olds" campaign.[113]

In Tibet, Buddhism, Tibetan culture, and other remnants of the national identity were once again the targets of attack. One of the first actions of the Red Guards was the storming and ransacking of Lhasa's central cathedral, the Tsugla Khang. This was followed by the destruction of the few remaining monasteries, temples, and historic buildings in the country.[114] The power struggle launched by the Red Guards was primarily Chinese, and the open fighting that erupted in 1966 and lasted for three years involved rival Chinese factions in Tibet.[115] On one side stood the Revolutionary Rebels, who attacked Zhang Guohua and the established Chinese authorities in Lhasa. On the other stood the Great Alliance, a rival Red Guard organization allegedly organized by Zhang Guohua himself. The PLA, though initially backing only Zhang, eventually also joined in the fighting, causing it to escalate greatly.[116] The weaponry used was heavy and the casualties were high. But, on balance, casualties were the highest among the Tibetan people for they were caught in the middle. Moreover, it was the Tibetans who were the object of the "Destroy the Four Olds" campaigns implemented with a vengeance by both Chinese factions, each trying to outdo the other to prove its revolutionary zeal.[117]

Fighting was so serious in Tibet that the restoration of any kind of order took much longer there than in China. Thus, together with Xinjiang, Tibet was the last region to set up a Revolutionary Committee. "Amidst the storm of class struggle," the New China News Agency reported, the Revolutionary Committee was established as Tibet's new government on 5 September 1968.[118] It consisted of twelve Chinese and four Tibetan members and was headed by General Zeng Yungya, Zhang Guohua's deputy (Zhang himself having been transferred to Sichuan in order to protect him from Red Guard attack). Despite the Committee's establishment, fighting continued for another year.[119]

By 1976, when China's three top leaders, Zhou Enlai, Jhu De, and Mao Zedong had passed away, practically all external manifestations of Tibetan identity had been destroyed. With the "upper strata" and the clergy eliminated and the rural life radically transformed by the establishment of communes, Tibet's social structure had been replaced by a socialist one.[120] Furthermore, Tibetans had experienced unprecedented famine, bringing the total number of Tibetans who died as a direct result of the Chinese invasion close to the 1 million mark—over one-seventh of the entire population.[121]

In only one respect was China's occupation of Tibet a success. Tibet's Himalayan border was turned into what appears to be an impregnable fortress. Especially since the 1962 Sino-Indian War, the defense of Tibet's southern and western borders has been a priority in China's Tibet policy.[122] But all of Tibet is highly militarized. China transferred its principal nuclear base to Tibet in 1962 and built nine airfields and an extensive network of roads used almost exclusively by the military.[123] However, the military presence in Tibet is intended not so much to protect the borders from external attack as to prevent another rebellion. Ever since the outbreak of fighting in Eastern Tibet in the early 1950s, the Chinese have had to contend with attacks from Tibetan guerrilla forces and other resistance movements. Most estimates put the strength of the PLA in the TAR alone at 300,000 men, and only 50,000 are thought to be posted along the borders.[124]

After the revolt in Lhasa had been crushed in March of 1959, the Tibetan National Volunteer Defence Army (NVDA) held control over the Lhoka region and other areas in south and east Tibet for several months. A year later, they were still holding out in parts of the Chang-tang (the Northern plains, deep in the interior), in Amdo, and even in parts of Western Tibet.[125] For the next two decades, reports continued to reach India of sabotage, ambushes, and armed clashes between guerrilla units and the PLA.[126] In addition, a number of underground resistance organizations have been operating in Lhasa and other cities and towns. Unlike the guerrillas who operate as military units these organizations do not generally engage the Chinese in open battle. The total number of underground movements is not known. An indication is provided, however, by the discovery of nine such organizations by the Chinese authorities between 1962 and 1976. In the same period alone, at least forty-four known cases of resistance flared up into open revolts.[127] The Panchen Lama's arrest, for example, set off a revolt, and a number of others broke out in 1965.[128] During the Cultural Revolution, the guerrilla forces stepped up their attacks on the PLA, and the underground movements provoked open rebellions and clashes between rival Red Guard groups. Then, in 1972, a revolt affecting over two-thirds of the Autonomous Region broke out, claiming the lives of 12,000 Tibetans.[129] In fact, not a year has passed without reports of popular rebellions coming out of Tibet.[130]

In exile, the Gushi Gandruk guerrilla forces regrouped and set up their main base of operations in Mustang, a small dependent principality of Nepal on the Tibetan border. From there raids were regularly carried out against Chinese convoys and military bases. To some extent, these activities were being supported by the CIA with the tacit approval of Pakistan and, after 1962, with the help of India.[131] At the end of 1962, the Special Frontier Force, an entirely Tibetan force under the command of the Research and Analysis Wing of the India Intelligence department, was secretly deployed near the Tibetan borders. With a troop strength of over 10,000 men and an entirely Tibetan officer corps below the highest ranks, for all practical purposes a fully Tibetan army now existed and, in fact, is still being kept in readiness through the joint efforts of the Indian and exile Tibetan governments.[132]

In 1971, as part of efforts for a U.S. rapprochement with the PRC, the CIA discontinued its support of the Tibetan guerrillas. At the same time, Nepal, under strong pressure from Beijing, forced the Tibetans to abandon their Mustang base in 1974.[133] Although this was an important setback, it did not mean an end to all guerrilla activity in Tibet. Thus, for example, a large convoy of 100 PLA vehicles was reportedly ambushed, raided, and burnt three years later, in 1977.[134]

China's Tibet policy entered a new phase sometime after Mao Zedong's death and of the arrest of his widow, Jiang Qing, and of the other radical members of the so-called Gang of Four. Deng Xiaoping gradually steered China on a more moderate and pragmatic course. Although Tibet was too remote to experience the immediate effects of the liberalization policies initiated in Beijing, indications that some improvement was forthcoming were already apparent in 1978.[135] In that year, as a gesture of leniency, a number of Tibetan prisoners who had been jailed in 1959 were released, some Tibetans were allowed to visit relatives in exile, and Tibetan refugees were gradually permitted into the country. These positive changes were somewhat overshadowed by the major transfer of Chinese officials to Tibet in June.[136] An important breakthrough did take place, however, when Sino-Tibetan talks resulted in three extensive visits to Tibet by official fact-finding delegations sent by the Dalai Lama.

It was the findings of these Tibetan delegations—shocking in their complete condemnation of Chinese past and current policies in Tibet and, more especially, in their descriptions of the overwhelming display of loyalty to the Dalai Lama occasioned by these visits—that prompted the General Secretary of the CCP, Hu Yaobang, and the Deputy Prime Minister, Wan Li, to personally inspect Tibet.[137]

While in Lhasa, Hu Yaobang conceded publicly that Tibet had been severely maladministered, that the Tibetan people had been subjected to suffering, and that in nearly thirty years of Chinese rule "no marked improvement had been brought about in the people's livelihood."[138] He promised to restore Tibet's economy to the pre–1959 level within three years and announced measures to create a "new, united, prosperous, and highly cultured Xizang [Tibet]."[139] The new measures included some liberalization to stimulate the local economy, a temporary tax exemption for farmers, and a promise to replace 85 percent of the Chinese administrators with Tibetans and to send the former back to China.[140]

It soon appeared that the government had second thoughts about the advisability of drastically reducing the Chinese presence in Tibet, and the modest reduction that took place in the first year was promptly offset by the arrival of 20,000 new PLA troops.[141] The other measures announced were partly implemented, but the result was not as significant as expected. In 1983, economic conditions were still characterized as disastrous by the Chinese; and, in May 1984, Beijing, once again admitting that little had changed in Tibet, announced more reforms to encourage Tibetan peasants to revert to their own self-sufficient farming methods, with the declared aim of shifting within a few years "from basically solving the food and clothing problem to the goal of getting rich and prosperous."[142]

The moderate liberalization policy has undeniably had some positive effects, as Tibetans in exile have admitted, especially in Lhasa and other major cities.[143] It has not diminished the population's opposition to Chinese rule, however. In fact, according to some Tibetans, the liberalization has merely served to encourage the public articulation of anti-Chinese sentiments, and there are indications that underground organizations, some of which have contacts with the Tibetan Youth Congress in India and with the government-in-exile, are better organized and more extensive than before.[144] Two such organizations have sent written messages to the Youth Congress, and Western visitors to Lhasa have repeatedly reported receiving secret letters and memoranda from the underground condemning Chinese oppression, demanding the independence of Tibet, and pleading for United Nations intervention.[145] These same visitors reported seeing official posters throughout the city warning against armed subversion, and the Chinese authorities, as well, have occasionally admitted the existence of underground activity.[146] In 1979 and 1981, widespread unrest was reported in Tibet, and a year later more than 100 demonstrators were arrested in Shigatse, in the south.[147] Arrested in 1983 were an estimated 3,000 persons, many of whom were executed between August and November.[148]

The twentieth anniversary of the establishment of the TAR, officially celebrated in Lhasa on 1 September 1985, was marked by heightened tension prior to that day. Many Tibetans were arrested and stern warnings were broadcast over the radio to ensure that no disturbance might occur. Three bombs were found, two of which had been placed in the stadium where celebrations were to have taken place. Although the celebrations had been organized as a mass media event, at the last moment foreign correspondents and tourists were refused entry to Lhasa, and large numbers of troops conspicuously patrolled the streets and staked out rooftops with machine guns.[149]

In short, despite the new leadership in Beijing and a dramatic change in Chinese national policy orientations, including a more tolerant attitude toward religious practice and cultural pursuits,[150] the fundamental issues in Tibet remain unchanged. The Chinese authorities still lack the confidence to hand over any significant responsibility to the Tibetans, and the latter still refuse to accept, much less trust, this or any Chinese regime intent on maintaining China's hold on Tibet at all costs.[151] Indeed, the tensions between the two peoples thirty-five years after the Chinese invasion are serious enough to warrant the deployment of an occupation army of close to 500,000 men on the plateau.[152]

Michael Weisskopf echoed the observations of many recent Western visitors to Tibet when he concluded that an unofficial view of the country revealed "an uneasy society in desperate search of the independence it lost when China occupied it in 1951."[153]

The Present Status of Tibet

The previous chapter established that the People's Republic of China did not acquire a legal title to sovereignty over Tibet by virtue of the 1951 Seventeen-Point Agreement. The purpose of the present chapter is, therefore, to determine whether any other circumstances resulted in the transfer of sovereignty to the People's Republic.

As international law, by its very nature, is a system developed and enforced by independent States in order to protect their interests, and, consequently, as its most fundamental function is the protection of those States' very existence, "[the extinction of a State] is neither easily presumed nor lightly accepted."[154] Once established, the statehood of a political entity is buttressed by strong presumptions in its favor, despite very extensive loss of actual authority at times. A State's formal independence is therefore not lost unless and until the source or validity of its government has indisputably been transferred from that State to the government of another State. Similarly, actual independence is not lost unless the effective governmental authority of the independent State has been totally extinguished and replaced by that of the controlling State. In the present investigation, in order to ascertain the validity or falsity of the Chinese claim that Tibet today forms an integral part of the PRC, we must therefore identify specific events or circumstances that could have brought about the extinction of the State of Tibet and its incorporation into the People's Republic. In other words, the question that must be answered is whether or not the PRC acquired a legal title to the State of Tibet (i.e., to sovereignty over that State) and, if so, by what means.

A brief review of the law governing the modes of acquisition of territory will be helpful in reaching valid conclusions. Two elements stand out as the most important: the creation of a title and its maintenance.[155] The balancing of these aspects where conflicting claims exist can be a delicate task, as the International Court cases suggest. Thus, on the one hand as

Judge M. Huber noted in the *Island of Palmas* case: "International law, the structure of which is not based on any super-State organization, cannot be presumed to reduce a right such as territorial sovereignty, with which almost all international relations are bound up, to the category of an abstract right, without concrete manifestations."[156] On the other hand, the law does recognize an abstract title where other principles of international law prevail— for example, in the case of belligerent occupation. Furthermore, the Permanent Court of International Justice held, in the *Eastern Greenland* case, that where international tribunals have to decide between two competing claims to sovereignty, "in many cases the tribunal has been satisfied with very little in the way of the actual exercise of sovereign rights, provided that the other State could not make out a superior claim."[157]

But as R.Y. Jennings has noted, "of course the assumption . . . is that however little sovereign activity had to be shown, it was nevertheless activity that was unambiguously *a titre de souverain*."[158]

Acquisition of Territory in International Law

The classical theory of international law recognized five modes by which a State could acquire a legal title to territory: accretion, prescription, conquest (or subjugation), cession, and *occupatio*.[159] Of these, only conquest and prescription need to be discussed in the present study.[160]

Conquest can be described, essentially, as the incorporation of foreign territory "after its subjugation by armed forces."[161] The legality of this mode of territorial acquisition was not seriously contested among the classical publicists; by the middle of the nineteenth century, however, it was no longer universally accepted and in the early part of this century it was being seriously questioned and limited. Since the Second World War, it is at least doubtful whether conquest can still legitimately be listed as a mode of acquisition.[162]

There are basically two approaches to this question. The first, deriving from the classical theory, still recognizes conquest as a valid mode of acquisition but subjects it to important limitations.[163] Supporters of this approach are mainly from the Anglo-American school. The other has its origin in the writings of continental European and Latin American publicists, particularly those of the current century, and draws its support, also, from newly independent States and socialist States, including the PRC. This latter approach rejects the legal validity of conquest altogether, as being obviously incompatible with both the right to self-preservation and the inviolability of national territorial integrity.[164] Thus, the Chinese jurist Xin Wu calls conquest "a savage and aggressive act . . . used by imperialists to plunder the territory of colonized countries and weak and small countries," and denounces this method of territorial acquisition.[165] The results arrived at by applying either approach to a given situation hardly differ in practice.

Legal authorities generally distinguish between the act of taking possession of foreign territory through military force and the formal annexation of the territory that occurs after the conqueror has firmly established control.[166] In other words, conquest in the military sense is distinguished from conquest in the legal sense.[167] There is no disagreement regarding the premise that from the former the conqueror cannot derive a legal title. Thus, as L. Oppenheim has stated: "Conquered enemy territory, although actually in possession and under the sway of the conqueror, remains legally under the sovereignty of the enemy until through annexation it comes under the sovereignty of the conqueror."[168] It is the continued validity of the second assertion in this quotation—that formal annexation following military conquest can give the conqueror a title—that is still the subject of disagreement among jurists.

Whereas, between the World Wars, a strong body of legal opinion existed opposing the validity of conquest as a basis for acquiring a title to territory, the fact of conquests still prevented the greater number of authorities from rejecting its validity absolutely.[169] International law's outright condemnation of wars of aggression or aggrandizement—indeed, of all use or threat of force in violation of the Charter of the United Nations, embodied in that Charter—has rendered virtually untenable the notion that conquest can still be accepted as a valid mode of acquiring territory at least since the close of the Second World War.[170]

Writing before this time, in 1940, M. McMahon concluded in his comprehensive study entitled *Conquest and Modern International Law* that, regardless of existing differences in definitions and theories of conquest, it is the element of seizure and force that characterizes the act of conquest. He accordingly defines conquest as "a coercive act whereby territory is acquired by one State from another State through belligerent operations, or by measures short of war, such as a display of force or threat of the use of force."[171] As the basic element of conquest is undeniably the use or threat of force, the condemnation of such conduct in modern international law would seem effectively to undermine this mode of territorial acquisition.[172]

The argument is nevertheless advanced that, although the use of force is illegal and the act of military conquest *per se* cannot create any rights over the forcibly occupied territory for the conqueror, the subsequent annexation thereof can still do so.[173]

In the eighteenth century, E. de Vattel formulated as the requirements for the transfer of sovereignty over occupied territory either the conclusion of a peace treaty or final subjugation—that is, *debellatio*.[174] Hardly any comment is necessary with regard to the first of these, the conclusion of a peace treaty, where the treaty is imposed on a defeated State as a result of the illegal use of force. Modern international law on the subject was reviewed earlier.[175] Only where a peace treaty is imposed by States that have used force in self-defense against an agressor or otherwise done so in accordance with international law (i.e., on the basis of a U.N. Security Council Resolution), invalidity does not follow. With regard to the second alternative, final subjugation and annexation, a more detailed discussion is in order.

Annexation is a unilateral act expressing a State's intention to appropriate territory. This act is universally considered illegal and is devoid of legal effect if undertaken *pendente bello*—that is, before the victory of the conqueror is so final that the possibility of its expulsion can reasonably be excluded.[176] In outlawing premature annexation and upholding the continued legal existence of an occupied State in these circumstances, international law acts not on a certainty of the State's actual restoration but on uncertainty of its extinction. K. Marek adds: "There can be no more telling proof of the international law's inherent tendency to postpone—even at a risk—the passing of a death sentence on a State until the moment of absolute and incontrovertible finality."[177]

The consequence of this rule, it can be argued, is that once invaded territory is fully subjugated (i.e., once the conqueror has incontrovertibly and finally crushed organized opposition, leaving no reasonable possibility of his expulsion), the subsequent annexation "will necessarily result in the extinction of the conquered State and the extension of the conqueror's sovereignty over its territory."[178]

The inconsistency inherent in such reasoning is evident and has been pointed out by numerous writers.[179] By this theory, an illegal act—the use or threat of force by the conqueror or aggressor—that the law punishes by denying the action the desired legal effect (e.g., the transfer of sovereignty of occupied territory to the violator), would be legitimized and would therefore create the desired effect on the sole basis that the force used or threatened is so overpowering that the legitimate government and the people of the victim State are no longer able to effectively oppose it. Thus, the very function of the law is denied where it is most needed. It is not the existence of illegal acts that form the supreme challenge to international law but the possibility of their giving rise to legal titles on an equal footing with lawful acts. Marek aptly condemns the illegal attempt against the independence of a State as the most drastic illegality that can be committed— "a supreme attempt against the highest of the internationally protected interests of a State: its existence."[180] It is inconceivable that such illegality would be sanctioned with legal validity only because it is pursued with enough force to achieve a measure of effectiveness. In the past, this traditional theory was merely a corollary of the attitude toward war, which the law was obliged to tolerate as a method of settling disputes.[181] In modern (post-1945) international law it lacks both moral and logical validity. Jennings summarizes this point in the following words:

To brand as illegal the use of force against the "territorial integrity" of a State, and yet at the same time to recognize a rape of another's territory by illegal force as being itself a root of legal title to the sovereignty over it, is surely to risk bringing the law into comtempt. For it is not simply a question whether it is possible to allow a title which cannot be pleaded without incidentally exhibiting the illegality. Nor is it merely a question of the limits of the maxim *ex injuria jus non oritur*. The question is whether an international crime of the first order can itself be pleaded as title because its perpetration has been attended with success.[182]

He then concludes that "one is driven to accept the position that conquest as a title to territorial sovereignty has ceased to be a part of the law."[183]

This conclusion is supported by the adoption by the United Nations General Assembly, in 1970, of the "Declaration on Principles of International Law Concerning Friendly Relations and Cooperation Among States in Accordance with the Charter of the United Nations," which proclaims that "the territory of a State shall not be the object of acquisition by another State resulting from the threat or use of force. No territorial acquisition resulting from the threat or use of force shall be recognized as legal."[184]

It is, nonetheless, often argued that an action, illegal though it might be when committed, may under some circumstances bring about a legal effect over time. This argument derives principally from the need to reconcile tensions between the law and the facts, in the interest of international order and stability, for there is a limit to the legal system's ability to tolerate significant discrepancies between the two.[185] In the case of illegal use of force and invasion of another State, the tension is between the illegality of the aggressor's action and the effectiveness of his control over the territory he occupies over time.

The conflict in concrete situations between the two principles, Ex iniuria ius non oritur and Ex factis ius oritur, is most difficult to reconcile (1) where the international law that regulates a particular area of inter-State relations is no longer in accordance with the general practice of States or (2) in areas that ought to be regulated by international law but are not. Where an area of international relations is regulated by international law and the general practice of States is in accordance with the legal principles, concrete situations "can be judged on the grounds of clear objective standards."[186] The starting point in that situation should be to accord no legal consequences to the illegal act:

[A] territorial claim contrary to really valid rules of international law ought to be rejected. Rejection should be maintained even if the claim is supported by effective exercise of sovereignty by the claiming State. For the effective exercise of an act contrary to international law by no means justifies the existence of a right. It remains a claim but does not become a right by virtue of the effective exercise of State authority.[187]

The question of acquisitive prescription nevertheless arises when a situation clearly contrary to such objective standards of international law persists. Scholars often contend that legal effects may eventually result from an illegal act by virtue of the fact that the factual situation has been maintained over a long period of time and that it is undisputed by the other States:

The application of *Ex iniuria ius non oritur* is limited to the areas in relation to which an obvious agreement about what is valid exists among States, while [the criterion *Ex factis ius oritur*] is of greater importance with regard to areas where such objective standards are absent. Finally, *Ex factis ius oritur* can even be applied if a State violates an objective standard of international law on condition that [after the violation] the claiming State maintained its claim and the other States acquiesce in it. In this way the latter criterion contributes to legal security among nations. Consequently, it is impossible to state in general whether *Ex iniuria ius non oritur* or *Ex factis ius oritur* is the right criterion. Rather, the attending circumstances are relevant in deciding what criterion has to be applied.[188]

It was shown above that the illegal use of force by a State to acquire a part or the whole of the territory of another State is regarded as a supreme violation of international law by the international community as a whole. What is more, a clear and objective standard exists in international law in this regard.

One can certainly accept the proposition that where the lapse of time brings about the gradual acceptance of a new situation by the government or population of a conquered State, the fact, illegal in its origin, may thus gradually be legalized. This might conceivably occur if the conquered government or people consider that the benefits of the new state of affairs (e.g., economic advancement or increased long-term security) outweigh the advantages of restoring the *status quo ante*. Similarly, there can be little point in withholding title to sovereignty over conquered territory where the lapse of time has eliminated or virtually eliminated any challenge to the conqueror's claim, above all, by the conquered.[189]

Where the lapse of time has not had either of these effects, can the illegal use of force against a State nonetheless result in the transfer of the legal title? The maintenance of a claim and the exercise of a measure of effective control are in themselves inconclusive where the claim is challenged and the possession is not peaceable or the degree of control is brought into question.[190] The use of violence against the conqueror is not the only means of interrupting his peaceful possession and thereby impeding his claim by prescription. As early as 1910–1911, the Arbitral Tribunal in the *Chamizal* arbitration between the United States and Mexico held that the decision to desist from action that might lead to violence cannot be held against the State threatened by a prescriptive claim. The State against which the claim is being made, the Tribunal therefore held, "cannot be blamed for resorting to the milder forms of protest contained in its diplomatic correspondence."[191]

Acquiescence by third States has little more than evidentiary value, particularly where it is not universal: Recognition, it was pointed out earlier, is conclusive only against recognizing States themselves.[192] Recognition by a third State, far from being a legal act based on legal criteria, is an act of policy, which is incapable in itself of legalizing the illegal actions of States: Recognition cannot bring about the extinction of a State, just as it cannot create a new one. Nonrecognition similarly indicates, at most, only the disapproval of individual States.[193]

History is replete with examples of conquests and annexations of entire States that, regardless of their acceptance or continued challenge, have permanently transformed international political boundaries. State practice since the coming into force of the United Nations Charter, however, has confirmed the legal norm that rejects the acquisition of title over territory following the illegal use of force.

Since 1945, the illegal invasion of States for the purpose of their annexation has not occurred with any frequency. A significant case of annexation that took place shortly before that time, in 1940, is that of the Baltic States by the Soviet Union.[194] This case sheds little light on the problem for, on the whole, few States have so far recognized the annexation of the Baltic States. President Ronald Reagan of the United States, for example, recently declared: "The United States has never recognized the forcible incorporation of the Baltic States into the Soviet Union, and it will not do so in the future."[195]

A more recent case, even though it does not involve the conquest of an entire State, is Israel's annexation of Jerusalem in 1967. Israel's action is still condemned by the overwhelming majority of States and by the United Nations as a violation of international law and, more specifically, in terms of "the inadmissibility of the acquisition of territory by war."[196] Repeatedly, in the debates and resolutions of the United Nations Security Council and General Assembly on this question, the member States have "reaffirm[ed] that no territorial acquisition resulting from the threat or use of force shall be recognized."[197] What these two cases reveal is that to the extent annexations are perceived by other States to result from the illegal use or threat of force, they are today given no international legal effect.

Although force has been used by States since 1945 for the purpose of territorial aggrandizement or political expansion, the conduct of States in this respect is significant because they have deliberately not claimed a title to invaded territory on the basis of conquest or of protracted effective control. On the contrary, invading States either claim the existence of a prior title to the territory in question as the basis for their action or they limit such action to the securement of the victim State's political and military allegiance. The latter type of action most frequently results in the establishment of a so-called satellite relationship.[198] In neither case is a claim to title by conquest advanced.[199]

The conclusion that may be drawn is that claims to territory based solely on the effective but illegal use or threat of force are rejected by the overwhelming majority of States as contrary to modern international law. Furthermore, the time which has elapsed since the adoption of the United Nations Charter has proved insufficient to establish any title to invaded territory by prescription. Thus, the two decades since the annexation of Jerusalem and even the almost 50-year period since the incorporation of the Baltic States are generally not considered sufficiently long to give a legal effect to the acts of Israel and the Soviet Union with respect to those territories. What effect a longer period of time might have in closing the gap between law and fact cannot be conclusively established.[200]

Even the classic writers, such as Grotius, argued that more than one hundred years was required for the establishment of a prescriptive title, while other, more recent authorities such as F. de Martens and A. Rivier required "immemorial possession."[201] Some States, notably the People's Republic of China, take the view that no amount of time can legitimize illegal acquisition of territory and, hence, that conquered States can never be deprived of the legal title to sovereignty over their territory. This view was reiterated on numerous occasions with regard to China's "resumption of sovereignty" over Hong Kong.[202]

As the foregoing analysis shows, contemporary international law is extremely reluctant, at best, to consider conquest, even where it is followed by subjugation and annexation and by the exercise of effective control over a period of time, to be a valid mode of acquisition of territory. International law is even less willing to accept the proposition that such illegal action can effectuate the extinction of a whole State.[203]

Conclusions

From the review of post–1951 developments presented in this chapter, a number of relevant facts emerge that allow certain conclusions to be drawn concerning Tibet's extinction or continued existence.

First, and perhaps foremost, it is clear that neither the Tibetan government, in Lhasa until 1959 and in exile since then, nor the people of Tibet have accepted the imposition of Chinese rule over Tibet. To this day, the Dalai Lama and his government challenge the legitimacy of the Chinese presence in Tibet and claim to be the sole legitimate government of that country. Indeed, their desire for the restoration of Tibet's independence is not diminished. This stand is supported not only by the exile community, but, more important, by the overwhelming majority of Tibetans in Tibet.

It is admittedly difficult, under the present circumstances, accurately to ascertain the extent of support the Dalai Lama and his government enjoy in Tibet today. Nevertheless, the evidence presented above, especially the dramatic display of loyalty and support witnessed by the Dalai Lama's delegations to Tibet between 1979 and 1985, leaves little doubt as to the well-nigh universal devotion among Tibetans to the religious person of the Dalai Lama and the overwhelming support for the political ideal of *rangzen*, the popular Tibetan term for freedom and independence, that he represents.[204] It is not possible, in fact, to separate the religious from the political sentiments in Tibet, for the distinction is rarely made by the Tibetans themselves, who regard the Dalai Lama as the ultimate symbol of both. Franz Michael's conclusion effectively reflects the opinion of most observers and visitors to Tibet: "Recent events have clearly demonstrated that the large majority of the six million Tibetans at home has not abandoned its faith or its loyalty to the Dalai Lama who has come to personify more than ever the Tibetan religio-political order and national identity."[205]

On the other hand, the opposition to Chinese communist rule in Tibet is also widespread. The Tibetan dislike for the Chinese has historical roots— a dislike only aggravated by Zhao Erfeng's invasion of Tibet in 1910 and the communist invasion in 1949. The Chinese communists are regarded by the Tibetans as an alien and atheist people with whom they have hardly anything in common. Most important, the invasion of Tibet and, especially, the subsequent attempts to suppress the Tibetan identity were brutal: In short, the Tibetans have experienced little benefit from the Chinese presence in Tibet, while they have had to endure a tremendous amount of hardship and suffering under their rule.

Beyond establishing the fact that the Tibetan people and their government clearly do not accept but, instead, continue to reject the Chinese presence in Tibet, the evidence presented in this chapter casts doubt even on the degree of effectiveness or control of China's regime in Tibet. Most analysts would agree that the guerrilla operations, which declined after 1974, and the underground resistance movements, which have expanded since then, do not pose a serious threat to China's physical hold on Tibet. Nonetheless, the threat is serious enough to warrant a massive military presence in Tibet. At the very least, this continuing opposition represents a constant challenge to Chinese authority in Tibet; it is a source of grave embarrassment to Beijing; and it constitutes a certain reminder to the Tibetan population and the Chinese authorities that the struggle is not over. The overall position of the Chinese in Tibet is, consequently, far from peaceable, stable, or undisputed.

The attitude of other States to China's claims is inconclusive, at best. The initial reaction of noncommunist States to the events of 1959 was extremely sympathetic. But even today, over twenty-five years later, the position taken by many States is noncommittal.

In the course of debates at the U.N. General Assembly between 1960 and 1965, noncommunist governments made statements that reflected their view of Tibet's pre–1951 independent status. In particular, the delegates referred to the "military aggression" and "invasion" of Tibet by foreign forces, and denounced the 1951 Seventeen-Point Agreement as having been imposed on Tibet by force.[206]

The Philippines' government referred to Tibet "as an independent nation" and voiced support for the Tibetan people's "fight against foreign domination." "[I]t is clear," the delegate from the Philippines declared, "that on the eve of the Chinese invasion in 1950, Tibet was not under the rule of any foreign country." He stated that China's occupation of Tibet conformed to "the worst type of imperialism, and colonialism past or present."[207] The Nicaraguan representative spoke for other governments of the Americas also when he characterized the Chinese action as "an act of aggression . . . perpetrated by a large State against a small and weak one."[208] The representative from Thailand similarly reminded the Assembly that the majority of States "refute the contention that Tibet is part of China."[209]

The Irish representative, Frank Aiken, also expressed his country's indignation at the oppression to which the Tibetans were being subjected. "Tibet has fallen into the hands of the Chinese People's Republic for the last few years," he pointed out, but "[f]or thousands of years, or for a couple of thousand years at any rate, it was as free and as fully in control of its own affairs as any nation in this Assembly, and a thousand times more free to look after its own affairs than many of the nations here."[210] In 1965, Aiken repeated his government's position and specified that "Tibet can rightly claim to be historically an independent country."[211] El Salvador, which sponsored the inclusion in the General Assembly's agenda of the item entitled "Invasion of Tibet by Foreign Forces" in 1950, maintained that "the question of Tibet has not been finally settled simply because Communist China has succeeded in achieving domination over the small country of Tibet."[212]

During the debates in the General Assembly, the United States, which had earlier denounced the 1951 agreement and Chinese claims to sovereignty over Tibet, also condemned Chinese "aggression" and their "invasion" of Tibet.[213] Despite the development of friendly relations with the PRC and the abandonment of aid to the Tibetan resistance, the United States has been careful to avoid taking a stand on the question of China's sovereignty. Thus, the official U.S. position goes no further than "not to recognize that Tibet is not a part of China."[214] The German government in Bonn recently stated that it was not indifferent to the fate of Tibet and the Tibetans despite the fact that "Tibet is not recognized as a sovereign nation by a large majority of all countries." The statement continued: The Federal Government is of the opinion that a clarification of the century-old changing relation between China and Tibet can only be achieved through a mutual agreement between the two people."[215] During the General Assembly debates on the subject, the Soviet Union and Eastern European countries supported the Chinese position regarding the status of Tibet. They have subsequently abandoned this position and have expressed support for the Tibetans.[216]

Whether time will resolve the decades-long struggle of attrition in favor of China or of Tibet remains to be seen. Almost thirty-five years of domination, and over twenty-five years of subjection to China's direct and mostly military rule, have not succeeded in securing the final submission of the Tibetan people. As one recent visitor to Tibet concluded, "The Chinese have found Tibet easy to invade but impossible to conquer."[217] In the absence of conclusive evidence of the acquiescence of the Tibetan people and also of other States, the total extinction and incorporation of Tibet into the PRC can certainly not be presumed.

The continuation of the State is further supported by the continued existence and activity of the Tibetan government-in-exile. Its effectiveness, a concept normally associated with the exercise of territorial jurisdiction of governments, "may be wholly lacking in the case of a government in exile," P. Jessup points out.[218] But "nothing illustrates [the] dynamic aspect of the continuity of the occupied State better than the existence and activity of exiled governments or, as is sometimes more radically said, States in exile."[219] This fact was first tangibly demonstrated during the First World War, by the physical existence on foreign soil of the governments and armies of occupied States, such as those of Belgium, Serbia, and Montenegro.[220] It was confirmed on a greater scale during the Second World War, when a large number of governments of States incorporated into the German and Italian empires, including those of the Netherlands, Norway, Yugoslavia, and Greece, continued their activities in London.[221] At the present time, the exiled government of Kampuchea is still widely regarded as the legitimate government of that country despite Vietnam's invasion and the installation of a new regime in Phnom Penh. It is the exiled government, for example, that occupies the seat of Kampuchea at the United Nations. Arnold McNair formulated the accepted view thus:

> The mere fact that a foreign Government has been deprived of the control of a part or the whole of its territory by an enemy in no way invalidates legislation passed or other acts of sovereignty done by it outside its normal territory. . . . There is no principle of International Law which says that a Government cannot act validly upon foreign territory with the consent of the local sovereign.[222]

Moreover, "the term 'exiled' or 'refugee' government," F.E. Oppenheimer pointed out, "is not very appropriate since it does not express clearly that such government is the only *de jure* sovereign power of the country."[223]

The Government of Tibet in Exile is not a new body established outside the territory of Tibet but, rather, the continuation of the legitimate and recognized Government of Tibet in Lhasa. In exile, that government has functioned, and still functions, effectively to the extent that this is possible on foreign soil and without official political recognition. At the very least, the Dalai Lama's presence in exile and the functioning of his government there act as a continuous challenge to the legitimacy of the Chinese administration in Lhasa. The successful reconstruction and advancement of the exile community as a whole, moreover, present a tangible and viable alternative to the highly unsucccessful and tragic attempt at transformation of the Tibetan plateau. Both these elements constitute the dynamic aspect of the continuity of the Tibetan State.

In conclusion, the foregoing analysis reveals that the People's Republic of China could not have obtained a legal title to sovereignty over Tibet on the basis either of the military invasion of that State or of the subsequent exercise of a measure of effective control. The continued support for the Dalai Lama among the overwhelming majority of the population, the active resistance to Chinese rule in Tibet, the successful development of the Tibetan polity in exile, and the functioning of a government in exile are all factors that contribute to the continuity of the Tibetan State. On the other hand, in view of the illegality of China's invasion of Tibet and the nullity of the Seventeen-Point Agreement, neither the degree of control exercised by China through the maintenance of a strong military presence in Tibet, nor the amount of time that has elasped since the invasion has been sufficient to permit the conclusion that China has legally acquired the whole territory of Tibet. To the present time, nothing has occurred that, according to generally accepted norms of international law, can justify the conclusion that the State of Tibet has been totally extinguished and legally incorporated to form an integral part of the People's Republic of China. It is indeed significant to note, once again, that the Chinese government does not itself recognize conquest, annexation, or prescription as modes of valid territorial acquisition and, furthermore, that it has never claimed to have acquired a title to Tibet through any of these modes. Instead, Beijing has maintained that Tibet is an integral part of China only by virtue of its prior possession of a legal title to sovereignty over Tibet. Yet the historical analysis contained in the first part of this study has conclusively demonstrated that prior to the invasion of Tibet, in 1950, no such title existed and Tibet was an independent State.

As Tibet was fully independent prior to 1950, and as no sufficient legal grounds can be found to support the contention that since that time the Tibetan State ceased to exist and was legally incorporated to form an integral part of the People's Repubic of China, the State of Tibet still exists at the time of this writing as an independent legal entity, with a legitimate government, in exile in Dharmsala, to represent it. Accordingly, that government and the people of Tibet have the right to resumé the exercise of sovereignty over their own territory, free from the interference of other States.

11

Beyond the Status Quo: Toward an Equitable Resolution

On the basis of Tibet's past and present legal status, it was concluded in the previous chapter that the government and people of Tibet themselves have the right to "resume the exercise of sovereignty" over their own territory. This conclusion would seem to be in keeping with recent pronouncements of the government of the People's Republic of China in reference to China's recovery of Hong Kong, after well over a century of British rule.[1]

The Dalai Lama recently called on Tibetans everywhere to "struggle with greater determination and dedication to regain the right which is justly ours and enjoyed by people the world over—the right to govern ourselves."[2] But, he consistently stresses, this demand is, and should be, based solely on the wishes of the 6 million Tibetans inside and outside Tibet. Any resolution of the future status of Tibet and the political, social, and economic system of the country must be in accordance with the declared wishes of the Tibetan masses. In order to determine those wishes, the Dalai Lama has demanded that an internationally supervised plebiscite be held.[3] Ultimately, he maintains, "the final solution is self-determination,"[4] and he is confident that the Chinese government "will sooner or later realistically recognise the reasonable desires and aspirations of the Tibetan people."[5]

The question of the Tibetan people's right to self-determination is one that can be resolved apart from and irrespective of the past and present status of Tibet, although that status does, to some extent, affect the outcome of a discussion on the subject. For one thing, the Tibetans' right to resume sovereignty over their territory implies *a fortiori* their right to determine their own future.

The implementation of the Tibetan's right to resume sovereignty over their country or to exercise self-determination could have a number of outcomes. Some alternatives for the nature of Sino-Tibetan relations that might result will be touched upon in this chapter, although such a discussion merits far more attention than the present work can spare.

The Legitimacy of the Tibetan People's Claim
to Self-Determination in International Law

On 13 October 1975, at the World Peace Through Law Conference, the President of the International Court of Justice proudly referred to the court's reaffirmation of the principle of self-determination as its greatest jurisprudential accomplishment.[6] Although definitions of self-determination vary somewhat, it is generally considered to be the right of a people to determine their own political, economic, and cultural destinies. This "inalienable right," as it is described in numerous United Nations resolutions, has been laid down in some of the principal international instruments, including the Charter of the United Nations.[7]

Self-Determination in International Law

The fundamental notion that government should rest on the consent of the governed, the basis of democracy, is also the basis for self-determination—and it is as old as government itself.[8] The First World War brought the principle of self-determination to the fore of international politics. As President Wilson declared in 1917, "No peace can last or ought to last, which does not accept the principle that governments derive all their just powers from the consent of the governed, and that no right anywhere exists to hand peoples about from sovereignty to sovereignty as if they were property."[9] In addition, Lenin held that the forcible retention of one nation within the State frontiers of another was a form of political oppression. He considered the right to self-determination to be as applicable in a socialist society as in any other society: "It would be a betrayal of socialism not to implement the self-determination of nations under socialism."[10]

These statements of policy became "an imperative principle of action which statesmen would henceforth ignore at their peril" following the First World War, when the political map of Europe was redrawn on the basis of self-determination of nationalities.[11] Austria, Hungary, and Czechoslovakia emerged as separate States; Finland, Estonia, Latvia, Lithuania, and Poland became independent States; and Yugoslavia, Greece, and Rumania grew in size. A number of plebiscites were provided for in the peace treaty, and eight of them were actually held.[12]

In the early years of the revolution in China, the ideals of Chinese unification and national self-determination were important slogans of the Communist Party, which expected the "autonomous states" of Mongolia, Tibet, and Turkestan to voluntarily unite with China in a federal republic.[13] The "Constitution of the [Chinese] Soviet Republic," adopted in 1931, for example, "categorically and unconditionally" recognized the right of national minorities to self-determination, meaning

> [the] right to complete separation from China, and to the formation of an independent state for each national minority. All Mongolians, Tibetans, Miao, Yao, Koreans, and others living on the territory of China shall enjoy the full

right to self-determination, i.e., they may either join the Union of Chinese Soviets or secede from it and form their own state as they may prefer.[14]

Following the Second World War, the right of self-determination was codified in numerous international instruments. The very first article of the Charter of the United Nations declares that one of the paramount purposes of the United Nations is "to develop friendly relations among nations based on respect for the principles of equal rights and self-determination of peoples, and to take other appropriate measures to strengthen universal peace."[15] The "Declaration on the Granting of Independence to Colonial Countries and Peoples," adopted in 1960 without a dissenting vote, denounces the subjection of peoples to alien governance as contrary to the Charter of the United Nations. Three paragraphs may be singled out:

2. All peoples have the right to self-determination; by virtue of that right they freely determine their political status and freely pursue their economic, social, and cultural development.
3. Inadequacy of political, economic, social, or education preparedness should never serve as a pretext for delayed independence.
4. All armed action or repressive measures of all kinds directed against dependent peoples shall cease in order to enable them to exercise peacefully and freely their right to complete independence, and the integrity of their national territories shall be respected.[16]

As a result of the universal support the Declaration received from Member States and of the decisive language used in it, the Declaration is the most frequently cited resolution in the United Nations and is considered by most of the African and Asian Nations to be "a document only slightly less sacred than the Charter."[17] It is indeed argued that the Declaration makes the right to self-determination not only legally binding and obligatory but also directly enforceable.[18]

In 1966 the two Human Rights Covenants were adopted by the General Assembly; the Article 1 they have in common defines the right of all peoples to self-determination in exactly the same words as does the 1960 Declaration.[19] Adopted four years later was the "Declaration on Principles of International Law Concerning Friendly Relations and Co-operation Among States in Accordance with the Charter of the United Nations," which once again emphasized the right to self-determination.[20]

A consideration of the frequency and consistency of the language of the Charter, the resolutions and declarations, the coming into force of the Human Rights Covenants, as well as the United Nations' impact on the implementation of the right to self-determination, particularly in the field of de-colonization, leads to the conclusion that the already strong principle of self-determination has been elevated to the status of a right, legally binding on all States and enforceable in international law.[21]

This view is confirmed by the pronouncements of the International Court of Justice in the *Western Sahara* case, which called for respect for "the right of the population of Western Sahara to determine their future political status by their own freely expressed will."[22] With regard to non-self-governing territories, the International Court of Justice had already affirmed the right to self-determination in its "Advisory Opinion on Legal Consequences for States of the Continued Presence of South Africa in Namibia (South West Africa) Not-withstanding Security Council Resolution 276 (1970)."[23]

The practice of States, as manifested through the organs of the United Nations, is consistent with the view "that the right of self-determination has become, in the last generation, an integral part of . . . international law."[24] Thus, the United Nations' involvement in the conflict between the Netherlands' forces in Indonesia (then Dutch East Indies) and Indonesia's nationalist forces resulted in Indonesia's independence. The United Nations also supported the struggles for self-determination of the Moroccan, Tunisian, and Algerian peoples.[25] The Special Committee on the Implementation of the Declaration of the Granting of Independence to Colonial Countries and Peoples became entrusted with the task of establishing independence and majority rule in Angola, Mozambique, Rhodesia, and Namibia.[26] In Namibia, efforts are still being made, whereas the other territories have achieved independence. The right to self-determination has not been accorded readily since the Second World War in non-colonial situations. Nonetheless, claims to self-determination have been made outside the context of decolonization that have been recognized and supported by the United Nations and by States individually.

In 1950, when the government in Beijing recognized the independence of the Mongolian People's Republic, this recognition ostensibly occurred "as a result of the referendum held in Outer Mongolia in 1945 which confirmed [the country's] desire for independence"[27] and, therefore, could be regarded as an implementation of self-determination. The creation of Bangladesh is a good example of a successful assertion and exercise of the right to self-determination, which was promptly recognized both by the United Nations and by individual States.[28] In Eritrea, Tibet, and Portuguese Timor the United Nations explicitly recognized the people's right to self-determination but has been unsuccessful in engendering its implementation.[29] A recent outstanding example is also the explicit recognition by the United Nations and many individual States of the "inalienable right" of the Palestinian people to self-determination. If any doubts remained with regard to the general acceptance of the right to self-determination as a legally enforceable right, they were removed by the wording and frequency of Security Council and General Assembly resolutions on the question of Palestinian rights.[30]

A recent reaffirmation of the universal right to self-determination of peoples is contained in the Helsinki Declaration, which stipulates, in part: "By virtue of the principle of equal rights and self-determination of peoples, all peoples always have the right, in full freedom, to determine, when and as they wish, their internal and external political status, without external interference, and to pursue as they wish their political, economic, social and cultural development."[31]

It is evident that the right to self-determination is not absolute. Where it conflicts with other rights or principles recognized by international law, a process of balancing these rights and their underlying values must take place. The emphasis placed by the United Nations on the right to self-determination in the context of human rights is significant in this respect.[32] The United Nations considers the right to self-determination to be a fundamental "collective right, appertaining to all peoples and nations, and . . . a prerequisite of the enjoyment of all the rights and freedoms of the individual."[33] It is with this understanding that the conflicting principles and rights should be viewed. This is particularly true when, at times, the right of self-determination conflicts with the principle of territorial integrity. As neither is absolute, neither should be dogmatically applied; rather, they should be seen as a pair of complementary opposites subservient to the concern for human rights and dignity.[34]

The Declaration on Principles of International Law cautions that the right to self-determination should not be construed

> as authorizing or encouraging any action which would dismember or impair, totally or in part, the territorial integrity or political unity of sovereign and independent States conducting themselves in compliance with the principle of equal rights and self-determination of peoples as described above and thus possessed of a government representing the whole people belonging to the territory without distinction as to race, creed or colour.[35]

Thus, in deciding the legitimacy of a claim to self-determination, the reasonableness test must be taken as the determining factor.[36] The critical questions are whether the people's disidentification with the larger unit, of which it politically forms a part, is real and whether its demands are compatible with basic community interests. The determining factors in resolving such claims are, therefore, (1) the nature and extent of the common characteristics and values of a people and of their disidentification with the dominant group; (2) the stability of expectations and extent of public support; (3) the viability of the anticipated end and its compatibility with the dominant group's vital interests and those of the region and world community as a whole; and, above all, (4) its contribution to the furtherance of human rights and dignity.

The common values of a people are the product of its common characteristics, traditions, and history. The more cohesive the group and the greater the intensity of disidentification with the dominant group, the more reasonable the claim for self-determination and the greater the need to honor it.

Stability of expectations, defined as the relationship between a people's expectations and its past and present situation, enables a projection of how reasonable and persistent these expectations will be in the immediate and long-range future.[37] Clearly, the isolated demand for self-determination, bearing no relation to past experience and having no foreseeable continuity, cannot carry the weight of one that does. Similarly, such a demand carries little weight when it originates and is supported only by a small segment of the population.

The viability of the political units that emerge from the exercise of self-determination and their compatibility with regional and world community interests must also be considered. The size of territory and population are irrelevant in this regard, but there are no clear-cut rules. The most one can say is that the concentration of a people whose members constitute a clear majority of the population within a particular area may significantly contribute to the viability of independent existence.[38]

The people exercising self-determination must also project an identity compatible with the dominant, or ruling, group's interest, such that the latter also remains a viable unit. In addition, the new situation should contribute to rather than disrupt world and regional peace and order.

Self-determination is increasingly being recognized as both a fundamental human right and a prerequisite to the enjoyment of other human rights and freedoms. Thus, the Declaration on the Granting of Independence, cited earlier, reads, in part: "The subjection of Peoples to alien subjugation, domination and exploitation constitutes a denial of fundamental human rights, is contrary to the Charter of the U.N. and is an impediment to the promotion of World peace and co-operation."[39]

Deprivation of human rights of a people and non-compliance with the principle of equal rights and discrimination are important grounds for the exercise of the right to self-determination. In fact, although there is some disagreement among jurists with respect to circumstances under which the right can be exercised, it is generally agreed that "if one of the constituent peoples of a state is denied equal rights and is discriminated against, . . . their full right of self-determination will revive."[40]

On 20 December 1961, the United Nations General Assembly passed a resolution calling, *inter alia*, "for the cessation of practices which deprive the Tibetan people of . . . their right to self-determination."[41] From the debates leading up to its adoption, it is evident that the resolution was primarily based on Articles 1 and 55 of the U.N. Charter, on the Universal Declaration of Human Rights and on the Declaration on Granting Independence to Colonial Countries and Peoples.[42]

The approximately 6 million Tibetans inhabiting the Tibetan plateau are a distinct race or ethnic group with their own language, culture, religion, and historical heritage. Although each of the neighboring civilizations in India, China, Mongolia and Nepal had their effect on Tibetan life, culture, and history, "whatever was borrowed from outside was adopted to suit local conditions and the native Tibetan character and mentality, with a result that remains strikingly original and homogenous."[43] Thus, "there can be no doubt as to the distinct characteristics of the Tibetan race, language, religion, culture, historical development, and political structure from that of any other country."[44] The Chinese, commenting on a statement made by the Dalai Lama, declared: "The statement, does . . . enunciate a truth: The Tibetans are different from the Hans [i.e., Chinese]."[45] Most important, the Tibetans have throughout history considered themselves as one people, distinct from any of the neighboring peoples.

The common characteristics and background of the Tibetan people not only helps prove peoplehood; they also go a long way toward suggesting the reasonableness and legitimacy of their claim for self-determination. The history of the Tibetans and their continued resistance to domination by the Chinese, as evidenced by popular uprisings, underground resistance movements, and protracted guerrilla activity illustrate the people's extreme and real disidentification with the dominant Chinese group. Their disidentification is based both on the many differences of the two distinct peoples and on the incompatibility of these differences—in particular, their religious and ideological values, considered of paramount importance by both peoples.[46]

Only a plebiscite would conclusively establish the extent of popular support for the claim of self-determination in Tibet. But, as was shown in the previous chapter, among the overwhelming majority of Tibetans inside and outside Tibet, strong feelings of nationalism, expressed in terms of loyalty to the Dalai Lama and demands for Tibetan independence, are abundantly evident.

The stability of expectations can be assumed from Tibet's past and recent history. The Tibetans have governed themselves for centuries and have always shown a strong dislike for foreign intervention. Their demand for self-determination is therefore aimed at regaining what was lost rather than at creating a new situation with unforeseeable consequences.

The Tibetan claim poses few problems in terms of the country's geographic and economic viability, as the existence of an independent State of Tibet, which functioned adequately prior to the 1950 invasion, goes a long way toward proving viability. Certainly, its striking natural borders only enhance the viability of the State. The tremendous mineral resources of the Tibetan plateau, as well as the traditional farming and trading, and perhaps even tourism, would also give Tibet a viable economy in the twentieth century.[47] The success of the Tibetan community in exile, particularly as compared to the lack of progress in Tibet under the Chinese, supports this conclusion.

China's strategic interest in Tibet is clear from the geography of the region and the heavy Chinese military concentration.[48] Undoubtedly, Tibet contributes to China's military security. And the economic interest, though of some significance, is at least partly offset by the tremendous cost of maintaining the PLA forces in Tibet and is not of great importance to China's overall economy. Neither of these two interests are vital to China's continued existence or viability, and various arrangements between an independent Tibet and China could satisfactorily ensure the latter's security interests. Moreover, the existence of a large independent State of Tibet in Central Asia could well be in the best interests of India and Nepal, and would contribute to the stability and peace of the area rather than endangering it.[49]

In 1959, 1961, and again in 1965, the United Nations General Assembly passed resolutions expressing "grave concern" over the "violation of fundamental human rights of the Tibetan people" and the suppression of the distinctive cultural and religious life and autonomy that the Tibetans had traditionally enjoyed.[50] The most complete of these resolutions declared, in part:

The General Assembly, . . .

> *Gravely concerned* at the continuation of events in Tibet, including the violation of the fundamental human rights of the Tibetan people and the suppression of the distinctive cultural and religious life which they have traditionally enjoyed,
> *Noting with deep anxiety* the severe hardships which these events have inflicted on the Tibetan people, as evidenced by the large-scale exodus of Tibetan refugees to the neighboring countries,
> *Considering* that these events violate fundamental human rights and freedoms set out in the Charter of the United Nations and the Universal Declaration of Human Rights, including the principle of self-determination of people and nations, and have the deplorable effect of increasing international tension and embittering relations between the peoples. . . .

> 2. *Solemnly renews* its call for the cessation of practices which deprive the Tibetan people of the fundamental Human Rights and freedoms, including their right to self-determination;
> 3. *Expresses the hope* that Member States will make all possible efforts, as appropriate, towards achieving the purposes of the present resolution.[51]

In 1960, the International Commission of Jurists found, after an extensive investigation, "that acts of genocide had been committed in Tibet in an attempt to destroy the Tibetans as a religious group, and that such acts are acts of genocide independently of any conventional obligation."[52] The Commission also came to the conclusion that the Chinese authorities in Tibet had violated sixteen articles of the Universal Declaration of Human Rights.[53] Since these findings were published, and since the United Nations Resolutions were passed, violations of human rights in Tibet have continued. In the past twenty-five years, the Chinese have carried out a harsh and ruthless policy in Tibet, with the manifest purpose of eradicating the Tibetan political entity as well as its cultural, religious and ethnic personality.[54] Thus, the Tibetans have been denied equal political rights, they have been severely restricted in their right to travel, and they have been granted no freedom of expression. Thousands of people have been sent to prisons and labor camps, and many have been executed for alleged anti-Chinese activities.[55] Some Tibetans have been forced to marry Chinese. Food has been confiscated and rationed, and religious persecution has been intensive.[56] Alexander Solzhenitsyn has described the communist Chinese regime in Tibet as "more brutal and inhuman than any other communist regime in the world."[57] Since that regime recently introduced some liberalization, conditions in Tibet have improved somewhat. Nevertheless, Tibetans are still deprived of many fundamental human rights and freedoms, including religious and political freedoms, and are treated as second-class citizens in a manner typical of all colonial regimes.[58]

Conclusion

Irrespective of the independent legal status of Tibet, the Tibetans as a people unquestionably have the right to self-determination, and their demand to exercise that right is both justified and reasonable.

This was the shared opinion of the Member States of the United Nations, when they called for the implementation of the Tibetan people's right to self-determination and declared the continual denial thereof to be a violation of the United Nations Charter and the Universal Declaration of Human Rights.[59]

Toward a Solution

On the basis of both the Tibetan people's right to self-determination and Tibet's past and present legal status, the Tibetans unquestionably have the right to resume sovereignty over their territory, to independently determine their future political status, and to freely pursue their economic, social, and cultural development. What the future status of Tibet should be, and what economic and social system would be most appropriate is a question that would best be left to the Tibetan people themselves to determine—for example, by means of a plebiscite.

It is unlikely, however, that the Government of the People's Republic of China could, under the present circumstances, be persuaded to unconditionally comply with the demands of international law in this regard. China's stand was reiterated recently by Yang Jingren, head of the CCP's United Front Work Department, who stated: "It will never do for anyone to play with the idea of an independent Tibet."[60] It is certainly conceivable, however, that China may eventually find it advantageous to reconsider its stand on the question of Tibet's future status in favor of one that is more acceptable to the Tibetans.

Some indication already does exist that the leaders in Beijing desire to come to an understanding with the Dalai Lama and his exiled government, and that both sides are indeed hopeful of bringing about a rapprochement. In 1979, a Tibetan delegation traveled to Tibet on a fact-finding mission. Two more delegations toured Tibet in the year that followed. These unprecedented contacts were followed by four rounds of discussions between a Tibetan cabinet-level delegation and senior Chinese officials in Beijing between April and June 1982. Unlike the earlier Tibetan visitors, the purpose of these envoys "was not to obtain facts, but to tackle the real business," according to the Dalai Lama.[61] The talks were exploratory in nature, and the delegates did not enter into substantive negotiations. They paved the way, however, for a second round of talks, held at the end of 1984.[62]

Following these negotiations, both sides released a statement clarifying their respective positions. The Chinese statement conveys the impression that the Tibetan issue principally concerns the Dalai Lama's return to Tibet. It includes a five-point proposal,[63] of which the first two points contain the reassurance that China has entered "a new stage of long-term political stability" and the stipulation that "there should be no more quibbling over the events in 1959." Under the third point, the Dalai Lama and exiled Tibetans are encouraged to live in the PRC, "based on the hope that they will contribute to upholding China's unity and promoting solidarity between the Han and Tibetan nationalities." Point four reads: "The Dalai Lama will enjoy the same political status and living conditions as he had before 1959. It is suggested that he not go to live in Tibet or hold local posts there."

When Yang Jingren made these proposals public, he added a clear warning against anyone raising the question of Tibetan independence.[64] The Tibetan statement sets forth the basic terms of an eventual resolution acceptable to the exiled government. After opening with a reminder of the international nature of the Tibetan issue, the statement stipulates, in part: "First and foremost, the Chinese Government must accept the separate historical identity of Tibet and the right of the Tibetan people to self-determination and the unification of the entire Tibetan area known as *Chol-Kha-Sum* [i.e., the three provinces: U-Tsang, Kham and Amdo]."[65] The statement then concedes that "for the mutual benefit of the Tibetans and the Chinese, the establishment of a special relationship or alliance on equal footing could be explored"; it also proposes that the whole of Tibet be transformed into a "zone of peace." In their reply to the five-point Chinese proposal, the Tibetans stated that the Dalai Lama's residence in Beijing would be "totally unacceptable to the Tibetan people and . . . against Tibet's historical tradition."

Upon the delegates' return to India, the Dalai Lama described the discussions as beneficial from a "human relations point of view" and expressed the hope that the maintenance of contacts between his government and that of the Chinese, desired by both parties, would eventually lead to a solution.[66]

At the time of this writing, little, if any, headway has been made toward resolution of the fundamental question concerning the future status of Tibet and the nature of future relations between that country and China. A number of alternatives have been suggested at one time or another, either within the existing framework of the PRC or outside of it. Given the status and rights of the Tibetan people, the future status of Tibet could take on one of three (forms as suggested by the United Nations General Assembly classification): (a) actual reemergence of Tibet as a sovereign independent State; (b) free association with an independent State; or (c) integration with an independent State.[67] Here, three viable alternatives corresponding to this classification will be summarily reviewed (in reverse order) as an indication of the range and diversity of options available to Tibet.

In the absence of any change in either the structure of the Chinese State or the formal claims of China over Tibet, the Tibetans should, at the very least, be granted actual, rather than merely nominal, autonomy. The term "autonomy" is often used in a restrictive sense, to mean only cultural or religious autonomy. It should here be understood to mean general political or governmental autonomy—that is, self-government, as well as cultural, religious, and economic autonomy.

Generally, self-government or governmental autonomy refers to the actual, as well as formal, independence of the autonomous entity in its political decisionmaking process on the internal or domestic level. Foreign affairs and defense are normally in the hands of the central, or national, government. In some cases, however, the power to conclude international agreements concerning cultural or economic matters may also reside with the autonomous entity.[68] In the People's Republic of China, this kind of autonomy is made possible in the Constitution—not under the general provisions regulating the administration of "National Autonomous Areas" but under Article 31, which allows for the establishment of "special administrative regions when necessary."[69]

The significance of Article 31 has become evident with the adoption of the "important state policy of 'one country, two systems'"[70] and, more specifically, in that policy's implementation with regard to Hong Kong and Taiwan. The Sino-British Joint Declaration on the question of Hong Kong, of 18 December 1984, and the nine-point proposal for the reunification with Taiwan, made public on 30 September 1981, both envisage a high degree of governmental autonomy for the respective regions, even though, as Deng Xiaoping has warned, "complete autonomy is simply out of the question, [for] 'complete autonomy' means 'two Chinas', not one China."[71] The Central Government recognizes the right of the local government of Taiwan and Hong Kong to determine and administer their own internal policies and to maintain different (i.e., capitalist) social and economic systems. These special administrative regions are to be allowed to keep their own judicial systems and separate executive and legislative organs. According to the declarations made with respect to Hong Kong and Taiwan, those regions may maintain independent international economic and cultural relations, and enter into agreements with States and international organizations in those fields. Taiwan may even keep its own armed forces "so long as they do not constitute a threat to the mainland."[72] The Central Government, moreover, pledged to station neither its own troops nor administrative personnel in Taiwan.[73]

The Chinese press claims that any thought of granting Tibet a similar special administrative zone status is out of the question. As Tibet was "reunified" with China over three decades ago, so the argument goes, the special zone system cannot apply as it does to regions yet to be reunified.[74] Most Tibetans reject the idea because such an arrangement would not go far enough and, more specifically, because Tibet would still be regarded as an integral part of China. They also argue that their situation is wholly different from that of either Taiwan or Hong Kong, for although those areas have political, social, and economic systems different from those of the mainland, their populations, with the exception of the native minority on Taiwan, are Chinese and there is no fundamental disagreement over the notion that they are part of China.[75]

The PRC's rejection of the special administrative zone formula for Tibet has been interpreted in Taiwan to suggest that the nine-point proposal the Beijing government offered Taipei is "just a transitional policy to entice Taiwan to unify with the PRC."[76] President Chiang Ching-kuo [Jiang Jingguo] called on the people of the Republic of China to regard the tragedy of Tibet as an objective lesson in dealing with Beijing's peace overture.[77] Officials in Taiwan recall that the communist government concluded an agreement to respect the autonomy of Tibet in 1951 and then proceeded to take complete control.[78] Hungdah Chiu concludes that "after unification, the terms [of the nine-point proposal] could easily be nullified and Taiwan turned into another Tibet, i.e., under tight control of the PRC with autonomy in name only."[79] In Hong Kong also, the experience of Tibet was used by opponents of the Anglo-Chinese Joint Declaration to support their contention that the PRC could not be trusted to honor their agreements.[80]

There is an indication that the leadership in Beijing may be prepared to modify its stand. An article published in the 26 August 1985 issue of the Beijing publication *Liaowang* contains an excerpt of a speech by a "leading comrade" of the Chinese Communist Party Central Committee. This speech states in part:

> There are two kinds of special zones in [the PRC]: one is in the coastal areas and another is in Tibet. Special zones should be run in a special way. In all our work we should proceed from Tibet's special features and adopt special policies and flexible measures. The special characteristics of Tibet find expression in the following two aspects: first, it is most special in that it is more special than not only the other provinces but also the Inner Mongolia and Xinjiang national autonomous regions. Secondly, these special characteristics have been formed over the years, will go on for a very long time, and will not disappear in a short time.[81]

What the acknowledgment of Tibet's "special status" might entail in practical terms is not clear from the article. What it does suggest, however, is that there is room for negotiation on substantive aspects of autonomy.

The granting of a high degree of formal as well as actual autonomy to Tibet, if accompanied by effective guarantees, would undoubtedly represent a substantial improvement over the present state of affairs. It would be lawful, however, only if this autonomy were granted in accordance with the principle of self-determination, as emphasized in Principle 9 of General Assembly Resolution 1541 of 1960:[82]

> (b) The integration should be the result of the freely expressed wishes of the territory's people acting with full knowledge of the change in their status, their wishes having been expressed through informed and democratic processes,

impartially conducted and based on universal adult suffrage. The United Nations could, when it deems it necessary, supervise these processes.

Resolution 1541 is particularly instructive because it was adopted on the same day as the historic Declaration on the Granting of Independence to Colonial Countries and Peoples, referred to earlier. Hence it can be viewed as an authoritative explanation of the lawful means of granting independence.[83]

An arrangement that would be far more satisfactory to the Tibetans, while still safeguarding China's primary interests, is the free association relationship, also explained in the 1960 Resolution.

The concept of association is legally acceptable and realistic in that it recognizes the fundamental legal principle of sovereign equality of States while taking account of the factual inequalities among them.[84] Where two States of unequal power establish formal and durable links, their relationship may be regarded as one of "association": "A relationship of association in contemporary international law is characterized by recognition of the significant subordination of and delegations of competence by one of the parties (the associate) to the other (the principal) but maintenance of the continuing international status of statehood of each component."[85] The critical factors in determining the international lawfulness of a relationship of association are enumerated in Principle 7 of Resolution 1541:

(a) Free association should be the result of a free voluntary choice by the peoples of the territory concerned expressed through informed and democratic processes. It should be one which respects the individuality and the cultural characteristics of the territory and its peoples, and retains for the peoples of the territory which is associated with an independent State the freedom to modify the status of that territory through the expression of their will by democratic means and through constitutional processes.

(b) The associated territory should have the right to determine its internal constitution without outside interference, in accordance with due constitutional processes and the freely expressed wishes of the people. This does not preclude consultations as appropriate or necessary under the terms of the free association agreed upon.

The important features of free association can accordingly be listed as follows: (1) the relationship must be a consensual one between two sovereign States, and the terms must be clearly and fully set down, in a form binding on the parties. The relationship is governed by international law; therefore, ongoing relations between the principal and the associate State are not a matter within the domestic jurisdiction of the former. (2) The association must be the result of a "free and voluntary choice" of the population of the associate State, expressed through informed and democratic methods. (3) The associate State retains international personality but delegates certain functions of government—generally, but not necessarily, the overall conduct of international relations and defense—to the principal. The former may nevertheless retain the competence to enter into international relations and conclude treaties with respect to specific areas of national interest, for example, in the domain of economic, cultural, educational, or scientific affairs. The associate can also be a member of international organizations concerned with these affairs and might even be a member of the United Nations. (4) The government and people of the associate State exercise full autonomy in their internal affairs free from intervention by the principal. They consequently adopt their own constitution and freely determine their social and economic systems. (5) Last, but not least, the people of the associate State always retain the right to modify the status of their territory, including the right to terminate the relationship of association altogether.[86]

Free association is very similar to the protectorate relationship, but there is one important distinction: The emphasis that contemporary international law places on the popular will as determined by a plebiscite or an equally reliable mode of popular expression "indicates that dispositions of territorial communities can be effected lawfully only with the free and informed consent of the members of that community."[87]

James Crawford is of the opinion that "[a]ssociation represents one of the more significant possibilities of self-government for the future,"[88] and W. M. Reisman feels that "insufficient attention may have been given to the potential contribution of associate status to public order." Reisman adds: "Association involves a recognition of the political dependence of an entity, but at the same time an insistence on its continuing discrete identity under the international scrutiny accorded to all states. This becomes an increasingly important status for small states which find themselves in the comparatively uncontested sphere of one of the Great Powers."[89] Association arrangements have not been undividedly successful in the past, but, on balance, they have had a very positive impact on the movement of the emancipation of nations.[90]

The conclusion of an agreement of association between Tibet and the PRC would fulfill the basic requirements of both States and fully accord with the demands of international law. Tibet would thereby resume the exercise of its sovereignty, but China could assume the desired degree of responsibility for Tibet's foreign relations and defense. What this would entail in concrete terms—for example, in terms of Chinese military presence in Tibet, Tibetan participation in international organizations, and any other delimitations of competences—is a matter that should be laid down in the binding agreement of association. The establishment of a free association relationship would have the added advantage that it bears significant similarities to the traditional Chö-yön (Priest-Patron) relationship entered into by Tibetan rulers with powerful neighbors in past history.

The most satisfactory resolution of the Sino-Tibetan question in the long run, however, would be, to paraphrase the first of the alternatives presented in General Assembly Resolution 1541, the reemergence of Tibet as a sovereign independent State in law and fact.

The reemergence and reconstruction of an independent Tibetan State need not run contrary to China's interests and could well have a decisively positive impact on the reduction of international tension and the promotion of peace and stability in Asia. There is, no doubt, more than one way to achieve this result, but the neutralization of Tibet would seem to be the most obvious as well as the most effective means of doing so.

Permanent neutrality can rest on the entirely independent decision of the State concerned, or it could be imposed upon that State by an international instrument, typically at the request or with the consent of the State so neutralized. Examples of the first category are the decisions of Iceland under the Dano-Icelandic *Forbundslov* of 30 November 1918 and of Honduras under the 1907 General Treaty of Peace and Amity between the Central American Republics. Austrian neutrality, though proclaimed by Austria unilaterally in 1955, was, in fact, a precondition for the treaty concluded by the four Great Powers to restore Austria's sovereign status. A good example of imposed neutrality is that of Switzerland, since 1815. The Swiss Confederation accepted the declaration by which the Great Powers of Europe, assembled at the Congress of Vienna, decided to recognize and guarantee the permanent neutrality of Switzerland.[91]

Substantively, the neutralized State is under obligation "not to engage in war, nor to enter into alliances, nor to act in a partial manner in favour of one State or group of States to the prejudice of another, either in view of possible future conflict or in the actual case of war."[92]

The geographical location of Tibet at the heart of Asia and its close proximity to the major powers of that continent make Tibet one of the most strategically placed countries of Asia, but also the ideal country for neutralization. The high tensions among China, India, and the Soviet Union could be considerably reduced if Tibet were permanently neutralized. The Chinese would no longer be constrained to keep close to a half-million troops in Tibet, and the Indians could greatly reduce their armed forces. As Tibet would certainly not pose a threat to those powers, India's northern frontier and much of China's western frontier would be unexposed to outside threat. Tibet could join Switzerland and Austria in fulfilling the important task of hosting international organizations and promoting international negotiation and reconciliation. Finally, the transformation of Tibet into such a zone of peace would, more than any other solution, fulfill the desire of the Tibetans both to govern themselves and to play a meaningful role in advancement of world peace.

Conclusion

This much is clear: that the present state of affairs is both unsatisfactory in terms of the promotion of friendly international and regional relations and peace, and distressing in terms of the disregard for human rights and dignity. Furthermore, China's continued presence in Tibet constitutes a serious violation of international law.

The maintenance of the *status quo* in the "Land of Snows," as the Tibetans refer to their country, is clearly not a goal to be pursued. The goal is, instead, the promotion and fulfillment of the requirements for a dignified existence of all peoples in and around Tibet. As John Stuart Mill wrote over a century ago, "One hardly knows what any division of the human race should be free to do, if not to determine, within which of the various collective bodies of human beings they choose to associate themselves."[93]

Notes

Notes to Chapter 1

1. A Sino-Tibetan glossary from Dunhuang attests that the Tibetan term "Tsanpo" (*btsan-po*) meant emperor. The glossary translates the term as *tianzi* (Wade-Giles: *t'ien-tzu*) or "son of heaven," a Chinese expression reserved only for the emperor. See P. Pelliot, *Histoire Ancienne du Tibet* (Paris, 1961), p. 143. E. Sperling further notes that "in the Tibetan text, the Chinese emperor is often referred to as just the lord of China, while the Tibetan emperor is always noted as being the emperor, *btsan-po*. In the Chinese text the Tibetan ruler is always referred to in Chinese as the *tsan-p'u* which is simply a transcription of the Tibetan word *btsan-po*." See E. Sperling, "The Status of Tibet According to Tibetan and Chinese Sources," *Tibetan Messenger* 9, No. 1 (1980), p. 12.

2. For discussions of this treaty, see H.E. Richardson, "The Sino-Tibetan Treaty Inscription of A.D. 821/823 at Lhasa," JRAS, No. 2 (1978), pp. 137–162; Fang-kuei Li (F. Li), "The Inscription of the Sino-Tibetan Treaty of 821–822," *T'oung Pao* 44 (1956), pp. 1–99. Because the treaty-signing ceremony was first held in Chang'an in 821, and then in Lhasa in 822 or 823, this treaty is generally referred to as the 821/823 treaty.

3. The first treaty was signed around A.D. 705/710. Treaties were also concluded in 730, 756, 765, 766, 783, and 784. See Tieh-tseng Li (T. Li), *Tibet: Today and Yesterday* (New York, 1960), p. 7. Important treaties are those of 730 (Pelliot, pp. 19–21) and 783, which established the boundaries between China and Tibet (Pelliot, pp. 41–46). The 783 boundaries are presumed to be the ones to which the Treaty of 821 referred (F. Li, "Inscriptions," p. 7).

4. The latter treaties were concluded around 750–754 and 810, respectively. See W. Wood, *A History of Siam from Earliest Times to the Year A.D. 1781* (London, 1926), pp. 33; L. Petech, *A Study on the Chronicles of Ladakh* [hereafter, *Chronicles*] (Calcutta, 1939), p. 78.

5. The "maternal uncle" or rather "father-in-law" (Tib. *Zhang-po*) and "nephew" or rather "son-in-law" (Tib. *dBon-zhang*) relationship evidently refers to the marriage of two Chinese princesses to Tibetan emperors: Wen Cheng to Songtsen Gampo in 641 and Jin Cheng to Tride Tsugtsen in 710. F.W. Thomas writes that in a polyandrous country, the position of "uncle" has special aspects not necessarily denoting the existence of an actual nephew and uncle relationship. He compares it to the use of "cousin" in Old English. See F.W. Thomas, *Tibetan Literary Texts and Documents Concerning Chinese Turkestan* (London, 1951), Vol. 2, pp. 5–6.

6. For the full text of this treaty, see Appendix 1.

7. For the full text of this edict, see Richardson, "Treaty Inscription," pp. 140–148.

8. The Dunhuang Annals are the most important and reliable Tibetan history of the period. See primarily J. Bacot, F.W. Thomas, and C. Toussaint, *Documents*

de Touen-Houang Relatifs a l'Histoire du Tibet (Paris, 1940) [hereafter, Documents de Touen-Houang]; see also F.W. Thomas and S. Konow, Two Medieval Documents from Tun-Huang (Oslo, 1929); L. Petech, "Glosse agli Annali di Tun-Huang," Rivista degli Studi Orientali 42, Fasc. 3 (1967). Other Tibetan chronicles include G.N. Roerich, The Blue Annals, a translation of Bod-kyi yul-du chos-dan chos-smra-ba ji-ltar byun-ba'i rim-pa Deb-ther sngon-po, or "The Blue Annals, the Stages of the Appearance of the Doctrine and Preachers in the Land of Tibet" [hereafter, Blue Annals], 2nd ed. (Delhi, 1976). The Jiu Tang Shu (Old History of the Tang), Chs. 196A and 196B, and the Xin Tang Shu (New History of the Tang), Chs. 216A and 216B, constitute the official Chinese record of recognized authority; for translations, see Pelliot, Histoire Ancienne du Tibet.

9. Pelliot, p. 77 [translated by M. Lutz].

10. In fact, Songtsen Gampo's father, Namri Songtsen (also known as Trisongtsen, ca. 602–609), started the unification of Tibet, although he was probably little more than the head of a tribal confederation. It was Songtsen Gampo and the later emperor, Trisong Detsen, who centralized, consolidated, and expanded the power.

11. For accounts of Tibetan conquests to the north, see the "Saka Document" in Thomas and Konow, pp. 131–160; see also Petech, "Glosse."

12. G. Tucci, "Deb t'er dmar po gsar ma: Tibetan Chronicles by bSod nams grags pa," Vol. 1, Serie Orientale Roma 24 (Rome, 1971), pp. 146–147. There has been some discussion as to the exact identity of the Nepalese Princess. See, for example, D.R. Regmi, Ancient Nepal (Calcutta, 1969), pp. 214–216. Following prolonged fighting between Tibet and China, the Chinese Emperor was persuaded to give a member of the Imperial family in marriage to the Tibetan sovereign (Documents de Touen-Houang, pp. 8–9).

13. Tucci, Deb t'er, p. 148. The Tibetans ultimately adopted the Indian school of Buddhism following a major religious debate, organized in the presence of the Tibetan Emperor between the Chan Buddhists of China and the Indian Kamalashila school, in 792–794. The losing Chinese were consequently forced to leave the country. See M. Tatz, "T'ang Dynasty Influences on the Early Spread of Buddhism in Tibet," The Tibet Journal 3, No. 2 (Summer 1978).

14. The Tang Annals and Dunhuang Documents record continuous Tibetan advances into China during the 740s and 750s. These advances were only briefly halted by peace treaties.

15. See the text of the inscription from the southern face of the stone pillar below the Potala in Appendix 2 of C.A. Bell, Tibet: Past and Present (1924; reprinted in [rpt.] Oxford, 1968), pp. 273–274.

16. The Chinese text of the 783 treaty is recorded in the Jiu Tang Shu, Ch. 196B, and is translated in Pelliot, pp. 43–45. The following extract conveys the essence thereof:

"The Tang formed matrimonial alliances with the Tibetan Tsanpo for generations. As neighbors, they built up a strong friendship; the two countries acted as one in time of both peace and danger. They were kingdoms closely linked through uncles and nephews—a system which lasted almost two hundred years. But generosity was at times forgotten in the name of petty grievances and the people acted in enmity. The border territories were so troubled that soon not one year passed peacefully. . . Envoys came and went, proclaiming the sovereign orders one after the other, preventing the people from carrying out treacherous schemes or using weapons of war. In order to determine once and for all what was essential to the two kingdoms, they proposed to revert to the alliance which had been agreed upon previously. In a commitment to ensure peace for the border inhabitants, the empire renounced its old territory; it abandoned its interests to pursue the goal of public well being, and solemnly swore to uphold the treaty. The empire's present borders are [a description of the Sino-Tibetan boundary follows.] As for those areas not mentioned in the alliance pact, the areas which contain Tibetan troops will remain occupied by the Tibetans; those areas which contain Chinese troops will continue to be occupied by the Chinese. In both cases, the new ownership status will be agreed upon so that trespassing is not necessary. In areas where there have as yet been no troops, none shall be placed, nor shall walls or entrenchments be constructed or developed." [translated by M. Lutz]. See also, F. Li, "Inscription," pp. 7–8.

17. W.D. Shakabpa, *Tibet: A Political History* (New Haven, 1967), pp. 51–61. See also G. Tucci, *Tibetan Painted Scrolls* [hereafter, TPS] (1949; rpt. Kyoto, 1980), pp. 3–7.

18. TPS, pp. 405; *Blue Annals*, pp. 60–62.

19. H. Hoffmann, *Tibet: A Handbook* (Bloomington, Indiana, 1977), p. 51.

20. F.W. Thomas, *Tibetan Literary Texts and Documents Concerning Chinese Turkestan*, Vol. 2, p. 417. Nepal shook off Tibetan overlordship by the beginning of the Nepalese calendar, *Nepal Samvat*, in A.D. 879. Note that the Nepalese historian D. R. Regmi argues that Nepal had done so earlier. See D.R. Regmi, *Medieval Nepal* (Calcutta, 1966), Vol. 1, p. 58. This view is shared by G. Jain, *India Meets China in Nepal* (Bombay, 1959), p. 88. Jain cites the year A.D. 702. See also S. Levy, *Le Nepal* (Paris, 1909), Vol. 2, pp. 158, 163, 173–177.

21. *Blue Annals*, p. 54.

22. J. Kolmas, *Tibet and Imperial China*, Australian National University Center of Oriental Studies, Occasional Paper No. 7 (Canberra, 1967), p. 12.

23. This conclusion is supported by the comparatively small space allotted to Tibet in the Chinese Dynastic histories of this period. In the *Ju Wudai Shi* (Old History of the Five Dynasties), the section on Tibet was reduced from two large chapters in each of the Tang histories to a section of less than one thousand Chinese characters. At the time, Tibet posed no threat to China, and much more attention was given to the Mongol tribes to the north who threatened invasion. See Kolmas, pp. 12–14. See also T. Li, *Tibet*, p. 15.

24. D. Sinor, *Inner Asia*, 2nd ed. (Bloomington, Indiana, 1971), p. 163.

25. Sinor, pp. 163–167, 169–174.

26. T.V. Wylie, "The First Mongol Conquest of Tibet Reinterpreted," *HJAS* 37, No. 1 (1977), pp. 103–133. The *dPag bSam lJon bZang* actually records that the Tibetan rulers separately submitted to different Mongol princes, who in turn became their particular patrons (TPS, p. 651).

27. Wylie, pp. 106–112. For a translation of the letter summoning Sakya Pandita, see D. Schuh, *Erlasse und Sendschreiben Mongolischer Herrscher fur Tibetische Geistliche*, Vol. 3, No. 1 of *Monumenta Historica Tibetica*, eds. D. Schuh et al. (St. Augustin, Germany, 1977), pp. 31–41.

28. For a summary of the agreement between Sakya Pandita and Prince Goden, see Schuh, p. xvii.

29. Translated by G. Tucci in TPS, p. 649.

30. Wylie, p. 119.

31. Ngawang Lobsang Gyatso [hereafter, Dalai Lama V], *Deb ther rdzogs ldan gzhou nu'i dga' ston* (Varanasi, India, 1967), p. 128. Mongol authority in Tibet is evidenced by the censuses that they conducted as well as by the military expedition that Kubilai Khagan sent (TPS, pp. 12–13).

32. P. Ratchnevsky, "Die Mongolischen Grosskhane und die Buddhistiche Kirche," *Asiatica* 32, pp. 493–494.

33. H. Franke, "Tibetans in Yuan China," in *China under Mongol Rule*, ed. J.D. Langlois, Jr. (Princeton, 1981), p. 306. The Mongol Emperors' concern for such legitimation was already evident in the name chosen for their dynasty. By choosing Yuan, a title derived from *Qianyuan*, "the original creative force" in the Book of Changes, they avoided the customary use of a place name, which would have reminded the Chinese subjects of the foreign origin of the regime of conquest (J.D. Langlois, "Introduction" to *China under Mongol Rule*, pp. 3–5).

34. For a translation of an extract from the *Yuan Shi* showing this relationship, see *TPS*, pp. 31–34.

35. See Franke, pp. 306–309.

36. The *Xuan Zheng Yuan* was a unique office that existed only under the Mongol Dynasty. For a discussion of the administration of Tibet at the time, see Franke, pp. 299–301; see also *TPS*, pp. 15–17, 31–39.

37. Franke, p. 302.

38. *TPS*, pp. 17–23, 637–638.

39. When the Yuan Dynasty collapsed, the Mongol ruling house did not disappear but moved north still intact. The Chinese clearly despised being ruled by the Mongol barbarians; the founder of the Ming, Zhu Yuanzhang, issued a proclamation asserting that Mongol rule was a cause for "shame." The edict is quoted in Wu Han, *Zhu Yuanzhang Zhuan*, pp. 128–130, and translated in H. Serruys, *The Mongols in China During the Hung-Wu Period* (Bruges, Belgium, 1959) pp. 44–45, 56–57. Modern historians of the PRC deny the "alien" character of the Yuan Dynasty, arguing that the Mongols are also a Chinese people.

40. *TPS*, p. 34.

41. *TPS*, p. 24.

42. Kolmas, pp. 27–28. The monographs on Tibet in the *Ming Shi* are placed in the section concerned with the "western regions," including places such as Samarkand, Bukhara, and other regions of the Timurid Empire (Sperling, "The Status of Tibet," p. 15).

43. *Ming Shi*, Ch. 331, translated in *TPS*, p. 685.

44. E. Sperling, "Did the Early Ming Emperors Attempt to Implement a 'Divide and Rule' Policy in Tibet?" Paper presented at the Csoma de Körös Symposium, Velm, Austria (Sept. 1981), pp. 3–13. The Chinese exerted some control in the frontier areas of the northeastern Tibetan region of Amdo. See *TPS*, p. 33. At the time, Chinese chroniclers complained that the Tibetans made great profits during missions that these chroniclers purported to be "tributary" in nature. See portions of the *Ming Shi* translated in *TPS*, p. 685, note 89; p. 689, note 141; pp. 692–693, note 255.

45. Sperling, "Early Ming Emperors," pp. 5–6.

46. Regarding Nepal; all the Kathmandu Valley Kingdoms in fact maintained diplomatic representatives (Nep. *Vakil*) and trade officers in Tibet. For a translation of the Nepalese Chronicle, or *Vansavali*, see D. Wright, ed. *History of Nepal* (1871; rpt. Kathmandu, 1972), pp. 177–178, 180, 211, 237. See also D.R. Regmi, *Medieval Nepal* (Calcutta, 1968), Vol. 2, pp. 454, 533. In the seventeenth century, a treaty between Tibet and Kathmandu, regulating trade and the treatment of Nepalese traders in Tibet, was reportedly concluded by Bhim Malla. See T.R. Manandhar, "Crisis with Tibet (1883–84)," *Voice of History* 3 (1977), p. 7. Regarding Kashmir, see P.N. Bamzai, *A History of Kashmir* (Delhi, 1962).

47. Unlike the older schools of Tibetan Buddhism (the Ningmapa, Sakyapa, and Kagyupa), the Gelugpa clergy used yellow instead of red monastic hats. The Gelugpa is consequently often referred to as the "Yellow Church." For details on the founding

of the Gelugpa and the line of Tsonkapa, see C.A. Bell, *The Religion of Tibet* (1931; rpt., Oxford, 1968), pp. 95–101.

48. C.A. Bell, *The Religion of Tibet*, pp. 108–109.

49. Z. Ahmad, "Sino-Tibetan Relations in the Seventeenth Century," *Serie Orientale Roma* 40 (Rome, 1970), pp. 85–99.

50. An exchange of titles actually took place. Sonam Gyatso received the title Dalai Lama Dorje Chang (the all-embracing or "Ocean" Lama, the holder of the Thunderbolt; Sanskrit: *Vajradhara*). In turn, he conferred on Altan Khan the title Chökyi Gyalpo Lhai Tsangpa Chenpo (The King-according-to-the-Faith, the Divine Maha-Brahman) (Shakabpa, p. 95). In a proclamation made by Altan Khan contained in the *dNgos-grub Shing-rta* (a biography of Sonam Gyatso), the Khan recalls that "the Buddhist religion first came to our country in the earlier times, when we gave our patronage to Skaya Pandita. . . . Your visit to us has helped the Buddhist religion to revive. Our relation of patron and Lama can be likened to that of the Sun and the Moon." (Shakabpa, p. 94).

51. Shakabpa, pp. 84–85.

52. See the passages of the *Ming Shi* translated in TPS, p. 255, note 97. One such passage states: "From this time the Western countries acknowledged themselves obedient to this monk."

53. TPS, p. 50.

Notes to Chapter 2

1. The first four Dalai Lamas could not be said to have been national leaders while the struggle with the Karmapa was unresolved.

2. G. Tucci, *Tibetan Painted Scrolls* [hereafter, TPS] (1949; rpt. Kyoto, 1980), p. 63.

3. Z. Ahmad, "Sino-Tibetan Relations in the Seventeenth Century," *Serie Orientale Roma* 40 (Rome, 1970), pp. 130–138.

4. L. Petech, *China and Tibet in the Early XVIIIth Century* (Leiden, 1972), pp. 236–237.

5. Initially the Desi was nominated by Gushri Khan, but not for long. See Petech, *China and Tibet*, pp. 8, 237. In actual fact, the Dalai Lama also controlled the troops and issued the orders for movements (Ahmad, pp. 147–149).

6. The Mongolians, for example, regularly petitioned the Dalai Lama to appoint and confirm Khans among them. The rulers of Nepal, Ladakh, and various Indian states sent envoys to the Dalai Lama (Ahmad, pp. 146–147).

7. The Manchus, a people related to the Mongols, were unified by Nurachi in the late sixteenth century. Under his successor, Tian Zong, they conquered the Korean State and the Chahar Mongols, and subsequently declared war on China in 1618. It was not until 1644, however, that the Manchus captured Beijing and established the Qing Dynasty. The conquest of China was not complete until the anti-Manchu rebellions had been put down in the southern and southwestern provinces of China (1674–1681).

8. O. Lattimore, *Studies in Frontier History* (New York, 1962), p. 77.

9. Lattimore shows that despite the widespread knowledge that "for twenty centuries or so China has been subject to barbarian conquests from the north . . . alternated with periods of Chinese recovery . . . [the] importance [of the barbarian conquests] is always neglected." The use of Chinese names for the dynasties (Wei, Tang, Liao, Jin, Yuan, and Qing) conceals the fact that they were founded by conquerors of China and not by the Chinese. Lattimore writes: "The importance

of these foreigners from beyond the Great Wall is that they ruled large parts of China, and sometimes the whole of it, for some 850 out of the last 1500 years. . . . We increase the illusion of the Chineseness of China by uncritical acceptance of the dogma that the Chinese absorb all their conquerors, but similarly, the barbarian, in barbarian territory, has absorbed or modified the Chinese as decisively as the Chinese has absorbed the barbarian within China." See *Studies in Frontier History*, pp. 76–77. For a good history of the origin of Manchu rule, see also F. Michael, *The Origin of Manchu Rule in China* (Baltimore, 1942).

10. Tai Zong sent the following letter: "Forgiving, Gentle, Magnanimous and Divine Emperor of the Great Ch'ing State sends this letter to the great Lama, who is an Upholder of the Buddhist Faith. We cannot bear to see suppressed the laws [i.e., the Buddhist Teachings] which have come down from ancient times. Neither do we wish that they should be extinguished without transmission to posterity. Therefore, we are sending specially envoys to invite [you], the high priest, in order to propagate the growth of the Buddhist Faith and to benefit all living beings." See *Da Qing Lichao Shilu* (The Veritable Records of the Great Qing Dynasty), translated in Ahmad, pp. 157–158; see also pp. 156–162.

11. The delegation's reception is recorded in the Chinese chronicle *Donghua Quanlu*, extracts of which are translated in W.W. Rockhill, "The Dalai Lamas of Lhasa and Their Relations with the Manchu Emperors of China, 1644–1908," *T'oung Pao* 11 (1910), pp. 9–13, 17. See also Ahmad, pp. 176–177.

12. His authority did not extend westward beyond the provinces of China proper, and little or no contact existed with the Mongols at this time. See K.M. Pannikar, *Asia and Western Dominance* (London, 1959), p. 61.

13. For a discussion of the Chinese and Tibetan sources regarding this invitation, see Rockhill, p. 13.

14. In particular, see the autobiography of the Fifth Dalai Lama, *Du ku la'i gos-bzang*, Vol. 1; *Donghua Lu* (the annals of the reigns of the Qing emperors, arranged chronologically); and the *Qing Shilu* ("Veritable Records" or "Complete Annals") of the Qing Dynasty).

15. See Ahmad, pp. 176, 178. It is clear from the correspondence between the Dalai Lama and the Manchu Emperor that Shun Zhi had actually decided to travel beyond the Great Wall to Taika, to await the Dalai Lama there. See the letter from Shun Zhi to the Dalai Lama in Ahmad, p. 170. Upon the advice of the Chinese members of his court, the Emperor finally decided to travel a lesser distance (Ahmad, pp. 168–177; Rockhill, pp. 15–18).

16. See Rockhill, p. 18. See also H.E. Richardson, *A Short History of Tibet* (New York, 1962), p. 45; C.A. Bell, *Tibet: Past and Present* (1924; rpt. Oxford, 1968), p. 36; H. Hoffmann, *Tibet: A Handbook* (Bloomington, Indiana, 1977), p. 57. But see also Tieh-seng Li (T. Li), *Tibet: Today and Yesterday* (New York, 1960), pp. 35–37; Wang Furen and Suo Wenqing, *Highlights of Tibetan History* (Beijing, 1984), pp. 93–94.

17. See in particular the accounts in Ahmad, pp. 166–191. That the Dalai Lama himself was highly aware of his sovereign status and the recognition thereof is clear from his account of the visit in his autobiography.

18. The Dalai Lama received the title "The very Virtuous, Bliss-abiding Buddha of the Western Heaven; the one Securer of Buddha's Word for all beings beneath the sky, the Immutable *Vajradhara* Dalai Lama" (*Nub kyi lha gnas ches dge ba bde par gnas pa'i sangs rgyas bka' lung gnam 'og gi skye 'gro thams ca d btsan pa gcid tu gyur pa 'gyur med rdo rje 'chang rgya mtsho bla ma*). In turn, the Emperor received the title "The Great Master, Spiritual one, Emperor of the Heavens, Manjusri Incarnate" (*Gnam gyi lha 'jam dbyangs gong ma bdag po chenpo*).

19. J. Kolmas, *Tibet and Imperial China*, Australian National University Center of Oriental Studies, Occasional Paper No. 7 (Canberra, 1967), p. 34.

20. See Ahmad, pp. 95–98.

21. D. Farquhar, "Emperor as Bodhisattva in the Governance of the Ch'ing Empire," *HJAS* 38, No. 1 (June 1978), pp. 5–34.

22. Rockhill, pp. 14–15, 18; M. Courant, *L'Asie Centrale aux XVIIe et XVIIIe Siecles* (Paris, 1912), pp. 24–25. It was feared that failure to properly greet the Dalai Lama might prevent the Mongols from submitting to the Emperor.

23. Ahmad, pp. 205–230; Rockhill, pp. 20–23.

24. Petech, *China and Tibet*, p. 9.

25. For a full text of this treaty, see Appendix 2. See also Ahmad, pp. 267–283; L. Petech, *A Study on the Chronicles of Ladakh* [hereafter *Chronicles*] (Calcutta, 1939), pp. 151–156.

26. *TPS*, pp. 68, 71, 73–75.

27. This is evident from a number of Imperial edicts, particularly those directed to the Depa denouncing conspiratorial relations with the Dzungars (Ahmad, pp. 305–309).

28. In 1703, the Qoshot Prince Lhazang took up the nominal office of Chökyi Gyalpo or Chögyal (*Chos-rgyal*) of Tibet, succeeding Gushri Khan, Tenzin Dalai Khan, and Dayan Khan. Not satisfied with this nominal role, however, Lhazang Khan sent his troops into Lhasa in 1706 with the approval, if not encouragement, of the Kangxi Emperor, who saw him as a valuable ally against the Dzungars. In fact, Kangxi recognized him as Tibet's ruler after the coup and bestowed on him the title "Religious, helpful, submissive Khan" (Rockhill, pp. 33–34).

29. Petech, *China and Tibet*, pp. 15–16; "Rappresentanza del 1738," in L. Petech, ed., *I Missionari Italiani nel Tibet e nel Nepal* [hereafter, *MITN*], *Il Nuovo Ramusio* 2 (Rome, 1952–1956), Vol. 3, p. 145; K. Dhondup, *Songs of the Sixth Dalai Lama* (Dharmsala, 1981), pp. 26–27. The Board of Dependencies in Beijing reported to the Emperor (29 Jan. 1707) that the Dalai Lama had died of a disease on his way to Beijing (Ahmad, p. 332). The popular belief was that he was murdered or executed by the Chinese ("Relazione del Padre F.O. della Penna," *MITN*, Vol. 3, p. 62).

30. Ngawang Yeshe was a young monk from Lhasa's medical college. Some believed him to be Lhazang's own son (*TPS*, p. 78). For the life of the Sixth Dalai Lama, see Dhondup, pp. 1–35.

31. Rockhill, p. 37. As the administrative official, He Shou, remained in Tibet only from 1709–1711 and was not replaced, the opinion expressed by some that he was in fact the first in the line of Manchu Residents in Tibet is inaccurate. See Petech, *China and Tibet*, pp. 19–20. See also "Breve Relazione del P. Domenico da Fano," *MITN*, Vol. 3, p. 7.

32. See Rockhill, pp. 35–37. The child, Kelsang Gyatso (1708–1757), was discovered in Kham province in accordance with a prophecy of the deceased Sixth Dalai Lama (Dhondup, pp. 1, 27). See also "Relazione del Padre F.O. Della Penna," *MITN*, Vol. 3, pp. 62–63.

33. Petech, *China and Tibet*, pp. 32–34, 51–54. The attempt of the Dzungars to free the Dalai Lama from Kumbum and take him to Lhasa had failed after their army was defeated by the Manchus. See W. Heissig, "Ein Mongolischer zeitgenossicher Bericht uber den Oloteneinfall in Tibet und die Plunderung von Lhasa 1717," *Zeitschrift der Deutschen Morgenlandischen Gesellschaft* (1954), pp. 391–411. For descriptions of the Dzungar invasion, see the letter of P. Domenico da Fano dated 2 February 1719, in *MITN*, Vol. 1, pp. 114–115; Ippolito Desideri, "Notizie Della

Natura, Costume, e Governo Civile del Thibet" in *MITN*, Vol. 6, pp. 51–66. In addition, Desideri reported resistance to the Dzungars ("Notizie," pp. 64–66).

34. E. Haenisch, "Bruchstucke aus der Geshichte Chinas unter der Gegenwartigen Dynastie," *T'oung Pao* 12 (1911), p. 207; Hoffmann, p. 60.

35. See extracts from the *Donghua Lu* in Haenisch, pp. 375–377, 40, 421–422; and Emperor Kangxi's edict in Haenisch, pp. 392–395.

36. In 1718, the men who acted for the Dalai Lama made the initial request to the Manchu emperor for the Dalai Lama's protection and escort to Lhasa, and it is evident that the Dalai Lama and his court completely supported the Manchu military expedition (Petech, *China and Tibet*, pp. 69–73).

37. Ibid., p. 74. This provisional administration consisted of two Tibetan noblemen, two Khalka princes, and two Qoshot chiefs and was presided over by the Manchu commander, General Yan Xin (Desideri, *MITN*, Vol. 6, p. 75).

38. Petech, *China and Tibet*, pp. 78–80; Desideri, *MITN*, Vol. 6, pp. 75–76. Besides the four Kalons comprising the official Council, the Dalai Lama's father and Polhanas were highly influential informal members thereof.

39. Kolmas, pp. 40–41. The garrison was originally manned by 3,000 imperial troops, but by 1747 their number had been reduced to 100. Some 15,000 troops were temporarily sent to Tibet after the Civil War in 1727–1928 (ibid., pp. 40–55).

40. Petech, *China and Tibet*, pp. 81–82.

41. As a rule all higher officials sent to Tibet were Manchus. The Imperial representatives stationed in Tibet at the time were commonly addressed with the Manchu title "Amban," which, Petech explains, was "a mode of address more or less like His Excellency in Europe and had nothing to do with the office of the Imperial Resident, which was established only after the Civil War of 1727–1928, as expressly stated by the Chinese texts" (ibid., p. 87).

42. Some of these imperial orders, particularly those concerning internal matters, were ignored, however. For examples, see ibid., pp. 106–109, 113.

43. Ibid., pp. 95–98.

44. For an account of this civil war and the events leading up to it, see ibid., pp. 114–140.

45. See Documents 2, 3, 5, and 6 from the *Shih Zong Shi Lu* in ibid, pp. 265–266, 268–270. See also H.E. Richardson, "Ch'ing Dynasty Inscriptions at Lhasa," *Serie Orientale Roma* 47 (Rome, 1974), p. 21.

46. See Documents 1 and 7 in Petech, *China and Tibet*, pp. 264, 270; see also pp. 151–153.

47. Petech concludes that "the duties of the ambans consisted mainly in holding the command of the small garrison, ensuring communications with Peking and reporting to the Emperor the doings" of the Tibetan ruler (*China and Tibet*, p. 256). Richardson writes that although it was not their function to take part in the actual government of Tibet, the presence of the Ambans in command of a substantial escort "provided the Emperor with some assurance that if ever his advice on matters of policy should become necessary, it would be respected" (*A Short History*, p. 52). Kolmas also concludes that although the Manchu official's presence must have had some influence, the Tibetan administration was left unaffected and the Ambans were therefore little more than observers (*Tibet and Imperial China*, p. 43).

48. Since 1729 the Dalai Lama had been in East Tibet, where he was watched over and his movements restricted. A rescript, issued by the Emperor on 18 August 1734, was the first official justification for the exile. The Dzungar threat was given as the reason; but with stability restored by Polhanas, and the threat almost eradicated, there was little reason to prolong the exile (Petech, *China and Tibet*, pp. 173–174).

49. Ibid., p. 169.

50. Quoted in ibid., p. 238.

51. Gyume Namgyal's ambitions were obvious from a letter he wrote to the Emperor, requesting, among other things, the further reduction of the Amban's escort to 100 men (which the Emperor approved) and the return of those Tibetan territories annexed by the Kangxi Emperor (Richardson, *A Short History*, p. 56).

52. See Petech, *China and Tibet*, pp. 216–222; M. Klaproth, ed., "Description du Tubet," *Journal Asiatique* (August 1829), pp. 126–127.

53. Petech, *China and Tibet*, pp. 223–232, 238–239; Documents 11, 12, pp. 275–281. Petech also quotes passages from other Tibetan texts confirming the Dalai Lama to be sovereign in the temporal as well as spiritual affairs of Tibet.

54. Ibid., p. 256.

55. Hoffmann, p. 61. At the same time, Tibet's contacts with Christian missionaries became frequent. In fact, these Jesuit and Capuchin missionaries set up missions in Lhasa. See Richardson, *A Short History*, pp. 61–62; Petech, *MITN*, Vols. 1–6.

56. After 1646, numerous conflicts with Bhutan took place (1647, 1668, 1669, 1671, 1676, 1714, 1730). Bhutan's rulers sent regular missions to Lhasa until 1950. See W.D. Shakabpa, *Tibet: A Political History* (New Haven, 1967), pp. 113, 119, 122; TPS, pp. 68, 71, 73.

57. TPS, pp. 71, 73–75.

58. Rockhill, pp. 66, 69; M. Huc, *Recollections of a Journey Through Tartary, Thibet and China* (London, 1852), pp. 258, 261.

59. Richardson, *A Short History*, pp. 60, 68. This reduction of influence did not mean the end of Manchu interest in Tibet altogether. As the Qianlong Emperor (1736–1796) stated himself: "As the Yellow Church inside and outside [of China] is under the supreme rule of these two men [the Dalai Lama and the Panchen Lama], all the tribes bear allegiance to them. By patronizing the Yellow Church we maintain peace among the Mongols. This being an important task, we cannot but protect this religion." Quoted in Ramakant, *Nepal-China and India* (New Delhi, 1976), p. 7.

60. George Bogle was sent to Bhutan and Tibet in 1774. The purpose of his mission was described in his official appointment by Warren Hastings on 13 May 1774: "The design of your mission is to open up a mutual and equal communication of Trade between the inhabitants of [Tibet] and Bengal." C.R. Markham, ed., *Narratives of the Mission of George Bogle to Tibet, and of the Journey of Thomas Manning to Lhasa* (London, 1879), p. 6.

61. The Fifth Dalai Lama granted Lobsang Chöky Gyaltsen (1567–1662), who was his teacher and the abbot of Tashi Lhunpo, the title of Panchen Rinpoche and recognized him as the incarnation of Amitabha Buddha (Tibetan: Od-dpag-med). See TPS, pp. 72–73; Hoffmann, p. 58.

62. Markham, pp. 195–197, 207. In 1870, the Emperor's profound devotion was lavishly displayed during the Panchen Lama's visit, at the invitation of the Emperor, to his court. See the letter from the Qianlong Emperor to the Dalai Lama in Turner, pp. 443–448.

63. "General Report by Mr. Bogle on his Return from Tibet," in Markham, p. 195; see also pp. 45, 191–206. In addition, see Rockhill, pp. 46–47; S. Turner, *An Account of an Embassy to the Teshoo Lama, in Tibet* (London, 1830), pp. 363, 365.

64. Turner, pp. 253, 245, respectively.

65. Letter from Bogle to Hastings, 15 December 1774, in D.B. Diskalkar, "Bogle's Embassy to Tibet," *Indian Historical Quarterly* 9, No. 2 (June 1933), p. 424.

66. Markham, pp. 45, 148, 151; Turner, pp. 249, 253.

67. For discussions of the structure and importance of the trade relations between the Nepalese Kingdoms and Tibet, and between the Indian Kingdoms and Tibet, particularly in the seventeenth and eighteenth centuries, see L. Rose, *Nepal: Strategy for Survival* (Berkeley, 1971); S. Camman, *Trade through the Himalaya* (Princeton, 1951).

68. The terms of the treaty are summarized in P.R. Uprety, *Nepal-Tibet Relations, 1850–1930* (Kathmandu, 1980), pp. 21–22.

69. Ibid., p. 22.

70. Ibid.

71. Ibid., pp. 26–28; Markham, pp. 157–158.

72. A treaty (*gacha patra*) concluded in August 1775 in Kuti on the Tibet-Nepal border stipulated as follows: "(1) The rate of exchange between gold and silver would be either fixed jointly between the two governments or determined by the merchants, who would settle their own rates and conduct their own transactions. (2) Coins of the proper (i.e., traditional) alloy would be sent to Tibet by the Nepal government and accepted there. (3) The position of the Newari *Mahajans* (merchants) and shopkeepers in Lhasa should be unchanged. (4) The eastern and western *Madesh-parbat* (plains-mountains) routes to Tibet should be closed even for *Sanyasis* (Gosains), Indians, and merchants." See the summary in Rose, p. 32. Rose attributes the final outbreak of war to the great changes of political leadership in the region: The Panchen Lama had died, and the Dalai Lama reached majority; the Regent Bahadur Shah came to power in Nepal; and Hastings was replaced by Cornwallis in India (Rose, pp. 35–39).

73. The text based on records of the *Jaisi Kotha* (Tibet-China Relations Office) of the Nepal Foreign Ministry is reproduced in Y. Naraharinath, *Itihas Prakash ma Sandhi Patra Sangraha* (Kathmandu, 1966), Vol. 1, p. 20; for the Tibetan version, see Shakabpa, p. 161; for the Chinese version, see Rose, pp. 42–43. The Dalai Lama refused to pay the tribute "agreed" upon in the treaty. See C. Imbault-Huart, "Histoire de la Conquete du Nepal," *Journal Asiatique* 12 (1878), pp. 361, 363–364; Rockhill, p. 51.

74. Rose, pp. 53–54.

75. Ibid., pp. 54–55. No authoritative text of the treaty, which appears to have been embodied in a series of letters between the parties, is available. The terms listed here are based on a Nepalese version, the essence of which is in Naraharinath, *Itihas Prakas ma Sandhi Patra Sangraha*, Vol. 2. This version is used by Uprety (pp. 42–43) and Rose (p. 65). Shakabpa (p. 168) gives the terms as recorded by the Tibetan signatory Kalon Doring in his memoirs. A pillar commemorating the Manchu victory was erected by Amban He Lin in Lhasa; it said little about the treaty except that the Gorkhas submitted to the Emperor. For a text of the inscription, see Bell, pp. 275–278.

76. Uprety, pp. 43–44.

77. Rose, p. 73; Rockhill, p. 53; Kolmas, p. 47.

78. See Imperial Edict of February/March 1793, from the *Donghu Quanlu* in Rockhill, pp. 55–57. Tibetan affairs in Beijing were now entrusted to the *Li Fan Yuan*. This office, principally concerned with the administration of Eastern Turkestan and Mongolia, was created in 1638 by reorganizing a similar institution, the *Menggu Yamen* (Kolmas, p. 49).

79. See Imperial Edict in Rockhill, pp. 55–57.

80. Bell, pp. 52–53.

81. The accounts herein of the numerous travelers, including missionaries, to Tibet indicate that until then Tibet had not been a "closed" country.

82. The "big three" monasteries, Ganden, Sera, and Drepung, took the threat to the religion and institutions most seriously. See Shakabpa, p. 173. Note, however, that some Europeans did travel to Lhasa and reported that the Tibetans themselves did not profess the Manchu and Chinese principle of exclusion. They did confirm a widespread mistrust of the British, who were suspected of having helped the Gorkhas in the past war. Huc wrote that the Manchus were jealous of the foreigners' popularity in Tibet and feared the influence outsiders might one day acquire in Tibet (Huc, *Recollections*, pp. 255, 295).

83. Rockhill, p. 63; Rose, pp. 111–112.

84. D. Snellgrove and H.E. Richardson, *A Cultural History of Tibet* (New York, 1968), p. 226.

85. Rockhill, p. 63. The Emperor was clearly displeased and ordered future selections to be made in accordance with the Qianlong Emperor's edict. On the next occasion, the tenth incarnation of the Dalai Lama was also selected without regard to the decree. The Emperor's protest, however, caused the authorities to confirm their choice *pro forma* by means of the urn procedure.

86. Rose, pp. 111–112, 121.

87. M. Huc, *Decouverte du Thibet, 1845-1846* (1933), pp. 50–51 (translated from the French by M. Lutz). See also Huc, *Recollections of a Journey*, pp. 296–297.

88. Western accounts have incorrectly described the Tibetan Commander Shatra's forces as Chinese, when in fact they were exclusively Tibetan (Richardson, *A Short History*, p. 72; T. Li, p. 60).

89. For the full text of this treaty, see Appendix 3. In the version of the treaty published in C.V. Aitchison, *A Collection of Treaties, Engagements and Sanads Relating to India and Neighbouring Countries*, Vol. 14 (New Delhi, 1929), p. 15, there is a reference to the overlords of the Dogra Raja of Jammu and of the Dalai Lama. This version states that the parties "have arranged and agreed that relations of peace, friendship and unity between Sri Khalsaji and Sri Maharaj Sahib Bahadur Raja Gulab Singhji and the Emperor of China and the Lama Guru of Lhasa will henceforward remain firmly established forever." The treaty confirmed the boundary fixed by the previous treaty of 1683 between Tibet and Ladakh (Shakabpa, p. 79).

90. For the full text of this new treaty, see Appendix 4. See also the translation of the Tibetan original in Shakabpa, pp. 328–329.

91. Rose, pp. 108, 112, 122.

92. Ibid., pp. 108–116; Uprety, pp. 65–66.

93. The British, however, did allow Nepalese troops to pass through British territory to facilitate the invasion. See Secret Consultation No. 42, 27 Oct. 1854, Ramsay to Edmondstone, cited in Uprety, p. 68.

94. Uprety, p. 76; Rose, pp. 110–116. After the war, the Amban demanded to know whether the Nepalese had been at war with China or only with Tibet, and whether the Darbar still respected the Emperor (Rose, p. 117).

95. For the full text of the Nepalese version of this treaty, see Appendix 5. The treaty included two provisions to the effect that (1) The Tibetan government promised to make an annual *salami* (payment) of Rs. 10,000 to Nepal. (2) Nepal promised to come to the aid of Tibet, as far as possible, if it was attacked by a foreign power.

96. Rose, pp. 116–117.

97. For the Tibetan version of this treaty, translated by Bell, see Appendix 6. For a translation of the Nepalese version, see Aitchison, *A Collection of Treaties*, Vol. 14, pp. 49–50. A translation by O'Connor from the Tibetan version is in L/P&S/10/1078, 14 April 1910. The preamble's wording has been the subject of some discussion. Most translations of the treaty from the Tibetan and Nepali texts have

used the expression "the Emperor shall continue to be regarded with respect," but others have translated the same part as "the Emperor of China shall be obeyed by both states as before." Bell and O'Connor use the former phrasing, whereas Aitchison uses the latter. Rose states that the official Nepali text published in *Itihas Prakas*, Vol. 2 (Kathmandu, 1955), uses *"lai aghi dekhi mani aya Bamojim mane rahanu,"* which he translates as "will be respected (or honored) as he has been respected (or honored) in the past" and does not connote "shall be obeyed" (*Nepal: Strategy for Survival*, p. 117).

98. Translated in Bell, p. 279.

99. The Tibetans did not accept this interpretation; and they attempted to invoke the treaty twice: against the Manchus in 1910 and the Chinese in 1949–1950 (Rose, p. 117).

100. Article 5 of the Treaty reads: "Henceforth the Gorkha government will keep a high officer [of the Gorkha government], and not a Newar, to hold Charge at Lhasa." The *Vakil* (Ambassador, plenipotentiary, representative) at Lhasa was therefore no longer to be a representative of the trading community of Kathmandu (a Newar) but, rather, was to be a high civil or military officer of the Gorkha government and, hence, also of the ruling Gorkha aristocracy (a Bahadar). For official Nepalese references to this Bahadar, see A.S. Bhasin, ed., *Documents on Nepal's Relations with India and China, 1949–66* (New Delhi, 1970), p. 20, and Article 5 of the 1856 Treaty as reproduced on p. 21 of Bhasin.

101. Rose, p. 122.

102. For details on this period, see Uprety, pp. 91–103.

103. Rose, pp. 121–122.

104. Shakabpa, p. 190; Huc, *Decouverte*, pp. 50–51. In fact, the little interest shown Tibet in Beijing is reflected in the lack of Chinese documents relating to Tibetan affairs published between 1859 and 1877 (Rockhill, pp. 69–70).

105. Uprety, p. 119.

106. E. Sperling, "The Status of Tibet According to Tibetan and Chinese Sources," *Tibetan Messenger* 9, No. 1 (1980), p. 15.

Notes to Chapter 3

1. "Translation of a letter from Teshoo Lama to Warren Hastings," in S. Turner, *An Account of an Embassy to the Court of the Teshoo Lama, in Tibet* (London, 1800), pp. ix–xii; "Minute by Warren Hastings," 4 May 1774, and "Letter from Warren Hastings to the Court of Directors," n.d., in C.R. Markham, ed., *Narratives of the Mission of George Bogle to Tibet, and the Journey of Thomas Manning to Lhasa* (London, 1879), pp. 3–6. In 1772, the Bhutanese, under Deb Judhur Rajah, descended into the plains and overran Chooch Behar. Warren Hastings, the Governor of Bengal, sent forces to push them back into Bhutan. The Bhutanese appealed to the Panchen Lama, who in turn wrote to Hastings in an effort to mediate.

2. See "Appointment of Mr. Bogle," by Warren Hastings, 13 May 1774, in Markham, pp. 6–7; see also pp. 124–129, 167–168. The British also hoped that Tibet might help to solve Britain's conflicts with the Himalayan states (Markham, pp. 207–210).

3. "General Report by Mr. Bogle on his Return from Tibet," in Markham, pp. 195–197. In fairness, it must be said that trade did increase for a time as a result of Bogle's mission, and that the Panchen Lama was reported to have spoken in favor of opening communications to the Qian Long Emperor for the British.

4. Relations were established after the British defeated the Chinese in the Opium War of 1842.

5. Turner has noted that the Tibetans, being "little versed in the arts of war, and thinly scattered over a mountainous region, derive from their local situation their only means of defense against invaders; an advantage which they would inevitably lose, if they were to allow free passage through their territories" (Turner, p. v).

6. Such rumors were reportedly encouraged by the Manchus. See Turner, p. 440; H.E. Richardson, *A Short History of Tibet* (New York, 1962), p. 71; C.A. Bell, *Tibet: Past and Present* (1924; rpt. Oxford, 1968), p. 45.

7. The Commercial Treaty between the East India Company and Nepal, in 1792, reopened the trade route through Nepal to Tibet. The Treaty of Segauli, in March of 1816, was concluded at the close of the Nepal-British War. For an account of British aid to the Gorkhas, see P.R. Uprety, *Nepal-Tibet Relations, 1850-1930* (Kathmandu, 1980), p. 68. The close friendship that Sir Jang Bahadur Rana developed with the British caused Tibet concern during crises with Nepal in 1873-1874 and 1883. A. Lamb, *Britain and Chinese Central Asia* (London, 1960), pp. 135-137.

8. Persistent attempts by the British to enter Tibet as government agents or private adventurers, especially the secret explorations of Sarat Chandra Das, only increased Tibetan suspicions (Bell, p. 59).

9. Lamb, pp. 49, 87-89.

10. The British government's misconception about Manchu authority in Tibet should be attributed primarily to the lack of information from inside Tibet as well as to mistaken information provided by British officials. For example, Cunningham reported from Ladakh that it was "Chinese armies" that had pushed back the Dogra's army from Tibet in 1842. The attitude of the Tibetan border officials, who undoubtedly contributed to this view, claimed it was the Manchus who prevented Tibet from having relations with British India. On the other hand, the British minister in Beijing should have been better informed as to the extent of Manchu authority in Tibet, inasmuch as the *Zongli Yamen* ("Office for General Administration" of foreign affairs in Beijing) had told the British that the Imperial government had no power to impose its wishes on the government of the Dalai Lama. See IO records *Secret Letters*, Vol. 88, No. 30, Cunningham to Clerk, 26 June 1842; Vol. 90, No. 52, Cunningham to Clerk, 24 Sept. 1842; Vol. 90, Incl., Secret Department Confidential News Letter No. 3, 22 Jan. 1842.

11. For the text of this special article, see Appendix 7. The Convention was concluded on 17 September 1876.

12. "Treaty Between H.M. the Queen of the U.K. of Great Britain and Ireland and H.M. the Emperor of China," signed at Tianjin, 26 June 1858, Article 9. For the full text, see D.C. Boulger, *History of China*, Vol. 3 (London, 1884), pp. 773-786. From the terms of this treaty, especially Articles 6, 7, and 52, it is clear that its provisions apply to all dominions of the Qing Emperor and to those of the British Sovereign.

13. See Lamb, p. 116, citing FO report, Bruce to GOI, 13 July 1861. See also FO 405/24, No. 73, Sir T. Wade to FO, 3 Oct. 1879.

14. See Lamb, p. 148; W.D. Shakabpa, *Tibet: A Political History* (New Haven, 1967), pp. 198-199. See also FO 405/50, Confidential Paper 5949, "Memorandum on Difficulties Connected with Frontier Between Sikkim and Tibet," 10 May 1890, pp. 1-2.

15. The Manchu authorities strongly rebuked the Tibetans in 1886 (after the mission was abandoned) for opposing a mission expressly allowed by the Emperor.

In a further demonstrative gesture, the Tibetans closed all passes into Sikkim, sent reinforcements south to Lingtu, and demanded a promise from the British never again to attempt such a mission, nor to allow Europeans beyond that town (Lamb, p. 180).

16. FO 405/30, No. 86, Incl. in FO to Sir J. Walsham (Minister in Beijing), 29 June 1886.

17. "Convention Relating to Burmah and Thibet," 24 July 1886, Article 4. For the full text, see Appendix 8.

18. FO 405/50, Confidential Paper 5949, p. 4.

19. Ibid., pp. 2–3. The British advanced after realizing that all requests to Beijing for the withdrawal of the Tibetan were to no avail.

20. For the full text, see Appendix 9.

21. This clause, taken from Article 2, was typical of Britain's position vis-à-vis "colonial protectorates."

22. For the full text of this treaty, see Appendix 9.

23. Article 1. The British had wanted to position the mart further into Tibet at Phari; they also wanted the right for British subjects to travel freely in the whole country. See *Papers Relating to Tibet* [hereafter, *Papers*] (Cd. 1920), No. 9, GOI to IO, 4 July 1893.

24. J.C. White, the Political Officer in Sikkim, reported from Dromo shortly after the conclusion of the Trade Regulations that "the Tibetans repudiate the treaty and assert that it was signed by the British Government and the Chinese, and therefore they have nothing to do with it." See *Papers* (Cd. 1920), No. 13, Incl. 1, Ann. 2, White to GOB, 9 June 1894. P. Nolan, the Commissioner of the Rajshahi Division, similarly reported from Tibet that a Tibetan government official, Tenzin Wangpu, deputed from Lhasa, had "made the important statement that the Tibetans do not consider themselves bound by the Convention with China, as they were not a party to it." See *Papers* (Cd. 1920), No. 18, Incl. 1, Ann., Nolan to GOB, 24 Nov. 1895.

25. *Papers* (Cd. 1920): No. 13, Incl. 1, GOB to GOI, 25 June 1894; No. 13, GOI to IO, 25 June 1895; Bell, p. 61.

26. During the treaty negotiations, James Hart, who represented the Amban, assured his British counterparts that "China will be quite able to enforce in Tibet the terms of the Treaty." See *Papers* (Cd. 1920), No. 1, Hart to A.W. Paul, 23 Sept. 1889. But Li Hongzhang admitted to E. Goschen in Beijing that although the Yamen could promise as it wished, "it is quite impossible in the present state of relations between China and Tibet for [it] to carry out [its] promise. People talk of China's influence in Tibet—but it is only nominal, as the Lamas are all powerful there." See FO 17/1056, E. Goschen to Sir P. Currie, 8 Dec. 1887. Edmund Candler later lamented: "Our ignorance of the Tibetans, their Government and their relations with China was at this time so profound that we took our cue from the Chinese who always referred to the Lhasa authorities as the 'barbarians.'" Things would be different, he added, "had we realized that the Chinese authority was practically non-existent in Lhasa, and that the temporal affairs of Tibet were mainly directed by the four Shapes [or Kalons] and the Tsong-du (the very existence of which, by the way, was unknown to us)." See E. Candler, *The Unveiling of Lhasa* (London, 1905), pp. 25–26.

27. *Papers* (Cd. 1920), No. 13, Incl. 1, Ann. 2, White to GOB, 9 June 1894. H.J.S. Cotton, Chief Secretary to GOB, wrote: "These observations of Mr. White on the weakness of the Chinese authority in Tibet . . . corroborate what has been reported on this subject from other sources, and explain the extreme difficulty

involved in giving effect to the provisions which have been concluded with the Chinese Government." See *Papers* (Cd. 1920), No. 13, Incl. 1, GOB to GOI, 25 June 1894. White also wrote that the Manchus had "practically no authority over the Tibetans . . . the Tibetans are asserting themselves and wish to throw off [their] yoke. The Chinese acknowledge that they have no authority, and the Tibetans say [the Chinese] have no right to treat for them." See *Papers* (Cd. 1920), No. 26, Incl. 7, Ann. 2, White to GOB.

28. Bell, pp. 206–207.

29. Lord Curzon wrote: "What we are concerned to examine is not the mere settlement of a border dispute, or even the amelioration of our future trading relations with Tibet, but the question of our entire political relations with that country, and the degree to which we can permit the influence of another great Power to be exercised for the first time in Tibetan affairs." See *Papers* (Cd. 1920), No. 66, GOI to IO, 8 Jan. 1903. For H.M.G.'s concurrence, see also *Papers* (Cd. 1920), No. 78, IO to GOI, 27 Feb. 1903.

30. Candler, p. 277.

31. For a history of Russian expansion in Asia, see D. Sinor, *Inner Asia* (Bloomington, Indiana, 1969), pp. 184–186, 199–203, 215–218.

32. FO 535/1, No. 16, Spring-Rice (Charge d'Affaires, St. Petersburg) to FO, 12 Nov. 1903. For a history of Russian interests in Central Asia, see P. Tang, *Russian and Soviet Policy in Manchuria and Outer Mongolia 1911–31* (Durham, N.C., 1959).

33. Lamb, pp. 206–207, 185.

34. The Marquess of Salisbury (Robert, Cecil) quoted in Lamb, p. 242. Lamb also quotes Captain Bower, who crossed Tibet with the support of British Military Intelligence, on the Manchu presence in Tibet: "A power which is incapable of protecting anyone or applying the most insignificant rules of police, does not deserve the name of a Government" (pp. 206–207).

35. See *Papers* (Cd. 1920), No. 66, GOI to IO, 8 Jan. 1903. See also Lamb, p. 238.

36. *Papers* (Cd. 1920), No. 66, GOI to IO, 8 Jan. 1903.

37. Ibid.; *Papers* (Cd. 1920): No. 26, Incl. 7, Ann. 2, White to GOB, 23 Nov. 1898; No. 27, IO to GOI, 2 June 1899; No. 29, GOI to IO, 26 Oct. 1899.

38. Bell, pp. 45–46.

39. *Papers* (Cd. 1920): No. 18, Incl. 1, Ann., Nolan to GOB, 24 Nov. 1895; see also No. 129, Incl. 56, Political Diary of Colonel Younghusband, 6 Sept. 1903.

40. *Papers* (Cd. 1920), No. 66, GOI to IO, 8 Jan. 1903.

41. Lamb, pp. 228–229, 255.

42. Richardson, pp. 79–81; Lamb, p. 240; Bell, pp. 62–63.

43. *Papers* (Cd. 1920), No. 31, Incl., Hardinge (British Minister, St. Petersburg) to FO, 17 Oct. 1900.

44. Cited in *Papers* (Cd. 1920), No. 36, Sir C. Scott (British Minister, St. Petersburg) to FO, 10 July 1901.

45. This was not the only disquieting information that reached the British. A number of rumors, in particular the reports originating in the Chinese press that a secret agreement had been signed between Russia and China regarding Tibet, alarmed the British government. It was also rumored that such a treaty had been concluded between Russia and Tibet. The main import of these alleged treaties was the establishment of a Russian protectorate over Tibet. In fact, it is highly unlikely that these agreements were ever concluded, and the existence of any such agreement was officially denied. See the extract from the *China Times*, 18 July 1902, in *Papers* (Cd. 1920), No. 49, Incl., Sir E. Satow (British Minister, Beijing) to FO, 5 Aug.

1902, *Papers* (Cd. 1920), No. 66, GOI to IO, 8 Jan. 1903; FO 535/3, No. 90, Hardinge to FO, 20 June 1904; Lamb, p. 268. The twelve clauses of the alleged treaty provided, *inter alia*, for the Manchu Emperor's relinquishment of his entire interest in Tibet to the Czar, in exchange for Russian support and assistance in maintaining the integrity of the former's Empire; and the establishment of Russian officers in Tibet to control the affairs of the country.

46. *Papers* (Cd. 1920), No. 36, Scott to FO, 10 July 1901.

47. The British authorities took reports of the alleged treaties and the subsequent rumors of Russian arms shipments to Tibet seriously. Whatever the truth of the information reaching the British, it is clear that communications of an official character existed between Lhasa and St. Petersburg, from which both countries hoped to reap some benefit. Regarding Russian arms, see Candler, p. 277; FO 535/4, No. 19, Incl., GOI to IO, 30 June 1904. For Tibetan-Russian contacts, see Lamb, pp. 229, 253, 256–258, 314–317.

48. See *Papers* (Cd. 1920), Nos. 13, 24, and 26; see also No. 44, Incl. 1, GOB to GOI, 21 June 1901. Lord Curzon bitterly complained about Tibet's isolationist policy: "It is indeed, the most extraordinary anachronism of the 20th century that there should exist within less than 300 miles of the borders of British India a State and a Government with whom political relations do not so much as exist, and with whom it is impossible even to exchange a written communication." See *Papers* (Cd. 1920), No. 44, GOI to IO, 13 Feb. 1902.

49. Quoted in Lamb, p. 241.

50. *Papers* (Cd. 1920), No. 37, Incl. 3, Ann., letter from Viceroy and Governor General of India to the Dalai Lama, 11 Aug. 1900. In this letter, the Viceroy requested the Dalai Lama to depute a delegate to India to discuss matters "for the mutual advantage, both commercial and political, of Tibet and India." A second letter to the Dalai Lama contained a warning that if the British overtures were still treated with indifference, "we reserve the right to take such steps as may be necessary and proper to enforce the terms of the treaty of 1890 and to ensure that the trade regulations are observed." See *Papers* (Cd. 1920), No. 37, GOI to IO, 25 July 1901.

51. *Papers* (Cd. 1920): No. 37, GOI to IO, 25 July 1901; No. 41, GOI to IO, 29 Oct. 1901; No. 42, GOI to IO, 3 Nov. 1901.

52. Political Officer White complained that the Imperial Manchu or Chinese officials played the Tibetans off against the British and vice versa: "The Chinese aver they have no authority over the Tibetans, the Tibetans say the Chinese have no authority to make treaties for them. They, however, also say they cannot act without the Chinese, the result being a deadlock." See *Papers* (Cd. 1920), No. 26, Incl. 8, Ann. 2, White to GOB, 9 Dec. 1898.

53. *Papers* (Cd. 1920), No. 66, GOI to IO, 8 Jan. 1903.

54. Ibid.

55. *Papers* (Cd. 1920), No. 78, IO to GOI, 27 Feb. 1903.

56. Lamb, pp. 206, 260–261.

57. *Papers* (Cd. 1920): No. 72, FO to Scott, 11 Feb. 1903; No. 73, FO to Scott, 18 Feb. 1903; No. 83, FO to Scott, 8 April 1903.

58. *Papers* (Cd. 1920): No. 74, IO to GOI, 20 Feb. 1903; No. 78, IO to GOI, 27 Feb. 1903.

59. Lamb, p. 242. As Khamba Dzong was so close to the Indian border, the hope was that a mission sent there would not provoke strong reactions from St. Petersburg or Beijing. See Lamb, pp. 288–289. Beijing was duly notified. See *Papers* (Cd. 1920), No. 91, Incl., Townley (British Charge d'Affaires, Beijing) to Prince Qing, 12 May 1903.

60. *Papers* (Cd. 1920), No. 99, Incl., GOI to Younghusband, 3 June 1903.

61. FO 535/3, No. 92, Incl., GOI to Younghusband, 26 June 1904.

62. Beijing's agreement is evident from *Papers* (Cd. 1920), No. 103, Incl., Waiwu Bu (Foreign Ministry, Beijing) to Townley, 13 July 1903. That the Tibetans did not agree can be deduced from FO 535/1, No. 19, Incl. 3. Despite what is said in *Papers* (Cd. 1920), No. 129, GOI to IO, 5 Nov. 1903, there is no evidence that either the Dalai Lama or the Tibetan government agreed. See also *Papers* (Cd. 1920): No. 129, Incl. 58, Younghusband to GOI, 9 Sept. 1903; No. 112, GOI to IO, 16 Sept. 1903.

63. See *Papers* (Cd. 1920): No. 103, Incl., Waiwu Bu to Townley, 13 July 1903; No. 129, Incl. 69, Political Diary of Younghusband, 26 Sept. 1903; No. 112, GOI to IO, 16 Sept. 1903. See also FO 535/2: No. 10, IO to FO, 11 Jan. 1904; No. 20, Incl. GOI to IO, 27 Jan. 1904.

64. Altogether, there were some 1,700 Tibetans killed in the fighting. See Candler, pp. 171–245. See also FO 535/4, No. 21, IO to FO, 19 July 1904, Incl., correspondence between the Dalai Lama and Tsonga Penlop; FO 535/4, No. 76, Incls. 3, 4.

65. The Tsongdu wrote as follows to the Amban: "It is recorded in our records that by a concession made to us in the twentieth year of the reign of the Emperor Dhakon [1840] we can ask the assistance of the Chinese troops that are stationed this side of Tarchindo [Dartsedo or Dajianlu], in case of emergency, so we beg you to kindly make, without fail, the necessary representations before His Majesty the Emperor of China, so that we may have all the necessary assistance in case of a big war breaking out." See FO 535/1, No. 19, Incl. 3, Tsongdu to Amban, n.d. The Amban refused to forward the request, arguing that the Emperor had forbidden the Tibetans to fight the British. See also FO 535/4, No. 36, Incl. 2, letters from Amban to Dalai Lama.

66. FO 535/4, No. 36, Incl. 2, Amban to Dalai Lama, approximately 29 July 1905.

67. FO 535/4, No. 46, Incl. 2, Nepal *Vakil* to government of Nepal, in British Resident, Kathmandu, to GOI, 7 July 1904.

68. *Papers* (Cd. 1920), No. 129, Incl. 51, Ann., Prime Minister of Nepal to *Kazis* (Ministers) of Lhasa, dated *Samvat* 1960.

69. FO 535/4, No. 76, Incls. 3–4, Dalai Lama to Tsonga Penlop.

70. Lamb, p. 302. It was suggested that the British, with the help of the Manchus, could set up a new government in Tibet favorable to British interests. See FO 535/4, No. 19, Incl., GOI to IO, 30 June 1904. For a report of the reaction to the deposition, see FO 535/5, No. 91, Incl. 3, Ravenshaw to GOI, 15 Nov. 1904, which states: "The Proclamation of the Chinese *Amban* at Lhasa, deposing the Dalai Lama and placing the Digarcha Lama [i.e. the Panchen Lama] in his place is reported to be not only most unpopular, but is considered *ultra vires*, and will never be accepted, and the Proclamations have been spat at and torn down. The Amban is said to be disturbed at this behavior, and is strengthening his Chinese troops, and has asked for 500 of the latest rifles from the Emperor of China."

71. For the full text of the Lhasa Convention, see Appendix 10. Originally a tripartite agreement was envisaged. See FO 535/4, No. 16, Incl, GOI to IO, 13 July 1904. For the decision in favor of a bilateral treaty, see FO 535/4, No. 29, Incl. 2, IO to GOI, 26 July 1904. See also Lamb, p. 302; *Further Papers Relating to Tibet* (Cd. 2370), No. 168, GOI to IO, 30 Sept. 1904.

72. Lamb (pp. 308–309) points out that this provision was aimed primarily at Russia.

73. FO 535/5, No. 20, Incl. 17, Younghusband to GOI, 28 Aug. 1904. The only official mention of the *eclaircissement* was that made in a speech delivered at the conclusion of the signing ceremony by Younghusband, who stated that "[the British Government] fully recognize the continued suzerainty of the Chinese Government." See FO 535/5, No. 53, Incl. 2, speech delivered by Younghusband, 7 Sept. 1904.

74. F0 535/4, No. 109, Incl. 1, GOI to IO quoting telegram from Waiwu Bu to Amban received on 15 Sept. 1904. In fact, an amendment proposed by the Amban before the signing of the Convention, expressly stating that China, being the suzerain of Tibet, was not to be included in the term "foreign Power" or in Article 9, was not accepted for inclusion in the final agreement. See FO 535/5, No. 20, Incl. 3, "Suggested Amendments Made by the Amban," 21 Aug. 1904. For Younghusband's reply, see Incl. 5 to No. 20.

75. F0 535/4, No. 78, Satow to FO, 9 Sept. 1904.

76. F0 535/4, No. 102, Satow to FO, 22 Sept. 1904.

77. FO 535/4, No. 119, Incl., GOI to IO, 29 Sept. 1904.

78. For information concerning the British administration of the Chumbi Valley, see Bell, pp. 73–81. Charles Bell was in charge of this administration from the summer of 1904 to November 1905. The indemnity was reduced by two-thirds at the time of the treaty's ratification. See *Further Papers* (Cd. 2370), No. 194, Incl. 3, letter of Viceroy to Ganden Tri Rimpoche (Regent of Tibet), 15 Nov. 1904.

79. FO 535/4: No. 97, Satow to FO, 20 Sept. 1904; No. 104, Satow to FO, 23 Sept. 1904.

80. FO 535/4, No. 106, FO to IO, 24 Sept. 1904; No. 107, "Memorandum by Mr. Montgomery Respecting the Agreement with Tibet: Russian Protests." See Richardson, p. 95. Aside from losing face, the Manchus feared, with good reason, the establishment of British influence in Tibet. When the Panchen Lama visited India in 1905, the Manchus' determination to remove all British influence in Tibet and to replace it with their own became an urgent priority.

81. See L/P&S/10/148, GOI to IO, 15 Nov. 1905. See also FO 535/4: No. 120, Satow to FO, 30 Sept. 1904; No. 3, FO to Satow, 1 Oct. 1904; No. 98, FO to Satow, 20 Sept. 1904; FO 535/5, No. 67, Satow to FO, 29 Sept. 1904.

82. FO 535/4, No. 109, Incl. 1, GOI to IO, 24 Sept. 1904.

83. FO 535/6: No. 7, Satow to FO, 29 Nov. 1904; No. 37, Incl., GOI to IO, 11 May 1905; No. 50, Incl., GOI to IO, 10 July 1905.

84. FO 535/6, No. 37, Incl., GOI to IO, 11 May 1905.

85. FO 535/4, No. 119, Incl., GOI to IO, 29 Sept. 1904.

86. FO 535/5, No. 5, IO to FO, 3 Oct. 1904.

87. For the full text of this agreement, see Appendix 11. The agreement was ratified in London on 23 July 1906.

88. FO 535/6, No. 70, Incl., GOI to IO, 8 Aug. 1905.

89. Lamb, p. 311. Note that this modification was also made to appease the Russians. See FO 535/7, No. 24, FO to IO, 5 Feb. 1906. Officially H.M.G. did not concede that the Adhesion Agreement altered the stipulation of the Lhasa Convention (FO 535/7, No. 72, FO to Spring-Rice, 24 April 1906).

90. FO 405/179, Confidential Memorandum 9098, 3 Dec. 1907, pp. 2–3; L/P&S/10/137, GOI to IO, 22 Oct. 1907. Note also that, at Beijing's request, the phrase "Government of Tibet" was replaced by "Tibet" throughout the Adhesion Agreement (FO 535/7: No. 63, Incl., IO to GOI, 3 April 1906; No. 70, IO to FO, 17 April 1906).

91. L/P&S/10/147, Bell to GOI, 16 May 1910, Incl., Tsongdu to Bell.

92. FO 535/5, No. 13, FO to Hardinge, 5 Oct. 1904.

93. The Russians did in fact react by advancing into Mongolia. See Bell, p. 71. For a discussion and evidence of Russia's continued interest in Tibet, see Lamb, pp. 313–317. For the full text of the "Convention Between Great Britain and Russia Relating to Persia, Afghanistan, and Thibet," 31 Aug. 1907, see Appendix 12.

94. L/P&S/10/148, Nicholson to FO, 20 Aug. 1907, Incl., Aide Memoire, 6 Aug. 1907 [translated from the French by M. Lutz].

95. Bell, p. 71.

96. The Dalai Lama returned to Tibet in 1909 after a prolonged exile in Mongolia and a visit to Beijing.

97. FO 535/6: No. 125, Satow to FO, 14 Nov. 1905; No. 126, FO to IO, 15 Nov. 1905; No. 142, Incl., GOI to IO, 30 Nov. 1905.

98. FO 535/6, No. 126, FO to IO, 15 Nov. 1905.

99. FO 535/7, No. 20, Incl., Satow to Prince Qing, 7 Dec. 1905.

100. FO 535/7, No. 34, IO to GOI, 22 Feb. 1906; FO 535/8, No. 104, FO to Jordan, 24 Dec. 1906.

101. L/P&S/10/149, FO to IO, 30 Jan. 1908; Lamb, p. 311. The Tibetans felt that the Emperor's gesture compensated for his inability to help the Tibetans militarily against the British (FO 535/6, No. 32, Incl. 4, Bell to White, 22 Feb. 1905).

102. L/P&S/10/148, Extract from the *Zhongwai Ribao*, 14 Feb. 1906.

103. L.T. Sigel, *Ch'ing Tibetan Policy*, East Asian Research Center, Harvard University, Papers on China Vol. 20 (Cambridge, Mass. 1966), pp. 181–185; FO 535/9, No. 37, Incl. 2, Bell to GOI, 13 Dec. 1906; L/P&S/10/149, Bailey to Bell, 11 Feb. 1909, Incl.; *Bahua Guanbao* (official Chinese Lhasan newspaper) of Aug. and Sept. 1908; L/P&S/10/148, GOI to IO, 3 Feb. 1907.

104. FO 535/9: No. 71, Jordan to FO, 5 Jan. 1907; No. 57, FO to Jordan, 9 Feb. 1907.

105. FO 535/8, No. 77, Incl., White to GOI, 29 Aug. 1906.

106. E. Teichman, *Travels of a Consular Officer in Eastern Tibet* (Cambridge, 1922), pp. 20–21.

107. Ibid., pp. 21–24; *Further Papers* (Cd. 2370), No. 15, Goffe to Satow, 25 April 1905; L/P&S/10/138, Bell to GOI, 26 March 1910, Incl. list of monasteries, etc., plundered and destroyed by Zhao Erfeng and his troops. See also L/P&S/10/137, MacDonald to GOI, 17 Sept. 1908, Incl. (b), letter from Nepal *Vakil*, Lhasa, to King of Nepal, 15 June 1908.

108. FO 535/6: No. 6, Incl. 1, Pol. O. Chumbi to Pol. O. Sikkim, 10 Dec. 1904; No. 6, Incl. 3, Deputy Commissioner, Darjeeling to GOB, 15 Dec. 1905; No. 25, Incl. 1, Bell to White, 7 Feb. 1905.

109. See FO records FO 535/6, FO 535/7, FO 535/8, for the years 1905 and 1906 and IO records, L/P&S/10/147 for 1906.

110. W.W. Rockhill, "The Dalai Lamas of Lhasa and Their Relations with the Manchu Emperors of China, 1644–1908," *T'oung Pao* 11 (1910), pp. 76–77; L/P&S/10/147, Jordan to FO, 9 July 1908.

111. Bell, p. 111; FO 535/12, No. 3, Incl. 1, Rockhill to President Roosevelt, 8 Nov. 1908; L/P&S/10/147, Jordan to FO, 12 Oct. 1908 and 25 Oct. 1908. Note that the Waiwu Bu took measures to restrict meetings between the Dalai Lama and foreign diplomats. In a memorandum, the Waiwu Bu announced: "If any of the members of the Staffs of the foreign Legations desires to visit the Dalai Lama, they should proceed to the Yellow Temple on any day except Sunday, between the hours of 12 noon and 3" (FO 535/11, No. 114, Incl., "Memorandum from Waiwu Bu to Doyen of Diplomatic Body," 8 Oct. 1908). Eric Teichman, a member of the British Legation at that time, remarked that this memorandum was worded as though

it referred to a public exhibition rather than to the reception of the Representatives of the Great Powers of Europe and the United States by the Ruler of Tibet and Pope of Lamaism, whose religious authority extended over half of Asia (*Travels of a Consular Officer*, p. 14).

112. L/P&S/10/147, Jordan to FO, 12 Oct. 1908. As Fairbank and Teng have noted: "It should be emphasized that the relationship to the Son of Heaven expressed by the kowtow was shared by all mankind, Chinese and barbarian alike. The highest dignitaries of the empire performed the ceremony on appropriate occasions—as did the Emperor himself when paying reverence to Heaven (pai-t'ien) [*baitian*]. The kowtow performed unilaterally, on the other hand, expressed an inferiority of status in the universal order, without which there could be no order. It was therefore appropriate, honorable, and indeed good manners when performed in the right context. Other contexts might require less elaborate ceremonies, such as one kneeling and three prostrations." See J.K. Fairbank and S.Y. Teng, "On the Ch'ing Tributary System," in *Ch'ing Administration: Three Studies* (Cambridge, Massachusetts, 1961), p. 138. Ultimately, the Dalai Lama was required only to make genuflections. He was also given, for example, the rank of Prince of the First Class, the highest that could be given (Rockhill, pp. 79, 84).

113. L/P&S/10/147, Jordan to FO, 2 Nov. 1908. For the original title given by the Shun Zhi Emperor, see Note 18 in Chapter 2 of this book.

114. L/P&S/10/147, Jordan to FO, 2 Nov. 1908.

115. Ibid.; L/P&S/10/147, Jordan to FO, 25 Oct. 1908; FO 535/12, No. 3, Incl. 1, Rockhill to President Roosevelt, 8 Nov. 1908.

116. FO 535/12, No. 3, Incl. 1, Rockhill to President Roosevelt, 8 Nov. 1908.

117. This plan, however, was never officially approved by the court. In fact, Zhao Erfeng wanted Xikang to extend to Giamda, only about sixty miles east of Lhasa (Hoffmann, p. 69).

118. See, Appendix 10.

119. 535/5, No. 1, Incl. 2, GOI to IO, 30 Sept. 1904; 535/6, No. 18, Incl. 1, GOI to IO, 29 Dec. 1904.

120. L/P&S/10/137, GOI to IO, 22 Oct. 1907; 535/9, No. 155, FO to Jordan, 8 May 1907. In order to stress the similarity between the status of Tibet and India vis-à-vis the Qing Emperor and the British Crown, the Waiwu Bu had actually proposed that the negotiations be held by Tibetan and Indian authorities and then be submitted to Commissioner Zhang and the Viceroy for approval and signing. See FO 535/10, No. 12, Incl. 1, Memorandum by Waiwu Bu to Jordan, 21 May 1907.

121. L/P&S/10/137: GOI to IO, 22 Oct. 1907; GOI to FO, 14 Feb. 1908; Jordan to FO, 11 Jan. 1908; Jordan to FO, 22 Jan. 1908, Incl. 1, Prince Qing to Jordan, 9 Jan. 1908.

122. For the full text of the Trade Regulations, see Appendix 13. See also L/P&S/10/137, GOI to FO, 27 June 1907; Godley to FO, 4 July 1907. As Lamb writes: "Had the Indian Government been given a free hand in these negotiations, it would never have accepted the final text which was signed at Calcutta on 20 April 1908. Lord Minto, however, was throughout under great pressure from London to come to some kind of agreement, and he probably realised that if he permitted the negotiations to break down in India they would only be transferred to Peking or London." Such a change of venue would have led to even more favorable terms for the Manchus, as had been the case in 1905/06. See A. Lamb, *The McMahon Line* (London, 1966), Vol. 1, p. 147.

123. This designation of the Tibetan delegate was a compromise between the British and Manchu positions (Lamb, *The McMahon Line*, Vol. 1, p. 146).

124. L/P&S/10/137, Jordan to FO, 15 Oct. 1908, Incl.

125. Kashag Document 11(4)11.

126. The British were very concerned about the acceptability of the Tibetan credentials. See L/P&S/10/137: GOI to IO, 27 June 1907; IO to FO, 23 July 1907. For the text of the credentials, a sealed certificate from the Regent, Tri Rimpoche, see FO 535/10, No. 104, Incls. 15, 18.

127. See FO 535/10, No. 104, Incls. 15, 16, 17.

128. Kashag Document 11(4)11.

129. FO 405/187, Confidential Memorandum 9344, 31 Dec. 1908, p. 1; FO 535/10, No. 104, IO to FO, 7 Nov. 1907; No. 104, Incls. 1-12. The British Trade Agent in Gyantse wrote: "[The delegates'] whole attitude is most unsatisfactory and they are completely under the influence of the Chinese. Selected delegates are certainly representative men, but are mere puppets as long as they are associated with Chang, or any other Chinese official" (L/P&S/10/137, GOI to IO, 20 July 1907).

130. Kashag Document 11(4)11.

131. L/P&S/10/137, Jordan to FO, 15 Oct. 1908.

132. For the Dalai Lama's conversations with U.S. Diplomat Rockhill, see L/P&S/10/147, Jordan to FO, 24 Oct. 1908 and 9 July 1908.

133. Although it is not clear whether Zhao's advance was officially sanctioned by the Imperial Court in Beijing, it appears that the government was somewhat uneasy about the effect it might have (FO 535/13, No. 3, Jordan to FO, 29 Nov. 1909).

134. Richardson, p. 98. The Tibetan government decided to police the streets of Lhasa in response to allegations that 1,000 Imperial troops were needed for this purpose. See L/P&S/10/147, British Resident, Nepal, to GOI, 25 Dec. 1909, Incl., letter from Nepal *Vakil*, Lhasa, 19 Nov. 1909. The Waiwu Bu maintained that, "since the conclusion of the [Tibet Trade Regulations], all matters in connection with the opening of new trade marts and the maintenance of peace in that country are of such great importance that it has been found necessary to dispatch 2,000 soldiers from Szechuan to Tibet for the purpose of preserving order." See L/P&S/10/149, translation of telegram from Waiwu Bu to H.M.G., 25 Feb. 1910. See also FO 535/12: No. 47, Jordan to FO, 12 Nov. 1909; No. 50, IO to FO, 25 Nov. 1909.

135. L/P&S/10/147: P.M. Nepal to British Resident, Nepal, 2 Jan. 1910; Bell to GOI, 21 Jan. 1910; FO to IO, 12 Feb. 1910; *Kashag* to P.M. Nepal, 23 Nov. 1909; L/P&S/10/138, P.M. Nepal to British Resident, Nepal, 24 Feb. 1910, Incl., Nepal *Vakil*, Lhasa, to P.M. Nepal; Bell, p. 96.

136. L/P&S/10/138, P.M. Nepal to British Resident, Nepal, Incl., Nepal *Vakil*, Lhasa to P.M. Nepal.

137. L/P&S/10/147, Bell to GOI, 17 Jan. 1910 and Incls., Sidkeong Tulku to Bell, Tangme-Pa to Sidkeong Tulku, 5 Jan. 1910.

138. The Tibetan government had sent a considerable force to Chamdo, but it was sent to intimidate and not to fight. See Bell, p. 97. See also GOI to IO, 12 March 1910, Incl., Amban to Dalai Lama, 10 Feb. 1910.

139. L/P&S/10/138, GOI to IO, 3 March 1910. As Wang Furen and Suo Wenqing have noted: "The deputy Amban Wen Zongyao assured the Dalai Lama that the Sichuan troops would maintain strict discipline and keep peace and order when in the Tibetan capital. But in fact the Sichuan troops were badly disciplined. After entering Lhasa they looted and threw the whole city into chaos." See *Highlights of Tibetan History* (Beijing, 1984), p. 147. For the Dalai Lama's account of these events, see the letter from the Dalai Lama to Lo Ti-t'ai [Whang Bu Phul], quoted in Shakabpa, pp. 234-237. The letter is in Shakabpa's possession.

140. Tibet Blue Book 1910, No. 311, cited in Bell, p. 109.

141. L/P&S/10/149, translation of telegram from Waiwu Bu to H.M.G., 25 Feb. 1910. In answer to a query by the Russian government, the Waiwu Bu stated that the Dalai Lama was deposed because he had not filled his duty as a vassal; he no longer recognized the Manchu overlordship; and he interfered in the internal administration of Tibet, rather than limiting himself to spiritual matters. See L/P&S/10/149, Count Beckendorff (Russian Minister, London) to FO, 8 March 1910. See also L/P&S/10/138, Bell to GOI, 26 March 1910; L/P&S/10/147, Bell to GOI, 10 May 1910; L/P&S/10/149, Bell to GOI, 2 April 1910.

142. L/P&S/10/147, GOI to IO, 5 March 1910; L/P&S/10/138, Bell to GOI, 26 March 1910.

143. Bell, p. 111. Charles Bell, the British official appointed to act as liaison to the Dalai Lama and his ministers, writes that these Tibetan officials "denied" Chinese suzerainty. Bell quotes the ministers: "The relations between the two are those between a layman and his priest. The priest receives help from the layman but does not become his subordinate" (p. 111).

144. The Amban sent delegations to invite the Dalai Lama to return and assured the Lama that no harm would be done him. See FO 535/13, No. 62, Incl. 3, GOI to IO, 11 April 1910.

145. Even the Dalai Lama's offer to conclude a protectorate treaty with the British was not given much attention. The IO wrote the GOI: "Dalai Lama should now be definitely informed that His Majesty's Government cannot interfere between them and the Chinese Government" (L/P&S/10/147, telegram from Secretary of State for India to Viceroy, 4 May 1910).

146. L/P&S/10/265, FO to IO, 13 Jan. 1912.

147. L/P&S/10/138: GOI to IO, 12 March 1910; and telegram from Viceroy to Secretary of State for India, 12 March 1910. The Convention of 1904 recognized the Tibetan government, and Article 1 of the 1906 Convention between Britain and China bound the Qing government thereto. Therefore, one of the most significant violations was the replacement of the Tibetan government by one administered by the Qing.

148. L/P&S/10/265, FO to IO, 13 Jan. 1912; FO 535/13, No. 60, FO to Max Muller, 8 April 1910. Significantly, written replies were not as explicit as were the oral denials.

149. L/P&S/10/138, GOI to IO, 12 March 1910.

150. L/P&S/10/265, Jordan to Grey, 27 April 1912, Incl., telegram from Yin Changheng to Zhang Peijue, 5 April 1912.

Notes to Chapter 4

1. E. Teichman, *Travels of a Consular Officer in Eastern Tibet* (Cambridge, 1922), p. 17.

2. Sir John Jordan wrote of Amban Lian: "In [Lian's] opinion, the Tibetan Government would never again agree to the presence of Chinese troops in Lhasa. The recent excesses had, he said, exasperated the whole population" (FO 535/16, No. 125, Jordan to FO, 6 March 1913). The Assistant Amban, Wen Zongyao, complained that the Manchus and Chinese had alienated the Tibetans (L/P&S/10/340, Jordan to FO, 28 June 1912, Incl. 2).

3. Much of the Tibetan military action was directed by officials of the Dalai Lama, who had set up a secret War Department. See W.D. Shakabpa, *Tibet: A*

Political History (New Haven, 1967), p. 239. See also L. Rapgay, "The Thirteenth Dalai Lama," *Bulletin of Tibetology,* New Series, No. 2 (1977), p. 28.

4. W.J. Calhoun, the American Minister in Beijing, wrote to the Secretary of State that it was "common hatred of [the Manchus] which forms the bond of union among the seceding provinces." See FRUS, *China* (1912), p. 53. According to Chinese historiographers, the revolution was the result of 250 years of suffering by the Chinese people under alien Manchu rule. See F. Wakeman, *The Fall of Imperial China* (New York, 1975), pp. 225–227.

5. L/P&S/10/147, Jordan to FO, 14 Dec. 1912; L/P&S/10/265, Jordan to FO, 18 May 1912, Incl., Yuan Shikai to Yun and Chang (Governor and Lieutenant Governor of Sichuan), 12 April 1912; 535/15, No. 318, Incl., Extract from *Bing Bao,* 11 Dec. 1912; L/P&S/10/393, intercepted telegram from Lu Xingji to Beijing, 13 May 1913. General Zhong complained that "the Tibetans have strongly urged me to leave Lhasa as they say I have violated the agreement by staying in Tibet. I explained to them the previous customs and rules [regarding the position of Resident], but they do not understand me, and, moreover, they do not respect me." See FO 535/15, No. 284, Incl. 2, Chinese General Officer Commanding, Lhasa, to British Trade Agent, Gyantse, n.d.

6. See FO 535/15, No. 138, Incl., GOI to IO, 3 July 1912. See also FO 535/15, No. 81, Incl. 2, *Lonchens* to Bell, 13 April 1912.

7. FO 535/15, No. 81, Incl. 2, *Lonchens* to Bell, 13 April 1912. The Chinese also wanted British mediation as they mistrusted the Tibetans. See FO 535/15: No. 139, IO to FO, 5 July 1912; No. 110, Incl., GOI to IO, 18 June 1912.

8. FO 535/15, No. 92, Incl., Manners-Smith, British Resident, Nepal, to GOI, 22 April 1912.

9. For the full text of the Sino-Tibetan Agreement of 12 August 1912, see Appendix 14. The initiative was taken by the Chinese; with few reinforcements and supplies, they contacted the Tibetan War Department through the Nepal Vakil. A truce had been arranged in April, but it had lasted only three days (Shakabpa, p. 243).

10. For the full text of the Sino-Tibetan Agreement of 14 December 1912, see Appendix 15. Once again, the Nepalese mediated, as the British refused to do so. See FO 535/15, No. 300, Incls. 1 and 2, GOI to IO, 29 Nov. 1912 and 3 Dec. 1912. See also FO 535/15: No. 221, IO to FO, 21 Sept. 1912; No. 225, Incl., GOI to IO, 17 Oct. 1912; No. 231, Incl., GOI to IO, 28 Sept. 1912. General Zhong himself left Lhasa on 19 December; but he stayed in the Chumbi Valley, delaying his departure from Tibet even further. At the end of March, he finally left under a renewed threat of the use of force (FO 535/16, No. 150, IO to FO, 25 March 1913).

11. FO 535/16, No. 27, Jordan to FO, 28 Dec. 1912. Although the Dalai Lama had already crossed into Tibet in June 1912, he stayed in Phari and delayed his return to Lhasa until all troops had left the city.

12. For the full text of this proclamation, see Appendix 16. The text was copied from the declaration in the archives of the district of Senge Dzong by Tsepon W.D. Shakabpa, who was on duty in that district in 1927. That copy is in his possession.

13. Letter from Dalai Lama to Lo Ti-t'ai [Wang Bu Phul], Sept. 1910, quoted in Shakabpa, pp. 234–237. The letter is in Shakabpa's possession.

14. See FO 535/15, No. 228, Incl. 2, GOI to IO, 26 Oct. 1912. See also FO 535/15, No. 284, Incl. 11, British Trade Agent, Gyantse, 19 Oct. 1912. These statements by the Tibetans were indeed regarded by the British government as constituting a declaration of independence. Thus, they referred to the "Thibetan

Declaration of Independence" in their own documents. For an example, see FO 535/16, No. 126, IO to FO, 7 March 1913.

15. FO 535/15, No. 39, Incl. 2, Dalai Lama to Czar of Russia, Feb. 1912. The Dalai Lama also asked for Russia's support in an earlier letter sent to the Czar at the end of 1911. The Czar responded by expressing sympathy for Tibet in its efforts to defend its rights "insofar as these rights are based on the system of existing treaties." At the same time, he specifically referred to the 1907 Anglo-Russian Treaty (FO 535/14, No. 108, Aide-Memoire from Count Beckendorff to H.M.G., 18 Dec. 1911).

16. FO 535/15, No. 198, Incl., GOI to IO, 4 Sept. 1912.

17. FO 535/16, No. 58, Jordan to FO, 17 Jan. 1913.

18. FO 535/16, No. 58, Incl. 1, extract from the *Guomin Gongbao*, 6 Jan. 1913.

19. FO 535/16, No. 181, Incl. 3, letter from Haji Ghulam Muhammad, Lhasa, to British Trade Agent, Gyantse, 14 Feb. 1913. See also L/P&S/10/147, Jordan to FO, 4 Nov. 1912, Incl., Presidential Order published in the Government *Gazette*, 28 Oct. 1912. Note that the Chinese government did acknowledge that Tibet declared its independence in 1912. See Chinese Ministry of Information, *China Handbook, 1937–45* (New York, 1947), p. 30; see also the 1950 issue, p. 66.

20. For the full text of the Tibetan-Mongolian Treaty of 11 January 1913, see Appendix 17. The independence of Mongolia was recognized by Russia in the Russo-Mongolian Agreement of 3 Nov. 1912, and by the Republic of China in 1945. Owen Lattimore describes Outer Mongolia as a satellite of Russia and "independent in fact" from China between 1911 and 1920. From then on it was a "constitutional monarchy," and then a "People's Republic" and satellite of the Soviet Union. See O. Lattimore, *Studies in Frontier History* (New York, 1962), pp. 175, 279–288. Some scholars question the authority of the Tibetan delegate Dorjieff to conclude the treaty. Based on a letter from Lonchen Shatra to C.A. Bell, McMahon concluded that "the terms of [Dorjieff's] powers are as full and explicit as those conferred upon Lonchen Shatra himself for the present Conference." McMahon continues by saying that "Dorjieff claims in the preamble [of the treaty] that he was acting with full powers." See L/P&S/10/138, *Tibet Conference: Final Memorandum*, 8 July 1914 [hereafter, *Final Memorandum*], Incl. 2, p. 7. The Fourteenth Dalai Lama confirmed the validity of the treaty in a written statement in 1959: "Dorjieff was an accredited representative of the Dalai Lama." See International Commission of Jurists, Legal Inquiry Committee on Tibet, *Tibet and the Chinese People's Republic* (Geneva, 1960), p. 309.

21. See C.A. Bell, *Portrait of the Dalai Lama* (London, 1956), p. 173. See also -Shakabpa, p. 249.

22. Teichman, p. 2.

23. L/P&S/10/265, Jordan to FO, 27 April 1912, Incl., translation of Presidential Order, 21 April 1912.

24. FO 535/15, No. 53*, Jordan to FO, 31 March 1912.

25. Note that as early as December 1911, the Conference of Imperialist and Revolutionary Representatives had decided that China's future National Assembly should include delegates from Tibet, Mongolia, and Turkestan, as well as from the eighteen provinces of China. See L/P&S/10/265, FO to IO, 13 Jan. 1912. The Republican flag was composed of five color bars, each of which represented a "race." The Tibetans were represented by the black bar. For the text of the provisional constitution, see *FRUS, China* (1912), p. 38. See also the "Constitutional Compact of the Chung-Hua Min Kuo [Zhonghoa Minguo]," in *FRUS, China* (1914), p. 56.

26. FO 535/16, No. 167, Incl. 1, GOI to IO, 28 March 1913. (Information was gathered from intercepted telegrams.) General Zhong Yin bitterly complained to the

President that "the Tibetans object to the Republic." See FO 535/15, No. 318, Incl., extract from *Bing Bao*, 11 Dec. 1912.

27. L/P&S/10/265, Jordan to FO, 27 April 1912, Incl., telegram from Governors Yin Changheng and Zhang Peijue to Yuan Shikai, 5 April 1912. The President responded by acknowledging Tibet to be "of the very greatest importance," and that "the Marches and Thibet are to Szechuan [Sichuan] as the lips to the jaw." See L/P&S/10/265, Jordan to FO, 18 May 1912, Incl. 3, Yuan Shikai to Yin Changheng and Zhang Peijue, 12 April 1912.

28. L/P&S/10/265, Jordan to FO, 6 June 1912, Incl.

29. See L/P&S/10/265, Jordan to FO, 26 June 1912, Incl., 23 June 1912. See also L/P&S/10/265, GOI to IO, 23 March 1912.

30. L/P&S/10/340, Secret Report, *Tibet*, 27 Jan. 1913, pp. 2–3.

31. FO 535/15, No. 198, Incl., GOI to IO, 4 Sept. 1912.

32. C.A. Bell, *Tibet: Past and Present* (1924; rpt. Oxford, 1968), p. 148; FO 535/16: No. 172, Inc. 4, British Trade Agent, Gyantse, to GOI, 28 Feb. 1913; No. 240, Incl., GOI to IO, 29 May 1913; L/P&S/10/147, Minute Paper, 28 Nov. 1912.

33. L/P&S/10/147, FO to Jordan, Incls., Government *Gazette*, 27 Oct. 1912 and 15 Nov. 1912; L/P&S/10/147, Minute Paper, 28 Nov. 1912.

34. FO 535/16, No. 26, Incl., GOI to IO, 16 Jan. 1913; FO 535/15, No. 294, Incl. 3, British Trade Agent, Gyantse, to GOI, 8 Nov. 1912, quoting telegram from Yang Fen to Dalai Lama, 4 Nov. 1912; L/P&S/10/147, British Trade Agent, Gyantse, to GOI, 30 Nov. 1912, Incl., telegram from Yang Fen to Dalai Lama, 29 Nov. 1912; FO 535/15, No. 228, Incl. 2, GOI to IO, 26 Sept. 1912.

35. L/P&S/10/147, Jordan to FO, 28 Oct. 1912 and 4 Nov. 1912; Shakabpa, pp. 250–251; Bell, *Tibet: Past and Present*, p. 151; P. Hyer, "Yashiro Yajima—The Japanese Military Advisor to Tibet," *TR* 17, No. 6 (June 1982), pp. 8–11; FO 535/16, No. 269, Incl., GOI to IO, intercepted telegrams, Lu Xingji to Beijing, 7 May 1913 and Suez to Beijing, 10 May 1913; *Final Memorandum*, Incl. 1, p. 2.

36. FO 535/15, No. 284, Incl. 4, Lamen Kempo to Laden La, 4 Oct. 1912; L/P&S/10/340, GOI to IO, 1 May 1913; FO 535/16, No. 270, IO to FO, 18 June 1913.

37. L/P&S/10/265: Jordan to FO, 26 June 1912, Incl., minutes of the meeting between Jordan and the President, 23 June 1912; Jordan to FO, 17 Aug. 1912. The British protests, however, were generally relatively mild, owing to the Britons' concern not to harm trade relations with China and to their efforts not to displease the Russians (L/P&S/10/340, Jordan to FO, 16 Dec. 1912).

38. For the full text of the "17th August Memorandum," see L/P&S/10/147, Jordan to FO, 17 Aug. 1912, Incl. 1, Memorandum to Waijiao Bu. For a discussion of the modifications regarding the use of suzerainty and sovereignty in the memorandum, see L/P&S/10/265: IO to FO, 11 July 1912; FO to IO, 15 Aug. 1912. Jordan was later instructed to make clear to the Chinese "the distinction between suzerainty, which we acknowledge, and sovereignty, which we have never admitted" (FO 535/15, No. 218, FO to Jordan, 17 Sept. 1912).

39. L/P&S/10/147, FO to Jordan, 12 Dec. 1912.

40. L/P&S/10/340, Jordan to FO, 16 Dec. 1912; Jordan to FO, Incl., memorandum from Waijiao Bu, 23 Dec. 1912.

41. L/P&S/10/340, Jordan to FO, 16 Dec. 1912, Incl., memorandum of conversation with Dr. Yen, 14 Dec. 1912.

42. L/P&S/10/340, Jordan to FO, 4 Feb. 1913.

43. FO 535/16: No. 172, Incl. 13, Dalai Lama to Bell, 16 Feb. 1913; No. 177, Incl., GOI to IO, 2 March 1913; No. 240, Incl., GOI to IO, 29 May 1913. The

Chinese threatened the Tibetans with extinction if they failed to submit (FO 535/16, No. 204, Incl., GOI to IO, 28 April 1913).

44. For the text of the communications to the British, see FO 535/16, No. 172, Incls. 4, 12, and 18.

45. L/P&S/10/340, FO to Jordan, 3 March 1913; FO 535/16: No. 125, Jordan to FO, 6 March 1913; No. 206, FO to IO, 30 April 1913; No. 291, IO to FO, 1 July 1913; L/P&S/10/340: FO to Jordan, 5 April 1913; Jordan to FO, 10 April 1913. Initially, H.M.G. favored British participation in the negotiations, as a benevolent assistant to both parties, as it feared that becoming a signatory would impose new responsibility upon Britain (FO 535/16, No. 132, FO to IO, 13 March 1913).

46. L/P&S/10/340, Jordan to FO, 29 May 1913.

47. *Final Memorandum*, p. 3. The Chinese had already lost their influence in Mongolia to the Russians and feared losing Tibet to Britain. See L/P&S/10/340, Jordan to FO, 16 Dec. 1912. When the Chinese plenipotentiary to the conference again objected to the equal status of the Tibetan delegate, he was told by the British that "the status of Tibet was that of an independent nation recognizing no allegiance to China." See *The Boundary Question between China and Tibet* (Peking, 1940), p. 102.

48. L/P&S/10/340, GOI to IO, 23 Feb. 1913; 535/16, No. 213, Incl., GOI to IO, 30 April 1913; L/P&S/10/393, intercepted telegrams, Lu Xingji to President and Cabinet, 13 May 1913, 6 June 1913, 9 June 1913, and 15 July 1913; FO535/16: No. 315, Incl. 1, GOI to IO, 15 July 1913; No. 213, Incl. 1, GOI to IO, 30 April 1913.

49. Note, however, that even after the Three Power Conference had started in India, the Chinese were still intriguing to get the Tibetan government to agree to bilateral talks at Chamdo in Kham. Also, throughout the conference, the Chinese continued military operations in and threats to Eastern Tibet. See the correspondence throughout the period of the conference in FO 535/16.

50. FO 535/16: No. 381, Incl., GOI to IO, 3 Oct. 1913; No. 326, FO to Alston, 27 July 1913; No. 318, IO to FO, 18 July 1913, Incl., GOI to IO; No. 370, Incl. 1, Waijiao Bu to Alston, 7 Aug. 1913.

51. For the full text of the statement of the Tibetan claims, made 10 Oct. 1913, see *The Boundary Question*, pp. 1-6. The complete, unpublished Tibetan record of the negotiations at Simla, kept by Teji Trimon, "The Jewel-Treasure of the People of the Land of the Snows," is in the possession of W.D. Shakabpa.

52. For the full text of the Chinese counterproposals, see *The Boundary Question*, pp. 7-11.

53. *Final Memorandum*, Incl. 1, p. 1.

54. *Final Memorandum*, Incl. 2, pp. 4-5; *Final Memorandum*, pp. 3-4.

55. *Final Memorandum*, p. 4. See also the "British statement on the limits of Tibet," made by McMahon on the meeting of 17 Feb. 1914, reproduced in *The Boundary Question*, pp. 88-90. McMahon acknowledged "that a measure of Chinese control was established during the 18th Century," but he added that there existed "a well defined line between the sphere of periodical Chinese intervention in Tibet, and the sphere in which Chinese dictation was of a purely nominal nature."

56. *The Boundary Question*, p. 90. McMahon concluded that "the whole country with both zones is still and has always been Tibetan. At the time of our treaty with Tibet in 1904, there was no Chinese administration in either Inner or Outer Tibet—this was admitted by Fu Sung-mu" (L/P&S/10/343, "Verbal Statement by Sir Henry McMahon," 9 March 1914).

57. H.E. Richardson, *A Short History of Tibet* (New York, 1962), p. 109.

58. Ibid.; L/P&S/10/343: "Statement by Lonchen Shatra," 5 March 1914; "Statement by Mr. Ivan Chen," 7 March 1914.

59. The convention was to be initialed rather than signed at this stage, as Great Britain felt that reference must be made to Russia, in light of the Anglo-Russian Treaty of 1907, before it could be signed (FO 535/17, No. 94, Incl., IO to GOI, 21 April 1914).

60. The Tibetans resisted this stipulation very strongly, but ultimately agreed when a provision allowing a British Trade Agent to travel to Lhasa for discussion was added. See L/P&S/10/344, "Proceedings of the 7th meeting of the Tibet Conference held at Simla on 22 and 27 April 1914," p. 1.

61. The Tibetans had pressed for a British representative to be stationed at Lhasa to counter the one stationed there by the Chinese. H.M.G., however, believed that Russia would never consent to such a provision, which was contrary to the Anglo-Russian Treaty of 1907 (*Final Memorandum*, Incl. 1, p. 3).

62. The Foreign Office considered the notes to be an annex to and not an "integral part of the convention." Nonetheless, it was "presumed that they would, if exchanged, be considered as equally binding" (Shakabpa, p. 255).

63. For a discussion of "nominal suzerainty," see Chapter 7 of this book.

64. *Final Memorandum*, Incl. 4, p. 2.

65. Chen officially communicated his Government's stand on April 26 as follows: "With the exception of Article 9 of the draft Convention [relating to the Sino-Tibetan boundary], we are prepared to take the main principles, embodied in the other articles, into our favourable consideration." See L/P&S/10/344, "Proceedings of the 7th meeting of the Tibet Conference," Ann. 3, Chen to McMahon, 26 April 1914.

66. *Final Memorandum*, p. 4.

67. Ibid.; L/P&S/10/344: Waijiao Bu to Chinese Legation, 28 April 1914; Memorandum from Chinese Legation to FO, 1 May 1914. In a communication to the British, the Chinese wrote: "[The] Chinese Government give their adhesion to [the] major articles of the convention. But they are unable to agree to the boundary arrangement" (L/P&S/10/344, Jordan to FO, 30 June 1914).

68. Richardson, p. 113.

69. *Final Memorandum*, Incl. 4; L/P&S/10/344, Memorandum from FO to Chinese Minister, 5 June 1914.

70. L/P&S/10/344, Memorandum from FO to Chinese Minister, 25 June 1914.

71. *Final Memorandum*, Incl. 4, p. 3. For the full text of this declaration, see Appendix 18. At the last minute, the FO was not in favor of a separate signature with Tibet, fearing a negative reaction from Russia. Later, however, London expressly approved McMahon's signing the Anglo-Tibetan Agreement (FO 535/17, No. 214, FO to IO, 14 July 1914). The six Tibetan seals that were attached to the declaration were those of the Dalai Lama, the Tibetan Plenipotentiary, the Tsongdu, or National Assembly, and the Three Great Monasteries (Sera, Drepung, and Ganden) (FO 535/17, No. 261*, IO to FO, 24 Dec. 1914).

72. For the full texts of these documents, see Appendix 19. Changes were made in the tripartite agreement originally initialed by all three plenipotentiaries, in order to keep it in harmony with the 1907 Anglo-Russian Convention. After the Anglo-Russian talks, Article 10, which had provided that Great Britain should act as arbitrator in all disputes between Tibet and China, was altered to a simple provision stating that the English text should be considered authoritative in case of need. An eleventh article, stating that the convention should take effect from the date of signature, was also inserted (*Final Memorandum*, p. 5).

73. *Final Memorandum*, Incl. 4, p. 3.

74. For the full text of the Tibetan Trade Regulations, see Appendix 20.

75. For the text of the boundary agreement, in the form of an exchange of notes, see Appendix 21. See also *Final Memorandum*, p. 7; W.F. Van Eekelen, *Indian Foreign Policy and the Border Dispute with China* (The Hague, 1965), pp. 16–17.

76. *The Boundary Question*, p. 147.

77. Offical Document, Mongolian and Tibetan Affairs Commission, Taipei, reproduced in Hengtse Tu, *A Study of the Treaties and Agreements Relating to Tibet* (Taichung, Taiwan, 1971), p. 79.

78. *Final Memorandum*, Incl. 4, p. 3.

79. Richardson, pp. 116, 115. See also the Chinese President's explanation to Jordan in FO 535/17, No. 249, Jordan to FO, 29 Sept. 1914.

80. *Final Memorandum*, pp. 6, 10.

Notes to Chapter 5

1. FO 535/20, No. 6, Incl., *Memorandum on Thibetan Question*, 21 Sept. 1916.

2. See the third section in Chapter 4.

3. See L/P&S/10/344, Incl. in Bell to GOI, 28 Oct. 1915: Dalai Lama to Bell, 15 Sept. 1915 and Shapes to Bell, 16 Sept. 1915.

4. See FO 535/17, No. 235, Incl., GOI to IO, 10 Sept. 1914: citing Bell to GOI, 7 Sept. 1914. See also 535/18, No. 15, Incl. 2, GOI to IO, 9 April 1915.

5. FO 535/20, No. 6, Incl., *Memorandum on Thibetan Question* 21 Sept. 1916; FO 535/21, No. 3, Incl. 3, Chief Ministers of Tibet to MacDonald, 26 Nov. 1917.

6. FO 535/17, No. 169, Jordan to FO, 13 June 1914.

7. FO 535/18, No. 19, Incl., GOI to IO, 25 March 1915; FO 535/17, No. 240, Incl., GOI to IO, 16 Sept. 1914.

8. FO 535/18, No. 44, Incl. 2, GOI to Bell, 3 Sept. 1915. In January 1918, the GOI agreed to supply 500,000 rounds of ammunition if it was considered truly necessary. See FO 535/21, No. 4, GOI to Bell, 9 Jan. 1918. At first the British pleaded that no war materials could be spared for Tibet during the World War. Later, the British argued that the Arms Traffic Convention of September 1919 precluded the sale of military armaments to Tibet, as Tibet was not a party to that convention.

9. L/P&S/10/344, statement made by Chamberlain in House of Commons, 20 Oct. 1915, published in India, 22 Oct. 1915.

10. FO 535/17 No. 248, Incl., Jordan to Chinese Minister of Foreign Affairs, 19 Sept. 1914; FO 535/17, No. 237, FO to Jordan, 17 Sept. 1914.

11. FO 535/17, No. 229, FO to Lew Yuk Lin (Chinese Minister, London), 8 Aug. 1914. Both the Tibetans and the British considered the terms now offered by China to be totally inadmissible. As reported by Jordan, these terms were as follows: "(1) If a statement of fact that Tibet forms a part of Chinese territory now included in the notes to be exchanged could be inserted in [the Simla] convention itself, the Chinese Government would agree to the inclusion of Chamdo within "Outer Tibet" and would withdraw Chinese troops and officials now stationed within a year. (2) Chinese trade agents to be stationed at Chamdo, Gyantse, Shigatze, Yatung, Gartok, and other places which may be opened to trade in the future. Their ranks and guards to be the same as those of British agents. (3) The insertion of a clause in the convention to the effect that Outer Tibet recognizes China's suzerainty" (FO 535/18, No. 35, Jordan to FO, 2 Aug. 1915). Apparently, the Chinese wanted to

negotiate a treaty with the British to which the Tibetans would later be made to adhere (FO 535/20 No. 1, Incl., extract from *Peking Daily News*, 27 Dec. 1916).

12. FO 535/20, No. 8, FO to IO, 7 Aug. 1917; FO 535/21, No. 7, Jordan to FO, 13 Dec. 1917, citing reports from Teichman; E. Teichman, *Travels of a Consular Officer in Eastern Tibet* (Cambridge, 1922), pp. 50–51.

13. Teichman, p. 52; FO 535/21, No. 7, Incl. 2, Teichman to Jordan, 21 Nov. 1917. In reply to conciliatory letters from Kalon Lama, Commander of the Tibetan forces, Peng wrote: "Your country of Tibet was for long subject to the Emperor of China, and now, although you are still subject to the President [of the Republic], you have behaved as evil servants acting against their masters. . . . Further evil thoughts have entered your hearts and your tongues have uttered falsehoods regarding the so-called mediation of the British Government between Tibet and China. As our Emperor affords protection to his dominions, there is no need to mention the British Government. . . . Now we, the leaders and troops, will continue our advance to Lhasa, so do you, leaders and troops, prepare for this" (FO 535/21, No. 11, Incl. 9, Peng to Kalon Lama, 4 Jan. 1918).

14. L/P&S/10/714, Teichman to Jordan, 11 Oct. 1918.

15. See Teichman, pp. 57–58; see also pp. 53–56.

16. FO 535/21, No. 16, Jordan to FO, 5 July 1918.

17. For the text of the Sino-Tibetan Peace Treaty of 19 Aug. 1918, see Appendix 22.

18. For the text of the Rongbatsa Agreement of 10 Oct. 1918, see Appendix 23.

19. L/P&S/10/714, Teichman to Jordan, 21 Aug. 1918.

20. L/P&S/10/714, Jordan to FO, 6 July 1918.

21. Ibid.

22. On the boundary question China suggested "a reversion to the old Eighteenth Century line as the boundary of Autonomous Tibet and the creation of an 'Inner Tibet' consisting of Derge, Nyarong, and the southern portion of the Kokonor territory" (L/P&S/10/715, Jordan to FO, 1 June 1919).

23. B. Alston, the British Charge d'Affaires in Beijing, reported an article from the Chinese press representing the view of a considerable portion of the Chinese public and possibly of the military authorities as well. He summarized the ideas expressed therein as follows: "Mongolia having been recovered, China can make no treaty with Great Britain recognizing the autonomy of Tibet and denying China's sovereign (as opposed to suzerain) rights in that country; but if the Tibetans will turn of their own accord to the Chinese Government and beg for favorable treatment and a certain measure of autonomy, it will be graciously granted to them: the Tibetans are members of the Chinese nation, and no interference in Sino-Tibetan affairs by an outside party, such as Great Britain, should be tolerated" (FO 535/23, No. 32, Alston to FO, 24 April 1920). The Tibetan government was not informed of the Sino-British talks until they had broken down. Jordan was of the opinion that a "stable and satisfactory" settlement could be reached only by England and China—a settlement that the Tibetans would then sign. Members of Tibetan government, however, were furious; moreover, the Tsongdu rejected the Chinese proposals outright and demanded that tripartite negotiations be opened in Tibet without delay (L/P&S/10/715, Jordan to FO, 1 June 1919; L/P&S/10/715, GOI to IO, 29 Aug. 1919, citing letter from the Tsongdu and the three Great Monasteries).

24. Tibetan impatience is clear from the following letter from the Kashag to the British government: "Unless we are allowed to purchase soon about Rupees 15 lakhs of rounds of rifle ammunition and a few machine guns, according to the request we have been making for months and months and years and years the case may become a matter of regret to the Tibetans and a disgrace to the good name

of the British Government." See L/P&S/10/716 (part 1), GOI to IO, 23 April 1920. By 1921, news had reached the British that firearms from Russia and Japan were finding their way to Tibet via Mongolia (FO 535/24, No. 26, Incl. 11, Bell to GOI, 29 Jan. 1921).

25. See Inclosures to L/P&S/10/716 (part 1), Bell to GOI, 13 March 1920. Note that the Chinese government denied that the Gansu Mission represented the Central Government (FO 535/23, No. 1, Jordan to FO, 27 Dec. 1919).

26. See Inclosures to L/P&S/10/716 (part 1), Campbell to GOI, 8 Dec. 1919. It is possible that some kind of agreement on the principles for improving Sino-Tibetan relations was drafted, but this fact has not been confirmed.

27. The Tibetan government had sent repeated invitations to the British, but the latter considered themselves precluded from accepting by the terms of the 1907 Treaty with Russia, until the Soviet government formally denounced it shortly after the Bolshevik revolution.

28. FO 535/25, No. 13, Memorandum by Teichman, 12 Aug. 1921.

29. For the full text of this ultimatum, see FO 535/25, No. 24, FO to Alston, 27 Aug. 1921.

30. L/P&S/10/717, FO to Alston, 26 Aug. 1921.

31. H.E. Richardson, *A Short History of Tibet* (New York, 1962), p. 123. Teichman stated in a memorandum that "the object of making this communication was twofold: firstly, to make a final appeal to the Chinese Government to come to terms; and secondly, to show them clearly that in the event of their being unable to do so His Majesty's Government considered that they had a free hand to take what action they pleased in relation to autonomous Tibet without further reference to China, and thus justify themselves in carrying out their long-standing promise to furnish the Tibetans with additional supplies of arms and ammunition strictly for purposes of self-defense" (FO 535/25, No. 41, *Memorandum Respecting Tibet*, 10 Oct. 1921).

32. L/P&S/10/717, Bell to GOI, 21 Feb. 1921; L/P&S/10/718, *Lhasa Mission 1920-21*, p. 4.

33. See L/P&S/10/717, Bell to GOI, 12 Oct. 1921. See also L/P&S/10/717, Bell to GOI, 22 Oct. 1921. The exchange of declarations between the two countries can also be found in these two communications.

34. L/P&S/10/1088, Baily to GOI, 6 June 1927.

35. L/P&S/10/1078, Weir to GOI, 4 April 1930; L/P&S/10/1078, *Latest News From Lhasa*, Incl. in Daukes to GOI, 30 April 1930; L/P&S/10/1088, Laden-La to Pol. O. Sikkim [Weir], 26 May 1930.

36. A list of the questions posed by the President and the Dalai Lama's replies can be found in Tieh-tseng Li (T. Li), *Tibet: Today and Yesterday* (New York, 1960), pp. 153-155. This document is said to have come from the archives of the Mongolian and Tibetan Affairs Commission. It is also referred to in Richardson, *A Short History*, p. 132.

37. L/P&S/10/1228, Pol. O. Sikkim to GOI, 19 June 1931. The Dalai Lama transferred the necessary funds for the upkeep of Jungas and his staff in Nanjing. See L/P&S/10/1088, report from Laden-La to Pol. O. Sikkim [Weir], 26 May 1930.

38. See L/P&S/10/1228, translation of an extract from *Tibet-Mongolia Weekly News* 1, No. 3 (Nov. 1929).

39. L/P&S/10/1228, *Foreign Policy of Mongolia and Tibet*, from *Kuo Min [Guomin] News Agency*, 22 May 1930.

40. Memorandum of conversation, by Hornbeck, 28 Sept. 1943, FRUS, *China* (1943), p. 134.

41. L/P&S/12/4194, Gould to GOI, 23 March 1940. A clear example of misrepresentation of facts by the Chinese is their accounts of the installation of the fourteenth Dalai Lama documented in Note 62 below.

42. L/P&S/10/715, Jordan to FO, 4 Dec. 1919; L/P&S/10/716 (part 1), Alston to FO, 21 May 1920.

43. For a text of the agreement, see L/P&S/10/1228, Toller to Lampson, 25 Jan. 1932. The agreement reached in November 1931 was amended to make the wording less offensive to Chinese public opinion. The essence of the new agreement remained the same: It stipulated that Tibet was to retain control over occupied lands and that China was to pay Tibet an indemnity. However, further truce agreements of 10 Oct. 1932 and 15 June 1933, which regarded the eastern and northeastern Tibet-China borders respectively, reinstituted the boundaries that had existed before the fighting (T. Li, pp. 164–165).

44. L/P&S/10/1113, *Report on Mission to Lhasa*, Baily to GOI, 28 Oct. 1924.

45. The Fourteenth Dalai Lama, lecture delivered to the Austrian Buddhist Society (Nov. 1973). See also T. Li, p. 154 and p. 274, note 105, citing Chinese sources.

46. "The Nature of the Office of the Panchen Lama," Kashag Document 11(4)4; P. Mehra, *Tibetan Polity, 1904–37* (Wiesbaden, 1976), pp. 1–11.

47. For example, on both occasions in which the Dalai Lama fled the country (in 1904 and 1910), the Manchus had urged the Panchen Lama in vain to take his place (Richardson, *A Short History*, pp. 126–127).

48. L/P&S/12/4197, *Lhasa Mission 1936–37*. For a letter to this effect from the Kashag to the Chinese, see L/P&S/10/4197, GOI to IO, 22 July 1936.

49. L/P&S/10/1113, IO Minute Paper, by H. Rumbold, 27 April 1929; L/P&S/12/4197, GOI to IO, 21 July 1936.

50. For the text of the testament, see F. Michael, *Rule by Incarnation* (Boulder, Colorado, 1982), Appendix 1, pp. 171–174.

51. L/P&S/12/4177, telegram from "All the High Monk and Lay Officials and the Public of Tibet," Incl. to Pol. O. Sikkim to GOI, 21 Dec. 1933.

52. L/P&S/12/4177, *National Government Mandate*, 21 Dec. 1933, published in *National Government Gazette*, No. 1319, 22 Dec. 1933.

53. L/P&S/12/4177, Extract, *National Government Gazette*, No. 1335, 13 Jan. 1934.

54. See L/P&S/12/4177, Williamson to GOI, 19 Oct. 1934; and Williamson to GOI, 10 Nov. 1934. See also T. Li, pp. 168–172.

55. L/P&S/12/4177, Williamson to GOI, 22 Nov. 1934, citing report from Rai Bahadur Norbu.

56. Ibid.

57. L/P&S/12/4197, *The Lhasa Mission, 1936–37*: Appendix A, *The Treaty Position*, p. 18.

58. Richardson, *A Short History*, p. 145.

59. L/P&S/12/4194, letter from Pol. O. Sikkim [Gould]; 30 Oct. 1940.

60. The Fourteenth Dalai Lama, *My Land and My People* (New York, 1977), pp. 28–29; L/P&S/12/4197, Gould to GOI, 14 Nov. 1939; L/P&S/12/4194, Gould to GOI, 23 March 1940.

61. L/P&S/12/4194, letter from Pol. O. Sikkim [Gould], 30 Oct. 1940, enclosing letter from Ministers of Tibet to Rai Bahadur Norbu.

62. See W.D. Shakabpa, "Refutation of Chinese Allegations," *Sheja* (Oct. 1980), pp. 7–10; (Nov. 1980), pp. 4–7; Richardson, *A Short History*, pp. 150–151. For accounts of the installation by Basil J. Gould, who was present as a British

representative, see his *Jewel in the Lotus* (London, 1957), pp. 217–229. See also Note 61 above. Gould reported to his government: "As to Mr. Wu Chung Hsin's alleged participation in the installation ceremony of the 22nd February, [it is clear] that the Chinese put out an advance account of events which were not likely to take place and did not take place. This represents one form of tendentious statement" (L/P&S/12/4194, Gould to GOI, 23 March 1940). See also L/P&S/12/4194, Political Department, *Tibet: Chinese Policy in Tibet and the Installation of the Dalai Lama*, Harrison, 18 April 1940.

63. See L/P&S/12/4194, GOI to IO, 14 May 1940, citing telegram from Gould, 10 April 1940. See also Richardson, *A Short History*, p. 155.

64. See Note 61 above.

65. L/P&S/12/4613, FO Secret Report, Oct. 1940.

66. L/P&S/12/4613, *Memorandum from the Ministry of Foreign Affairs*, 22 Feb. 1941; L/P&S/12/4613, Kerr to FO, 25 Feb. 1941.

67. L/P&S/12/4613, British Ambassador (Chongqing) to Ministry of Foreign Affairs, 6 June 1941.

68. L/P&S/12/4613, GOI to IO, 25 July 1941; L/P&S/12/4613, Rai Bahadur to Pol. O. Sikkim, 29 Dec. 1941.

69. L/P&S/12/4613: FO to Chongqing, 30 July 1941; British Embassy, Chongqing, to Chinese Ministry of Foreign Affairs, 16 Aug. 1941; L/P&S/12/4613, GOI to IO, 30 Sept. 1941.

70. L/P&S/12/4613, GOI to Chongqing, 2 April 1942.

71. L/P&S/12/4614, Chongqing to FO, 20 May 1942.

72. L/P&S/12/4614, War Cabinet Distribution to China, FO to Chongqing, 7 June 1942.

73. L/P&S/12/4614, War Cabinet Distribution to the United States, FO to Washington, 19 June 1942.

74. L/P&S/12/4614, GOI to IO, 17 July 1942; L/P&S/12/4614, War Cabinet Distribution to the United States, FO to Washington, 15 Aug. 1942.

75. L/P&S/12/4614, Tibetan FO to Ludlow, 11 Dec. 1942.

76. L/P&S/12/4614, GOI to IO, 23 April 1943; L/P&S/12/4201, *Lhasa Letter*, 28 Feb. 1943.

77. Memorandum by Chief of Division of Far Eastern Affairs (Hamilton), 20 May 1942, FRUS, *China* (1942), pp. 51–54; Amb. Gauss to Sec. of State, 8 May 1942, FRUS, *China* (1942), pp. 42–43.

78. L/P&S/12/4201, *Lhasa Letter*, 24 Aug. 1942; L/P&S/12/4229, Ludlow to GOI, 25 Aug. 1942; L/P&S/12/4229, Ludlow to Pol. O. Sikkim, 4 April 1943.

79. President Roosevelt to the Dalai Lama of Tibet, 3 July 1942, FRUS, *China* (1942), p. 625.

80. L/P&S/12/4229, Dalai Lama to President Roosevelt, 24 Feb. 1943; L/P&S/12/4229, Regent of Tibet to President Roosevelt, 15 Feb. 1943.

81. L/P&S/12/4229, British Missions, Lhasa, to Pol. O. Sikkim, 14 March 1943; L/P&S/12/4229, *A Note on Capt. I. Tolstoy's and Lieut. Brooke Dolan's Visit to Lhasa*, Ludlow to Pol. O. Sikkim [Gould], 4 April 1943.

82. Tibetan FO to Capt. Tolstoy and Lt. Dolan, Feb. 1934, FRUS, *China* (1943), p. 622. In fact, the British representative in Lhasa, Ludlow, reported that the Kashag granted the permission in the hope that the United States would help Tibet to maintain its independence (L/P&S/12/4229, Ludlow to Pol. O. Sikkim [Gould], 4 April 1943).

83. Two more instances in which Tibet asserted its neutrality should be mentioned: The Tibetan government permitted two prisoners of war who had escaped from a

British prison camp to remain in Tibet despite British demands for their extradition; and they requested that U.S. Air Force planes refrain from flying over Tibetan airspace on their flights between China and India. See, respectively, H. Harrer, *Seven Years in Tibet* (London, 1953); and L/P&S/12/4201, *Lhasa Letter*, 2 Jan. 1944.

84. L/P&S/12/4201, *Lhasa Letter*, 24 Aug. 1942; Richardson, *A Short History*, p. 156.

85. C.A. Bell, *Tibet: Past and Present* (1924; rpt. Oxford, 1968), p. 225; FO 535/23, No. 57, Incl., *Report on a Visit to Urga by Mr. Teichman, Aug. 1920*. Teichman wrote that originally the *Bogdo Khans* were Mongols. Under the Manchus, however, the Dalai Lama started to appoint Tibetans; Beijing encouraged these appointments in order to check national and separatist tendencies among the Mongols.

86. Bell, *Tibet*, p. 228.

87. See ibid.; see also FO 535/24, No. 43, Incl., Bell to GOI, 14 March 1921.

88. For the details of these incidents, see FO 535/23, No. 57, Incl., *Report on a Visit to Urga by Mr. Teichman, Aug. 1920*; P. Tang, *Russian and Soviet Policy in Manchuria and Outer Mongolia, 1911–31* (Durham, N.C., 1959), pp. 359–368.

89. FO 535/25, No. 42, *Memorandum Respecting Mongolia*, 10 Oct. 1921.

90. See the last testament of the Thirteenth Dalai Lama in Michael, *Rule by Incarnation*, p. 173. See also Tang, pp. 371–398.

91. L/P&S/10/1113, Political Department, *Note on the Soviet Agent at Lhasa*, 30 March 1930; L/P&S/10/1088, *News Report*, Pol. O. Sikkim to GOI, 10 Jan. 1928.

92. Interviews by the author with Kungo Yeshe and Kalon P. Takla, Dharmsala, Jan. 1981; L/P&S/10/1088, *News Report*, Pol. O. Sikkim to GOI, 10 Jan. 1928.

93. L/P&S/10/1113, Letter from Pol. O. Sikkim, 18 Nov. 1930.

94. L/P&S/10/1113, Minute Paper by Rumbold, 27 April 1929; L/P&S/10/1113, Political Department, *Note on the Soviet Agent at Lhasa*, 30 March 1930.

95. L/P&S/10/1128, Pol. O. Sikkim to GOI, 8 Jan. 1931. The official, Tsetrung Ngawang Trapka, was the Dalai Lama's A.D.C.

96. See P.R. Uprety, *Nepal Tibet Relations, 1850–1930* (Kathmandu, 1980), pp. 134–139.

97. FO 535/16, No. 198, Incl. 2, Chinese Resident of Tibet [Gen. Zhong] to Maharaja of Nepal, Feb. 1913.

98. FO 535/16, No. 201, Incl. 2, Gen. Chung [Pinyin: Zhong] to Thinyik Company, 1 Feb. 1913.

99. FO 535/16, No. 198, Incl. 3, Chinese Resident of Tibet [Gen. Zhong] to President of China, 1 Feb. 1913. The Chinese government encouraged General Zhong's efforts (FO 535/16, No. 201, Incl. 3, intercepted telegram from Peking to Thinyik Company for transmission to Gen. Chung, n.d.).

100. FO 535/16, No. 340, Incl. 6, Prime Minister of Nepal to Gen. Chung, 16 March 1913.

101. Ramakant, *Nepal-China and India* (New Delhi, 1976), p. 27.

102. FO 535/24, No. 59, Incl., Bell to GOI, 22 April 1921.

103. For details, see Bell, *Tibet*, pp. 233–234.

104. L/P&S/10/1078, Prime Minister of Nepal to Dalai Lama, 3 Oct. 1929. For details, see Uprety, pp. 141–145.

105. L/P&S/10/1078, Prime Minister of Nepal to Dalai Lama, 3 Oct. 1929; L/P&S/10/1078, GOI to IO, 10 Oct. 1929; L/P&S/10/1078, GOI to Pol. O. Sikkim, 21 March 1930.

106. See Uprety, pp. 145–150.

107. L/P&S/10/1078, President of National Government of the Republic of China to the King of Nepal, Incl. in British Envoy, Nepal, to GOI, 13 Sept. 1930.

108. L/P&S/10/1078, British Envoy, Nepal, to GOI, 9 Sept. 1930.

109. Memorandum by E. Drumright (Division of Far Eastern Affairs), 26 Oct. 1942, FRUS, China (1942), p. 688.

110. Memorandum by Chief of Division of Far Eastern Affairs, China's War Potential, 17 June 1942, FRUS, China (1942), p. 71.

111. Clarke (FO) to Matthews (U.S. Ambassador, London), 7 Aug. 1942, FRUS, China (1942), p. 145.

112. Memorandum from Division of Far Eastern Affairs (Hamilton), 15 Sept. 1942, FRUS, China (1942), cited in note at p. 631.

113. Berle (Asst. Sec. of State) to Donovan (Director of OSS), 23 April 1943, FRUS, China (1943), p. 629.

114. For example, the United States agreed to purchase surplus wool from Tibet and provided Tibet with wireless sets. Sir Olaf Caroe, Foreign Secretary of the GOI, remarked that in presenting the wireless sets, "no suggestion was made that these should be presented through the Chinese Government" (L/P&S/12/4194, GOI to IO, 7 Aug. 1944). Regarding the surplus wool, see Sec. of State to Currie, 9 June 1944, FRUS, China (1944), pp. 976–977.

115. For a discussion of the establishment of permanent or incidental U.S. representation in Lhasa, see Memorandum by Drumright (Division of Far Eastern Affairs), 26 Oct. 1942, FRUS, China (1942), pp. 687–693; Memorandum by Clubb, 21 April 1944, FRUS, China (1944), p. 963. Clubb cautioned, however, that "it is felt that any action which the U.S. might take in this general connection should be designed carefully to avoid U.S. involvement in international politics respecting the status of Tibet."

116. L/P&S/12/4194, British Embassy, Washington, Aide memoire, 19 April 1943.

117. L/P&S/12/4194, IO to FO, 7 May 1943.

118. L/P&S/12/4194, DO to Governments of Canada, Australia, New Zealand, South Africa, sent at 11:45 p.m., 4 June 1943.

119. L/P&S/12/4195 B, Eden to Seymour, 22 July 1943, Incl.

120. L/P&S/12/4232, memorandum presented by Eden to Dr. Soong, 5 Aug. 1943.

121. L/P&S/12/4217 Aide memoire, Pol. O. Sikkim [Gould] to Kashag and Tibetan FO, 22 Dec. 1944.

122. Bell, Tibet, p. 243, pp. 99–106. Through a series of Anglo-Bhutanese treaties in 1865 and 1910, Bhutan became a protectorate of the British Empire and surrendered the conduct of its foreign relations to the British.

123. See T. Li, who cites Japanese Foreign Office Archives documents at the Library of Congress (pp. 124–125): Reel S. 656 S 1.6.1. 3–4, Chibetto Mondai Oyobi Jijo Kandei Zassan.

124. Ibid., p. 158; pp. 276–277, notes 124 and 125. Citing Japanese FO Archives at the Library of Congress: Reel 126, T. 1.6.1.4–7, Report of Sakai (Japanese Consul Gen. at Shanghai) to K. Uchida (Japanese Foreign Minister), 8 Sept. 1932.

125. Ibid., pp. 193–194, citing Japanese FO Archives at Library of Congress: Reel S 656 S 1.6.1.3–4, Report of Tibetan Affairs, by Bunkyo Aoki, Sept. 1944.

126. L/P&S/12/4201, Lhasa Letter, 15 Oct. 1944.

127. L/P&S/12/4217, Gould to GOI, 15 Nov. 1944; L/P&S/12/4217, Aide memoire, Gould to Kashag and Tibetan FO, 22 Dec. 1944.

Notes to Chapter 6

1. The new Chinese representative in Lhasa, former Presidential Adviser Shen Zonglian, informed the Kashag in October 1945 that there would be an important

conference in Nanjing to deal with the postwar settlement and constitutional arrangements. On behalf of his government, he extended to the Tibetans an invitation to send a high-level delegation to the conference, which was, in fact, China's National Assembly. The Tibetan government declined the invitation, suggesting instead that it would send an official Good Will Mission to New Delhi and Nanjing. See L/P&S/12/4226, GOI to IO, 8 Nov. 1945.

2. L/P&S/12/4226, *Tibetan Government Good Will Mission*, Minute Paper, 27 March 1946.

3. L/P&S/12/4226, IO to GOI, 22 Nov. 1945; L/P&S/12/4195B, IO to GOI, 5 March 1946.

4. L/P&S/12/4226, report quoting a Central News Agency release, Seymour to FO, 1 May 1946.

5. See Note 2 above.

6. In 1944, a delegation from Labrang in Gansu Province was much publicized as a "Tibetan delegation" in order to create the impression that it was from Tibet (L/P&S/12/4196: British Embassy, Chonqing, to FO, 3 Feb. 1944; extract from confidential report, Menon, 4 April 1944). There was no Tibetan representation in the National Assembly until 1913, when ten ethnic Tibetans living in China were appointed by the Chinese government to each house of the Assembly. See FRUS, *China* (1913), p. 89; L/P&S/10/341, Alston to FO, 2 July 1913.

7. L/P&S/12/4226: Hopkinson [Pol. O. Sikkim] to GOI, 30 Jan. 1946; *Tibetan Government Good Will Mission*, Minute Paper, 27 March 1946.

8. L/P&S/12/4226, GOI to Pol. O. Sikkim, 15 June 1946.

9. "The 9-Point Communiqué, 1945" is a document translated by and in the possession of Lobsang Lhalungpa. The letter required, among other things, that Chinese wishing to travel to Tibet apply for an entry visa, and it suggested that this requirement be made reciprocal. The Tibetans also demanded the closing of the Chinese Mission in Lhasa, suggesting that the two governments maintain contact by means of the new wireless system to be installed in Tibet shortly thereafter. See also L/P&S/12/4226, British Embassy, Nanjing, to GOI, 25 October 1946.

10. L/P&S/12/4226: Brit. Trade Agent, Gyantse [Richardson] to Pol. O. Sikkim [Hopkinson], 16 July 1946; Brit. Trade Agent, Gyantse to Pol. O. Sikkim, 4 Aug. 1946; H.E. Richardson, *A Short History of Tibet* (New York, 1962), p. 167.

11. See Note 10 above; see also L/P&S/12/4226, British Embassy, Nanjing, to GOI, 25 Oct. 1946.

12. Tieh-tseng Li (T. Li), *Tibet: Today and Yesterday* (New York, 1960), p. 191.

13. L/P&S/12/4226, Brit. Trade Agent, Gyantse, to Pol. O. Sikkim, 9 Dec. 1946.

14. Ibid.

15. Tibet was mentioned, however, in several articles of the 1946 and 1948 Constitutions. See M.M. Whiteman, ed., *Digest of International Law*, Vol. 1 (Washington, 1963), p. 462. See also Kashag Document 11(4)12; Richardson, p. 167; T. Li, p. 191.

16. L/P&S/12/4226, Lamb, British Embassy, Nanjing, to FO, 28 Feb. 1947. It was reported in April of 1946 that delegations to the National Assembly had arrived in China from the United Kingdom, Cuba, the Philippines, and elsewhere (L/P&S/12/4226, Seymour to FO, 1 May 1946).

17. W.F. van Eekelen, *Indian Foreign Policy and the Border Dispute with China* (The Hague, 1964), p. 24.

18. Quoted in N. Sinha, "Asian Relations and Gandhi," *Indian Yearbook of International Affairs* 17 (1974), p. 511.

19. L/P&S/12/4197, GOI to Pol. O. Sikkim, 23 July 1947.

20. L/P&S/12/4197, U.K. High Commissioner, New Delhi, to CRO, 7 Nov. 1947; Richardson, p. 174.

21. Quoted in *Letter from Prime Minister of India to the Prime Minister of China*, 26 Sept. 1959, *White Paper*, No. 2 (1959), p. 39.

22. The Chinese, in an apparent test of India's policy, suggested that the 1908 Trade Regulations were due for revision. The Indian government replied that it recognized only the validity of the 1914 agreements with Tibet, which had canceled the earlier Trade Regulations (Richardson, p. 176).

23. Richardson, pp. 174–175.

24. W.D. Shakabpa, *Tibet: A Political History* (New Haven, 1967), p. 295.

25. L/P&S/12/4230, British Embassy, Nanjing, to FO, 19 May 1948. The Central News Agency in Nanjing reported the purpose of the Trade Mission as being to "negotiate with the authorities on the problem of improving trade relations between Tibet and other provinces" (quoted in L/P&S/12/4230, British Embassy, Nanjing, to FO, 25 Feb. 1948).

26. See ibid.; and Kashag Document 11(4)12. For the Chinese view, see T. Li, p. 191.

27. Grady to Sec. of State, 21 Aug. 1947, *FRUS* 7 (1947), p. 599; L/P&S/12/4230, British Embassy, Washington, to FO, 5 Nov. 1948.

28. Sec. of State to Stuart (U.S. Ambassador, Nanjing), 28 July 1948, *FRUS* 7 (1948), p. 767. Note that in its statements, the U.S. government indiscriminately used the terms "suzerainty" and "sovereignty," because the former term was not generally accepted in U.S. political terminology as it was by the British. To avoid controversy, the suggestion was therefore made that Chinese *de jure* authority over Tibet or some similar term be used to denote the purely nominal character of that authority. See memorandum by R. Bacon to Sprouse, 12 April 1949, *FRUS* 9 (1949), p. 1069.

29. Sec. of State to Stuart, 28 July 1948, *FRUS* 7 (1948), p. 767. The present author has added prepositions and articles to correct telegraphic style.

30. Memorandum of Conversation, by Sprouse, 31 July 1948, *FRUS* 7 (1948), pp. 768–769; Memorandum of Conversation, by Freeman, 2 Feb. 1948, *FRUS* 7 (1948), pp. 770–771. See also *Tibetan Trade Delegation Report, 1948*, unpublished document from the Office of His Holiness the Dalai Lama, Dharmsala.

31. Sec. of State to Stuart, 4 Aug. 1948, *FRUS* 7 (1948), p. 773. For the text of the complimentary letters from the Dalai Lama, the Regent, and the Kashag to President Truman, see *FRUS* 7 (1948), pp. 773–774.

32. The Charge d'Affaires in India to the Sec. of State, 30 Dec. 1947, *FRUS* 7 (1947), p. 605; Sec. of State to Sec. of Treasury, 27 Aug. 1948, *FRUS* 7 (1948), p. 780. The sale of gold had to be postponed until the Tibetan foreign exchange problem was resolved.

33. L/P&S/12/4195B, CRO to FO, 16 Nov. 1948.

34. Ibid; L/P&S/12/4230, CRO to U.K. High Commissioner, India, 17 Dec. 1948; L/P&S/12/4230, J. Mark to Shakabpa, 9 Dec. 1948.

35. L/P&S/12/4230: J. Mark to Shakabpa, 9 Dec. 1948; FO to Stevenson, 23 Dec. 1948; British Embassy, Washington, to FO, 11 Aug. 1948; L/P&S/12/4234, Richardson to Pol. O. Sikkim, 1 Aug. 1948. Italy, too, expressed an interest in establishing trade relations with Tibet (*Tibetan Trade Delegation Report, 1948*).

36. The original passports of some of the Trade Mission members are still in their possession. That of Shakabpa was reproduced in the 1967 edition of *Tibet: A Political History*. Both the United States and the United Kingdom initially had some misgivings about recognizing the travel documents, as doing so was sure to

offend China. They contemplated using separate forms, but ultimately the visas were stamped directly on the passports. The Chinese had demanded that the Tibetans use Chinese passports and even offered them financial rewards. China protested the recognition by the other governments of the Tibetan passports. See Memorandum of Conversation, by Sprouse, 12 July 1948, FRUS 7 (1948), pp. 759–760; L/P&S/ 12/4230: FO to Nanjing, 17 July 1948; British Embassy, Washington, to FO, 11 Aug. 1948.

37. *An Outline History of China* (Beijing: Foreign Languages Press, 1958), pp. 434–435.

38. C. Brandt, B. Schwartz, J.K. Fairbank, *A Documentary History of Chinese Communism* (Cambridge, Massachusetts, 1952), p. 64.

39. V. Yakhontoff, *The Chinese Soviets* (New York, 1934), p. 277.

40. As a preliminary to this move, the Kashag called a number of troops to Lhasa. See L/P&S/12/4232, Indian Trade Agent, Gyantse [Richardson] to Pol. O. Sikkim, 1 Aug. 1949. The Tibetan government also felt that if the Nationalist Chinese Mission were allowed to stay, the communists would expect the same privileges once they came into power. See Kashag Document 11(4)10. Thus, in addition to the official reason given, the move was undoubtedly meant as a demonstration of Tibet's independence in the face of the new Chinese threat.

41. L/P&S/12/4232, FO to Singapore, 6 Sept. 1949, quoting the Beijing Radio Broadcast.

42. L/P&S/12/4232, Tibetan FO to Chairman Mao Zedong, 2 Nov. 1949.

43. L/P&S/12/4232, Tibetan FO to Bevin, 4 Nov. 1949.

44. *Continuation of Paper on China*, British Embassy to Department of State, 10 Jan. 1949, FRUS 9 (1949), p. 9; Henderson to Sec. of State, 12 April 1949, FRUS 9 (1949), pp. 1071–1072.

45. L/P&S/12/4232, U.K. High Commissioner, India, to CRO, 17 Nov. 1949; L/P&S/12/4232, U.K. High Commissioner, India, to CRO, 26 Nov. 1949; Donovan to Sec. of State, 23 Nov. 1949, FRUS 9 (1949), p. 1084.

46. Henderson to Sec. of State, 10 Jan. 1950, FRUS 6 (1950), pp. 272–273.

47. Henderson to Sec. of State, 30 Dec. 1949, FRUS 9 (1949), p. 1097; Donovan to Sec. of State, 21 Nov. 1949, telegrams sent at 10 a.m. and 3 p.m., FRUS 9 (1949), pp. 1080–1083; Donovan to Sec. of State, 7 Nov. 1949, FRUS 9 (1949), pp. 177–178.

48. L/P&S/12/4232, U.K. High Commissioner, India, to CRO, 17 Nov. 1949.

49. L/P&S/12/4232, Intel from FO to H.M.'s Representatives abroad [all British Diplomatic posts are listed in the document], 5 Dec. 1949.

50. L/P&S/12/4232, British Embassy, Washington, to FO, 1 Dec. 1949; Memorandum by Bacon to Sprouse, 12 April 1949, FRUS 9 (1949), pp. 1065–1071.

51. Henderson to Sec. of State, 14 Dec. 1949, FRUS 9 (1949), pp. 1091–1092; Sec. of State to Embassy, New Delhi, 12 Jan. 1950, FRUS 6 (1950), p. 276. In fact the Chinese did threaten that "any country receiving such illegal 'missions' [would] be regarded as harbouring hostile intentions towards the People's Republic of China." See "Statement by the Spokesman of the Chinese Foreign Ministry Regarding 'Good Will Missions' of Lhasa Authorities," 20 Jan. 1950, in R.K. Jain, *China-South Asian Relations* (New Delhi, 1981), Vol. 1, p. 17.

52. Henderson to Sec. of State, 9 June 1950, FRUS 6 (1950), pp. 361–362; Sec. of State to Henderson, 19 April 1950, FRUS 6 (1950), pp. 330–331.

53. Shakabpa, pp. 299–300.

54. Ibid., p. 300.

55. Sec. of State to Henderson, 1 March 1950, *FRUS* 6 (1950), p. 314; Henderson to Sec. of State, 8 March 1950, *FRUS* 6 (1950), pp. 317–318; Sec. of State to Henderson, 16 June 1950, *FRUS* 6 (1950), pp. 364–365.

56. Sec. of State to Henderson, 19 April 1950, *FRUS* 6 (1950), p. 331.

57. Editorial note, *FRUS* 6 (1950), p. 367; Henderson to Sec. of State, 7 Aug. 1950, *FRUS* 6 (1950), pp. 424–426.

58. Douglas to Sec. of State, 12 Aug. 1950, *FRUS* 6 (1950), pp. 430–431; Henderson to Sec. of State, 25 Aug. 1950, *FRUS* 6 (1950), p. 449.

59. Shakabpa, p. 300.

60. *Military Communiqué on Entry of Chinese Army into Tibet*, NCNA, 8 Nov. 1950, in Union Research Institute (URI), *Tibet, 1950–1967* (Hong Kong, 1968), p. 2; Shakabpa, p. 301. Note that, in June of 1950 and even in 1949, China had already made incursions into Tibetan territory. See Henderson to Sec. of State, 9 June 1950, *FRUS* 6 (1950), p. 362.

Notes to Chapter 7

1. J. Crawford, "The Criteria for Statehood in International Law," *BYIL* 48 (1976–1977), p. 93; P. Cobbett, *Cases and Opinions on International Law*, 3rd ed. (London, 1909), Vol. 1, pp. 44–45.

2. L. Oppenheim, *International Law*, ed. H. Lauterpacht, 8th ed. (London, 1955), Vol. 1, pp. 118–119; P.C. Jessup, *A Modern Law of Nations* (New York, 1968), p. 46. For the discussion of the elements of statehood, the present author is much indebted to the comprehensive works of Marek and Crawford: K. Marek, *Identity and Continuity of States in Public International Law* (Geneva, 1968); and J. Crawford, *The Creation of States in International Law* (Oxford, 1979).

3. Permanent Court of Arbitration, *North Atlantic Fisheries* case, Great Britain v. U.S.A. (1910), in *AJIL* 4 (1910), p. 956. See also I. Delupis, *International Law and the Independent State* (New York, 1974), p. 4.

4. Judge Anzilotti wrote of this principle that none was more well grounded in international law. See D. Anzilotti, "La formazione del regno d'Italia nei riguardi del diritto internazionale," *Rivista di Diritto Internazionale* (1912), p. 9. See also the Mixed Arbitral Tribunal, *Deutsche Continental Gas-Gesellschaft v. Poland* case, in *Tribunaux Arbitraux Mixtes* 9 (1930), p. 346.

5. Crawford, p. 37; see also pp. 38–39.

6. Oppenheim uses the term "a people," but does so within the meaning of a population. See Oppenheim, p. 118. See also Cobbett, p. 45.

7. See H. Kelsen, "La Naissance de l'Etat et la formation de sa nationalite," *Revue de Droit International* (1929), p. 614; Crawford, p. 42.

8. See the *Lighthouses in Crete and Samos* case (France v. Greece), P.C.I.J. (1937), Series A/B, No. 71, p. 136; and the case concerning *Serbian Loans Issued in France*, P.C.I.J. (1929), Series A, Nos. 20/1, Judgement No. 14, p. 44.

9. Crawford, p. 42.

10. Ibid., pp. 46–47.

11. See F. Despagnet, *Essai sur les Protectorats* (Paris, 1896), p. 8; C.C. Hyde, *International Law: Chiefly as Interpreted and Applied by the United States* (Boston, 1945), Vol. 1, pp. 22–23.

12. See Oppenheim, pp. 118–119; H. Kelsen, "Recognition in International Law," *AJIL* 35 (1941), p. 608; *Case of the S.S. Lotus*, Judge Weiss, Dissenting Opinion, in P.C.I.J. (1927), Series A, No. 10, p. 44. But also see Hyde and Westlake, who do

not consider independence to be a necessary element of statehood: Hyde, p. 22; J. Westlake, *International Law* (Cambridge, 1910), Vol. 1, p. 21.

13. R. Lansing, *Notes on Sovereignty* (Washington, 1921), pp. 30, 38.

14. Permanent Court of Arbitration, *Island of Palmas* case (1928), in R.I.A.A. 2, p. 823. In the court's definition, the positive and negative aspects of sovereignty are evident: The positive concern the exercise of domestic jurisdiction and the determination of the State's foreign policy, whereas the negative concern independence from other States in these areas. See G. Schwartzenberger, *International Law*, 3rd ed. (London, 1957), Vol. 1, pp. 118–119.

15. Delupis, pp. 21–23; Schwartzenberger, p. 121.

16. Schwartzenberger, p. 121; Crawford, p. 48; Jessup, pp. 40–41.

17. Independent Opinion, *Customs Regime Between Austria and Germany*, P.C.I.J. (1931), Series B, No. 41, p. 58. Anzilotti's definition contains two elements found in most definitions of independence: the "separateness" of the State and its direct subordination to international law. The two elements can hardly be separated. Only a separate State—that is, one that is not part of or subordinate to another state, can be directly subordinate to international law. The Majority Opinion in the *Customs Regime Between Austria and Germany* case (at p. 45) is at times cited as a definition of independence, but it is far too absolute to serve as a general definition of independence. See Crawford, p. 51.

18. Crawford, pp. 52, 54–56; Marek, p. 168; Kelsen, p. 608; Delupis, pp. 21–22; Hyde, p. 22.

19. P.C.I.J. (1920), Series A, No. 1, p. 25. For confirmation thereof, see *Jurisdiction of the European Commission of the Danube Between Galatz and Braila*, P.C.I.J. (1927), Series B, No. 14, p. 36.

20. J.H.W. Verzijl, *International Law in Historical Perspective*, Vol. 2 (Leiden, 1969), pp. 482–488. Note that the "capitulation treaties" even provided that certain judicial functions would be exercised by the consuls of foreign powers. See also I. Detter, "The Problem of Unequal Treaties," *International and Comparative Law Quarterly* (1966), pp. 1073 ff.

21. Crawford, pp. 54–55, 295–297.

22. Separate opinion, P.C.I.J. (1937), Series A/B, No. 71 p. 127.

23. Schwartzenberger, p. 120.

24. See the *Charkieh* case (1873) and *Mighell v. Sultan of Johore* (1894) cited in Cobbett, pp. 41–43; Judge Seferiades, Dissenting opinion, *Lighthouses in Crete and Samos* case, P.C.I.J., Series A, Nos. 20/1, Judgment 14 (1929), p. 44.

25. Crawford, pp. 44, 247–270.

26. Ibid., pp. 42–44. For a discussion of devolution, see Verzijl, pp. 66–86.

27. A. McNair and A.D. Watts, *The Legal Effects of War*, 4th ed. (Cambridge, 1966), p. 426; Crawford, pp. 57–58. Marek writes: "Belligerent occupation is precisely the classical case, where the principle of effectiveness is relegated to the background and yields its place to contrary rules of international law." See Marek, p. 88 and pp. 87, 73–126, 266–267. See also J.S. Pictet, e.d., *Commentary: IV Geneva Convention Relative to the Protection of Persons in Time of War* (Geneva, 1958), p. 257.

28. Hyde, p. 392.

29. The other three Baltic States declared their independence at the same time, and Soviet Russia recognized that fact in four treaties in 1920. On 14 October 1920, a treaty was signed with Finland. See Martens, *Nouveau Recueil*, 3rd Series, Vol. 12, p. 37.

30. L.N.O.J., Special Supplement No. 3 (Oct. 1920), p. 9.

31. I. Brownlie, *Principles of Public International Law*, p. 76.

244   Notes to Chapter 7

32. Crawford, pp. 60–69.

33. Similarly, Denmark found itself under a considerable degree of influence from Napoleon's France. Nevertheless, arbitrators investigated this relationship early in the last century and rightly concluded that "the kingdom of Denmark was then, as now, independent. . . ." See J.B. Moore, *History and Digest of the International Arbitrations to Which the United States Has Been a Party* (1898), Vol. 5, pp. 4475–4476.

34. The Allied forces occupied Iran to forestall fears of an impending German takeover. But throughout the occupation the Allies emphasized their intention not to impair in any way the legal independence and territorial integrity of Iran (Crawford, p. 69).

35. Crawford, p. 72; Marek, p. 243. Crawford points out that the Mali Federation lasted only two months and British Somaliland only five days. The short existence of these States, however, did not affect their statehood while they were in existence (Crawford, p. 72).

36. Jessup, p. 43.

37. Ibid.

38. See G.H. Hackworth, e.d., *Digest of International Law*, Vol. 1 (Washington, 1940), p. 161. See also Article 2 of Draft No. 6, American Institute of International Law, *AJIL* Official Document, Special Number (Oct. 1926).

39. Marek, p. 8.

40. J.F. Williams, "Some Thoughts on the Doctrine of Recognition in International Law," *Harvard Law Review* 47 (1934), p. 779; J.L. Brierly, *The Law of Nations*, 4th ed. (Oxford, 1949), pp. 124–125.

41. "The Inter-American Convention on Rights and Duties of States," Montevideo, 1933, *U.S.T.S.* No. 881.

42. Oppenheim, p. 146; Hackworth, pp. 166–168.

43. Lansing, p. 34. See also Hyde, p. 190, note 15. The Mixed Arbitral Tribunal confirmed this conclusion in *Deutsche Continental Gas-Gesellschaft v. Poland*, in TAM 9 (1929), p. 344.

44. H. Kelsen, "La naissance de l'Etat et la formation de sa nationalite," *Revue de Droit International* (1929), p. 618 (translated by M. Lutz).

45. *Deutsche Continental Gas-Gesellschaft v. Poland*, TAM 9 (1929), p. 344; Oppenheim, p. 148; Cobbett, p. 49; P. Brown, "The Legal Effects of Recognition," *AJIL* 44 (1950), p. 633.

46. P.C.I.J. (1933), Series A/B, No. 53, pp. 68–69; T. Baty, "So-Called 'De Facto' Recognition," *Yale Law Journal* (1922), pp. 469–470; C.C. Hyde, "Status of the Republic of Indonesia in International Law," *Columbia Law Review* 49 (1949), p. 964.

47. A.M. Stuyt, *The General Principles of Law* (The Hague, 1946), p. 204; Kelsen, "La Naissance de l'Etat," p. 617; J.L. Brierly, "Regles Generales du Droit de la Paix," *Recueil Des Cours* 58 (1936), p. 60. Van Roijen remarks that one must avoid confusing the notions of *de facto* or *de jure* recognition, and *de facto* or *de jure* States or governments, for the only point of agreement among international lawyers is that there is no relation whatsoever between the two notions. See J. van Roijen, *De Rechtspositie en de Volkenrechtelijke Erkenning van Nieuwe Staten en De-Facto Regeringen* (1929), p. 43; see also pp. 44–46.

48. This conduct is also referred to as "acts falling short of recognition" (Hyde, p. 157; Hackworth, p. 327). Marek (p. 142) shows how the existence of States has time and again been confirmed by the practice of States that, notwithstanding their own non-recognition, have engaged in active intercourse with such allegedly non-existent entities.

49. In support of this view, see the *Eastern Greenland* case, P.C.I.J. (1933), Series A/B, No. 53, pp. 45–46. But also see Marek (pp. 129, 142–145, 216–217), who suggests that such a perception can be admitted only to a limited extent as a controvertible piece of evidence.

50. Crawford, pp. 94–106.

51. Ibid., p. 68.

52. This presumption is reflected in Article 2, paragraph 7, of the U.N. Charter, which protects a State's territorial integrity and independence. See Schwartzenberger, p. 119, 123–126; Morgenthau, pp. 343–344; *Case of the S.S. Lotus*, P.C.I.J. (1927), Series A, No. 10, pp. 18, 34.

53. Crawford, pp. 70–71; Marek, pp. 188–189; Cobbett, p. 49.

54. Marek, pp. 279, 302, 310–311, 553–556, 589, 592.

55. Marek, pp. 103–104. Upon liberation, a new State is not created, but the old State continues following a temporary suspension of effective independence. See ibid., pp. 80–81, 98–99; see also pp. 102–103.

56. Ibid., pp. 103–110, 263–282; see also p. 86, note 1.

57. J. Westlake, *The Collected Papers of John Westlake on Public International Law*, ed. L. Oppenheim (1914), p. 87.

58. Dissenting Opinion of Judges Adatci et al., *Customs Regime Between Austria and Germany*, Advisory Opinion, P.C.I.J. (1931), Series A/B, No. 41, p. 77.

59. E.D. Dickinson, *The Equality of States in International Law*, Harvard Studies in Jurisprudence No. 3 (Cambridge, Massachusetts, 1920), pp. 34–99; H. Grotius, *De Jure Belli et Pacis* (Cambridge, 1853), Vol. 1, pp. 151–162; pp. 136–137.

60. Dickinson, p. 58; Grotius, Vol. 1, pp. 113–114, 151–162; pp. 136–137.

61. L. Rose, *Nepal: Strategy for Survival* (Berkeley, 1971), p. 115.

62. Westlake, *Papers*, p. 86.

63. Verzijl, pp. 412–413, 425.

64. Statement made on 17 March 1884, quoted in G. Venturini, *Il Protettorato Internazionale* (Milan, 1939), p. 20.

65. Quoted in Verzijl, p. 414. Translated by M. Lutz.

66. Crawford, p. 186.

67. Ibid.; see also Oppenheim, p. 192.

68. Regarding the first point, see Judge Anzilotti, Individual Opinion, *Customs Regime between Austria and Germany*, P.C.I.J. (1931), Series B, No. 41, p. 57. Regarding the second point, see Hyde, p. 44.

69. *Nationality Decrees in Tunis and Morocco*, Advisory Opinion, P.C.I.J. (1923), Series B, No. 4, p. 27.

70. This position is virtually unanimously accepted. See Verzijl, pp. 413–415. See also Venturini, pp. 9–10; D. Anzilotti, *Corso di Diritto Internazionale* (Rome, 1928), p. 215.

71. G.B. Davis, *The Elements of International Law* (1908), p. 38. Oppenheim defines the protectorate as follows: "A Protectorate arises when a weak State surrenders itself by treaty to the protection of a strong State in such a way that it transfers the management of all its more important international affairs to the protecting State. Through such a treaty an international union is called into existence between two States, and the relation is called protectorate." See Oppenheim, p. 92; see also Despagnet, p. 51.

72. Venturini, pp. 62, 83–84; J. Westlake, *International Law*, 2nd ed. (Cambridge, 1910), Vol. 1, pp. 21–24; Crawford, p. 187; Marek, pp. 283–287, 299; Oppenheim, pp. 192–193; Verzijl, pp. 417–418, 438.

73. Westlake, *International Law*, pp. 21–24; Oppenheim, p. 192; Anzilotti, p. 206; Venturini, pp. 97–98, 106–107. The British Order of Council of 18 December 1914 stipulated: "His Majesty's Government will adopt all measures necessary for the defence of Egypt and the protection of its inhabitants and interests." See B.F.S.P., Vol. 109, p. 109. The *Protocol Between Corea and Japan Concerning Friendly Relations*, signed at Seoul, 23 Feb. 1904, and the *Treaty of Protectorate between France and Annam*, signed at Hue, 6 June 1884, both contain similar stipulations.

74. Venturini, pp. 20–21; Verzijl, pp. 416–418.

75. Venturini, pp. 13–14, 97–100; Verzijl, p. 419. The *Treaty of Protectorate Between France and Annam* (1884) and the *Protocol Between Corea and Japan* (1904) both include such a provision.

76. Verzijl, p. 418; Venturini, pp. 15–16, citing many authors.

77. Despagnet, pp. 317 ff.; Venturini, pp. 106–107. Whereas the commission of an international wrong by a protected State engages the responsibility of the protecting State, the performance of juridical acts by the latter on behalf of the former binds the protected State (Verzijl, p. 419).

78. Venturini, p. 17.

79. Verzijl, p. 418. According to Article 3 of the *Peace Treaty of Gandamak*, "His Highness the Amir of Afganistan and its dependencies agrees to conduct his relations with foreign States in accordance with the advice and wishes of the British Government" (Martens, *Nouveau Recueil*, 2nd Series, Vol. 4, p. 536). The *Treaty of Guarantee Between France and Tunis* (1881) and the *Treaty of Peace and Alliance Between France and Annam* (1874) both gave France similar powers. Venturini, however, doubts whether this is sufficient control to qualify as a protectorate relationship (Venturini, pp. 17, 20, 111–114).

80. Venturini, pp. 111–112, 115–136; Anzilotti, p. 206. Some examples are the *Treaty of Protectorate Between France and Annam* (1884), the *Treaty Between France and Morocco for the Organisation of the Protectorate* (1912), and the *Treaty Between France and Madagascar* (1885).

81. For examples of indirect rather than direct intervention, see the *Convention Between France and Tunisia* (1883), and the *Treaty Betweeen France and Morocco* (1912). On the other hand, the *Treaty of Protectorate Between France and Annam* (1884) allowed considerable direct French intervention in the domestic affairs of Annam in order to effect reforms in the organization of the judicial system, public works, and customs. Article 10 also granted France extrajudicial rights, thus giving it jurisdiction over foreigners (Martens, *Nouveau Receuil*, 2nd Series, Vol. 12, p. 634; Venturini, p. 92; Verzijl, p. 426).

82. The *Protocol Between Corea and Japan* (1904) permitted the Imperial government of Japan to occupy "such places as may be necessary from strategical points of view" to protect Korea and its Imperial House (B.F.S.P., Vol. 98, p. 842). Article 4 of the *Protectorate Between France and Annam* (1884) is similar in this regard.

83. The 1815 treaty establishing the protectorate over the Ionian Islands provided for the appointment of a British Lord-Commissioner, invested with all authority (B.F.S.P., Vol. 3, p. 250). Article 5 of the *Treaty of Guarantee Between France and Tunis* (1881) gave France similar powers. See also Venturini, p. 104.

84. Venturini, p. 132. This is evident from the provisions of the above-mentioned treaties.

85. This retention of status is illustrated by the status of the Ionian Islands vis-à-vis their British protectorate (Verzijl, pp. 421–422). For the position of Zanzibar and Morocco, see also pp. 425–426. See Crawford, pp. 188–189; Oppenheim, p.

193; Venturini, pp. 51–52; and the *Case Concerning Rights of Nationals of the U.S.A. in Morocco*, in I.C.J., *Reports* (1952), p. 185.

86. Venturini, pp. 51–52, 61; Despagnet, pp. 369–370. Oppenheim characterizes the protectorate as an international union between two States (Oppenheim, Vol. 1, p. 192). See the *Case Concerning Rights of Nationals of the U.S.A. in Morocco*, in I.C.J., *Reports* (1952), pp. 185–188. See also J. Westlake, *Chapters on the Principles of International Law* (Cambridge, 1894), p. 178. Protecting and protected States generally continue to regulate or modify their mutual relations by means of international treaties. Japan's protectorate over Korea and France's protectorate over Annam are two such examples. Despagnet concludes that wars between the Protector and Protected are necessarily international and not civil wars (Despagnet, p. 372).

87. See *Case Concerning the Rights of Nationals of the U.S.A. in Morocco*, note 85; Venturini, pp. 132–134; Despagnet, pp. 370–371. The British, for example, concluded treaties for Zanzibar on behalf of and in the name of the protected State, by using the formula: "The Government of Her British Majesty, acting on behalf of His Highness the Sultan of Zanzibar," [translated by M. Lutz]. See Verzijl, p. 427; for other examples, see p. 441.

88. Marek, p. 301.

89. I.C.J. *Reports*, (1952), pp. 185, 188.

90. This situation often leads to the creation of the so-called colonial protectorate. Judge Huber, in the *Island of Palmas* case, distinguished between international and colonial protectorates, reserving for the former the title of "true protectorate." See *Arbitral Award Concerning the Island of Palmas*, AJIL 22 (1928), p. 898. See also T. Baty, "Protectorates and Mandates," BYIL 2 (1921–22), pp. 113–115; Venturini, pp. 147, 149. Notable examples are provided by the gradual consolidation of the powers of France over its protectorates in South-East Asia. Relations between the two States are regulated by the municipal law (colonial legislation) of the colonizing State and not international law (Verzijl, p. 415; for a list of examples, see p. 414).

91. Venturini, p. 149.

92. Despagnet, pp. 361–362; Venturini, pp. 151–152. The outbreaks of war in Transvaal in 1902, in Madagascar in 1896, and in Abyssinia in the same year serve as examples (Venturini, p. 151).

93. Oppenheim, p. 188; Dickinson, p. 236.

94. Verzijl, pp. 339–340; Crawford, p. 209. With the advent of colonialism, the use of the term "suzerainty" was modified yet again to suit the interests of the colonial powers. See C.H. Alexandrowicz-Alexander, "The Legal Position of Tibet," AJIL 48 (1954), pp. 265–266; Westlake, *International Law*, pp. 25–26; H.M. Albaharna, *The Legal Position of Arabian Gulf States* (Manchester, 1968), pp. 61–62.

95. Verzijl, pp. 339–340. The Overlordship of the Kings of England over the Kings of Scotland in the twelfth and thirteenth centuries provides an example of a relationship with all of these characteristics (ibid., pp. 341–342).

96. Alexandrowicz, p. 266; Dickinson, p. 236.

97. Westlake, *Papers*, p. 90. For example, see Article 8 of the *Treaty of Osnabruck* between the Holy Roman Emperor and Sweden, in Dickinson, pp. 231–232.

98. Verzijl, pp. 340–343; see also pp. 348–350. The situation often developed in which a ruler, who was independent with regard to his own domain, was simultaneously the vassal of another independent ruler with respect to territories held from the latter in fief. A ruler might even be placed, as a vassal, in a state of subordination to himself, in the capacity of liege lord.

99. Westlake, *International Law*, p. 25; Verzijl, pp. 359–360. The establishment of the suzerainty relationship was generally accomplished through a consensual transaction (Crawford, p. 210).

100. Despagnet, pp. 46–47.

101. Despagnet (p. 47) draws a similar conclusion. See also Marek, p. 295.

102. This conclusion follows from both the presumption in favor of the independence of States and that derived from the effective exercise of governmental authority over the relevant territory, both discussed earlier.

103. Despagnet, p. 47. This notion, derived from the conception of States as unequal subjects of international law, had become an anachronism by the nineteenth century (Verzijl, p. 344).

104. Despagnet, p. 47; Cobbett, p. 60; Westlake, *International Law,* p. 90.

105. Verzijl, pp. 389–391, 353–354; see also pp. 374–377, 385.

106. Bulgaria's relation to the Porte, between 1878 and 1908, is often cited as an example (Verzijl, pp. 381 ff.). Egypt's relation to the Porte in the latter half of the nineteenth century serves as an example of an even higher degree of reliance on the suzerain (Cobbett, pp. 42–43; Despagnet, p. 47).

107. See Oppenheim, pp. 188–189; Crawford, p. 209; H.M. Albaharna, p. 61; Venturini, p. 149; Verzijl, pp. 355, 420.

108. Oppenheim, pp. 189–90; Alexandrowicz, p. 266.

109. Oppenheim, p. 191; Verzijl, p. 363; Marek, pp. 189–190; Venturini, p. 116.

110. See Oppenheim, p. 191; see also pp. 362–363. For examples, see Verzijl, pp. 361–363. Nonpolitical treaties with Egypt had to be communicated to the Sultan. Such a role for the suzerain was a feature often found in suzerainty relationships (Hyde, p. 49).

111. J.B. Moore, ed., *Digest of International Law,* Vol. 1 (Washington, 1906), pp. 27–28. One exception was Bulgaria, which, between 1878 and 1908, did maintain direct diplomatic relations with, *inter alia,* the United States (Hyde, p. 49).

112. When Serbia invaded Turkey's vassal, Bulgaria, the latter protested against this aggression on the grounds that, in its legal status as a vassal, it could not counter that invasion with a declaration of war against Serbia. See Bulgarian note of 17 November 1885, cited in Verzijl, p. 365.

113. See Oppenheim, p. 191. For examples of and exceptions to this condition, see also Verzijl, pp. 364–365.

114. Moore, *Digest of International Law,* p. 27.

115. An example of the colonial powers' use of the term to describe what was essentially the incorporation of a State into an Empire is provided by Britain's reference to its suzerainty over the Native States of India. The entire organization of British India was theoretically built upon treaties of vassalage with the rajaships or princedoms of the subcontinent. See Crawford, pp. 210–211; Verzijl, pp. 354, 364.

116. For examples and discussion, see Verzijl, pp. 352–353, 369.

117. Despagnet, p. 49 (Translated by M. Lutz).

118. Westlake, *Papers,* p. 90.

119. G. Rutherford, "Spheres of Influence: An Aspect of Semi-Suzerainty," *AJIL* 20 (1926), p. 300.

120. Crawford, p. 214.

121. Rutherford, p. 300.

122. Ibid., p. 301.

123. Ibid., pp. 300–304.

124. Ibid. For example, see the Anglo-Egyptian Treaty of 1936, discussed in some detail in Verzijl, pp. 428–434.

125. See Rutherford, pp. 304–307; Verzijl, pp. 428–434.

126. See Rutherford, pp. 309, 316; see also pp. 317–325.

127. See ibid., p. 316. See also C. P. Ilbert, *Government of India* (Oxford, 1913), p. 369, note 2.

128. This point is clearly illustrated by Britain's formal recognition of Egyptian independence and sovereignty and simultaneous establishment of its sphere of influence over that State in 1920. See Rutherford, p. 318; Verzijl, pp. 427–428, 430.

129. Crawford, pp. 238–246.

130. Imperial Conference, 1926, "Summary of Proceedings," Cd. 2768, p. 14, quoted in Hyde, pp. 52–53.

131. Hyde, p. 54; R. Stewart, "Treaty Making Procedure in the British Dominions," *AJIL* 32 (1938), pp. 486–487.

132. Hyde, pp. 52–56; Crawford, pp. 238–246.

133. Crawford, p. 290. See also Verzijl, p. 158.

134. Rivier, *Principes du Droit des Gens* (1896), p. 77, quoted in Crawford, p. 290. For examples of such unions, see Verzijl, pp. 133–140.

135. Crawford, p. 290. Judge Basdevant in his Individual Opinion in the *Minquiers and Erechos* case observed: "The Duke of Normandy's conquest of England in 1066 and his acquisition of the title of King of that country cannot have conferred upon the King of England, as such, any title to the possessions of the Duke of Normandy. The two crowns, one royal, the other ducal, were vested in the same person, but legally they remained distinct" (I.C.J., *Reports* [1953], p. 74).

136. Crawford, p. 290; Verzijl, p. 140.

137. The *Delimitation of the Polish-Czechoslovakian Frontier*, Advisory Opinion, P.C.I.J. (1923), Series B, No. 8, pp. 42–43. Although a real union sometimes entered into treaties with third States as one composite juridical entity, its members often continued to conclude treaties separately. For examples of such unions and treaties, see Verzijl, pp. 143–158.

138. The relationship resulted in the presence of a "Lord Protector" in the person of the Earl of Leicester and two English members in the Netherlands "Council of State" as well as British garrisons in two Netherlands towns (Verzijl, p. 412).

139. By the treaty of 17 July 1918, the Principality of Monaco placed itself under the protection of France, but it was expressly not a protectorate of France. Although Monaco submitted to the defense of its independence and territorial integrity by France, it continued to be recognized as a sovereign State by France and by third States (Verzijl, p. 461). San Marino's relation to Italy, governed by the treaty of 1897, precluded the principality neither from entertaining direct diplomatic and consular relations nor from directly concluding treaties with third States. It was expressly recognized by Italy as a sovereign State in 1923. See ibid., p. 462. See also Venturini, p. 17.

140. See Venturini, pp. 21–23. See also Hyde, pp. 56–60.

141. J.K. Fairbank and Ssu-yu Teng, "On the Ch'ing Tributary System," in *Ch'ing Administration: Three Studies* (Cambridge, Massachusetts, 1961), p. 135; R. Jung, *The Sino-Burmese War, 1766–1770* (1971), p. 74. China's view of the world order was not only Confucian in origin; it included the thought of other philosophers such as Mengzi (Mencius), Xunzi (Hsun Tzu), and Laozi (Lao Tzu), all of whom also influenced it. See A.K. Pavithran, *Substance of International Law, Western and Eastern* (Madras, India, 1965), pp. 725–738.

142. The *Collected Statutes* used in "On the Ch'ing Tributary System" are *Daming Huidian* or *Qinding Daqing Huidian.*

143. See O. Lattimore, *Studies in Frontier History* (New York, 1962), p. 130. Chinese terms used are *Fan*, in reference to countries outside China, and *Man*, *Yi*, *Rong*, and *Di*, in reference to the barbarians from the four directions, south,

east, west, and north respectively. Yi also serves as a generic term for all barbarians; Si Yi (literally "Four barbarians") is a collective term for all barbarians living in the four directions outside the center of the civilized world, i.e., China (Fairbank and Teng, p. 137, note 4).

144. See Fairbank and Teng, pp. 137–139. See also Jung, pp. 74–75; Lattimore, p. 130.

145. T.F. Tsiang, "China and European Expansion," quoted in Fairbank and Teng, p. 140.

146. Jung, p. 75.

147. Fairbank and Teng, p. 141. Thus under whatever pretext for whatever purpose, imperial envoys were sent abroad, but always according to the ceremony or protocol of the system: "As in European experience, very practical results were achieved within this cloak of ritual. Mourning for the dead being a major ceremony of the Confucian life, the Emperor could properly send his envoys abroad on the death of a foreign ruler, at just the right time when it was desirable to have information as to the new ruler and perhaps exert pressure upon affairs in the foreign state. . . [and] bestowal of an imperial seal upon a new ruler has obvious analogies to the recognition of new governments practiced in the West" (ibid., p. 148).

148. Ibid., pp. 174–190.

149. See Kang Xi Huidian in Fairbank and Teng, pp. 178–179. The first Dutch Embassy was allowed an audience with the Qing Emperor in 1655. Their intention was to secure trading privileges with China. Both envoys performed the ketou, or "kowtow," before the Emperor, as the only means of obtaining an audience. See J. Nieuhof, Het Gezantschap der Nederlandsche Oost Indie Campagnie aan den Grooten Tatarischen Cham (1665); J. Vixeboxse, Een Hollandsch Gezantschap naar China in de Zeventiende Eeuw, 1685–1687 (1946). With reference to England it is worth mentioning the well-known letters of Emperor Qianlong to George III at the time of Lord Macartney's mission to China in 1793. The Emperor addressed the King as a humble and devout suppliant and exhorted him to obey reverently the imperial instructions. See H. Macnair, Modern Chinese History (Shanghai, 1927), pp. 2–9.

150. Fairbank and Teng, p. 140.

151. Quoted in Macnair, pp. 532–534.

152. J.A. Cohen and H. Chiu, People's China and International Law: A Documentary Study (Princeton, 1974), Vol. 1, p. 5. This exposure was partly a result of the Manchu's dealings with the representatives of the Dutch East India Company discussed earlier.

153. Cohen and Chiu, pp. 6–10, 12. In 1874, a Sino-Japanese dispute was argued in terms of western international law (ibid., p. 9). China joined the Universal Postal Union and the International Institute of Agriculture; more important, it sent representatives to the Association for Reform and Codification of the Law of Nations (ibid., p. 12).

154. Quoted in Cohen and Chiu, p. 12.

155. Ibid, p. 12. In a 1967 message to an international conference of Jurists, President Chiang Kai-shek stated that "we Chinese share a belief that national security and world peace can be reassured only by the rule of law" (Free China Weekly, 16 July 1967, p. 1). In 1924, the Supreme Court of China explicitly stated that "the validity of an international agreement is superior to municipal law." See H. Chiu, "The Position of International Law in Chinese Law," Annals of the Chinese Society of International Law 3 (July 1966), p. 94; for other examples, see pp. 88–89.

156. This proposal was made at the San Francisco Conference that launched the United Nations, but it was successfully opposed by the United States and the Soviet Union. See *China and the United Nations*, report of a Study Group set up by the China Institute of International Affairs (New York, 1959), pp. 36–37.

157. For the text of the Chinese declaration accepting such jurisdiction on 26 Oct. 1946, see I.C.J., *Yearbook 1969–70* 24 (1970), p. 56.

158. Cohen and Chiu, p. 13.

159. Huang Tsen-ming, *The Annals of the Chinese Society of International Law* 1 (July 1964), pp. 41–42.

160. Thus the Chinese Ambassador to the U.N. Security Council, Liu Jie, said: "In line with the policy laid down some decades ago by Dr. Sun Yat-sen, founder of the Republic of China, my government has consistently upheld the right of colonial peoples to political independence and freedom" (*Free China Weekly*, 17 Dec. 1967, p. 1).

161. H. Chiu, "Communist China's Attitude Toward International Law," *AJIL* 60 (1966), p. 246.

162. Their criticism essentially was based on the premise that international law possesses class character. Thus, conventional law reflects the will of the ruling classes of the States taking part in the respective agreements. See He Wushuang and Ma Zhun, "A Criticism of Ch'en T'i-ch'iang on the Sciences of International Law," *Zhengfa Yanjiu* (Political-legal research) 6 (1957), in Cohen and Chiu, pp. 33–36.

163. As an expression of its support for the principles of the U.N., the Chinese Communist party appointed a representative to China's delegation to the San Francisco Conference. See Mao Zedong, *Selected Works of Mao Tse-tung* (Beijing, 1965), Vol. 3, pp. 306–307. See also Telegram from Minister for Foreign Affairs of the Central People's Government of the PRC (Zhou Enlai) to U.N. Secretary General, 26 August 1950, U.N. Document A/1364, 14 Sept. 1950; Zhou Gengsheng, "China's Legitimate Rights in the United Nations Must be Restored," in Cohen and Chiu, pp. 126, 272–274, 283–299, 126 and 1291–1298; "Sino-Afghanistan Treaty of Friendship and Mutual Non-Aggression," 26 Aug. 1960, Preamble; *Peking Review*, 20 Sept. 1960, p. 18; and the "Joint Communiqué of the Bandung Conference," 24 April 1955, SCMP, No. 1033, 24 April 1955, in Cohen and Chiu, pp. 123–124.

164. See Zhou Fulun, "An Inquiry into the Nature of Modern International Law," *Jiaoxue Yu Yanjiu* (Teaching and Research), No. 3, p. 52; and Lin Hsin, "A Discovery of the Post World War II Systems of International Law," *Jiaoxue Yu Yanjiu*, No. 1, p. 34. Both can be found in Chiu, "Communist China's Attitude Toward Int'l Law," p. 248. But also see Zhu Lilu, "Refute the Absurd Theory Concerning International Law by Ch'en T'i-ch'iang," *Renmin Ribao*, 18 Sept. 1957, also in Chiu, p. 249, note 15. Zhu Lilu argues that international law, as an instrument for settling international disputes, should be followed where useful for the PRC and socialism, and that it should be replaced by a new instrument where it is not.

165. In 1979, the first article on international law was published in *Renmin Ribao* on 30 March; it urged the strengthening of the study of international law. A university textbook, *Guoji fa* [International Law], eds. Wang Treya and Wei Min, was published a year later; and a treatise, *Guoji fa*, written many years earlier by Zhou Gengsheng, was also published. See also Chiu, "Communist China's Attitude Toward International Law," pp. 263–267.

166. J.C. Hsiung, *Law and Policy in China's Foreign Relations* (New York, 1972), p. 72.

167. Kong Meng, "A Criticism of the Theories of Bourgeois International Law Concerning the Subjects of International Law and Recognition of States," *Guoji*

Wenti Yanjiu [Studies in International Problems] 2 (1960), pp. 51–53, in Cohen and Chiu, p. 249.

168. According to Communist Chinese legal doctrine, the subjects of international law generally can be only States; therefore, only States can enter into contractual relations. See Hsiung, p. 76; Shao Jinfu, "The Absurd Theory of 'Two Chinas' and Principles of International Law," *Guoji Wenti Yanjiu* 1 (1959), in Cohen and Chiu, pp. 231–237.

169. Kong Meng, in Cohen and Chiu, p. 249; see also pp. 246–250.

170. Shao Jinfu, in Cohen and Chiu, p. 234. Shao quotes (a) Oppenheim, *International Law*; (b) Tunkin, *Osnovy Sovremennogo Mezhdunarodnogo Prava* [The Thesis of Modern International Law]; and (c) Anzilotti, *Cours de Droit International*.

171. Hsiung, p. 72. The Soviet Union introduced a theory of "limited sovereignty" in 1969 to defend its intervention in Czechoslovakia (ibid).

172. Shi Song et al., "An Initial Investigation into the Old Law Viewpoint in the Teaching of International Law," *Jiaoxue Yu Yanjiu* 4 (1958), in Cohen and Chiu, p. 334. Thus, the Chinese also often refer to Article 1 of the Five Principles of Peaceful Coexistence, which prescribes "mutual respect for each other's territorial integrity and sovereignty," and to the 1955 Asian-African (Bandung) Conference Communiqué, which calls for "respect for the sovereignty and territorial integrity of all Nations" (ibid.). The PRC not only refuses to tolerate any violations or infringements of its own sovereignty by other States; it also respects the sovereign prerogatives of other States. Thus, Beijing condemned not only U.S. intervention in Vietnam, Laos, and Cuba but also the U.S.S.R.'s intervention in Czechoslovakia and Afghanistan, as well as Vietnam's invasion of Kampuchea and Laos. See Zheng Weizhi, "Independence is the Basic Canon: An Analysis of China's Foreign Policy," *Beijing Review*, 7 Jan. 1985; Hsiung, p. 74.

173. See Jin Fu, "China's Recovery of Xianggang (Hong Kong) Area Fully Accords with International Law," *Beijing Review*, 26 Sept. 1983, p. 17. See also Yu Fan, "Speaking About the Relationship Between China and the Tibetan Region from the Viewpoint of Sovereignty and Suzerainty," *Renmin Ribao*, 5 June 1959, in Cohen and Chiu, p. 395.

174. Academy of Sciences of the U.S.S.R., Institute of State and Law, *International Law* (Moscow, 1961), p. 97. Jin Fu writes: "True 'divisibility of sovereignty' was advocated by some people. But that is a reactionary doctrine concocted by Western powers for encroaching on other countries' territory and sovereignty" (Jin Fu, p. 17).

175. The principle of true equality has been emphasized in many official speeches and documents. It is mentioned in the Common Program (Article 56) and in the 1954 Constitution, and also in the preamble to the 1982 Constitution. According to Hsiung the doctrine "follows generally the Soviet position, except that the Chinese have used even stronger language in its behalf" (Hsiung, p. 82).

176. Wang Yaotian, *Guoji maoyi tiaoyue he xieding* [International Trade Treaties and Agreements] (Beijing, 1958), p. 10, quoted in H. Chiu, *The People's Republic of China and the Law of Treaties* (Cambridge, Massachusetts, 1972), pp. 61–62.

177. Quoted in Jin Fu, p. 14. For a discussion of the PRC's concept of "unequal treaties," see G.L. Scott, *Chinese Treaties* (Dobbs Ferry, N.Y., 1975), pp. 60, 85–99.

178. Hsiung, p. 82.

179. Ibid., p. 85.

180. See H. Chiu, "Comparison of the Nationalist and Communist Chinese Views of Unequal Treaties," in *China's Practice of International Law: Some Case*

Studies, ed. J. Cohen (Cambridge, Massachusetts, 1972), p. 267; see also pp. 248–258.

181. At the Bandung Conference of 1955, Zhou Enlai stated that his government believed: "Countries, whether big or small, strong or weak, should all enjoy equal rights in International relations. Their territorial integrity and sovereignty should be respected and not violated." See statement made on 19 April 1955, quoted in Yang Xin and Chen Jian, "Expose and Criticize the Absurd Theories of the Imperialists Concerning the Question of State Sovereignty," *Zhengfa Yanjiu* (Political legal research), No. 4, (1964), in Cohen and Chiu, p. 111.

182. Xin Wu, "A Criticism of Bourgeois International Law on the Question of State Territory," *Guoji Wenti Yanjiu* [Studies in International Problems] 7 (1960), in Cohen and Chiu, p. 325.

183. Ibid., pp. 327–328. Jin Fu writes: "According to a basic principle of international law, wars of aggression are unjust and unlawful, 'ex injuria jus non oritur.' Therefore, treaties concluded in connection with the spoils of such wars are invalid" (Jin Fu, p. 15).

184. Xin Wu, in Cohen and Chiu, p. 33. With regard to puppet states, the Chinese communist view is the same as that current in the West. See "Considerations of 'Bangla Desh's' Application for U.N. Membership Opposed," *Peking Review*, 18 Aug. 1972, P. 12.

185. Yu Fan, in Cohen and Chiu, pp. 395–401.

186. Ibid., p. 395. With regard to the terms "sovereignty" and "suzerainty," Alistair Lamb writes: "*Chu Kuo* is an old Chinese term going back to the period of the Warring States, and was generally used in the sense of 'part of the political entity which made up China.' *Shang Kuo*, I am informed by Dr. Wang Gungwu, who has made a special study of the concepts of Chinese political structure, is not really a translation of "Suzerainty" as the British understood that word. The expression *Shang Kuo* is sometimes used to mean a Foreign Power in the general framework of traditional Chinese ideas about Foreign Powers, that is to say, Powers in a tributary relationship to China, but not under Chinese rule. In orthodox Ch'ing political thought Great Britain would have been *Shang Kuo* and so would Siam. "Suzerainty," in fact, would have been a concept quite foreign to Chinese brought up in traditions of Ch'ing diplomacy" (A. Lamb, *The McMahon Line* [London, 1966], p. 44, note 18).

187. Yu Fan, in Cohen and Chiu, p. 397.

188. Ibid.

189. Ibid., p. 400.

190. Shi Song et al., in Cohen and Chiu, p. 335.

Notes to Chapter 8

1. See Chapter 1 of the present book and quotation from the *Jiu Tang Shu* in Note 16 to Chapter 1.

2. See Wang Furen and Suo Wenqing, *Highlights of Tibetan History* (Beijing, 1984), pp. 14–21; Nationalities Affairs Commission of the People's Republic of China, *Bod ljongs hi krung cha shas yin* (Tibet is an Integral Part of China) (Beijing, 1981), pp. 9–12. The latter publication cites Tride Tsugten's wedding to the Tang Princess Jin Cheng in 710 as additional evidence in support of this view.

3. Wang and Suo even present the Peace Treaty of A.D. 821 as evidence of "the unity and friendship between Hans and Tibetans," which they claim "points to the close ties between ancient Tibet, as part of the motherland, and the central regime

in interior China" (Highlights of Tibetan History, p. 32). In fact, the treaty language speaks for itself (see Appendix 1).

4. Tang Shu, translated by S.W. Bushell, "The Early History of Tibet from Chinese Sources," JRAS (1880), pp. 486–487, quoted in Tieh-tseng Li (T. Li), Tibet: Today and Yesterday (New York, 1960), pp. 12–13.

5. W.D. Shakabpa, Tibet: A Political History (New Haven, 1967), p. 54.

6. See Chapter 1 at Note 28.

7. This is true even though relations with the Emperor had to be conducted according to the formalities prescribed by the Confucian perception of international relations. See Wang and Suo, p. 71.

8. Z. Ahmad, "Sino-Tibetan Relations in the Seventeenth Century," Serie Orientale Roma 40 (Rome, 1970), p. 85.

9. I. Desideri, An Account of Tibet, ed. F. De Filippi (London, 1932), pp. 201, 205–206.

10. For the text of the treaty with Ladakh, see Appendix 2.

11. Quoted in Ahmad, p. 157.

12. Ibid., p. 159.

13. Ibid.

14. For a recent interpretation of Chinese documents concerning Dalai Lama V, see A.S. Martynov, "On the Status of the Fifth Dalai Lama," in Proceedings of the Csoma De Körös Symposium, ed. L. Ligeti (Budapest, 1978), pp. 289–294.

15. See Chapter 2, Note 18.

16. See T. Li, Tibet, pp. 36–37.

17. This view is confirmed by the fact that the Dalai Lama turned down Imperial requests for military assistance against rebels in Yunnan. To quote Desideri writing from Lhasa: "It is impossible to describe the reverence shown by all Tibetans, Tartars, Nepalese, and Chinese to the Grand Lama of Thibet. Successive [Manchu] Emperors of China have always shown him great respect, some even going to meet him and escort him with pomp to Peking, and they often send their ambassadors to him with presents" (An Account of Tibet, p. 209).

18. Indirect intervention was already apparent in the Emperor's support of Lhazang Khan in 1703 and in the Manchu involvement in the subsequent exile of the Sixth Dalai Lama.

19. The Dzungar occupation was temporary and therefore did not extinguish the Tibetan State or otherwise alter its legal status.

20. See the Kangxi or Dzungar Edict of 1721, reproduced and translated in H.E. Richardson, "Chi'ing Dynasty Inscriptions at Lhasa," Serie Orientale Roma 47 (Rome, 1974), pp. 10–16.

21. Shi Zong Shilu, quoted in L. Petech, China and Tibet in the Early XVIIIth Century (Leiden, 1972), p. 94. Abbe Huc wrote that the Amban himself stated he had been sent to Lhasa by the Emperor to protect the Dalai Lama; thus, he was to "remove every person that might be inimical to [the Dalai Lama]." See M. Huc, Recollections of a Journey Through Tartary, Thibet, and China (London, 1852), p. 296. Therefore, the Amban's duties in Lhasa were derived from his position there to protect the Dalai Lama.

22. This view is not shared by some scholars who consider the Imperial intervention to signify the incorporation of Tibet into the Empire or the establishment of Manchu suzerainty, or protectorate, over Tibet. For examples, see Tieh-tseng Li, "The Legal Position of Tibet," AJIL 55 (1956); J. Kolmas, Tibet and Imperial China, Australian National University Center of Oriental Studies, Occasional Paper No. 7 (Canberra, 1967), p. 33; Petech, China and Tibet, p. 260.

23. The stone pillar inscription at Kundeling, dated 1794, praises the Emperor's intervention on behalf of Tibet in terms of his role as protector of the faith: "The Emperor 'Jam-dpal-dbyangs [i.e., the incarnation of the Bodhisattva Manjushri], our great master, is truly Buddha. He gives loving protection to all under heaven. He defends the religion of Buddha" (translated in Richardson, *Ch'ing Inscriptions*, p. 63).

24. See Chapter 2, Note 78.

25. Petech, p. 256.

26. Richardson, *Ch'ing Inscriptions*, p. 51. On a formal protocol level, these reforms meant that the Amban was no longer required to kowtow before the Dalai Lama.

27. From the attitude of many Tibetans, as reported by Bogle and Turner, the Emperor appears to have been highly esteemed; moreover, in some sense, he may have been regarded at the time as overlord as well as protector of Tibet and Nepal. See C.R. Markham, ed., *Narratives of the Mission of George Bogle to Tibet* (London, 1879); S. Turner, *An Account of an Embassy to the Teshoo Lama, in Tibet* (London, 1830).

28. Petech, p. 238. The Dalai Lama's sovereignty over Tibet was never questioned, even when the actual exercise of governmental power was obstructed or denied.

29. Shakabpa, p. 128.

30. From 1770, both the Dalai Lama and Panchen Lama paid a regular tribute to the Emperor. The significance of this tribute, however, was minimal, in light of the above discussion of the Qing tributary system. Nepal and Burma, for instance, continued regularly to sent tribute missions to the Emperor into the twentieth century, although the Emperor had no influence over either country.

31. *China and Tibet in the Early XVIIIth Century.*

32. Note, however, that the notion of tributary relations is insufficient to explain Manchu intervention in Tibetan affairs. In this connection, see the declaration of war made by the Qing Emperor against Japan in 1894. In it the Emperor states that "although we have been in the habit of assisting our tributaries, we have never interfered with their internal government." See H.F. MacNair, *Modern Chinese History* (Shanghai, 1927), pp. 532–534.

33. M. Huc, *Decouverte du Thibet, 1845–1846* (1933), p. 50. As Rose has noted, the Amban's influence drastically declined after 1793 and his advice was neither sought nor followed. See L. Rose, *Nepal: Strategy for Survival* (Berkeley, 1971), pp. 111–112.

34. *Tibet: Today and Yesterday*, p. 61.

35. Rose writes: "Indeed, the Chinese were hard put to retain any position of influence in Tibet, as there was a substantial body of opinions at both Lhasa and Kathmandu favoring their expulsion from the area" (*Nepal: Strategy for Survival*, p. 112).

36. For the full text of these treaties, see Appendixes 3, 4, 5, and 6.

37. In fact, the Manchus voiced their displeasure over the treaty because they felt it was inconsistent with the tributary relations they claimed to have with Tibet (Rose, pp. 116–117).

38. C.A. Bell, *Tibet: Past and Present* (1924; rpt. Oxford, 1968), p. 278. Note also that although the Tibetan version of the Dogra Treaty does not mention the Emperor, he is mentioned in the version published in C. Aitchinson, *A Collection of Treaties, Engagements and Sanads Relating to India and Neighbouring Countries*, Vol. 14 (New Delhi, 1929). Compare Appendix 3 with the version in H.E. Richardson, *A Short History of Tibet* (New York, 1962), pp. 246–247.

39. As reported by Captain O'Connor in *Papers Relating to Tibet* (Cd. 1920), No. 129, Incl., Diary of Capt. O'Connor, 4 Sept. 1903.

40. For the text of these agreements, see Appendixes 7, 8, and 9.

41. See Appendix 10.

42. The invalidity of such treaties in Tibet was confirmed on a number of other occasions. See FO 535/4, No. 119, Incl. GOI to IO, 29 Sept. 1904; FO 535/5, No. 25, Incl., GOI to IO, Oct. 1904. Thus, the British Foreign Office stated: "The evidence available seems to show that in point of fact, the treaties which have hitherto been executed by China with foreign Powers have not been operative in Tibet" (FO 535/5, No. 33 FO to IO 20 Oct. 1904).

43. An essential characteristic of "modern suzerainty," as Oppenheim chooses to call the relationship defined as suzerainty in the international law of the nineteenth and twentieth centuries, is that "all international treaties concluded by the suzerain State are *ipso facto* concluded for the vassal if an exception is not expressly mentioned or is not self-evident." See L. Oppenheim, *International Law*, ed. H. Lauterpacht, 8th ed. (London, 1955), Vol. 1, p. 191.

44. G. Schwarzenberger, *International Law*, 3rd ed. (London, 1957), Vol. 1, pp. 130–131.

45. For the text of the Adhesion Agreement, see Appendix 11. In view of the rules of the interpretation of treaties applicable at the time, condensed in Vattel's maxim, "La premiere maxime generale est qu'il n'est pas permis d'interpreter ce qui n'a pas besoin d'interpreter," Younghusband's statements that Britain recognized the Qing Empire's suzerainty over Tibet cannot be considered to form a part of the treaty. See E. Vattel, *Le Droit des Gens ou Principes de la Loi Naturelle* (1758), Vol. 2, Ch. 17, para. 262. For Younghusband's verbal statements, see Note 73 in Chapter 3 of the present book.

46. In this respect, the situation was not unlike that created by Britain's establishment of an effective protectorate over Egypt while, at the same time, recognizing the Sultan's continued suzerainty over that country. See J. Verzijl, *International Law in Historical Perspective*, Vol. 2 (Leiden, 1969), pp. 395, 427–434.

47. For the texts of these treaties, see Appendixes 11 and 12.

48. *German Interests in Polish Upper Silesia*, P.C.I.J. (1926), Series A, No. 7, p. 29.

49. FO 535/5, No. 3, FO to Satow, 1 Oct. 1904; FO 535/6, No. 61, FO to Satow, 23 July 1905.

50. L/P&S/10/148, GOI to IO, 15 Nov. 1905.

51. There are few rules of international law as well established and clear as the rule that a treaty cannot impose obligations upon a third State (*pacta tertiis nec nocent nec prosunt*). Article 34 of the Vienna Convention on the Law of Treaties states: "A treaty does not create either obligations or rights for a third State without its consent." Articles 35 and 36 then go on to specify that although such consent can be presumed where rights arise for a third State, obligations can arise only where the State expressly accepts that obligation in writing. These articles are declaratory of the international law in effect well before the turn of the century.

52. Yu Fan, "Speaking About the Relationship Between China and the Tibetan Region from the Viewpoint of Sovereignty and Suzerainty," *Renmin Ribao*, 5 June 1959, in J. Cohen and H. Chiu, *People's China and International Law* (Princeton, 1974), Vol. 1, p. 397.

53. L/P&S/10/147, Bell to GOI, 10 May 1910, enclosing letter from Tibetan Ministers and National Assembly to the Viceroy of India.

54. T. Shen and S. Liu, *Tibet and the Tibetans* (New York, 1973), p. 46. Bhushan wrote: "The relationship operated on a personal level and only insofar as the 'chela'

or patron conformed to the Buddhist pattern of Kingship, i.e., a king who patronises the Buddhist religion, endows it, maintains it, and protects it from its enemies." See S. Bhushan, *China: The Myth of a Superpower* (New Delhi, 1976), p. 159.

55. Vienna Convention on the Law of Treaties, in I. Brownlie, ed., *Basic Documents in International Law*, 3rd ed. (Oxford, 1983), p. 373.

56. E. Teichman, *Travels of a Consular Officer in Eastern Tibet* (Cambridge, 1922), p. 2; J. Escarra, *La Chine et le Dtroit International* (Paris 1931), p. 230. See also, P. Mehra, *Tibetan Polity, 1904–37* (Wiesbaden, 1976), p. 9; Bell, *Tibet: Past and Present*, p. 213. Regarding the Tibetan-Manchu relationship, Sperling writes that it was "exclusive of Chinese interference, for it was between the Manchu sovereign of a Manchu empire and a subject Tibetan head of State. This framework was not altered throughout the duration of the Ch'ing dynasty, in spite of the progressively intense acculturation that occurred during the period among Manchu circles. Tibet's status, as well as that of Mongolia and other regions, was not tied to China." See E. Sperling, "The Status of Tibet According to Tibetan and Chinese Sources," *Tibetan Messenger* 11, No. 1 (1980), p. 16.

57. J.L. Brierly, *The Law of Nations*, 4th ed. (Oxford, 1949), pp. 237–239.

58. F. Michael, *Rule by Incarnation* (Boulder, Colorado, 1982).

59. See Shakabpa, *Tibet: A Political History*, pp. 246 ff.; Dalai Lama XIV, *My Land and My People* (1962; rpt. New York, 1977); Shen and Liu, *Tibet and the Tibetans*; T. Li, *Tibet: Today and Yesterday*, pp. 130 ff.; Bell, *Tibet: Past and Present*, pp. 123 ff.; Richardson, *A Short History of Tibet*, pp. 101 ff.; B.J. Gould, *Jewel in the Lotus* (London, 1957); H. Harrer, *Seven Years in Tibet* (London, 1953); I. Tolstoy, "Across Tibet from India to China," *National Geographic* 90, No. 2 (Aug. 1949), pp. 169 ff.

60. Teichman, p. 51.

61. Ibid., p. x. Shen and Liu write: "[Tibet] has seen how China has been embroiled in continual war since the founding of the Republic in 1911 and how much her people have suffered. Lhasa believes that to be politically attached to China is more a liability than an asset" (Shen and Liu, p. 62).

62. For a text of this treaty, see Appendix 17.

63. *The Boundary Question Between China and Tibet* (Beijing, 1940), p. 102.

64. *Tribunaux Arbitraux Mixtes* 9 (1930), p. 344.

65. Strictly speaking, recognition could have been implied neither from the earlier negotiations and conclusions of the 1912 armistice agreements in Lhasa for the surrender of Manchu and Chinese troops nor from the subsequent peace agreements of Rongbatsa in 1918, given the limited scope of those negotiations and treaties. The Simla Conference, on the other hand, was convened to resolve comprehensively all major issues affecting the status of Tibet and its relations with other States, including territorial and boundary questions, trade and commerce, and the political status of Tibet, particularly with respect to China and the British Empire. For the Agreements of 1912 and 1918, see Appendixes 14 and 15; see also Appendix 23.

66. Note from Ivan Chen to McMahon, 6 July 1914, in Hengtse Tu, *A Study of the Treaties and Agreements Relating to Tibet* (Taichung, Taiwan, 1971), p. 79.

67. For the full text of these agreements, see Appendixes 18, 19, and 20.

68. At the same time, the declaration rejected both the notion that China had a right to interfere in the Tibetan area described as Inner Tibet and the notion that it had a right to send a representative to Lhasa. Although China could have accrued all such privileges had it signed, it would thereby also have bound itself to accept and respect the full autonomy of "Outer" Tibet and the existence of the greater Tibetan State; in addition, it would have had to withdraw from a number

of occupied border areas and relinquish any claim to sovereignty over Tibet. Those were among the most important conditions under which the Tibetans and the British were prepared to recognize any role for China in any part of Tibet.

69. Schwarzenberger, p. 127.

70. Britain's earlier recognition of the Qing government's suzerainty, implied by the 1906 Adhesion Agreement, as well as the reaffirmation of that stand to the Chinese government in August of 1912, was legitimately reversed for three reasons: first, the change of circumstances brought about by the Dalai Lama's renunciation of his ties with Beijing, the fall of the Qing Dynasty, and the effective reassertion of Tibet's independence; second, the state of war betwen Tibet and China created by the latter; and, finally, China's own recognition of Tibet's equal status at the Simla Conference. For the Memorandum of 7 August 1912, see L/P&S/10/147, Jordan to Grey, 17 Aug. 1912, Incl. Memorandum communicated to Waijiao Bu by Jordan.

71. Note to the government of the PRC, 12 Feb. 1960, White Paper, No. 3 (1960), pp. 94–95.

72. See U.N. Security Council Document S/C2/16, 8 Aug. 1949, and Enclosures 1–6 as appended to it, reproduced in A.S. Bhasin, ed., Documents on Nepal's Relations with India and China, 1949–66 (New Delhi, 1970), pp. 1–22.

73. See Shen and Liu, p. 62; see also International Commission of Jurists, Legal Inquiry Committee on Tibet, Tibet and the Chinese People's Republic (Geneva, 1960), pp. 5–6; C.H. Alexandrowicz, "The Legal Position of Tibet," AJIL 48, No. 2 (April 1954), pp. 265–274.

74. This conclusion is also supported by the International Commission of Jurists in The Question of Tibet and the Rule of Law (Geneva, 1959), p. 85. See also Chapter 7 of the present book for a discussion of the concept of de facto and de jure existence of the State, a distinction this author rejects.

Notes to Chapter 9

1. Quoted in C. Sen, Tibet Disappears (Bombay, 1960), p. 65.

2. Union Research Institute [hereafter, URI], Tibet, 1950–1967 (Hong Kong, 1968) pp. 2, 765; Kashag Document 11(4)3; Guanmin Ribao, Beijing, 19 May 1977; W.D. Shakabpa, Tibet: A Political History (New Haven, 1967), p. 301.

3. Henderson to Sec. of State, 26 Oct. 1950, FRUS 6 (1950), p. 540, note 2.

4. G. Jain, India Meets China in Nepal (Bombay, 1959), pp. 18–19.

5. Deputy Premier V. Patel to J. Nehru, 7 Nov. 1950, in R.K. Jain, e.d., China-South Asian Relations, 1947–1980 (Bombay, 1981), Vol. 1, pp. 29–30. The Indian newspaper, The Statesman, voiced a slightly different opinion, which was widespread at the time, that Ambassador Panikkar "was principally responsible for misleading Mr. Nehru" on the question (The Statesman, 29 Oct. 1950).

6. NCNA, 21 Nov. 1950, Government of India to Government of PRC, 26 Oct. 1950.

7. The United States also did not want to pressure India to follow a course of action for which the United States would later be blamed. See Henderson to Sec. of State, 3 Nov. 1950, FRUS 6 (1950), pp. 550–551. India did not want to be drawn into an East-West confrontation should the Western powers enter on the side of Tibet. Nehru also asked the United States to persuade the Republic of China not to raise the matter of Tibet at the United Nations.

8. "Nehru's Note on China and Tibet," 18 Nov. 1950, in China-South Asian Relations, Vol. 1, p. 46.

9. Ibid., p. 45. India was also discouraged from playing an active role on account of the Korean War. To take issue with China over Tibet would, India felt, oblige it to move closer to the United States, which it did not want to do. See S.P. Varma, *Struggle for the Himalayas* (Jullundur, India, 1971), p. 66.

10. Henderson to Sec. of State, 26 Oct. 1950, FRUS 6 (1950), pp. 540–541.

11. "Chinese Note to India on the Question of Tibet," 16 Nov. 1950, in *China-South Asian Relations*, pp. 39–41.

12. "Southwest Bureau of the CCP Central Committee, Southwest Military Region Command, and Command Headquarters of the 2nd Field Army Jointly Issue Political Mobilization Directive on the Military Expedition into Tibet," NCNA, Beijing, 1 Nov. 1950, in URI, pp. 6–7.

13. "Southwest Military and Administrative Committee and Southwest Military Region Command Issue Notice on Various Policies Connected with the Military Expedition into Tibet," NCNA, Chongqing, 10 Nov. 1950, in URI, pp. 8–9.

14. Shakabpa, p. 301.

15. See Henderson to Sec. of State, 12 Jan. 1951, FRUS 7(1951), p. 1507.

16. Henderson to Sec. of State, 27 Dec. 1950, FRUS 6 (1950), p. 611; Shakabpa, p. 301.

17. For the full text of this first appeal, see Appendix 24.

18. See "Request for the Inclusion of an Additional Item in the Agenda of the Fifth Regular Session," letter from the Chairman of the Delegation of El Salvador to the President of the General Assembly, 17 Nov. 1950, G.A. Doc. A/1534 (1950). See also Sec. of State to U.S. Mission at the U.N., 16 Nov. 1950, FRUS 6 (1950), p. 578.

19. "Invasion of Tibet by Foreign Forces," El Salvador: Draft Resolution, G.A. Doc. A/1534 (1950).

20. Sec. of State to Henderson, 28 Nov. 1950, FRUS 6 (1950), p. 583; Henderson to Sec. of State, 30 Nov. 1950 and 18 Dec. 1950, FRUS 6 (1950), pp. 584 and 603, respectively. The Indian government's action was all the more surprising given that it was this government that had originally advised the Tibetans to appeal to the United Nations. See Henderson to Sec. of State, 31 Oct. 1950, FRUS 6 (1950), p. 546. See also "Nehru's note on China and Tibet," 18 Nov. 1950, in *China-South Asian Relations*, Vol. 1, pp. 46–47.

21. Regarding the reference to the Chinese note of 16 Nov. 1950, see Note 11 in this chapter. See also "Statement by Indian Representative Jam Saheb . . .," 24 Nov. 1950, in *China-South Asian Relations*, Vol. 1, pp. 47–48.

22. See Statement by Gross, U.S. Mission to the U.N., U.N. General Assembly Fifth Session, General Committee 73rd meeting, 24 Nov. 1950.

23. "Note by Secretary General," communicating text of a cablegram dated 8 Dec. 1950 from the Tibetan Delegation, G.A. Doc. A/1658 (1950).

24. Henderson to Sec. of State, 30 Dec. 1950, FRUS 6 (1950), p. 612.

25. Sec. of State to Henderson, 6 Jan. 1951, FRUS 6 (1950), p. 618; memorandum by Strong to Clubb, 24 Jan. 1951, FRUS 7 (1951), p. 1528.

26. Department of State to British Embassy, Aide-Memoire, 30 Dec. 1950, FRUS 6 (1950), p. 613.

27. URI, pp. 735, 766, 767; Kashag Documents 11(4)1, 11(4)3. The first mission was the one sent to join Shakabpa in India.

28. Henderson to Sec. of State, 31 Oct. 1950, FRUS 6 (1950), p. 546; Dalai Lama XIV, *My Land and My People* (1962; rpt. New York, 1977), p. 87.

29. These instructions were reported to Ambassador Henderson in New Delhi by Heinrich Harrer, a few days after he had left Dromo, where he had a last

meeting with the Dalai Lama (Henderson to Mathews, 29 March 1951, *FRUS* 7 [1951], p. 1611). This was confirmed on 13 May by *Dzasa* Liushar, the Tibetan Foreign Secretary. (Steere to Sec. of State, 29 May 1951, *FRUS* 7 [1951], p. 1690). Shakabpa too confirmed the Dalai Lama's instructions. (Henderson to Sec. of State, 11 June 1951, *FRUS* 7 [1951], pp. 1707–1708).

30. Wilson to Sec. of State, 3 July 1951 and 10 July 1951, *FRUS* 7 (1951), pp. 1729 and 1735 respectively; Kashag Document 11(4)1.

31. Kashag Document 11(4)1; Wilson to Sec. of State, 10 July 1951, *FRUS* 7 (1951), p. 1735.

32. For the full text of this agreement, see Appendix 25. See also Dalai Lama, p. 88.

33. A significant feature of this agreement was the attempt to increase the prestige of the Panchen Lama. The new incarnation of this Lama had been chosen and installed by the Chinese in Amdo in 1949, against the wishes of the Tibetan authorities, who did not recognize him. The 1951 Agreement did not preclude the Dalai Lama's status from being altered by the Tibetans themselves. The position of the Panchen Lama, however, was to be maintained unconditionally.

34. Henderson to Sec. of State, 11 June 1951, *FRUS* 7 (1951), pp. 1707–1708. The Dalai Lama's elder brother, Thubten Norbu, arrived in India bearing a letter from the Dalai Lama that authorized him to speak for the Tibetan leader (ibid., p. 1710). Norbu stated that neither the Dalai Lama nor his government approved the agreement (Wilson to Sec. of State, 26 June 1951, *FRUS* 7 [1951], p. 1718).

35. Kennedy to McGhee, 11 July 1951, *FRUS* 7 (1951), pp. 1745–1747; Steere to Sec. of State, 11 July 1951, transmitting secret letter to the Dalai Lama, *FRUS* 7 (1951), pp. 1744–1745. Ambassador Henderson had already sent secret letters to the Dalai Lama in March. They warned him not to accept an agreement conceding to China the right to post officials in Tibet, as such an agreement would only speed up the seizure of all of Tibet by the Chinese communists. Henderson also advised the Dalai Lama not to return to Lhasa; instead, arrangements were to be made for an eventual asylum in a friendly country, such as the United States or Ceylon. See Henderson to Matthews, 29 March 1951, Incl., *FRUS* 7 (1951), pp. 1612–1613. See also Steele to Sec. of State, 29 May 1951, *FRUS* 7 (1951), pp. 1687–1691.

36. Bajpai was quoted as saying: "It was inevitable that the present Chinese Government should gain control of Tibet, and there was nothing the Government of India could do about it." See Henderson to Sec. of State, 31 May 1951, *FRUS* 7 (1951), pp. 1691–1693.

37. Henderson to Sec. of State, 3 June 1951, *FRUS* 7 (1951), p. 1696.

38. Wilson to Sec. of State, 12 July 1957, *FRUS* 7 (1951), pp. 1747–1748; Dalai Lama, p. 90; interview with the Dalai Lama, Santa Barbara, 26 Oct. 1984. The United States continued to make plans for the Dalai Lama's escape, should he choose to make one. They were under the impression that he was "under very strong pressure to return to Lhasa." See Wilson to Sec. of State, 17 July 1951, *FRUS* 7 (1951), pp. 1754–1755.

39. Dalai Lama, p. 91; Varma, pp. 20–21.

40. Steere to Sec. of State, 30 Oct. 1951, *FRUS* 7 (1951), p. 1839, note 2; Bowles to Sec. of State, 15 Nov. 1951, *FRUS* 7 (1951), p. 1848. See the Dalai Lama's telegram to Mao Dzedong, published by NCNA, 25 April, 1959, which the Dalai Lama denies having sent himself. For the U.S. legal opinion regarding Tibetan acceptance, see Memorandum to Merchant by Perkins, 6 Sept. 1951, *FRUS* 7 (1951), pp. 1800–1801.

41. Dalai Lama's statement of 20 June 1959, Mussoorie, India, in *N.Y. Times*, 21 June 1959; and *The Sunday Statesman*, 21 June 1959.

42. M. McMahon, *Conquest and Modern International Law* (Washington, 1940), p. 112. The treaty was signed on 27 August 1928. See L.N.T.S. 94 (1929), pp. 57–64.

43. A number of regional treaties were concluded following this pact, confirming its provisions outlawing wars of aggression. See McMahon, pp. 110–120. Under the Covenant of the League of Nations, Articles 10–16, members had already renounced the use of force until they had submitted the dispute to arbitration or council inquiry. The Kellogg-Briand Pact therefore went much further than the Covenant and was more universal. See J.H.W. Verzijl, *International Law in Historical Perspective*, Vol. 1 (Leiden, 1968), pp. 217–219. Appeals to the provisions of the Pact were frequent, especially during the years immediately preceding the outbreak of the Second World War. China, for example, accused Japan in 1937 of violating international law and the Kellogg-Briand Pact, a pronouncement that was also made by the League of Nations. See FRUS 3 (1938), p. 35, cited in I. Brownlie, *International Law and the Use of Force by States* (Oxford, 1963), p. 78.

44. "Agreement for the Prosecution and Punishment of the Major War Criminals of the European Axis," *U.N.T.S.* 82 (1951), p. 279.

45. Article 5 of the "Charter of the International Military Tribunal of the Far East" defined crimes against peace in the same terms (U.S. Department of State publication No. 2613, Far Eastern Series 12, p. 40).

46. Brownlie, *Use of Force*, pp. 130–213; Verzijl, p. 221.

47. For numerous examples, see J.A. Cohen and H. Chiu, eds., *People's China and International Law* (Princeton, 1974), Vol. 2, pp. 1457–1496. A recent reiteration of this point can be found in Jin Fu, "China's Recovery of Xianggang (Hong Kong) Area Fully Accords with International Law," *Beijing Review*, 26 Sept. 1983, p. 15.

48. Shen Chun-ju, "On the Indictment and Punishment of War Criminals," *People's China*, No. 4 (Supp.), 16 Sept. 1951, in Cohen and Chiu, pp. 1471–1473.

49. See G.A. Res. 95(I), adopted 11 Dec. 1946. See also Brownlie, *Use of Force*, p. 116. Numerous other agreements that strengthen this agreement have been concluded. (Brownlie, pp. 188–194).

50. See M.K. Nawaz, "The Doctrine of the Outlawry of War," *Indian Yearbook of International Affairs* 13 (1964), pp. 80–111. For international attempts to agree on a definition of aggression, see Brownlie, *Use of Force*, pp. 351–358; see also pp. 361–378. See article 2 of "Conventions for the Definition of Aggression," signed in London on 3, 4, and 5 July 1933, ibid., p. 360.

51. See U.N. Charter, Articles 51 and 42.

52. "Declaration on Principles of International Law Concerning Friendly Relations and Cooperation Among States in Accordance with the Charter of the U.N.," G.A. Res. 2625(XXV).

53. Letter from J. Nehru, in R.H. Fifield, *The Diplomacy of Southeast Asia* (New York, 1958), pp. 510–511. The name *Panch Shila* (or *Panchasheel*) was applied *ex post facto* by the Indian Prime Minister as an analogy to the title given to the basic principles of the Indonesian Constitution, and the substance is related to Buddhist precepts.

54. See Brownlie, *Use of Force*, p. 119; see also p. 118. For a list of eighty international instruments affirming the Principles, see Brownlie, pp. 123–126; Cohen and Chiu, pp. 123–124. The Final Communiqué of the Afro-Asian Conference at Bandung of 24 April 1955, in which twenty-nine States, including the PRC, participated, laid down ten principles for the conduct of international relations, *inte alia*: "(1) Respect for fundamental human rights and principles of the Charter of the United Nations; (2) Respect for the sovereignty and territorial integrity of all

nations; (5) Respect for the right of each nation to defend itself singly or collectively, in conformity with the Charter of the United Nations; (7) Refraining from acts or threats of aggression or the use of force against the territorial integrity or political independence of any country; (8) Settlement of all international disputes by peaceful means . . . in conformity with the Charter of the United Nations" (Cohen and Chiu, pp. 123–124). Since then, the nonaligned States have repeatedly espoused similar principles. See, for example, Havana Summit, *Documents of the Sixth Conference of Heads of State or Government of Nonaligned Countries* (1979).

55. M. Akehurst, *A Modern Introduction to International Law* (London, 1984), pp. 219–220; Brownlie, *Use of Force*, 214–215, 357.

56. I.C.J., *Reports* (1949), p. 35.

57. Brownlie, *Use of Force*, pp. 214, 425; R.Y. Jennings, *The Acquisition of Territory in International Law* (Manchester, 1963), p. 60.

58. Brownlie, *Use of Force*, p. 214.

59. Ibid., p. 424; see also p. 428.

60. Shi Song et al., "An Initial Investigation into the Old Law Viewpoint in the Teaching of International Law," *Jiaoxue Yu Yanjiu* [Teaching and Research], No. 4 (1958), in Cohen and Chiu, p. 335.

61. Sir Hersch Lauterpacht wrote: "It follows [from the changes that brought about such instruments as the Kellogg-Briand Pact and the U.N. Charter] that a treaty imposed by or as the result of force or threat of force resorted to in violation of the principles of these instruments of a fundamental character is invalid by virtue of the operation of the general principle of law which postulates freedom of consent as an essential condition of the validity of consensual undertakings. The reasons which in the past have rendered that principle inoperative in the international sphere have now disappeared." See International Law Commission, *Report on the Law of Treaties*, H. Lauterpacht, Special Rapporteur, G.A. Doc. A/CN.4/63, in *Yearbook of the International Law Commission* (1953), Vol. 2, p. 148. See also F. Nozari, *Unequal Treaties in International Law* (Stockholm, 1971), pp. 31, 64–65. In the preamble to the *Vienna Convention on the Law of Treaties* the principles of free consent and good faith are declared to be "universally recognized" (I.L.C., *Report on the Law of Treaties*, G.G. Fitzmaurice, Special Rapporteur, G.A. Doc. A/CN.4/101, p. 16).

62. Nozari, p. 66; I. Sinclair, *The Vienna Convention on the Law of Treaties* (Manchester, 1984), pp. 176–177. Today, this rule is embodied in Article 51 of the Vienna Convention. See I. Brownlie, ed., *Basic Documents in International Law* (Oxford, 1983), p. 370.

63. Sinclair, pp. 176–177.

64. Ibid, p. 177.

65. Quoted in Sinclair, p. 177. Lauterpacht wrote in his report to the I.L.C: "[In] so far as war or force or threats of force constitute an internationally illegal act, the result of that illegality—namely, a treaty imposed in connection with or in consequence thereof—[is] governed by the principle that an illegal act cannot produce legal rights for the benefit of the law-breaker. The principle—ex injuria ius non oritur—recognized by the doctrine of international law and by international tribunals, including the highest international tribunal, is in itself a general principle of law." See Lauterpacht, *Report on the Law of Treaties*, *Yearbook of the I.L.C.* (1953), Vol. 2, p. 148.

66. See the *Fisheries Jurisdiction* case, in I.C.J., *Reports* (1973), pp. 13, 14 and throughout.

67. See Brownlie, *Basic Documents*, p. 370.

68. The Charter entered into force on 24 October 1945. The I.L.C., in its commentary to Article 52, found that it would be illogical and unacceptable to formulate the rule as applicable only from the date of conclusion of the Convention on the Law of Treaties, as the invalidity of a treaty procured by the illegal threat or use of force was a principle that was *lex lata*. The Commission thus held that "[Article 52], by its formulation, recognizes by implication that the rule which it lays down is applicable at any rate to all treaties concluded since the entry into force of the Charter." See *Yearbook of the I.L.C.* (1966), Vol. 2, p. 247.

69. See Jin Fu, "China's Recovery of Xianggang (Hong Kong) Area Fully Accords with International Law," *Beijing Review*, 26 Sept. 1983, p. 15; *Renmin Ribao* editorial reprinted in *Beijing Review*, 1 Oct. 1984, p. 14. See also Cohen and Chiu, pp. 62–63.

70. E.J. de Arechaga, "International law in the Past Third of a Century," *Recueil Des Cours* 159 (1978), pp. 68–69.

71. Ibid., p. 68. See also Akehurst, pp. 132–133; Nozari, pp. 274, 284. Whereas the validity of the rule, as expressed in Article 52 of the Vienna Convention, is no longer disputed, the interpretation of the word "force" still is. Most States and jurists hold that it refers only to physical or armed force. A number of African, Asian, and Latin American countries, as well as communist ones, including the People's Republic of China, interpret the prohibition of force to include, besides physical force, any economic or political pressure. Without passing judgment on this disagreement, this author finds it clear that, at any rate, the resort to physical or military force and the threat to do so as an instrument of policy is absolutely prohibited by law, and that the violator, the aggressor, is guilty of an international crime.

72. For a discussion of attempts to agree on a definition of aggression, see Brownlie, *Use of Force*, pp. 351–358. "The Conventions for the Definition of Aggression," signed in London on 3, 4 and 5 July 1933; defined the aggressor, in Article 2, "to be that State which is the first to commit any of the following actions: (1) Declaration of War upon another State; (2) Invasion by its armed forces, with or without a declaration of war, of the territory of another State; (3) Attack by its land, naval or air forces, with or without a declaration of war, on the territory, vessels or aircraft of another state; (4) Naval blockade of the coasts or ports of another state; (5) Provision of support to armed bands formed on its territory which have invaded the territory of another state, or refusal, notwithstanding the request of the invaded state, to take, in its own territory, all the measures in its power to deprive those lands of all assistance or protection." Article 3: "No political, military, economic or other considerations may serve as an excuse or justification for the aggression referred to in Article 2" (Brownlie, *Use of Force*, p. 360).

73. Article 2 of the Seventeen-Point Agreement.

74. For official documents reflecting this Chinese stand, see Union Research Institute *Tibet, 1950–1967* (Hong Kong, 1968), pp. 2–9.

75. Answer to a question posed by the author, Santa Barbara, 26 Oct. 1984.

76. Statement issued at press conference, Mussoorie, India, 20 June 1959; in N.Y. *Times*, 21 June 1959; and *The Sunday Statesman*, 21 June 1959.

77. This conclusion was also reached by the International Commission of Jurists, who concluded after investigation that "the inference from the circumstances in which it was signed, is obviously that Tibet signed at pistol-point." See International Commission of Jurists, *The Question of Tibet and the Rule of Law* (Geneva, 1959), p. 96.

Notes to Chapter 10

1. *The Constitution of the People's Republic of China*, adopted 4 Dec. 1982, Preamble.

2. The Tibet Autonomous Region (TAR) includes less than half the surface area of historic Tibet. The bulk of Kham and all of Amdo have been incorporated into eleven autonomous districts, or prefectures, and into two autonomous counties appended to Sichuan, Yunnan, and Gansu, as well as into an entire province, Qinghai.

3. The provision was adopted at the Second Session of the Sixth National People's Congress in Beijing.

4. Ngapo Ngawang Jigme, "Explaining Regional Autonomy Law," *Beijing Review*, 25 June 1984, p. 17.

5. Ibid., pp. 17–18.

6. Emphasizing this point, Deng Xiaoping declared that, in relation to the possible reunification of Taiwan, within the PRC "autonomy has its limits and, so, 'complete autonomy' is simply out of the question." See *Deng Xiaoping on China's Reunification*, *Beijing Review*, 9 Aug. 1983, p. 5.

7. See *Dalai Lama's Report at the Inaugural Meeting of the Preparatory Committee of the Autonomous Region of Tibet*, Renmin Ribao, 25 April 1956, in Union Research Institute [hereafter, URI], *Tibet, 1950–1967* (Hong Kong, 1968), pp. 144–155; Dalai Lama's telegram to Mao Dzedong, published by the NCNA, 25 April, 1959.

8. Interview with the Dalai Lama, Santa Barbara, 26 Oct. 1984. See also, International Commission of Jurists, Legal Inquiry Committee on Tibet, *Tibet and the Chinese Peoples Republic* (Geneva, 1960), p. 290.

9. Upon his arrival in Lhasa, the Chinese commander, Zhang Guohua, and his colleagues called on the Tibetan Prime Ministers, Lukangwa and Lobsang Tashi, whom he described as "the actual rulers of the Tibetan local government." Zhang reported that the attitude of these men was hostile and their rejection of the Sino-Tibetan agreement blatant. He reminded them of their duty, by the terms of that agreement, to "actively help the Liberation Army in its entry into Tibet" and handed the Tibetans the Tibetan text of the Seventeen-Point Agreement to emphasize his position. Zhang later wrote: "Under the eyes of all around him, this bandit chief [Lukangwa] took up the document as if his fingers were burned by it. Shaking with rage he suddenly cried as if he was ill: 'you whose surname is Zhang, how dare you bring in your troops.' We could not help laughing at the man's hysterical outbreak. The day-dreamer now finally spoke from his inner mind." See Zhang Guohua, "Tibet Returns to the Bosom of the Motherland," *Renmin Ribao*, Beijing, 25 Oct. 1962, in SCMP, No. 2854, 6 Nov. 1962.

10. J. Avedon, *In Exile from the Land of the Snows* (New York, 1984), p. 37.

11. "Summary of Basic Experience in Promoting Regional Autonomy Among Minority Nationalities," *Renmin Ribao*, 9 Sept. 1953, in URI, p. 31.

12. *Guanmin Ribao*, Beijing, 19 May 1977, in SPRCP, No. 6362, 16 June 1977.

13. G. Ginsburgs and M. Mathos, *Communist China and Tibet* (the Hague, 1964), chapter 2.

14. CNA, No. 270, 3 April 1959, p. 1; Kashag Document 11(4)3. See also *Tibet and the Chinese People's Republic*, pp. 295–297.

15. Ginsburgs and Mathos, p. 41

16. Zhang Jingwu, "Report on the Work in the Tibet Area as Approved by the 7th Plenary Session of the State Council," 9 March 1955, published in *Renmin*

Ribao, 13 March 1955, in URI, p. 108; Ginsburgs and Mathos, pp. 60, 61; URI, p. 99.

17. H. Hoffman, *Tibet: A Handbook* (Bloomington, Indiana, 1977), pp. 78–79; Dalai Lama XIV, *My Land and My People* (1962; rpt. New York, 1977), p. 95.

18. Ginsburgs and Mathos, pp. 65–66. In Northeastern and Eastern Tibet (i.e., Amdo and Kham), nearly 5 million Chinese had settled. The Tibetan government suspected that some 4 million were going to be sent to Central Tibet (Kashag Documents 11[4]17 and 11[4]9). A directive issued by Mao Zedong on 8 Oct. 1952 suggests that the Chinese were indeed contemplating a massive colonization of Tibet. See "Radio Address by Leosha Thubten Tarpa," published in *Renmin Ribao,* 22 Nov. 1952, in URI, p. 45.

19. Avedon, pp. 44–45. The existence of discontent and open clashes was already admitted by the Chinese in 1953, although it was blamed on "imperialist" and "counter-revolutionary" plots. The Chinese also admitted, however, that "some of the minority nationalities thought . . . that they could live separately from the Hans." See "Summary of Basic Experience . . .," in URI, pp. 31, 29. See also "Facts on the 'Khamba Rebellion,'" NCNA, English, Beijing, 24 June 1959, in URI pp. 359–361. In the summer of 1954, 40,000 persons were reported to have taken part in an uprising in Southeast Tibet (N.Y. *Times,* 28 Aug. 1954; *Guardian,* 2 Sept. 1954). The rebellion in Xikang (Eastern Tibet) was admitted by the official Chinese news agency, NCNA (*Hindustan Times,* 20 April 1959). For a number of accounts of the guerrilla war in Tibet, see G. Patterson, *Tibet in Revolt* (London, 1960); M. Peissel, *Cavaliers of Kham* (London, 1972); J. Norbu, *Horsemen in the Snow* (Dharmsala, 1979); G. T. Andrugtsang, *Four Rivers, Six Ranges* (Dharmsala, 1973).

20. NCNA, Lhasa, 29 Nov. 1954, in URI, p. 54; *China News Service,* Lhasa, 19 Dec. 1954, in URI, p. 55. In 1957, the Xinjiang-Tibet highway was completed (*Guanmin Ribao,* 6 Oct. 1957, in URI, p. 263).

21. J.T. Dreyer, *China's Forty Millions* (Cambridge, Massachusetts, 1976), p. 133. For claims made by the Chinese regarding membership, see "Report of the Work Committee on Problems Relating to the Nationalities Policy," *Xizang Ribao,* 15 Oct. 1957, in URI, p. 224.

22. "Report on the Work . . .," in URI, pp. 105–115; "Report of Chairman Chantung Jijigme of the Panchen Kanpo Lija Committee," *Renmin Ribao,* 13 March 1955, in URI, p. 123. See *Tibet and the Chinese People's Republic,* p. 301; URI, pp. 306–313. More than 30,000 children were sent to China between 1952 and 1969. See Minority Rights Group [hereafter, MRG], *The Tibetans,* Report No. 49, by C. Mullin and P. Wangyal (London, 1983), p. 17.

23. Avedon, p. 38; Dalai Lama, pp. 91–93; Dreyer, pp. 134–135; interview with Kungo Kundeling, Dehra Dun, India, 4 Jan. 1981. In addition to a six-point petition, General Zhang Jingwu was handed a memorandum, dated 6 March 1952, that stated in part: "To us Tibetans, the phrase 'the liberation of Tibet,' in its moral and spiritual implications, is a deadly mockery. The country of a free people was invaded and forcefully occupied under the pretext of Liberation. . . . Thus, we unequivocally demand that all the Chinese quit Tibet" (quoted in *Brief Survey of History and Present-Day Conditions in Tibet,* published by Information and Publicity Office of His Holiness the Dalai Lama [Dharmsala, 1977], pp. 13–14).

24. Ginsburgs and Mathos, pp. 78–80. For the Dalai Lama's account of the Congress, which he described as a "mere formality," and his reasons for attending, see *My Land and My People,* pp. 100, 121–122.

25. *Constitution of the People's Republic of China,* adopted 20 Sept. 1954. Two earlier documents reflect the same view of the status of minorities in the PRC:

266 Notes to Chapter 10

The Common Programme (1949) and The General Programme for the Implementation of Regional Autonomy for Nationalities in the PRC (1954).

26. See the full text of this resolution, "State Council Resolution on the Establishment of the Preparatory Committee for the Autonomous Region of Tibet," Renmin Ribao, 13 March 1955, in URI, pp. 141–143. The resolution itself refers to the Sino-Tibetan agreement of 1951 as the basis for the new committee's establishment. According to the Dalai Lama, the Chinese had intended to take over the Tibetan administration totally and to govern the country directly from Beijing, but the confidence he was able to instill in the Chinese leaders during his visit in 1954 resulted in the creation of what was, at least nominally, an autonomous institution (Avedon, p. 41; Dalai Lama, p. 125).

27. See Dalai Lama, pp. 125–126, 133; "Decree of the People's Republic of China Promulgating Outline Regulations Governing Organization of Preparatory Committee for Tibet Autonomous Region," Renmin Ribao, 27 Sept. 1956, in URI, pp. 171–176; "State Council Resolution . . .," in URI, pp. 141–143. The composition of the 51-person committee broke down as follows: 15 for the Local Government of Tibet; 10 for the Chamdo PLC; 10 for the Panchen Lama's Council of Kenpo; 11 for the larger monasteries, religious sects and mass organizations; and 5 recruited from Chinese personnel in Tibet.

28. See "State Council Resolution . . .," and "Decree of the PRC . . ." in Note 27. See also Dreyer, p. 135; Ginsburgs and Mathos, p. 89.

29. Dalai Lama, p. 133. See also MRG, p. 6; Ginsburgs and Mathos, p. 89; Kashag Document 11(4)8. In 1951, the Chinese set up the Work Committee of the CCP for the Tibet Area. The Secretary General was Zhang Jingwu, and Zhang Guohua was a Deputy Secretary (URI, p. 743). Zhang Guohua later blamed the Tibetans for PCART's lack of progress (CB No. 565, 29 May 1959, p. 1). At the Press Conference in Mussoorie, India, 20 June 1959, the Dalai Lama stated: "The Preparatory Committee . . . is nothing but nominal, with all powers concentrated in the hands of the Chinese"(U.S. News & World Report, 6 July 1959, pp. 60–61).

30. MRG, p. 6; Ginsburgs and Mathos, p. 89.

31. See Kashag Documents 11(4)7, 11(4)16, and 11(4)17. See also Dagong Bao, Tianjin, 24 July 1955 in URI p. 41; Renmin Ribao, 11 and 24 March 1959, in CNA, No. 282, 26 June 1959.

32. Interview with Kungo Kundeling, Dehra Dun, India, 4 Jan. 1981; Ginsburgs and Mathos, p. 190; Dalai Lama, pp. 134–135.

33. The principal guerrilla organization took the name Gushi Gandruk (four rivers, six ranges), the traditional epithet for Kham and Amdo provinces. For Chinese references to fighting in these provinces, see Liu Zexi, "Herdsmen on the Tsinghai Pastures Advance Bravely with Flying Red Flags," Minzu Tuanjie, No. 11, 6 Nov. 1958, in URI, pp. 325–329; "Facts on the Khamba Rebellion," NCNA English, Beijing, 26 April 1959, in URI, p. 359; CNA, No. 270, 3 April 1959, p. 1. Repeated references were made in official speeches in 1956 regarding the need for heightened vigilance against elements attempting to undermine the unity between the Han and Tibetan peoples. See Zhen Yi, "Summing-up Report of Central Government Delegation to Tibet," Guanmin Ribao, 15 Sept. 1956, in URI, pp. 166, 170.

34. On 23 March 1957, the People's Daily (Renmin Ribao) reported: "Last year in the Tibetan area of Sichuan province and at Teko and other places on the eastern side of Chingsha River, during the introduction of Reforms—although the policy of the Central Government cannot be erroneous—the cadres carrying out the policy erred, and since the reform was badly done, it caused consternation in the whole area, and rich and poor fled to the Western side of the River and many fled to Lhasa" (in CNA, No. 270, 3 April 1959, p. 4).

35. In April 1956, Nehru invited the Dalai Lama and the Panchen Lama to India to take part in ceremonies commemorating the 2,500th anniversary of the *Nirvana* of the Lord Buddha. After initial refusals, the Chinese consented to let them go (Dalai Lama, pp. 141–142; URI, p. 177). The Dalai Lama invited Nehru to return the visit, but despite the latter's acceptance, the Chinese did not allow it (Kashag Documents 11[4]7, 11[4]16; Dalai Lama, pp. 157–158).

36. Avedon, pp. 47–48; Dalai Lama, pp. 147–150, 157–158.

37. "Outline of Propaganda for CCP Tibet Work Committee . . .," *Xizang Ribao,* 2 Aug. 1957, in URI, p. 207.

38. "20th Standing Committee Meeting . . .," *Xizang Ribao,* 18 June 1957, in URI, pp. 219–221.

39. URI, p. 178.

40. "Outline of Propaganda . . .," in URI, p. 211.

41. Avedon, pp. 48–49; *Brief Survey of History,* pp. 17–18. See also CNA, No. 270, 3 April 1959, pp. 6–7; CNA No. 282, 26 June 1959, citing *Renmin Ribao,* 12, 17, 26 April 1959 and 1, 2 May 1959; *Guanmin Ribao,* 25 April 1959.

42. See "Manifesto by Tibetan Leaders," "Letter from Tibetan Leaders to Mr. Jawaharlal Nehru," and "Memorandum by Tibetan Leaders," Documents 12, 11, and 13, respectively, in International Commission of Jurists, *The Question of Tibet and the Rule of Law* (Geneva, 1959), pp. 143–162.

43. *Renmin Ribao,* 1 March 1958 and 12 Nov. 1958, in URI, p. 178, notes 6 and 7.

44. The inauguration of a "Rectification Campaign" by the Chinese to "weed out" members of so-called reactionary movements, once defined as "any nationality movement which seeks to separate from the Chinese People's Republic to become independent," further raised the tension in Tibet. See CB, No. 490, 7 Feb. 1958, citing NCNA, Lhasa, 1 Jan. 1958 and 16 Jan. 1958. Although the withdrawal of many cadres was confirmed by Chinese sources and by the Dalai Lama (CNA, No. 270, 3 April 1959, p. 7; CB, No. 490, 7 Feb. 1958, p. 7), the government called for the reinforcement of the PLA and National Defense in Tibet (*Xizang Ribao,* 1 Aug. 1957).

45. On 28 March 1959, while the uprising in Tibet was being put down, Premier Zhou Enlai made the following statement: "Most of the Kaloons of the Tibet Local Government and the upper strata reactionary clique colluded with imperialism, assembled rebellious bandits, carried out rebellion, ravaged the people, put the Dalai Lama under duress, tore up the 17-Article Agreement on Measures for the Peaceful Liberation of Tibet and, on the night of March 19, directed the Tibetan local Army and rebellious elements to launch a general offensive against the People's Liberation Army garrison in Lhasa." See "Order of the State Council of the Chinese People's Republic," NCNA, Beijing, 28 March 1959, in URI, p. 357. See also *Tibet and the Chinese People's Republic,* p. 290; Foreign Languages Press, *Concerning the Question of Tibet* (Beijing, 1959), pp. 166–174.

46. A week later, the press reported: "Today Lhasa is under Chinese martial Law. For two days thousands of killed Tibetans were given mass cremation. . . . The Tibetan Army has been killed or disbanded. Four thousand Tibetans have been arrested" (*The Organiser,* 6 April 1959).

47. See Chinese PLA, Xizang Junqu Zhengzhibu [Tibetan Military District Political Department], *Xizang Xingshi he Renwu Jiaoyu de Jiben Jiaocai* [Fundamental Teaching Material and Task Education on the Tibetan Situation] (1960). See also H. Goldberg, "Remember Tibet," *AFL-CIO Free Trade Union News* (March 1966).

48. "Order of the State Council of the People's Republic of China," NCNA, Beijing, 28 March 1959, in URI, p. 357.

49. Dalai Lama, p. 212.

50. Press Conference, Mussoorie, India, 20 June 1959, reported in *U.S. News & World Report*, 6 July 1959, pp. 60–61.

51. Dalai Lama, pp. 97–98, 155–170; *Tibet and the Chinese People's Republic*, pp. 289–290; *Brief Survey of History*, pp. 16–18; Avedon, p. 34. In 1958 also, the Chinese reportedly threatened the Dalai Lama with imprisonment if he did not go along with their policies (*Brief Survey of History*, p. 17).

52. Dalai Lama, p. 133; see also p. 148.

53. Interview with the Dalai Lama, Santa Barbara, California, 26 Oct. 1984; Interview with members of the Kashag, Dharmsala, Jan. 1981.

54. Mao Zedong, *Selected Works of Mao Tse-tung*, Vol. 5 (Beijing, 1965), p. 75.

55. Statement issued by the Chinese Embassy in New Delhi, 1 April 1959, Institute of International Affairs, *Dalai Lama and India*, p. 27.

56. Zhang Guohua, "Tibet Returns to the Bosom of the Motherland," *Renmin Ribao*, Beijing, 25 Oct. 1962, in SCMP, No. 2854, 6 Nov. 1962, pp. 6–7, 11.

57. NCNA, English, Lhasa, 23 April 1959, in CB, No. 565, 29 May 1959, p. 2.

58. *Times of India*, 30 March 1959.

59. I.L.C., *Report on the Law of Treaties*, Lauterpacht, Special Rapporteur, U.N. Document A/Cn.4/63, p. 148.

60. "Thus [the Judge continues] Czechoslovakia could invoke in 1973 the invalidity of the Munich Agreement of 29 September 1938, obtained through the threat of force on the Czechoslovak Republic by the Nazi regime, even if it was not a party to that agreement." See E. Jimenez de Arechaga, "International Law in the Past Third of a Century," *Recueil Des Cours* 159 (1978), p. 69.

61. F. Nozari, *Unequal Treaties in International Law* (Stockholm, 1971), p. 286.

62. Ibid., p. 279.

63. The Information Office of His Holiness the Dalai Lama, *Tibetans in Exile, 1959–1980* (Dharmsala, 1981), pp. 101–206; U.S. Congress, Senate Committee on the Judiciary, *World Refugee Crisis: The International Community's Response*, 96th Cong., 1st sess., 1979, pp. 147–150; F. Michael, "Survival of a Culture: Tibetan Refugees in India," *Asian Survey* 25, No. 7 (July 1985).

64. Hoffman, p. 233. F. Michael stresses the important rise of the "new force to cement Tibetan unity in exile. . . : modern nationalism." See Michael, *Rule by Incarnation* (Boulder, Colorado, 1982), p. 169.

65. *Tibetans in Exile*, pp. 3–16.

66. Avedon, p. 107.

67. *Constitution of Tibet*, promulgated by His Holiness the Dalai Lama, 10 March 1963, published by the Bureau of H.H. the Dalai Lama, New Delhi; see specifically the foreword by the Dalai Lama.

68. Quoted in Avedon, p. 106.

69. See *Tibetans in Exile*, pp. 3–4. Together, this body and the Kashag form the National Working Committee, the highest policy-making organ of the government.

70. Ibid., pp. 3–14.

71. Ibid., pp. 209–235, 101–185, 23–66. See also S. Narayan, Education of Tibetan Refugee Children in India, *News Tibet* 19, No. 1 (Jan.-Aug. 1984), pp. 23–25. Note also, that a new Tibetan University is being established.

72. Avedon, p. 101.

73. Governments as diverse as those of the United States, Thailand, and Yugoslavia came out in favor of Tibet. For the Chinese reaction to such sympathy, see NCNA,

Beijing, 23 April 1959, in CB, No. 564, 27 April 1959. See also Raja Hutheesing, ed., *Tibet Fights For Freedom* (Bombay, 1960), pp. 125–161.

74. Prime Minister Nehru declared: "Whatever our respect for the Dalai Lama and whatever our reaction to the events in Tibet, it would be improper and not justified for us to recognize any kind of Tibetan Government on Indian soil. That we have made clear. For the rest, it is for the Dalai Lama to decide what he likes to do" (*The Statesman*, 8 July 1959). Nehru formulated his government's stand succinctly at a press conference on 5 April 1959. He said that India had to keep a number of factors in view: "The major factor being, of course, our own security . . . the second factor: our desire to have and continue to have friendly relations with China. The third factor: our strong feeling about developments in Tibet." See "Statement in Lok Sabha," 4 Sept. 1959, quoted in NCNA, Beijing, 9 April 1959, in SCMP, No. 1992, 14 April 1959. See also Ministry of External Affairs, India, *Prime Minister on Sino-Indian Relations*, Vol. 1, p. 118.

75. See the press reports reproduced in *Tibet Fights for Freedom*, pp. 125–161.

76. R.K. Jain, *China-South Asian Relations, 1947–1980* (New Delhi, 1981), Vol. 1, pp. 61–67.

77. "China-Nepal Joint Communiqué on the Establishment of Diplomatic Relations," 1 Aug. 1955; and "The China-Nepal Agreement to Maintain Friendly Relations and on Trade and Intercourse," signed 20 Sept. 1956, effective from 17 Jan. 1958, Documents 254 and 259 respectively, in *China-South Asian Relations, 1947–1980*, Vol. 2, pp. 285, 287–294.

78. See report from Kathmandu, 3 May 1959, in *The Statesman*, 5 May 1959. Nepal wanted to undertake joint diplomatic action with India (*Free Press Journal*, 27 March 1959).

79. See the reports from London quoted in *Indian Express*, 25 March 1959, and *Times of India*, 21 April 1959.

80. Department of State, *Bulletin*, 40, No. 1033, 13 Apr. 1959, p. 515. Cited in M.M. Whiteman, ed., *Digest of International Law*, Vol. 5 (Washington, 1965), p. 202.

81. Assistant Sec. of State Morton to Senator Wiley, 29 April 1953, Department of State, file 611.936/4–1753; transcript of press and radio news conference, 11 Sept. 1959. Quoted in M.M. Whiteman, ed., *Digest of International Law*, Vol. 1 (Washington, 1963), p. 464.

82. Yugoslavia also condemned the Chinese action. See NAFEN Message, 11 April 1959, in *Tibet Fights for Freedom*, p. 193. Malaya, statement by Minister of External Affairs, in *Tibet Fights for Freedom*, p. 189; President Nasser of Egypt, in *Times of India*, 21 April 1959; Thailand, statement by Foreign Minister, 12 April 1959, in *Indian Express*, 13 April 1959; Prime Minister Sihanouk of Cambodia, interviewed in *The Statesman*, 7 April 1959; Maharaj-Kumar of Sikkim, in *Hindustan Standard*, 7 April 1959; Netherlands' delegate to Inter-Parliamentary Union, in *Indian Express*, 3 Sept. 1959. See also Sington, "The World Condemns Chinese Aggression," *The Listener*, 9 April 1959.

83. See Afro-Asian Council, *Report of the Afro-Asian Convention on Tibet and Against Colonialism in Asia and Africa* (New Delhi, 1960).

84. *The Question of Tibet and the Rule of Law*, p. 71. The International Commission of Jurists (I.C. Jur.) is a nonpolitical organization of eminent jurists, supported by more than 30,000 lawyers and judges in more than 50 countries, and has consultative status with the U.N. In its final report, *Tibet and the Chinese People's Republic*, the I.C. Jur. found the Chinese guilty of genocide.

85. See "Message from His Holiness the Dalai Lama to Secretary General Dag Hammarskjold," 9 Sept. 1959, in Bureau of H.H. the Dalai Lama, *Tibet in the United Nations, 1950–1961* (New Delhi, 1961), p. 17.

86. G.A. Res. 1353 (XIV); G.A. Res. 1723 (XVI); GA Res. 2079 (XX). For a full text of these resolutions, see Appendix 26. For a summary of the debates, see *Yearbook of the United Nations* [Y.U.N.], 1959, pp. 67–69; Y.U.N., 1960, pp. 173–174; Y.U.N., 1961, pp. 138–140; Y.U.N. 1964, pp. 149–150; Y.U.N. 1965, pp. 191–194.

87. See Tibetan Affairs Coordination Office (TACO) Documents.

88. NCNA, Tokyo, 11 Oct. 1967.

89. *Le Monde*, 6 Oct. 1982; TR 17, No. 10 (Oct. 1982), pp. 22–23. In fact the Chinese have registered protests with the Dalai Lama's hosts on every occasion (TACO Documents). See also *Beijing Review*, 14 Dec. 1982, which states that the Chinese government "cannot agree" to the Dalai Lama "conducting political activities in exile" or meeting with officials abroad.

90. See TACO Documents. See also TR 10, Nos. 7 & 8 (July/Aug. 1975), p. 8.

91. Sweeney, "Keeping the Gentle Faith," *Sheffield Morning Telegraph*, 23 June 1983.

92. See Michael, "Survival of a Culture," p. 738.

93. *Tibet and the Chinese People's Republic*, p. 3.

94. G.P. Deshpande, "Towards Integration: Tibet Since the Revolt," *International Studies* 10, No. 4 (April 1969), pp. 511–515. Ginsburgs and Mathos, pp. 130–135.

95. See *Tibet and the Chinese People's Republic*, p. 13. Regarding the Tibetans' religious beliefs, the *People's Daily* explained on 18 May 1959 that "faith is free, but we must distinguish vigorously between religion of the masses on the one hand, and, on the other, the use of religion by the reactionary class against the people, against the revolution. Since religion is a mental attitude, it cannot be treated by mere administrative measures and mere prohibition: it is the mind of the masses which has to be dealt with" (quoted in Deshpande, p. 514).

96. Ginsburgs and Mathos, p. 134.

97. See "Communiqué on Revolt," NCNA Beijing, 28 March 1959, in URI, p. 348; "Order of the State Council of the PRC," Beijing, 28 March 1959, in URI, p. 357.

98. Cited in *Hindustan Times*, 11 Nov. 1964.

99. NCNA, Lhasa, 20 July 1959, in URI, pp. 392–393. See also NCNA, Lhasa, 5 April 1959, in SCMP, No. 1988, 8 April 1959.

100. *Brief Survey of History*, pp. 20–28; Deshpande, pp. 515–516.

101. For examples, see "Tibet in 1960," *Renmin Ribao*, 15 Dec. 1960, in URI, p. 408; *The Hindustan Times*, 29 June 1962; CNA, No. 378, 30 June 1961; *Times of India*, 14 Sept. 1970, 22 Sept. 1970, 31 Oct. 1970; *The Statesman*, 24 Aug. 1972; *Intelligence Digest*, 1 Aug. 1975. See also P.H. Lehmann and J. Ullal, *Tibet: Das Stille Drama auf dem Dach der Erde* (Hamburg, 1981).

102. CNA, No. 378, 30 June 1961. By the end of November, it was reported that 80 percent of the rural population had "gone through land reform." See *China Reconstructs*, No. 2 (Feb. 1961). See also "Report on Work in Tibet," *Renmin Ribao*, 15 Dec. 1960, in URI, p. 414.

103. *Sunday Standard*, 10 Dec. 1960; *The Statesman*, 14 April 1961, 15 May 1961, 25 March 1962; *Times of India*, 18 Nov. 1961; *Hindustan Times*, 15 March 1961, 6 Sept. 1962, 5 Feb. 1964; *N.Y. Times*, 19 July 1964; *Hindustan Standard*, 18 Jan. 1970, 4 Sept. 1973. See also Avedon, pp. 237–238.

104. Ginsburgs and Mathos, p. 134.

105. Hoffmann, p. 81; G. Patterson, "Why the Panchen Lama Was Sacked," *Hindustan Times*, 1 Feb. 1965; K. Dhondup, "Panchen Lama, the Enigmatic Tibetan," TR 13, Nos. 2/3 (Feb./March 1978), pp. 13–17; Avedon, pp. 274–276; *Times of India*, 30 July 1965; N.Y. *Times*, 24 Jan. 1965; URI, p. 448.

106. CNA, No. 378, 30 June 1961, p. 3; Avedon, pp. 270–271; *Hindustan Times*, 3 Aug. 1965; *Brief Survey of History*, pp. 27–28.

107. URI, p. 516; Avedon, p. 271. The Chinese authorities admitted the process was "a torturous hard, road . . . the quelling of the Dalai traitorous clique plot, and that of the Panchen clique of reactionary serf owners . . . for controlling, striking against, winning over, and buying over revolutionary youths and cadres" (*Minzu Tuanjie* [Nationalities Unity], Aug. 1965, SCMM, No. 489, 16 Nov. 1965).

108. Avedon, p. 271.

109. CB, No. 771, 27 Sept. 1965; URI, pp. 757–758.

110. Deshpande, p. 520.

111. Speech by Zhang Guohua, 2 Sept. 1965, in URI, pp. 482–488. See also speech by Xie Fuzhi, 2 Sept. 1965, in URI, pp. 468–473.

112. NCNA, 8 Sept. 1965, cited in Deshpande, p. 520.

113. Avedon, pp. 280–281; Dreyer, pp. 205–206.

114. See "Revolutionary Masses of Various Nationalities in Lhasa Thoroughly Smash the 'Four Olds,'" NCNA, Lhasa, 28 Aug. 1966, in URI, pp. 604–605.

115. CNA, No. 782, 21 Nov. 1969; TR 1, No. 12 (Dec. 1968), p. 7, quoting *The Times*. But also see MRG, p. 10: Mullin argues that Tibetan youths, albeit under instruction from the Chinese, took part in the destruction.

116. "Inauguration Declaration of the Lhasa Revolutionary Headquarters" (a Red Guard leaflet), in URI, pp. 633–637; "Behold, How Chang Kuo-hua and Others Fanned up Evil Winds and Set Vicious Fire," *Red News*, No. 3, 22 Jan. 1967, in URI, pp. 643–650. See also other documents in URI, pp. 600–700; Dreyer, p. 218.

117. TR 1, No. 3 (March 1968), pp. 4–5; *Hindustan Times*, 17 April 1967; *The Statesman*, 20 April 1967; *Indian Express*, 13 Jan. 1968.

118. NCNA, Lhasa, 6 Sept. 1968, in SCMP, No. 4256, 12 Sept. 1968. On 7 Sept., *People's Daily* was printed in red, and the following editorial was announced in oversized characters: "Overall Victory of Proletarian Cultural Revolution" (CNA, No. 730, 25 Oct. 1968).

119. See NCNA, Lhasa, 6 Sept. 1968, in note 117; NCNA, Beijing, 8 Sept. 1968 in SCMP, No. 4257, 13 Sept. 1968; Avedon, p. 293. Fierce fighting was still being reported in the summer of 1969 (*The Statesman*, 12 July 1969). Some reports indicate that fighting did not stop until 1971 (Information Office, Tibetan Government in Exile, "Political Developments in Chinese Occupied Tibet, 1950–1972," n.d.).

120. PRC Mission to the U.N., Press Release No. 155, 30 Sept. 1974; *Brief Survey of History*, p. 26.

121. Avedon, p. 299. In 1983, the figure was given as 1,278,387. The breakdown released by the Information Office included those who died in prison or labor camps and those who were executed, died in battle, starved, or committed suicide (*Hindustan Times*, 28 June 1984).

122. For a discussion of the Sino-Tibetan border dispute and the war, see W.F. Van Eekelen, *Indian Foreign Policy and the Border Dispute with China* (The Hague, 1965), chapter 6. For numerous articles on Chinese military deployments, see TR 10, Nos. 9/10 (Sept./Oct. 1975).

123. *The Tribune*, Chandigarh, 22 Feb. 1970; "Nuclear Base in Tibet," TR 10, Nos. 9/10 (Sept./Oct. 1975), pp. 27–31. According to the CIA, road transport has

been the key to Chinese control in Tibet. See CIA, "The Integration of Tibet: China's Progress and Problems," in *TR* 14, No. 11 (Nov. 1979), p. 15.

124. Deshpande, pp. 520–521. For various estimates, see N.Y. *Times*, 19 July 1964, 24 Jan. 1965; *Intelligence Digest*, 1 Aug. 1975; *Tashkent International Service*, 5 and 11 Sept. 1968, cited in R. Vaidyanath, "The Soviet View of the Tibetan Situation," *International Studies* 10, No. 4 (April 1969), p. 603. *The Times of India*, 14 May 1966, quoted India's defense minister as stating that China holds between 125,000 and 150,000 troops on the borders. Some have estimated troop strength in the TAR at 500,000: Avedon, p. 317; MRG, p. 20; and some even higher: J. Sweeney, "Keeping the Gentle Faith," *Sheffield Morning Telegraph*, 23 June 1983.

125. In June and July 1960, numerous articles in the Indian press reported widespread Tibetan revolt. For example, see *Hindustan Times*, 9 and 11 June 1960. The Chinese admitted the continued existence of armed hostility. See *The Statesman*, 30 June 1960; see also the Panchen Lama's announcement that fresh blows had been dealt against remnant "reactionary forces," in URI, pp. 410–411; "Tibet in 1960," *Renmin Ribao*, 15 Dec. 1960, in URI, pp. 423–424.

126. N.Y. *Times*, 27 Sept. 1961; *Sunday Standard*, 14 Jan. 1962; *Hindustan Times*, 10 Nov. 1964; *Red Flag*, 30 July 1964; *Hindustan Times*, 29 June 1962 and 11 Nov. 1964, quoting Chinese media. Zhang Guohua warned that "reactionary" forces would be "smashed," in URI, pp. 447–448; NCNA, Lhasa, 13 Dec. 1964, in SCMP, No. 3359, 17 Dec. 1964; *Hindustan Times*, 15 Nov. 1968; *The Times*, 23 Dec. 1970; *People's Daily*, Beijing, 24 June 1974, cited in *Sunday Standard*, 30 June 1974; *The News World*, 17 May 1977; Tiwari, "Unrest in Tibet Continues," *TR* 9, Nos. 6/7 (July/Aug. 1974), pp. 28–29.

127. *Brief Survey of History*, pp. 35, 37. In 1970, a 200-member underground organization in south Tibet was unearthed; 60 Tibetans were arrested and many were executed. In the same year, 190 members of the underground were arrested after violent clashes in Shigatse. In 1972, a demonstration was staged, a convoy ambushed, and a meteorological station destroyed. The next year, the discovery of another organization in Lhasa led to violent clashes and many casualties. In 1974, Chinese offices were set on fire for seven days by an underground organization. See Information Office, Tibetan Government in Exile, *Report* (1975). See also *TR* 7, Nos. 6/7 (June/July 1972), p. 3; "Founding and Unearthing a Nationalist Underground Organization in Phari," *TR* 10, No. 4 (April 1975), pp. 5–7.

128. V. Marchetti and J. Marks, *The CIA and the Cult of Intelligence* (New York, 1974), p. 131; *Newsweek*, 2 Aug. 1965; *The Statesman*, 17 July 1965; *Hindustan Times*, 21 July 1965, citing Radio Lhasa, 13, 14, and 15 July 1965.

129. Soon after the start of the Cultural Revolution, 7,000 Tibetans took part in an uprising. See *Indian Express*, 2 Dec. 1966; V. Bogoslovsky, "Tibet and the Cultural Revolution," *Far Eastern Affairs*, No. 1 (1976), p. 119. In 1968, two revolts took place, leaving 200 Tibetans killed (Vaidyanath, p. 604, citing Radio Moscow, Nov. 1968). In June of that year, a demonstration turned violent in Lhasa (*Brief Survey of History*, p. 37). See also *Times of India*, 18 June 1968; *The Statesman*, 17 Sept. 1973; *Hindustan Times*, 9 Nov. 1973, citing *Literaturnaya Gazeta* [a Soviet weekly], 7 Nov. 1973.

130. For example, in 1969, the *Tibet Daily* admitted serious trouble (*Hindustan Times*, 7 Dec. 1969). A widespread revolt, inflicting over 1,000 casualties among the PLA, was reported in 1970 (Bogoslovsky, pp. 119–120). See also *The Statesman*, 7 Aug. 1970; *Amrita Bazar Patrika*, 2 Aug. 1970; *The Free Press Journal*, 29 July 1970. In 1976, Radio Lhasa complained about the continuing activities of "class enemies" 26 times in 8 months (*TR* 11, No. 10 [Oct. 1976], pp. 6–7).

131. Avedon, pp. 114–130; D. Norbu, "Who Aided Khampas and Why?" *TR* 9, Nos. 6/7 (July/Aug. 1974), pp. 19–23; Mullin, "How the CIA Went to War in Tibet," *The Guardian*, 19 Jan. 1976. The CIA's involvement started in 1955. The training of Tibetans lasted until 1964, and small amounts of money and weapons were supplied until 1971. As Mullin writes, "[this aid] was, however, never really forthcoming on a scale big enough to influence events" (MRG, p. 8; see also Peissel, *Cavaliers of Kham*).

132. Avedon, pp. 121, 129. The present author also interviewed members of the Special Frontier Force in India in 1981.

133. *TR* 9, Nos. 6/7 (July/Aug. 1974), pp. 3–4; *TR* 9, No. 8 (Sept. 1974), pp. 9–10; *TR* 10, No. 1 (Jan. 1975), editorial; *TR* 9, No. 6/7 (July/Aug. 1974). In fact, the dismantling of the base was due as much to internal factionalism as to external pressure (Avedon, pp. 125–129). According to Marchetti and Marks (pp. 131, 157), the CIA had already discontinued most of its aid by the late 1960s.

134. *Brief Survey of History*, p. 39; *The News World*, 17 May 1977.

135. "Tibet Remains a Vast Prison," interview with the Dalai Lama, *Newsweek*, 18 June 1979.

136. NCNA, Beijing, 15 Nov. 1978; *TR* 13, No. 11 (Nov. 1978), pp. 5–6; *TR* 13, No. 6 (June 1978); *TR* 14, No. 1 (Jan. 1979); T. Mathews, "China Starts Big Transfer of Bureaucrats to Tibet," *Washington Post*, 14 June 1979.

137. See T. Dorjee, "Observations of the Second Delegation to Tibet," *Tibetan Messenger* 9, No. 3 (1980), pp. 3–21. Dorjee concluded on p. 20 that: "it would . . . not be unfair or overly critical to say that in 20 years the Chinese have destroyed a priceless age-old culture and have not replaced it with anything worthwhile by any standards." For the full report, see *Tibetan Messenger* 9, No. 3 (1980), pp. 22–41. See also D. Bonavia, "Mistakes on the Roof of the World," *Far Eastern Economic Review*, 8 Aug. 1980; B. Johnson, "Tibetan Protests Undermine China Talks with Dalai Lama," *Christian Science Monitor*, 18 Aug. 1980; N. Nash, "Clenched Fists in the Mountains," *Far Eastern Economic Review*, 22 Aug. 1980; Lehmann and Ullal, pp. 338–353.

138. Xinhua, Beijing, 30 May 1980; *Washington Post*, 7 June 1980, citing NCNA report. According to a vice-chairman of the Tibetan People's Government, at least one third of Tibetans had a lower per capita income in 1980 than in 1959, and another third had experienced no improvement. He also revealed an 80 percent illiteracy rate (M. Kelly, "Tibet and China on the Roof of the World," *America*, 31 Jan. 1981).

139. Xinhua, Beijing, 30 May 1980.

140. Ibid.; *Tibetan Messenger* 9, No. 2 (1980); Kulkarni, "Tibetans Adopt Wait and See Stance on Chinese Reforms," *Christian Science Monitor* July 1, 1981; Jiang Shu, "New Changes on the Plateau," *Beijing Review*, 25 May 1981.

141. Wren, "The Han Chinese in Tibet," *Amrita Bazar Patrika*, 10 May 1983; *Chicago Tribune*, 10 Aug. 1980; NRC *Handlesblad*, 14 Jan. 1984.

142. These reforms were disclosed by Yin Fatang, first secretary of the Regional CCP Committee, quoted in *The Statesman*, 20 June 1984. See also *The Statesman*, 27 June 1984; D. Bonavia, "Tibetan Troubles," *Far Eastern Economic Review*, 27 Oct. 1983.

143. In 1983, the Dalai Lama agreed that conditions in Tibet had improved to some extent since 1979–1980; but he also stressed that "99 percent of the Tibetans are not at all happy, not at all happy" (*The Telegraph*, Calcutta, 1 May 1983).

144. See S. Ali, "Two-Line Struggle," *Far Eastern Economic Review*, 27 Oct. 1983. According to Phuntsog Wangyal, a member of the second delegation to Tibet

who was contacted by members of such organizations, many such organizations exist throughout Tibet. Some have up to 500 members, with branches in different areas. See "Tibetans in Tibet Today," *Tibet News Review* 1, Nos. 3/4 (Winter 1980/1981), pp. 26–27. The names of six such organizations with whom Tibetans in exile have contact were published in *TR* 15, No. 9 (Sept. 1980), p. 8. Estimates of the size of the underground vary. See *U.S. News and World Report,* 29 Aug. 1983; M. Weisskopf, "Separatists Keep up Struggle for Free Tibet," *Washington Post,* 13 Aug. 1983; M. Liu, "Tensions in a High Place," *Newsweek,* 29 Aug. 1983.

145. For the text of messages from the "Tiger-Dragon Youth Association of Tibet" and the "Three Provinces Youth Organization of Tibet," see *TR* 17, No. 10 (Oct. 1982), pp. 4–5; and *TR* 18, No. 10 (Oct. 1983), pp. 5–6. See also the letter from the "Tibetan People's Patriotic Association," 14 Oct. 1982, handed to a visitor in Lhasa, in TACO Documents; McNulty, "Unsigned Letters Appeal for Tibetan Independence," *Chicago Tribune,* 10 Aug. 1980; B. Johnson, *Christian Science Monitor,* 18 Oct. 1980.

146. See Weisskopf, "Separatists Keep up Struggle for Free Tibet," Note 144 above; Liu, "Tensions in a High Place," Note 144 above. In January 1981, Radio Lhasa broadcast orders by Yin Fatang to government officials and the PLA to "resolutely struggle against the counter-revolutionary, criminal and sabotage activities," and charged that "bad elements" had sown discord among the nationalities (*Arab News,* Jiddah, 1 Feb. 1981). Chinese officials also warned the second Tibetan delegation of underground organizations causing trouble in Lhasa. (Wangyal, "Tibetans in Tibet Today").

147. *Times of India,* 31 Jan. 1981; *TR* 17, No. 6 (June 1982), p. 4.

148. See Office of Tibet, New York, "Summary of Recent Events in Tibet," 30 Oct. 1983; and "News Release", 28 Oct. 1983. Some arrests and executions, specifically those held in public, were reported in the press (*N.Y. Times,* 3 Oct. 1983; *N.Y. Tribune,* 1 Oct. 1983). See the articles by Bonavia and Ali in *Far Eastern Economic Review,* 27 Oct. 1983. But also see *Beijing Review,* 17 Oct. 1983. The arrests and executions were apparently made possible under the penal law revised in September 1983, which called for severe punishment, including the death sentence, for offenders "who cause grave harm to the social order." Under the same law, the death sentence was to be imposed on persons "who illegally manufacture, traffic in, transport, steal, or seize firearms, ammunitions, or explosives in serious cases, and those who teach others to commit serious crimes" ("On Capital Punishment," *Beijing Review,* 7 Nov. 1983, editorial).

149. See *Daily Telegraph,* 2 Sept. 1985; see also Radio Lhasa Broadcast, 26 June 1985, regarding meeting to ensure "law and order" is kept during the 20th anniversary celebration; Security Office Documents, n.d., Tibetan Government in Exile, Dharmsala.

150. Note, however, that freedom of religion is very restrictively defined by the Chinese. This is evidenced by the official publication called *"Lobjung Che Zhi—Basic Study Guide No. 55,"* which contains guidelines for Communist Party and Youth League members and officers. It states *inter alia:* "Religion is a tranquilizing poison used by capitalists to oppress people. So why does the Communist Party have to tolerate freedom of religion? The existence of religion—its development and decline—is a fact. That the people who believe in religion come mainly from the ordinary people is also an undeniable fact. We have to stop religion in that it is blind faith, against the law, and counter-revolutionary." The publication then lists the specific practices that are forbidden: "reciting things, doing circumambulations, and asking Lamas for help when someone is sick and dying; . . . induc[ing] minors

to do anything religious or take them to a religious service; . . . try[ing] to revive the power of religion that has already been destroyed." It is strictly forbidden for the Communist Party and Youth League members to practice religion in any form; instead, they are urged to propagate atheism. The full text is published in MRG, Appendix 2.

151. The Dalai Lama expressed the Tibetans' fears thus: "Frankly speaking, it is difficult to trust the Chinese. Once bitten by a snake, you feel suspicious even when you see a piece of rope" (MRG, p. 12).

152. A recent visitor to Lhasa described the troop presence there as "massive" and wrote that "guards with bayonets are posted at bridges leading to the city and soldiers regularly patrol the old Tibetan quarter of the city" (M. Ross, "Tibetan Dissidents Resist Chinese," *The Dispatch*, 13 Aug. 1983).

153. Weisskopf, "Separatists Keep up Struggle for Free Tibet," Note 144 above. Taylor wrote: "Here in this breathtakingly beautiful corner of Asia, an indomitable spirit of independence and religious fervor endures among the Tibetan people despite 33 years of Chinese Communist rule" (*U.S. News and World Report*, 29 Aug. 1983). Sweeney wrote: "Like the Russians in Afghanistan, the Chinese have found Tibet easy to invade, but impossible to conquer" (Sweeney, "Keeping the Gentle Faith" Note 124 above). Ross concluded: "Fear and animosity still separate the Tibetan people from the Chinese who conquered them 33 years ago" (Ross, "Tibetan Dissidents Resist Chinese," Note 152 above). Finally, Earnshaw wrote from Lhasa: "Virtually everyone said they wanted the Dalai Lama back and Tibet independent" (*Daily Telegraph*, 10 Aug. 1983).

154. K. Marek, *Identity and Continuity of States in Public International Law* (Geneva, 1968), p. 548.

155. These two elements, in Roman Law terms, pertain to the presence of *corpus* and *animus*. See R.Y. Jennings, *The Acquisition of Territory in International Law* (Manchester, 1963), p. 4.

156. Permanent Court of Arbitration, *U.S.A. v. the Netherlands*, Arbitral Award, 4 April 1928, in J.B. Scott, ed., *The Hague Court Reports*, Second Series (New York, 1932), p. 93.

157. P.C.I.J. (1933), Series A/B, No. 53, p. 46.

158. Jennings, p. 6.

159. A.S. Hershey, *The Essentials of International Public Law* (New York, 1927), pp. 276–284; W.E. Hall, *International Law*, 7th ed. (Oxford, 1917), p. 103; M. Akehurst, *A Modern Introduction to International Law*, 5th ed. (London, 1984), pp. 141–155.

160. *Occupatio* is used to mean "the act of appropriation by a State by which it intentionally acquires sovereignty over such territory as is at the time not under the sovereignty of another State [i.e., *terra nullius*]." See L. Oppenheim, *International Law*, ed. H. Lauterpacht, 8th ed. (London, 1955), Vol. 1, p. 555. See also N. Hill, *Claims to Territory in International Law* (London, 1945), pp. 146–147.

161. Hershey, p. 277.

162. Akehurst, pp. 146–147. For a historical survey of conquest, see M. McMahon, *Conquest in Modern International Law* (Washington, 1940), pp. 3–92.

163. For the evolution of this approach, see McMahon.

164. Ibid., pp. 83–92.

165. Xin Wu, "A Criticism of Bourgeois International Law on the Question of State Territory," *Guoji Wenti Yanjiu*, No. 7 (1960), in J. Cohen and H. Chiu, eds., *People's China and International Law* (Princeton, 1974), Vol. 1, pp. 326–328.

276

46 J.L. Brierly, *The Law of Nations*, 4th ed. (Oxford, 1949), p. 147.

166. McMahon, pp. 8–12; Oppenheim, pp. 566–570; J.L. Brierly, *The Law of Nations*, 4th ed. (Oxford, 1949), p. 147.

167. T.J. Lawrence, *The Principles of International Law*, 7th ed. (London, 1923), p. 159, cited in McMahon, p. 12.

168. Oppenheim, p. 567.

169. McMahon, pp. 89–90; Brierly, pp. 147–149.

170. See "Declaration on Principles of International Law Concerning Friendly Relations Among States in Accordance with the Charter of the United Nations," G.A. Res. 2625 (XXV), adopted 24 Oct. 1970, for an expression of the community of Nations. Unless one is to reject completely the rule of international law, which, as Jennings states, "there is neither authority nor reason to do," titles by conquest pre-dating the condemnation of the use of force must still remain valid (*The Acquisition of Territory*, p. 53).

171. McMahon, p. 14.

172. Ibid., p. 15; Akehurst, pp. 146–147, see also "Declaration on Principles of International Law," in Note 170 above.

173. See McMahon, p. 10, quoting Oppenheim.

174. E. de Vattel, *The Law of Nations or the Principles of Natural Law* (1758; rpt. New York, 1964), p. 308.

175. See Jennings, p. 67. The view that such treaties cannot transfer sovereignty is supported in two Dutch municipal court decisions: *Amato Narodni Podnik v. Julius Keilwerth Musikinstrumentenfabrik*, in International Law Reports (1957), pp. 435–439; *Ratz-Lienert and Klein v. Nederlands Beheers-Institut*, International Law Reports (1957), pp. 536–542.

176. Marek, pp. 105–106; J. Crawford, *The Creation of States in International Law* (Oxford, 1979), p. 407.

177. Marek, p. 566.

178. Ibid, p. 104.

179. For examples, see McMahon, p. 13; Jennings, p. 54.

180. Marek, p. 554. For a similar Chinese view, see Shi Song et al., "An Initial Investigation into the Old Law Viewpoint in the Teaching of International Law," *Jiaoxue Yu Yanjiu*, No. 4 (1958), in Cohen and Chiu, p. 335.

181. Brierly, pp. 147–148.

182. Jennings, p. 54.

183. Ibid., p. 56.

184. See Note 170 above. "The legal significance of the Declaration lies in the fact that it provides evidence of the consensus among Member States of the United Nations on the meaning and elaboration of the principles of the Charter" (I. Brownlie, *Basic Documents in International Law*, 3rd ed. [Oxford, 1983], p. 35).

185. D.H.N. Johnson, "Acquisitive Prescription in International Law," BYIL (1950), p. 333.

186. L.J. Bouchez, "The Concept of Effectiveness as Applied to Territorial Sovereignty over Sea-Areas, Air Space and Outer Space," *Nederlands Tijdschrift voor Internationaal Recht* (1962), p. 159.

187. Ibid. See also I. Brownlie, *Principles of Public International Law*, 3rd ed. (1979), p. 83.

188. Bouchez, p. 159. See also McMahon, p. 9, quoting Hall; Johnson, pp. 334–335.

189. For a similar view, see P. Fiore, *International Law Codified and Its Legal Sanction* (New York, 1918), pp. 431–432. Strictly speaking, it is the consent given

by the conquered State and not the conquest that gives legal effect to the action of the conqueror.

190. See the *Chamizal* Arbitration between the United States and Mexico in 1910-1911, in *AJIL* 5 (1911), pp. 782-833. The United States claimed title to the Chamizal tract, *inter alia*, on the grounds of prescription. The arbitrators from Canada, the United States, and Mexico were unanimous on this point: that the claim of the United States failed simply because the possession had not been "undisturbed, uninterrupted and unchallenged" since 1848 (Johnson, pp. 340-341).

191. *AJIL* 5 (1911), p. 807. For further discussion, see Johnson, p. 34.

192. Marek, pp. 556-563.

193. Nonrecognition may derive some additional significance as a sanction by penalizing the law-breaker to the extent that the intended result of the violation is denied (Marek, pp. 558-561). Similarly, it could be argued that recognition of annexation of territory by the international community as a whole might constitute evidence that the new situation has acquired at least a degree of legitimacy. See H. Lauterpacht, *Recognition in International Law* (Cambridge, 1947), p. 429; Akehurst, pp. 148-150. But even this contention cannot be lightly presumed in the face of contrary State practice. Of particular interest are the cases of annexation of entire States by force that occurred, with some frequency, in the period from 1935 to 1940. The States of Ethiopia, Austria, Czechoslovakia, and Albania, effectively submerged by external illegal force, were reconstituted by the Allies during, or at the termination of, the Second World War. Despite the extension of recognition of the Italian and German annexations of these States by the international community, the reconstituted States were considered to be not new entities but continuations of the earlier independent States. For a detailed discussion of these cases, see Marek, pp. 269-282, 343-368, 287-330, 333-337. See also Crawford, p. 418.

194. For a discussion of the occupation and incorporation of Latvia, Estonia, and Lithuania by the U.S.S.R., see Marek, pp. 379-382.

195. See Proclamation by the President of the United States of America, No. 5209, 14 June 1984, and Proclamation by the President of the United States of America, No. 5302, 16 Feb. 1985. For similar recent statements, see also letter from Department of External Affairs, Ottawa, Canada (B.M. Mawhinney) to Act-Hon. Council of Latvia (E. Upenicks), 12 July 1984; Message from the Prime Minister of Australia (R.J.L. Hawke), in *Baltic News* 10, No. 1., March 1984, p. 1; message from the Auswartiges Amt (Dr. A. Arnot) in Bonn, West Germany, to the Baltic World Conference, 21 April 1983; answer to question in Assemblee Nationale by the Minister of External Affairs of France, 3 May 1982, in *Journal Officiel*, 3 May 1982; letter from the Foreign and Commonwealth Office, London (S.J. Butt) to Chairman, Latvian National Council in Great Britain (A. Abakuks), 10 March 1980; letter from Ministere des Affaires Etrangeres, Bruxelles, Belgium (H. Simonet) to President of the Supreme Committee for the Liberation of Lithuania (C.K. Bobelis), Nov. 1979.

196. Security Council Resolution 242 (XXII), adopted 22 Nov. 1967. For a discussion of the series of Security Council and General Assembly resolutions that followed, see Le Morzellec, *La Question de Jerusalem Devant l'Organisation des Nations Unies* (Brussels, 1979).

197. G.A. Res. 2628 (XXV), adopted 4 Nov. 1970. See "Resolutions and Decisions of the General Assembly and the Security Council Relating to the Question of Palestine," G.A. Doc. A/AC.183/L.2 (1976) and G.A. Doc. A/AC.183/L.2/ Add.1(1980). Security Council Resolution 242 and General Assembly Resolution 2628 can both be found in the first document, on pp. 215 and 91 respectively.

198. An example is provided by the U.S.S.R.'s intervention in Mongolia, Eastern Europe, and, more recently, Afghanistan.

199. Official statements of the Israeli government defended Israel's action in terms of the historical claim to Jerusalem as "the capital of Israel in the days of David" (statement by Bengurion, 20 June 1967). See also statement by General Moshe Dayan, 8 June 1967. Both are quoted in Ataov, "The Status of Jerusalem as a Question of International Law," in *Legal Aspects of the Palestine Problem*, H. Kochler, ed., (Vienna, 1981), p. 138. The annexation of the Baltic states was presented as a voluntary merger. For further discussion, see Marek, pp. 383–387. In other cases, actions have been taken ostensibly to redress unjust colonial situations. An example is provided by India's recovery of Goa and other colonial enclaves. For details on the PRC's support of India's action, see "Statement of the Chinese Government [in Support of India's Recovery of Goa]," in *Peking Review*, 22 Dec. 1961, pp. 10–11; Jin Fu, "China's Recovery of Xianggang (Hong Kong) Area Fully Accords with International Law," *Beijing Review*, 26 Sept. 1983, p. 17. Shi Song and others state: "In order to rectify the unjust situation created by history, a state must recover sovereignty over its own territory. This is confirmed by the practice of modern international law." Shi Song et al., in Cohen and Chiu, p. 335.

200. See Crawford, pp. 419–420.

201. Johnson, p. 347.

202. Despite over 100 years of effective, undisputed, and universally recognized British control over Hong Kong, the Chinese government asserts that this territory has always remained a part of China and that China has never lost its sovereignty over it. Thus, as the Chinese have clarified, by the "recovery of Hong Kong" is meant only "the resumption of the exercise of sovereignty." This view is reflected in the "Joint Declaration of the Government of the PRC and the Government of the United Kingdom of Great Britain and Northern Ireland on the Question of Hong Kong," Article 1. For the text, see *Beijing Review*, 1 Oct. 1984. See also Jin Fu, "China's Recovery of Xianggang," pp. 15–17.

203. Crawford, pp. 407, 417.

204. See the quotations by Taylor, Sweeney, Ross, and Earnshaw in Note 153 above. See also *N.Y. Times*, 19 July 1979, articles on p. A1; *The Times*, 27 July 1983.

205. F. Michael, "Survival of a Culture," *Asian Survey* 24, No. 7 (July 1985), p. 744.

206. For the various reactions in the United Nations, see the following General Assembly Documents: Philippines, A/PV.1394 (1965), p. 27; El Salvador, A/PV.898 (1960), pp. 36–37, A/PV.1401 (1965), p. 17; Ireland, A/PV.898 (1960), pp. 47–50; Nicaragua, A/PV.1401 (1965), pp. 52–56; New Zealand, A/PV.1401 (1965), p. 2; U.S.A., A/PV.1401 (1965), pp. 42–50. The U.S.S.R., Poland, Romania, and Albania all contended that, as Tibet was a part of China, the topic ought not be discussed in the United Nations. See Albania, A/PV.1401 (1965), p. 417, and A/PV.1403 (1965), pp. 33–36; Romania, A/PV.1401 (1965), pp. 32–36, and A/PV.898 (1960), pp. 42–55; U.S.S.R., A/PV.1401 (1965), pp. 48–50, 52–55; Poland, A/PV.1401 (1965), pp. 63–65; Czechoslovakia, A/PV.1401 (1965), pp. 67–70; Hungary, A/PV.1401 (1965), pp. 58–60. For the text of the debates, see U.N. Documents and *Tibet in the United Nations, 1950–1961*, published by the Bureau of His Holiness the Dalai Lama, New Delhi.

207. G.A. Doc. A/PV.1394 (1965), pp. 2–25, 37.

208. G.A. Doc. A/PV.1401 (1965), pp. 52–55. For a similar statement by New Zealand, see G.A. Doc. A/PV.1401 (1965), p. 2.

209. G.A. Doc. A/PV.1394 (1965), p. 52.

210. G.A. Doc. A/PV.898 (1960), p. 52.

211. G.A. Doc. A/PV.1394 (1965), p. 61.

212. G.A. Doc. A/PV.898 (1960), p. 46. See "Invasion of Tibet by Foreign Forces," G.A. Doc. A/1534 (1950).

213. G.A. Doc. A/PV.1401 (1965), pp. 42–50.

214. T.R 17, No. 12 (Dec. 1982), p. 4. The State Department still regards Tibet as an entity that, in some respects, is separate from China. The Foreign Assistance Legislation for Fiscal Year 1983, Parts 4 and 5, states that "the People's Republic of China and Tibet" are to be deleted from the list of "countries" that are prohibited from receiving U.S. foreign aid (ibid.). See also TR 12, No. 6 (June, 1977), pp. 5–6, quoting the U.S. State Department; "China Denounces U.S. on Tibetans," N.Y. *Times*, 15 Oct. 1975, p. 9.

215. German Foreign Office letter, quoted in TR 19, No. 4 (April 1984), p. 6.

216. I. Epstein, *Tibet Transformed* (Beijing, 1983), pp. 517–519. The Soviet Union's attitude has changed to the point where it has offered its support to the exiled Tibetan government (*Indian Express*, 1 May 1980; *Times of India*, 1 May 1980).

217. J. Sweeney, "Keeping the Gentle Faith," *Sheffield Morning Telegraph*, 23 June 1983.

218. P. Jessup, *Transnational Law* (New Haven, 1956), p. 62.

219. Marek, p. 86.

220. Ibid., pp. 86–87.

221. See C.N. Okeke, *Controversial Subjects of Contemporary International Law* (Rotterdam, 1973), p. 137. See also F.E. Oppenheimer, "Governments and Authorities in Exile," AJIL 36 (1942), pp. 556–595; M.M. Whiteman, ed., *Digest of International Law*, Vol. 1 (Washington, 1963), pp. 925–930.

222. McNair, A. and Watts, A.D., *Legal Effects of War*, 4th ed. (Cambridge, 1966), pp. 426–427.

223. Oppenheimer, "Governments and Authorities in Exile," p. 568.

Notes to Chapter 11

1. See the "Joint Declaration of the Government of the PRC and the Government of the United Kingdom of Great Britain and Northern Ireland on the Question of Hong Kong," Article 1, in *Beijing Review*, 1 Oct. 1984.

2. Statement made by H.H. the Dalai Lama on the occasion of the twenty-fifth anniversary of the Tibetan National Uprising Day, Dharmsala, 10 March 1984. On behalf of the Tibetan people, the Dalai Lama asked: "Why should an alien rule be forced upon them? Why shouldn't they have the choice of holding their own beliefs, traditions, culture, and identity?" (Dalai Lama, "The Dalai Lama Speaks Out His Mind," *Asian Wall Street Journal*, 25 August 1977).

3. Dalai Lama, "The Dalai Lama Speaks Out His Mind." See also Dalai Lama, "China and the Future of Tibet," *Wall Street Journal*, 8 Nov. 1979.

4. *The Telegraph*, 1 May 1983.

5. G. Earnshaw, "Dalai Lama Calls for 'Tibetan Autonomy,'" *Daily Telegraph*, 13 Dec. 1982.

6. Y. Alexander and R.A. Friedlander, eds., *Self Determination: National, Regional and Global Dimensions* (Boulder, Colorado, 1980), p. xiii.

7. Alexander and Friedlander, p. xiii.

8. U. Umozurike, *Self-Determination in International Law* (Hamden, Connecticut, 1972), p. 4; International Commission of Jurists, "East Pakistan Staff Study," *The Review*, No. 8 (June 1972), p. 47. See for a discussion, M.C. van Walt van Praag,

"Tibet and the Right to Self-Determination," *Wayne Law Review* 26, No. 1 (Nov. 1979).

9. J.B. Scott, ed., *Official Statements of War Aims and Peace Proposals* (Westport, Connecticut, 1921), p. 52. See also V. van Dyke, *International Politics* (New York, 1972), pp. 41–42.

10. V.I. Lenin, "Socialism and Self-Determination of Nations," in *Collected Works* (Moscow, 1964), Vol. 31, p. 321.

11. President Wilson quoted in Van Dyke, p. 41.

12. Umozurike, p. 21.

13. J.T. Dreyer, *China's Forty Millions* (Cambridge, Massachusetts, 1976), p. 63. In the "Ten Great Political Programs," adopted in 1930, minority nationalities were given the right to secede or federate.

14. C. Brandt, B. Schwartz, and J.K. Fairbank, *A Documentary History of Chinese Communism* (New York, 1967), pp. 220–224.

15. U.N. Charter, Article 1, paragraph 2.

16. G.A. Res. 1541 (XV), adopted 14 Dec. 1960, in I. Brownlie, ed., *Basic Documents in International Law*, 3rd ed. (Oxford, 1983), pp. 299–301.

17. R. Rosenstock, "The Declaration of Principles of International Law Concerning Friendly Relations: A Survey," *AJIL* 65 (1971), p. 730.

18. M. El Kayal, *The Role of the United Nations in the Protection of Human Rights*, unpublished dissertation, University of Illinois at Urbana, 1975, p. 314. The same view is supported by Resolution 1654 (XXI), adopted one year later. See R. Higgins, *The Development of International Law Through the Political Organs of the United Nations* (London, 1963), p. 100.

19. The *International Covenant on Economic, Social and Cultural Rights* and the *International Covenant on Civil and Political Rights* [hereafter referred to as the Human Rights Covenants], in Brownlie, *Basic Documents*, pp. 257–292. The first Covenant entered into force on 3 Jan. 1976, the second on 23 March 1972. Paragraph 2 of the common Article 1 states: "All peoples may, for their own ends, freely dispose of their natural wealth and resources without prejudice to any obligations arising out of international economic cooperation, based upon the principle of mutual benefits, and international law. In no case may a people be deprived of its own means of subsistence."

20. G.A. Res. 2625 (XXV), [hereafter referred to as the Declaration on Principles of International Law], adopted without vote on 24 Oct. 1970, in Brownlie, *Basic Documents*, pp. 35–44.

21. A growing number of commentators have come to this conclusion. See El Kayal, p. 34; Umozurike, p. 272; H. Bokor-Szego, *New States in International Law* (Budapest, 1970), p. 16. Using the emphasis on decolonization in many of the U.N. resolutions as evidence, some analysts have suggested that self-determination is applicable only to colonies. The history of the principle and its application in noncolonial as well as colonial situations since 1945 shows this view to be incorrect.

22. Advisory Opinion on Western Sahara, I.C.J., *Reports* (1975), pp. 35–36.

23. The court stated that "the subsequent development of International Law in regard to non-self-governing territories, as enshrined in the Charter of the United Nations, made the principle of self-determination applicable to all of them" (I.C.J., *Reports* [1971], p. 31).

24. See Y. Dinstein, "Collective Human Rights of Peoples and Minorities," *International Legal and Comparative Law Quarterly* 25 (Jan. 1976), p. 106. See also El Kayal, p. 315.

25. See G.A. Res. 612 (VII), adopted 19 Dec. 1952; G.A. Res. 611 (VII), adopted 17 Dec. 1952; G.A. Res. 1573 (XV), adopted 19 Dec. 1960; G.A. Res. 1724 (XVI), adopted 20 Dec. 1961.

26. The committee had expanded to twenty-four members by the 17th General Assembly.

27. Official note from Zhou Enlai to A. Vyshinsky, Minister of Foreign Affairs of the U.S.S.R., 14 Feb. 1950, in "Exchange of Notes Concerning . . . the Recognition of the Independence of the Mongolian People's Republic," *U.N.T.S.* 226 (1956), pp. 16–18.

28. For a detailed discussion of this topic, see I.C. Jur., "East Pakistan Staff Study."

29. See G.A. Res. 390 (V), adopted 2 Dec. 1950, regarding Eritrea; G.A. Res. 1723 (XVI), adopted 20 Dec. 1961, regarding Tibet; Security Council Resolutions 384 (XXX), adopted 22 Dec. 1975, and 389 (XXXI), adopted 22 April 1976, regarding Timor. See also G.A. Res. 34/44, adopted 23 Nov. 1979, "Importance of the Universal Realization of the Right of Peoples to Self-determination and of the Speedy Granting of Independence to Colonial Countries and Peoples for the Effective Guarantee and Observance of Human Rights."

30. In 1974 the General Assembly adopted a complete statement of its conception of Palestinian rights, which has since been reaffirmed numerous times. In relevant part, this resolution states: "*The General Assembly, Recalling* its relevant resolutions which affirm the right of the Palestinian people to self-determination, (1.) *Reaffirms* the inalienable rights of the Palestinian people in Palestine including: (a) The right of self-determination without external interference; (b) The right to national independence and sovereignty; (2.) *Reaffirms* also the inalienable right of the Palestinians to return to their homes and property from which they have been displaced and uprooted, and calls for their return." See G.A. Res. 3236 (XXIX), adopted 22 Nov. 1974. See also "Resolutions and Decisions of the General Assembly and the Security Council Relating to the Question of Palestine," G.A. Doc. A/AC.183/L.2 (1976) and G.A. Doc. A/AC.183/L.2/Add.1 (1980).

31. Quoted in A. Cassese, "The Helsinki Declaration and Self-Determination," in *Human Rights, International Law and the Helsinki Accord,* ed. T. Buergenthal (Montclair, N.J., 1977), pp. 99–100. It is interesting to note that the right to self-determination is also being recognized in a different context, namely, in the field of Humanitarian Law of War. Article 1, paragraph 4, and Article 96, paragraph 3 of "Protocol I Additional to the Geneva Convention of 1949" (opened for signature on 12 Dec. 1977) refer to the right of self-determination of peoples and regard struggles for self-determination as international armed conflicts, thereby granting the participants belligerent rights heretofore granted only to sovereign states.

32. E. Suzuki, "Self-Determination and World Public Order: Community Response to Territorial Separation," *Virginia Journal of International Law*" 16, No. 4 (Summer 1976), p. 862. Note that many legal instruments of the U.N. that establish the right of self-determination concern human rights (e.g., the Covenants on Human Rights).

33. 10 U.N. GAOR, Annexes (Agenda Item No. 28(11)), 14 U.N. Doc. A/2929 (1955).

34. Suzuki, pp. 801–802, 848. For this reason, the U.N. organs do not permit Article 2, paragraph 7, of the Charter to impede discussion and decision when the right to self-determination is at issue.

35. Brownlie, *Basic Documents,* p. 43.

36. Suzuki, p. 784.

37. Ibid. p. 795.

38. It could be argued that where no previous territory existed, the creation of a new state may still not be incompatible with regional interests.

39. Brownlie, *Basic Documents*, p. 300.

40. I.C. Jur., "East Pakistan Staff Study," p. 46.

41. G.A. Res. 1723 (XVI). For the full text, see Appendix 26.

42. See the debates on agenda item "Question of Tibet," during the 16th Session of the General Assembly, in *Tibet in the United Nations, 1950–1961*, published by the Bureau of His Holiness the Dalai Lama, New Delhi, pp. 253–311.

43. H.E. Richardson, *A Short History of Tibet* (New York, 1962), p. 13.

44. "Editorial," *Tibetan Messenger* 7, No. 2, Special Commemoration Issue (1978), p. 6.

45. NCNA, Beijing, 20 April 1959, "Commentary on the So-called Statement of the Dalai Lama."

46. Although Marxist ideology is not necessarily wholly incompatible with Buddhist teachings, the Chinese attempt to destroy Buddhism by forbidding its practice and by attacking its doctrine, institutions, and priests obviously is.

47. See P. Karan, *The Changing Face of Tibet* (Lexington, Kentucky, 1976), p. 50.

48. See R. Sawhny, "China's Control of Tibet and Its Implications for India's Defense," *International Studies* 10, No. 4 (April 1960), pp. 486–494; G.H. Corr, *The Chinese Red Army* (Reading, 1976), p. 62.

49. R. Rahul, *The Government and Politics of Tibet* (1969), p. 121; C. Sen, "Tibet and the Sino-Indian Impasse," *International Studies* 10, No. 4 (April 1960), pp. 523–541.

50. G.A. Res. 1353 (XIV); G.A. Res. 1723 (XVI); G.A. Res. 2079 (XX). The texts of these resolutions are in Appendix 26.

51. G.A. Res. 1723 (XVI). For the text, see Appendix 26.

52. International Commission of Jurists, Legal Inquiry Committee on Tibet, *Tibet and the Chinese People's Republic* (Geneva, 1960), p. 3.

53. Ibid. pp. 4–5. In an earlier report, the commission stated: "On the basis of the available evidence, it would seem difficult to recall a case in which ruthless suppression of man's essential dignity had been more systematically and efficiently carried out." See International Commission of Jurists, *The Question of Tibet and the Rule of Law* (Geneva, 1959), p. 59.

54. See Prince Peter of Greece and Denmark, "The Chinese Colonisation of Tibet," *TR* 13, No. 4 (April 1978), p. 24. See also Karan, pp. 81–84.

55. See Chapter 10 of the present book.

56. See *Time*, 13 Sept. 1968, The *London Observer* of 4 Feb. 1969 stated that famine in Tibet had become so threatening that the Chinese were suppressing Tibetan food marches. Most of the available local food had been commandeered by the Chinese occupation authorities for the Chinese troops. The *Statesman* of 4 April 1969 reported that the Chinese retained three-fourths of the harvested crops.

57. Address delivered in Tokyo, 9 Oct. 1982, "The Choice for Modern Japan," quoted in Minority Rights Group, *The Tibetans*, Report No. 49, by C. Mullin and P. Wangyal (London, 1983), p. 22.

58. From Lhasa in 1979, John Fraser reported: "On top of all this [evidence of Maoism everywhere] is the sinister sheen of classical colonial rule by the Chinese over the Tibetans, in direct refutation to all the propaganda claims of respect for minority cultures and values. Even in those areas where the Chinese make a show of Tibetaness, the purpose appears designed to assert the correctness of Chinese authority" (*Vancouver Sun*, 25 July 1979).

59. G.A. Res. 1723 (XVI). The resolution was adopted by a vote of 56 to 11 with 29 abstentions.

60. Quoted in "Beijing Receives Dalai Lama's Envoys," *Beijing Review*, 3 Dec. 1984.

61. "Dalai Lama Speaks Out on Contacts with Peking," *Far Eastern Economic Review*, 16 July 1982, p. 29.

62. Ibid.; Tibetan Affairs Coordination Office press release, 11 Sept. 1984.

63. "Beijing Receives Dalai Lama's Envoys," *Beijing Review*, 3 Dec. 1984. From Yang Jingren's statement, it appears that "the same political status" refers only to the Dalai Lama's positions in the National People's Congress and the Consultative Conference, which are Central Government organs in Beijing.

64. Ibid.

65. Reprinted in TR 20, No. 1 (Jan. 1985), p. 6.

66. Statement of H.H. the Dalai Lama, 16 Dec. 1984.

67. See G.A. Res. 1541 (XV), adopted 14 Dec. 1960.

68. H. Hannum and R.B. Lillich, "The Concept of Autonomy in International Law," *AJIL* 74 (1980), p. 860.

69. *Constitution of the People's Republic of China*, adopted 4 Dec. 1982. Article 31 reads: "The State may establish special administrative regions when necessary. The systems to be instituted in special administrative regions shall be prescribed by law enacted by the National People's Congress in the light of the specific conditions." See also Article 30 and Section 6 of the Constitution.

70. *Renmin Ribao* editorial, reprinted in *Beijing Reviw*, 1 Oct. 1984.

71. "Deng Xiaoping on China's Reunification," *Beijing Review*, 8 Aug. 1983, p. 5.

72. Ibid.

73. Ibid.

74. "Policy Towards Dalai Lama," *Beijing Review*, 15 Nov. 1982.

75. Editorial, "The Madness and the Method," TR 17, No. 7 (July 1982), p. 3; "Tibetans Seek Complete Independence," *The Statesman*, 27 Oct. 1984.

76. H. Chiu, "Prospects for the Unification of China: An Analysis of the Views of the Republic of China on Taiwan," paper presented at the 35th Annual Meeting of the Association for Asian Studies, San Francisco (March 1983).

77. "Tragedy of Tibet Provides Objective Lesson for Republic of China, President Chiang Warns," *Free China Weekly*, 19 Dec. 1982. In view of the ROC's concern over the Tibetan case, the PRC put out three lengthy articles to defend the government's policy. One article noted: "Following more than 30 years of liberation, Xizang [i.e., Tibet] accomplished its democratic and socialist reforms and abolished the serf system. Under the direct leadership of the central people's government, Xizang practices national autonomy, [and] the people will never allow the wheels of history to be turned back. This is why earlier this year, when the Dalai Lama said the Xizang autonomous region must also be allowed to enjoy autonomous rights like those of Taiwan, which will become a special administrative region after its return to the motherland, the CPC flatly refused. This is understandable and it meets with the people's approval." "Commentary by Chen Guoshao: The Trilogy that Fishes in Muddied Waters," *Beijing Zhongguo Cinwen She*, 7 Jan. 1983, in FBIS, 21 Jan. 1983.

78. Huang Bengxiao, "Trilogy of the Fall of Tibet," *Zhongyang Ribao*, 14 Dec. 1982; Dr. J. Soong, government spokesman of the Republic of China, quoted in *Tibetan Bulletin* 13, No. 1 (Jan.-Feb. 1982), p. 9.

79. Chiu, "Prospects for the Unification of China."

80. Report of the Assessment Office, Nov. 1984, cited in *Tibetan Bulletin* 15, No. 5 (Dec.-Jan. 1985), p. 24.

81. "Chinese Leaders on New Policy for Tibet's Construction," reproduced in Tibetan Affairs Coordination Office, "Excerpts from Broadcasts by Radio Lhasa and Other Chinese Radio Sources," 5 Sept. 1985.

82. G.A. Res. 1541 (XV), adopted 14 Dec. 1960.

83. W.M. Reisman, *Puerto Rico and the International Process: New Roles in Association* (Washington, 1975), p. 11.

84. U.N. Charter, Article 2, paragraph 1.

85. Reisman, p. 10.

86. "A freely associated State . . . may terminate [the relationship of association] unilaterally only after a plebiscite has demonstrated the freely expressed will of the people." See A.J. Armstrong, "Negotiations for the Future Political Status of Micronesia," *AJIL* 74 (1980), p. 691. See also Reisman, pp. 10–13; J. Crawford, *The Creation of States in International Law* (Oxford, 1979), pp. 376–377. Hannum and Lillich summarize the status of associated states thus: "In essence, associated states have all the powers and prerogatives of sovereign independent states, except for those powers they unilaterally choose to delegate to the principal government (typically foreign affairs and defense). An associated state's control over its internal affairs is unlimited and it retains the power not only to alter unilaterally its own constitution, but also to sever its relationship with the principal entity" ("The Concept of Autonomy in International Law," p. 888).

87. Reisman, p. 12.

88. Crawford, p. 371.

89. Reisman, p. 19.

90. For example, see the book by Reisman regarding Puerto Rico. See also Crawford, regarding the Cook Islands and Western Samoa (pp. 372–374 and 295, respectively); and the article by Armstrong regarding Micronesia.

91. For discussion of these examples of permanent neutrality, see J.H.W. Verzijl, *International Law in Historical Perspective*, Vol. 2 (Leiden, 1969), pp. 455–457. The treaty regarding Honduras, concluded in Washington, 20 Dec. 1907, contained the following declaration: "Taking into account the central geographical position of Honduras and the facilities which owing to this circumstance have made its territory most often the theatre of Central-American conflicts, Honduras declares from now on its absolute neutrality in the event of any conflict between the other Republics; and the latter, in their turn, provided such neutrality be observed, bind themselves to respect it and in no case to violate the Honduranean territory" (Quoted in ibid. p. 456). The States of Belgium and Luxembourg were neutralized in a fashion similar to that pertaining to Switzerland, in 1837 and 1867, respectively. Their neutralities were both violated by Germany in 1914 and abolished in 1919 (Ibid. pp. 456–457).

92. Ibid. pp. 458–459. Nevertheless, the State is permitted to take necessary measures for self-defense, including the acceptance of a promise of military aid in case of aggression.

93. J.S. Mill, *On Representative Government* (1873), p. 120.

Appendixes

APPENDIX 1:
THE SINO-TIBETAN TREATY OF 821/823 A.D.

*Translated from the inscription on the
west face of the stone pillar at Lhasa*

The great king of Tibet, the Divine Manifestation, the *bTsan-po* and the great king of China, the Chinese ruler Hwang Te, Nephew and Uncle, having consulted about the alliance of their dominions have made a great treaty and ratified the agreement. In order that it may never be changed, all gods and men have been made aware of it and taken as witnesses; and so that it may be celebrated in every age and in every generation the terms of the agreement have been inscribed on a stone pillar.

The Divine Manifestation, the *bTsan-po*, Khri gTsug-lde-brtsan himself and the Chinese Ruler, B'un B'u, He'u Tig Hwang Te, their majesties the Nephew and Uncle, through the great profundity of their minds know whatsoever is good and ill for present and future alike. With great compassion, making no distinction between outer and inner in sheltering all with kindness, they have agreed in their counsel on a great purpose of lasting good—the single thought of causing happiness for the whole population— and have renewed the respectful courtesies of their old friendship. Having consulted to consolidate still further the measure of neighbourly contentment they have made a great treaty. Both Tibet and China shall keep the country and frontiers of which they are now in possession. The whole region to the east of that being the country of Great China and the whole region to the west being assuredly the country of Great Tibet, from either side of that frontier there shall be no warfare, no hostile invasions, and no seizure of territory. If there be any suspicious person, he shall be arrested and an investigation made and, having been suitably provided for, he shall be sent back.

Now that the dominions are allied and a great treaty of peace has been made in this way, since it is necessary also to continue the communication of pleasant messages between Nephew and Uncle, envoys setting out from either side shall follow the old established route. According to former custom their horses shall be changed at Tsang Kun Yog, which is between Tibet and China. Beyond sTse Zhung Cheg, where Chinese territory is met, the Chinese shall provide all facilities; westwards, beyond Tseng Shu Hywan, where Tibetan territory is met, the Tibetans shall provide all facilities. According to the close and friendly relationship between Nephew and Uncle the customary courtesy and respect shall be practised. Between the two countries no smoke or dust shall appear. Not even a word of sudden alarm or of enmity shall be spoken and, from those who guard the frontier upwards, all shall live at ease without suspicion or fear, their land being their land and their bed their bed. Dwelling in peace they shall win the blessing of happiness for ten thousand generations. The sound of praise shall extend to every place reached by the sun and moon. And in order that this agreement establishing a great era when Tibetans shall be happy in Tibet and Chinese shall be happy in China shall never be changed, the Three Jewels, the body of saints, the sun and moon, planets and stars have been invoked as witnesses; its purport has been expounded in solemn words; the oath has been sworn with the sacrifice of animals; and the agreement has been solemnized.

If the parties do not act in accordance with this agreement or if it is violated, whether it be Tibet or China that is first guilty of an offence against it, whatever stratagem or deceit is used in retaliation shall not be considered a breach of the agreement.

Thus the rulers and ministers of both Tibet and China declared and swore the oath; and the text having been written in detail it was sealed with the seals of both great kings. It was inscribed with the signatures of those ministers who took part in the agreement and the text of the agreement was deposited in the archives of each party.

Notes

1. Source: H.E. Richardson, "The Sino-Tibetan Treaty Inscription of A.D. 821/ 23 at Lhasa," *JRAS* 2 (1978), pp. 153–154. Reprinted by permission. Other translations of the Tibetan and Chinese texts can be found in L/P&S/10/343, "Proceedings of the 3rd Meeting of the Tibet Conference at Delhi on 12 January 1914," Incl. 2, "Tibetan Statement on Limits of Tibet," Docs. 1 to 7.

APPENDIX 2:
PEACE TREATY BETWEEN LADAKH AND TIBET AT TINGMOSGANG (1684)

The Drukpa (red sect) Omniscient Lama, named Mee-pham-wang-po, who in his former incarnations had always been the patron Lama of the kings of Ladak, from generation to generation, was sent from Lhasa to Tashis-gang, to arrange the conditions of a treaty of peace—for the Ladak king could never refuse to abide by the decision of the Omniscient One. It was agreed as follows:

1. The boundaries fixed, in the beginning, when king Skyed-lda-ngeema-gon gave a kingdom to each of his three sons, shall still be maintained.
2. Only Ladakis shall be permitted to enter into Ngarees-khor-sum wool trade.

3. No person from Ladak, except the royal trader of the Ladak Court, shall be permitted to enter Rudok.
4. A royal trader shall be sent by the Deywa Zhung (*i.e.*, the Grand Lama of Lhasa), from Lhasa to Ladak, once a year, with 200 horse-loads of tea.
5. A "Lo-chhak" shall be sent every third year from Leh to Lhasa with presents. As regards the quality and value of presents brought for all ordinary Lamas, the matter is of no consequence, but to the Labrang Chhakdzot shall be given the following articles, *viz.*: (a) *Gold dust*—the weight of 1 zho 10 times. (b) *Saffron*—the weight of 1 srang (or thoorsrang) 10 times. (c) Yarkhand cotton cloths—6 pieces. (d) Thin cotton cloth—1 piece.

The members of the Lapchak Mission shall be provided with provisions, free of cost, during their stay at Lhasa, and for the journey they shall be similarly provided with 200 baggage animals, 25 riding ponies, and 10 servants. For the uninhabited portion of the journey, tents will be supplied for the use of the Mission.

6. The country of Ngarees-khor-sum shall be given to the Omniscient Drukpa Lama, Mee-pham-wang-po, and in lieu thereof the Deywa Zhung will give to the Ladak king three other districts (in Great Tibet).
7. The revenue of the Ngarees-khor-sum shall be set aside for the purpose of defraying the cost of sacrificial lamps, and of religious ceremonies to be performed at Lhasa.
8. But the king of Ladak reserves to himself the village (or district?) of Monthser (*i.e.*, Minsar) in Ngarees-khor-sum, that he may be independent there; and he sets aside its revenue for the purpose of meeting the expense involved in keeping up the sacrificial lights at Kang-ree (*i.e.*, Kailas), and the Holy Lakes of Manasarwar and Rakas Tal.

With reference to the first clause of the treaty, it may be explained that, roughly speaking, king Skyed-lda-ngeema-gon gave the following territories to his sons:

a. To the eldest son—The countries now known as Ladak and Purig, extending from Hanley on the east to the Zojila Pass on the west, and including Rudok and the Gogpo gold district.
b. To the second son—Goo gey, Poorang and certain other small districts.
c. To the third son—Zangskar, Spiti, and certain other small districts.

Notes

1. Source: The Indian Society of International Law, *The Sino-Indian Boundary* (New Delhi, 1962), pp. 1–2. Reprinted by permission.

APPENDIX 3:
LADAKHI LETTER OF AGREEMENT, 1842

Translations of the original letters
written in Tibetan

Shri Khalsaji Apsarani Shri Maharajah; Lhasa representative Kalon Surk-hang; investigator Dapon Peshi, commander of forces; Balana, the representative of Gulam Kahandin; and the interpreter Amir Shah, have written this letter after sitting together. We have agreed that we have no ill-feelings because of the past war. The two kings will henceforth remain friends forever. The relationship between Maharajah Gulab Singh of Kashmir and the Lama Guru of Lhasa (Dalai Lama) is now established. The Maharajah Sahib, with God (Kunchok) as his witness, promises to recognize ancient boundaries, which should be looked after by each side without resorting to warfare. When the descendants of the early kings, who fled from Ladakh to Tibet, now return, they will be restored to their former stations. The annual envoy from Ladakh to Lhasa will not be stopped by Shri Maharajah. Trade between Ladakh and Tibet will continue as usual. Tibetan government traders coming into Ladakh will receive free transport and accommodations as before, and the Ladakhi envoy will, in turn, receive the same facilities in Lhasa. The Ladakhis take an oath before God (Kunchok) that they will not intrigue or create new troubles in Tibetan territory. We have agreed, with God as witness, that Shri Maharajah Sahib and the Lama Guru of Lhasa (Dalai Lama) will live together as members of the same household. We have written the above on the second of Assura, Sambhat 1899 (17 September 1842).

Sealed by the Wazir, Dewan,
Balana, and Amir Shah.

Tibetan Letter of Agreement, 1842

This agreement is made in the interests of the friendship between the Lhasa authorities and Shri Maharajah Sahib and Maharajah Gulab Singh. On the thirteenth day of the eighth month of the Water-Tiger year (September 17, 1842), the Lhasa representative Kalon Surkang, investigator Dapon Peshi, Shri Raja Sahib Dewan Hari Chand and Wazir Ratun Sahib, the representative of Shri Maharajah Sahib, sat together amicably with Kunchok (God) as witness. This document has been drawn up to ensure the lasting friendship of the Tibetans and the Ladakhis. We have agreed not to harm each other in any way, and to look after the interests of our own territories. We agree to continue trading in tea and cloth on the same terms as in the past, and will not harm Ladakhi traders coming into Tibet. If any of our subjects stray into your country, they should not be protected. We will forget past differences between the Lhasa authority and Shri Maharajah. The agreement arrived at today will remain firmly established forever. Kunchok (God), Mount Kailash, Lake Manasarowar, and Khochag Jowo have been called as witnesses to this treaty.

Sealed by Kalon Surkhang
and Dapon Peshi

Notes

1. Source: W.D. Shakabpa, *Tibet: A Political History* (New Haven, 1967), pp. 327–328.

APPENDIX 4:
AGREEMENT BETWEEN TIBET
AND KASHMIR (1852)

*Concluded between the two Garpons
or provincial Governors appointed by the Dalai Lama
and the representatives of the Maharaja of Kashmir*

This is dated the third day of the month of the Water Bull Year (apparently 1852).

The Ladakis refusing to supply the Tibetan Government trader Ke-Sang Gyurme with the usual transport animals on account of the decreased tea trade, the Nyer-pas of the Garpons were deputed to enquire about this matter and to investigate the boundary dispute between Ladak and Tibet. A meeting was accordingly arranged between Ladak Thanadar Sahib Bastiram and Kalon Rinzin accompanied by his servant Yeshe Wangyal and an agreement was made as follows:

In future the Ladakis will supply the Tibetan Government traders with the usual transport requirements without any demur. The joint Te-Jis ["*Teji*" is a Tibetan title which the then Garpons might have held] will request their Government to appoint only intelligent and capable men to take the annual tribute to Tibet. The Ladakis shall provide the Tibetan Government traders with accommodation and servants as usual and render them any further assistance according to the old-established custom. The Garpons will issue orders to the effect that tea and woollen goods arriving at Nagari shall only be sent to Ladak and not to any other place. The boundary between Ladak and Tibet will remain the same as before. No restriction shall be laid by the people of Rudok on the export of salt and woollen goods and the import of barley flour and barley. Neither party shall contravene the existing rules and the rates of Customs duties and market supplies shall be fixed by both parties concerned. The above rules shall apply also to the Rongpas [people inhabiting the valley countries], who export salt. The travellers from North and West who come through Rong are given passports by the Thanadar. They are liable to Customs duties as prescribed in their passports. Should any of them be unable to produce his passport, he shall be made to pay fifty times the amount ordinarily recoverable from him. No case will be heard against such recoveries made by the Customs Officer. In deciding all important matters the ruler shall take into consideration the manners and customs of both sides and observe the old-established rules regarding supply of transport, etc. There shall be no restriction in grazing animals in the pasture reserved for the animals of the Government traders, but the people shall not be allowed to abuse this privilege by bringing animals from outside to graze on it. Both parties shall adhere strictly to the agreement thus arrived at between Tibet and Singpas (Kashmiris), and the two frontier officers shall act in perfect accord and co-operation.

Notes

1. Source: The Indian Society of International Law, *The Sino-Indian Boundary* (New Delhi, 1962), pp. 4–5. Reprinted by permission. This Treaty was signed and sealed by Thanedar Bisram and *Kalon* Rigzin of Ladakh, and two stewards of the Tibetan governor at Gartok; witnessed by Yeshe Wangyal.

APPENDIX 5:
TREATY BETWEEN NEPAL AND TIBET, MARCH 1856

Translation of the Nepalese version of the Text of the Treaty of Chaitra Sudi 3, 1912 [V.E.], i.e., March 1856

The *Bhardars* (Nobles) of Gorkha Government and those of the Government of Bhot (Tibet) have by our own free will decided to sign this document. If war commences on account of the fact that one party to this treaty breaks the *ahad* (agreement), then the violator of the *ahad* will have sinned against God. We have signed this *ahad* with God as a witness.

Clauses of the Treaty

1. *Pratham Kura* (Article One): The Government of Bhot is to give to the Gorkha Government a *salami* of rupees 10,000 annually.

2. *Doshro Kura* (Article Two): Gorkha is to render assistance to Tibet, as far as possible, if she is invaded by a foreign power.
3. *Teshro Kura* (Article Three): Bhot is not to impose *jagat mahasul* (custom duties) that had been hitherto levied upon the Gorkha subjects throughout the territory of Tibet.
4. *Chouthon Kura* (Article Four): The Government of Gorkha is to withdraw its troops from the occupied territories of Kuti and Kerong and Jhung and return to the Tibetans the sepoys, sheep, and yaks captured during the war, when the conditions of the treaty were fulfilled. The Tibetans, in return, are also to give back to the Gorkhali cannons and also the Sikh prisoners-of-war who had been captured in 1841 in the war between Bhot and the Dogra ruler.
5. *Panchoun Kura* (Article Five): Gorkha is permitted to station a *Bhardar* (envoy) in Tibet, instead of a *Nayak* that had been stationed there previously.
6. *Chhaithoun Kura* (Article Six): Gorkha is allowed to keep their *kothis* (trade-marts) in Lhasa with the right to trade in jewels, ornaments, grains, and clothes.
7. *Satoun Kura* (Article Seven): The Gorkha Bhardar in Bhot is authorized to settle disputes between the Gorkha subjects and the Gorkha Kashmiris. But the disputes between the Gorkha subjects and the Bhotes are to be settled by the representatives of both Governments. The Nepalese *Bhardar* was prohibited from settling disputes between the Bhotes.
8. *Athoun Kura* (Article Eight): Gorkha and Bhote Governments are henceforth to return the criminals that escaped into each other's territory.
9. *Nawoan Kura* (Article Nine): The life and property of the Gorkha merchants were to be protected by the Government of Bhot. If the Bhote looter cannot restore the looted articles of the Gorkhalis the Bhot Government would compensate for the loot. The Gorkha Government was to act in a similar fashion and protect the property of the Bhotes in the country of the Gorkha.
10. *Dasaun Kurar* (Article Ten): The Gorkha and Bhote Governments are to protect the life and property of those subjects who had helped the enemy during the war.

Notes

1. Source: P. Uprety, *Nepal-Tibet Relations, 1850–1930* (Kathmandu, 1980), pp. 213–214. Reprinted by permission. This treaty is extracted from a copy of the *Ahad* preserved in the Ministry of Foreign Affairs, Kathmandu. See New Unnumbered *Poka* (Bundle) titled "Correspondence with China and Lhasa." The sub-*Poka* (Bho 5), which contains the treaty, is labeled as "The Conversation between *Maharaja* Jang Bahadur Rana and the Resident Ramsay."

APPENDIX 6:
TREATY BETWEEN TIBET AND NEPAL, 1856

Translation of the Tibetan text

The undermentioned gentlemen, monks and laymen, of the Gurkha and Tibetan Governments held a conference and mutually agreed upon and concluded a Treaty of ten Articles, and invoked the Supreme Being as their witness, and affixed their seals to it. They have agreed to regard the Chinese Emperor as heretofore with respect, in accordance with what has been written, and to keep both the States in agreement and to treat each other like brothers. If either of them violate the Treaty, may the Precious Ones not allow that State to prosper. Should either State violate the terms of the Treaty, the other State shall be exempt from all sin in making war upon it. (Here follow the names of the signatories and their seals.)

List of Articles of the Treaty

1. The Tibetan Government shall pay the sum of ten thousand rupees annually as a present to the Gurkha Government.

2. Gurkha and Tibet have been regarding the Great Emperor with respect. Tibet being the country of monasteries, hermits, and celibates, devoted to religion, the Gurkha Government have agreed henceforth to afford help and protection to it as far as they can, if any foreign country attacks it.

3. Henceforth Tibet shall not levy taxes on trade or taxes on roads or taxes of any other kind on the merchants or other subjects of the Gurkha Government.

4. The Government of Tibet agrees to return to the Gurkha Government the Sikh soldiers captured by Tibet, and all the Gurkha soldiers, officers, servants, women, and cannon captured in the war. The Gurkha Government agrees to return to the Tibetan Government the Tibetan troops, weapons, yaks, and whatever articles may have been left behind by the Tibetan subjects residing at Kyi-rong, Nya-nang, Dzong-ga, Pu-rang, and Rong-shar. And on the completion of the Treaty all the Gurkha troops in Pu-rang, Rong-shar, Kyi-rong, Dzong-ga, Nya-nang, Tar-ling, and La-tse will be withdrawn and the country evacuated.

5. Henceforth the Gurkha Government will keep a high officer [a *Bahadar*], and not a Newar, to hold charge at Lhasa.

6. The Gurkha Government will open shops at Lhasa, where they can freely trade in gems, jewellery, clothing, food, and different articles.

7. The Gurkha officer is not allowed to try any case arising from quarrels amongst Lhasa subjects and merchants, and the Tibetan Government is

not allowed to try any case arising from quarrels amongst the Gurkha subjects and traders and the Mahomedans of Khatmandu who may be residing in the jurisdiction of Lhasa. In the event of quarrels between Tibetan and Gurkha subjects the high officials of the two Governments will sit together and will jointly try the cases; the fines imposed upon the Tibetan subjects as punishments will be taken by the Tibetan official, and the fines imposed upon Gurkha subjects, merchants, and Mahomedans as punishments will be taken by the Gurkha official.

8. Should any Gurkha subject, after committing a murder, go to the country of Tibet, he shall be surrendered by Tibet to Gurkha; and should any Tibetan subject, after committing a murder, go to the country of Gurkha, he shall be surrendered by Gurkha to Tibet.

9. If the property of a Gurkha merchant or other subject be plundered by a Tibetan subject, the Tibetan officials after inquiry will compel the restoration of such property to the owner. Should the plunderer not be able to restore such property, he shall be compelled by the Tibetan official to draw up an agreement to make good such property within an extended time. If the property of a Tibetan merchant or other subject be plundered by a Gurkha subject, the Gurkha official after inquiry will compel the restoration of such property to the owner. Should the plunderer not be able to restore such property, he shall be compelled by the Gurkha official to draw up an agreement to make good such property within an extended time.

10. After the completion of the Treaty neither Government will take vengeance [Lit. 'be angry with'] on the persons or property of Tibetan subjects who may have joined the Gurkha Government during the recent war, or on the persons or property of Gurkha subjects who may have so joined the Tibetan Government.

Dated the 18th day of the 2nd month of the Fire-Dragon Year.

Notes

1. Source: C.A. Bell, *Tibet: Past and Present* (1924; rpt. Oxford, 1968), pp. 278–280. Reprinted by permission. Translated from the original, which was shown to him by the Dalai Lama in 1920. (L/P&S/10/718, Lhasa Mission, Nov. 1920 to Oct. 1921, Final Report, p. 3.)

APPENDIX 7:
THE CHEFOO CONVENTION, 1876

Between the British Government
and the Government of China (Extract)

Her Majesty's Government having it in contemplation to send a mission of exploration next year, by way of Peking, through Kansuh and Kokonor, or by way of Szechuan to Thibet, and thence to India, the Tsungli Yamen, having due regard to the circumstances, will, when the time arrives, issue the necessary passports, and will address letters to the High Provincial Authorities and the Residents in Thibet. If the Mission should not be sent by these routes but should be proceeding across the Indian frontier to Thibet, the Tsungli Yamen, on receipt of a communication to that effect from the British Minister, will write to the Chinese Resident in Thibet, and the Resident, with due regard to the circumstances, will send officers to take care of the Mission, and passports for the Mission will be issued by the Tsungli Yamen, that its passage be not obstructed.

Notes

1. Source: H.E. Richardson, *A Short History of Tibet* (New York, 1962), p. 249. The above is a separate article. The main body of the Convention did not concern Tibet.

APPENDIX 8:
CONVENTION RELATING TO BURMAH
AND THIBET, 24 JULY 1886

*Between the British Government
and the Government of China (Extract)*

Inasmuch as inquiry into the circumstances, by the Chinese Government, has shown the existence of many obstacles to the Mission to Thibet provided for in the separate article of the Chefoo Agreement, England consents to countermand the Mission forthwith. With regard to the desire of the British Government to consider arrangements for frontier trade between India and Thibet, it will be the duty of the Chinese Government, after careful inquiry into the circumstances, to adopt measures to exhort and encourage the people with a view to the promotion and development of trade. Should it be practicable, the Chinese Government shall then proceed carefully to consider trade regulations; but if insuperable obstacles should be found to exist, the British Government will not press the matter unduly.

Notes

1. Source: H.E. Richardson, *A Short History of Tibet* (New York, 1962) p. 250. The remainder of the Convention was concerned with the recognition of British supremacy in Burma and the above clause about Tibet appears to be in the nature of a concession to facilitate the principal object of the Convention.

APPENDIX 9:
CONVENTION BETWEEN GREAT BRITAIN AND CHINA
RELATING TO SIKKIM AND TIBET

Signed at Calcutta, 17 March 1890
Ratified at London, 27 August 1890

Whereas Her Majesty the Queen of the United Kingdom of Great Britain and Ireland, Empress of India, and His Majesty the Emperor of China, are sincerely desirous to maintain and perpetuate the relations of friendship and good understanding which now exist between their respective Empires; and whereas recent occurrences have tended towards a disturbance of the said relations, and it is desirable to clearly define and permanently settle certain matters connected with the boundary between Sikkim and Tibet, Her Britannic Majesty and His Majesty the Emperor of China have resolved to conclude a Convention on this subject, and have, for this purpose, named Plenipotentiaries, that is to say:

Her Majesty the Queen of Great Britain and Ireland, his Excellency the Most Honourable Henry Charles Keith Petty Fitzmaurice, G.M.S.I., G.C.M.G., G.M.I.E., Marquess of Lansdowne, Viceroy and Governor-General of India;

And His Majesty the Emperor of China, his Excellency Sheng Tai, Imperial Associate Resident in Tibet, Military Deputy Lieutenant-Governor;

Who, having met and communicated to each other their full powers, and finding these to be in proper form, have agreed upon the following Convention in eight Articles:—

I. The boundary of Sikkim and Tibet shall be the crest of the mountain-range separating the waters flowing into the Sikkim Teesta and its affluents from the waters flowing into the Tibetan Mochu and northwards into other rivers of Tibet. The line commences at Mount Gipmochi on the Bhutan frontier, and follows the above-mentioned water-parting to the point where it meets Nipal territory.

II. It is admitted that the British Government, whose Protectorate over the Sikkim State is hereby recognized, has direct and exclusive control over the internal administration and foreign relations of that State, and except through and with the permission of the British Government neither the Ruler of the State nor any of its officers shall have official relations of any kind, formal or informal, with any other country.

III. The Government of Great Britain and Ireland and the Government of China engage reciprocally to respect the boundary as defined in Article I, and to prevent acts of aggression from their respective sides of the frontier.

IV. The question of providing increased facilities for trade across the Sikkim-Tibet frontier will hereafter be discussed with a view to a mutually satisfactory arrangement by the High Contracting Powers.

V. The question of pasturage on the Sikkim side of the frontier is reserved for further examination and future adjustment.

VI. The High Contracting Powers reserve for discussion and arrangement the method in which official communications between the British authorities in India and the authorities in Tibet shall be conducted.

VII. Two joint Commissioners shall, within six months from the ratification of this Convention, be appointed, one by the British Government in India, the other by the Chinese Resident in Tibet. The said Commissioners shall meet and discuss the questions which, by the last three preceding Articles, have been reserved.

VIII. The present Convention shall be ratified, and the ratifications shall be exchanged in London as soon as possible after the date of the signature thereof.

In witness whereof the respective negotiators have signed the same, and affixed thereunto the seals of their arms.

Done in quadruplicate at Calcutta, this 17th day of March, in the year of our Lord 1890, corresponding with the Chinese date, the 27th day of the second moon of the 16th year of Kuang Hsu.

Landsdowne
Signature of the Chinese Plenipotentiary

Regulations Regarding Trade, Communications and Pasturage Appended to the Convention Between Great Britain and China Relating to Sikkim and Tibet of 1890

Signed at Darjeeling, India, 5 December 1893

I. A trade mart shall be established at Yatung on the Tibetan side of the frontier, and shall be open to all British subjects for purposes of trade from the first day of May, 1894. The Government of India shall be free to send officers to reside at Yatung to watch the conditions of British trade at that mart.

II. British subjects trading at Yatung shall be at liberty to travel freely to and fro between the frontier and Yatung, to reside at Yatung, and to rent houses and godowns for their own accommodation, and the storage of their goods. The Chinese Government undertake that suitable buildings for the above purposes shall be provided for British subjects, and also that a special and fitting residence shall be provided for the officer or officers appointed by the Government of India under Regulation I to reside at Yatung. British subjects shall be at liberty to sell their goods to whomsoever they please, to purchase native commodities in kind or in money, to hire transport of any kind, and in general to conduct their business transactions in conformity with local usage, and without any vexatious restrictions. Such British subjects shall receive efficient protection for their persons and property.

At Lang-jo and Ta-chun, between the frontier and Yatung, where rest-houses have been built by the Tibetan authorities, British subjects can break their journey in consideration of a daily rent.

III. Import and export trade in the following articles—arms, ammunition, military stores, salt, liquors, and intoxicating or narcotic drugs, may at the option of either Government be entirely prohibited, or permitted only on such conditions as either Government on their own side may think fit to impose.

IV. Goods, other than goods of the descriptions enumerated in Regulation III, entering Tibet from British India, across the Sikkim-Tibet frontier, or *vice versa*, whatever their origin, shall be exempt from duty for a period of five years commencing from the date of the opening of Yatung to trade; but after the expiration of this term, if found desirable, a tariff may be mutually agreed upon and enforced.

Indian tea may be imported into Tibet at a rate of duty not exceeding that at which Chinese tea is imported into England, but trade in Indian tea shall not be engaged in during the five years for which other commodities are exempt.

V. All goods on arrival at Yatung, whether from British India or from Tibet, must be reported at the Customs Station there for examination, and the report must give full particulars of the description, quantity, and value of the goods.

VI. In the event of trade disputes arising between British and Chinese or Tibetan subjects in Tibet, they shall be inquired into and settled in personal conference by the Political Officer for Sikkim and the Chinese Frontier Officer. The object of personal conference being to ascertain facts and do justice, where there is a divergence of views the law of the country to which the defendant belongs shall guide.

VII. Dispatches from the Government of India to the Chinese Imperial Resident in Tibet shall be handed over by the Political Officer for Sikkim to the Chinese Frontier Officer, who will forward them by special courier.

Dispatches from the Chinese Imperial Resident in Tibet to the Government of India will be handed over by the Chinese Frontier Officer to the Political Officer for Sikkim, who will forward them as quickly as possible.

VIII. Dispatches between the Chinese and Indian officials must be treated with due respect, and couriers will be assisted in passing to and fro by the officers of each Government.

IX. After the expiration of one year from the date of the opening of Yatung, such Tibetans as continue to graze their cattle in Sikkim will be subject to such Regulations as the British Government may from time to time enact for the general conduct of grazing in Sikkim. Due notice will be given of such regulations.

General Articles

I. In the event of disagreement between the Political Officer for Sikkim and the Chinese Frontier Officer, each official shall report the matter to his immediate superior, who, in turn, if a settlement is not arrived at between them, shall refer such matter to their respective Governments for disposal.

II. After the lapse of five years from the date on which these Regulations shall come into force, and on six months' notice given by either party, these Regulations shall be subject to revision by Commissioners appointed on both sides for this purpose who shall be empowered to decide on and adopt such amendments and extensions as experience shall prove to be desirable.

III. It having been stipulated that Joint Commissioners should be appointed by the British and Chinese Governments under the seventh article of the Sikkim-Tibet Convention to meet and discuss, with a view to the final settlement of the questions reserved under Articles 4, 5, and 6 of the said Convention; and the Commissioners thus appointed having met and discussed the questions referred to, namely, Trade, Communication, and Pasturage, have been further appointed to sign the agreement in nine Regulations and three General Articles now arrived at, and to declare that the said nine Regulations and the three General Articles form part of the Convention.

In witness whereof the respective Commissioners have hereto subscribed their names.

Done in quadruplicate at Darjeeling this 5th day of December, in the year one thousand eight hundred and ninety-three, corresponding with the Chinese date the 28th day of the 10th moon of the 19th year of Kuang Hsu.

A. W. PAUL,
British Commissioner

Ho Chang-Jung, James H. Hart,
Chinese Commissioners

Notes

1. Source for 1890 document: B.F.S.P., 1889–1890, Vol. 82, pp. 9–11.
2. Source for 1893 document: B.F.S.P., 1892–1893, Vol. 85, pp. 1235–1237.

APPENDIX 10:
CONVENTION BETWEEN GREAT BRITAIN AND THIBET

Signed at Lhasa, 7 September, 1904

Whereas doubts and difficulties have arisen as to the meaning and validity of the Anglo-Chinese Convention of 1890, and the Trade Regulations of

1893, and as to the liabilities of the Thibetan Government under these Agreements; and whereas recent occurrences have tended towards a disturbance of the relations of friendship and good understanding which have existed between the British Government and the Government of Thibet; and whereas it is desirable to restore peace and amicable relations, and to resolve and determine the doubts and difficulties as aforesaid, the said Governments have resolved to conclude a Convention with these objects, and the following Articles have been agreed upon by Colonel F.E. Younghusband, C.I.E., in virtue of full powers vested in him by His Britannic Majesty's Government and on behalf of that said Government, and Lo-Sang Gyal-Tsen, the Ga-den Ti-Rimpoche, and the Representatives of the Council of the three monasteries, Se-ra, Dre-pung, and Ga-den, and of the ecclesiastical and lay officials of the National Assembly on behalf of the Government of Thibet.

I. The Government of Thibet engages to respect the Anglo-Chinese Convention of 1890 and to recognize the frontier between Sikkim and Thibet, as defined in Article I of the said Convention, and to erect boundary pillars accordingly.

II. The Thibetan Government undertakes to open forthwith trade marts to which all British and Thibetan subjects shall have free right of access at Gyangtse and Gartok, as well as at Yatung.

The Regulations applicable to the trade mart at Yatung, under the Anglo-Chinese Agreement of 1893, shall, subject to such amendments as may hereafter be agreed upon by common consent between the British and Thibetan Governments, apply to the marts above mentioned.

In addition to establishing trade marts at the places mentioned, the Thibetan Government undertakes to place no restrictions on the trade by existing routes, and to consider the question of establishing fresh trade marts under similar conditions if development of trade requires it.

III. The question of the amendment of the Regulations of 1893 is reserved for separate consideration, and the Thibetan Government undertakes to appoint fully authorized Delegates to negotiate with the Representatives of the British Government as to the details of the amendments required.

IV. The Thibetan Government undertakes to levy no dues of any kind other than those provided for in the tariff to be mutually agreed upon.

V. The Thibetan Government undertakes to keep the roads to Gyangtse and Gartok from the frontier clear of all obstruction and in a state of repair suited to the needs of the trade, and to establish at Yatung, Gyangtse, and Gartok, and at each of the other trade marts that may hereafter be established, a Thibetan Agent, who shall receive from the British Agent appointed to watch over British trade at the marts in question any letter which the latter may desire to send to the Tibetan or to the Chinese authorities. The Thibetan Agent shall also be responsible for the due delivery of such communications and for the transmission of replies.

VI. As an indemnity to the British Government for the expense incurred in the dispatch of armed troops to Lhasa, to exact reparation for breaches of Treaty obligations and for the insults offered to and attacks upon the British Commissioner and his following and escort, the Thibetan Government engages to pay a sum of 500,000l.—equivalent to 75 lakhs of rupees—to the British Government.

The indemnity shall be payable at such places as the British Government may from time to time, after due notice, indicate, whether in Thibet or in the British districts of Darjeeling or Jalpaiguri, in seventy-five annual instalments of 1 lakh of rupees each, on the 1st January in each year, beginning from the 1st January, 1906.

VII. As security for the payment of the above-mentioned indemnity and for the fulfilment of the provisions relative to trade marts specified in Articles II, III, IV and V, the British Government shall continue to occupy the Chumbi Valley until the indemnity has been paid, and until the trade marts have been effectively opened for three years, whichever date may be the later.

VIII. The Thibetan Government agrees to raze all forts and fortifications and remove all armaments which might impede the course of free communication between the British frontier and the towns of Gyangtse and Lhassa.

IX. The Government of Thibet engages that, without the previous consent of the British Government—

a. No portion of Thibetan territory shall be ceded, sold, leased, mortgaged or otherwise given for occupation, to any foreign Power;
b. No such Power shall be permitted to intervene in Thibetan affairs;
c. No Representatives or Agents of any foreign Power shall be admitted to Thibet;
d. No concessions for railways, roads, telegraphs, mining or other rights, shall be granted to any foreign Power, or the subject of any foreign Power. In the event of consent to such concessions being granted, similar or equivalent concessions shall be granted to the British Government;
e. No Thibetan revenues, whether in kind or in cash, shall be pledged or assigned to any foreign Power, or to the subject of any foreign Power.

X. In witness whereof the negotiators have signed the same, and affixed thereunto the seals of their arms.

Done in quintuplicate at Lhassa, this 7th day of September, in the year of our Lord 1904, corresponding with the Thibetan date, the 27th of the 7th month of the Wood Dragon year.

(Seal of Dalai Lama, affixed by the Ga-den Ti-Rimpoche)
(Seal of Thibet Frontier Commission)
(Seal of British Commissioner)

(Seal of Council)
(Seal of the Dre-pung Monastery)
(Seal of Se-ra Monastery)
(Seal of Ga-den Monastery)
(Seal of National Assembly)

F. E. *Younghusband*, Colonel,
British Commissioner

In proceeding to the signature of the Convention, dated this day, the Representatives of Great Britain and Thibet declare that the English text shall be binding.

(Seal of Dalai Lama, affixed by the Ga-den Ti-Rimpoche)
(Seal of Thibet Frontier Commission)
(Seal of British Commissioner)
(Seal of Council)
(Seal of Dre-pung Monastery)
(Seal of Se-ra Monastery)
(Seal of Ga-den Monastery)
(Seal of National Assembly)

F. E. *Younghusband*, Colonel,
British Commissioner

Ampthill,
Viceroy and Governor-General of India

This Convention was ratified by the Viceroy and Governor-General of India in Council at Simla on the 11th day of November, A.D. 1904.

S. M. *Fraser*
Secretary to the Government of India
(Foreign Department)

Declaration Signed by his Excellency the Viceroy and Governor-General of India on the 11 November, 1904, and Appended to the Ratified Convention of 7 September, 1904

His Excellency the Viceroy and Governor-General of India, having ratified the Convention which was concluded at Lhassa on 7th September, 1904, by Colonel Younghusband, C.I.E., British Commissioner for Tibet Frontier Matters, on behalf of His Britannic Majesty's Government; and by Lo-Sang Gyal-Tsen, the Ga-den Ti-Rimpoche, and the Representatives of the Council, of the three Monasteries Se-ra, Dre-pung, and Ga-den, and of the ecclesiastical and lay officials of the National Assembly, on behalf of the Government of Thibet, is pleased to direct as an act of grace that the sum of money which the Thibetan Government have bound themselves under the terms of Article VI of the said Convention to pay to His Majesty's Government as an indemnity for the expenses incurred by the latter in connection with the dispatch of armed forces to Lhassa be reduced from 75,00,000 rupees to 25,00,000 rupees; and to declare that the British occupation of the Chumbi valley shall cease after the due payment of three annual instalments of the said indemnity as fixed by the said Article: Provided, however, that the trade marts as stipulated in Article II of the Convention shall have been effectively opened for three years as provided in Article VI of the Convention; and that, in the meantime, the Tibetans shall have faithfully complied with the terms of the said Convention in all other respects.

Ampthill
Viceroy and Governor-General of India

Notes

1. Source for 7 September document: B.F.S.P., 1904–1905, Vol. 98, pp. 148–151.
2. (Source for 11 November document: Crown-copyright document, FO 405/179, Confidential Memorandum Respecting Negotiations for Regulations for Trade between India and Tibet, 31 December 1907, Appendix I. Crown-copyright documents in the India Office Records and the Public Record Office reproduced and/or transcribed in this publication appear by permission of the Controller of Her Majesty's Stationery Office.

APPENDIX 11:
CONVENTION BETWEEN GREAT BRITAIN
AND CHINA RESPECTING TIBET

Signed at Peking, 27 April 1906
Ratified at London, 23 July 1906

Whereas His Majesty the King of Great Britain and Ireland and of the British Dominions beyond the Seas, Emperor of India, and His Majesty the Emperor of China are sincerely desirous to maintain and perpetuate the relations of friendship and good understanding which now exist between their respective Empires;

And whereas the refusal of Tibet to recognise the validity of or to carry into full effect the provisions of the Anglo-Chinese Conventions of March 17, 1890 and Regulations of December 5, 1893 placed the British Government under the necessity of taking steps to secure their rights and interests under the said Convention and Regulations;

And whereas a Convention of ten Articles was signed at Lhasa on September 7, 1904 on behalf of Great Britain and Tibet, and was ratified by the Viceroy and Governor-General of India on behalf of Great Britain on November 11, 1904, a declaration on behalf of Great Britain modifying its terms under certain conditions being appended thereto;

His Britannic Majesty and His Majesty the Emperor of China have resolved to conclude a Convention on this subject and have for this purpose named Plenipotentiaries, that is to say—His Majesty the King of Great Britain and Ireland: Sir Ernest Mason Satow, Knight Grand Cross of the Most Distinguished Order of Saint Michael and Saint George, His said Majesty's Envoy Extraordinary and Minister Plenipotentiary to His Majesty the Emperor of China; And His Majesty the Emperor of China: His Excellency Tong Shoa-yi, His said Majesty's High Commissioner Plenipotentiary and a Vice-President of the Board of Foreign Affairs—who having communicated to each other their respective full powers and finding them to be in good and true form have agreed upon and concluded the following Convention in six Articles.

Art. I. The Convention concluded on September 7, 1904 by Great Britain and Tibet, the texts of which in English and Chinese are attached to the present Convention as an annex, is hereby confirmed, subject to the modification stated in the declaration appended thereto, and both of the High Contracting Parties engage to take at all times such steps as may be necessary to secure the due fulfilment of the terms specified therein.

II. The Government of Great Britain engages not to annex Tibetan territory or to interfere in the administration of Tibet. The Government of China also undertakes not to permit any other foreign State to interfere with the territory or internal administration of Tibet.

III. The Concessions which are mentioned in Article IX (d) of the Convention concluded on September 7, 1904 by Great Britain and Tibet are denied to any State or to the subject of any State other than China, but it has been arranged with China that at the trade marts specified in Article II of the aforesaid Convention Great Britain shall be entitled to lay down telegraph lines connecting with India.

IV. The provisions of the Anglo-Chinese Convention of 1890 and Regulations of 1893 shall, subject to the terms of this present Convention and annex thereto, remain in full force.

V. The English and Chinese texts of the present Convention have been carefully compared and found to correspond but in the event of there being any difference of meaning between them the English text shall be authoritative.

VI. This Convention shall be ratified by the Sovereigns of both countries and ratifications shall be exchanged at London within three months after the date of signature by the Plenipotentiaries of both Powers.

In token whereof the respective Plenipotentiaries have signed and sealed this Convention, four copies in English and four in Chinese.

Done at Peking this twenty-seventh day of April, one thousand nine hundred and six, being the fourth day of the fourth month of the thirty-second year of the reign of Kuang-hsu.

(L.S.) *Ernest Satow*
(Signature and Seal
of the Chinese Plenipotentiary)

Exchange of Notes Between Great Britain and China Respecting the Non-Employment of Foreigners in Tibet, Peking, April 27, 1906

Tong Shoa-yi to Sir E. Satow

Your Excellency,

With reference to the Convention relating to Tibet which was signed to-day by your Excellency and myself on behalf of our respective Governments, I have the honour to declare formally that the Government of China undertakes not to employ any one not a Chinese subject and not of Chinese nationality in any capacity whatsoever in Tibet.

I avail, &c.

Tong Shoa-yi

Sir E. Satow to Tong Shoa-yi

Your Excellency,

I have the honor to acknowledge the receipt of your Excellency's note of this day's date, in which you declare formally, with reference to the Convention relating to Tibet which was signed to-day by your Excellency and myself on behalf of our respective Governments, that the Government of China undertakes not to employ any one not a Chinese subject and not of Chinese nationality in any capacity whatsoever in Tibet.

I avail, &c.

Ernest Satow

Notes

1. Source: B.F.S.P., 1905-1906, Vol. 99, pp. 171-173.

APPENDIX 12:
CONVENTION BETWEEN GREAT BRITAIN
AND RUSSIA, 1907

*Signed at St. Petersburg
on the 18th (31st) August 1907*

His Majesty the King of the United Kingdom of Great Britain and Ireland and of the British Dominions beyond the Seas, Emperor of India, and His Majesty the Emperor of All the Russias, animated by the sincere desire to settle by mutual agreement different questions concerning the interests of their States on the Continent of Asia, have determined to conclude Agreements destined to prevent all cause of misunderstanding between Great Britain and Russia in regard to the questions referred to, and have nominated for this purpose their respective Plenipotentiaries, to wit:

His Majesty the King of the United Kingdom of Great Britain and Ireland and of the British Dominions beyond the Seas, Emperor of India, the Right Honorable Sir Arthur Nicolson, His Majesty's Ambassador Extraordinary and Plenipotentiary to His Majesty the Emperor of All the Russias;

His Majesty the Emperor of All the Russias, the Master of his Court Alexander Iswolsky, Minister for Foreign Affairs;

Who, having communicated to each other their full powers, found in good and due form, have agreed on the following.

Arrangement Concerning Thibet

The Governments of Great Britain and Russia recognizing the suzerain rights of China in Thibet, and considering the fact that Great Britain, by reason of her geographical position, has a special interest in the maintenance of the *status quo* in the external relations of Thibet, have made the following arrangement.

Article I. The two High Contracting Parties engage to respect the territorial integrity of Thibet and to abstain from all interference in the internal administration.

Article II. In conformity with the admitted principle of the suzerainty of China over Thibet, Great Britain and Russia engage not to enter into negotiations with Thibet except through the intermediary of the Chinese Government. This engagement does not exclude the direct relations between British Commercial Agents and the Thibetan authorities provided for in Article V of the Convention between Great Britain and Thibet of the 7th

September 1904, and confirmed by the Convention between Great Britain and China of the 27th April 1906; nor does it modify the engagements entered into by Great Britain and China in Article I of the said Convention of 1906.

It is clearly understood that Buddhists, subjects of Great Britain or of Russia, may enter into direct relations on strictly religious matters with the Dalai Lama and the other representatives of Buddhism in Thibet; the Governments of Great Britain and Russia engage, as far as they are concerned, not to allow those relations to infringe the stipulations of the present arrangement.

Article III. The British and Russian Governments respectively engage not to send Representatives to Lhassa.

Article IV. The two High Contracting Parties engage neither to seek nor to obtain, whether for themselves or their subjects, any Concessions for railways, roads, telegraphs, and mines, or other rights in Thibet.

Article V. The two Governments agree that no part of the revenues of Thibet, whether in kind or in cash, shall be pledged or assigned to Great Britain or Russia or to any of their subjects.

Annex to the Arrangement Between Great Britain and Russia Concerning Thibet

Great Britain reaffirms the declaration, signed by His Excellency the Viceroy and Governor-General of India and appended to the ratification of the Convention of the 7th September 1904, to the effect that the occupation of the Chumbi Valley by British forces shall cease after the payment of three annual instalments of the indemnity of 25,00,000 rupees, provided that the trade marts mentioned in Article II of that Convention have been effectively opened for three years, and that in the meantime the Thibetan authorities have faithfully complied in all respects with the terms of the said Convention of 1904. It is clearly understood that if the occupation of the Chumbi Valley by the British forces has, for any reason, not been terminated at the time anticipated in the above Declaration, the British and Russian Governments will enter upon a friendly exchange of views on this subject.

The present Convention shall be ratified, and the ratifications exchanged at St. Petersburgh as soon as possible.

In witness whereof the respective Plenipotentiaries have signed the present Convention and affixed thereto their seals.

Done in duplicate at St. Petersburgh, the 18th (31st) of August, 1907.

Notes

1. Source: C.A. Bell, *Tibet: Past and Present* (1924; rpt. Oxford, 1968), pp. 289–291. Reprinted by permission.

APPENDIX 13:
AGREEMENT BETWEEN GREAT BRITAIN, CHINA
AND TIBET AMENDING TRADE REGULATIONS
IN TIBET OF 1893

Signed at Calcutta, 20 April 1908
Ratified at Peking, 14 October 1908

Tibet Trade Regulations

Preamble

Whereas by Article I of the Convention between Great Britain and China on the 27th April, 1906, that is the 4th day of the 4th moon of the 32nd year of Kwang Hsu, it was provided that both the High Contracting Parties should engage to take at all times such steps as might be necessary to secure the due fulfilment of the terms specified in the Lhassa convention of the 7th September, 1904, between Great Britain and Tibet, the text of which in English and Chinese was attached as an annex to the above-named Convention;

And whereas it was stipulated in Article III of the said Lhassa convention that the question of the amendment of the Tibet Trade Regulations which were signed by the British and Chinese Commissioners on the 5th day of December, 1893, should be reserved for separate consideration, and whereas the amendment of these Regulations is now necessary;

His Majesty the King of the United Kingdom of Great Britain and Ireland and of the British Dominions beyond the Seas, Emperor of India, and His Majesty the Emperor of the Chinese Empire have for this purpose named as their plenipotentiaries, that is to say—His Majesty the King of Great Britain and Ireland and of the British Dominions beyond the Seas, Emperor of India: Mr. E.C. Wilton, C.M.G.; His Majesty the Emperor of the Chinese Empire: His Majesty's Special Commissioner Chang Yin Tang— And the High Authorities of Tibet have named as their fully authorized representative to act under the directions of Chang Tachen and take part in the negotiations, the Tsarong Shape, Wang-Chuk Gyalpo.

And whereas Mr. E.C. Wilton and Chang Tachen have communicated to each other since their respective full powers and have found them to be in good and true form and have found the authorization of the Tibetan Delegate to be also in good and true form, the following amended Regulations have been agreed upon.

1. The Trade Regulations of 1893 shall remain in force in so far as they are not inconsistent with these Regulations.

2. The following places shall form, and be included within, the boundaries of the Gyantse mart.

A. The line begins at the Chumig Dangsang (Chhu-Mig-Dangs-Sangs) north-east of the Gyantse Fort, and thence it runs in a curved line, passing behind the Pekor Chode (Dpal-Hkhor-Choos-Sde), down to Chag-Dong-Gang (Phyag-Gdong-Sgang); thence passing straight over the Nyan Chu, it reaches the Zamsa (Zam-Srag).

B. From the Zamsa the line continues to run, in a south-eastern direction, round to Lachi-To (Gla-Dkyii-Stod), embracing all the farms on its way, viz., the Lahong, the Hogtso (Hog-Mtsho), the Tong-Chung-shi (Grong-Chhung-Cshis), and the Rabgang (Rab-Sgang), &c.

C. From Lachi-To the line runs to the Yutog (Gyu-Thog), and thence runs straight, passing through the whole area of Gamkar-Shi (Ragal-Mkhar-Gshis), to Chumig Dangsang.

As difficulty is experienced in obtaining suitable houses and godowns at some of the marts, it is agreed that British subjects may also lease lands for the building of houses and godowns at the marts, the locality for such building sites to be marked out specially at each mart by the Chinese and Tibetan authorities in consultation with the British Trade Agent. The British Trade Agents and British subjects shall not build houses and godowns except in such localities, and this arrangement shall not be held to prejudice in any way the administration of the Chinese and Tibetan local authorities over such localities, or the right of British subjects to rent houses and godowns outside such localities for their own accommodation and the storage of their goods.

British subjects desiring to lease building sites shall apply through the British Trade Agent to the municipal office at the mart for a permit to lease. The amount of rent, or the period or conditions of the lease, shall then be settled in a friendly way by the lessee and the owner themselves. In the event of a disagreement between the owner and lessee as to the amount of rent or the period or conditions of the lease, the case will be settled by the Chinese and Tibetan authorities, in consultation with the British Trade Agent. After the lease is settled, the sites shall be verified by the Chinese and Tibetan officers of the municipal office conjointly with the British Trade Agent. No building is to be commenced by the lessee on a site before the municipal office has issued him a permit to build, but it is agreed that there shall be no vexatious delays in the issue of such permit.

3. The administration of the trade marts shall remain with the Tibetan officers, under the Chinese officers' supervision and directions.

The Trade Agents at the marts and Frontier Officers shall be of suitable rank, and shall hold personal intercourse and correspondence one with another on terms of mutual respect and friendly treatment.

Questions which cannot be decided by agreement between the Trade Agents and the local authorities shall be referred for settlement to the

Government of India and the Tibetan High Authorities at Lhassa. The purport of a reference by the Government of India will be communicated to the Chinese Imperial Resident at Lhassa. Questions which cannot be decided by agreement between the Government of India and the Tibetan High Authorities at Lhassa shall, in accordance with the terms of Article I of the Peking Convention of 1906, be referred for settlement to the Governments of Great Britain and China.

4. In the event of disputes arising at the marts between British subjects and persons of Chinese and Tibetan nationalities, they shall be inquired into and settled in personal conferences between the British Trade Agent at the nearest mart and the Chinese and Tibetan authorities of the Judicial Court at the mart, the object of personal conference being to ascertain facts and to do justice. Where there is a divergence of view the law of the country to which the defendant belongs shall guide. In any of such mixed cases, the officer or officers of the defendant's nationality shall preside at the trial, the officer or officers of the plaintiff's country merely attending to watch the course of the trial.

All questions in regard to rights, whether of property or person, arising between British subjects, shall be subject to the jurisdiction of the British authorities.

British subjects who may commit any crime at the marts or on the routes to the marts shall be handed over by the local authorities to the British Trade Agent at the mart nearest to the scene of offence, to be tried and punished according to the laws of India, but such British subjects shall not be subjected by the local authorities to any ill-usage in excess of necessary restraint.

Chinese and Tibetan subjects, who may be guilty of any criminal act towards British subjects at the marts or on the routes thereto, shall be arrested and punished by the Chinese and Tibetan authorities according to law.

Justice shall be equitably and impartially administered on both sides.

Should it happen that Chinese or Tibetan subjects bring a criminal complaint against a British subject before the British Trade Agent, the Chinese or Tibetan authorities shall have the right to send a representative, or representatives, to watch the course of trial in the British Trade Agent's Court. Similarly, in cases in which a British subject has reason to complain of a Chinese or Tibetan subject in the Judicial Court at the mart, the British Trade Agent shall have the right to send a representative to the Judicial Court to watch the course of trial.

5. The Tibetan authorities, in obedience to the instructions of the Peking Government, having a strong desire to reform the judicial system of Tibet, and to bring it into accord with that of Western nations, Great Britain agrees to relinquish her rights of extra-territoriality in Tibet, whenever such rights are relinquished in China, and when she is satisfied that the state of the Tibetan laws and the arrangements for their administration and other considerations warrant her in so doing.

6. After the withdrawal of the British troops, all the rest-houses, eleven in number, built by Great Britain upon the routes leading from the Indian frontier to Gyantse, shall be taken over at original cost by China and rented to the Government of India at a fair rate. One-half of each rest-house will be reserved for the use of the British officials employed on the inspection and maintenance of the telegraph lines from the marts to the Indian frontier and for the storage of their materials, but the rest-houses shall otherwise be available for occupation by British, Chinese, and Tibetan officers of respectability who may proceed to and from the marts.

Great Britain is prepared to consider the transfer to China of the telegraph lines from the Indian frontier to Gyantse when the telegraph lines from China reach that mart, and in the meantime Chinese and Tibetan messages will be duly received and transmitted by the line constructed by the Government of India.

In the meantime China shall be responsible for the due protection of the telegraph lines from the marts to the Indian frontier, and it is agreed that all persons damaging the lines or interfering in any way with them or with the officials engaged in the inspection or maintenance thereof shall at once be severely punished by the local authorities.

7. In law suits involving cases of debt on account of loans, commercial failure, and bankruptcy, the authorities concerned shall grant a hearing and take steps necessary to enforce payment; but, if the debtor plead poverty and be without means, the authorities concerned shall not be held responsible for the said debts, nor shall any public or official property be distrained upon in order to satisfy these debts.

8. The British Trade Agents at the various trade marts now or hereafter to be established in Tibet may make arrangements for the carriage and transmission of their posts to and from the frontier of India. The couriers employed in conveying these posts shall receive all possible assistance from the local authorities whose districts they traverse and shall be accorded the same protection as the persons employed in carrying the despatches of the Tibetan authorities. When efficient arrangements have been made by China in Tibet for a postal service, the question of the abolition of the Trade Agents' couriers will be taken into consideration by Great Britain and China. No restrictions whatever shall be placed on the employment by British officers and traders of Chinese and Tibetan subjects in any lawful capacity. The persons so employed shall not be exposed to any kind of molestation or suffer any loss of civil rights to which they may be entitled as Tibetan subjects, but they shall not be exempted from all lawful taxation. If they be guilty of any criminal act, they shall be dealt with by the local authorities according to law without any attempt on the part of their employer to screen or conceal them.

9. British officers and subjects, as well as goods, proceeding to the trade marts, must adhere to the trade routes from the frontier of India. They shall not, without permission, proceed beyond the marts, or to Gartok from Yatung and Gyantse, or from Gartok to Yatung and Gyantse, by any

route through the interior of Tibet, but natives of the Indian frontier, who have already by usage traded and resided in Tibet, elsewhere than at the mart shall be at liberty to continue their trade, in accordance with the existing practice, but when so trading or residing they shall remain, as heretofore, amenable to the local jurisdiction.

10. In cases where officials or traders, *en route* to and from India or Tibet, are robbed of treasure or merchandise, public or private, they shall forthwith report to the police officers, who shall take immediate measures to arrest the robbers and hand them to the local authorities. The local authorities shall bring them to instant trial, and shall also recover and restore the stolen property. But if the robbers flee to places out of the jurisdiction and influence of Tibet, and cannot be arrested, the police and the local authorities shall not be held responsible for such losses.

11. For public safety, tanks or stores of kerosene oil or any other combustible or dangerous articles in bulk must be placed far away from inhabited places at the marts.

British or Indian merchants wishing to build such tanks or stores may not do so until, as provided in Regulation 2, they have made application for a suitable site.

12. British subjects shall be at liberty to deal in kind or in money, to sell their goods to whomsoever they please, to purchase native commodities from whomsoever they please, to hire transport of any kind, and to conduct in general their business transactions in conformity with local usage and without any vexations restrictions or oppressive exactions whatever.

It being the duty of the police and local authorities to afford efficient protection at all times to the persons and property of the British subjects at the marts, and along the routes to the marts, China engages to arrange effective police measures at the marts and along the routes to the marts. On due fulfilment of these arrangements, Great Britain undertakes to withdraw the Trade Agents' guards at the marts and to station no troops in Tibet, so as to remove all cause for suspicion and disturbance among the inhabitants. The Chinese authorities will not prevent the British Trade Agents holding personal intercourse and correspondence with the Tibetan officers and people.

Tibetan subjects trading, travelling, or residing in India shall receive equal advantages to those accorded by this Regulation to British subjects in Tibet.

13. The present Regulations shall be in force for a period of ten years reckoned from the date of signature by the two Plenipotentiaries as well as by the Tibetan Delegate; but if no demand for revision be made by either side within six months after the end of the first ten years, then the Regulations shall remain in force for another ten years from the end of the first ten years; and so it shall be at the end of each successive ten years.

14. The English, Chinese, and Tibetan texts of the present Regulations have been carefully compared, and, in the event of any question arising as

to the interpretation of these Regulations, the sense as expressed in the English text shall be held to be the correct sense.

15. The ratifications of the present Regulations under the hand of His Majesty the King of Great Britain and Ireland, and of His Majesty the Emperor of the Chinese Empire, respectively, shall be exchanged at London and Peking within six months from the date of signature.

In witness whereof the two Plenipotentiaries and the Tibetan Delegate have signed and sealed the present Regulations.

Done in quadruplicate at Calcutta this 20th day of April, in the year of our Lord 1908, corresponding with the Chinese date, the 20th day of the 3rd moon of the 34th year of Kuang Hsu.

(L.S.) *E.C. Wilton,*
British Commissioner.

(L.S.) *Chang Yin Tang,*
Chinese Special Commissioner.

(L.S.) *Wang Chuk Gyalpo,*
Tibetan Delegate.

Notes

1. Source: B.F.P.S., 1907–1908, Vol. 101, pp. 170–175.

APPENDIX 14:
AGREEMENT BETWEEN THE CHINESE
AND TIBETANS, 12 AUGUST 1912

Translation of the Tibetan version

The representatives of the Chinese and the Tibetans met together in the presence of the Gorkha witnesses to discuss the three-point proposals, approved by the Dalai Lama in his answer to the letter submitted by Ambans Len and Chung on the 29th day of the 6th month. On the 30th the parties carefully discussed the matter and decided to have the three-point proposals drawn up in the Chinese, Tibetan and Nepali languages, and to sign and seal them.

Point 1. All the arms and equipment including field guns and Maxim guns in the possession of the Chinese at Dabshi and Tseling in Lhasa shall be sealed in the presence of the representatives of the two sides and witnesses and entrusted to the custody of the Government of Tibet. Before the departure of the Chinese officials and soldiers from Tibet, all the arms and equipment shall be removed to the Yabshi Lang Dun house within fifteen days; the bullets and gunpowder shall be collected and deposited in the Doring house. All the arms and ammunition shall be removed to the Doring house on the expiry of the fifteen-day limit, and the witnessing Gorkha envoy shall arrange to guard the house.

Point II. The Chinese officials and soldiers shall leave Tibet within fifteen days. According to the dates given by them for their departure in three batches, Tibetans will depute an official to accompany the different batches and will arrange to supply the necessary pack animals and riding ponies. The Tibetans will supply against adequate payment and according to local rates foodstuffs such as rice, flour, tsampa, meat, butter and tea to the Chinese at the halting stages up to the frontier, through the Tibetans escorting them. There shall not be any delay in supplying pack animals and riding ponies on the way. The Chinese shall not take by force any pack or riding animals beyond the frontier.

Point III. The two representatives shall remove all Chinese officials and soldiers from the Yapshi house and the Tibetan soldiers from the Doring house tomorrow in order to keep the arms and ammunition in these houses.

All the arms and ammunition belonging to the Chinese government at Dabshi and Tseling in Lhasa, including those in the possession of the Chinese private traders from China, shall, according to the letter of the 29th day of the 6th month from Ambans Len and Chung, be produced before the representatives of the two parties and witnesses on the 1st day of the 7th month together with an inventory. No part of these arms and ammunition shall be given away, sold, hidden or thrown away. Ambans Len and Chung for their protection shall, as suggested by the witnesses, be allowed to retain sixty rifles and ammunition. All other arms and equipment shall be kept in the Doring and Yabshi houses, which shall be sealed by the two representatives and the witnesses. The two representatives and witnesses shall arrange to place guards as stated above. After all arms, equipment, field-guns, and Maxim guns from Lhasa, Dabshi, and Tseling and from the Chinese government and private traders have been collected, they shall be deposited, without giving away, selling, hiding, or leaving out any. A list will be made of the arms genuinely belonging to the private Chinese traders, and the representatives and the witnesses shall discuss matters concerning their return to them.

This agreement, signed and sealed by the two parties and witnessed this day, will be considered void in the event of any party infringing any of its provisions.

Joint seal of the Dalai Lama's representatives:
Sertsa Thitul and Tsedon Tangyal

Seals of the representatives of Ambans Len and Chung:
Luchang Krang Lungrin
Yulji Lu Langrin
U Yon Krephu Hai Kru

Krephu Wang Chiujin
Thung Krikung Buhu Hai
Sru Phun
LuLu Kon Kon
Ngan Khru

Seals of Five Sris' witnesses:
Envoy of the Gorkha Darbar
Major-Captain Jit Bahadur Khatri Chhetri
Lieutenant Lal Bahadur Basnyat Chhetri
Dittha Kul Prasad Upadhyay
Subedar Ratna Gambhir Singh
Khatri Chhetri

30th day of the 6th month of the Water-Mouse Year.

Notes

1. Source: Ram Rahul, "The 1912 Agreement Between The Chinese and Tibetans," *Tibetan Review* (Feb. 1979), pp. 20–21. Reprinted by permission. The text of this treaty is kept in the archives of The School of International Studies, New Delhi, India. Compare to the version in FO 535/16, No. 258, Inclosure 4.

APPENDIX 15:
AGREEMENT OF THE CHINESE AND THIBETANS,
14 DECEMBER, 1912

ARTICLES of the Agreement made in the
Water-mouse year, i.e., the 6th Sudee
of the Magh month of the year 1969 (translation of the Nepalese version)

On account of the fighting between the Chinese and the Thibetans, the representatives of the Chinese and of the Thibetans met together in the presence of the Nepalese representatives as a witness, and in his office, in order to satisfy the respective parties. The representatives discussed the matters which were in dispute, and finally decided as follows.

1. First, to count consecutively all the arms which had been stored in Yapshi house, to see whether the number of arms stored there is correct. After this, to set apart from the arms which were kept in Yapshi house, and also from the arms which are to be collected hereafter, and to hand over to the Thibetans, the Thibetan prong-guns, the newly manufactured five-shot magazine U-shang guns, and the Nu-chhau-u or Martini-Henri guns which bear Thibetan marks. The cannon, and all the big and small guns (without bolts), and the powder and the cartridges, which belong to

the Chinese, shall be kept in the Sho store room. The (door of the) store room shall be sealed by the representatives of the Chinese, Thibetans and Nepalese, and it shall be guarded by the Nepalese until the Chinese have crossed the Tromo (Chumbi Valley) frontier. After this the Nepalese shall hand over the sealed (store room) to (the custody of) the Thibetans, and shall obtain proper receipt from them.

2. Until the Chinese leave Lhassa, the Thibetans shall send Thibetan merchants daily with sufficient food to sell to the Chinese. Should any Chinese require to go towards the Thibetan side, he shall receive a letter from Tungling, and should any articles have been left with the Thibetans, the owners, whether Thibetan or Chinese, can take them.

3. The Thibetans shall arrange to supply riding ponies and transport to the (Chinese) officials and soldiers during their march according to the list. (a). The Thibetans shall supply riding ponies and transport to the (Chinese) traders and subjects, on payment of 10 tankas for each riding pony and 6 tankas for each transport animal from one jong to the next jong, *i.e.*, at each of the changing places for animals.

4. The Tungling and the (Chinese) officials and soldiers and subjects will start from here (Lhassa) on the 8th of this month (December 16th, 1913). They will not molest the Thibetan subjects, nor loot their property on the way, and they (Chinese) will return direct (to China) *via* India without delaying on their way.

5. Should any arms and ammunition other than bolts be found among the baggage of the Chinese at the place of inspection, the Thibetan Government will take possession of them.

6. The Thibetans will supply on proper payment sufficient food for the Chinese at halting places and stages on their way.

7. The Thibetans have promised not to injure the lives or loot the property of Tungling, or of the Chinese officials and soldiers, traders and subjects, who are leaving Thibet, or of the Chinese traders and subjects living in Thibet.

8. The houses in the neighbourhood of the Yamen are to be handed over to the Thibetans. The wooden boxes, and utensils, according to the list written in a book, will be kept in a separate house, the door of which shall be sealed by the representatives of the Chinese and Thibetans. The Thibetans will look after the house.

9. As regards the monks of the Tengyeling monastery. At the time when the first agreement was made, His Holiness the Dalai Lama promised to protect the lives of the monks should they behave well. The representatives undertake to observe this promise.

Both the parties (Chinese and Thibetans) are satisfied and have agreed (to the above).

(Sign and seal of the Thibetan Representative
Teji Timon)
(Sign and seal of Kempo (Professor) Trung-yik Chempo

(Chief Secretary Trepa Gyal-tsen)
(Sign and seal of Kenchung Lobsang Gyatso, Interpreter)
(Sign and seal of the Sera, Drepung and Ganden
Monasteries and of the National Assembly)
(Seals of the Chinese Representatives)
(Sign and seal of Jha-ka Mu-yon Gyo-khun)
(Sign and seal of Lhassa Li-si-kwan Cha-del)
(Sign and seal of De-si-kwan Ka-ra-kwan)

Witnesses:
(Sign and seal of Lieutenant Lal Bahadur Chetri,
Officiating Nepalese Representative at Lhassa)
(Sign and seal of Dittha Kal Persad Upadia)
(Sign and seal of Se-Ku-sho Rana Gambhir
Singh Gharti Chetri)

Notes

1. Source: FO 535/15, No. 181, Inclosure 6.

APPENDIX 16:
PROCLAMATION ISSUED BY H.H. THE DALAI LAMA XIII,
ON THE EIGHTH DAY OF THE FIRST MONTH
OF THE WATER-OX YEAR (1913)

Translation of the Tibetan Text

I, the Dalai Lama, most omniscient possessor of the Buddhist faith,
whose title was conferred by the Lord Buddha's command from the glorious
land of India, speak to you as follows:

I am speaking to all classes of Tibetan people. Lord Buddha, from the
glorious country of India, prophesied that the reincarnations of Avalokitesvara, through successive rulers from the early religious kings to the
present day, would look after the welfare of Tibet.

During the time of Genghis Khan and Altan Khan of the Mongols, the
Ming dynasty of the Chinese, and the Ch'ing Dynasty of the Manchus,
Tibet and China co-operated on the basis of benefactor and priest relationship.
A few years ago, the Chinese authorities in Szechuan and Yunnan endeavored
to colonize our territory. They brought large numbers of troops into central
Tibet on the pretext of policing the trade marts. I, therefore, left Lhasa
with my ministers for the Indo-Tibetan border, hoping to clarify to the
Manchu emperor by wire that the existing relationship between Tibet and
China had been that of patron and priest and had not been based on the
subordination of one to the other. There was no other choice for me but

to cross the border, because Chinese troops were following with the intention of taking me alive or dead.

On my arrival in India, I dispatched several telegrams to the Emperor; but his reply to my demands was delayed by corrupt officials at Peking. Meanwhile, the Manchu empire collapsed. The Tibetans were encouraged to expel the Chinese from central Tibet. I, too, returned safely to my rightful and sacred country, and I am now in the course of driving out the remnants of Chinese troops from DoKham in Eastern Tibet. Now, the Chinese intention of colonizing Tibet under the patron-priest relationship has faded like a rainbow in the sky. Having once again achieved for ourselves a period of happiness and peace, I have now allotted to all of you the following duties to be carried out without negligence:

1. Peace and happiness in this world can only be maintained by preserving the faith of Buddhism. It is, therefore, essential to preserve all Buddhist institutions in Tibet, such as the Jokhang temple and Ramoche in Lhasa, Samye, and Traduk in southern Tibet, and the three great monasteries, etc.

2. The various Buddhist sects in Tibet should be kept in a distinct and pure form. Buddhism should be taught, learned, and meditated upon properly. Except for special persons, the administrators of monasteries are forbidden to trade, loan money, deal in any kind of livestock, and/or subjugate another's subjects.

3. The Tibetan government's civil and military officials, when collecting taxes or dealing with their subject citizens, should carry out their duties with fair and honest judgment so as to benefit the government without hurting the interests of the subject citizens. Some of the central government officials posted at Ngari Korsum in western Tibet, and Do Kham in eastern Tibet, are coercing their subject citizens to purchase commercial goods at high prices and have imposed transportation rights exceeding the limit permitted by the government. Houses, properties and lands belonging to subject citizens have been confiscated on the pretext of minor breaches of the law. Furthermore, the amputation of citizens' limbs has been carried out as a form of punishment. Henceforth, such severe punishments are forbidden.

4. Tibet is a country with rich natural resources; but it is not scientifically advanced like other lands. We are a small, religious, and independent nation. To keep up with the rest of the world, we must defend our country. In view of past invasions by foreigners, our people may have to face certain difficulties, which they must disregard. To safeguard and maintain the independence of our country, one and all should voluntarily work hard. Our subject citizens residing near the borders should be alert and keep the government informed by special messenger of any suspicious developments. Our subjects must not create major clashes between two nations because of minor incidents.

5. Tibet, although thinly populated, is an extensive country. Some local officials and landholders are jealously obstructing other people from developing vacant lands, even though they are not doing so themselves. People

with such intentions are enemies of the State and our progress. From now on, no one is allowed to obstruct anyone else from cultivating whatever vacant lands are available. Land taxes will not be collected until three years have passed; after that the land cultivator will have to pay taxes to the government and to the landlord every year, proportionate to the rent. The land will belong to the cultivator.

Your duties to the government and to the people will have been achieved when you have executed all that I have said here. This letter must be posted and proclaimed in every district of Tibet, and a copy kept in the records of the offices in every district.

From the Potala Palace.
(Seal of the Dalai Lama)

Notes

1. Source: W.D. Shakabpa, *Tibet: A Political History* (New Haven, 1967), pp. 246–248.

APPENDIX 17:
TREATY OF FRIENDSHIP AND ALLIANCE

*Concluded Between the Government
of Mongolia and Tibet at Urga
29 December 1912 (11 January 1913)
(translation of the Tibetan text)*

Mongolia and Thibet, having freed themselves from the dynasty of the Manchus and separated from China, have formed their own independent States, and, having in view that both States from time immemorial have professed one and the same religion, with a view to strengthening their historic and mutual friendship the Minister for Foreign Affairs, Nikta Biliktu Da-Lama Rabdan, and the Assistant Minister, General and Manlai baatyr beiseh Damdinsurun, as plenipotentiaries of the Government of the ruler of the Mongol people, and gudjir tsanshib kanchen-Lubsan-Agvan, donir Agvan Choinzin, director of the Bank Ishichjamtso, and the clerk Gendun Galsan, as plenipotentiaries of the Dalai Lama, the ruler of Thibet, have made the following agreement.

Article 1. The ruler of Thibet, Dalai Lama, approves and recognises the formation of an independent Mongol State, and the proclamation, in the year of the pig and the ninth day of the eleventh month, of Chjebzun Damba Lama of the yellow faith as ruler of the country.

Article 2. The ruler of the Mongol people, Chjebzun Damba Lama, approves and recognises the formation of an independent (Thibetan) State and the proclamation of the Dalai Lama as ruler of Thibet.

Article 3. Both States will work by joint consideration for the well-being of the Buddhist faith.

Article 4. Both States, Mongolia and Thibet, from now and for all time will afford each other assistance against external and internal dangers.

Article 5. Each State within its own territory will afford assistance to the subjects of the other travelling officially or privately on affairs of religion or State.

Article 6. Both States, Mongolia and Thibet, as formerly, will carry on a reciprocal trade in the products of their respective countries in wares, cattle, &c., and will also open industrial establishments.

Article 7. From now the granting of credit to anyone will be permitted only with the knowledge and sanction of official institutions. Without such sanction Government institutions will not consider claims.

As regards contracts made previous to the conclusion of the present treaty, where serious loss is being incurred through the inability of the two parties to come to terms, such debts may be recovered by (Government) institutions, but in no case shall the debt concern "shabinars" or "khoshuns."

Article 8. Should it prove necessary to supplement the articles of the present treaty, the Mongolian and Thibetan Governments must appoint special delegates, who will conclude such agreements as the conditions of the time shall demand.

Article 9. The present treaty shall come into force from the date of its signature.

Plenipotentiaries from the Mongolian Government for the conclusion of the treaty: Nikta Biliktu Da-Lama Rabdan, Minister for Foreign Affairs; and General and Manlai baatyr beiseh Damdinsurun, Assistant Minister.

Plenipotentiaries from the Dalai Lama, the ruler of Thibet, for the conclusion of the treaty: Gudjir tsanshib kanchen Lubsan-Agvan, Choinzin, the Director of the Bank of Thibet Ishichjamtsa, and the clerk, Gendun-Galsan.

Signed (by Mongol reckoning) in the fourth day of the twelfth month of the second year of the "Raised by the Many," and by Thibetan reckoning on the same day and month of the year of the "water-mouse."

Notes

1. Source: FO 535/16, No. 88, Inclosure 1, 1913.

APPENDIX 18:
ANGLO-TIBETAN DECLARATION OF 3 JULY 1914

We, the Plenipotentiaries of Great Britain and Thibet, hereby record the following declaration to the effect that we acknowledge the annexed convention as initialled to be binding on the Governments of Great Britain and Thibet, and we agree that so long as the Government of China withholds signature to the aforesaid convention she will be debarred from the enjoyment of all privileges accruing therefrom.

In token whereof we have signed and sealed this declaration, two copies in English and two in Thibetan.

Done at Simla this 3rd day of July, A.D. 1914, corresponding with the Thibetan date the 10th day of the 5th month of the Wood-Tiger year.

A. Henry McMahon,
British Plenipotentiary
(Seal of the British Plenipotentiary)
(Seal of the Dalai Lama)
(Signature of the Lonchen Shatra)
(Seal of the Lonchen Shatra)
(Seal of the Drepung Monastery)
(Seal of the Sera Monastery)
(Seal of the Gaden Monastery)
(Seal of the National Assembly)

Notes

1. Source: Crown-copyright document, FO 535/17, No. 231, Inclosure 7. Crown-copyright documents in the India Office Records and the Public Record Office reproduced and/or transcribed in this publication appear by permission of the Controller of Her Majesty's Stationery Office.

APPENDIX 19:
CONVENTION BETWEEN GREAT BRITAIN, CHINA, AND TIBET, SIMLA 1914

Attached to the Anglo-Tibetan Declaration
of 3 July 1914

His Majesty the King of the United Kingdom of Great Britain and Ireland and of the British Dominions beyond the Seas, Emperor of India, His Excellency the President of the Republic of China, and His Holiness the Dalai Lama of Tibet, being sincerely desirous to settle by mutual agreement various questions concerning the interests of their several States on the Continent of Asia, and further to regulate the relations of their several Governments, have resolved to conclude a Convention on this subject and have nominated for this purpose their respective Plenipotentiaries, that is to say:

His Majesty the King of the United Kingdom of Great Britain and Ireland and of the British Dominions beyond the Seas, Emperor of India, Sir Arthur Henry McMahon, Knight Grand Cross of the Royal Victorian Order, Knight Commander of the Most Eminent Order of the Indian Empire, Companion of the Most Exalted Order of the Star of India, Secretary to the Government of India, Foreign and Political Department;

His Excellency the President of the Republic of China, Monsieur Ivan Chen, Officer of the Order of the Chia Ho;

His Holiness the Dalai Lama of Tibet, Lonchen Ga-den Shatra Pal-jor Dorje; who having communicated to each other their respective full powers and finding them to be in good and due form have agreed upon and concluded the following Convention in eleven Articles.

Article 1. The Conventions specified in the Schedule to the present Convention shall, except in so far as they may have been modified by, or may be inconsistent with or repugnant to, any of the provisions of the present Convention, continue to be binding upon the High Contracting Parties.

Article 2. The Governments of Great Britain and China recognising that Tibet is under the suzerainty of China, and recognising also the autonomy of Outer Tibet, engage to respect the territorial integrity of the country, and to abstain from interference in the administration of Outer Tibet (including the selection and installation of the Dalai Lama), which shall remain in the hands of the Tibetan Government at Lhasa.

The Government of China engages not to convert Tibet into a Chinese province. The Government of Great Britain engages not to annex Tibet or any portion of it.

Article 3. Recognising the special interest of Great Britain, in virtue of the geographical position of Tibet, in the existence of an effective Tibetan Government, and in the maintenance of peace and order in the neighbourhood of the frontiers of India and adjoining States, the Government of China engages, except as provided in Article 4 of this Convention, not to send troops into Outer Tibet, nor to station civil or military officers, nor to establish Chinese colonies in the country. Should any such troops or officials remain in Outer Tibet at the date of the signature of this Convention, they shall be withdrawn within a period not exceeding three months.

The Government of Great Britain engages not to station military or civil officers in Tibet (except as provided in the Convention of September 7, 1904, between Great Britain and Tibet) nor troops (except the Agents' escorts), nor to establish colonies in that country.

Article 4. The foregoing Article shall not be held to preclude the continuance of the arrangement by which, in the past, a Chinese high official with suitable escort has been maintained at Lhasa, but it is hereby provided that the said escort shall in no circumstances exceed 300 men.

Article 5. The Governments of China and Tibet engage that they will not enter into any negotiations or agreements regarding Tibet with one another, or with any other Power, excepting such negotiations and agreements between Great Britain and Tibet as are provided for by the Convention of September 7, 1904, between Great Britain and Tibet and the Convention of April 27, 1906, between Great Britain and China.

Article 6. Article III of the Convention of April 27, 1906, between Great Britain and China is hereby cancelled, and it is understood that in Article IX(d) of the Convention of September 7, 1904, between Great Britain and Tibet the term 'Foreign Power' does not include China.

Not less favourable treatment shall be accorded to British commerce than to the commerce of China or the most favoured nation.

Article 7. a. The Tibet Trade Regulations of 1893 and 1908 are hereby cancelled.

b. The Tibetan Government engages to negotiate with the British Government new Trade Regulations for Outer Tibet to give effect to Articles II, IV and V of the Convention of September 7, 1904, between Great Britain and Tibet without delay; provided always that such Regulations shall in no way modify the present Convention except with the consent of the Chinese Government.

Article 8. The British Agent who resides at Gyantse may visit Lhasa with his escort whenever it is necessary to consult with the Tibetan Government regarding matters arising out of the Convention of September 7, 1904, between Great Britain and Tibet, which it has been found impossible to settle at Gyantse by correspondence or otherwise.

Article 9. For the purpose of the present Convention the borders of Tibet, and the boundary between Outer and Inner Tibet, shall be as shown in red and blue respectively on the map attached hereto.[1]

Nothing in the present Convention shall be held to prejudice the existing rights of the Tibetan Government in Inner Tibet, which include the power to select and appoint the high priests of monasteries and to retain full control in all matters affecting religious institutions.

Article 10. The English, Chinese and Tibetan texts of the present Convention have been carefully examined and found to correspond, but in the event of there being any difference of meaning between them the English text shall be authoritative.

Article 11. The present Convention will take effect from the date of signature.

In token whereof the respective Plenipotentiaries have signed and sealed this Convention, three copies in English, three in Chinese and three in Tibetan.

Done at Simla this third day of July, A.D., one thousand nine hundred and fourteen, corresponding with the Chinese date, the third day of the seventh month of the third year of the Republic, and the Tibetan date, the tenth day of the fifth month of the Wood-Tiger year.

Initial of the Lonchen Shatra[2]
Seal of the Lonchen Shatra

A.H.M.
Seal of the British
Plenipotentiary

Schedule

1. Convention between Great Britain and China relating to Sikkim and Tibet, signed at Calcutta the 17th March 1890.
2. Convention between Great Britain and Tibet, signed at Lhasa the 7th September 1904.
3. Convention between Great Britain and China respecting Tibet, signed at Peking the 27th April 1906.

The notes exchanged are to the following effect:

1. It is understood by the High Contracting Parties that Tibet forms part of Chinese territory.
2. After the selection and installation of the Dalai Lama by the Tibetan Government, the latter will notify the installation to the Chinese Government whose representative at Lhasa will then formally communicate to His Holiness the titles consistent with his dignity, which have been conferred by the Chinese Government.
3. It is also understood that the selection and appointment of all officers in Outer Tibet will rest with the Tibetan Government.
4. Outer Tibet shall not be represented in the Chinese Parliament or in any other similar body.
5. It is understood that the escorts attached to the British Trade Agencies in Tibet shall not exceed seventy-five per centum of the escort of the Chinese Representative at Lhasa.
6. The Government of China is hereby released from its engagements under Article III of the Convention of March 17, 1890, between Great Britain and China to prevent acts of aggression from the Tibetan side of the Tibet-Sikkim frontier.
7. The Chinese high official referred to in Article 4 will be free to enter Tibet as soon as the terms of Article 3 have been fulfilled to the satisfaction of representatives of the three signatories to this Convention, who will investigate and report without delay.

Initial of the Lonchen Shatra
Seal of the Lonchen Shatra

(Initialled) A.H.M.
Seal of the British
Plenipotentiary

Notes

1. Published for the first time by the Government of India in *An Atlas of the Northern Frontier of India*, 15 January, 1960. Source: Crown-copyright Document,

FO 535/17, No. 231, Inclosure 8. Crown-copyright documents in the India Office Records and the Public Record Office reproduced and/or transcribed in this publication appear by permission of the Controller of Her Majesty's Stationery Office.

2. Owing to the impossibility of writing initials in Tibetan, the mark of the Lonchen at this place is his signature.

APPENDIX 20:
ANGLO-TIBETAN TRADE REGULATIONS,
3 JULY 1914

Whereas by Article 7 of the Convention concluded between the Governments of Great Britain, China and Tibet on the third day of July, A.D., 1914, the Trade Regulations of 1893 and 1908 were cancelled and the Tibetan Government engaged to negotiate with the British Government new Trade Regulations for Outer Tibet to give effect to Articles II, IV and V of the Convention of 1904;

His Majesty the King of the United Kingdom of Great Britain and Ireland, and the British Dominions beyond the Seas, Emperor of India, and His Holiness the Dalai Lama of Tibet have for this purpose named as their Plenipotentiaries, that is to say: His Majesty the King of Great Britain and Ireland and of the British Dominions beyond the Seas, Emperor of India, Sir A. H. McMahon, G.C.V.O., K.C.I.E., C.S.I.; His Holiness the Dalai Lama of Tibet—Lonchen Ga-den Shatra Pal-jor Dorje.

And whereas Sir A. H. McMahon and Lonchen Ga-den Shatra Pal-jor Dorje have communicated to each other since their respective full powers and have found them to be in good and true form, the following Regulations have been agreed upon.

I. The area falling within a radius of three miles from the British Trade Agency site will be considered as the area of such Trade Mart.

It is agreed that British subjects may lease lands for the building of houses and godowns at the Marts. This arrangement shall not be held to prejudice the right of British subjects to rent houses and godowns outside the Marts for their own accommodation and the storage of their goods. British subjects desiring to lease building sites shall apply through the British Trade Agent to the Tibetan Trade Agent. In consultation with the British Trade Agent the Tibetan Trade Agent will assign such or other suitable building sites without unnecessary delay. They shall fix the terms of the leases in conformity with the existing laws and rates.

II. The administration of the Trade Marts shall remain with the Tibetan Authorities, with the exception of the British Trade Agency sites and compounds of the rest-houses, which will be under the exclusive control of the British Trade Agents.

The Trade Agents at the Marts and Frontier Officers shall be of suitable rank, and shall hold personal intercourse and correspondence with one another on terms of mutual respect and friendly treatment.

III. In the event of disputes arising at the Marts or on the routes to the Marts between British subjects and subjects of other nationalities, they shall be enquired into and settled in personal conference between the British and Tibetan Trade Agents at the nearest Mart. Where there is a divergence of view the law of the country to which the defendant belongs shall guide.

All questions in regard to rights, whether of property or person, arising between British subjects, shall be subject to the jurisdiction of the British Authorities.

British subjects, who may commit any crime at the Marts or on the routes to the Marts, shall be handed over by the Local Authorities to the British Trade Agent at the Mart nearest to the scene of the offence, to be tried and punished according to the laws of India, but such British subjects shall not be subjected by the Local Authorities to any ill-usage in excess of necessary restraint.

Tibetan subjects, who may be guilty of any criminal act towards British subjects, shall be arrested and punished by the Tibetan Authorities according to law.

Should it happen that a Tibetan subject or subjects bring a criminal complaint against a British subject or subjects before the British Trade Agent, the Tibetan Authorities shall have the right to send a representative or representatives of suitable rank to attend the trial in the British Trade Agent's Court. Similarly in cases in which a British subject or subjects have reason to complain against a Tibetan subject or subjects, the British Trade Agent shall have the right to send a representative or representatives to the Tibetan Trade Agent's Court to attend the trial.

IV. The Government of India shall retain the right to maintain the telegraph lines from the Indian frontier to the Marts. Tibetan messages will be duly received and transmitted by these lines. The Tibetan Authorities shall be responsible for the due protection of the telegraph lines from the Marts to the Indian frontier, and it is agreed that all persons damaging the lines or interfering with them in any way or with the officials engaged in the inspection or maintainance thereof shall at once be severely punished.

V. The British Trade Agents at the various Trade Marts now or hereafter to be established in Tibet may make arrangements for the carriage and transport of their posts to and from the frontier of India. The couriers employed in conveying these posts shall receive all possible assistance from the Local Authorities, whose districts they traverse, and shall be accorded the same protection and facilities as the persons employed in carrying the despatches of the Tibetan Government.

No restrictions whatever shall be placed on the employment by British officers and traders of Tibetan subjects in any lawful capacity. The persons so employed shall not be exposed to any kind of molestation or suffer any loss of civil rights, to which they may be entitled as Tibetan subjects, but they shall not be exempted from lawful taxation. If they be guilty of any criminal act, they shall be dealt with by the Local Authorities according to law without any attempt on the part of their employer to screen them.

VI. No rights of monopoly as regards commerce or industry shall be granted to any official or private company, institution, or individual in Tibet. It is of course understood that companies and individuals, who have already received such monopolies from the Tibetan Government previous to the conclusions of this agreement, shall retain their rights and privileges until the expiry of the period fixed.

VII. British subjects shall be at liberty to deal in kind or in money, to sell their goods to whomsoever they please, to hire transport of any kind, and to conduct in general their business transactions in conformity with local usage and without any vexation, restrictions or oppressive exactions whatever. The Tibetan Authorities will not hinder the British Trade Agents or other British subjects from holding personal intercourse or correspondence with the inhabitants of the country.

It being the duty of the Police and the Local Authorities to afford efficient protection at all times to the persons and property of the British subjects at the Marts and along the routes to the Marts, Tibet engages to arrange effective Police measures at the Marts and along the routes to the Marts.

VIII. Import and export in the following Articles:—arms, ammunition, military stores, liquors and intoxicating or narcotic drugs, may at the option of either Government be entirely prohibited, or permitted only on such conditions as either Government on their own side may think fit to impose.

IX. The present Regulations shall be in force for a period of ten years reckoned from the date of signature by the two Plenipotentiaries; but, if no demand for revision be made on either side within six months after the end of the first ten years the Regulations shall remain in force for another ten years from the end of the first ten years; and so it shall be at the end of each successive ten years.

X. The English and Tibetan texts of the present Regulations have been carefully compared, but in the event of there being any difference of meaning between them the English text shall be authoritative.

XI. The present Regulations shall come into force from the date of signature.

Done at Simla this third day of July, A.D., one thousand nine hundred and fourteen, corresponding with the Tibetan date, the tenth day of the fifth month of the Wood-Tiger year.

Seal of the Dalai Lama

Signature of the Lonchen Shatra

A. HENRY MCMAHON,
British Plenipotentiary

Seal of the
Lonchen Shatra

Seal of the British
Plenipotentiary

Seal of the	Seal of the	Seal of the	Seal of the
Drepung	Sera	Gaden	National
Monastery	Monastery	Monastery	Assembly

Negotiated and signed only by the British and Tibetan plenipotentiaries.

Notes

1. Source: International Commission of Jurists, *The Question of Tibet and the Rule of Law* (Geneva, 1959), pp. 128–131.

APPENDIX 21:
INDIA-TIBET FRONTIER 1914:
EXCHANGE OF NOTES BETWEEN
THE BRITISH AND TIBETAN PLENIPOTENTIARIES

To Lonchen Shatra, Tibetan Plenipotentiary:

In February last you accepted the India-Tibet frontier from the Isu Razi Pass to the Bhutan frontier, as given in the map (two sheets), of which two copies are herewith attached, subject to the confirmation of your Government and the following conditions:

a. The Tibetan ownership in private estates on the British side of the frontier will not be disturbed.
b. If the sacred places of Tso Karpo and Tsari Sarpa fall within a day's march of the British side of the frontier, they will be included in Tibetan territory and the frontier modified accordingly.

I understand that your Government have now agreed to this frontier subject to the above two conditions. I shall be glad to learn definitely from you that this is the case.

You wished to know whether certain dues now collected by the Tibetan Government at Tsona Jong and in Kongbu and Kham from the Monpas and Lopas for articles sold may still be collected. Mr. Bell has informed you that such details will be settled in a friendly spirit, when you have furnished him the further information, which you have promised.

The final settlement of this India-Tibet frontier will help to prevent causes of future dispute and thus cannot fail to be of great advantage to both Governments.

A. H. McMANON,
British Plenipotentiary
Delhi
24th March 1914

[*Translation*]

To Sir Henry McMahon, British Plenipotentiary
to the China-Tibet Conference:

As it was feared that there might be friction in future unless the boundary between India and Tibet is clearly defined, I submitted the map, which you sent to me in February last, to the Tibetan Government at Lhasa for orders. I have now received orders from Lhasa, and I accordingly agree to the boundary as marked in red in the two copies of the maps signed by you, subject to the condition mentioned in your letter, dated 24th March, sent to me through Mr. Bell. I have signed and sealed the two copies of the maps. I have kept one copy here and return herewith the other.

Sent on the 29th day of the 1st Month of the Wood-Tiger year (25th March 1914) by Lonchen Shatra, the Tibetan Plenipotentiary.

Seal of Lochen Shatra

Notes

1. The map referred to in these notes has been published in *An Atlas of the Northern Frontier of India* issued on 15 January 1960 by the Ministry of External Affairs of the Government of India.

2. Source: Crown-copyright document in the India Office Records, L/P&S/10/343. Crown-copyright documents in the India Office Records and the Public Record Office reproduced and/or transcribed in this publication appear by permission of the Controller of Her Majesty's Stationery Office.

APPENDIX 22:
AGREEMENT FOR THE RESTORATION
OF PEACEFUL RELATIONS AND THE
DELIMITATION OF A PROVISIONAL FRONTIER
BETWEEN CHINA AND TIBET, 19 AUGUST 1918

1. Whereas a state of hostilities arose last year between Chinese and Tibetans owing to an attack by Chinese troops on Tibetan troops on account of a trifling dispute near Leiwuchi and Chiamdo; and whereas the leaders on both sides are now desirous of a restoration of peaceful relations on the general basis of both sides retaining the territories they now occupy; and whereas the British Government has consented to mediate in the dispute; the following arrangement for a complete cessation of hostilities has been agreed upon between the undersigned, namely, General Liu Tsanting, commanding the Chinese troops at Batang, and acting on behalf of China. The Kalon Lama, commanding the Tibetan troops on the frontier, and acting on behalf of Tibet, and Mr. Eric Teichman, of His Britannic Majesty's Consular Service, acting on behalf of the British Government.

2. This agreement is of a temporary nature and shall only remain in force until such time as the Governments of China, Tibet, and Great Britain shall have arrived at a final and permanent tripartite settlement; but in the meantime it cannot be modified in any way except with the unanimous consent of all three contracting parties.

3. It is agreed that the provisional boundary line between Chinese and Tibetan controlled territory shall be as follows: The districts of Batang (Baan), Yenching (Tsakalo), Itun (Sanpa or Taso), Tejung (a), Litang, (Lihua), Kantze, Nyarong (Chantui or Chanhua), Luho (Changku or Drango)(b), Taofu (Taowu), Hokou (Nyachuka or Yachiang), Tachienlu (Dartsendo or Kangting), Tanpa (Romidrango)(c), Lutingchiao (Jazamaka)(e), Chiulung (Jez-erong)(d), Hsiangcheng (Tinghsiang)(f), and Taocheng(g), and the country lying to the east of them, shall be under the control of the Chinese; no Tibetan troops or civil or military officials being permitted to reside therein; while the districts of Riwoche (Leiwuchi), Enta(h), Chiamdo (Changtu), Draya (Chaya), Markam-Gartok (Chiangka or Ningching), Gonjo (Kung-chueh), Sangen (Sangai or Wucheng), Tungpu (i), Tengko (k),* Seshu (Shihchu), Derge (Teko), and Beyu (Paiyu), and the country lying to the west of them, shall be under the control of the Tibetans; no Chinese troops or civil or military officials being permitted to reside therein. As soon as the Governments of China and Tibet shall have formally accepted this agreement, all the Tibetan troops and civil and military officials at present in Kantze and Nyarong (Chantui) districts shall be withdrawn; the Chinese civil and military authorities engaging not to oppress or in any way maltreat the natives of those parts, including the Lamas of Dargye Gomba and other monasteries, after the withdrawal of the Tibetan troops. The existing boundaries of Yunnan Province and of the Kokonor (*i.e.,* the territory at present under the control of the Sining officials) shall remain for the present unchanged.

4. It is agreed that, apart from local constabulary necessary for the maintenance of law and order, no Tibetan troops shall be stationed to the east of the river Yangtze (Dre Chu or Chin Sha Chiang); and it is likewise agreed that, with the exception of one hundred local constabulary, the Chinese troops stationed on the south and north roads shall not cross to the West of the Yangtze and Yalung rivers respectively; both sides engaging to withdraw their troops in accordance with the above arrangements as soon as the Governments of China and Tibet shall have formally accepted this agreement.

5. It is agreed that the control of all the monasteries in the above-mentioned Chinese governed districts, as well as the right of appointing high Lamas and other monastic functionaries, and the control of all matters appertaining to the Buddhist religion, shall be in the hands of the Dalai Lama; the Chinese authorities not interfering in any way therein; but the

---

*(a) De-Rong (b) Traog-Go (c) Rong-Ming-Trag-Go (d) Gyal-Tso-Rong (e) Chag-Sam-Ka (f) Cha-Trong (g) Taotria (h) Ngenda (i) Teng-Pug (k) Ten-Pog.

Lamas, on the other hand, shall not interfere in the territorial authority of the Chinese officials.

6. The Chinese and Tibetan authorities on both sides of the border shall be responsible for and shall take all possible steps to prevent raids by members of their forces or by others under their respective jurisdictions across the temporary boundary line laid down in Article 3; and will render one another reciprocal assistance in the maintenance of order, suppression of brigandage, and apprehension of evil-doers. Peaceful traders and travellers, however, shall be permitted to cross the border without interference.

7. When the Governments of China and Tibet shall have formally accepted this agreement, all the Chinese prisoners in the hands of Tibetans, and all the Tibetan prisoners in the hands of the Chinese, shall be released and permitted to return home if they so desire.

8. It is agreed that no Tibetans or Chinese will be punished or in any way maltreated for having adhered to or supported the Tibetan or Chinese cause in the past before the conclusion of this agreement, a general and complete amnesty in this respect coming into force immediately. The Tibetan and Chinese authorities further undertake that all Chinese in Tibetan controlled territory, and all Tibetans in Chinese controlled territory, whether lamas or laymen, agriculturalists, merchants, or others, shall be properly protected, well and fairly treated, and in no way oppressed.

9. In the event of any dispute arising between the Tibetan and Chinese authorities on the frontier after the conclusion of this agreement, there shall be no recourse to arms; but both sides agree to refer the matter in dispute to the British Consul for his arbitration. In order to enable the British Consul to carry out satisfactorily his duties of arbitrator and middleman under this agreement, the Chinese and Tibetan authorities engage to render him all possible assistance in visiting the frontier officials and travelling through the frontier districts.

10. Inasmuch as the natives of Eastern Tibet have suffered greatly of recent years from the large numbers of troops stationed in the country, and since now that peace has been arranged under this agreement there is no longer any need for soldiers beyond those necessary for the maintenance of law and order, the Chinese and Tibetan authorities express their willingness to reduce their frontier garrisons; and in accordance with this policy it is agreed that not more than two hundred Chinese troops shall be stationed at Batang and Kantze, respectively, and that not more than two hundred Tibetan troops shall be stationed at Chiamdo and Gartok (Chiangka) respectively; but the authorities on either side shall be at liberty to take what military action they please in case of disturbances of the peace in their respective territories.

11. It is agreed that no Chinese troops shall be stationed in the districts known as Hsiangcheng (Tinghsiang) [Cha-Treng] and Nyarong (Chantui or Chanhua) so long as the natives of those regions remain peacefully within their own borders and abstain from raiding other parts, but in the event of their causing trouble; the Tibetan authorities shall not interfere with any action the Chinese authorities may take.

12. When the Governments of China and Tibet shall have formally accepted this agreement, its provisions shall be widely made known by proclamations in Tibetan and Chinese throughout the districts on both sides of the frontier with a view to pacifying the minds of the inhabitants of the border after the recent years of fighting and unrest.

13. Eighteen copies of this agreement having been drawn up and signed, six in Chinese, six in Tibetan, and six in English, each of the three signatories shall retain two Chinese, two Tibetan, and two English copies. As the British representative has acted as mediator in the matter the English text shall, in the event of disputes arising, be considered authoritative. Each signatory engages to report the provisions of this agreement to his Government with the least possible delay for their approval. Both Chinese and Tibetan authorities engage not to move troops or open hostilities pending the receipt of the decisions of the three Governments.

Signed and sealed at Chiamdo, this Nineteenth Day of August, Nineteen Hundred and Eighteen.

Liu Tsan-Ting   *Eric Teichman*   *Chamba Denda,*
                                                  The Kalon Lama

Notes

1. Source: Crown-copyright document in the India Office Records, L/P&S/10/714, E. Teichman to J. Jordan, 21 Aug. 1918, Inclosure. Crown-copyright documents in the India Office Records and the Public Record Office reproduced and/or transcribed in this publication appear by permission of the Controller of Her Majesty's Stationery Office.

APPENDIX 23:
SUPPLEMENTARY AGREEMENT REGARDING MUTUAL WITHDRAWAL OF TROOPS AND CESSATION OF HOSTILITIES BETWEEN CHINESE AND TIBETANS, 10 OCTOBER, 1918

Translation from Chinese and Tibetan texts

1. The Chinese and Tibetan leaders are equally desirous of peace. The Chinese troops will withdraw to Kantze. The Tibetan troops will withdraw to within the boundary of Derge district. Both Chinese and Tibetans undertake not to advance their forces along either the Northern or Southern Roads and to cease all hostilities for a year from the date of the mutual withdrawal of troops pending the receipt of the decisions of the President of the republic and the Dalai Lama regarding the Chiamdo negotiations.

2. This agreement only concerns the mutual withdrawal of troops and cessation of hostilities, and is not a definite settlement of the questions at issue.

3. The mutual withdrawal of troops to commence on October 17, (12th day of 9th Moon) and to be completed by October 31, (26th day of 9th Moon).

4. This agreement is concluded between Han Kuang-chun and the Chala Chief, special representatives of the Szechuan Frontier Commissioner, on the one hand, and the Kenchung Lama and Chungrang and Drentong Dapons, representing the Kalon Lama of Tibet, on the other, and is witnessed by Mr. Eric Teichman, British Vice-Consul, as middleman. The signatories engage to report the matter to their respective Governments as soon as possible.

Signed and sealed by the Chinese, Tibetan, and British Representatives, at Rangbatsa, October the 10th, 1918.

Additional Article

The Chinese troops shall withdraw to Kantze, but they shall be at liberty to occupy the strategic point of Beri—beyond which point, however, they must not advance during the cessation of hostilities.

(Signed by the three parties)

Notes

1. Source: Crown-copyright document in the India Office Records, L/P&S/10/714, E. Teichman to J. Jordan, 11.10.1918, Inclosure 3. Crown-copyright documents in the India Office Records and the Public Record Office reproduced and/or transcribed in this publication appear by permission of the Controller of Her Majesty's Stationery Office.

APPENDIX 24:
APPEAL BY HIS HOLINESS THE DALAI LAMA
OF TIBET TO THE UNITED NATIONS

U. N. Document A/1549
11 November 1950, Kalimpong

The attention of the world is riveted on Korea where aggression is being resisted by an international force. Similar happenings in remote Tibet are passing without notice. It is in the belief that aggression will not go unchecked and freedom unprotected in any part of the world that we have assumed the responsibility of reporting to the United Nations Organization, through you, recent happenings in the border area of Tibet.

As you are aware, the problem of Tibet has taken on alarming proportions in recent times. This problem is not of Tibet's own making but is largely the outcome of unthwarted Chinese ambition to bring weaker nations on its periphery under its active domination. Tibetans have for long lived a cloistered life in their mountain fastnesses, remote and aloof from the rest of the world, except in so far as His Holiness the Dalai Lama, as the acknowledged head of the Buddhist Church, confers benediction and receives homage from followers in many countries.

In the years preceding 1912, there were indeed close friendly relations of a personal nature between the Emperor of China and His Holiness the Dalai Lama. The connection was essentially born of belief in a common faith and may correctly be described as the relationship between a spiritual guide and his lay followers; it had no political implications. As a people devoted to the tenets of Buddhism, Tibetans had long eschewed the art of warfare, practiced peace and tolerance, and for the defense of their country relied on its geographical configuration and on noninvolvement in the affairs of other nations. There were times when Tibet sought but seldom received the protection of the Chinese Emperor. The Chinese, however, in their natural urge for expansion, have wholly misconstrued the significance of the ties of friendship and interdependence that existed between China and Tibet as between neighbors. To them China was suzerain and Tibet a vassal State. It is this which first aroused legitimate apprehension in the mind of Tibet regarding China's designs on its independent status.

The conduct of the Chinese during their expedition of 1910 completed the rupture between the two countries. In 1911–1912, Tibet, under the Thirteenth Dalai Lama, declared its complete independence—even Nepal simultaneously broke away from allegiance to China—while the Chinese revolution of 1911, which dethroned the last Manchurian Emperor, snapped the last of the sentimental and religious bonds that Tibet had with China. Tibet thereafter depended entirely on its isolation, its faith in the wisdom of the Lord Buddha, and occasionally on the support of the British in India for its protection. No doubt in these circumstances the latter could also claim suzerainty over Tibet. Tibet, notwithstanding Anglo-Chinese influence from time to time, maintained its separate existence, in justification of which it may be pointed out that it has been able to keep peace and order within the country and remain at peace with the world. It continued to maintain neighborly good will and friendship with the people of China, but never acceded to the Chinese claim of suzerainty in 1914.

It was British persuasion which led Tibet to sign a treaty which superimposed on it the nominal (noninterfering) suzerainty of China and by which China was accorded the right to maintain a mission in Lhasa, though it was strictly forbidden to meddle in the internal affairs of Tibet. Apart from that fact, even the nominal suzerainty which Tibet conceded to China is not enforceable because of the nonsignature of the treaty of

1914 by the Chinese. It will be seen that Tibet maintained independent relations with other neighboring countries, such as India and Nepal. Furthermore, despite friendly British overtures, it did not compromise its position by throwing in its forces in the Second World War on the side of China. Thus it asserted and maintained its complete independence. The treaty of 1914 still guides relations between Tibet and India, and China not being a party to it may be taken to have renounced the benefits that would have otherwise accrued to it from the treaty. Tibet's independence thereby reassumed *de jure* status.

The slender tie that Tibet maintained with China after the 1911 revolution became less justifiable when China underwent a further revolution and turned into a full-fledged Communist State. There can be no kinship or sympathy between such divergent creeds as those espoused by China and Tibet. Foreseeing future complications, the Tibetan Government broke off diplomatic relations with China and made a Chinese representative in Lhasa depart from Tibet in July, 1949. Since then, Tibet has not even maintained formal relations with the Chinese Government and people. It desires to live apart, uncontaminated by the germ of a highly materialistic creed, but China is bent on not allowing Tibet to live in peace. Since the establishment of the People's Republic of China, the Chinese have hurled threats of liberating Tibet and have used devious methods to intimidate and undermine the Government of Tibet. Tibet recognizes that it is in no position to resist. It is thus that it agreed to negotiate on friendly terms with the Chinese Government.

It is unfortunate that the Tibetan mission to China was unable to leave India through no fault of its own, but for want of British visas, which were required for transit through Hong Kong. At the kind intervention of the Government of India, the Chinese People's Republic condescended to allow the Tibetan mission to have preliminary negotiations with the Chinese Ambassador to India, who arrived in New Delhi only in September. While these negotiations were proceeding in Delhi, Chinese troops, without warning or provocation, crossed the Di Chu river, which has for long been the boundary of Tibetan territory, at a number of places on October 7, 1950. In quick succession, places of strategic importance such as Demar, Kamto, Tunga, Tshame, Rimochegotyu, Yakalo, and Markham, fell to the Chinese. Tibetan frontier garrisons in Kham, which were maintained not with any aggressive design, but as a nominal protective measure, were all wiped out. Communist troops converged in great force from five directions on Chamdo, the capital of Kham, which fell soon after. Nothing is known of the fate of a minister of the Tibetan Government posted there.

Little is known in the outside world of this sneak invasion. Long after the invasion had taken place, China announced to the world that it had asked its armies to march into Tibet. This unwarranted act of aggression has not only disturbed the peace of Tibet, but it is also in complete disregard of a solemn assurance given by China to the Government of India, and it has created a grave situation in Tibet and may eventually deprive Tibet of its long-cherished independence. We can assure you, Mr. Secretary-General, that Tibet will not go down without a fight, though there is little hope that a nation dedicated to peace will be able to resist the brutal effort of men trained to war, but we understand that the United Nations has decided to stop aggression whenever it takes place.

The armed invasion of Tibet for the incorporation of Tibet in Communist China through sheer physical force is a clear case of aggression. As long as the people of Tibet are compelled by force to become a part of China against their will and consent, the present invasion of Tibet will be the grossest instance of the violation of the weak by the strong. We therefore appeal through you to the nations of the world to intercede in our behalf and restrain Chinese aggression.

The problem is simple. The Chinese claim Tibet as a part of China. Tibetans feel that racially, culturally, and geographically they are far apart from the Chinese. If the Chinese find the reactions of the Tibetans to their unnatural claim not acceptable, there are other civilized methods by which they could ascertain the views of the people of Tibet; or, should the issue be surely juridical, they are open to seek redress in an international court of law. The conquest of Tibet by China will only enlarge the area of conflict and increase the threat to the independence and stability of other Asian countries.

We Ministers, with the approval of His Holiness the Dalai Lama, entrust the problem of Tibet in this emergency to the ultimate decision of the United Nations, hoping that the conscience of the world will not allow the disruption of our State by methods reminiscent of the jungle.

The Kashag (Cabinet) and National Assembly of Tibet, Tibetan delegation, Shakabpa House, Kalimpong.

Dated Lhasa, the twenty-seventh day of the ninth Tibetan month of The Iron Tiger Year (November 7, 1950).

APPENDIX 25:
THE AGREEMENT OF THE CENTRAL PEOPLE'S GOVERNMENT AND THE LOCAL GOVERNMENT OF TIBET ON MEASURES FOR THE PEACEFUL LIBERATION OF TIBET, 23 MAY 1951

The Tibetan nationality is one of the nationalities with a long history within the boundaries of China and, like many other nationalities, it has done its glorious duty in the course of the creation and development of the great motherland. But over the last hundred years and more, imperialist forces penetrated into China, and in consequence, also penetrated into the

Tibetan region and carried out all kinds of deceptions and provocations. Like previous reactionary Governments, the KMT [Guomindang] reactionary government continued to carry out a policy of oppression and sowing dissension among the nationalities, causing division and disunity among the Tibetan people. The Local Government of Tibet did not oppose imperialist deception and provocations, but adopted an unpatriotic attitude towards the great motherland. Under such conditions, the Tibetan nationality and people were plunged into the depths of enslavement and suffering. In 1949, basic victory was achieved on a nation-wide scale in the Chinese people's war of liberation; the common domestic enemy of all nationalities—the KMT reactionary government—was overthrown; and the common foreign enemy of all nationalities—the aggressive imperialist forces—was driven out. On this basis, the founding of the People's Republic of China and of the Central People's Government was announced. In accordance with the Common Programme passed by the Chinese People's Political Consultative Conference, the Central People's Government declared that all nationalities within the boundaries of the People's Republic of China are equal, and that they shall establish unity and mutual aid and oppose imperialism and their own public enemies, so that the People's Republic of China may become one big family of fraternity and cooperation, composed of all its nationalities. Within this big family of nationalities of the People's Republic of China, national regional autonomy is to be exercised in areas where national minorities are concentrated, and all national minorities are to have freedom to develop their spoken and written languages and to preserve or reform their customs, habits, and religious beliefs, and the Central People's Government will assist all national minorities to develop their political, economic, cultural, and educational construction work. Since then, all nationalities within the country, with the exception of those in the areas of Tibet and Taiwan, have gained liberation. Under the unified leadership of the Central People's Government and the direct leadership of the higher levels of People's Governments, all national minorities have fully enjoyed the right of national equality and have exercised, or are exercising, national regional autonomy. In order that the influences of aggressive imperialist forces in Tibet may be successfully eliminated, the unification of the territory and sovereignty of the People's Republic of China accomplished, and national defence safeguarded; in order that the Tibetan nationality and people may be freed and return to the big family of the People's Republic of China to enjoy the same rights of national equality as all other nationalities in the country and develop their political, economic, cultural, and educational work, the Central People's Government, when it ordered the People's Liberation Army to march into Tibet, notified the local government of Tibet to send delegates to the Central Authorities to hold talks for the conclusion of an agreement on measures for the peaceful liberation of Tibet. At the latter part of April, 1951, the delegates with full powers from the Local Government of Tibet arrived in Peking. The Central People's Government appointed representatives with full powers to conduct talks on a friendly basis with the delegates of the Local Government of Tibet. The result of the talks is that both parties have agreed to establish this agreement and ensure that it be carried into effect.

1. The Tibetan people shall be united and drive out the imperialist aggressive forces from Tibet; that the Tibetan people shall return to the big family of the motherland—the People's Republic of China.

2. The Local Government of Tibet shall actively assist the People's Liberation Army to enter Tibet and consolidate the national defences.

3. In accordance with the policy towards nationalities laid down in the Common Programme of the Chinese People's Political Consultative Conference, the Tibetan people have the right of exercising national regional autonomy under the unified leadership of the Central People's Government.

4. The Central Authorities will not alter the existing political system in Tibet. The Central Authorities also will not alter the established status, functions and powers of the Dalai Lama. Officials of various ranks shall hold office as usual.

5. The established status, functions, and powers of the Panchen Ngoerhtehni shall be maintained.

6. By the established status, functions and powers of the Dalai Lama and of the Panchen Ngoerhtehni is meant the status, functions and powers of the 13th Dalai Lama and of the 9th Panchen Ngoerhtehni when they were in friendly and amicable relations with each other.

7. The policy of freedom of religious belief laid down in the Common Programme of the Chinese People's Political Consultative Conference will be protected. The Central Authorities will not effect any change in the income of the monasteries.

8. The Tibetan troops will be reorganised step by step into the People's Liberation Army, and become a part of the national defence forces of the Central People's Government.

9. The spoken and written language and school education of the Tibetan nationality will be developed step by step in accordance with the actual conditions in Tibet.

10. Tibetan agriculture, livestock raising, industry and commerce will be developed step by step, and the people's livelihood shall be improved step by step in accordance with the actual conditions in Tibet.

11. In matters related to various reforms in Tibet, there will be no compulsion on the part of the Central Authorities. The Local Government of Tibet should carry out reforms of its own accord, and when the people raise demands for reform, they must be settled through consultation with the leading personnel of Tibet.

12. In so far as former pro-imperialist and pro-KMT officials resolutely sever relations with imperialism and the KMT and do not engage in sabotage or resistance, they may continue to hold office irrespective of their past.

13. The People's Liberation Army entering Tibet will abide by the above-mentioned policies and will also be fair in all buying and selling and will not arbitrarily take even a needle or a thread from the people.

14. The Central People's Government will handle all external affairs of the area of Tibet; and there will be peaceful co-existence with neighbouring

countries and the establishment and development of fair commercial and trading relations with them on the basis of equality, mutual benefit and mutual respect for territory and sovereignty.

15. In order to ensure the implementation of this agreement, the Central People's Government will set up a military and administrative committee and a military area headquarters in Tibet, and apart from the personnel sent there by the Central People's Government it will absorb as many local Tibetan personnel as possible to take part in the work. Local Tibetan personnel taking part in the military and administrative committee may include patriotic elements from the Local Government of Tibet, various district and various principal monasteries; the namelist is to be prepared after consultation between the representatives designated by the Central People's Government and various quarters concerned, and is to be submitted to the Central People's Government for approval.

16. Funds needed by the military and administrative committee, the military area headquarters and the People's Liberation Army entering Tibet will be provided by the Central People's Government. The Local Government of Tibet should assist the People's Liberation Army in the purchases and transportation of food, fodder, and other daily necessities.

17. This agreement shall come into force immediately after signatures and seals are affixed to it.

Signed and sealed by delegates of the Central People's Government with full powers:

Chief Delegate: Li Wei-han (Chairman of the Commission of Nationalities Affairs);
Delegates: Chang Ching-wu, Chang Kuo-hua, Sun Chih-yuan
Delegates with full powers of the Local Government of Tibet:
Chief Delegate: Kaloon Ngabou Ngawang Jigme (Ngabo Shape)
Delegates: Dzasak Khemey Sonam Wangdi, Khentrung Thuptan, Tenthar, Khenchung Thupten Lekmuun Rimshi, Samposey Tenzin Thundup

Notes

1. Source: Union Research Institute, *Tibet, 1950–1967* (Hong Kong, 1968), *Document* 6, pp. 19–23.

APPENDIX 26:
RESOLUTIONS ADOPTED
BY THE UNITED NATIONS GENERAL ASSEMBLY

Resolution 1353 (XIV)

The General Assembly,

Recalling the principles regarding fundamental human rights and freedoms set out in the Charter of the United Nations and in the Universal Declaration of Human Rights adopted by the General Assembly on 10 December 1948,

Considering that the fundamental human rights and freedoms to which the Tibetan people, like all others, are entitled include the right to civil and religious liberty for all without distinction,

Mindful also of the distinctive cultural and religious heritage of the people of Tibet and of the autonomy which they have traditionally enjoyed,

Gravely concerned at reports, including the official statements of His Holiness the Dalai Lama, to the effect that the fundamental human rights and freedoms of the people of Tibet have been forcibly denied them,

Deploring the effect of these events in increasing international tension and in embittering the relations between peoples at a time when earnest and positive efforts are being made by responsible leaders to reduce tension and improve international relations,

1. *Affirms its belief* that respect for the principles of the Charter of the United Nations and of the Universal Declaration of Human Rights is essential for the evolution of a peaceful world order based on the rule of law;

2. *Calls* for respect for the fundamental human rights of the Tibetan people and for their distinctive cultural and religious life.

Resolution 1723 (XVI)

The General Assembly,

Recalling its resolution 1353 (XIV) of 21 October 1959 on the question of Tibet,

Gravely concerned at the continuation of events in Tibet, including the violation of the fundamental human rights of the Tibetan people and the suppression of the distinctive cultural and religious life which they have traditionally enjoyed,

Noting with deep anxiety the severe hardships which these events have inflicted on the Tibetan people, as evidenced by the large-scale exodus of Tibetan refugees to the neighbouring countries,

Considering that these events violate fundamental human rights and freedoms set out in the Charter of the United Nations and the Universal Declaration of Human Rights, including the principle of self-determination of peoples and nations, and have the deplorable effect of increasing international tension and embittering relations between peoples,

1. *Reaffirms its conviction* that respect for the principles of the Charter of the United Nations and of the Universal Declaration of Human Rights is essential for the evolution of a peaceful world order based on the rule of law;

2. *Solemnly renews* its call for the cessation of practices which deprive the Tibetan people of their fundamental human rights and freedoms, including their right to self-determination;

3. *Expresses the hope* that Member States will make all possible efforts, as appropriate, towards achieving the purposes of the present resolution.

Resolution 2079 (XX)

The General Assembly

Bearing in mind the principles relating to human rights and fundamental freedoms set forth in the Charter of the United Nations and proclaimed in the Universal Declaration of Human Rights,

Reaffirming its resolutions 1353 (XIV) of 21 October 1959 and 1723 (XVI) of 20 December 1961 on the question of Tibet,

Gravely concerned at the continued violation of the fundamental rights and freedoms of the people of Tibet and the continued suppression of their distinctive cultural and religious life, as evidenced by the exodus of refugees to the neighbouring countries,

1. *Deplores* the continued violation of the fundamental rights and freedoms of the people of Tibet;

2. *Reaffirms* that respect for the principles of the Charter of the United Nations and of the Universal Declaration of Human Rights is essential for the evolution of a peaceful world order based on the rule of law;

3. *Declares its conviction* that the violation of human rights and fundamental freedoms in Tibet and the suppression of the distinctive cultural and religious life of its people increase international tension and embitter relations between peoples;

4. *Solemnly renews* its call for the cessation of all practices which deprive the Tibetan people of the human rights and fundamental freedoms which they have always enjoyed;

5. *Appeals* to all States to use their best endeavours to achieve the purposes of the present resolution.

Selected Bibliography

Unpublished Records

British Public Record Office. (1) Foreign Office 535. Confidential Print: Tibet and Mongolia, 1903–1923. (2) Foreign Office 405. Confidential Print: China, 1848–1922. (3) Foreign Office 17. General Correspondence: China, 1815–1905.

Chinese People's Liberation Army (PLA), Xizang Junqu Zhengzhibu [Tibetan Military District Political Department], *Xizang Xinqshi he Renwu Jiaoyu de Jiben Jiaocai* [Fundamental Teaching Materials and Task Education on the Tibetan Situation]. 1960.

India Office Records. Dispatches to India (Political Department); Secret Letters from India; Foreign Letters from India; Enclosures to Secret Letters; Secret and Political Letters from India.

Kashag (Tibetan Cabinet) Documents from the Kashag Archives, Dharmsala.

Documents at the Library of Tibetan Works and Archives and Tibetan documents in the possession of private persons.

Tibetan Affairs Coordination Office documents.

Rockhill (William Woodville) Papers. Collection of Letters and Manuscripts at the Houghton Library, Harvard University.

Published Records

British and Foreign State papers (B.F.S.P.). Published for the Foreign and Commonwealth Office.

Government of His Holiness the Dalai Lama. *The International Position of Tibet.* 1959.

Imperial Gazetteer of India.

Nationalities Affairs Commission of the People's Republic of China, *Bod. ljongs. ni. krung.go'i. cha. shas. yin.* [Tibet is an Integral Part of China]. Beijing, 1981.

National Government Gazette. Beijing and Nanjing, 1925–1949.

Ministry of External Affairs, India. *Report of the Officials of the Governments of India and the People's Republic of China on the Boundary Question.* New Delhi, 1961.

Ministry of External Affairs, India. *Prime Minister on Chinese Aggression.* New Delhi, 1963.

Ministry of External Affairs, India. *Prime Minister on Sino-Indian Relations.* Vol. 1 in Parliament. This volume covers the period from 17 March to 12 September 1959.

Ministry of External Affairs, India. *Notes, Memoranda and Letters Exchanged and Agreements Signed by the Governments of India and China.* 14 Vols. 1959–1968. Referred to as *White Paper.*

Papers Relating to the Foreign Relations of the United States (FRUS). Documents
    relating to the foreign relations of the United States, published by the Department
    of State.
Papers Relating to Tibet 1904 (Cd. 1920). Commissioned for Parliament.
Further Papers Relating to Tibet 1904 (Cd. 2054). Commissioned for Parliament.
Further Papers Relating to Tibet 1905 (Cd. 2370). Commissioned for Parliament.

United Nations and Legal Sources

International Court of Justice. Reports of Judgements, Advisory Opinions and Orders
    (I.C.J., Reports).
League of Nations Official Journal (L.N.O.J.).
League of Nations Treaty Series (L.N.T.S.).
Permanent Court of International Justice (P.C.I.J.).
Reports of International Arbitral Awards (R.I.A.A.).
United Nations Documents and Resolutions.
United Nations Treaty Series (U.N.T.S.).
Yearbook of the International Law Commission.
Yearbook of the United Nations.

Newspapers and Other Publications

Daily Telegraph. London.
Hindustan Standard. Calcutta.
Hindustan Times. New Delhi.
New York Times. New York.
Renmin Ribao (People's Daily). Beijing.
Indian Express. Madras.
The Statesman. Calcutta.
The Telegraph. Calcutta.
The Times. London.
The Tribune. Chandigarh.
Times of India. New Delhi.
United States Consulate General, Hong Kong. (1) Current Background (CB). (2)
    Survey of China Mainland Press (SCMP). (3) Selections from China Mainland
    Magazine (SCMM). (4) Survey of People's Republic of China Press (SPRCP).
China News Analysis (CNA). Hong Kong.
New China News Agency (NCNA) [Xinhua She]. Beijing and other locations.
Beijing Review (formerly Peking Review).
Tibetan Bulletin. Dharmsala.
Tibetan Messenger. Utrecht, the Netherlands.
Tibetan Review (TR). New Delhi.
Far Eastern Economic Review. Hong Kong.

Books and Journal Articles

Aacharya, Babu Ram. Shree 5 (His Majesty) Bada Maharajadhiraja Prithivi Narayan
    Shah Biography. 4 Vols. Kathmandu, (1969).
Academy of Sciences of the USSR, Institute of State and Law. International Law.
    Moscow, 1961.

Afro-Asian Council. *Report of the Afro-Asian Convention on Tibet and Against Colonialism in Asia and Africa.* New Delhi, 1960.

Ahmad, Z. *China and Tibet, 1708–1959: A Resume of Facts.* Distributed for the Royal Institute of International Affairs by the Oxford University Press, February 1960.

"New Light on the Tibet-Ladakh-Mughal War of 1679–1684." *East and West* 18 (1968).

————. "Sino-Tibetan Relations in the Seventeenth Century." *Serie Orientale Roma* 40 (1970).

Aitchinson, C. *A Collection of Treaties, Engagements and Sanads Relating to India and Neighbouring Countries.* Vol. 14. New Delhi, 1929.

Akehurst, M. *A Modern Introduction to International Law.* 5th ed. London, 1984.

Albaharna, H.M. *The Legal Status of the Arabian Gulf States.* Manchester, 1968.

A Letter from Fr. A. De Andrada, S.J. (Tibet, August 29, 1627), and from Fr. Gaspar Diaz, S.J. (Annam, 1627). Translated and edited by the Rev. H. Hosten, S.J.

Alexander, Y., and Friedlander, R.A., eds. *Self Determination: National, Regional and Global Dimensions.* Boulder, Colorado, 1980.

Alexandrowicz-Alexander, C.H. "The Legal Position of Tibet." *AJIL* 48 (1954).

Allen, J.L. "Chinese Communist Policy in Tibet." Dissertation, University of California, Berkeley, 1967.

Ambekar, G.V., and Divekar, V.D., eds. *Documents on China's Relations with South and South-East Asia (1949–1962).* Bombay, 1964.

American Institute of International Law. *American Journal of International Law,* Official Document, Special Number (Oct. 1926).

————. *Restatement of the Law: The Foreign Relations Law of the United States.* Philadelphia, 1962.

Amnesty International. *Political Imprisonment in the People's Republic of China.* London, 1978.

————. *1980 Annual Report.* London, 1981.

————. *China: Violations of Human Rights.* London, 1984.

Anand, R.P. *Asian States and the Development of Universal International Law.* Delhi, 1972.

————. "The Status of Tibet in International Law." *International Studies* 10, No. 4 (April 1969).

Andrugtsang, G.T. *Four Rivers, Six Ranges.* Dharmsala, 1973.

Anzilotti, D. "La formazione del Regno d'Italia nei riguardi del diritto internazionale." *Rivista di Diritto Internazionale* (1912).

————. *Corso di Diritto Internazionale.* Rome, 1928.

Armstrong, A.J. "The Negotiations for the Future Political Status of Micronesia." *AJIL* 74 (1980).

Aryal, I.R., and Dhungyal, T.P. *A New History of Nepal.* 2nd ed. Kathmandu, 1975.

Avedon, J.F. *In Exile from the Land of Snows.* New York, 1984.

Bacot, J. "Le Mariage Chinois du Roi Tibetain de Sron bcan sqan po." *Melanges Chinois et Bouddhiques* 3 (July 1935). [A translation of the "Mani Bka 'Bum," a Tibetan Chronicle.]

————. *Introduction a L'Histoire du Tibet.* Paris, 1962.

Bacot, J.; Thomas, F.U.; and Touissaint, C. *Documents de Touen-Houang Relatifs a L'Histoire de Tibet.* Paris, 1940.

Balkrishna, P., ed. *Panch Saya Barsha.* Kathmandu, 1975 (BS 2031).

Balladore-Pallieri, C. *La Guerra.* Padova, 1935.

Bamzai, P.N. *A History of Kashmir.* Delhi, 1962.

Baratashvili, D.I. *Novye Gacuarctva Azii i Afriki i Mezhdunarodnoe Pravo*. Moscow, 1968.

Basnet, Lal Bahadur. *Sikkim: A Short Political History*. New Delhi, 1974.

Baty, T. "Protectorates and Mandates." *BYIL* 2 (1921-1922).

―――. "So Called 'De Facto' Recognition." *Yale Law Journal* 31 (1922).

Bell, C.A. *Tibet: Past and Present*. 1924; rpt. Oxford, 1968.

―――. *The People of Tibet*. 1928; rpt. Oxford, 1968.

―――. *The Religion of Tibet*. 1931; rpt. Oxford, 1968.

―――. *Portrait of the Dalai Lama*. London, 1956.

Bernier, I. *International Legal Aspects of Federalism*. London, 1973.

Bhasin, A.S., ed. *Documents on Nepal's Relations with India and China, 1949-66*. New Delhi, 1970.

Bhushan, S. *China: The Myth of a Super Power*. New Delhi, 1976.

Bisconti, G. "Sulla condizione giuridica del Protettorato di Boemia e Moravia." *Rivista di Diritto Internazionale* (1941).

Bishop, W. *International Law*. 2nd ed. Boston, 1962.

Bluntschli, J. *The Theory of the State*. 3rd ed. London, 1901.

Bogoslovskii, V.A. *Ocherk Istorii Tibetskovo Naroda*. Moscow, 1962.

―――. "Tibet and the Cultural Revolution." *Far Eastern Affairs*, No. 1 (1976).

Bokor-Szego, H. *New States in International Law*. Budapest, 1970.

Bot, B. *Non-Recognition and Treaty Relations*. Dobbs Ferry, New York, 1968.

Bouchez, L.J. "The Concept of Effectiveness as Applied to Territorial Sovereignty over Sea-Areas, Air Space and Outer Space." *Nederlands Tidjschrift voor Internationaal Recht* (1962).

Bourg D'Anvill, J.B. *Nouvel Atlas de la Chine, de la Tartarie Chinoise et du Tibet*. Amsterdam, 1785.

Brandt, C.; Schwartz, B.; and Fairbank, J.K. *A Documentary History of Chinese Communism*. Cambridge, Massachusetts, 1952.

Brauen, M. *Heinrich Harrers Impressionen Aus Tibet*. Innsbruck, 1974.

Brierly, J. "Regles Generales du Droit de la Paix." *Recueil des Cours* 58 (1936).

―――. *The Law of Nations*. 4th ed. Oxford, 1949.

Broderick, M. "Associated Statehood—A New Form of Decolonisation." *International and Comparative Law Quarterly* 17 (Sept. 1968).

Brossard, J. "Le Droit du Peuple Quebecois de Disposer de lui-meme au Regard du Droit International." *The Canadian Yearbook of International Law* 91 (1977).

Brown, P. "The Legal Effects of Recognition." *AJIL* 44 (1950).

Brownlie, I. *International Law and the Use of Force by States*. Oxford, 1963.

―――. *Principles of Public International Law*. 2nd ed. Oxford, 1973.

―――, ed. *Basic Documents in International Law*. 3rd ed. Oxford, 1983.

Buchan, J., ed. *India: The Nations of Today*. London, 1923.

Buergenthal, T., ed. *Human Rights, International Law and the Helsinki Accord*. New York, 1977.

Bureau of His Holiness the Dalai Lama. *Tibet in the United Nations, 1950-1961*. New Delhi, n.d.

Bushell, J.W. "The Early History of Tibet From Chinese Sources." *JRAS* 12 (1980).

Camman, S. *Trade Through the Himalayas: The Early British Attempts to Open Tibet*. Princeton, 1951.

Candler, E. *The Unveiling of Lhasa*. London, 1905.

Carrasco, P. *Land and Polity in Tibet*. Seattle, 1959.

Cavare, L. *Le Droit International Public Positif*. 2 Vols. Paris, 1951.

Central Intelligence Agency. *The Integration of Tibet: China's Progress and Problems.* Released, 1979.

C.E.S. *'t Verwaerloosde Formosa.* n.d.

Chand, A. *Tibet: Past and Present, 1660–1981.* New Delhi, 1982.

Chang, Chih-i. *The Party and the National Question.* Translated by George Mosely. Cambridge, 1966.

Changchub Gyalsten (Byang-chub rGyal-mtshan). *Lha rigs rlangs kyi rnam thar.* New Delhi, 1974.

Chavannes, E. *Documents sur les Tou-Kive (Turcs) Occidentaux.* St. Petersburg, 1903.

Chen, T. *The International Law of Recognition.* London, 1951.

Chiang, Kai-Shek. *China's Destiny.* New York, 1947.

China and the United Nations. Report of a study group set up by the China Institute of International Affairs. New York, 1959.

Chinese Ministry of Information. *China Handbook, 1937–1945.* New York, 1947.

Chiu, H. "Communist China's Attitude Toward International Law." *AJIL* 60 (1966).

———. "The Position of International Law in Chinese Law." *The Annals of the Chinese Society on International Law* 3 (July 1966).

———. "Chinese Contemporary Practices and Judicial Decisions Relating to International Law (April 1967 to March 1968)." *The Annals of the Chinese Society of International Law* 5 (Aug. 1968).

———. "Comparison of the Nationalist and Communist View of Unequal Treaties." In *China's Practice of International Law: Some Case Studies,* ed. J. Cohen. Cambridge, Massachusetts, 1972.

———. *The People's Republic of China and the Law of Treaties.* Cambridge, Massachusetts, 1972.

———, ed. *The Legal Aspects of the Palestine Problem with Special Regard to the Question of Jerusalem.* International Progress Organization, Studies in International Relations, Vol. 4. Vienna, 1981.

———. "Prospects for Unification of China—An Analysis of the Views of the Republic of China on Taiwan." Presented at the 35th Annual Meeting of the Association for Asian Studies, San Francisco, March 1983.

Chou, En-Lai (Zhou Enlai). *Premier Chou En-Lai's Letter to the Leaders of Asian and African Countries on the Sino-Indian Boundary Question, Nov. 15, 1962.* Beijing, 1974.

Churchill, R.P. *The Anglo-Russian Convention of 1907.* Cedar Rapids, Iowa, 1939.

Clark, G. *Tibet, China and Great Britain.* Peking, 1924.

Clark, J.J. "Chinese Communist Administration in Tibet, 1950–1961." Dissertation, Tufts University, 1962.

Cobban, A. *National Self-Determination.* London, 1945.

Cobbett, P. *Cases and Opinions on International Law.* 2 Vols. 3rd ed. London, 1909.

Cohen, J.A., and Chiu, H. *People's China and International Law: A Documentary Study.* 2 Vols. Princeton, 1974.

Constantopoulos, D. "Deux notions fondamentales de la souverainete." In *Grundprobleme des Internationalen Recht,* eds. D. Constantopoulos, C. Eustathiades, and C.N. Fragistas. Bonn, 1957.

Cooper, T.T. *Travels of a Pioneer of Commerce.* London, 1871.

Corr, G.H. *The Chinese Red Army.* Reading, 1976.

Courant, M. *L'Asie Centrale au XVIIe et XVIIIe Siecles.* Paris, 1912.

Crawford, J. "The Criteria for Statehood in International Law." *BYIL* 48 (1976–77).

———. *The Creation of States in International Law.* Oxford, 1979.

Dalai Lama V. "Chronicles of the Fifth Dalai Lama." In *The Early History of Tibet,* ed. Ngawang Geleh Demo. New Delhi, 1967.

Dalai Lama XIV, H. H. Tenzin Gyatso. *My Land and My People.* 1962; rpt. New York, 1977.

Dallin, D.J. *The Rise of Russia in Asia.* New Haven, 1949.

Das, S.C. "Indian Pandits in Tibet." *Journal of the Buddhist Text Society of India,* Part 1 (1893).

————. *Journey to Lhasa and Central Tibet.* Ed. W.W. Rockhill. London, 1904.

Dastur, A. "The Tibetan Ordeal and India." *National Integration.* Independence Number (1964).

Datta, C.L. *Ladakh and Western Himalayan Politics, 1819–1848.* New Delhi, 1973.

Davis, G.B. *The Elements of International Law.* 3rd ed. New York, 1908.

Delupis, I. *International Law and the Independent State.* New York, 1974.

Demieville P. "Le Concile de Lhasa: Une Controverse sur le Quietisme Entre Bouddhistes de l'Inde et de la Chine au VIII Siecle de l'Ere Chretienne." *Biblioteque de l'Institut des Hautes Etudes Chinoises* 7 (Paris, 1952).

————. *La Situation Religieuse en Chine au Temps de Marco Polo.* (Rome, 1967).

Desgodin, E.H. *La Mission du Tibet de 1855 a 1870, Comprennant l'Expose des Affaires Religieuses et d'Apres les Lettres de M. L'Abbe Desgodins, Missionaire Apostolique.* Verdun, 1872.

Deshpande, G.P. "Towards Integration: Tibet Since the Revolt." *International Studies* 10, No. 4 (April 1969).

Desideri, I. *An Account of Tibet.* Ed. F. de Filippi. London, 1932.

Despagnet, F. *Essai sur les Protectorats.* Paris, 1896.

Detter, I. "The Problem of Unequal Treaties." *International and Comparative Law Quarterly* 15 (1966).

Dhanalaxmi, R. *British Attitude to Nepal's Relations with Tibet and China, 1814–1914.* New Delhi, 1981.

Dhondup, K. *Songs of the Sixth Dalai Lama.* Dharmsala, 1981.

Dickinson, E.D. *The Equality of States in International Law.* Harvard Studies in Jurisprudence No. 3. Cambridge, Massachusetts, 1920.

Dinstein, Y. "Collective Human Rights of Peoples and Minorities." *International and Comparative Law Quarterly* 25 (1976).

————, ed. *Models of Autonomy.* Tel Aviv, 1981.

Diskalkar, D.B. "Bogle's Embassy to Tibet." *The Indian Historical Quarterly* 9, No. 2 (June 1933).

————. *Tibeto-Nepalese War, 1788–1793.* Calcutta, 1933.

Dowell, H., ed. *The Cambridge History of India.* Cambridge, 1932.

Dreyer, J.T. *China's Forty Millions.* Cambridge, Massachusetts, 1976.

————. "A Thirty Year Assessment: China and Tibet." *Spearhead* (Autumn 1981).

Du Halde, J.B. *Description Geographique, Historique, Chronologique, Politique et Physique de l'Empire de la Chine et de la Tartarie Chinoise.* 4 Vols. Paris, 1735.

Dunnett, D. "Self-Determination and the Falklands." *International Affairs* 59, No. 3 (Summer 1983).

Eberhard, W. *A History of China.* London, 1950.

El-Kayal, M.I. "The Role of the United Nations in the Protection of Human Rights." Dissertation, University of Illinois at Urbana, 1975.

Emerson, R. "Political Development in the United Nations." *International Organization* 19 (1965).

————. "Self-Determination." *AJIL* 65 (1971).

Emmerick, R.E. "Tibetan Texts Concerning Khotan." *London Oriental Series* 19 (London, 1967).

Escarra, J. *La Chine et le Droit International.* Paris, 1931.

Fairbank, J.K., and Teng, S.Y. "On the Transmission of Ch'ing Documents." *HJAS* 4 (1939).

_____ . "On the Ch'ing Tributary System." In *Ch'ing Administration: Three Studies.* Cambridge, Massachusetts, 1961.

Farquhar, D.M. "Emperor as Bodhisattva in the Governance of the Ch'ing Empire." *HJAS* 38, No. 1 (June 1978).

_____ . "Structure and Functions in the Yuan Imperial Government." In *China Under Mongol Rule*, ed. J. Langlois. Princeton, 1981.

Fawcett, J. *The British Commonwealth in International Law.* London, 1963.

Fedozzi, P. *Corso di Diritto Internazionale.* Padova, 1930.

Fenwick, C.G. *International Law.* 4th ed. New York, 1965.

Fifield, R.H. *Diplomacy of Southeast Asia, 1945–58.* New York, 1958.

Fiore, P. *International Law Codified and Its Legal Sanction.* New York, 1918.

Foreign Languages Press. *An Outline History of China.* Beijing, 1958.

_____ . *Oppose the New U.S. Plot to Create "Two Chinas."* Beijing, 1962.

Francke, A.H. *Antiquities Of Indian Tibet.* Part 2, "The Chronicles of Ladakh and Minor Chronicles." Archeological Survey of India New Imperial Series, Vol. 50 (Calcutta, 1926).

_____ . *Ladakh the Mysterious Land.* 1907; rpt. New Delhi, 1978.

Franke, H. "Tibetans in Yuan China." In *China Under Mongol Rule*, ed. J.D. Langlois. Princeton, 1981.

Fraser, L.T. *India Under Curzon and After.* London, 1911.

Friters, G. *Outer Mongolia and Its International Position.* Baltimore, 1949.

Fuchs, W. "Der Jesuiten Atlas Der K'anghsi-Zeit." In *Monumenta Serica*, Monograph 4. Beijing, 1943.

Gashi, T.D. *New Tibet: Memoirs of a Graduate of the Peking Institute of National Minorities.* Translated from Tibetan by Samphel. Dharmsala, 1980.

Gemma, S. "Les Gouvernements De Fait." *Recueil des Cours* 3 (1924).

Ghosh, S.K. *Tibet in Sino-Indian Relations, 1899–1914.* New Delhi, 1977.

Ginsburgs, G., and Mathos, M. *Communist China and Tibet: The First Dozen Years.* The Hague, 1964.

Godinho, F. "A Letter of Father Francisco Godinho, S.J., From Western Tibet." Translated and edited by the Rev. H. Hosten, S.J. *Journal Of The Asiatic Society of Bengal* 21 (1925).

Gopal, R. *India-China-Tibet Triangle.* Lucknow, India, 1964.

Gould, B.J. *Jewel in the Lotus.* London, 1957.

Graber, D. *The Development of the Law of Belligerent Occupation, 1863–1914.* New York, 1949.

Green, L.D. "Legal Aspects of the Sino-Indian Border Dispute." *The China Quarterly* 3 (Jul.-Sept. 1960).

Grotius, H. *De Jure Belli Et Pacis.* 3 Vols. Cambridge, 1853.

Grousset, R. *L'Empire des Steppes.* Paris, 1941.

Guggenheim, P. *Lehrbuch des Volkerrechts.* 2 Vols. Basel, 1948, 1951.

Hackworth, G., ed. *Digest of International Law.* 8 Vols. Washington, 1940–1944.

Haenisch, E. "Bruchstucke aus der Geschichte Chinas Unter den Gegenwartigen Dynastie." *T'oung Pao* 12 (1911).

_____ . "Kaeserliches Vorwort zum Aktenwerk Uber den Krieg gegen G'aldan, aus dem Mandschu Ubersetzt." *Zeitschrift Der Deutschen Morgenlandischen Gesellschaft* 107 (1957).

Hall, W.E. *A Treatise on International Law.* 7th ed. Oxford, 1917.

Hambis, L. "L'histoire des Mongols a L'Epoque de Gengis-Khan et le dPag-bsam ljon-bzan de Sumpa-qutuqtu." In *Etudes Tibetaines.* Paris, 1971.

Hannum, H. and Lillich, R.B. "The Concept of Autonomy in International Law." *AJIL* 74 (1980).

Heilborn, P. *Das Volkerrechtliche Protectorat.* Berlin, 1891.

Heissig, W. "Ein Mongolischer zeitgenossischer Bericht uber den Oloteneinfall in Tibet und die Plunderung von Lhasa 1717." *Zeitschrift der Deutschen Morgenlandischen Gesellshaft* (1954).

Hershey, A.S. *The Essentials of International Public Law and Organization.* New York, 1927.

Higgins, R. *The Development of International Law Through the Political Organs of the United Nations.* London, 1963.

Hill, N. *Claims to Territory in International Law and Relations.* London, 1945.

Hoffmann, H. *Tibet: A Handbook.* Bloomington, Indiana, 1977.

Howorth, H. *History of the Mongols from the Ninth to the Nineteenth Century.* London, 1876.

Hsieh, P. *The Government of China, 1644–1911.* Baltimore, 1925.

Hsiung, J.D. *Law and Policy in China's Foreign Relations: A Study of Attitude and Practice.* New York, 1972.

Hsu, I. *China's Entrance into the Family of Nations: The Diplomatic Phase, 1858–1880.* Cambridge, Massachusetts, 1960.

Hsu, Shu-Hsi. *An Introduction to Sino-Foreign Relations.* Shanghai, 1941.

Huang, Tsen-ming. "Is the Policy of Non-Recognition Consistent with Rules of International Law?" *The Annals of the Chinese Society of International Law* 1 (July 1964).

Huber, M. *The Law of Nations in the History of Mankind.* The Hague, 1958.

Huc, M. *Decouverte du Tibet, 1845–1846.* 1933.

――――. *Recollections of a Journey Through Tartary, Thibet, and China.* London, 1852.

Hummel, A.W. *Eminent Chinese of the Ch'ing Period.* 2 Vols. Washington, 1943–1944.

Hutheesing, R., ed. *Tibet Fights For Freedom.* Bombay, 1960.

Hyde, C.C. *International Law: Chiefly As Interpreted and Applied by the United States.* 3 Vols. 2nd ed. Boston, 1945.

――――. "Status of the Republic of Indonesia in International Law." *Columbia Law Review* 49 (1949).

Hyer, P. "Yasujiro Yajima—The Japanese Military Advisor To Tibet." *Tibetan Review* 17, No. 6 (June 1982).

Ilbert, C.P. *Government of India.* Oxford, 1913.

Imbault-Huart, C. "Histoire de la Conquete du Nepal." *Journal Asiatique* 12 (Oct./Nov. 1878).

Important Documents Relating to China's Revolution. With English translations. Shanghai, 1912.

Indian Society of International Law. *The Sino-Indian Boundary.* New Delhi, 1962.

Indraji, B. *Twenty-Three Inscriptions From Nepal.* Translated by G. Buhler. Bombay, 1885.

Information and Publicity Office of His Holiness the Dalai Lama. *Brief Survey of History and Present-Day Conditions in Tibet.* Dharmsala, 1977.

Information Office of His Holiness the Dalai Lama. *Tibetans in Exile, 1959–1980.* Dharmsala, 1981.

Institut de Droit International. *Annuaire de l'Institut de Droit International* 2 (1936).
Institute of National Affairs. *Dalai Lama and India*. New Delhi, 1959.
International Commission of Jurists, Legal Inquiry Committee on Tibet. *Tibet and the Chinese People's Republic*. Geneva, 1960.
International Commission of Jurists. "East Pakistan Staff Study." *The Review*, No. 8 (June 1972).
_____. *The Question of Tibet and the Rule of Law*. Geneva, 1959.
International Council of World Affairs. *Asian Relations Conference 1947*. New Delhi, 1948.
International Law Association. *The Effect of Independence on Treaties: A Handbook*. Prepared by the Committee on State Succession to Treaties and Other Governmental Obligations. London, 1965.
International Studies (Indian School of). *Tibet*. Special Issue of *International Studies* 10, No. 4 (April 1969).
Jaffe, L. *Judicial Aspects of Foreign Relations*. Cambridge, Massachusetts, 1933.
Jain, G. *India Meets China in Nepal*. Bombay, 1959.
Jain, R.K., ed. *China-South Asian Relations 1947-1980*. 2 Vols. New Delhi, 1981.
Jametel, M. "Histoire de la Pacification du Tibet." *Revue de l'Extreme Orient* (1882).
Jennings, R.Y. *The Acquisition of Territory in International Law*. Manchester, 1963.
Jessup, P. *A Modern Law of Nations: An Introduction*. New York, 1968.
_____. *Transnational Law*. New Haven, 1956.
Jimenez de Arechaga, E. "International Law in the Past Third of a Century." *Recueil des Cours* 159 (1978).
Jin, Fu. "China's Recovery of Xianggang (Hong Kong) Area Fully Accords with International Law." *Beijing Review*, 23 Sept. 1983.
Johnson, D.H.N. "The Effect of Resolutions of the General Assembly of the United Nations." BYIL 32 (1955-56).
Johnson, H.S. *Self-Determination Within the Community of Nations*. Leiden, 1967.
Johnson, W. *Sovereignty and Protection: A Study of British Jurisdictional Imperialism in the Late Nineteenth Century*. Durham, North Carolina, 1973.
Jung, R. *The Sino-Burmese War, 1766-1770*. Cambridge, Massachusetts, 1971.
Karan, P. *The Changing Face of Tibet*. Lexington, Kentucky, 1976.
Kargl, R.C. "A Study of Sino-Tibetan Relations: 61 B.C. - 1952 A.D." Dissertation, University of Southern California, 1953.
Kaul, T.N. *Diplomacy in Peace and War: Recollections and Reflections*. New Delhi, 1979.
Kawaguchi, E. *Three Years in Tibet*. London, 1909.
Keith, A.B. *The Dominions as Sovereign States*. London, 1938.
Kelson, H. *Das Problem der Sourveranitat und die Theorie des Volkerrechts*. Tubingen, 1920.
_____. "La Naissance de L'Etat et la Formation de sa Nationalite." *Revue de Droit International* (1929).
_____. "Theorie Generale du Droit International Public." *Recueil Des Cours* 4 (1932).
_____. "Recognition in International Law." *AJIL* 35 (1941).
Kirkpatrick, W. *An Account of the Kingdom of Nepaul*. London, 1811.
Klaproth, M., ed. "Description du Tubet." *Journal Asiatique* (August 1829).
Kochler, H., ed. *The Legal Aspects of the Palestine Problem with Special Regard to the Question of Jerusalem*. Vienna, 1981.
Kolmas, J. "Ch'ing Shih Kao on Modern History of Tibet (1903-1912)." *Archiv Orientalni* 32 (1964).

———. *Tibet and Imperial China*. The Australian National University Center of Oriental Studies, Occasional Paper No. 7. Canberra, 1967.

———. "Tibetan Sources." In *Essays on the Sources for Chinese History*, eds. D. Leslie, C. Mackerras, W. Gungwu. Canberra, 1973.

Kvaerne, P. "Mongols and Khitans in a Fourteenth Century Tibetan Bonpo Test." *Acta Orientalia Hungarica* 34 (1980).

Kwanten, L. "Tibetan Mongol Relation During the Yuan." Dissertation, University of Southern California, 1972.

———. "Chingis Khan's Conquest of Tibet: Myth or Reality?" *Journal of Asian History* 7, No. 1 (1974).

Lamb, A. "Some Notes on Russian Intrigue in Tibet." *JRCAS* (1959).

———. *Britain and Chinese Central Asia: The Road to Lhasa (1767–1905)*. London, 1960.

———. *The McMahon Line*. 2 Vols. London, 1966.

Landon, P. *Lhasa*. London, 1905.

———. *Nepal*. Vols. 1–2. 1928; rpt. Kathmandu, 1976.

Langlois, J.D., ed. *China Under Mongol Rule*. Princeton, 1981.

Lansing, R. *Notes on Sovereignty: From the Standpoint of the State and of the World*. Washington, 1921.

Lattimore, O. "China and the Barbarians." In *Empire in the East*, ed. J. Barnes. New York, 1934.

———. *Inner Asian Frontiers of China*. 2nd ed. New York, 1951.

———. "Mongolia, Sinkiang and Tibet." In *The State of Asia*, ed. L.K. Rosinger. New York, 1951.

———. *Studies in Frontier History: Collected Papers, 1928–1958*. New York, 1962.

Lauterpacht, H. *Recognition in International Law*. Cambridge, 1947.

———. "Recognition of States." In *Essays on International Law From the Columbia Law Review*. New York, 1965.

———. *International Law: Collected Papers*. 3 Vols. Cambridge, 1970–1977.

Le Morzellec, J. *La Question de Jerusalem devant l'Organisation des Nations Unies*. Brussels, 1979.

Lee, Wei Kuo. "Tibet in Modern World Politics (1774–1922)." Dissertation, Columbia University, 1931.

Legge, J. *The Chinese Classics*. Hong Kong, 1960.

Lehmann, P.H. and Ullal, J. *Tibet: Das Stille Drama auf dem Dach der Erde*. Hamburg, 1981.

Leng, Shao-Chuang and Chiu, Hungdah, eds. *Law in Chinese Foreign Policy: Communist China and Selected Problems of International Law*. Dobbs Ferry, New York, 1972.

Lenin, V.I. *Collected Works*. 34 Vols. Moscow, 1964.

———. "The Right of Nations to Self Determination." *National Liberation, Socialism and Imperialism* 72 (1968).

Levi, S. *Le Nepal: Etude Historique d'un Royaume Hindou*. 3 Vols. Paris, 1909.

Lhalungpa, L. "Chronicle." In *Tibet: The Sacred Realm*. Philadelphia Museum of Art, 1983.

Li, Fang-Kuei. "The Inscription of the Sino-Tibetan Treaty of 821–822." *T'oung Pao* 44 (1956).

Li, Tieh-tseng. "The Legal Position of Tibet." *AJIL* 50, No. 2 (1952).

———. *Tibet: Today and Yesterday*. New York, 1960.

Ligeti, L. "Histoire Secrete des Mongols." *Monumenta Linguae Mongoligae Collecta* 1 (1971).

Lurie, J.H. "Through a Harsh Dawn: Communist China and Tibet; The First Decade, 1950-1960." Masters Thesis, University of Wisconsin.

MacDonald, D. *The Land of the Lama.* London, 1929.

Mackerras, C. *The Uighur Empire According to T'ang Dynastic Histories.* Canberra, 1972.

Macnair, H. *Modern Chinese History.* Shanghai, 1927.

Manandhar, T.R. "Crisis with Tibet (1883-84)." *Voice of History* 3 (1977).

Mansergh, N. "The Asian Conference." *International Affairs* (July 1947).

———, ed. *Documents and Speeches on British Commonwealth Affairs, 1931-1952.* London, New York, 1953.

Mao, Tse-tung. *Selected Works of Mao Tse-tung.* 5 Vols. Beijing, 1965.

Marchetti, V., and Marks, J.D. *The CIA and the Cult of Intelligence.* New York, 1978.

Marek, K. *Identity and Continuity of States in Public International Law.* Geneva, 1968.

Markham, C.R., ed. *Narratives of the Mission of George Bogle to Tibet, and of the Journey of Thomas Manning to Lhasa.* London, 1879.

Martens, G. de. *Nouveau Recueil General des Traites:* 1st Ser., 20 Vols. (Gottingen, 1843-75); 2nd Ser., 35 Vols. (Gottingen, Leipzig, 1876-1908); 3rd Ser., 41 Vols. (Leipzig, Greifswald, 1915-1944).

———. *Precis du Droit des Gens de l'Europe.* 3rd ed. Gottingue, Dieterich, 1821.

Martynov, A.S. "On the Status of the Fifth Dalai Lama: An Attempt at an Interpretation of His Diploma and Title." In *Proceedings of the Csoma de Körös Memorial Symposium,* ed. L. Ligeti. Budapest, 1978.

Mayers, W.F. *The Chinese Government.* 3rd ed. Taipei, 1966.

McMahon, M. *Conquest and Modern International Law: Legal Limitations on the Acquisition of Territory by Conquest.* Washington, 1940.

McNair, A. *International Law Opinions.* Cambridge, 1956.

———. *The Law of Treaties.* Oxford, 1961.

McNair, A. and Lauterpacht, H., eds. *Annual Digest of Public International Law Cases, 1925-26.* London, 1929.

McNair, A. and Watts, A.D. *The Legal Effects of War.* 4th ed. Cambridge, 1966.

Mehra, P. "Beginnings of the Lhasa Expedition: Younghusband's Own Words." *Bulletin of Tibetology* 4, No. 3 (November 1967).

———. *The McMahon Line and After.* Delhi, 1974.

———. *Tibetan Policy, 1904-37.* Wiesbaden, 1976.

Michael, F. *The Origin of Manchu Rule in China: Frontier and Border as Interacting Forces in the Chinese Empire.* Baltimore, 1942.

———. *Rule By Incarnation.* Boulder, Colorado, 1982.

———. "Survival of a Culture: Tibetan Refugees in India." *Asian Survey* 25, No. 7 (July 1982).

Mill, J.S. *On Representative Government.* London, 1873.

Mojumdar, K. *Anglo-Nepalese Relations in the Nineteenth Century.* Calcutta, 1973.

Mole, G. "The T'u-yu-hun from the Northern Wei to the Time of the Five Dynasties." *Serie Orientale Roma* 41 (1970).

Monger, G. *The End of Isolation: British Foreign Policy, 1900-1907.* London, 1963.

Moore, J.B. *History and Digest of the International Arbitrations to Which the United States Has Been a Party.* Washington, 1898.

———, ed. *Digest of International Law.* 8 Vols. Washington, 1906.

Morgenthau, H. "The Problem of Sovereignty Reconsidered." In *Essays On International Law from the Columbia Law Review.* New York, 1965.

Morris, R. *China and Inner Asia: From 1368 to the Present Day.* New York, 1975.

Morrison, G.E. *The Correspondence of G.E. Morrison.* Ed. Lo Hui-Min. Vols. 1–2. Cambridge, 1976.

Morse, H.B. *International Relations of the Chinese Empire.* 3 Vols. London, 1918.

Moseley, G. *The Consolidation of the South China Frontiers.* Berkeley, 1973.

Namgyal Institute of Tibetology. *The Red Annals.* Part One (Tibetan Text). Gangtok, Sikkim (1961).

Naraharinath, Y. *Itihas Prakash ma Sandhi Patra Sangraha* (A Collection of Treaties in the Illumination of History). Vol. 14. Kathmandu, 1966 (V.E. 2022).

Nawaz, M. "The Doctrine of the Outlawry of War." *Indian Yearbook of International Affairs* 13 (1964).

Nepali, C.R. "Nepal ra Tibbat ko Sambandha" (Nepal-Tibet Relations). *Pragati*, Year II, Issue 4, No. 10 (1956).

———. "Nepal-Chin Yuddha" (Nepal-China War). *Sharadai* 21 (1956).

Norbu, D. *Red Star over Tibet.* London, 1974.

———. *Horseman in the Snow.* Dharmsala, 1979.

———. "The 1959 Tibetan Rebellion: An Interpretation." *The China Quarterly*, No. 77 (March 1979).

———. "National Determinism and Hanman's Burden: Chinese Communist Views on Self-Determination." Unpublished paper. June 1979.

Okeke, C.N. *Controversial Subjects of Contemporary International Law.* Rotterdam, 1973.

Oppenheim, L. *International Law.* Ed. H. Lauterpacht. 2 Vols. 8th ed. London, 1955.

Oppenheimer, F.E. "Governments and Authorities in Exile." *AJIL* 36 (1942).

Panikkar, K.M. *In Two Chinas.* London, 1955.

Parker, E.H. "Campaigns of K'ang-hi, Yuung-cheng and K'ien-lung." *China Review* 16 (1887/88).

———. "Nepal and China in Asia." *Quarterly Review* (1899).

Patterson, G.N. *Tibet in Revolt.* London, 1960.

Pavithran, A.K. *Substance of International Law Western and Eastern.* Madras, 1965.

Peaslee, A.J. and Peaslee, D. *Constitutions of Nations.* 2nd ed. The Hague, 1956.

Pelliot, P. *Histoire Ancienne du Tibet.* Paris, 1961.

Petech, L. *A Study on the Chronicles of Ladakh.* Calcutta, 1939.

———. "Il Tibet nella Geografia Musulmana." *Atti della Accademia Nazionale dei Lincei*, 8th Series, Vol. 2. Rome, 1947.

———. "The Tibetan-Ladakhi-Moghul War of 1681–83." *The Indian Historical Quarterly* 23, No. 3 (1947).

———. "Notes on Ladakhi History." *The Indian Historical Quarterly* 24, No. 3 (1948).

———, ed. "The Missions of Bogle and Turner According to the Tibetan Texts." *T'oung Pao* 39 (1949–50).

———. *I Missionari Italiani nel Tibet e nel Nepal.* Il Nuovo Ramusio 2 (1952–56).

———. "Notes on Tibetan History of the Eighteenth Century." *T'oung Pao* 52 (1965–66).

———. "Glosse agli Annali di Tun-Huang." *Rivista degli Studi Orientali* 42, Fasc. 3 (1967).

———. *China and Tibet In the Early XVIIIth Century.* Leiden, 1972.

———. "The Kingdom of Ladakh, C.950–1842 A.D." *Serie Orientale Roma* 51 (1977).

Phur-lcog yongs-'dzin Byams-pa tshul-khrims. *Rin-po-che'i 'phreng-ba* (a biography of Dalai Lama XIII, Thub-bstan rgya-mtsho). n.d.

Pomerance, M. *Self Determination in Law and Practice: the New Doctrine in the United Nations.* The Hague, 1982.

Raestad, A. "La Cessation des Etats d'apres le Droit des Gens." *Revue Generale de Droit International Public* (1939).

Rahul, R. "The Sino-Tibetan Agreement of 1951." Dissertation, Columbia University, 1954.

———. *Government and Politics of Tibet.* Delhi, 1969.

———. *The Himalaya As A Frontier.* New Delhi, 1978.

———. "The 1912 Agreement Between the Chinese and Tibetans." *Tibetan Review* 12, No. 2 (Feb. 1979).

Ramakant. *Nepal-China and India.* New Delhi, 1976.

Rapgay, L. "The Thirteenth Dalai Lama." *Bulletin of Tibetology* NS, No. 2, 1977.

Ratchnevsky, P. "Die Mongolische Grosskhane und die Buddhistische Kirche." 2 *Asiatica* 32.

Regmi, D.R. *Medieval Nepal.* 2 Vols. Calcutta, 1966.

———. *Ancient Nepal.* 3rd ed. Calcutta, 1969.

———. *Modern Nepal.* 2nd ed. Calcutta, 1975.

Reisman, W.M. *Puerto Rico and the International Process: New Roles in Association.* Washington, 1975.

Richardson, H.E. "Three Ancient Inscriptions from Tibet." *JRAS* (1949).

———. *Ancient Historical Edicts at Lhasa and the Mutsung Khri Gtsug Lde Brtsan Treaty of A.D. 821–822 from the Inscription at Lhasa.* London, 1952.

———. "A Tibetan Inscription from Rgyal Lha Khang; and a Note on Tibetan Chronology from A.D. 841 to A.D. 1042." *JRAS* (April 1957).

———. *A Short History of Tibet.* New York, 1962.

———. "Who Was Yun-brtan?" In *Etudes Tibetaines.* Paris, 1971.

———. "Ch'ing Dynasty Inscriptions at Lhasa." *Serie Orientale Roma* 47 (1974).

———. "General Huang Mu-sung at Lhasa, 1934." *Bulletin of Tibetology* NS, No. 2 (1977).

———. "The Sino-Tibetan Treaty Inscription of A.D. 821–823 at Lhasa." *JRAS*, No. 2 (1978).

———. "Regurgitating an Imperial Political Myth." *Tibetan Review* 17, No. 9 (Sept. 1982).

Rivier, A. *Principes du Droit des Gens.* 2 Vols. Paris, 1896.

Rockhill, W.W. *Diplomatic Audiences at the Court of China.* London, 1905.

———. "The Dalai Lamas of Lhasa and Their Relations with the Emperors of China 1644–1908." *T'oung Pao* 11 (1910).

Roerich, G.N. *Mongolo-Tibetskie Otnoshenija v XIII i XIV vv* [Mongolian-Tibetan Relations in the 16th and Early 17th Century]. Moscow, 1959.

———. *The Blue Annals.* Full title: *Bod-kyi yul du chos-dan chos-smra-ba ji-ltar byun-ba'i rim-pa Deb-ther sngon-po,* or *The Blue Annals, The Stages of the Appearance of the Doctrine and Preachers in the Land of Tibet.* 2nd ed. Delhi, 1979.

Rose, L. *Nepal: Strategy for Survival.* Berkeley, 1971.

Rosenstock, R. "The Declaration of Principles of International Law Concerning Friendly Relations: A Survey." *AJIL* 65 (1971).

Rossabi, M. "The Tea and Horse Trade with Inner Asia During the Ming." *Journal of Asian History* 4 (1970).

———. *China and Inner Asia.* London, 1975.

Rubin, A.P. "The Position of Tibet in International Law." *The China Quarterly*, No. 35 (July/Sept. 1968).

Rutherford, G.W. "Spheres of Influence: An Aspect of Semi-suzerainty." *AJIL* 20 (1926).

Sastroamidjojo, A. and Delson, R. "The Status of the Republic of Indonesia in International Law." *Columbia Law Review* 49 (1949).

Sawhny, R. "China's Control of Tibet and Its Implications for India's Defence." *International Studies* 10, No. 4 (April 1969).

Schoeborn, W. "La Nature Juridique du Territoire." *Recueil des Cours* 5 (1929).

Schuh, D. "Erlasse und Sendschreiben Mongolischer Herrscher fur Tibetische Geistliche." Vol. 3, No. 1 of *Monumenta Historica Tibetica*, eds. D. Schuh et al. St. Augustin, Germany, 1977.

Schurmann, F., and Schell, O. *Republican China: Nationalism, War and the Rise of Communism 1911-1949*. New York, 1967.

———. *Imperial China: The Decline of the Last Dynasty and the Origins of Modern China; the 18th and 19th Centuries*. New York, 1967.

Schwarzenberger, G. *International Law*. 2 Vols. 3rd ed. London, 1957.

Scientific Buddhist Association. *Tibet: The Facts*. Report prepared for the U.N. Commission on Human Rights. London, 1984.

Scott, J.B., ed. *The Hague Court Reports*. 2nd Ser. New York, 1932.

———. *Official Statements of War Aims and Peace Proposals, December 1916 to November 1918*. Westport, Connecticut, 1984.

Sen, C. *Tibet Disappears*. New York, 1960.

———. "Tibet and the Sino-Indian Impasse." *International Studies* 10, No. 4 (April 1969).

Serruys, H. *The Mongols in China During the Hung-Wu Period*. Bruges, Belgium, 1959.

———. "The Tribute System and Diplomatic Missions (1400-1600)." Vol. 2 of "Sino-Mongol Relations During the Ming." *Melanges Chinois et Bouddhiques* 14 (Brussels, 1967).

———. "Trade Relations: The Horse Fairs (1400-1600)." Vol. 3 of "Sino-Mongol Relations During the Ming." *Melanges Chinois et Bouddhiques* 17 (Brussels, 1973-75).

Shakabpa, Tsepon W.D. *Tibet: A Political History*. New Haven, 1967.

———. "Refutation of Chinese Allegations." *Sheja* (Oct. and Nov. 1980).

———. "Seeking Truth from Facts." *Tibetan Bulletin* 15, No. 2 (June-July 1984).

Sharma, S.P. "The India China Border Dispute: An Indian Perspective." *AJIL* 59 (1965).

Shen, Shih-hsing et al. *Ming Hui-tien*. Taipei, 1968.

Shen, T., and Liu, S. *Tibet and the Tibetans*. New York, 1973.

Sigel, L.T. *Ch'ing Tibetan Policy*. East Asian Research Center, Harvard University, Papers on China, Vol. 20. Cambridge, Massachusetts, 1966.

Sinclair, I.M. *The Vienna Convention on the Law of Treaties*. Manchester, 1973.

Sinha, N. "Tibet's Status During the World War." *Bulletin of Tibetology* 2, No. 2 (August 1965).

———. "Was the Simla Convention Not Signed?" *Bulletin of Tibetology* 3, No. 1 (Feb. 1966).

———. *Tibet: Considerations on Inner Asian History*. Calcutta, 1967.

———. "The Simla Convention 1914: A Chinese Puzzle." *Bulletin of Tibetology* NS, No. 1 (1977).

_____. "India and Tibet: Geographical Considerations." *Bulletin of Tibetology* NS, No. 3 (1977).

Sinor, D. *Inner Asia*. Bloomington, Indiana, 1969.

Snellgrove, D., and Richardson, H.E. *A Cultural History of Tibet*. New York, 1968.

Sperling, E. "The Fifth Karma-pa and Some Aspects of the Relationship Between Tibet and the Early Ming." In *Tibetan Studies in Honor of Hugh Richardson*, eds. M. Aris and Aung San Suu Kyi. New Delhi, 1980.

_____. "The Status of Tibet According to Tibetan and Chinese Sources." *Tibetan Messenger* 9, No. 1 (1980).

_____. "Did the Early Ming Emperors Attempt to Implement a Divide and Rule Policy in Tibet?" Paper presented at Csoma de Körös Symposium, Velm, Austria, Sept. 1981.

Stein, R.A. *Une Chronique Ancienne de bSam-yas: sBa-bzed*. Paris, 1961.

_____. *Tibetan Civilization*. Stanford, 1972.

Stewart, R. "Treaty-Making Procedure in the British Dominions." *AJIL* 32 (1938).

Stiller, F.S. *The Rise of the House of Gorkha*. New Delhi, 1973.

Stuyt, A.M. *Survey of International Arbitrations, 1794–1938*. The Hague, 1939.

_____. *The General Principles of Law as Applied by International Tribunals to Disputes on Attribution and Exercise of State Jurisdiction*. The Hague, 1946.

Suzuki, E. "Self-Determination and World Public Order: Community Response to Territorial Separation." *Virginia Journal of International Law* 16, No. 4 (Summer 1976).

Svarlien, O. *An Introduction to the Law of Nations*. New York, 1955.

Svontausta, T. "La Souverainete des Etats." *Ius Finlandiae* 2. Helsinki, 1956.

Szerb, J. "Glosses on the Oeuvre of bLa-ma 'Phangs-pa: Part I, On the Activity of Sa-skya Pandita." In *Tibetan Studies in Honor of Hugh E. Richardson*, eds. M. Aris and Aung San Suu Kyi. New Delhi, 1980.

_____. "Glosses on the Oeuvre of bLa-ma 'Phags-pa: Part II, Some Notes on the Events of the Years 1251–1254." *Acta Orientalia Hungarica* 34 (1980).

Tada, T. *The Thirteenth Dalai Lama*. Tokyo, 1965.

Tang, P. *Russian and Soviet Policy in Manchuria and Outer Mongolia, 1911–31*. Durham, North Carolina, 1959.

Taracouzio, T.A. *The Soviet Union and International Law*. New York, 1935.

Tatz, M. "T'ang Dynasty Influences on Early Spread of Buddhism in Tibet." *The Tibet Journal* 3, No. 2 (1978).

Teichman, E. *Travels of a Consular Officer in Eastern Tibet*. Cambridge, 1922.

The Boundary Question Between China and Tibet. Beijing, 1940.

The China White Papers, Aug. 1949. Vols. 1–2. Stanford, 1967.

Thomas, F.W. *Tibetan Literary Texts and Documents Concerning Chinese Turkestan*. Vol. 2. London, 1951.

Thomas, F.W., and Konow, S. *Two Medieval Documents from Tun-Huang*. Oslo, 1929.

Tiwari, B. "Unrest in Tibet Continues." *Tibetan Review* 9, Nos. 6–7 (July/Aug. 1974).

Tolstoy, I. "Across Tibet from India to China." *The National Geographic Magazine* 90, No. 2 (August 1946).

Touscoz, T. *Le Principe d'Effectivite dans l'Ordre International*. Paris, 1964.

Tu, H. "The Legal Status of Tibet." *The Annals of the Chinese Society of International Law* 7 (August 1970).

_____. *A Study of the Treaties and Agreements Relating to Tibet*. Taichung, Taiwan, 1971.

Tucci, G. "Tombs of the Tibetan Kings." *Serie Orientale Roma* 1 (1950).
————. "The Validity of Tibetan Historical Tradition." *India Antiqua* (1957).
————. "The Wives of Sron btsam sgam Po." *Oriens Extremus* 9 (1962).
————. "Deb t'er dmar po gsar ma: Tibetan Chronicles by bSod nams grags pa." Vol. 1. *Serie Orientale Roma* 24 (1971).
————. *Tibetan Painted Scrolls.* 1949; rpt. Kyoto, 1980.
Turner, S. *An Account of an Embassy to the Court of the Teshoo Lama in Tibet.* London, 1800.
United States Naval War College. *International Law Situations.* Washington, 1902.
U.S. State Department, *Charter, Indictment and Opening Statement, Trial of the Japanese War Criminals.* Department of State Publication No. 2613, Far Eastern Series 12, Washington, 1946.
Umozurike, U. *Self-Determination In International Law.* Hamden, Connecticut, 1972.
Union Research Institute (URI). *Tibet, 1950–1967.* Hong Kong, 1968.
Uprety, P.R. *Nepal-Tibet Relations 1850–1930.* Kathmandu, 1980.
Uray, G. "Notes on a Tibetan Military Document from Tun-Huang." *Acta Orientalia Hungarica* 12 (1961).
Vaidyanath, R. "The Soviet View of the Tibetan Situation." *International Studies* 10, No. 4 (April 1969).
Van Dyke, V. *International Politics.* New York, 1972.
Van Eekelen, W.F. *Indian Foreign Policy and the Border Dispute with China.* The Hague, 1964.
Van Roijen, J. *De Rechtspositie en de Volkenrechtelijke Erkenning van Nieuwe Staten en De-Facto-Regeringen.* 's-Gravenhage, 1929.
Van Walt, M.C. "Tibet and the Right to Self Determination." *Wayne Law Review* 26, No. 1 (Nov. 1979).
————. "A Note on China's Claims to Tibet." *News Tibet* 19 (Jan.-Aug. 1984).
————. "Whose Game? Records of the India Office Concerning Events Leading up to the Simla Conference." In *Soundings in Tibetan Civilization.* Eds. B. Aziz and M. Kapstein. New Delhi, 1985.
Varma, S. *Struggle for the Himalayas.* 2nd ed. Jullundur, India, 1971.
Vattel, E. de. *The Law of Nations or the Principles of Natural Law.* 1758; rpt. New York, 1964.
Venturini, G. *Il Protettorato Internazionale.* Milan, 1939.
Verdoss, A. *Volkerrecht.* 2nd ed. Vienna, 1950.
Verzijl, J.H.W. *International Law in Historical Perspective.* Vols. 1–2. Leiden, 1968–1969.
Visscher, C. de. *Theories et Realites en Droit International Public.* 4th ed. Paris, 1974.
Viswanatha, S.V. *International Law in Ancient India.* Bombay, London, 1925.
Vixeboxse, J. *Een Hollandsch Gezantschap naar China in de Zeventiende Eeuw, (1685–1687).* Leiden, 1946.
Von Glahn, G. *Law Among Nations.* 4th ed. New York, 1981.
Von Wolff, C. *Jus Gentium Methodo Scientifica Pertractatum.* Frankfurt, 1764.
Waddell, L.A. "Ancient Historical Edicts at Lhasa." *JRAS* (1910).
————. "Tibetan Invasion of India in 647 A.D. and Its Results." *Asiatic Quarterly Review* (1911).
Wakeman, F. *The Fall of Imperial China.* New York, 1975.
Wang, F. and Suo, W. *Highlights of Tibetan History.* Beijing, 1984.
Wangdu, S. *The Discovery of the Fourteenth Dalai Lama.* Translated by Bikkhu Thupten et al. Bangkok, 1975.

Wessels, C. *Early Jesuit Travellers in Central Asia, 1603–1721*. The Hague, 1924.

Westlake, J. *Chapters on the Principles of International Law*. Cambridge, 1894.

––––––. *International Law*. 2 Vols. 2nd ed. Cambridge, 1910.

––––––. *The Collected Papers of John Westlake*. Ed. L. Oppenheim. Cambridge, 1914.

Wheaton, H. *Elements of International Law*. Ed. H.B. Keith. 6th ed. London, 1929.

White, P. "Silencing The Dalai Lama." Press Release from the Tibetan Affairs Coordination Office, the Netherlands, Nov. 1982.

Whiteman, M., ed. *Digest of International Law*. 14 Vols. Washington, 1963–1973.

Williams, E.T. "Tibet And Her Neighbors." University of California Publications, Bureau of International Relations, Vol. 3, No. 2 (July 19, 1937).

Williams, J.F. "Some Thoughts on the Doctrine of Recognition in International Law." *Harvard Law Review* 47 (1934).

Williams, S.W. *The Middle Kingdom: A Survey of Geography, Government, Literature, Social Life, Arts, and History of the Chinese Empire and Its Inhabitants*. Vols. 1–2. 1895; rpt. New York, 1966.

Willoughby, W.W., and Fenwick, C.G. *Types of Restricted Sovereignty and of Colonial Autonomy*. Washington, 1919.

Wood, W.A.R. *A History of Siam from Earliest Times to the Year A.D. 1781*. London, 1926.

Woodman, D. *Himalayan Frontiers: A Political Review of British Chinese, Indian and Russian Rivalries*. London, 1969.

Wright, D., ed. *History of Nepal*. 1871; rpt. Kathmandu, 1972.

Wylie, T.V. "The First Mongol Conquest Of Tibet Reinterpreted." *HJAS* 37, No. 1 (1977).

Yakhontoff, V. *The Chinese Soviets*. New York, 1934.

Yang, Tsang-hao. "The Reality of the Power Seizure in Tibet." *Chinese Communist Affairs* 4, No. 3 (June 1967).

Younghusband, F. "A Cloud in Tibet: British Action and Its Results." *The Times*. 3 August 1910.

––––––. "A Cloud in Tibet: British Policy—A Suggestion." *The Times*. 4 August 1910.

––––––. *India and Tibet*. London, 1910.

Table of Cases

Abbreviations

AJIL	*American Journal of International Law*
Ann.	Annexure
B.F.S.P.	British and Foreign State Papers
BYIL	*British Yearbook of International Law*
Cd.	Commissioned for Parliament
CB	*Current Background*
CNA	*China News Analysis*
CCP	Chinese Communist Party
CRO	Commonwealth Relations Office
DO	Dominion Office
FO	Foreign Office
FRUS	*Papers Relating to the Foreign Relations of the United States*
Further Papers	*Further Papers Relating to Tibet*
G.A. Doc.	General Assembly Document
G.A. Res.	General Assembly Resolution
GAOR	*General Assembly Official Records*
GOB	Government of Bengal
GOI	Government of India
HJAS	*Harvard Journal of Asiatic Studies*
H.M.G.	His/Her Majesty's Government
Incl.	Inclosure
IO	India Office
I.C. Jur.	International Commission of Jurists
I.C.J., *Reports*	International Court of Justice, *Reports of Judgments, Advisory Opinions and Orders*
I.L.C.	International Law Commission
JRAS	*Journal of the Royal Central Asiatic Society*
KMT	Kuomintang
L.N.O.J.	*League of Nations Official Journal*
L.N.T.S.	*League of Nations Treaty Series*
L/P&S	Political and Secret Files of the India Office, London

MITN	Petech, *I Missionari Italiani nel Tibet e nel Nepal*
MRG	Minority Rights Group
NCNA	New China News Agency
n.d.	not dated
Nouveau Recueil	Martens, *Nouveau Recueil General des Traites*
NVDA	Tibetan National Volunteer Defence Army
Papers	*Papers Relating to Tibet*
PCART	Preparatory Committee for the Autonomous Region of Tibet
P.C.I.J.	Permanent Court of International Justice
PLA	People's Liberation Army
Pol. O.	Political Officer
P.M.	Prime Minister
PRC	The People's Republic of China
R.I.A.A.	*Reports of International Arbitral Awards*
Sec.	Secretary
SCMM	*Selections From China Mainland Magazines*
SCMP	*Survey of China Mainland Press*
SPRCP	*Survey of People's Republic of China Press*
TAM	*Recueil des Decisions des Tribunaux Arbiraux Mixtes*
TAR	Tibet Autonomous Region
TPS	TUCCI, *Tibetan Painted Scrolls*
TR	*Tibetan Review*
URI	Union Research Institute, *Tibet 1950–1967*
U.N.T.S.	*United Nations Treaty Series*
U.S.T.S.	*United States Treaty Series*
White Paper	Ministry of External Affairs, India, *Notes, Memoranda and Letters Exchanged and Agreements Signed by the Governments of India and China*

Index